Ready
To *Fly*

Ready To Fly

STORIES OF
STRENGTH AND
COURAGE TO

Inspire Your Journey Forward

CRYSTAL BLUE

ANA♥HATA
PUBLISHING

Ready to Fly: Stories of Strength and Courage to Inspire Your Journey Forward

Published by Ana Hata Publishing, Castle Rock, CO.

Library of Congress Control Number: 2017962109

ISBN: 978-0-9992558-0-3

SELF-HELP / Personal Growth / Happiness

Cover design: Victoria Wolf of Red Wolf Marketing

QUANTITY PURCHASES: Schools, companies, professional groups, clubs, and other organizations may qualify for special terms when ordering quantities of this title.

For information, email Info@AnaHataPublishing.com.

This book is printed in the United States of America.

To all of you who read these words, thank you for supporting this project. Thank you for being a part of this movement to support and encourage women of all ages… in all stages…sages and mages… maidens, mothers, and crones… queen bees and drones… in caves or on thrones…

This book is for you.

May these stories shine a light through your darkness. May you find healing and hope. May you find your own light.

May you be the light.

Contents

Introduction   i

Stories

Free to Fly by Kate Hagerty   1

No Regrets by Phoenix Sagen   23

Power as One by Claire Kadlecek   32

Trusting Blindly by Karen Montoya   48

In Life as in Sex by Kristen Gentala   57

Flavor with Intention by Sherry Hess   66

If I Only Had a Brain by Lisa Martins   89

Picture Great Health by Donna Wade   99

Love Hard and Live Well by Kristin Schooler   113

The Broken Dish by Renee Salway   130

Creating My Joy Journey by Lynnette Adams   144

See Only Love by Andrea Rahlf   158

Shine by Lindsey Robinson   177

Way of the Warrior Princess by Aundrea De Leon   191

Forgive and Flourish by Jennifer Knoble   212

The Sound of Truth by Crystal Blue   227

About the Author   256

Acknowledgments   257

Introduction

"If you want to fly, give up everything that weighs you down."
– Buddha

But first, you need to figure out what those things are...

The first time I read the quote above, it resonated deep within my soul. There was something deep within me that wanted to be heard. To be released and set free. But where would I even begin? What does letting go really mean? I had so many questions and ultimately decided to start listening to my own answer: *Just start writing.*

Over the past several years, I have discovered that my journey has taken a pivotal turn. One that involves reflection, releasing, and healing. It was time for me to look at all the pieces of my life that were weighing me down. Not just the "easy" things like the career that was unfulfilling, or the one-sided relationships. I'm talking about the deep things. The things within. The pieces of *me* that were unfulfilling. My relationship with myself.

After a magnificent transformation, I was ready to share my story. But I realized that I didn't want to do it alone. I had connected with so many strong and vibrant women who all had amazing stories to tell… and I wanted to give them a voice. I wanted to create a space that could hold all of us together while we supported and carried each other through this journey, with hopes of empowering others with our words. I was anxious and excited. Terrified, yet determined.

And so, the Anthology was born.

This has definitely been a challenging project. On many occasions, I wanted to give up. I often thought that I would quietly put down my pen and just focus on managing the project without writing a chapter. That would certainly have been a hell of a lot safer than diving deep into the darkness to face my shadows. It would have felt much more comfortable to keep this monster of a story locked inside, even though it has been clawing at my soul for years. I could have backed down when I felt a rush of anxiety, regret, anger, sadness, guilt, fear… or when my PTSD got triggered as I approached the turning point of my story. It would have been easier for me to keep things just as they were, to stay quiet and small and feel weighed down… but I wanted to be free once and for all. *I wanted to fly.*

As you read the following stories of strength and courage, transformation and triumph, know that you are supported, understood, held, and loved. Even though I may not know you, I believe in you. Even though I may not be at your side, I hold you in my heart. It is my hope that one or more of these stories will resonate with you and where you are today, and ultimately provide you with hope, inspiration, power, freedom, and strength. We will walk side by side, hand in hand, as none of us should face this journey alone.

Are you ready to set yourself free?

Are you *Ready to Fly?*

Free to Fly

by Kate Hagerty

At first, I said no to participating in this book.

To be honest, I was a little intimidated by the strict deadlines to get it all done. I loved the idea of contributing to a women's anthology, but when I take on a new project I like to feel confident about being able to give it my all. I didn't think I would have the time or energy for all of the meetings that would be required with my current work schedule. I have been teased over the years about burning the candle at both ends—so I have made it a habit to keep that top of mind when making decisions about taking on new commitments.

But one morning in January 2017, I opened my inbox as I always do and there was an email from the lovely Crystal Blue.

She wrote that she had made "a cool connection over the weekend" at the initial brainstorm meeting for this book. She continued

to say that during the initial introductions, one of the women had mentioned that she was working with a fantastic Life Purpose & Relationship Intuitive Coach. She couldn't say enough about this coach and raved about the experience and how much her life had changed as a result of working with her.

Next, unexpectedly, Crystal shared with me that another participant in the group had asked the woman who this infamous coach was—and she proudly offered:

"Kate Hagerty."

Then three other women piped up and said they also knew me. WHAT?! It turns out that all of them had either worked with me personally, heard me speak at an event, or had attended one of my workshops. And I was truly touched when she told me they all thought I was "fabulous".

This just blew me away. What an email to wake up to!

When I read those words, I was struck with the realization, humility and gratitude that my work was making an impact. People were starting to know my name and they were beginning to refer me to others without me asking them to. I remember almost crying at the very thought because I recognized that I had made real progress in my professional life. After years of hard work and a lot of soul-searching, I was finally starting to see (and hear!) the results.

I couldn't believe that this amazing group of women, each of whom I knew from different parts of my life, had all found their way to the same meeting and had all decided to participate in this project. I decided right then and there that I should at least revisit the idea of participating in the book with Crystal.

So, I emailed her that I was interested in talking about the book content. After all, I believe that things happen for a reason when and how they should (also known as the Law of Divine Timing and the Law of Divine Order). I also believe that we have spirit guides, guardian angels and archangels that watch over us and provide us with signs or what I like to call Love Nudges from the Universe when

we are supposed to pay attention, take action, and/or change course.

How could this miraculous chain of events not be in alignment with these two universal laws?

More proof? After our virtual exchange, I ran into Crystal the next day at a networking event. Again, I felt that the Universe was urging me to move forward.

CHOOSING YES

I meditate every morning and work with a deck of cards afterward. Sometimes I use a deck of angel cards; sometimes it's a deck of goddess or fairy cards; or it may be a deck of fractal art image cards. I have a collection of over 14 different decks to choose from and I usually select the one that resonates with me the most each morning.

The next day, I chose to work with Cheryl Lee Harnish's *Return of Spirit* deck. It is a deck composed of 44 cards, each with a fractal art image and a significant word that accompanies it. Cheryl describes fractals and her fractal art images as: "A type of geometry." She goes on to say, "Everything in our natural world is created from fractal geometry, including us, right down to our DNA. The artwork is a visual representation of the fractal mathematics."

Cheryl creates her images using a fractal generating software. She applies multiple formulas to the same image until she intuitively feels it is complete. She can apply one hundred to five hundred formulas to a single fractal image. The deck comes with a guidebook that provides general meanings for each card.

The card I picked that morning was incredible—it was the WRITE card. I read the description in the guidebook and it said: "By drawing this card, Spirit is affirming to you that you need to get your words written down on paper. Do not put it off any longer. If you are having doubts, that's fine. Just acknowledge them and take action anyway. You can do this. Your words are needed." WOW!

When I opened my inbox later that day, I found an email from Crystal that included a link to learn more about the Women's

Anthology Project (the original title of this book), how she had arrived at her vision for the inspirational book, guidelines for the participating writers, FAQs, etc.

When I clicked on the link, I was greeted by a spectacular image. It was a large heart composed of butterflies—and it was not clear upon first glance whether the butterflies were joining or leaving the heart or both.

I love butterflies and never get tired of watching them. They are very symbolic to me. I have one on my business card as a representation of how my work helps people transform into who they are meant to be.

To me, the Universe had already clearly communicated in numerous ways that I needed to change my initial answer about contributing to this book from a no to a YES. And this image only solidified everything for me. Talk about synchronicity!

I emailed Crystal and told her that between pulling the WRITE card and coming across the butterfly heart image, I now had numerous signs from my spirit guides and guardian angels that I was supposed to be a part of this project and that she should add my name to the list of participating writers. She replied that she had gotten chills as she read my confirmation and agreed that the chain of events was indeed magical. It was official. I had chosen YES.

THE ROTOR RIDE

I grew up in a family where my parents had four children under the age of five by the time they were 30 years old. My dad lost his job repeatedly, resulting in many years of financial uncertainty and high stress in the house.

My parents' marriage was not the happiest either—and I grew up not feeling seen, heard or valued because it was such a strained, emotionally unstable environment. In fact, I felt alone a lot and found it a constant challenge not to feel invisible.

While parts of my childhood were painful, I believe that it also

cultivated my sensitivity and ability to truly understand others. I have true compassion for people and possess a strong desire to help others who experienced similar challenges growing up (or are experiencing them now).

I also believe that we are all born with unique traits, talents, and capabilities that we are meant to share with the world. When we align our life with our true purpose, these traits, talents, and capabilities are at their strongest. As you can probably tell by now, I am very passionate about helping others discover their unique traits and talents so that they can feel truly seen and heard, too. In other words, I help people get to the point where they realize their value and feel confident enough to share their gifts with the world.

Before I arrived at this realization, however, I spent over thirty years in corporate America trying to prove my worth to myself and to others. I was also determined not to struggle financially like I had during my childhood, so I set my sights on earning a six-figure income early on in my career. In fact, I decided that I was going to be a Vice President of Marketing or even a Chief Marketing Officer one day. I remember feeling very certain that this was the right path for me to take at the time.

I worked very hard and was on my way up that ladder when something unexpected happened. Right after I turned 47, that long-term goal of mine to reach those senior positions became meaningless to me.

What had once been so important to me all of a sudden felt completely hollow. Each day it felt more and more like my soul was literally drying up into a prune. It became harder and harder to focus. Most mornings on my way to the office I would cry as I drove downtown, dreading the day and how much energy I knew it was going to take for me to get through it.

Every morning when I entered the parking garage at my office, I would give myself a pep talk and tell myself: *"You can do this! You can go up to your corporate job today and you can try to make it the best day possible."*

When I'd get up to the 22nd floor, I would put my hand on the front door of my office and say a silent prayer, *"Please God, help me get through this day. Help me last here long enough to save up enough money to quit."*

Along with the unsettling realization that I just didn't care about those corporate titles or goals anymore, a thick fog of anxiety, panic, and discomfort started to roll in and completely engulf what I had *thought* my life plan entailed.

What I *did* know was that I wanted to do something that made a difference in the world. I wanted to feel things in my heart and soul, not just in my head. I felt that I was being called to do something much bigger with my life, but I had no idea what that was or how to figure it out. As trite as this all sounds, at this point in my life, trite WAS my truth.

Once I acknowledged that the floor of my lifelong plan had dropped out from beneath me—like that amusement park ride "The Rotor," that leaves you pinned to the wall by centrifugal force—the questions, *"What am I really supposed to be doing with my life?"* and *"What is my true purpose?"* began to follow me around 24/7.

So, I started sword fighting with my anxiety and panic in an effort to calm down enough to come up with a new plan of action.

THE CHANGING TIDES

My plight to find the answers to these questions led me to ask others at networking events if there were specific conferences or workshops they could recommend that focused on how to start a business, how to tap into your true passion or life purpose, how to discover your unique traits and talents, etc. I began reading books on purpose, calling, and intuition. I even consulted a few select intuitives to help me get on track.

Each of them reminded me of something that I'd been told over 20 years ago by two established psychic mediums—one in Chicago and one in Seattle. I had been told that I was intuitively gifted and

had inherited those gifts from my paternal grandmother.

No one in my family had ever mentioned anything about my grandmother being intuitive or gifted growing up. Perhaps she wasn't aware that she was gifted, didn't know what it meant, or she chose to ignore it.

But to my amazement, both psychic mediums encouraged me to begin strengthening my own gifts immediately.

How did I receive this encouragement? Well, initially, I was completely stunned that I might be intuitively gifted, so I just nodded and smiled and then immediately dismissed it. I had my eye on the corporate ladder and felt confident that possessing intuitive or psychic gifts would not be looked at as a strength within the industry I worked in at the time. In fact, I was concerned I would be completely removed from the rungs on the corporate ladder altogether should this news get out, or even worse, be labeled as weird. Why did I think this?

Here are a few examples that crossed my mind:

First, who doesn't remember how badly Nancy Reagan was mocked for consulting an astrologer over a seven-year period while President Reagan was in the White House? And how she admitted, at least initially, to being highly embarrassed by the revelation.

How about Barbara Walters calling well-known clairvoyant and psychic medium James Van Praagh a fraud in 2008 when he warned her about her health and a potential heart condition. Her doctors gave her a clean bill of health in 2008 but in 2010, Barbara *did* need to have heart surgery.

And finally, the insinuation and negative hype by the media that Princess Diana was mentally unstable when it was revealed that she had consulted with various astrologers and gifted intuitives during the many years of her unhappy marriage to Prince Charles.

YES, in light of those examples, when I considered the suggestion that had been made to me that I *"look into and strengthen my gifts"* I was silently adamant in my own mind. I thought to myself:

"Well that's nice, but I am in corporate America. I cannot be weird and still reach my goals."

But the truth is I *had* been given that advice over two decades ago and here I was being reminded of it once again in 2011. It occurred to me that perhaps I should look into whether I had intuitive gifts or not, what they were and if they could help me now to figure out the answers to those two nagging questions: *"What am I **really** supposed to be doing with my life?"* and *"What **is** my true purpose?"*

In addition to reading a lot of books, and attending several pertinent workshops and conferences, I decided it was worth a little more time and effort to figure this out. What did it all mean? So, while I remained at my day job, I tried to learn as much as I could about how to confirm for myself that I had intuitive gifts—and upon confirmation I wanted to learn what these gifts were, where they came from, and how they worked. I also wanted to see if I could use them to help other people.

I had graduated with a degree in psychology, so I was very clear that coaches were different from therapists, psychologists or psychiatrists. That was what I knew for sure. The rest was still a mystery to me, but I was determined to solve it.

Therapists, psychologists and psychiatrists obtain Masters and/ or Doctorate degrees. I knew that those educational paths would not include a focus on or celebration of spirituality or intuitive gifts, and I was confident that a different direction was going to be a better fit for me.

Starting in 2011, my growing curiosity inspired me to investigate my intuitive gifts further by becoming a Certified Life Purpose, Relationship and Grief Intuitive Coach. I completed these three certification programs over a three-year period with Sue Frederick, author of *I See Your Dream Job*. I used my vacation time at work to accomplish this and to attend the necessary conferences and workshops referenced earlier.

There are many different coaching certification programs available in this industry. I asked every one of my friends who were working in corporate America at the time if their company offered any type of coaching program, and if so, what type of certification the coaches needed to have to be able to participate in the program.

I discovered the companies that did offer their employees some kind of coaching programs (personal, executive, etc.) required their coaches to take specific certification programs before they were considered to be qualified. Interestingly, I never heard the same program mentioned more than once.

I also asked my friends if they personally wanted to work with a coach—and whether it mattered to them if that individual had completed any specific coaching certification program. This is where I did find some consistency. The unanimous answer? They did *not* care if a coach was certified or not. They only cared if the person truly helped them. Hmm, interesting…

With each certification program I attended, the participating students were paired up with individuals who were already certified coaches and working in the field. Each program focused on providing the students with tools on how to access, strengthen, and apply their intuitive senses to their intuitive coaching sessions. Every student was also provided with the opportunity to conduct live practice sessions.

Sue taught us to prepare for our practice intuitive coaching sessions by meditating for 20 minutes on the person we were going to "read" for—and asking the following questions:

- "What is this soul here to accomplish?"
- "How can I help [insert first name here] to reach their greatest potential?"
- "What specific next step does [first name] need to take now to align his/her life with his/her true life purpose, and with what he/she really came here to do?"

Each time I prepared for a practice intuitive coaching session, I'd sit at my dining room table with a stack white paper in front of me and ask those same questions. (This is still my process today.) I found out immediately that I didn't need to meditate for 20 minutes. Instead I began receiving information in about *20 seconds.*

First, I would "see" images like they were scenes from a movie. These "scenes" would show specific parts of that other person's life—typically from their childhood and/or emotional incidents they had experienced with their parents and other family members growing up.

Next, I would "hear" messages in my ear—very direct statements regarding what specific next steps that particular person needed to take.

For example, *"John needs to begin meditating every day, read the book The Secret by Rhonda Byrne, and take The Hero's Journey workshop offered by... "* YES, the steps I received were always *that* specific but varied significantly depending on whom I was channeling information for. I found that on average I would "receive" five to nine next steps for each person to take that were totally unique to their life goals or situation.

After completing my first program and becoming a Certified Life Purpose Intuitive Coach, I decided to have a business card designed and launch my website. At this time, I was also conducting intuitive coach sessions and readings—but on a referral basis only.

By continuing to work at the day job, I felt like I had one foot on the dock and one in the boat so to speak, and it was becoming increasingly painful to live that way. Something had to change.

THE CLAIRS

In every coaching program, I found it fascinating that each student possessed their own set of intuitive gifts and talents. This intrigued me, so I decided to do some research around the different types of intuitive gifts and how they "work" or show up.

I discovered that information can be received either intuitively (psychic abilities) or from Spirit (mediumship abilities).

While there are many ways that individuals can experience their own gifts, here are the most common intuitive senses that I came across during my research. They are also referred to as the Clairs. Let me explain.

The four main intuitive senses include:

- **Clairvoyance**: People with the intuitive gift of clairvoyance or "clear seeing" receive information in the form of pictures, symbols, words, and/or colors.
- **Clairaudience**: People with the gift of clairaudience or "clear hearing" have the ability to clearly hear the voice of Spirit speak to them within their own mind or their environment.
- **Clairsentience**: People with the intuitive gift of clairsentience or "clear feeling" are able to feel the present, past or future physical and emotional states of others without using the normal five senses.
- **Claircognizance**: People with the gift of claircognizance or "clear knowing" obtain psychic knowledge without knowing how or why they know it. It just comes to their mind. It can be knowledge about a person, an event, an object or a place.

Before I learned about the Clairs, I honestly had no idea where the information I had been getting was coming from—and I was pretty freaked out. Later, I met an older woman at an event who had worked with other people on a spiritual level for years, and she told me: "Oh honey, you channel."

At the time I remember thinking: "Um, really? What does *that* mean?"

After digging a little deeper, I discovered that I was receiving my information through all four of the main intuitive senses. Although I do not describe myself as religious, I do believe that my abilities to receive information through these intuitive senses are a gift from

God. The specific intuitive senses that I receive information through can and do vary depending on what I am doing at the time. For example, I may be preparing for an intuitive coaching session, or talking with a client during a follow up call, or listening to people talk about emotional times in their lives, etc.

I do not have control over which senses show up. I am just very grateful that they do because of how much they enable me to help others—those who feel stuck and are trying to sort through their thoughts, feelings or emotions so they can gain clarity around what next steps to take to begin aligning their lives with their true purpose.

Looking back, it all seems to make sense now. In 2010, I began working at my day job in marketing, initially as an independent contractor. In 2011, I was offered and accepted a full-time marketing position at the company. Later that same year, I began doing intuitive coaching sessions and readings, but on a referral basis only. In 2014, after an evening out celebrating my 50th birthday, I went in to the office the next day and learned that the company had decided to conduct employee layoffs.

The financial status of this private, family-owned company had been wobbly at best even before I started working there as an independent contractor in 2010. However, after continuing to pour millions into the company, the largest investor had decided enough was enough.

Remember when I said that I believe in the Law of Divine Timing and the Law of Divine Order, and that the Universe provides us with signs or Love Nudges when we are supposed to pay attention, take action, and/or change course? Well, I also believe that if we miss or ignore these signs and Love Nudges, they transform into something much stronger. They transform into a Love Shove.

On that fateful day, August 29, 2014, I discovered that I was included in the first group of employees to be laid off. Talk about a Love Shove!

When I received my severance package the next month, I had no

doubt that it was time for me to dedicate myself 100 percent to my Soul Purpose business and to begin working with clients on a full-time, paid basis.

I *knew* that there were many successful people who were still in full-time positions in corporate America and like me were earning a great income. I also knew that many of them were completely miserable in their own personal and professional lives. So miserable in fact that they were beginning to struggle with depression and/or experience some serious health issues.

What excited me was that I knew I could help them because of my own personal experience. It took years and a lot of work, but today, I can honestly say that I am the most "me" I've ever been.

I have since built a business where I work privately with clients one-on-one for three to six months. I use the information I "receive" during my initial meditative preparation to customize a program for each client based on their individual needs and the area(s) of their lives where they feel the most stuck and would like some help. Together we focus on one or more of these three areas:

- Life Purpose
- Relationships
- Grief

Let me tell you, when clients commit to making themselves (and their health and quality of life) a priority, real change begins to take place. When they show up fully—engage in and complete the steps that come through for them from their guardian angels and guides— *true life transformation* occurs.

THE PERFECT WOMAN

I love what I do and can't imagine doing anything else. But before I came to this realization there were some important (and genuinely challenging) stages I had to go through in order to arrive at where I am today.

By sharing these stages, coupled with my personal experiences, it is my hope that I can help others realize that they too are making progress even if they do not feel confident that they are doing so at the present moment.

1. Fear/Sheer Panic

Through my involvement with numerous networking groups over the years, I have learned that people do not always share what it is they are currently doing or have done to keep moving in the direction of their own dreams and ambitions. It's about sacrifice. It's about never giving up so that they can keep going and making consistent progress toward reaching their goals. I will share some of my own experiences shortly.

Encountering this behavior myself led to the following questions:

- What *if* we told the truth and showed our vulnerabilities all the time?
- How great would life be if more people realized that at that present moment they weren't actually that far off from their ultimate goals and ambitions?
- What would the world be like if we just all kept going and never allowed self-doubt to derail us?

Especially women.

We are socialized to be perfect. *The Perfect Woman* sits on our shoulder or banters in our ear 24/7 about what we need to do or be more or less of to be perfect. If we were only thinner, smarter, prettier—you know her—you've heard her. She doesn't even have a body. She isn't real, and yet, she can and will run our lives if we give her permission.

I'm sure we all know women who put a great deal of energy and effort into smiling and keeping up the perfect persona at all times.

When I was reflecting on this one day, I remembered that one of my dearest friends had been homeless *three* times and lived in a safe

house. She had sold her wedding ring to make ends meet. And another friend had lived in her car twice; and yet another friend had worked three jobs simultaneously to keep her business afloat. This made me realize that I was nowhere near what they had experienced and that I should keep going. In other words, I should stay focused on reaching my ultimate goals and vision and not allow self-doubt to derail me.

Just think of how free and empowered you'd feel if you didn't give up and always told the truth. You'd be an inspiration—particularly to other women. If we all showed our authentic self and talked about how we were really feeling—*while* we were struggling—we'd be able to help others do the same.

IT IS ALL ABOUT TIMING

After being laid off in 2014, I was 100 percent dedicated to my Soul Purpose business full-time—or at least, I wanted to be. It takes time to build up clientele, establish proof of concept, and make enough money to live worry-free.

During the early stages, I saw my savings go down, down, and yep, further down. I experienced excruciating and paralyzing fear and sheer panic. *What was I going to do?*

Well, I drove for Uber for a while and then I also drove for Lyft—two months later for both at the same time. I still have not shared that with many people. While I've heard others say they think it's fun and easy money, I was devastated at the thought that I needed to have a side job. I kept saying to myself: *"I know that my true life purpose isn't to be a full-time driver. Why is this happening to me?"*

However, during the five months that I drove for a living, the people I met and some of the situations they shared with me really moved me. Random strangers touched my heart and even made me cry. I was humbled, I was reminded of all I had to be grateful for and I slowly started to build my bank accounts back up again. Even though I wasn't excited about it, I remained a firm believer that

everything happens for a reason and that all of this was leading me to my next step.

Don't get me wrong though, there were still plenty of days where I struggled with my fear, panic, frustration and anger.

2. Anger/Frustration

As I shared earlier, I meditate every morning and work with a deck of oracle cards afterward. Oracle cards are an ancient, time-honored way for us to connect with our guardian angels and guides. By asking a question and having the question "answered" by the cards I select, I am able to receive their messages and guidance and gain clarity in every area of my life.

One day after completing both, I still didn't feel any better.

In exasperation, I started spewing my frustration at the ceiling by yelling: *"Why aren't you helping me? Why isn't this working?"* Later that afternoon, I got a new client. She signed up for my biggest program at the time. I was extremely grateful but still a little bewildered and frustrated over why it had to get to that point before there was a breakthrough.

I remember sitting at my dining room table, looking up at the ceiling, and saying: *"Now that's more like it. Do you think we can be a little more consistent?"* and immediately hearing in my ear, *"Can you?"*

I laughed out loud because I was finally getting it. My own thoughts, expectations and actions had played a part in all of it. Sure, I had read about the power of our thoughts in *The Secret* but at that moment it was delivered so personally that I now understood it on a new, much more evolved level.

Also during this time, I remember talking to one of my best friends—OK to be honest, I was whining and complaining to her—*not really talking.*

"I just don't understand why things aren't working for me! I've done so much to align my life with my true purpose. I've made huge changes

personally and professionally, invested my hard-earned money into training, working with a personal coach, promoting Soul Purpose, etc. Why isn't it happening?"

And my friend, who has been a successful entrepreneur for years, calmly replied: "Just because you're on your path, Kate, doesn't mean there won't be any more lessons to learn or struggles to deal with— those challenges are *part* of being on your path." And although I wanted to scream and shake her shoulders at that time—I knew she was right and today we still laugh about that conversation.

3. Finding Balance

During this particular stage, I often joked about trying to balance on a BOSU—but an upside-down BOSU—which is even more challenging. If you are not familiar with what a BOSU is, I'll explain. A BOSU is a piece of training equipment that is used to build balance and inner core strength. BOSU stands for "Both Sides Up." It looks like half of a blue dome or exercise ball attached to a platform. When the dome side is up, the BOSU provides an unstable surface to attempt to stand and/or balance on. When the device is flipped over so that the platform faces up, it is even harder to sustain your balance.

Today, when a tidal wave of fear or doubt is about to knock me off I think about balancing on the center of that hard platform. It takes some time to regain my balance of course and get "back to center" again. During this stage when close friends asked me how I was doing I'd answer, "I am trying to balance on an upside-down BOSU and when I fall off, seeing how quickly I can get back to center."

One morning as part of my daily practice, I chose to work with a favorite deck of mine, *Healing with the Angels*, created by Doreen Virtue. There are 44 cards in the deck, each with one or two words on them. One of the cards is SERENITY. In the guidebook that comes with the deck, part of the description for this card reads: "Peace of mind is within you. You can feel serene, even in the midst of great

turmoil. First, you work toward serenity and *then* your life challenges lessen and disappear."

It certainly offered a very different perspective on life. At the time, I thought that once the things we wanted most showed up in our lives *then* we would be happy and peaceful. While it has taken some time to get to a place of understanding the process, now when I get upset or frustrated I repeat to myself, "Go within. Serenity is within."

4. Self-Realization

One day I had an *aha* moment. I realized that the more people who step fully onto their path and align their life with their true purpose, the more others will see their example and be inspired to do the same. For example, let's say that you are really struggling and are thinking about giving up, but see someone else who didn't give up, and in fact, has reached a level that you would like to meet or exceed. You will *know* from their example that *it is* possible for you, too. Now *that* is inspiring.

If you think about it, those that we look up to as having "made it" most likely thought about giving up at some point as well. But they didn't. And because of that, they inspire us. And when you summon up the courage and strength to step fully onto your path and to fulfill your life purpose—you too will serve as an inspiration to others.

I sat for a moment and visualized how this cycle can and will result in a ripple effect of more and more people fulfilling their true life purpose and beginning to share their own unique traits and talents with the world. And, beyond that, how this ripple effect will ultimately expand to increase the overall vibration of the planet. I remember thinking, "*Wow! It doesn't get much bigger than that.*"

5. The Trust Walk

There were definitely chutes, ladders, and springboards during each stage but this one was about my building up faith and trust—in

myself, my gifts, my beliefs, and seeing proof that the world wanted what I had to offer. It was about gaining confidence that I was genuinely helping people.

I continued attending networking events, started posting more regularly on both my personal and Soul Purpose Facebook pages, launched a monthly newsletter called the Soul Purpose Insider, and began teaching at least two workshops each quarter.

During this particular stage, people started to tell me they looked forward to my newsletter each month. I also started getting asked to speak in front of groups—and I was pleasantly surprised to find out that I was working with 30 to 35 clients each year. Many of my clients had provided testimonials that touched me deeply. They mentioned how our work together was life changing. These and other encouraging incidents, signs, and YES you guessed it, Love Nudges, kept me moving forward on my trust walk.

6. Living From That Place

I believe we keep learning, changing and expanding until the day we die. This stage is still in play. It is about making it a daily practice to live from a place of faith, trust and positive expectation. It's about knowing when to let go and believing that I am always safe, provided for, taken care of and watched over by my guardian angels and spirit guides. It's all about believing that I have wings and should always go in the direction my heart tells me—and not to where my head may try to persuade me.

Some of the practices and tools I have used over the years to help me acquire a deep spiritual perspective include:

- Meditating every morning
- Working with angel oracle cards
- Reading Melody Beattie's daily entry in her book entitled *Journey to the Heart*
- Immersing myself in my favorite abundance affirmations
- Regularly revisiting certain parts of the following books:

The Secret, Money and the Law of Attraction, and *The Complete Works of Florence Scovel Shinn.*

I have also learned the immense power of gratitude and the magic that can accompany it.

My work is to help others discover their true life purpose—the unique traits and talents they were born with—and how to align their life with their purpose. The unique traits and talents we are born with shed light on what we have really come here to do and whom we have really come here to help. As I mentioned earlier, I believe my intuitive senses are a gift from God and I consider my calling to be an honor and a privilege.

Sometimes I tell people that I help my clients to discover their wings and remember how to fly. I believe we are born with that potential but that many of us just don't remember.

As I shared earlier, I grew up feeling invisible, not really seen, heard or valued. I never would have joined Toastmasters, hired a speaking coach, sought out opportunities to teach, speak onstage, write, be on the radio, etc., but I eventually realized that in order to find and connect with those I came here to help—I *had* to be seen, heard and valued.

It's fascinating how Divine Order works. Most of us have experienced things in the past that are now in the rearview mirror (so to speak) and we'd prefer that they stay there.

The truth is, however, that you have real gifts and can help others as a result of having gone through such painful and challenging experiences.

No one else but you is going to know what someone in that same situation is really going through or what they actually need to feel better. It goes far deeper than empathy. The pain, disappointment and/or sadness that you've experienced has not been just for you to suffer. No, the fact that you have experienced those things empowers you to really be able to help others who may still be in that situation.

Personally, I have found that many of my clients are here to help others who have endured, survived, or overcome what they themselves have experienced in their own lives—and that those experiences tie directly into why they are here and whom they really came here to help. They also shed significant light on those two powerful questions:

- *"What am I really supposed to be doing with my life?"*
- *"What is my true purpose?"*

YOU ARE NOT INVISIBLE

You are worthy of being seen, heard and valued for who you really are. You are worthy of love. You are perfect and you are enough—just as you are at this moment.

You were born with wings. You may just need some help discovering them and remembering how to fly.

But YES, you do have wings and *YES* you can fly.

I changed my answer to participate in this book and I am so glad I did. I decided to share my own journey with you with the hope that you will be inspired to say YES to yourself and YES to unleashing and sharing *your gifts* with the world. The people you came here to help are waiting for you.

"You were born with potential. You were born with goodness and trust. You were born with ideals and dreams. You were born with greatness. You were born with wings. You are not meant for crawling, so don't. You have wings. Learn to use them and fly."
– Rumi

And on that note, may your beautiful, purposeful flight begin today.

Namaste.

Kate Hagerty is a certified Life Purpose, Relationship, and Grief Intuitive Coach. She is also a gifted intuitive and certified Graphologist. After spending over 30 years in corporate America and realizing that she was not only on the wrong rung, but the wrong ladder, Kate took a leap of faith to seek her own life's purpose.

Today, Kate is a speaker, trainer and coach, and is passionate about helping other professionals who feel disconnected and are painfully aware that *something is missing* in their lives. Kate guides entrepreneurs, business owners and change leaders to discover their life's true purpose and realize that they, too, can fly.

Kate lives in Denver where she embraces her love of the great outdoors through running, hiking and skiing, and her weakness for dark chocolate, wine and dogs (but not necessarily in that order). To inquire about inviting Kate to present at your event, please visit SoulPurpose.biz.

No Regrets

by Phoenix Sagen

I learned some important facts about life at a very early age. When I was growing up in California my family owned a mortuary, and I remember playing hide-and-go-seek in the casket room. I know it might sound a little morbid, but this was normal for me. Before I was five, I understood what some people never quite grasp: No one gets out of life alive. It doesn't matter how old you are, what color you are, how big or skinny, how smart or brave… we all die at some point. We are not guaranteed tomorrow, so I learned that I had to live life *today*.

Another important life lesson came from what people shared with me at that tender age. During funerals, people would sit me down and share their thoughts, what I now consider wisdom. It was usually older people and grandparents saying things like, "I should

have done this with this person who had passed; I wish we had done that, but we didn't." I was too little then to understand why this was so important. I thought to myself, why wouldn't you just talk to this person, forgive this person, take that trip or whatever? I didn't fully comprehend the impact this would have on me at the time, but I promised myself that I would never grow up and say, "I shoulda, coulda, woulda… but I didn't." I promised myself that I would do my best to live every day to its fullest, to live a life of no regrets.

Thinking back now, my journey to "live my life to its fullest" began when I was about eight years old. My mom loved to travel but we didn't have a lot of money growing up. So, she started a separate savings account she called the "travel account." Every couple of years, we (my younger brother, my mom, and sometimes my dad and I) would pick a destination and save up enough so we could travel. This planning allowed us to do so much, so that when we did travel, we got to do it all.

When I was eight, my mom told my brother and I that she booked a cruise to Mexico for the four of us. She told me to pick an activity at one of the ports—I chose parasailing. She said, "OK, it's $50 per person to go parasailing, so it's your job over the next few years to save up enough money so that the whole family can go."

I started saving little by little—helping my mom by filing at her office, doing things around the house, helping my grandparents, and babysitting (because we could back then at that age). Let me tell you how empowering it was to know that at ten years old, I paid for my family to go parasailing in Mexico. It felt AMAZING! I felt like a part of the process, I got to participate, to share and to help. I loved that feeling. I loved to travel. I made a wish then that I could find a way to travel the world and get paid for it.

My parents were very busy when I was growing up. My mom was in nursing school and working full-time. My dad was a Marine, which meant he was gone a lot. When he was home, he worked for a movie studio, which was a two-hour drive away just to get there.

Neither parent was home much, and that left my younger brother and I at home alone most of the time. Looking back now, I see that I had one of two choices: I could either be home alone, feeling abandoned, or I could feel included, alive and happy traveling with my family. I preferred us together, happy and traveling. Being able to help plan our family's travel made me feel included and important.

I get emotional just thinking about this now. As I write this story tears are forming. I had no idea how impactful this really was for me as a child or what it would eventually mean for me as an adult years later.

Travel had been an important part of our family's culture going back generations. Hundreds of years ago, on my mom's side, we were Vikings, traveling and exploring the world by ship. My great-great grandfather wrote a book called "The American Pioneer," about our family making the trip across Canada down to California for the gold rush. My great grandmother loved road trips in the RV during summer vacations and my mom and grandmother still travel all over the world. They recently returned from the Arctic Circle and have already planned their next trip to Greece and the Holy Land.

As kids, we traveled often but we didn't always go far. Sometimes it was camping or a quick trip to the beach, a day trip to Magic Mountain or a weekend to Yosemite National Park. Other times we jetted around the world by air, land or sea to Alaska, the Caribbean or Mexico. I'd visited more places before I could drive than most people see in a lifetime. I don't have a single favorite place I like to go—I have many favorite places for different reasons. We continue to travel together as a family today and although I can't remember what I received as a child for Christmas every year, I can tell you about every trip we ever went on. Those memories I'll carry with me forever, whereas the material items came and went.

In my late teens, I was the assistant tour director on an escorted bus tour of Australia and New Zealand. We had 29 passengers in all, 11 of them were my family members. It was a bucket list trip for my

grandfather, and I was so excited to make it happen for him. I was in my element and I loved it!

The one thing I loved the most in the world was travel but I didn't know how to really make a living doing it. Didn't everyone want to travel the world and get paid? But who really made a living traveling and how did they do it? As I was wrapping up high school trying to figure out what exactly I wanted to do, I considered my options. I thought about working for a cruise ship, but unfortunately, they were not hiring at the time. I could have worked in the hospitality sector, but being a receptionist at a hotel wasn't really my idea of a fun job that would allow me to travel. So, what was I to do then?

I should have spent more time figuring out how to make a living in travel. I should have figured out a way to make money doing what I love… but I didn't. Instead of trying to find a way to get paid to travel, I went on to do other things, and although these other things taught me a great deal of business skills, over time I became unfulfilled.

I enrolled in college figuring that I would eventually find a way to make a living doing what I love. Instead I found myself struggling to pay the bills. I did what I thought I was "supposed to do" and got a job while still taking classes. I had many different types of jobs and usually more than one at a time.

I did things because they were easy to fit into a full load at school like being a server at a restaurant or working at the gym. I could easily pick my hours and work as little or as much as I needed to. Other jobs I did because honestly, I was money driven. Commission-based opportunities like being a mortgage broker or multi-level-marketer had promises of big payouts and being able to live the life I always dreamed of—having the time and money to travel the world. But instead of following my dreams, and figuring out a way to make money working *in* travel all along, I was following a dollar sign that I could never really catch. These jobs were exciting at first because they were new and challenging, both of which I like, but I still hadn't found my

purpose in life. No matter how hard I tried, I never felt truly fulfilled.

I went all the way through a Master's Program for International Business while I was working full-time. I had forgotten what made me happy. I had forgotten that feeling I had when I was traveling with my family as a child because I was in a place where I didn't get to do it as much. I was out on my own, didn't have the time or money to travel, and thinking about it now, I didn't have anyone to travel with. I had long veered off the path of trying to figure out how to make a living traveling the world.

Then I met Eric. An incredible man who is now my husband and the love of my life. One of the many reasons I fell in love with him is because he is a man of his word. When he said he would do something with me, he would. We all have those friends who, when we talk about going somewhere or doing something, will be like "yeah, let's do that." But then when it comes down to it, they always find a reason not to. Eric was never like that. He would say, "yeah, let's do it", and then he would actually go with me. Road trips, museums, food experiences and theater—it didn't matter what it was—he was game for it.

We did all kinds of things together, we visited Yellowstone National Park, drove all through the Colorado Rockies seeing places like the Great Dunes National Park, Indian Hot Springs and Durango for example. We had adventures that included things like sling shot bungees, snorkeling, hot air balloon rides, historic town tours, and seven-mile hikes.

My love for travel and adventure became invigorated with a new energy. I was being pulled to see the world again, and I found someone who wanted to come with me to see it—someone I could share my love for the world with, someone I could share my travel stories and experiences with. Now this was something I could do all day and not feel like I was working.

The feelings that I had as a child started to come back to me. I remembered how much I loved to travel and that I had once wanted

to figure out a way to make a living traveling the world. What happened next was almost a subconscious manifestation. "I can do this," I thought. That is when the door cracked open—the door of opportunity. The one the universe conspires to provide once we start believing in the possibilities. It didn't happen right away, but it did happen.

It started at a networking event in Dallas, Texas. That is where I met Lucinda. We connected first over her statement of what she did for a living. She said, "I specialize in chocolate cruises and food experiences"… Say what? What does that mean? We started talking and quickly bonded over our mutual love for travel. She had done many other things in her life, too, before she found her passion as a travel agent about four years earlier. She enjoyed the freedom that being a travel agent provides, the flexibility of traveling often and being able to have a mobile office to name a few.

She asked me then if I was a travel agent. I told her I wasn't, and she asked why. I said, "Why would I charge my friends and family for something I already do for free?" She laughed a bit and said, "You know it doesn't work that way anymore?"

No, I didn't know that. "How do travel agents get paid then?" I wondered.

As the internet started to really grow back in the 1990's, the way in which travel agents got paid started to change. Vendors and suppliers would pay travel agents; not customers. Basically, suppliers like cruise lines, hotel chains, shore excursion companies, and transportation suppliers pay travel agents to bring their clients to them. That means, it doesn't cost travelers anything to work with a travel agent.

Lucinda and I scheduled a time to meet for lunch and what was supposed to be an 30-60 minute "get to know you lunch", turned into a four-hour life-changing meeting. By the end of it, I was working as a travel agent for her travel agency. I had taken a purposeful step in the direction of my passion for the first time in my life!

I was so excited to be working in the travel industry. I was able to help people experience some of what I experienced in my travels. I

was now able to help people with their family's first trip, or a bucket list trip that someone had always wanted to do, but didn't think they could. It felt amazing.

I had been saying for years that I didn't feel fulfilled and that I needed to find my purpose. I didn't really know what that was though. Of course, I knew I loved travel and that I *wanted* to make a living traveling the world. But I didn't *really* know that being a travel agent was my purpose in life, until it was. Everything started to fall into place. The right people were coming into my life and I felt a peace I had never known before. I was where I was supposed to be.

All the places I have been, all the experiences I've had, have all lead me here. Even the many jobs I've had over the years have helped me prepare for this point in my life. They created a solid foundation of who I am as a person and the accumulation of all those many skills were now supporting me in what I was doing.

Even with those foundational skills, the first year as a travel agent was tough. I had to learn a lot of travel industry back-end systems, which are different than what a consumer uses and sees. I was taking class after class, workshop after workshop to learn everything I could as fast as I could. Something important struck me then: Even when I was doing the mundane day-to-day tasks, I wasn't bored; I was driven. I wasn't looking for another job or opportunity, I was looking to grow and expand on the one I had. That is when I knew I had stepped into my purpose and it felt empowering.

I was really happy booking travel for my friends and family. Over time they began suggesting I start my own company. I was in the right place, at the right time for me and this new business. I had been thinking about starting my own company for a while. I was extremely grateful for Lucinda and the opportunity she gave me, and I wanted to build on that for myself. I had envisioned a company that was my own, one that I could grow the way I wanted to, with my own branding and marketing. The seed of possibility had been planted.

My husband has always been supportive of everything I had ever

done, and I, too, of him. Not too long after we first discussed my idea of having my own travel agency, he got a job offer in Colorado Springs, Colorado. It was everything that he had ever wanted—it was his dream job. The offer was too good to pass up, so we sold our house in Garland, Texas and moved to Colorado Springs.

This move ended up being the perfect opportunity for me to start my own travel agency. New place, new people, new business—why not? I already had a database of clients and I had the support of my family and friends. In order to move forward I had to be brave enough to do it, and to believe in myself. To be all-in. *Truly all-in.* Not half-way or "kinda." Not just dipping my toe in the water. I had to give it my all.

I decided to give myself permission to do it, to start my own travel agency and follow my dreams. I let fear pass me by and grabbed the opportunity to be fulfilled by my greater causes and higher purposes in life.

I started my company MyTravel4Ever, a full-service travel agency, in November of 2016 and I have not looked back. And even as I type this now, I'm overrun with emotion. It has been the best thing I could have done for myself. I am truly fulfilled and living my purpose for the first time in my life.

My agency currently focuses on custom trips, family trips, cruises, group tours and retreats. Like most things, I know over time my company will evolve. I may team up with a tour operator or become a travel blogger. I could focus on a particular type of travel, like cruising or I could become specialized in a certain destination like Spain or Japan. The point is, now that I have found what I am supposed to be doing with my life, my focus can be on honing the skills I need to become the best in my field. I'm in the travel industry, which is where I am supposed to be. The sky is the limit as to what I decide to do with this company, now that I have found my purpose. I get to spend the rest of my life playing in an industry that I love and, by having my own company, I have the freedom to change, grow, and

become whatever my heart desires. I am now living that promise I made to my five-year-old self, to live life to its fullest, to live a life of no regrets.

Phoenix Sagen owns a full-service travel agency, MyTravel4Ever, in Colorado Springs, Colorado. She began her travel career planning vacations for her family and eventually began booking business trips for friends and hosting escorted tours around the world. She is a Travel Specialist, a certified Tour Director and Travel Agent specializing in custom trips, group tours and family vacations. While adventure travel is popular, she is also well-versed in luxury destinations. She thinks it's important to match the proper destination and product to the client. Over the years, she has traveled to many destinations and loves sharing her knowledge and experiences with her clientele via her blog on her website and her video blog on Facebook.

Both Phoenix and her husband Eric love to incorporate their love of biking and staying active into their vacations. Favorite vacations include zip-lining through Mexico, hiking in Canada and France, Glacier hopping in Alaska and snorkeling the beautiful waters of the Caribbean. Be it a scenic river cruise or a glamorous ocean liner, cruising remains one of her favorite means of travel. In fact, her bucket list includes taking a world cruise. Find Phoenix at: Facebook.com/MyTravel4Ever, MyTravel4Ever.com, or MyTravel4Ever@yahoo.com.

Power as One

by Claire Kadlecek

These are tumultuous times... There is awkwardness between friends where there use to be ease. I hear on the news that school and family reunion attendance is at an all-time low. I understand why... my sisters (in-laws, but I love them like sisters) visited last weekend and nothing major has changed for any of us. I have always been the city slicker, tree hugging, liberal yogi, who eats organically, and has a few too many hippie ideas. They are somewhat conservative from a small town in the Midwest who enjoy country music, hanging out, reading, gardening, motorcycles, and guns. But our different backgrounds have never been an issue, ever. Laughter, respect for each other, inside jokes, and support have been paramount to our relationships. Yet, something was different... simple conversations seemed to lead to paths that were off limits or might

bring up topics where we wouldn't agree… so there was silence instead of joyous laughter.

For me, it isn't just the current political environment, but also the fears brought up by going back to the 8-5 corporate world after 10 years of raising kids and trying to make a living as a yoga teacher. It's been interesting to watch the expectations of my family, my friends and my co-workers. We all see life from our own perspectives, but when things shift, it can become uncomfortable. My "shitty" perspective on life today leaves me feeling uncomfortable. No matter how open to change I think I am, in truth, I don't handle change well.

As I head back to the corporate work world, I find myself feeling like a failure. I tried for almost 10 years to "make it" as a yoga teacher, to live the life that I want to live, doing what I like to do, but no matter how I tried, the money wasn't there. I tried attracting abundance through positive thinking, changing my intentions, putting them out to the Universe, meditating on it, visualizing my abundance, creating vision boards… you name it, I've tried it.

Ten years ago, I was Vice President of Operations for a small Telecom Expense Management (TEM) company, and now… I'm 10 years older. I just accepted a job as an Inventory Manager at a large TEM company, earning not much more than I made 10 years ago. And, to add insult to injury, many of the folks that worked for me are now in higher up positions than me. Not exactly the success story I was hoping for!

Today's political environment coupled with whatever "situation" feels uncomfortable, has created a fear based society. I see it everywhere! Fear of finding a job at my age, fear of refugees who have religions that we don't understand, fear of whether to vaccinate our children, worrying about GMO food, whether the government is conspiring against us, or "fill in the blank" with whatever feels uncomfortable for you.

And when I get uncomfortable, doubt in my belief system follows. I believe on the surface, but underneath believe less and less as

scenario after scenario lead to what I deem "failure"... allowing my fears to grow. Eventually I get so angry that I ask myself, "WHAT IS THE POINT?"

Thankfully, most days I don't have my "shitty day" perspective from above, but lately, I seem to dip into those moments more than I'd like. Thus, I am grateful that I've been blessed with an amazing family and set of friends who don't let me fall into the hole of negative thoughts, depression, or addiction, but instead help me find the silver lining, the reason to laugh and to see my value. Demonstrating the Power as One.

Portia Nelson's poem spoke to me as she describes life's learning process of how to walk in to conscious flow.

"Chapter One of My Life: I walk down the street. There's a deep hole in the sidewalk. I fall in.

I am lost. I am helpless. It isn't my fault. It takes forever to find a way out.

Chapter Two: I walk down the same street. There's a deep hole in the sidewalk. I pretend I don't see it. I fall in again. I can't believe I'm in the same place! But it isn't my fault. And it still takes a long time to get out.

Chapter Three: I walk down the same street. There's a deep hole in the sidewalk. I see it there. I still fall in. It's a habit! My eyes are open. I know where I am. It is my fault. I get out immediately.

Chapter Four: I walk down the same street. There's a deep hole in the sidewalk. I walk around it.

Chapter Five: I walk down a different street."

My intention behind sharing the following stories is to remind myself how to step through my fears when I get in a space of doubt. I hope they also inspire others to step through fears that show up as boundaries and instead step into the harmonic, universal flow to more quickly get out of the holes in our lives.

Power as One – It is the philosophy of a single, intelligent Consciousness that pervades the entire Universe. It is all knowing, all powerful, all creative and always present. There is but One Consciousness of which your consciousness must be a part and "a part" you are, as am I. So, since we are all part of The Consciousness – no matter what you call it, God, Allah, Spirit, Universe, conclusively we are one. My actions towards myself or others directly affect everyone, as do yours. The ancient blessing Namaste says, "I honor the place in you where Spirit lives, I honor the place in you which is of Love, of Truth, of Light, of Peace. When you are in that place in you, and I am in that place in me, then we are One."

Recognize – Triggers in life, like feeling uncomfortable, stuck, dis-ease, bored, angry, complacent, abused, or hurt help me recognize that I need to stop and take a strong look at the situation. When I feel out of control, I remember that the one thing I control in life is my reaction, so if I am in a situation that doesn't serve or resonate with me, I can choose to remove myself; sometimes physically, emotionally, or just to collect my thoughts. I recognize the hole. I remember I have a choice in my action. No matter how hopeless the situation, I have the choice to consciously remain or to shift.

Leave the situation – Go on a trip, ask for help, find an adventure, drive a different way to work, emotionally or mentally shift, or choose a different street to walk down. After college, I went out west with my best friend, Lori. We drove from state to state, park to park (St. Louis arch, Garden of the Gods, Rocky Mountain National Park, Devil's Tower, Wall Drugs, Mount Rushmore, Yellowstone, Flaming Gorge, Great Salt Lake, La Brea tar pits, Yosemite and ended at the Grand Canyon), camping or staying with friends, relatives, friends of relatives, friends of friends… many we didn't know, but they all

welcomed us, and we enjoyed recounting our adventures and listening to theirs. It was all new, and all exciting! Nothing like the South where I grew up. We were pioneers in our own lives discovering the unknown and finding out more about life, ourselves, and each other as we went. Getting to know strangers in this way increases our tolerance for diversity and ties us more into the Power as One.

Open your mind – Pay attention to what shows up. There are so many new and exciting ideas and experiences available in our world. As a young person working three jobs, I had little time at home, so instead of paying rent, I gave up the walls and spent most of a year living out of a tent on the Mogollon Rim in Northern Arizona with several friends. I experienced many things that opened my mind more than I knew possible: Astrology, numerology, telepathy, UFOs, reiki, shiatsu massage, moxa, homeopathics, aromatherapy, acupuncture, cycling, hiking, climbing, yoga, and meditation. When I moved back inside for the winter from my tent adventure, I could still fit all my worldly possessions in a Toyota Camry. But still my rule remained: When I run out of shampoo, it's time to move on. Being flexible and going with what showed up allowed me to raft through the Grand Canyon three times and bike, yes pedal, over 900 miles, from Vancouver, Canada to San Francisco, California.

When I was 24, I spent two weeks house sitting in Calistoga, California alone. I knew no one, there was no Facebook or internet and long distance calls cost money, so I was really alone and there wasn't even a TV at the house. What an impact these experiences would have on being alone with myself and allowing necessary experiences to flow into my life. Being open frees not only the mind, but also the senses beyond limitations. Intuition, the sixth sense, is naturally enhanced from spending time outside! Outside is expansive and there aren't any walls to limit my ideas or imagination. Walls create boundaries and limits, so when I am feeling restricted, I go outside. While in Calistoga I read Richard Bach's book, *Illusions: The Adventures of*

a Reluctant Messiah. "I do not exist to impress the world. I exist to live my life in a way that will make me happy." This helped me learn how to be happy from my essence. I'd listen to my gut when meeting people or entering into new situations. In *Mutant Message Down Under* by Marlo Morgan, she gets to walk with aborigines and learn how they interact with land, nature, and the world outside of material possessions! So now when I'm feeling the fear of lack, I often ask myself, "what is really important and necessary to bring joy to my life?" More "things" require more work, more responsibility, and more stress to maintain that lifestyle.

Life is a mirror – When I keep getting the same lesson again and again, I ask myself, "What do *I* need to learn?" Recently, I lost a group of friends because of perspective. Our group did lots of fun things together, but there were underlying stories playing in the background. Stories of jealously, being left out, dishonesty and mistrust. As the group did more and more things together and members started spending time together in different capacities, individual "stories" started to show up more frequently. Instead of becoming closer to each other, insecurities and fears grew and eventually the uncomfortable circumstances exploded. Necessary conversations about perceived feelings weren't had, and the relationships ended with no discussion. Assumptions from one-sided perceptions clouded communication. People's own insecurities were projected onto the group. Interestingly, we all felt betrayed. Each of us did what we thought was right, however, since necessary conversations didn't take place, resentments, jealousy, and suspicion became reality.

Since "life is a mirror," I had to look in the mirror, understand how the shoe fit, try it on and then move forward with a better, more compassionate understanding of how to avoid the same lesson again. I re-evaluated who I was spending time with. I had more open conversations with my friends when something felt uncomfortable and talked openly about my intentions to avoid misunderstandings.

Often when we blame someone else, we need to hold up that mirror and understand that it is often a reflection of ourselves. Don't expect them to change! My husband, Craig, reminds me that I shouldn't apologize for who I am. He lets me be me. I am eternally grateful that I have a great guy who makes me laugh, and supports me in knowing that I am enough and worthy. For more on feeling like you are "not enough", seek the expert Brene Brown in her book, *The Gifts of Imperfection.*

Choose food wisely – My diet is often an indicator of how I feel. It took me until I had children to recognize my own low blood sugar issues. I didn't know that when I started my day with pancakes for breakfast that my blood sugar would spike and then tank. It's like the Snickers commercials that talk about not being yourself. Some of us eat when emotional, surround ourselves with weight as a barrier against the world or starve ourselves. For me, I would stand in front of the pantry full of food and not see anything worth eating. That's how I know that I'm not happy. Food is our essence. What we eat is indicative of how we nurture ourselves. I now recognize that I am worthy of eating the most nutritious food that helps feed my soul which shows that I truly love myself. Read *Mindful Eating* by Jan Chozen Bays for more on soulful eating.

Surround yourself with loving people – If you are constantly judgmental, angry, sad, or unhappy, look to see who you are surrounding yourself with. Are they constantly judgmental, angry, sad, or unhappy? Instead, choose traits that reflect how you would like to feel: positive, optimistic, adventurous, and energetic. I have always been blessed with groups of amazing friends. One group that sticks out was called Women's Journey. My friend, Laurel, started the group to bring a group of women closer on real topics. It couldn't have been timelier for me. I was new to Castle Rock, didn't have many close friends nearby, was at a new job, and was recently married. Lots of

"new" which is always uncomfortable for me. I couldn't have been more inspired, loved, or emotionally supported by and connected to this group of ladies. We are still close today, even though we don't see each other nearly enough. They are and will always be a blessing in my life!

Everyone is doing their best – Remembering that everyone is doing their best is the way that I come most quickly into a space of compassion. It is so very easy to get angry with others and see them as horrible, untrustworthy, or disappointing. I took the long road to realize that feeling this way just hardened me and closed my heart. When I'm in that place, I try instead to re-see the person or situation from a place of compassion, knowing that they are doing their best. As a parent, I have a new perspective on what my dad and mom went through, how tired they were at the end of the day and now I can look back and realize that they were doing their best to give me and my brother better opportunities than they had. No one is perfect, even though we often expect that of both ourselves and others. The ability to drop into a place of kindness and vulnerability in order to explain, rationalize, or forgive helps me see people as people who are doing their best. Rumi states, "Out beyond ideas of wrongdoing and right doing there is a field. I'll meet you there. When the soul lies down in that grass the world is too full to talk about."

Create a safe place – When things get tough (and they will get tough!), create a safe place or object that signifies safety. When I was little, I had a stuffed koala name Koley. He had milk chocolate fur and was about 10 inches long. I loved that bear and slept with him every night until college. He smelled safe. He had been loved so much that he needed to be fully "re-covered" so the only part that was original was his oatmeal colored ears, but they smelled like home. In college, I made the choice to give him to my first love to signify my love for him, but unfortunately, he didn't value Koley as I did. I didn't get

him back. Years later, my mom died of cancer and in order to deal with her loss, I started seeing a healer, who encouraged me to visualize my mom and myself doing something together where we were happy. The memory was lying in her bed in the morning, having a hot cup of tea, and talking. Then, afterwards, she encouraged me to think of a thing that might signify that happiness—it was my koala, even though I didn't have him anymore. My daughter heard me talking about the memory and bought me a small brown koala. My new koala is in my car, so I see him every day. My koala is my safe, happy place, just like my mom was for me. It helps me know how much she loved me, and signifies how much my daughter and my family love me.

Open your heart – We moved from England when I was almost four and my deepest memory is more of a feeling than a memory. It is of my Nana Pops. I heard stories of how she loved and played with me, and I saw tons of pictures, but I only "remember" her in my heart. I never saw her again after we moved to America because she died of cancer before we were able to return to visit. When we went back when I was five, I was crushed because I didn't understand why she wasn't there. I believe that experience, among others, hardened me. I became very independent because if I was strong and didn't need anyone then they couldn't hurt me or leave me. I was wrong. Be vulnerable. Be open. Ask for help and allow others to give to you without feeling like you owe them. This lesson is still hard for me, but with the unwavering support (and patience) of my husband, I have finally let my guard down. I learned over many years that I can't keep people away *and* expect to create an intimate connection. It doesn't work that way. It is one or the other. "It is better to have loved and lost, than to have never loved at all." Love is always worth it. The lessons sting, but I have learned to be open and honest with my feelings. They helped me to forgive and forget more quickly. It's what life is about. I now tell people how much I appreciate them

and what a good time I had with them. We all love to be appreciated. In yoga, we do heart-opening asanas. They are a great way to start opening your heart, but don't be surprised if they stir emotions that you didn't know you were hiding.

Synchronicity – Pay attention. Watch, look, and listen so that you don't miss the magic that shows up on your path. There are too many synchronistic experiences that have happened in my life for me to think that we aren't all connected as one. I don't believe there is one omnipotent plan, but I do believe that there is a universal energy that keeps us going down certain paths to learn a lesson or have an experience. This is one of my favorite parts of life. Like when you have been thinking of an old friend and they call. Or when you start reading a book that helps you see your current circumstance from a completely different perspective. Or when your house number shows up as the address locator for your favorite hike. It is all little, but for me it is the magic of life.

Meet them where they are – Recently, I ran into a situation where I couldn't find compassion. From my perspective, a person was abusing their dog. Keeping the dog in a 12x12 cage outside, not giving him any attention, and not letting him out. I called Animal Control, but they told me that the dog was more than likely a hunting dog, so not really seen as a pet. But after several days, I realized, that this person took care of the dog from his perspective: the dog had shelter, was safe from predators, and had food and water. What more did the dog need? This dog's purpose is to retrieve after a hunt. He isn't a pet as much as he is a tool to help with hunting. I can't expect the owner to personalize his dog or treat his dog in the manner that I would. I still don't think the way he treats the dog is right, but it is right from his perspective. It is not my job to change his mind to my way of thinking. I only control my behavior, not the behavior of others. I just have to shift my perspective to meet them where

they are. I can offer my perspective, but I shouldn't expect them to change. This is still tough for me and pushes my boundaries often. I believe that the best way to get someone to raise their vibration is through love, compassion and vulnerability. Another hunter helped me see that he values his dog, but the interaction isn't a warm loving interaction like I have with my animals. He sees the dog like a co-worker, but doesn't desire a relationship. Again, the only thing I control in life is my reaction.

Boundaries – Create some, if you don't have some! I thought that if I "trust" everyone and am nice to everyone, then everyone will be/do the same in return. Wrong! Boundaries are tied to intuition and to creating a level of protection with which to respect ourselves. When I encounter a boundary, I have to decide if I'm going to step in or step out, but either way, I need to pay close attention. I ask myself, "Why does this feel uncomfortable?" Do I feel the discomfort in my body? My gut, my throat, my chest? These triggers show up as discomfort and I often find lessons in the boundaries. And not all boundaries are bad. The older I get, the more I dislike crowds. I get very anxious. But I recognize that and I don't go to large indoor arenas for concerts. I go to Red Rocks, so that I am comfortable in the outdoors. Boundaries keep us safe. Which is why I say, if you don't have any, get some! But, they can also isolate us if we have too many. Find the balance.

Detach – Detach from outcomes, material things, and sometimes people. This is one of the most important lessons that I have come to "mostly" understand. We all have expectations, and when those expectations aren't met, we often get a little ruffled, or just down right pissed. But similar to meeting people where they are, I work on remembering to detach from how I think they "should" be. In fact, I have removed that nasty "should" word from my vocabulary. I have opinions. That doesn't make me right and other people

wrong. When it feels like I am pushing to make something happen, I back off because if it doesn't come from a sense of ease, then I'm not in Universal flow, I'm in ego. And if I can detach from my expectation, then I find that life is much more pleasant. Surrender—go with the flow, see what shows up and read the *Surrender Experiment* by Michael Singer. It helped me understand the need to detach, meditate, and surrender to the flow. I also loved, *How Yoga Works* by Geshe Michail Roach. It speaks more to abusive situations and shifting within them.

Receive – I came to realize that if I wasn't allowing others to give to me or vice versa, then I don't have a relationship. It is one sided. I have often felt the desire to do something nice for others, but for years, I realized that I had expectations tied to my giving. I wanted a thank you or appreciation. It was conditional. And I would often get annoyed when the person didn't react the way I wanted or didn't reciprocate. I was being needy. I was expecting them to fulfill my expectation. And worse, when someone gave me something or offered to help me, I would feel indebted to them so I wouldn't accept the help. These are one sided relationships, not letting anyone in or opening my heart. We need others, and nearly all of us desire love and acceptance from others. Needing others is human nature and helps us to see our human side, but it also requires us to be vulnerable – to give without expectations of receiving, to receive without the ability to give back. When we can do these things, our hearts open wider and we view the world more lovingly. We also need to receive guidance from our higher power. I listen daily, am open, intuitive, and receptive in order to be in the flow. As the flight attendants tell us, put the oxygen mask on yourself first and then help your loved ones. If we don't take care of ourselves, then how can we take care of others?

Be Soft – This is probably my greatest challenge. I have been so hard for so long that my re-action is to snap, yell, or be sarcastic. A healer taught me to look for the little girl within when I am in a mood and seem to be offending or angry at everyone. Obviously, that little girl got her feelings hurt and is now being defensive and having a temper tantrum. Recognizing why I am hurt and then picturing Little Claire will often allow me to drop back into my softer self so that I can apologize and admit why I was acting so pissy. We all have a Little Self. I found a great picture of myself when I was about five in pigtails, looking a little guilty and sullen. This is the picture I conjure in my mind to help me move through my shitty moments. I also try to remember that everyone has a little person within them and that when they act defensive, it is because something about the situation hurt them. It helps me drop into a space of compassion so much faster.

Ego and Pride – These shouldn't be allowed to rule your life. How do I know if it is? When I feel the need to be right, or convince others to see things my way. When I feel like I'm pushing to make something happen. When everything in life feels exhausting. How do I stop ego or my mind from ruling rather than my heart? First, I observe that I am in this place, have the desire to shift, and then ask to change. I take time daily to sit in meditation, reflection, with nature or in prayer. I listen to my guides, my spirit family, inner guidance (my daughter calls hers Antonio) and source (spirit, angels, God, Universe, or whatever you call the Source that pulls it all together). I quiet my monkey mind. And, if my thoughts or to-dos won't shut off, then I ask for my mind to be quiet and for the heart to speak. Be soft and receive. When I am unsure if my behavior comes from ego, I will watch nature or animals to see how they interact or what is the "norm" because animals don't have egos. Seeking balance is something that the planet, animals, and nature do constantly. Seek to find balance. Look up, "How wolves change rivers" to read about

how the reintroduction of wolves into Yellowstone park changed the entire park's balance. Animals work cooperatively, not competitively. They don't take more than they need and they step outside of their boundaries when needed to help another species. Look up, "How trees talk" for more examples. Alternate nostril breathing also helps me to calm my mind. It is a fantastic way to calm my nervous system so that I can be in rest and release rather than flight or fight.

Laughter – It is a gift and the best medicine! My son has the funniest sense of humor. I love just spending time with him because he lifts my spirits every time. The other night, we were having dinner in wine country. The restaurant told the kids to help themselves to the fruit juice bar, so Collin got his cranberry juice in a wine glass and proceeded to swirl it around and take a deep inhale before swishing it around in his mouth like he saw the other patrons doing with their wine. Our waitress took a double take to make sure he wasn't drinking alcohol… such a smart-aleck. My question earlier about, "What's the point?" is answered every time I laugh. It is about the relationships that are spent creating laughter. Whether I am in a foul mood and my friends pull me out or whether we are just hanging out. The best part of my life by far is laughing with my family and friends. I couldn't feel more blessed to have found a husband who makes me laugh. It is the number one quality that everyone should look for in a mate. The level of gratitude that I feel towards my groups (and they are many) of friends is too large for words. They are the reason I smile and how I muster the energy on shitty days to get on with life. And although, we sometimes trigger each other, staying in touch and reaching out to continue those relationships is worth all the time and effort in the world for what I get in return… the laughter.

I've been back at work now for two months and it certainly started

as a little bit of a roller coaster as I watched old patterns reemerge, but instead of re-acting, I found myself feeling pretty proud that I remembered to pause and think about the tools above. The first day of my new job, my boss and the guy that hired me got laid off as the company merged with another company... my new boss wasn't sure why I was hired and her new boss was still getting his arms around his new department... talk about change layered in chaotic change. As they were figuring out their new roles, I was sort of forgotten and given no information, so without the perspective of actually knowing how I could be of value, I became frustrated. I started to go back to my old re-actions—stepping in with a forceful, condescending attitude, taking charge because it didn't look to me like anyone else was and pushing forward. Thankfully, I recognized pretty quickly that I was going back to an old story.

Since I work from home, I was able to walk away from work for about an hour. I walked out back and sat with my son having lunch in the warm afternoon sun and gained perspective. My tools above came back to me and I was able to regroup, and remember my priorities—myself, family, friends, and the joy of being part of the flow. It occurred to me that all that positive energy, meditation, vision board stuff did help after all... it helped shape me into being mindful. After lunch, I went back to work with a new sense of calm. I let the situation play out and relaxed into the flow rather than forcing my way through it. Plus, my friend, Paula, reached out to check in on me and I became exceedingly grateful for going back to a situation with friends present. I've reconnected with several friends and we've had some pretty "real" conversations about stress and priorities. We've felt safe enough with each other to share our fears, to be "real" despite our differences and most importantly, we've agreed to support each other through the creation of healthy boundaries. The discomfort has passed and I actually like my new schedule, job, and co-workers. So, stepping past the boundaries that my mind had presented worked out. I'm not a failure. I feel such joy as I experience life

balance, love from my family, and laughter with new and old friends. Mostly, I'm pleased with myself for learning from my life lessons and loving myself. Gotta love perspective…

Many a healer has guided me to learn that the secret to combatting discomfort was with me all the time. That once I saw myself as "enough", as valuable, and as worthy, I had found "the point." Even though I deemed myself a failure, my new perspective is that I am valuable and I'll take my skills with me into the next lesson.

I know I don't have all the answers! There are still days when I play out my old stories and fall in the hole. And, even though I haven't quite learned to walk down a different street, at least I recognize the hole and I know how to get out. I am so thankful for the loving support of those who reach down into the hole and pull me out, so that I don't stay there long. I do know that the experiences that I mentioned above have made my life much happier and, I believe, my consciousness vibration higher. There is much more for me to learn and I can't wait to see what choices are ahead. My hope is that my lessons can bring us all closer to recognizing our Power as One.

Claire Kadlecek enjoys life in Castle Pines, Colorado with her two wonderful children and her husband. She tries to get outside daily to hike, bike, run, paddleboard or at least sit on the deck and watch the wildlife. Any activity that rewards her with being present like yoga, mountain biking or climbing are near and dear to her heart, but her favorite past time is laughing with her friends and family.

Trusting Blindly

by Karen Montoya

The wonderful things you will find when you aren't even looking...

This is a story based on love, hope, trust, and faith. It all began when my younger sister Helen asked me if I would like to go on a cruise with her in 1997 as she had found a great deal. Keep in mind, I was 24 years old and had never left my country, South Africa.

When she first asked, I was thinking we were going to Cape Town on a cruise, but OH NO! Helen had much bigger ideas for us. We were going to Miami on a Western Caribbean cruise! My initial thought was, are you CRAZY?! I am not going to travel for 18 hours and then be stuck on a ship for a week. You must be out of your mind, Helen! Although hesitant at first, you've probably already guessed she convinced me it would be a great adventure.

Boy o boy, little did I know at the time that by agreeing to go, both our lives would change in such a dramatic way that I could

never have imagined even in my wildest dreams—or maybe I did. So off we went, not knowing that this was the starting point that would put everything else in motion.

I recall being in my early twenties and looking out of my office window thinking how wonderful it would be to travel the world. I wanted to go to Italy, Paris, London, Switzerland and see it all. At the time I was not earning a lot of money. I was living with an abusive boyfriend and did not think I would ever be able to travel like that. Somehow since then, many years later, I have manifested that into my life and have been blessed to have traveled to all those places and more.

When my diabetic father passed away at the young age of 45 from organ failure, he left a little money for my sister and me. So, with the generosity of his gift, our adventure started in Miami. The first night we got to Miami, I was a bit nervous. Here we were, two young girls from South Africa, only knowing America from what I had seen in the movies or on TV. Of course, I told my sister we needed to walk on the opposite side of the road so that if those vans you see on TV try to kidnap us, it would not be so easy for "them." You know, those vans with the tinted windows that you cannot see into. The ones they use to kidnap people in the movies… Needless to say, we made it to the cruise ship the next day.

I remember having a conversation with my grandmother when I was very young. I must have been maybe 10 years old or so, asking her how do you know when you meet the right person to marry. How do you know if he is THE ONE? She told me that you just KNOW. I had forgotten about this conversation with my grandmother when I met my husband years later. As I am telling the story now, I remember that conversation.

We boarded the ship *Imagination,* and the first night of the cruise my sister met El's friend. El and his friend were going to go on a different cruise but as it turned out the person that was organizing their cruise was getting married and was no longer able to get them the

deal. As fate would have it, they instead ended up on the same cruise as Helen and I. It was unbelievable how all these things fell into place for us to meet. Back then I did not really think about it, but today it all makes sense. I do believe that nothing is coincidence and that everything happens for a reason.

I met El the second day of the cruise. As I was talking to him, getting to know him a bit, the only thing I could think was WOW, what a nice guy! I just really like this guy. Keep in mind I still had a boyfriend back home and was not really looking to meet anyone. I told El about my boyfriend, and he was the perfect gentleman.

We got to know each other over the week we spent together on the cruise, enjoying dinners together as a group and going on all the excursions. At the end of the week, we all exchanged emails. I did not have a computer or an email address at the time, so Helen exchanged her email. El mentioned that he would love to come to South Africa and visit me. I said, of course, no problem, thinking we would never see each other again. I mean come on, I lived on the other side of the world! It felt like it was a friendly farewell for him to say.

Once back in South Africa, El started to email and it was always such a treat when Helen called to tell me about it. She would proceed to read the message and then we would decide together what to reply. Eventually, El decided to start calling me. It worked out great as I was working night shifts and with the time difference it was perfect. El would call and we would talk for hours on the phone. To this day I am not sure how much his phone bills were.

Come to think of it, I never really thought of how blessed and lucky I am to have a man that traveled across the world to come and get me. The kicker of it is he does not even like flying, and it is about 18 hours to get to South Africa. So, as you can you see it must have been LOVE! You just never know where you will find love, especially when you are not looking.

I was still living with my verbally abusive boyfriend. This was a relationship that I had invested in for six years. I had tried to leave

him a few times before, but that did not work out so well. I knew one thing for sure, I was never going to marry that man. The first time he got physically abusive with me I decided that I was not going to accept that and finally got out of the relationship.

During all this, El was still phoning and once I told him that I left my boyfriend, he asked if he could come visit. We met in 1997 on the cruise for the first time, and he was now coming to visit me in South Africa in November 1998.

I was so nervous to see him in person, not knowing what to expect. He was coming to visit for a month. I asked my godmother if he could stay with her and she said absolutely not. He was my guest and my responsibility. We had been talking on the phone, but now we were going to be face to face. I was not sure I would recognize him or that he would recognize me!

My aunt and cousin accompanied me the day we went to the airport to pick him up. I showed my aunt his photo and she was going to be the welcoming committee. When I saw him again at the airport, I immediately recognized him. I was excited and scared at the same time.

I was afraid we would have nothing to say to each other. At first, it was a bit uncomfortable between us, but it did not take long for us to get back in the groove of our conversations. We were so comfortable with each other.

I was living in a small town that did not have much going for it in the way of tourist attractions, and not able to get the time off that I had hoped for to show him around South Africa. I did not want him coming all this way, and all he had to show for it was seeing my small town and my apartment. I was able to show him around Johannesburg, Pretoria, and we spent time at Sun City and also Pilansburg, a small game reserve.

He met my family, and they immediately liked him and spent weekends with us visiting what we could in the nearby vicinity. I really wanted him to see the wine country and Cape Town. We booked

him a tour for a week which he enjoyed immensely. It gave him a better idea of what South Africa was all about.

It was so nice to see him again and spend more time with him. It was lovely getting to know him a bit better. When he left, I knew I would see him again in January 1999 as we decided to go on another cruise to America with my family. I did not know what would happen with our relationship. The only thing I knew was that I would be seeing him again soon.

I had strong feelings for him, but did not even think about marriage. Before he left, he asked me if I had ever thought of living in America. I said no, I have never thought about it and why would I want to do that? Oh my, that one flew right over my head!

He asked if I would be willing to come to America and offered to purchase a return ticket for me. If I did not like America after the six months allowed by my visitor visa, I could always go back home to South Africa. Later I would find out that El had talked to my aunt and told her he wanted to marry me. He asked her if she thought I would say yes.

January arrived, and you will never guess the name of our ship for this Eastern Caribbean cruise. Wait for it… DESTINY! It was on this cruise that El asked me to marry him. Every day he would tie the ring in his swimming trunks so as not to lose it. On our last excursion to the island of Saint John, El decided that it was the right time to propose.

The group of us had been walking on the beach spending time enjoying the day. Right before we needed to get to the bus to return to the ship, El decided it was now or never and asked me to walk one last time with him on the beach alone. I said why do you want to do that? We just got back from walking on the beach, and I did not want to miss the bus. It took some convincing from him, my aunt and family as they knew what was up.

Of course, I was clueless. So, after huffing and puffing and making El promise we would not be that long we walked on the beach.

He got down on one knee as the tide was pulling him into the ocean and asked me to marry him. I said yes, and the wild ride began.

On March 1, 1999, I arrived in America with my suitcase in hand and a few Rand in my purse. Not much at all. I had sold my car, quit my job, gave up my apartment, sold all my furniture, left my sister and family behind in South Africa and off I went. I thought to myself at the time, if things did not work out, I could always go back home.

We got married on August 6, 1999, in the civil court in Colorado. I met his sisters for the first time the day of the wedding. They drove in from Albuquerque. It was a hot summer's day. El's best friend David, David's wife Chris, son, and El's three sisters and brother-in-law all attended our wedding along with a few more of his friends. I was very emotional and missed my family. El said we could have another wedding back in South Africa for my family.

We had our second wedding on October 9, 1999, in South Africa. I had a beautiful white wedding gown, my family and friends to share the day with, and we danced the night away. We celebrate the October 9 wedding day as we consider this date to be our REAL wedding day.

Let me tell you the first year in America was not easy. I am a very independent woman, and it was hard for me to not be able to earn money, drive, or have friends. I literally stepped into El's world. It was his home, his things. His friends. The only person I really knew was El. My whole life revolved around him. Not that it was bad or good, and El did everything he could to make me feel supported.

El was always very encouraging and said that everything he had was mine. I could decorate our townhome as I wished. If I wanted to work, I could, and if I wanted to stay home, he would be okay with that also.

We lived in Aurora, Colorado and traveled a lot that first year within the US with El's job. Much of it was a blur that I cannot remember. While the traveling was fun, I also remember feeling very lonely, missing my family, not liking the fact that I could not work,

and it bothered me that I was not contributing to the household.

I felt I had to work, I had to get out of the house and contribute, be my own person. Finally, I was able to get a work visa, I did get a job, I did make friends and met some of the most amazing people. I made a life for myself in a new country with a different culture far away from everything I knew with El cheering me on all along the way.

I started working in corporate America, and that gave us the means to travel. This had always been a dream of mine to travel the world, and we made it happen. I met a guy who loves to travel and see new places. How ironic that he does not like to fly.

I was far away from what I knew and from my family. I loved email and then when I found Skype it changed everything. Being able to talk to and see my family was great. You just have to love technology. Today I am so happy we have WhatsApp so that I can stay in touch with my family.

Some of the things that really stood out to me as I am thinking back now was the fact that I had a thick accent and people found it difficult to understand me. Initially, I got very frustrated, but then I learned to look at it in a different way—for me, everyone in America has an accent. I learned to be patient because at times I did not always understand them either. I also remember being surprised at first by the amount of food you get in restaurants – it really blew me away.

As time went on I learned what restaurants I liked and started to meet more like-minded people. Through it all I had El, and he had me. One thing I know now is that it takes a village. I realized that we need people to make our lives more colorful and interesting. While I love El, I believe it is healthy to have your own interests, shared interests, mutual friends and "girl" friends for me and "guy" friends for El.

After a few years, I decided I wanted to do something different. I went back to school at night to become an Esthetician. I am loving my journey and am always learning new things. I love how the right opportunities show up and how they take me on a different path.

I am now a Reiki Master and volunteer for a nonprofit organization called LifeSpark. They provide complimentary Reiki services to cancer patients. It has been very humbling for me to have an opportunity to give back in a meaningful way. I am so grateful for all the opportunities I have been given.

What I did not realize at the time, but is so clear to me now, is that I always had a choice of how I wanted to feel and respond to what was happening at any given moment. Just knowing this and questioning my own beliefs has helped me get through so much. I continue to grow and learn every day. I have grown so much and learned such a lot over the last nearly two decades. And yes, at times when I was ready to give up, the right people at the right time showed up in my life to help me through.

It is 18 years later, and El and I are still married. I will tell you it has not been all sunshine and roses. We have had our ups and downs, and all arounds, almost getting divorced in 2015. Thankfully, again, I met a fantastic lady. After working with her and doing my own inner work, El and I are still together.

We still have our moments and our days, but who doesn't? I've felt lucky and blessed to have met my ONE, THE ONE for me. My grandmother always used to say every pot has its lid, and I guess I found my lid in America. Who would have thunk? Life is such a spectacular journey with all its twists and turns.

This I know to be true, I never actually arrive, but rather just keep moving forward doing the best I can, learning and growing along the way, doing the inner and outer work required. Who knows what is next for El and me? I will take it one day at a time and for now, I am happy to be living in beautiful Colorado with my husband and my sister Helen close by.

Helen ended up working on the cruise ship once I left for America. As it turned out, the gentleman that was our waiter on the cruise ship when El and I got engaged in 1999, is Helen's husband now.

After her husband left the cruise ships, he had an opportunity to

transfer to Denver. I was so happy to have her move to Denver after 6 years of living in Miami. And now that she has her son, we can visit more often, and I can see my nephew grow up and be part of his life.

You never know how things are going to work out and where you might find love. Just trust that everything is working out exactly as it is supposed to, with all the challenges and blessings that life brings us. I do believe we create our lives and I am happy with what I have created so far.

Karen Montoya is highly intuitive and has a gift for helping guide those who are open to feel balanced, centered, peaceful and supported to find strength and clarity. She is an Neuro-Transformational Coach, Licensed Esthetician, and Reiki Master who believes in the power of transformative growth through one on one and group processes. Karen has hosted many workshops and loves going on retreat. She and her husband El live in Colorado. You can find her on Facebook.com/ ColoradoAllEyesOnU and AllEyesOnU.net.

In Life as in Sex

by Kristen Gentala

*"My life seemed divided between the upright Baptists and the proper
little girlfriends on one side, and all this earthiness on the other.
The clean and the dirty – I was caught in both worlds.
Maybe you have to be a bit of both to learn about life.
Life is certainly about both, isn't it?"* – Tina Turner

I am completely ordinary in the muddled, contradictory, "damned if you do damned if you don't" messages that I tucked
away in my psyche as I stumbled into womanhood. I had a strong
sense of my sexuality, so the innocent good girl didn't feel right, and
I had a judgmental streak that didn't give the vixen much room to
play. I found myself caught up in judging and being judged for don-
ning the mask of the prude or the jezebel, when in fact I was neither
of those things. And, underneath the loaded words, I was a little bit
of both of those things.

For far too long I didn't really know myself. From early childhood, I'd evolved into a master of malleability, contorting to please
and pacify those around me. As a coping method, being masterfully
malleable served its purpose, but left me with little clarity about who

I was outside of the real and perceived expectations of those around me. My sense of my value was inexorably attached to the desires and opinions of others, in nearly every aspect of my life.

Fortunately for me, my strong sense of my sexuality has been an exception and a refuge, even when it's sometimes tucked away for a while. It is a place for authenticity and play and release, connected directly to that illusory and mysterious self. And as a grown-ass woman who's been through some things, I'd like to propose that a healthy, fulfilling sex life and a healthy, fulfilling life have much in common. Kind of like that book, "All I Really Need to Know I Learned in Kindergarten"… but also definitely not like that.

Allow me to demonstrate…

~

In life as in sex, it's important to be vulnerable.

I grew up with much to appreciate. A canopy bed in my own little-girl pink room. Two younger brothers who were usually pretty fun to hang out with. My dad who worked hard and came home every night, and gifted us with a love of the outdoors. My mom who baked cookies for our teachers, was the leader of my Brownie troop, crafted homemade Christmas ornaments, and was a consummate caretaker. There were toys, books, and bicycles, and countless days of playing with the neighbor kids until the sun went down.

I also grew up with a childhood that was scattershot through with the typical and transformative dysfunctions of a family mired in alcoholism. And then my mom was diagnosed with cancer and died without seeing her 40th birthday. And then the alcoholism was more overt. Throw in a few more early traumas that I prefer not to elaborate on here… this is where the seeds were planted very early on, and the masterful malleability took root and served a purpose.

I used to grasp for safety in convincing people to like me, and then to validate me, and then to not reject me, and then to not leave

me. "Validation desperation" does not generally end well. It created an energy that was a magnet for people just as fractured and uncomfortable with themselves as I was. In my case we both put their needs first, and they validated what I really believed—that I was inadequate until somebody else decided otherwise.

Ultimately, the only opinion of me that should have that much power in my life is my own, and while I am a work in progress, I am in no way inadequate. I've learned to look within for validation, and to be discerning about who I choose to bring in close. This has been important in every aspect of my life, and an integral prerequisite to vulnerability.

It's impossible to have an unfiltered sexual connection when your objective is validation and approval over intimacy and mutual pleasure. If your most pressing thoughts in the heat of the moment are focused on if your thighs are too squishy, or if it's okay to ask for that thing that you like, or if you're good enough at all… you're not really experiencing the heat of that moment.

Do you feel safe enough to be vulnerable? If not, is it you or them or both? Feeling safe is sometimes still elusive for me; those roots run deep. I know, however, that vulnerability is a prerequisite to intimacy; without it we're often just role playing. Side note: Role playing, when done with healthy vulnerability, can be a whole lot of fun.

In life as in sex, it's important to be playful.

My chronic case of validation desperation tended to get in the way of unbridled play. Too self-conscious about wanting to do well and to be right, I would be the one reading the rulebook, or watching from the sidelines until I was sure I could hold my own.

Let's be honest though. Who doesn't love to be relaxed and silly and giggle and laugh until you snort? And then laugh harder because, omg you just snorted and now you have to catch your breath so you don't die from laughing, but didn't that feel really, *really* good?

It's hard to get to unbridled playfulness if you're caught up in

overthinking every move and every word, because maybe if you can get everything just right, if you can just be perfect in that moment, you'll get that taste of approval that you're longing for. When the approval comes from inside, and the chosen partners are people that like you and respect you and are emotionally healthy enough not to project their own shit onto you, it becomes safe to just be. To just be silly. To just be impulsive. To relax and to *play*.

Perfection is *not* playful. Aspire to do things well, with integrity and effort, and for the love of all that is holy, release the compulsive need to be perfect. Scrambled your words during an important presentation? Everybody listening has been there, too. Zit on your butt that time you were premiering the new super-cute thong undies? Chalk it up to the universe having a weird sense of humor and roll with it. Give that zit an amusing name if you like, and then forget about it and get busy getting busy. And when a peculiar noise of unusual volume sneaks in at the most inopportune time, be sure to laugh at that, too.

In life as in sex, it's important to be curious.

People who lack curiosity are a mystery. In this world, in this time, in any place that you may find yourself, there are discoveries to be made. How limiting it is to lock in to a very narrow comfort zone of what is acceptable to think and to do.

Or maybe a lack of curiosity isn't such a mystery after all. Our comfort zones are exactly that… comfortable. Sort of. There's a sense of comfort in "knowing" that your beliefs, however they arrived, are of course correct and thus superior to other perspectives. This is true both individually and collectively. It can feel dangerous to even begin to question the norms that were bestowed by family, religion, and culture.

Fear often plays a role as well. If we begin to push the walls out from our safe little comfort zones, we're basically stepping into discomfort zones, and we are hard-wired to avoid discomfort, even if

we're pretty sure that life will be more amazing on the other side.

Sometimes, curiosity requires courage. Especially when it's personal.

As a young woman, I clung tightly to what turned out to be a very narrow view of reality. I was certain that my perceptions of *everything* were of course correct, and stayed anchored in self-righteous victim-hood. I certainly didn't see it that way at the time, and it took too many painful experiences and a life-transforming therapist to nudge that narrow view of reality open. I had a pattern of refusing to be curious about what was right in front of me. Because if I found out what I knew I was likely to find out, I'd be an idiot to keep doing what I was doing. And I stayed uncomfortably comfortable in a number of unhealthy circumstances and relationships for far too long.

Be curious about the worlds around you; the tangible, the esoteric, the collective, the individual, and on and on. Be judicious about your sources and explore your own perspectives. Be curious about those around you, including those whose lives are quite different from your own. Be especially curious about those whose lives are interwoven with yours. Seek to know them as they are, not just as you want them to be. Most importantly, be curious about yourself. Learn to see, honor and work with both your light and your shadows.

Be curious about the sensual world as well. Learn about goddess archetypes, explore the Kama Sutra, go with a friend to the "naughty store" when you're not just shopping for bachelorette party penis straws. You're probably not a mind reader; ask your partner what takes them to their happiest hot and sweaty happy places. What takes you to your happiest hot and sweaty happy place? Curiosity can be very, *very* good.

In life as in sex, it's important to be communicative.

I regularly have fascinating, insightful, hilarious running dialogues in my head. Granted, that may totally be my fascinating, insightful, hilarious opinion, and my internal censor (usually) makes

sure that I remember that. From as early as I can remember, I've been so afraid of being wrong or unwelcome or misunderstood that I would take things in, but I would rarely speak out. Just another manifestation of the people-pleasing perfectionism that has been, at turns, a blessing and a curse. I still tend to overthink and worry, and sometimes literally have words catch in my throat—neglected emotions latching on uninvited.

My tendency towards extreme self-censorship has led me to be passive to a fault at times. For example, I was a young teenager on my first-ever subway ride when the man next to me passed the time by grinding his erection into my hip for miles. I said nothing. I didn't move. He felt entitled to non-consensually pleasure himself against me, and I didn't feel entitled to make a scene. Seriously?

My needs matter as much as anybody else's. So do yours. My thoughts are as relevant as anybody else's. So are yours. I matter as much as anybody else. So do you. My voice matters as much as anybody else's. And so does yours.

Use your voice. Not every thought warrants expression, but not every thought warrants a full internal investigation either. I love the five point Buddhist Canon suggesting that ideal communication "… is spoken at the right time. It is spoken in truth. It is spoken affectionately. It is spoken beneficially. It is spoken with a mind of goodwill." (Vaca Sutta: A Statement, AN 5.198, translated by Thanissaro Bhikkhu)

When you believe your words are true, timely, and well-intended, speak up. You can't expect people to read your mind, and those worthy of your inner circle will want to hear you and to be heard by you. Share your thoughts. Express your desires. Stand up for yourself. Speak truth to power. Honor your voice and make space for others to honor their own. Genuine communication feeds connection and intimacy in every aspect of life. That's the sweet spot; I'll meet you there.

In life as in sex, it's important to be present.

I have two excellent meditation and mindfulness apps on my phone right now. I tell myself that I'll fit at least one of them into my routine soon. You know… when I'm not quite so busy. When I take a moment to be curious about why this is my pattern, I know it's because I'm delaying my own growth to avoid potential discomfort. Curiosity leads to awareness, which ideally leads to right action, which in this case leads to me becoming present to myself. And I know that when I am present to myself, I'm more aware of my intuition, I'm less likely to make mistakes, life flows more easily, and I'm more actively engaged instead of just going through the motions.

Presence is an inside job. Practice mindfulness. Engage all of your senses. Be present to yourself. Feel and respond to the moment. Tune in to your own energy. Embrace your erotic energy, which is as natural and variable as any other manifestation of human energy, and deserving of respect and care.

Be present to those you're with. Tune in to their words, energy and body language, and grant them the respect and care that you would wish for yourself.

Of course, it should go without saying that sex is best when you're fully engaged; mind, body, and spirit. (This is as true alone as it is with a partner.) If it's sexy time and you're wondering when you can get the car in for that oil change, it's time to bring yourself back to your body to fully engage in whatever yumminess is going on there.

In life as in sex, it's important to be yourself.

I've granted too much space in my life to people whose affection required me to be a little more this or have a little less that. I've both tried to comply with and resented the qualifiers in somewhat equal measures. We all deserve to feel comfortable in our own skin, and we all deserve people in our lives who nurture and support us as we are, and as we strive to be. My challenge has been to find comfort in my own skin simply because it's my birthright, and not because someone

else has granted me permission.

It's *my* job to figure out who I am and what I want. The same is true for every other person in my life, and how delightful to come together from that place of authenticity. If you ever feel that you have to pretend to be anything that is not true to you, pay attention. You have a wicked, sarcastic sense of humor and have to temper that in your work as a kindergarten teacher? Yeah, that's reasonable. You have a wicked, sarcastic sense of humor and a narcissistic partner who's rarely engaged enough to banter? Screw that. Or, in the more literal sense, probably don't screw that.

Healthy self-regard and healthy relationships allow us to just be… us. That is beautiful. That is liberating. That is where I want to be.

"Sex is emotion in motion." – Mae West

I'm grateful that the realm of sex and sexuality is a place where I feel my own wildness. Where I feel organic and unencumbered by my lists and my burdens. Where I am privileged to dive into deep intimacy with myself and with another.

It's too easy to get stuck in the incomplete, shame-laced, conflicting messaging, or to be unable to detach from prior experiences of wounding. I believe that many women long for permission to explore their "earthiness." And just whose permission are they waiting for? If you feel called to do so, give yourself permission. With vulnerability, play, curiosity, communication, presence and authenticity, there is healing and self-knowledge to be found there.

In life as in sex, may we all find a playground where we can come to better know and love ourselves. May it be toe-curling, shuddering, ecstatic, raw and real. Clothing optional.

"When women reassert their relationship with the wildish nature, they are gifted with a permanent and internal watcher, a knower, a visionary, an oracle, an inspiratrice, an intuitive, a maker, a creator, an inventor, and a listener; who guide, suggest, and urge vibrant life in the inner and outer world." – Clarissa Pinkola Estes

Kristen Gentala has lived in Colorado, in various cities just west of the Rocky Mountains her whole life. She loves exploring those Rocky Mountains, and once learned the hard way that coolers are not smell-proof and bears love juice boxes. She is the Finance Director of a not-for-profit organization that champions the rights, safety, and well-being of children and youth.

Flavor with Intention

by Sherry Hess

Tasting our way back to individual health.

First, let me share with you how grateful I am to be included as an author of this fantastic anthology. I am so honored to be a part of it and to share space on paper and in spirit with so many amazing women. And, congratulations to you, the reader, who have chosen this book to guide and inspire you to be brave, strong, and authentic like the women in this book.

I'll never forget the first meeting of authors when I started to hear pieces of their stories and get a glimpse of their hearts. I just imagined all the people who would read it, relate to it, and have complete hope that they, too, can find the strength to change their paths. It was in that moment that I wondered… is my story enough? What in the world will my words do to inspire the people who read it?

It took some reflecting, envisioning, and recognition of self-worth

to realize that we all have stories, gifts, and purpose. And we all have words to inspire others. My message may not resonate with you as much as another story might in this book. However, my story will impact you if it is supposed to.

Where do I start? In New Jersey, where I grew up in what was truly "The Garden State," I lived a simple life. We had big yards and friends down the street. "Get outside and play" was a common theme for us.

I remember our big garden. To me, it seemed like it took up our whole yard. We had corn, green beans, tomatoes, peppers, onions, and huge carrots that I recall digging up and letting my dog eat like a bone. I always found that so funny: a dog, eating a carrot. It seemed weird, and yet now I know he was aware that it had the flavor and nutrition he needed.

We had rhubarb, and the yard was full of dandelions. We had a giant mulberry tree. I don't think I've even heard of a mulberry since leaving the home where I grew up. I'm guessing it has beneficial powers that I never knew. The food in my yard was absolutely magical to me. It was home. It was a treasure hunt at harvest time. Potatoes under the ground were like an earth-bound Easter egg hunt!

I don't particularly remember a lot about fantastic cooking in my household... but hands down, my mom made the best meatloaf (and still does). The funny thing is that the meals I remember enjoying most as a kid were all the new "up and coming" fad foods. Hamburger Helper and TV dinners were becoming the popular way to eat. And I liked them.

One of my fondest memories is of sitting in the living room and eating a TV dinner! Mind you, this was very special compared to the usual required sit-down family dinner in the kitchen. I think it was Salisbury Steak. I can still see the steam as I peeled back the foil to

reveal a whole meal right there! Although at first I was taken back by the sight of warm chocolate pudding, I could barely contain my excitement. At that moment, I looked up to see the opening credits of *The Wizard of Oz*. I was eating a TV dinner, the TV was on and the screen was glowing with one of my favorite movies! This was living! I really didn't care if I ever ate those garden stewed tomatoes in mason jars from our basement ever again. It felt so good to have this rare treat.

Now I sit and laugh at my fondness of this memory because of all the things I have come to know about food. At some point, everything that I knew to be true had changed. And when I thought I had it figured out, it changed again. The complicated woes of eating and cooking are a constant whirlwind for us all.

I know how to cook. I even went to culinary school. I am a certified expert (so says my culinary certificate). Until I bought a new house with a different, finicky, uncontrollable, electric stove. This thing didn't react to my commands instantly. It had a mind of its own, and it controlled the heat more than I did. Suddenly, I had no idea how to cook! Once again, I had to re-think all I knew about generating heat for cooking and its effects on food. The point is, we think we know… until we don't.

The big message revealing itself in my mind and soul, is… I believe as individuals we do know what foods are good for us and we've just been fooled our entire lives. Food. It's magical. It's poisonous. It's the very substance of our bodies. It's what we reach for three to five times a day for so many reasons. We're hungry. We're bored. We're weak. We're thirsty. We need comfort. It smells good. It looks good. We're craving something that we don't have. Food. It's essentially *who we are* in every sense of the word. It is relevant to our minds, our bodies, and our spirits. If food is our essence, our choices around it deserve our mindful attention.

That is my passionate introduction to where I'm going in this life. And, I suppose, a taste of where I've been. Let's fast forward to

present day. Right now, as I type, I am a single mom, approaching 50 very rapidly. I have a kind-hearted, sweet and loving son, an ex-husband (I much rather prefer the term "wasband" because "ex" sounds like I've crossed him out of my life and that's the farthest thing from the truth), and a very loving and supportive new man in my life.

Relationships are tricky when you are an empath like me who understands every emotion that anyone around you feels. However, I am now embracing this powerful strength and recognizing that it has allowed me to begin, as well as redefine, relationships without regrets or leaving people behind in a whirlwind of pain. This power I hold has brought me through a recent journey of divorce, a redefined career path, my constant role as loving mom, and a new relationship—where I get to trust my instincts, my intuition, and to believe in the connection of Oneness that we all share.

My divorce is still fresh and less than a year old. The separation was long, as smooth as it could be, and very confusing to people from the outside looking in. You'll probably read about some extremely challenging relationships in this book, and the incredible strength that some women muster up to leave horrible relationships. That was not my marriage. My marriage was textbook white picket fence.

I met this guy after college who was already successful, kind, generous, driven, and focused. He never questioned himself or the success that he would have in his life. I was the lucky Jersey country girl, who grew up with hand-me-down clothes from my cousin and a simple life. This guy was handsome, nice, and funny when he wanted to be. I was in awe that he wanted to marry me, and *that thought right there* ultimately became the demise of my marriage. The fact that I felt undeserving created unstable ground that became shakier over time. It's a recipe for the cliché of losing yourself in a relationship.

I've come to know that I am built to love, care, and nurture. It's part of why my kid is so sweet. My wasband didn't need or seem to want nurturing. He was a rock. He could stand on his own, and

didn't want to burden anyone with taking their love. He was strong-willed, successful, and fiercely independent. So much so that I didn't feel needed at all. He made the money, he was the caretaker, he made the decisions. My worth felt undefined. My gifts and strengths were simply seen as hobbies, and I allowed the value of my life to feel insignificant.

We had to redefine our relationship. After almost twenty years of marriage and a series of mistakes on both of our parts, it became apparent that neither one of us was happy. I left the comfort of my big beautiful house, the ease of never having to work, the jewelry, the Hawaiian vacations, and the black-tie galas. You know, those things that people think will make them happy, but actually don't. Fortunately, I believe we figured out how to divorce the right way and established a solid co-parenting friendship that is redefined, but still a solid relationship.

So here I am. In the first year of moving out and finding myself. I went whole hog into self- discovery and at the same time, decided I need to prove myself. I started a business, lost a few friends, bought a house, created a financial plan, embraced a new relationship, ensured my family was comfortable with my changes and then… traveled to India! All while navigating the stuff you need to do as a newly divorced single parent! What was I thinking?

The truth is, I was finally free to be me. I know that feeling like I couldn't be me previously was largely self-induced, however now I was free to fully embody my life. I did some reflecting on my strengths and what I'd been through. I found myself playing in the kitchen again, and doing it by the side of my new guy who seemed to have as much fun as I did. Crazily enough, he knew how to work that finicky stove. In this new space of freedom and love, I put together pieces of my life and created what I believe is my soul's purpose: My company, *Legendary Spice*.

I've always been comfortable being somehow woven into the tapestry of the food industry. In the early post-college years, I went through typical stints as a waitress, hostess, and restaurant manager. Even while pursuing my real job using my degree in graphic design, I worked in restaurants or wineries. There was always a draw to the social aspect, the understanding of good food, and my personal desire to create great experiences when I dined out. When I think back, restaurant blood was always in my veins. There was something about the life-affirming experience of eating food that kept me coming back.

When my son was born, it was easy for me to make the decision to be a stay at home mom. This was my chance to open my heart, give love away and have it received! I loved dedicating my time to raising him. But those darn kids grow so fast! As he got older and was gearing up for going to school full-time, the little voice in my head started telling me I needed something for me.

It seemed like perfect timing that a big-city style restaurant was opening in my quaint country neighborhood. The food was superb. The talented chef blew me away with his passion for food and his ability to coax flavors onto the plate, mastering both aesthetic design and appetite appeal. I was in awe of food again. This time, it became profound to me. I suddenly realized that it is only when you eat that you are truly engaging *all five of your physical senses.*

Think about that. We put so much value on our other senses. When we think of someone who has lost their sense of sight, we feel bad because they are blind. We usually consider them to be handicapped. The same goes for a deaf person. Oh, how awful to lose your sense of hearing. Imagine losing the ability to feel or touch. Can you imagine not being able to feel the softness of a baby's skin, the heat of a searing grill, the sting of a bee or a frostbitten nose?

What about smell? Can you close your eyes and smell that apple

pie cooking in your grandmother's kitchen and allow it to stir up fond memories and feelings of comfort? I wonder—if you were born without the sense of smell, would it be harder to recall memories because our sense of smell is connected to our recollection of events? Hmmm...

Our senses are critical to our experience here on earth. They provide us with the tools to interpret the physical world by seeing, feeling, hearing, tasting, and touching. The more acutely aware we are of the signals sent to us by our senses, the more apt we are to find a pathway to deeper spiritual connections and better communication with ourselves and others.

Senses can become superpowers! Most of us have heard of clairvoyance. This is the heightened sense of visual intuition. Clairvoyant people can see visions of past or future occurrences of others. Did you know that each sense has its own "clair"? There's clairaudience (clear hearing), clairsentience (clear feeling), clairalience (clear smelling), claircognizance (clear knowing) and clairgustance (clear tasting). *I believe that by heightening our sense of taste, we will cross the bridge to individual personalized nutrition.*

Taste. Taste. Taste. I would like to think that taste is the answer to the contradictory, mind-driven food confusion in our world today. Too many of us have lost our sense of taste. We have classified taste as a "non-sense". An unnecessary sense, if you will.

I am confident that if we collectively reconnect to our sense of taste, we will recognize that it is sending our bodies critical messages. This information is different for each of us. Why do you think some of us like some foods and dislike others? We were created with taste buds as the very first line of defense. These little suckers are telling our bodies something. Their message is worthy of attention. I suggest we start listening – very, very closely.

Many of us are so concerned with putting the *right food* into our bodies that we've convinced ourselves that tasting is insignificant. Sadly, we have come to associate something that tastes good with

something that is bad for us. Do you realize that sugar, salt, and fat were once the original, Paleolithic flavors that our bodies required for survival? Those flavors that we have come to fear were once indicative of our most beneficial nutrition. Try telling *that* to someone who is trying to navigate a healthy diet in today's world.

That said, I also believe that there are some critical things we need to recognize before we can allow ourselves to think we can just eat whatever tastes good. It runs much deeper than that. We need to train our bodies to recognize the individual reactions to food and the flavors that we feed it. We must start with food the way it is designed by nature.

I suppose there is another whole chapter here that I could delve into. If I did, it would center around the demise of our food system, the government-influenced failure of our agricultural system, and the stress-yourself-until-you-die expectations of our society. In a nutshell, those things have damaged the once critical, and now numb, connection between our taste buds and nutrition. It's almost surreal how we got to this point; however, here we are.

Let's reflect on the story of my glorious TV dinner memory. Thinking back, it was so symbolic. It was convenient: the start of a new world for my mother. By spending less time prepping meals, she now had more time to develop job skills to become a teacher.

She and many other newly career-driven women no longer had to plan dinner, prepare dinner, or even set the table. Feeding the family was less stressful, and she could balance her new dual roles. There was less family time, but more time for keeping busy! And what do you know... the kids liked eating it!

Honestly, I have no idea how they made Hungry Man TV dinners back in the day. I don't know what preservatives, processing, flavor additives or chemicals they added back then, but I can tell you, their popularity, convenience, and sales were the beginning of "chemically altered" flavorings. Flavorings like bleached iodized salt, MSG (do you remember *Accent* in your spice cabinet? I do!), processed

bleached flour, and refined white sugar were all part of this generation of altered food. Food began slowly drifting away from being earth designed to being scientifically altered for taste, shelf life, and convenience. It was like a magic wand was waved, and all the natural powers of experiencing food the way it was meant to be just disappeared in a decade. Poof!

These guys knew what they were doing. Food scientists are acutely aware of the inherent calling our bodies have for salt, fat, and sugar. As processed food developed, researchers knew about this natural appeal to taste. They found a way to let the taste buds think they were getting what they needed while altering what was actually crossing over them.

Fat was no longer coming from a natural source. Instead, it was a chemically created "better for you" margarine. Salt from the earth was inconvenient. It was clumpy and moist and varied in color. This just wouldn't do for the perfection of convenience food! It needed to be bleached, stripped of its minerals, and dried so that it would flow freely and coat food more evenly.

Sugar (a.k.a. sweetness) didn't have to come from its natural source anymore. Government subsidized crops made the production of alternative sweeteners (namely high-fructose corn syrup) cheaper and gave the food industry a convenient way to take the newly-demonized cane sugar off their ingredients list. And we, as consumers, bought it all.

We believed what they were telling us. The food seemed to taste good, so who were we to think otherwise? However, the flavors we were now experiencing were scientific flavors. They were altered, artificial, bleached, purified, perfect, like Mr. Clean! It all had such great appeal as everyone took on more stress and welcomed the convenience.

It seemed to taste right. The scientists and perfect mothers on TV who could bring home the bacon and fry it up in a pan were all so happy while they were telling us how healthy it was. Fruity Pebbles

has so many vitamins in it! And kids who eat cereal for breakfast do better in school! Wow, we were living high on the hog. We could get busier and busier because it was so cheap and easy to eat. Who needs time to sit down and eat? It was just food. That necessary evil thing…

We all lived very happily in this world of packaged foods for several decades. Priorities around food changed because the food magicians were making it cheaper, healthier (so they said) and easy to eat on the go. Taking time to eat was often seen as a selfish indulgence. Why would you ever take the time to make food from scratch, let alone grow food in your own garden? It was all right there in the colorful aisles of every grocery store. We all blindly followed what we were being driven by society to do: lower the standards of our food and practically eliminate the authentic experience of eating.

It was a utopia of convenience. However, utopias can be illusions, and the convenience was shielding what was manifesting in our bodies. We started seeing more and more health issues, and I was right in the mix of the quiet chaos. Eventually the scientifically produced foods find a way to remind you what they're made of, and it usually shows up as a health challenge. As diseases and health concerns mounted, we all searched for the answers again.

Enter the "right food for you" lessons. And holy cow, are there a gazillion people and theories out there telling you what you should and shouldn't eat. What the Hell?! Fat is bad! Eat carbs. Fat is good! Don't eat carbs! Eat Protein! Don't overeat protein! Protein powder is good! Protein powder is bad! Eat vegetarian! Wait, don't eat dairy! Eat Vegan! Umm, exactly why do we have incisors again? We are so lost! Everyone is telling us what to eat and then five minutes later changing their minds. I'm talking about people for whom I have the utmost respect. There are so many inspirational people out there who have changed their lives through food. And yes, those people totally inspire me, but man, am I dizzy with the ever-changing rules of eating! Aren't you?

The altering of food runs deep, so deep that most of us aren't

even aware of it all. As we navigate things we're told we should be eating, we owe it to ourselves to stop and look at who is telling us what to eat and why.

I'm sad to say it, but as I reflect on the food trends in my lifetime alone, I have become a skeptic of most science around food. As we diligently follow things like the food pyramid, the information that we are fed by the FDA, the EPA, the USDA and the agencies that we are supposed to trust to protect us, I am not seeing the benefits. As a matter of fact, it seems to be headed in the opposite direction.

Are you seeing the constant rise in chronic illnesses? Diabetes, fibromyalgia, autoimmune diseases, autism, cancer, Lyme disease, crazy viruses, and antibiotic resistance are skyrocketing. Have you experienced any of these things for yourself? I have.

If the complicated world of food and health has done one good thing in my life, it has driven me to find my highest and best self so that I might bring enlightenment to others. Like most personal growth experiences, mine came from a place of suffering and recovery. It's not a unique story. The more I've shared with others about why I became so passionate about food, the more I hear about similar paths. When you recognize your own dialog in the words of another, and the plot is repeated over and over – it's time to pay attention and recognize the significance. Our food is changing. Our health is declining. Let's figure this out.

I don't think there is anything more powerful than the energetics of food: its experience, its quality, its nutrition, its impact on our planet, its emotional ties, and the fact that it is the fuel of our existence makes it one of the most critical elements of our world. It's also what's making us sick. The natural healing energetics of food are being slowly destroyed by science and the capitalistic driven industries of agriculture, pharmaceuticals and big food. Yes, I know that's a bold statement, but the shoes I've walked in have led me to this conclusion at this stage of my life.

Sometimes I feel like parts of my life could be portrayed in a food

documentary on Netflix. Tell me you've seen some of them – there are so many! There's *Food Inc.*, *Fat, Sick and Nearly Dead*, and *Fed Up* just to name a few. Many of these films depict the demise of our food system and the ways that we have struggled as Americans to trust what we are being told is good for us. I can relate to so many of them.

My health journey started shortly after I graduated from culinary school. I remember being so excited to dive into my new playground of skills. I bought a pasta maker and a ravioli press. I dreamed of baking homemade baguettes for my family every day! Good-bye to azodicarbonamide (the chemical compound that we were discovering was being used in both white breads and yoga mats!). I was on my way to bringing "better food" to my family.

In my mind I had this amazing passion and a skill set that should be elevating me, but something was wrong. I was trying to take care of myself, and it wasn't working. I teamed up with a nutritionist to help me understand healthy eating, and I joined one of those crazy "training" gyms where you basically treat your body like it's in the military. I was willing to do *anything* to feel good.

Thinking back, I was once again doing what everyone *told* me I should be doing. Eat this, not that. Exercise like this, push, push, push and you'll be better! My anxiety levels were sky high. I felt myself snapping at my family over the slightest little things. Adding to the confusion was the irony of how I felt when I exercised. It made me feel worse. The endorphins you are supposed to feel when you work out were muted by the extreme racing heart that I got every time I did cardio. Was I *that* out of shape? Why isn't my heart getting stronger instead of letting me down all the time? I could barely catch my breath after a simple jog.

My daily routine of being the stay-at-home mom who was trying to be fit, happy, and healthy was exhausting me. The mean girls in my head were screaming, "You're a bad mom! You're a bad wife! You'll never lose weight! You don't know what you're doing in the kitchen! You're out of shape! No wonder you have no energy!" Sheesh… How

could I be doing everything the experts are telling me to do and still feel so awful?

One time I remember having an almost out of body experience. The details are foggy, but I know that the incident that prompted it was insignificant. I was in my kitchen, which was typically my happy place. I never follow recipes because creating food from my skill set comes easily for me. Although I tend to be a perfectionist when it comes to the food I'm serving, I can usually do it without rules or following recipes.

In this moment however, something very minor went wrong with the food I was creating. Something that could easily be overcome by anyone in a normal state of mind. This was not the case for me. I was freaking out! In my mind, I knew this was so incredibly insignificant and not worth the level of stress that I felt. However, it was like a freight train of anxiety was racing down the tracks, and everyone around me could feel the rumbling. HOW COULD I HAVE SCREWED THIS UP SO BADLY?! It was ridiculous how I reacted, and I knew it. And yet, the self-deprecating voices completely overpowered the part of me that was watching from above saying, "Sherry, this is no big deal. Get some help."

I was so fortunate to have divine timing and a perfect alignment of resources at the ready. The nutritionist that I worked with and my personal trainer independently—and at the same time—suggested that I have my thyroid checked. As a bonus, they both had enough knowledge to instruct me to ask for more than just the usual hormone level test. I was told to check for antibodies and levels of specific immunity responses from the thyroid itself. As they expected, the results showed that my thyroid was "attacking itself." I became one of the ever-growing statistics that was surely doomed to lose this organ to Hashimoto's disease.

I remember not fully understanding what it meant to test positive for thyroid antibodies. I called my nutritionist to share the results of my blood test and precisely recall her saying, "I'm so sorry!"

WHAT? What do you mean you're sorry? Am I dying?!

Fortunately, she assured me that people can manage thyroid autoimmune diseases, but she advised me to work with a different team of specialists that she knew could better serve me. I was sent to a chiropractor/neurologist with a team of nutritional experts that specialized in issues like mine. I took in everything they had to say about my blood tests and their recommendations.

If you had to take one guess as to the first thing they wanted me to do, what do you think it would be? Yep, change my diet! No gluten, no dairy, no nightshades, no grains, no legumes, no non-organic foods, no commercially processed meats. NO. NO. NO. NO. Are you kidding me? I'm a CHEF!!! I'm ALL ABOUT food! I already eat healthfully—or so I thought. I felt like an artist who was just told she could no longer use cadmium yellow, cerulean blue or alizarin crimson in her paintings. There were tears. A lot of them.

And yet, in this moment I saw more correlation in my life. You see, I had already bought into most of what they were suggesting about the quality of food I needed to eat. A few years prior, I had read Michael Pollan's *The Omnivore's Dilemma* in a book club. That book was life changing for me. It documented our food system, how it has changed, and the many choices we face as consumers. It opened my eyes to how our food is being altered and it boiled my blood. Reading this book was the reason why I chose the local organic food-focused culinary school that I did. Even though organic food choices were already important to me, I still found myself facing these new health problems and hearing that they were possibly a result of a poisonous diet and a toxic environment. It was happening again. I thought I was doing the right things and still I got the wrong results.

Because the thought of eliminating these foods from my diet seemed a bit extreme, and it still felt a little unreal that my failing thyroid could be improved with diet, I decided that I needed to make sure that this was indeed the best option. Lucky me, I had an executive at the best hospital in Colorado as my husband. I had an "in"

with the top cardiologist, endocrinologist, and functional medicine specialists. Surely, they would have some way to help me. There had to be an easier solution. Isn't that why we have doctors?

I did everything they asked. I wore a heart rate monitor, I took the test for celiac, and I met with their naturopathic doctor. I got "You're fine," and "It's just hormones," and "There's nothing to be done right now, we'll keep watching." Basically, their advice was to just carry on until I got sicker.

I became one of those mystery illness patients. It didn't matter to them that I felt like shit because none of my tests revealed a diagnosis that they could give me a prescription for, therefore there was nothing they could advise. I was told, "Your body is attacking itself, and there's nothing that can be done." What?! Well, then I guess all of those *"I suck"* voices in my head were right. Now I'm truly my own worst enemy because I'm attacking myself!

I didn't recognize it at the time, but now I know. The implication that an autoimmune disease is our bodies attacking ourselves is the worst possible mindset for healing. I wish I had never allowed that hopeless feeling that followed hearing those words. Our divine bodies were given to us to experience life and to elevate our souls to a higher level. My body is not its own enemy that subconsciously decides to attack itself. Even back then I heard a small voice in my head say, "I can reverse this."

After it was clear that the top docs didn't have an answer, making the choice to go down the path of a new diet was an easy one. In addition to food changes, the plan included starting with lots of gut and immunity healing supplements that were full of beneficial herbs and spices (*cue the singing angels guiding me to* **Legendary Spice**). These supplements were recommended based upon my individual responses to food and how my own immune system was reacting.

Wow. What do you know? It was individual treatment based on what was happening with me as a person. Isn't *that* a novel concept? I felt more like a human again and less like a statistic.

Lo and behold, it worked. I felt like a new person within months, and I never had to take thyroid medicine. This journey... of life, childhood, gardening, a random book-club book, my health, and some massive personal decision-making has put me right smack in the middle of my life.

You can see why I so passionately believe that food is our answer to health. However, we have a long, long way to go before we have our own answers. We need *our own answers* as individuals to our personal nutritional health. We also need to go back to understanding who we are as humans, why we are designed the way we are, and have a better understanding of why we were ever given those glorious little tasting bumps on our tongue to jump start what happens throughout the rest of our bodies.

And, (that's a huge AND) we need to not only understand our own bodies, but also recognize that if we are eating something that has been altered from the way the earth designed it, it is working against the laws of nature, and we are putting ourselves behind the eight-ball before we even put it in our mouths.

Please don't allow yourself to think for one minute that genetically modified foods, chemically altered flavors, recreated cholesterol-free vegetable oils, and that "harmless" herbicide that makes your front yard look like astroturf aren't destroying your body's ability to know what's right for it. We must go back to food the way Mother Nature created it before we will ever be able to trust our taste buds.

Figuring out how to start with food the way nature intended it is no small task. The good news is the trend is on the upswing! I've recently seen statistics showing that organic and natural food is growing at a great rate. There's hope. But there is still a long way to go. In the meantime, we can take steps to be more mindful of what we eat. We need naturally occurring foods and mindful eating. Those two

things, I believe, can lead us to the individual nutrition answers that we all seek.

I recently read *Mindful Eating: A Guide to Rediscovering a Healthy and Joyful Relationship with Food* by Jan Chozen Bays. The author talks about ways in which we can get back to fully recognizing what we are supposed to be putting into our bodies. I know, I know. It certainly seems like we have plenty of people telling us that already. Here's the difference: In my mind, her concepts reinforce my belief that everyone needs their *own* diet, nutrition, and plan for success. And, ideally, we will find that success by looking *within* instead of listening to the "shoulds". I once had a life coach who said, "Stop shoulding all over yourself." That was the day I became very aware of how *should* can be such a misleading and nearly meaningless word.

What I really loved was the awareness that Jan brings to different types of hungers. We can understand these hungers as our reasons for reaching for the food that we do. There is hunger of the eyes: "Ooh that looks good!" Similarly, there is hunger of smell when you think you want to eat something based upon its aroma alone. Then there is mouth hunger. This one is about the experience of food in our mouths. It's not just flavor, but texture and temperature and all the things you feel with your mouth (If you stop and think about why you're reaching for that fourth, fifth or tenth cookie… is it because your stomach is still empty or is it just a mouth experience?). She also refers to heart hunger, or an emotional emptiness that you may be trying to fulfill with food. It's a seeking of comfort. Haven't we all done that?

There are the two hungers that correspond to our nutritional biology. There is stomach hunger – where we are convinced that our bodies are empty based on the rumbling and churning of our seeming emptiness. If our stomach is calling, we must need food, right? Surprisingly she revealed that even our stomachs can dupe us. Evidently, it gets used to routine and can fool us into thinking we need food based solely upon the time it is used to being fed. My

interpretation of these hungers was that there was only one that was truly reliable in understanding what it is our bodies need. This powerful calling is cellular hunger. This is our bodies responding in a way where we can feel the nutrition at a cellular level and know it is being satiated. It's a powerful message from our bodies. This is awareness at a cellular level. It's where the answers lie to individual nutrition. Unfortunately, this critical messaging has gotten lost in our fast-paced, eat-what-we-are-told society.

If we recognize that our taste buds are the first receptors to the food that we are experiencing on a cellular level, their job becomes critical. In his article titled *An Evolutionary Perspective on Food and Human Taste,* Paul A.S. Breslin states, "Taste principally serves two functions: It enables the evaluation of foods for toxicity and nutrients while helping us decide what to ingest, and it prepares the body to metabolize foods once they have been ingested, [m]oreover, taste drives a primal sense of 'acceptable' or 'unacceptable' for what is sampled."

Our taste buds in their purest form are there to help us to determine the nutritional values of the foods we were consuming. Fat, salt, and sugar are all evolutionary tastes that used to tell our taste receptors that the food coming in was *good* for us, and was going to make us feel good. Yet we have been taught that these three things are the biggest evils there are. I'm not buying it. At least not as a blanket statement for *all things* salt, fat, and sugar.

I know, where do we go from here?! What could possibly be the answer to trusting salt, fat, and sugar again? What are we going to do to find and recognize that we are experiencing nutrition at a cellular level?! Is that even a thing? Yes. Yes it is.

We must look within ourselves and be *intentional* with our food. Mindful eating is paying attention to every little experience that you are having as you are putting food into your body. It's seeing it, hearing it (perhaps the crunch of a nut or the squeak a mushroom makes when it's sautéed in a hot pan), smelling it (which is a huge part of

our flavor experience), feeling it, and of course, tasting it. We have gotten so far removed from our actual experience of flavor in our mouths as we quickly shove in food. Most of the time it flies past the tongue so fast that if it's not offensive, we can't even recall what the flavor was. This sad reality has become our first step in not honoring our nutritional choices.

Think about a wine tasting. I'm talking about the true experience of tasting wine. When we are fully engaged with the experience, we start by admiring it visually – looking for color, legs, clarity. Then we experience the nose of the wine, sniffing it fully into our olfactory glands. Next is the taste. It's not a quick fly by (unless we're just in it for the quick sense of calm we think it will bring). We are savoring the sip. We send it all over our mouth; slurping, aerating and rolling it onto all the taste buds.

If you are a wine drinker and have experienced a wine tasting, you know. It is a process. And when you spend the time and make the effort, it changes your experience. The enjoyment level is lifted and the process is slowed. You are engaging with the wine as opposed to chugging it to wash away your bad day. It's more fulfilling, more enjoyable, and in this state of mind, can even be beneficial. It is mindful.

Fully experiencing a glass of wine is a great lesson in thinking of how to experience mindfulness with our food. Engage, if only for a few minutes when you start, as you would when tasting a glass of wine. Look for the subtleties in taste, the subtleties in spice, sweet, salt, sour. Engage all of your senses.

To reiterate:

1. Choose food the way nature designed it, without negative scientific alteration.
2. Practice mindful eating. This is a multi-part process and certainly takes practice. Ultimately the flavor of the food can have a direct correlation to the nutritional values it holds for you.

3. Tune into your body as you are consuming the food, as well as how your body feels across a time line. As you're eating, do you feel satiated? Do you feel your body responding on a cellular level to the nutrients it's taking in? Can you tell the difference in your body between eating an orange candy and eating an actual slice of an organic orange? How do you feel an hour later? Four hours later? The next day?

If all of that doesn't seem like a daunting enough task, let's take it one step further. I believe true happiness and the ultimate recognition of personal nutrition will come when we are able to recognize— as individuals—the feelings of satiation, joy, and nutrition *before* we eat. This is mindfulness leveled up! To borrow Wayne Dyer's phrase, "You'll see it when you believe it."

When we have personally experienced those feelings, and are sensitive to our own body's reactions to flavor, food, and nutrition, I believe we will serve our bodies best by feeling and recognizing those benefits even before we consume our food. By imagining and feeling what the food will do for us before we eat it, it will have a clearer, more defined path to serve us. Think of it like a little prayer or intention before you eat, a prayer coming from a place where you have already experienced the answer. Visualize, feel, and know that your body can heal, be energized by and positively experience the food that you are about to consume.

In *The Book of Joy*, by His Holiness the Dalai Lama and Archbishop Desmond Tutu with Douglas Abrams, the Dalai Lama said, "When we speak of experiencing happiness, we need to know there are actually two different kinds. The first is the enjoyment of pleasure through our senses. Here, sex [...] is one such experience. But we can also experience happiness at the deeper level through our mind, such as through love, compassion and generosity. What characterizes happiness at this deeper level is the sense of fulfillment that you experience. While the joy of the senses is brief, the joy at this deeper level is much longer lasting."

Substitute the word *taste* for *sex* and you have my point. Our senses are an amazing tool and a pathway to our higher selves. Use them to their greatest capacity and then find a way to recall those feelings by imagining your desired experiences rather than relying on your senses. You could also understand it as a form of using the law of attraction to guide you to personal nutrition.

In *The Secret: The 10ᵗʰ Anniversary Edition,* by Rhonda Byrne, she references a tip by Wallace Wattles about eating. He recommends that, "when you eat, make sure you are entirely focused on the experience of chewing the food. Keep your mind present and experience the sensation of eating food, and do not allow your mind to drift to other things. Be present in your body and enjoy all the sensations of chewing the food in your mouth and swallowing it. Try it the next time you are eating. When you are completely present as you eat, the flavor of food is so intense and magnificent; when you let your mind drift, the flavor virtually disappears. I am convinced that if we can eat our food in the present, entirely focused on the pleasurable experience of eating, the food is assimilated into our bodies perfectly and the result in our bodies must be perfection."

Here I am, in the thick of my mid-life awakening, being given amazing gifts of new friendships, new relationships, new opportunities, and the blessing of creating a business that is mindful, conscientious, and can change lives with flavor. The things that have fired me up, made me ill, or otherwise created discomfort have all been the pathways of learning. It's like a crazy river winding through life, but the cool part is that when you go with the flow and glimpse back at the twists and turns, it's all heading in the right direction.

Legendary Spice is new and exciting and I believe in the early stages of elevating food and flavor for health. It's the start of this phenomenal chapter in my life. It's a calling that just *feels right*. It's the result of revelations that show up in a flash; the ah-ha moments that remind us that those crazy, odd, seemingly disconnected times in our lives all have purpose. Suddenly, it all seems to make sense.

I created Legendary Spice, Flavor with Intention to give people

delicious, nutritious, easy to use spice blends. *The packages have written mindful intentions printed on them to guide you to simple mindfulness. Plus, no more Hungry Man dinners required, because these are an easy way to make food taste amazing.*

I create these blends to balance flavors and make food taste good. *Remember my lifetime of being enthralled with food and the importance of the sense of taste?*

I do it by starting with ingredients that have similar health benefits. *Wasn't it amazing how when I felt horrible and was diagnosed as incurable that I was given supplements that were full of herbs and spices?*

I use ingredients that are organic or sustainably sourced. *Spices are typically grown in parts of the world that have yet to be ruined by agricultural chemicals. Herbs that are grown here in the United States are sourced organically. The planet matters. Our bodies matter.*

My personal experiences and travels have shown me societies that have been using herbs and spices for lifetimes for both preventative and healing modalities. *Did I mention I traveled to India?*

Ultimately, the vision for Legendary Spice encompasses mindful eating retreats, with travel to cultures where herbs and spices are grown and are a prevalent part of life. These retreats will immerse the participants in the health and happiness of these communities. *Would you like to come along?*

It's going to be great! Eat natural food mindfully, and you'll never want warm chocolate pudding hiding under foil again – *even if* The Wizard of Oz is on TV in the living room!

Sherry Hess is the creator and founder of Legendary Spice where they believe in Flavor with Intention. She creates spice blends using both her culinary background and her personal experience of taking supplements for health. She has studied and visited cultures that have been using herbs and spices for both preventative and healing modalities for lifetimes. Inspired by her passion for mindful eating and experiencing flavor, she created her company with the belief that herbs and spices should be part of our daily tasting experience, not just buried in a capsule or hidden in a super powder.

Sherry's vision of this company extends beyond the spices themselves by providing educational guidance that enables us to trust our sense of taste again. By advocating naturally grown foods, experiencing flavor and setting intentions for our bodies, her philosophies create a mindset for recognizing proper nutrition on an individual basis. Her aspirations for Legendary Spice include mindful eating retreats, supporting organic/wildcrafted/biodynamic gardening, and traveling to cultures that embrace these values. You may read more about Sherry by visiting LegendarySpice.com.

If I Only Had a Brain

by *Lisa Martins*

My path to holistic health…

Sickness for me began at an early age. My first memory was when I was four. We lived in Illinois; my mom drove us to the Mayo clinic to get answers about my chronic constipation. I remember standing in line amongst all these adults towering over me, my hospital gown dragging on the floor. I was scared and confused as to why I was there, spending two days undergoing a multitude of tests. In the end, they said there was nothing wrong with me and sent us home.

I don't remember much of my early childhood, but my parents told me that weekly enemas became the norm. When I was six, we moved to Colorado and eventually I no longer needed enemas. I still had problems with constipation, but it had improved since our move from Illinois.

Our Midwestern dietary habits stayed the norm for our family, filled with heavy comfort foods – fried chicken, scalloped potatoes, canned peas, casseroles, custards, homemade cinnamon rolls and (oh the glory of it!) banana cream pie. The only time I ate fruit was in pie filling, fruit jello, or my favorite, canned fruit cocktail. My favorite snack was Wisconsin cheese. We would have blocks of it sitting on the kitchen counter. I would cut off huge chunks several times throughout the day, every day. It was the best cheese I ever tasted! If you're from the Midwest, you know what I'm talking about. My mom was an excellent cook, and entertaining was all about the food! We always boasted more desserts than other dishes during the holidays or at family reunions.

During my teenage years, burritos, cheeseburgers, soda, and gummy bears were my best friends. Considering all the crap I ate I wasn't overweight. I was like most kids in those days, playing outside all day and not coming home until it was time for supper. Despite my active lifestyle, I was bloated, depressed and lacked for energy. I continued to struggle with digestive distress, chronic hives, ear infections, and many other unexplained symptoms. I was on antibiotics more often than not.

Shortly after getting my driver's license I was in my first car accident. I totaled my parent's car and ended up in the emergency room with whiplash, a mild concussion and a badly bruised hip. As a teenager my injuries didn't seem to faze me a bit – and as far as the car? I was happy it was totaled! I hated that thing. It was big, ugly and I was embarrassed to be seen pulling into my high school parking lot. I nicknamed it the "big green machine". It was a 1967 pea green Chevy Impala with a 327 engine. It was ugly, but fast! I couldn't wait to go shopping for my new car! I bought a red, Nissan Pulsar that I was proud to be seen in and I paid for it myself! My parents were happy because I was no longer able to go from zero to 60 mph in less than 15 seconds!

In my early 20's a good friend wanted me to join a gym with her.

I hesitated. I thought, "Why do I need to work out? I'm not over-weight. In fact, I look great!" Then she told me about all the cute workout wear available, and I immediately signed up! That is what it's all about, right?! Fashion! After spending hundreds of dollars on cute, matching leotards, headbands and leggings, I was the next Jane Fonda! What started as my own personal fashion show quick-ly turned into two hours a day, five days a week of sweat and hard workouts that I loved. I looked lean, had defined muscles, and felt stronger than ever.

Although I looked fit on the outside, my insides were still a mess. I thought I was eating a normal healthy diet – chicken and beef, low-fat yogurt, bagels and pasta, some fruit and vegetables, diet soft drinks, and alcohol. I had no clue how damaging these foods were to my body. I did not believe there was a connection between the foods I ate and how I felt. During this time, I had my first health scare at only 24. A pearly looking mole on my nose turned out to be basal cell carcinoma skin cancer. I had to go through several surgeries to remove all the cancer. I thought I was good to go, that the doctor cut out my cancer. I went about my way, working out five days a week and eating my so-called healthy diet.

Soon after, I was in another car accident. Although not as bad as the first accident, I suffered yet another whiplash and mild concus-sion. This time I didn't bounce back as quickly as I did when I was a teenager. I was referred to a massage therapist for my whiplash. It took only a few sessions to start feeling relief, and within three months I had fully recovered. I decided I wanted to help others reha-bilitate from their injuries and I enrolled in massage therapy school. Little did I know this was the beginning of my life-long journey into alternative medicine and healthy eating.

My year in massage therapy school was not only filled with anat-omy classes and learning how to give someone a massage, it was also a lesson in understanding how my body worked. I found myself im-mersed in biology, physiology, nutrition, movement, psychology,

daily meditation, and learning about the human energy field. This was my first "ah-ha" moment about how the body could actually heal itself. It was the first time in my life I realized that the food we consume can either create disease or heal our bodies. I had lived so long with all of my symptoms that they had become normal to me. I had no idea what it really felt like to feel good. Learning from the experience in massage therapy school, I started to eat better, slowly adding more fruits and vegetables into my daily diet.

It was the best year of my life. I knew I was in the right place; I loved learning about the human body. This was, and remains, my passion. Over the next ten years I continued to work on my health and my massage therapy practice was thriving. In 2000, I opened a day spa on the heels of my success. My life was moving forward nicely, and I was in the best health of my life. Then in 2003, at the age of 37, I got the flu, or so I thought. As the days went on, my symptoms became worse with a high fever, terrible headaches, a strange pins and needles feeling all over my body and a rash on my thighs. I went to the doctor. After a few tests, the doctor said I contracted the West Nile Virus which turned into encephalitis, or commonly known as swelling of the brain.

The virus took over my health. I was unable to work for six months, my business was literally next door to my house, but I was too mentally and physically exhausted to make the short walk. It completely threw my body out of whack, I was zapped of energy, unaware of my surroundings, and my digestive system was a mess again, I began having symptoms of menopause, frequent hot flashes and my period completely stopped. I had neurological problems; I was hallucinating, everything was in slow motion, and I had to keep all of my blinds shut because light bothered my eyes. It was like having a never-ending migraine. And I was so weak. I couldn't even walk from my bedroom to the front door without nearly collapsing. I felt like I was on my death bed and this sure as hell wasn't the way I was gonna go!

The doctors explained that since it was a virus, there was nothing they could do. Being thrown into the medical world and feeling vulnerable and powerless, I realized I needed to take my health into my own hands. But, suffering from exhaustion and the symptoms of my illness, I was unable to take care of myself. Fortunately, my sister, who also knew a lot about holistic health, stayed with me for a couple months and fed me fresh green juices and shots of wheatgrass every 2-3 hours and loaded my body with the nutrients it needed to heal. My poop was the most colorful I've ever seen! Purple, red, green! OK, TMI… but poop is important!

Within a few short weeks, I was regaining my strength, my mind becoming more clear, alert and aware of my surroundings. I felt like I was back in my body. By no means was I out of the woods, but at least I didn't feel like I was on some crazy acid trip anymore!

Now I felt the need to dig deep and start understanding the root cause of my illness. My past experiences with food, nutrition and meditation that I learned in school had shown me the way to unlock the keys to my healing. I decided to change my life and take care of ME—mind, body and spirit. I chose to simplify EVERYTHING, so I sold my house and my day spa business, and moved in with family.

I started reading and taking classes on the healing benefits of herbs, essential oils, flower essences, raw food and energy healing. It took over two years of being mindful and living a healthy lifestyle for all my symptoms to finally disappear—something the doctors said would never happen. I felt so empowered! I felt that if I could conquer my health issues, I could conquer anything. I wasn't afraid of illnesses such as high blood pressure, diabetes, or even cancer. I knew I held the power within me to heal myself. I knew that if you give your body the right environment, you can heal yourself no matter what the diagnosis. Dis-ease is just that—it's your body feeling "not at ease". When you think of it that way, it's not so scary.

In 2009 I met a guy. He was intelligent, grounded, kind, and attentive and I fell head over heels for him. We decided to spend

Christmas 2015 in Mexico. I was thrilled, as this was our first vacation together, a time to connect and have fun together, just the two of us. Something we hadn't done in a very long time. What I didn't know was that my life was about to be changed forever.

Our trip to paradise turned into a disaster on our first day. We took a guided Segway tour around the resort. The helmet our guide gave me had a big chunk missing from the back. I looked for a different one, but they all seemed to be in bad shape. I thought to myself, "This can't be that dangerous, I saw people of all ages riding Segways," so I put on the helmet and off we went.

Everything was going great until we came to a narrow, wooded path that took us along the beach. The last thing I remember was coming up to a 90-degree turn. Barely moving, I made the turn, and next thing I felt was the back of my head slamming into a tree, it was so loud; it sounded like a walnut cracking. I was lying in the sand holding my head.

I could hear my boyfriend yelling my name and telling me to look at him. I couldn't focus, everything was blurry. I was nauseous and my head and neck hurt. I knew something was terribly wrong. I was rushed to Cancun hospital by ambulance, where they diagnosed me with whiplash and a moderate traumatic brain injury (TBI). My boyfriend called it the perfect storm. There were only three palm trees and I hit two of them, the rest was soft, forgiving sand.

I spent two days in the hospital and the rest of our vacation sleeping in our room. I tried to lie by the pool, but couldn't bear the humid heat and bright sunlight. We were stuck in Mexico until the hospital gave me permission to fly.

Finally we arrived home, only to find my symptoms became worse. I had brain fog so thick I couldn't think straight. I had trouble finding or remembering words. I often couldn't remember much of the day before or focus on the task at hand. Walking was a challenge, as I felt the floor was at a slant and I would constantly lose my balance. My vision was sensitive to light, making it difficult to

read, watch TV or spend much time on the computer. Any movement of my head sent the room spinning. The brain injury I was suffering made me realize that I couldn't drive, go back to work or finish school until I was healthy again.

Once again, most of my days became filled with doctor visits, from neurologists, to physical therapists and visual therapists. The doctors said I had vestibular (inner ear and brain) dysfunction, and post-concussion syndrome, and told me I may never fully recover. On days I didn't have doctor appointments, I just stared out the living room window until I was emotionally and physically exhausted, then I would go back to bed. I lived in my pajamas, not seeing any reason to get dressed. I was fatigued, anxious, and depressed. I just wanted my life back.

My relationship with my boyfriend suffered as well. Living with someone with a brain injury wasn't easy on him, and my moods were all over the place. I would get easily overwhelmed and start crying, which was completely out of character for me. Both of us dealing with my brain injury was putting a strain on our already uncertain relationship.

The hardest part for me was being dependent on my boyfriend to take care of me, not only financially, but driving me to all my doctor's appointments. As the weeks went on, I could feel him getting resentful. I could sense that he felt I was becoming one big inconvenience. He made references to my interference with his work schedule, but what he was actually saying was, "You're messing up my weekly happy hour with my co-workers."

I realized that he didn't think my brain injury was as serious as I was making it out to be. According to him, I was playing the victim, being over-emotional and claimed that I was faking it. Really? Who in their right mind (pun intended!) would pretend to have a TBI? I was feeling so very isolated, because other people cannot "see" the damage from a brain injury. He wasn't there for me emotionally and had no empathy. Feeling alone and isolated with no control threw

me into even deeper depression. I felt that if the man I loved couldn't be there for me during a health crisis, well, that says a lot! I suddenly realized he was not the man I wanted to spend my life with.

As weeks turned into months, my brain injury wasn't improving and I wasn't feeling better. I wondered if my doctor's visits were actually helping. I started to believe the doctors who said I may never fully recover. The emotional stress of having a brain injury, wondering if I would ever recover, and longing to feel normal again was overwhelming.

My digestive issue started to rear its ugly head again in a big way! I would wake up in the middle of the night with acid indigestion and heartburn so bad I thought it might be a heart attack. My right eye was swollen, and I had numbness down my face, neck and chest. This went on every night, to where I was afraid to fall asleep. Finally I went to urgent care. Fortunately, my heart was fine, although I was now diagnosed with gastroesophageal reflux disease (GERD) and Leaky Gut Syndrome.

The doctor wrote me a prescription and sent me on my way. The one thing I never had previously was heartburn or acid reflux, so how could I have GERD and Leaky Gut from a head injury? I then realized that traditional medicine could only take me so far and I needed to act as my own doctor to find alternative therapies. I took that prescription and threw it right in the trash! I knew I could heal this! I was determined to get my life back.

Once again, I researched, reading as much as I could with my head injury. I could only read about 20 minutes at a time, then I would need a nap. I did research on gut and brain health and how they are connected to the body's overall health. I learned Leaky Gut Syndrome is a condition known to be common with many conditions, including brain injuries and brain diseases. I dove into alternative medicine, treating myself with acupuncture, quantum neurology, and cranial sacral therapy. I was learning more every day, but still felt like the Scarecrow in *The Wizard of Oz*... if only I had a brain!

I immersed myself in learning about cranial nerves, the nerves that run from the base of the brain into different parts of the head. Cranial nerves can commonly be involved in traumatic injury, including injury to the brain itself. Unlike injuries to nerves and other parts of the body, injuries to the cranial nerves can also involve alteration or destruction of our senses, such as touch, sight, smell, hearing and taste. One or all of a person's senses can be injured with a TBI, and each has a specific job that controls different parts of the body.

For me, my cranial nerve ten (the vagus nerve) was the one most affected. The vagus nerve affects your heart, lungs and digestion. No wonder I was diagnosed with GERD and Leaky Gut Syndrome! I found it all so fascinating! Armed with this newfound information, I realized I first had to heal my digestion so that I could absorb the nutrients for my brain to heal.

I began rebuilding my gut with pre- and probiotics, fermented foods, juicing, and a high-fat diet to combat the effects of my damaged vagus nerve. Now, when I say high fat, I don't mean fried chicken and ice cream, but healthy fats such as avocados, coconut oil, and ghee, just to name a few. What I learned is that the brain needs healthy fats for fuel. Once I started practicing these alternative modalities by eating a high-fat diet, taking brain-specific supplements and changing my thought patterns, my body began to heal, and fast!

My increased energy, improved digestion and better brain function made me want to learn everything I could about gut and brain health. I treated my personal experience as a wake-up call and committed to transforming my life in every way possible, including letting go of my long term relationship and continuing my education through getting certified in health coaching and functional nutrition.

Today, for me it's an ongoing journey to discover what I need to keep myself healthy and ultimately happy. I'm so grateful for my life and this journey which has led me to my true calling. I've learned that our health is precious and it's not something that any of us should take for granted. We only have one body in this lifetime, and

to thoroughly enjoy this life—mind, body, and spirit—we need to nourish our bodies and take responsibility for our own health.

It is a very empowering feeling to do so. Focusing on those extra pounds, high blood pressure, diabetes, acid reflux, IBS or whatever health issue you may have is worth your personal attention. Personal lifestyle changes can be challenging and habits that contribute to illness may be hard to overcome, but the long-term benefits of these changes far outweigh any temporary resistance.

What I learned from my experiences is that you have to be your own health advocate. Honor your body and your spirit so you can live a wildly nourished life!

Lisa Martins, CMT, CNHC is a practicing Board Certified Holistic Health Practitioner, Aromatherapist, Herbalist and Energy Healer who has worked in the health & wellness industry since the late 1990's. She is a member of AADP—American Association of Drugless Practitioners and specializes in digestive wellness and brain health using a functional medicine approach. She currently lives in Denver, Colorado and loves to golf and paddle board. You can visit her website at WildlyNourishedLife.com.

Picture Great Health

by Donna Wade

Picture great health. That phrase conjures up a different image in everyone's mind, doesn't it? Take me for example. Not so long ago, if you'd asked me to describe a picture of great health, I'd have replied with a chuckle and a witty comment such as, "I'm lucky, I don't need to worry about that health stuff." I'd have given you the name of one of my granola-eating gym rat pals, and never given the subject another thought.

You see, I was often teased for being one of those skinny chicks surviving on junk food and candy bars. I went through life eating out of necessity, never taking a moment to consider if what I was consuming was actually good for me. I used to start my day with a pot of coffee and a cigarette or two, with a Snickers bar, Twix or a handful of M&M's. I was always in grab-and-go mode to stave off hunger

pangs, and there was frequently a drive-through, kiddie-sized lunch around Noon for quickness. I'd throw one of those "*healthy*" TV dinners into the microwave or reheat yesterday's leftovers to wrap up my day, sloshing it all down with a couple of cold beers or a glass of wine. That was unless I was going out for a late dinner and cocktails with clients. People would honestly joke about how it would take me weeks to notice if the stove happened to disappear. For goodness sakes, I used to keep extension cords, tools and cleaning supplies in the oven! I was simply way too busy running my real estate business to pay any attention to healthy eating choices, and nutrition was certainly not a word I ever considered in my constantly rushed and hectic schedule.

That was my life back in 2006. I was living in Denver, Colorado at the time. In due course, as the foreclosure market got worse, I sadly watched another dear friend lose her home. That's what prompted me to heed the sage advice of my teenage son. I decided to make a bold move to where snow boots were no longer required, and flip-flops became my new stylish footwear!

I decided to accept a job opportunity in Mexico that elicited high hopes of simplifying my rather stressful, overly demanding life. Unwittingly, I had only altered the geographical circumstances of my ridiculously lousy diet. I was living in paradise, yet I was working just as many hours (if not more), and juggling clients from all over the world in different time zones. This International Real Estate biz was taking its toll. Days off were something I only fantasized about late at night when I would drop into bed, typically still holding a computer on my lap. I was living the proverbial dream, yet it seemed I was under the weather more often than I cared to notice. However, I was on a roll and too focused on work to notice my deteriorating state of health. Looking back, I had several warning signs: long and painful periods; bouts of sheer exhaustion that would send me to the couch for days on end; annoying colds and sniffles that seemed to linger for ages… yet I still wasn't paying attention.

Even when a poisonous bug bite knocked me to my knees with the worst pain ever, I still didn't get it! I had a disgusting, quarter-inch deep, open and oozing wound that took several months to heal, which left me with a sizeable scar on my right leg. You would think a clear sign like that – a large, noticeable wound – would suggest that I was not taking care of myself! Yet, I was a dedicated, loyal worker bee and I just kept on going, plodding along, hobbling into work and putting everyone else's needs first. The universe was doing everything in its power to knock me over the head, shake up my world and slow me down so that I would wake up and realize that I desperately needed to take a break, recharge my batteries, and take care of myself. I was just too darn busy being a workaholic to notice that my entire body was silently screaming, "*stop constantly abusing me like this!*"

Shortly after recovering from the painful hole in my leg, by some sheer miracle, late one fall afternoon I met the man of my dreams, Tom. I fell head over heels in love. Happiness happens like that – when you're least expecting it. It bursts into your life like the first daffodils of Spring, and that genuine smile of sheer joy trickles deep into your very soul. "Me time" became a priority, for the first time in… quite possibly, ever. Life suddenly had new meaning. Delight and excitement filled my days, and I was giddy with happiness.

Shortly after we started dating, Tom and I went on a lovely trip together, I met his family and friends, and among many other firsts, I hugged a giant 400 year old Angel Oak tree. We had a sensational time at the most unforgettable performance by his favorite band, the Allman Brothers. That was an incredible show, for sure! Then, while flying home, Tom calmly asked me when I last had one of those woman's checkups. He said he had felt something, like a lump in my breast. "It's probably nothing," he remarked, but regardless, he thought I should at least get it checked out. I was only 49 years old, and annual screenings were not something I had honestly ever thought about. However, a week later, there I was getting my boobs

squashed between two cold metal plates thinking to myself, "I feel fine – really I do! It won't be anything serious. I'm so happy right now… but just in case, I really should start taking better care of myself." Little did I know that my world was about to be rocked to the very core. This was going to be a major turning point in my life – *a diagnosis for change.*

A few days later, I heard three terrifying, bone-shattering words: "*You've got cancer.*" Breast cancer to be exact. I instantly found myself having to make some pretty scary decisions, but I had no clue where to even begin! All sorts of ridiculous ideas immediately ran through my mind. Tom's place was under construction and we were planning on living together once the renovations were complete. The plans we were making didn't exactly include endless doctor visits and hospital appointments with me as the patient and him as the caregiver. No, that's not the movie I had playing in my mind at all! I had somewhat fancied a much more lively, fun and exciting future, akin to the theme of one of my many Hugh Grant DVDs. How unfair, how inconvenient, how unfortunate, and how could this be happening?! I was finally in a relationship with a wonderfully caring, intelligent man who made me laugh (*my top 3 attributes in a guy*), and I go and get cancer!

Well, after the initial shock wore off, I realized I wasn't so much scared of the cancer, but I was absolutely terrified of chemotherapy! As the disbelief, distress, and fear of this darn affliction lessened, I began to think that perhaps this dis-ease had shown up in my life for a reason. Perhaps to invoke a very necessary, whole health overhaul: Mind and body, heart and soul, top to bottom, inside and out. So, I took to the "worldwide wacky web" (as my father calls the Internet), and proceeded to lose myself in the labyrinth of cancer info, weeding through the plethora of medical advice, trying to figure out who and what to believe. This quickly became my full-time pre-occupation. The more confused and desperate I felt, the more frustrated I became. There is so much reading material out there in Internet land.

It was clear that I was going to have to take a deep breath, and then take several long, deep breaths, put on my big girl pants, have a little faith in my inner perceptions, listen to my heart, and make some serious life living decisions. I was beginning to understand that cancer didn't just appear out of nowhere, for no reason. Something had caused this cancer to grow inside of me, and whatever I had done to cause this mess, I was determined to remedy it – pronto.

Instinctively, I knew that I had to strengthen my body, take charge of my life and educate myself on the rudimentary basics of health. So, I took to the keyboard once again, this time with a real purpose. I intended to learn as much as I could to improve my chances of turning this cancer thing around. Instead of fighting, battling, and hating this annoyance that had entered my life, being all upset and angry with this cancer issue, I began to embrace the opportunity and open my mind to the possibility that this was a real second chance for me. Here was my motivation to strive towards ultimate health. After all, it was me who had unknowingly made those cancer cells go crazy. I realized that if my incredibly complex inner workings were capable of creating these problematic, pesky, wild, and out of control cells, I could most certainly do my utter best to bring a sense of balance and order back to my ravaged and distraught body. What was this cancer here to teach me anyway? I wondered. What kind of shift did my life need to take? "You've got time," I told myself. "Just breathe, do your research, and most importantly, stay positive!"

While searching for answers we got second, third, and even fourth opinions in hopes of some assurance, yet somehow each specialist put more fear into my head and each opinion was more alarming than the last. One oncologist even told me I didn't have eight months left. I kept thinking to myself, "This is not how my story is supposed to end!" Who gave him my timecard? That's when I got really angry. I have always believed that everything in life is a choice. What I was discovering was that the conventional medical route wasn't exactly giving me the warm and fuzzy comfort and reassurance I was

seeking. I desperately wanted to believe that I could reverse this situation. There just had to be an alternative course of action. Considering my immune system was non-existent, how the hell was I supposed to survive the harshness of drugs and toxins to rid my body of this inconvenient problem? Heck, I was the girl all my friends begrudged because I ate virtually anything and never gained so much as an ounce. Perhaps if I had been plagued by weight issues like so many other women, then maybe I'd have been a little more conscious, more aware of how I had so blatantly been mistreating my under-nourished, taxed to the max body.

Weeks after the initial shock of that heart-stopping diagnosis, I made a firm decision: to take a more natural view of what a body needs to totally heal physically, emotionally, and spiritually. It just made good sense. Fortunately, luck was on my side as with the greatest sigh of relief and optimism we stumbled across a small holistic clinic in México, not so far from where Tom and I lived. Doctor S. recommended a total diet overhaul and complete lifestyle do-over, along with a slew of natural, plant-based supplements that would nourish and strengthen my entire constitution before even contemplating the rigors of chemo and the likes. Overnight I went from junk food junkie to vegan vigilante. It was time to take charge of my own health, it was time to take responsibility for the outcome, and it was time to do what felt right and necessary for me.

Knowing in my gut that I had found a precise course of action, my new normal turned into weekly doctor visits, bi-weekly acupuncture sessions, Mayan energy healing therapies, as well as a myriad of other time-tested ancient healing modalities, including cannabis oil. I also received ozone treatments, which basically flooded my blood system with pure oxygen every Tuesday. The combination of all of these complementary treatments was fundamental to my overall whole health picture. Juggling his business as well as being my full-time driver, cook, and caregiver, Tom was my tower of power. Full of optimism and positivity every step of the way, with each

tedious hospital visit and every agonizing procedure, he never once complained. Always smiling, he took all of the crazy in stride.

Taking determined steps towards better health, I began to feel my body respond vigorously to all the proper nourishment that good clean food provides. I was slowly turning my body's immune system into a superpower machine, where dis-eased cells or any other destructive, unwelcome toxins didn't stand a chance. It was a monumental pivotal purging if you will. I let go of old habits, negative thoughts, anything and everything that was no longer beneficial to my physical or mental well-being. *"If it doesn't nourish your soul, get rid of it"* became my new mental mantra. I took heavy-duty nightly doses of cannabis oil which allowed me to rest while bringing balance to my digestive tract. It also helped to shrink those pesky cancer bits, as well as strengthen my immune system, preparing it for the blasts of chemo to come. My entire being was getting the critical boost it needed to reboot and begin functioning properly again. While transforming the interior sickly mess of my seriously ill body into a more stable semblance of health, Tom jokingly started to call me his Darkwing Duck (a cartoon superhero) and I began to believe I was actually going to get through this frightening situation.

I thrived on the words of Wayne Dyer, my long time daily motivator. Along with the inspiration and wisdom of so many other health authorities, from Mike Adams to Eric Zelinski, Kriss Carr, and Chris Wark… they are the heroes and heroines of my new health conscious world! They reassured, nurtured, and bolstered my mind; they filled my heart with optimism and motivation. Meanwhile, I drank gallons of fresh squeezed veggie juices packed with healing goodness, used comforting essential oils to calm my racing mind, prevent nausea, and lessen my headaches, and I began to practice gentle Hatha yoga postures. It's amazing how simple stretching and deep breathing exercises can give you a feeling of such wonderful peace and calm. Today, I love the more energetic Vinyasa style of yoga practice, and can't imagine starting my day any other way. Being stress free, soul

centered, and happy, getting out in nature and breathing the fresh air was, and still is the most vital, imperative component of my all around well-being.

How fortunate, how grateful I am to have been living on the beach in Mexico during all of this cancer nonsense. If you're gonna get cancer, Mexico is the best place to be, seriously! I was a mere step away from the most gorgeous warm blue Caribbean water and sugary white sand, the same beach they used to shoot the Corona commercials. Nothing quite compares to the salty fresh healing properties of the ocean, even if I was only able to splash my toes into its therapeutic shoreline. Plus, I had an awesome team of the best Eastern and Western medical minds right there in paradise—how could I not thrive through this bump in the boob moment of life? I consumed an abundance of fresh veggies and fruits every day and craved the occasional free range egg, fresh caught fish or portion of grass fed meat I was allowed to indulge in occasionally. It was exactly the kind of nutritious, delicious, biggie sized combo I needed to restore and repair from the inside out.

I was so weak and tired during the following arduous chemo months that to get through the harsher down days, I relied on the gamely practice of the energy bank. Each morning I mentally gave myself 10 energy credits. I had to prudently decide how I was going to mentally or physically spend them throughout the day and it really helped ease the frustration of being so darned weary and despondent feeling. You really do learn to appreciate the many, every day, simple actions you normally take for granted when chemo forces you to remain still for long, uncomfortable, extended periods of time. Chemo is not the most fun experience, but it doesn't have to be totally miserable, especially if you can complement those harsh treatments with other beneficial Eastern modalities as I did. I continued with my naturally organic whole mind and body healing regimen over the next several months. It was a rollercoaster of ups and downs, as each week seemed to blend and blur into the next. Did

you know that laughter really is the greatest of medicines? It's actually a scientific fact, no joke; so kids' cartoons, all sorts of funny comedy shows and stand up laughter makers became a part of my new mindfully nourished life. Darkwing was an anchor of optimism for me, I held onto those imaginary super powers with all my might and told myself, "You can do this girl!" Later, I decided to get certified as a laughter yoga leader (*hahahahaha!*). Chemo may have kicked my butt, but I purposefully, in true Darkwing style, kicked cancer's arse!

Cancer was the wake-up call my body finally found to make me stop, take heed and re-evaluate what's important in life. I lost so much more than just my hair, my strength, my appetite, and a few dress sizes. I also lost my job, my income, and my identity. I knew I couldn't go back to being my old gallons of coffee and candy bar devouring self. I barely recognized the scrawny person I saw in the mirror. Who the heck was I was going to be once this cancer crap was over? I had no idea what the rest of my life looked like, but I knew with every ounce of my being that I was going to get through this troublesome time. I was meant to thrive through the madness of disease and become an influential voice, a model of transformation that other people could be inspired by. How I would do this I had no idea, but I held on to the vision of being an empowering change maker for others. I was going to make a meaningful difference in the world.

Don't get me wrong, cancer is a horrible dis-ease that I wouldn't wish on anyone, but it can also be a very humbling bump in the road of life if you choose to see it in that way. A year and a half after that initial shocker *"you've got cancer"* diagnosis, I underwent a double mastectomy and reconstructive surgery. The good news is that there was no tumor whatsoever to be found anywhere in my body. What a relief! It took a few months to regain any real strength after the surgery, and there were still weekly checkups to attend, but all the fear and misery was over, finally over. Now all I had to do was gain some much-needed weight, grow some hair and get on with living that

great life Tom and I were supposed to have, or so I thought. As I regained a little weight, a little more energy and a smattering of hair began to grace my bald head, the unimaginable happened. Tom and I started to drift apart. We weren't the same two dreamers who began this unwelcomed, crazy cancer journey together. Neither of us had expected that it would be so challenging to just be us. Where was the fun and ease of simply being a normal cheerful couple? It devastated me beyond words. I wasn't the old Donna anymore, and Tom wasn't the happy-go-lucky guy he once was, either. Cancer gone—relationship over, wow! Didn't see that coming!

We had made it through the last two years of cancer hell and now we were going our separate ways. To say I was heartbroken was the understatement of the century. I went into survival mode, big time. I needed to get away, get some clarity, focus, meditate more, do something, anything to stop the agonizing realization of what was happening. I had been forced to sell the three properties I owned in order to cover the expense of all my medical bills. Fortunately, I still had a little bit of money left, so I sold off my belongings in Mexico, my trusty jeep included, and I flew to sunny Florida, just like that. I rented a little place overlooking the Banana River where I was going to take some time to contemplate what next, what now? Once again, I was going to have to put on my big girl pants and listen to my heart, really listen! This time I chose to take time in, no more taking time off. I had done enough lying around and feeling sorry for myself to last many lifetimes. I call this my self-imposed whole healing phase.

In this peaceful and quiet setting, as I watched the dolphins and manatees play, I began to take a good hard look within. I knew I wasn't ever going to get that sick again, ever. I had time, lots of it, and so I decided to use it wisely by enrolling in two first-class integrative health courses. As a full-time student, I was going to concentrate on a whole health education and I was also determined to teach myself how to cook properly in order to sustain my new found energy and sense of aliveness. So that's exactly what I did. There were torrents

of tears and plenty of soul searching days and nights, lots of self-induced alone time and mindful self-awareness weekends spent contemplating what it was I really wanted out of life. I was completely lost emotionally.

I acknowledged and accepted, revisited past mistakes, and recognized the teachable moments. I let go of all the unwarranted emotions I had been holding on to that were no longer necessary. There were many thoughts, feelings, and beliefs that needed to be addressed and expressed. It took time, it wasn't easy, there were many OMG and *aha* moments. I learned to truly appreciate the simple things in life again, like a gorgeous morning sunrise or a pleasurable bike ride on a sunny afternoon. I was allowing myself to truly heal mentally as well as physically, all with more love for myself and respect for others each and every day.

Over the next 10 months I was well on my way to becoming certified and qualified to take my place in the rewarding world of health and wellness, yet I couldn't lose the constant movie in my mind that was supposed to be. I was still stuck. Unable to move forward, let go and leave behind the life I had envisioned; a fulfilling life with Tom, our life. Throughout my damnable cancer situation, I had had such a vivid dream; this vision of a perfectly delightful, gratifying future together and I wasn't willing to let it fade. So I did what any girl lost and in love in today's modern world would do. I sent him a message on Facebook and we haven't looked back since.

Fast forward to today. We're taking things real slow this go around, laughing a lot and relishing the pleasure of getting to know each other again, for the first time really, with a bright sense of optimism and a vigorous zest for living. There are no guarantees in this life. It's early days in this newly rekindled romance of ours, but I can tell you this: Health and Happiness are uniquely precious commodities and we all deserve generous heapings of both! Who knows if the movie that played in my mind as I sat in that chemo chair is how this picture of great health will end. Right now all I know is

this: our hearts are lighter these days and Darkwing remains strong and steadfast. We keep each other smiling as we contemplate and explore the possibility of a future as yet unknown. And for now, that's enough. We're giving it our best shot and unreservedly enjoying the ride, so stay tuned!

Mine would be an entirely different story had it not been for the unwavering love and support of Tom, who was by my side every single step of the way, encouraging my diet, treatments and, at times, rather unusual cancer-ridding choices. I am eternally grateful for the heartening resilience of my incredibly amazing family and my true, loyal forever friends. Cancer affects those near and dear just as much as it does the patient, sometimes, actually, a lot of the time, even more so.

I'm honestly thankful to my cancer experience. It has empowered me to share the many life lessons I've learned along the way, the joys discovered, and the challenges that can be overcome. If you just put your mind to it and believe, then your heart's desire can be so. You know what else is true? Cancer puts everything into perspective — who's important, what's important. I am so genuinely appreciative for the awesome people I am so fortunate to have in my life. I take time to remind them, I make time to show them I care. I consciously celebrate every single glorious day I get to experience, and I'm positively grateful for the opportune occasions I have to guide and inspire others. Making deliberate, sensible choices towards a satisfying, stress-free lifestyle was more than just oddly intriguing and extremely necessary for me. My journey toward happy, whole health was also a journey of self-discovery, self-honesty and self-truth.

Today, I am most definitely the best version of myself that I have ever been. I look younger, have energy again like I did in my 20's, I feel so amazingly alive and I am eternally indebted to cancer for showing up in my life. My two-decade real estate career is not who I am anymore, but helping people has always been my passion, my forte. Now, I am able to offer experience, insight, and encouragement to

others as they embrace their own unique version of "a joyful, healthier ever after." Ultimately, we are all responsible for the state of our own personal health and wellbeing.

Cancer was a major teachable bump in the boob moment for me. A life-saving, life-giving shift, for which I am incessantly thankful. The best part is, I didn't lose my identity after all. I simply became who I was meant to be. The authentic Me... and you know what's so great about that? I like this new and improved Me, a lot!

I'm fully embracing this new lease on life, it's such a thrill to be content, strong, and disease free. It seems a lifetime ago that I was that happy meal, junk food guzzling girl. My desire to turn my health situation around has evolved into my true calling. Yes, you've guessed it. I started *Picture Great Health;* a personalized health coach and cannabis consulting service and I'm thoroughly enjoying every single minute of it! I have the honor of helping others hit the reset button of life, encouraging them to achieve their dreams and experience the high energy that only elevated whole health brings.

By choosing health and happiness I have gained a true sense of clarity and focus. Miracles really do happen, you just have to believe in the powers of Darkwing Duck my friends! If I can do this, anyone can. So live healthy, take time to laugh often and make time to truly appreciate the small things. In the words of a brilliant and unknown scribe:

"Time can be kept by clocks and calendars,
measured in inches and wrinkles,
and caught in images and photographs.
But if we are lucky,
it can also be counted in a life well spent,
full of learning, love, and laughter."

Originally from Scotland, Donna Wade has lived and worked in some rather interesting corners of the world in one capacity of service or another, happily helping people to live joyful, complete, and fulfilled lives. As a vibrantly alive cancer *thriver*, she is a budding natural health advocate, is an active member of several holistic health organizations, and her voice has been heard as a guest speaker, both live and virtually, as well as in print.

Drawing from her own personal life experiences and cancer healing journey, nothing brings Donna more joy than to help people make practical, lasting health changes in a fun and simple way. Bettering people's lives is what fuels her drive and making a positive difference in the quality of an individual's life is what she thrives on. When Donna is not inspiring lives she is either catching up with family and friends from around the world, down by the river with a good book, watching manatees and wild dolphins play, or dancing to the grooves of a funky live band. Family gatherings, long walks in nature, a *great* book, and the mystical flavors of exotic spices and tasty teas are just a few of her favorite things. If you're curious to know more about Donna's services and offerings, you're invited to visit her home on the web at PictureGreatHealth.com.

Love Hard and
Live Well

by Kristin Schooler

*"Grief is the last act of love we have to give to those we loved.
Where there is deep grief, there was great love."*
– Unknown

We all at some point in our lives will, unfortunately, face grief. Loss comes with life; it's a package deal. As universal as the experience of grief is, I have a feeling that every single person experiences grief differently. This is my story of grief. In 2016, I lost a man who was my hero. He was my stepdad. He was full of life and full of hell. In my eyes, he was as soft as a teddy bear, strong as an ox, ten feet tall and bullet proof, oh and he also hung the moon. He passed away at the young age of 56, in June of 2016. More than a year later, truthfully as I write this, I struggle with every sentence because, in some ways, I still have a lot of healing to do. But here it is, my journey.

Journal Entry – May 19, 2017
It's almost been a year since you died. Just writing that last

sentence brings tremendous heaviness to my heart. I miss you. Every. Single. Day. So much life can happen in a year. Another year of the planet rotating around the sun, another year of existence that you are no longer a part of. The world feels emptier without you in it, and sometimes I get so angry because no one else around me feels that emptiness like I do. I want everyone to know how amazing you were and how missed you are. It's true what they say about grieving – you definitely grieve alone.

We all have the people in our lives who shape the very core of who we are. Maybe it's a mom/dad/sister/friend. If we are lucky, some of us have more than one of these amazing people. You know what I'm talking about… the people who are a part of the very fabric of your being in this world. The people who have your back and keep you safe in their heart. The people who make you believe in love and goodness. Regardless of blood, these people are your family, your heart.

I have those people, too. Not many, but a few wonderful humans that make my soul so happy. One of the biggest pieces of my life fabric of love and goodness was my stepdad. Long story short, I didn't grow up in the most loving family, and as a child, he was the only one of my four parents that was genuinely nice to me. He was warm and kind. He was loving and supportive. He was encouraging and protective. He was also rough around the edges, in the most charming of ways, and a total badass. I loved him so much.

Randy died just shy of a year ago. I miss him, and some days, it still hurts just as bad as the day he died. On these days, I feel a physical pain in the core of my chest. Some days, I am still a complete mess, unable to remain grounded and stable in the world. It's getting better though, so I just try to take it day by day. Losing your father feels earth-shattering sometimes.

Today, and most days, I feel strong and accepting, understanding that life is ever-changing and eternal, and that energy just shifts.

On those days, I realize he isn't gone, he just isn't here in the same way. On those days, I feel close to him, in some ways closer than if he were still here. I swear that he talks to me in spirit. He's funny and encouraging, just like he used to be, but he is also different, younger, yet wiser, having lost the edge of living, but gained the spiritual depth that comes with dying.

To be honest, I don't know if grief ever goes away, I am only a year into this whole thing. I just think that the good days become bigger and better than the bad days. Especially in the beginning, for me, grief was isolating, lonely, painful and dark. No one knew how deeply my heart was broken, and I didn't have the vocabulary or the voice to be able to tell anyone.

Journal Entry – May 21, 2017

I miss you. I say and feel that all the time. To write those words doesn't do the feeling of missing you justice. You meant so much to me, and I am sure I didn't tell you that nearly enough. You were my family. I always felt like God had intentionally brought you to me as a child to be the bright spot, the guiding light in my life. At 35 years old, I ridiculously feel like an orphaned child. You were really the only stability I knew as a child, and now that feels gone, the foundation of my world feels shaken. I feel like I am drowning some days in the abyss of your loss, unable to comprehend how I can get through this life without you.

Miss doesn't even begin to describe how I feel. I miss him every day. A piece of my heart is gone, and a chapter of my life is over. I have asked God a thousand times or more over the last year, "What is the point of all of this?" I am not sure if I will ever know the answer, but a year later I would say something deep and spiritual like, the loss of love teaches us the lesson of what love really is. In my 35 years here on earth, I have a feeling that we are to learn lessons of love. We are

love, we come from love, and we will return to love. We are here to learn to love others and ourselves. But the mindless pursuit of money and power has made our world corrupt and we forget that whole love thing sometimes. We learn meaning by losing what really matters, we learn that love is eternal. We learn in the face of loss that life is precious and that connection and love are what really matter. With the lessons of loss, we learn to love harder, to be more present, and to live with more joy because this moment is all we really ever have.

Journal Entry – May 24, 2017
The eight-year-old in me didn't understand the gravity of the gift I had been given when you started dating my mother. You saved me in so many ways from the craziness of my fucked up family. You were kind, gentle and loving. You taught me about what a parent/child relationship could be. You made me feel seen and loved when my entire life I had been belittled or ignored. I want to go back in time. I want to say thank you. You were the best, and you brought so much light to my life.

I was born into chaos. I'm certain that I was unplanned and unwanted. My parents were way too young and definitely not in love. They got married because of my unexpected impending arrival in the world and then divorced almost immediately. My childhood was spent being dumped back and forth between each of my parent's households, constantly being told that I reminded them of the other. Then in my adolescence, both parents remarried and started families with their new spouses. At this point, I clearly didn't fit anywhere.

Let's just say that being unwanted and raised in chaos doesn't always make for a well-balanced, healthy mental outlook on life. Consequently, I can be really good at making bad decisions. I dropped out of college, I got pregnant young, and I have been married twice and divorced once. And I am a horrible perfectionist that feels all of my mistakes seem glaringly larger than they probably are. Despite

the tornado I was born into, I have spent my entire adulthood simultaneously working to heal myself and raise a healthy, well-adjusted daughter to change the cycle.

On top of a rough childhood and wildly poor decision-making early in adulthood, I have spent the last five years unexplainably ill, unable to be a functioning human for extended periods of time. I now know I have fibromyalgia and an autoimmune disorder, whatever both of those mean. To me, it has meant pain, confused doctors, a plethora of prescription drugs, mental health issues, and family and friends not understanding what in the world I am going through. To say the least, the last few years of my life have been a wild ride.

I don't want to be defined by just one part of my journey, and a sick, exhausted, barely functioning person is not who I am. It's a part of my story, but that isn't where it began nor where it ends, so enough about that.

Despite my rough start in life, I still ended up happy with a pretty amazing life. I have a beautiful daughter, incredible husband, and wonderful, supportive friends. I have had a great life filled with lots of meaning and love. For being raised around addiction and abuse, I suppose I turned out pretty freaking awesome.

I wasn't born into a loving situation. As a child, I didn't feel the love that a child is supposed to feel from their parents. As a child, I enjoyed retreating into the safety of myself, becoming very independent and always lost in my own head. I didn't make friends easily, which made school hard. I wasn't encouraged to pursue art or sports, so I didn't know what my talents were. But when Randy met my mom, everything changed. I wasn't a cute kid, but Randy never made me feel ugly like my parents did when they looked at me. He showed me how to play sports, and he taught me how to gamble at the horse races, which in hindsight was incredibly inappropriate and awesome. Randy complimented my school work, he encouraged me socially, and he even taught me how to drive. He made me laugh and he made life fun. He saw me when I didn't feel seen, and if that's not love, I don't know what is.

Journal Entry – May 26, 2017

Since you passed, some days I feel incredibly strong, like somehow your death gave me super powers of courage and resilience. Yet, other days I crumble, spending the day sobbing, not wanting to leave the comfort of my bed. Then there are the angry days when I am so pissed that you were taken from this world way too soon. The angry days might be the worst...

Death is, unfortunately, a package deal with life. When we are born, we receive this amazing gift of life. We get to come to earth in a physical body, and we get to experience love deeply, which is so incredible. Loss might be the worst part of life. Randy's death triggered deep anger in me. I have been so angry with Life, with God, and with the people closest to me. I have been angry with strangers and inanimate objects. Believe me, I know intellectually that my anger is completely irrational, yet the inner child within me is so angry that he's gone. I never wanted to lose him.

I am a yoga teacher (which is really just a fancy title for a yoga student that shares yoga with others). As a yoga teacher, learning the deeper lessons of life is kind of my jam. I see it as my job to study sacred texts and enlightened masters. As someone who has always been more spiritual than religious, it is super fun to be able to do that for my job. I love growing and integrating sacred wisdom into my life. Yet despite my spiritual focus and dedication, my reverence for the Divine, there have been many times over the past year that I have wavered from my spiritual path of goodness, of righteousness, of being a kind, accepting, loving human.

Being perpetually angry is not "yoga-like" at all, and it's not really being a good human either. Anger is not really that becoming on anyone either. I am ashamed at how angry I have been over the past year. The anger is finally subsiding, but I used to be so afraid that I would be angry forever and that my anger was going to ruin my life.

I now think I was so angry because of my deep suffering through the grieving process.

According to Buddhism, (and this is a simplified version), our suffering on earth is caused by our attachment to things. Suffering is caused by our inability to accept the constant change that is life. We attach to the things that bring us pleasure, and we don't like facing the things that bring us pain. Which makes our lives shittier than they have to be because we mentally/emotionally/energetically hold onto the change that hurts us and relive it over and over, thanks to the power of our minds. Buddhism approaches life as ever-changing and impermanent. Nothing lasts forever, nor is it meant to. I get it, but that's a hard pill to swallow when someone you love is ripped from your life.

The practice of yoga has been a healthy way for me to express the hell of grief that comes with loss. It has been a therapeutic way of gaining perspective on loss, life, energy, health, and happiness. It has taught me mindfulness of living in the moment, without getting carried away in the pain and regret of the past. Yoga has taught me that I can survive anything because of the connection I have to myself and the Divine.

Journal Entry – June 2, 2017
It's June here, and you have been gone almost a year. It rained yesterday. And the rain really got to me, pulling me into the ugly depths of isolating grief. The sad, grey clouds lulling me into the melancholy. I woke up, cried for a few hours, got my shit together long enough to teach my morning yoga class, went to therapy, cried some more, ate enough tacos to feed a small family, cried some more, got my shit together again to teach yoga again, ate some ice cream, and cried some more. Yea, so I guess you could say I am not always handling this so well. Today would be one of those days. I am trying to accept that some days are just going to be worse than others.

I'll try harder to keep my shit together tomorrow. I know you wouldn't want me to do this to myself. I know that you are cheering me on from Heaven hoping that a sad tear never falls down my face again. I know you are telling me to live each day with light in my eyes and fire in my soul. I know you want me to be happy and full of joy. I promise you, I am trying.

The day Randy died my life changed. Forever. On the morning of June 18, 2016, I woke up expecting another typical Saturday. I woke up naturally to the sunlight peeking through the blinds in my bedroom. My husband, always much more eager than myself to jump out of bed and start the day, said 'good morning' and rushed downstairs to make his morning coffee. I, being the snuggly, lazy one of the family, snuggled into my comfy bed, wrapping myself in my favorite down comforter, taking a few more peaceful moments surrounded by softness, and relished the quiet of dawn.

I love Saturdays. They are my lazy day, and if everything in my universe goes well, my Saturday includes having NO agenda except to exist and be present, just flow with life. I look forward to Saturdays, and this particular Saturday started like so many other previous ones.

After crawling out of bed, I got up to check my phone, and I saw a message from my brother. My family and I aren't exactly close, so it struck me as odd. In fact, I don't think my brother had ever messaged me before. Why was he all of the sudden reaching out?

The message from my brother asked if I was awake. I answered yes.

My heart dropped as I read his message. "Dad is dead."

I thought he was kidding.

I asked, begged him to stop joking around. He said he wasn't joking.

In some ways, my whole world crashed that day. In other ways, that day changed me beautifully. I gasped, cried, and screamed all at the same time. Feeling simultaneously devastated, regretful, alone,

abandoned, and angry. I also felt the worst and deepest pain in the core of my chest. A pain that was constant for a good four months following his death. That life-changing Saturday morning, I felt so fragile and weak. At 34 years old, I was unable to handle the tidal wave of pain, and the little girl in me was taken back to a life without Randy, feeling sad, lonely, and neglected all over again. I couldn't imagine a world without one of the most important men in my life part of it. The truth is, Randy's death shattered my heart. At the time, I didn't realize how shattered I was and what the process to piece it back together would look like.

I think about that day often. I reflect on this pain that I had never known before that day. On this journey, with time, the days get better and happier, and yet other days I slide right back into the grief. Sometimes I still don't want to get out of bed. Grieving is an act of love, and sometimes crawling back into the pain of the day Randy died is my way of transporting back to his last moments here on earth. Sometimes feeling happy makes me feel guilty because I am having fun and he isn't here anymore. But he wouldn't want me to think or feel that way. He would want me to never be sad again.

Journal Entry – June 4, 2017

I want to get better, so every day I am working on just that. Of course, the yoga is helping. And so is keeping busy with our Wild Souls Yoga project. I also started seeing a new therapist because I just don't think it hurts to get some professional advice. My first therapy session was so necessary and healing, much more so than I expected. I guess I shouldn't have waited a year to go.

I liked my therapist. He's older, with kind eyes. He's open-minded and uses alternative methods of healing, such as visualization and breathing exercises, which are right up my yoga alley. I made a promise to myself to be completely open and honest about how messed up I was feeling. He provided

a safe and comfortable space to let all the shit in my head out, and he didn't seem to judge me, which is great because I was sure he might make a phone call during our session and send me to the loony bin. He let me cry the pain out of my heart. Instead of offering me suggestions and therapy-like advice, he mostly just listened. He let me be angry without making me feel guilty. I went through an entire box of tissues in less than an hour. Maybe I should pick up a box of tissues before my next session for Mr. Therapist.

Making the decision to focus on health throughout this process has been crucial. My brain has the ability to intensely focus on things, and for a long time, I was intensely focusing on the pain and the loss following Randy's death instead of focusing on life, on the here and now. Everyone heals differently. For me, healing involved many things, including professional therapy and yoga. It also involved copious amounts of self-compassion, patience, healthy distractions, and the occasional cocktail with a friend.

The process of grieving is just that – a process. If you are grieving right now, be gentle on yourself. There is no right or wrong way to grieve, and no two people grieve in the same way. The grieving process from an outsider's perspective is probably like watching a train wreck. That's how I feel at least, about the higher me watching the earthly, dense me stumble through the grief. Some days it feels like a hurricane, or maybe a rollercoaster, or maybe more accurately like riding a rollercoaster through a hurricane.

GO EASY ON YOURSELF

> *"A moment of self-compassion can change your entire day.*
> *A string of moments can change the course of your life."*
> – Christopher Germer

I believe death and loss are some of the hardest parts of humanity. We experience such great love in physical form, experiencing love with all of our senses. We get to physically connect with other souls, which can truly be magical and life-changing. Then we can lose that physical connection in the blink of an eye, and just like that, we can never again experience that person the way we once did. That is a hard, harsh lesson.

The bottom line is you have to go easy on yourself through this process. Be strong and deeply loving to yourself. Show yourself immense amounts of love and grace. Chances are, you won't always handle your pain perfectly, and that's ok. You have to forgive yourself for the craziness you feel. You have to forgive yourself for not perfectly handling every situation, every day. There were MANY times I was an asshole to my husband or my friends, and over the last year, I have felt like a terrible mom. I have to apologize, forgive myself, and move on.

WALK YOUR OWN GRIEF JOURNEY

"Grief never ends... but it changes. It's a passage,
not a place to stay. Grief is not a sign of weakness,
nor a lack of faith... it's the price of love."
– Unknown

Experts and Google will both tell you there are set stages of grief. *The Five Stages of Grief* by Elizabeth Kubler-Ross is a popular theory. In the beginning of my own grieving, I researched these stages, frantically seeking answers as a way to help myself out of the abyss of suffering.

In my research, I found that the stages of grief are denial, anger, bargaining, depression, and acceptance. For me, it was more like denial, fury, withdrawal from friends and family, bitterness towards God, and a deep longing to check out of life, and then, some days

don't seem bad at all. Hey, I am handling this grief thing pretty well, you might say to yourself.

What I learned is that grief doesn't seem to be a linear process of checking off the boxes of the stages of grief to get to the end and achieve long-lost happiness and acceptance. It isn't a clean and neat path with a starting and ending point. That's not really how it works. It's sometimes two steps forward and 18 steps back. And then five steps forward. For some, it may be easy and profound. For me, it was UGLY, and mistakes were made.

I experienced denial in the beginning, but I assume this was because Randy's death was sudden and unexpected. Soon after he died, I often had the most vivid dreams about Randy, dreams where he was himself again, healthy, young, and full of joy. We would talk and hug in these dreams. He would show me how healthy and happy he was. And I would wake up in the morning, feeling in my heart that he was still alive, and yet within minutes of waking, the cold, hard truth would then again hit me. This period was the worst.

Following Randy's death, I tried to "out-busy" my grief. In fact, I started a yoga company with some friends to keep my mind off Randy and my screwed-up childhood that seemed to be haunting me in the wake of grief. Somehow the prospect of starting a business seemed less scary than facing what was in my own head. At the time, constantly staying mentally occupied appeared to work well. "Just stay busy," I would tell myself. But this just leads to exhaustion. Trust me.

I tried to help everyone else first. I wanted to check out, regularly. Finding healthy coping methods and focusing on mindfulness to stay present can help the healing process by learning to sit with the emotions that come up, and then learn to watch them pass. A year later, I would say balance is key. Lean into your grief when it comes. Let the tears stream down your face. Scream into a pillow. Write. Talk to a trusted friend or therapist. Then get back to "busy." But to avoid the emotions of grief is to do yourself a huge disservice. Emotions demand to be expressed, and if they aren't expressed, they can

come out in ugly and destructive ways.

I learned on my journey that grief cannot be healed without walking right through it, experiencing every pothole and puddle and hurdle and abyss and rays of sunshine. It absolutely feels better to outrun the memories and numb the pain, but I promise, the grief keeps knocking. But the sunshine does come, trust me.

Losing a loved one is kind of like losing a limb. Can you live without an arm? Yes. But your world is never the same. You adapt and adjust and learn how to be in a new way. Even though it won't always feel like it, you can learn how to live again without the presence of a soul so special to you that it felt almost a part of you. So, let the process be bumpy and ugly because there is no way out except through. Walk your own grief journey, regardless of what anyone else says. Because the truth is you can feel connected again to their soul, just in a different way.

FIND A NEW WAY TO CONNECT

"Do not stand at my grave and weep
I am not there, I do not sleep.
I am a thousand winds that blow.
I am the diamond glints on the snow.
I am the sunlight on ripened grain.
I am the gentle autumn rain.
When you awaken in the morning's hush
I am the swift uplifting rush
of quiet birds in circled flight.
I am the soft stars that shine at night.
Do not stand at my grave and cry;
I am not there, I did not die."

– Mary Elizabeth Frye

The interesting thing about the death of my beloved stepdad and what I learned along the way is that right after he died, I felt that his soul was gone, no longer here, his beautiful energy no longer buzzing about on this planet. I can't get the image of him at his viewing out of my head, wearing his favorite blue and white checkered button up shirt, pressed khakis, and his expensive brown leather belt. I remember seeing the wrinkles around his eyes that always framed his lighthearted expression when he would laugh, which was all the time. He looked like a wax version of himself, and even though the body resembled him, *it wasn't him.* I felt so devastatingly alone in that instant, just wanting to talk to him one more time, to connect with the soul that he is.

A year later, what I know for sure is that yes, his body is gone. I will never be able to call him on the phone or get a big bear hug from him, but he is still here. He is everywhere. He communicates through music and birds, mostly. But I can feel him. When I am needing him, I sit still and get quiet. Sometimes I might say something to him or ask him a question. I swear I can hear him tell me that he loves me and he's proud of me. I see him in my dreams, which is always so fun. I wake up with my heart a little fuller on those days.

I feel Randy all around me, cheering me on and supporting me from where he's at. Which is kind of cool, because I feel like I have a connection to an angel, of sorts, a connection to heaven and a connection to the Divine. I feel most connected when I am out in nature or connecting with a soulful friend. I feel connected when I say yes to new experiences and when I live well. I feel most connected when I am present, with an open heart, and face full of laughter.

DO HEALTHY THINGS

"Positive mind, positive vibes, positive life."
– Unknown

Staying healthy is super important to not getting sucked into the dark places of grief. I actually scheduled health into my planner. I would spend time and energy focusing on what I am grateful for in my life. I scheduled time with friends and family. Yoga was a huge healthy priority for me, as was my dog.

What are the things that make you feel good inside, and I don't mean booze, shopping, food, or drugs? What are the things that fill your soul up and make your heart warm? What are the things that are good for your body, good for your mind, and good for your heart? Know that all three are equally important.

Make yourself and your healing a priority. It's that cliché oxygen mask analogy-you cannot help anyone else if you don't help yourself first. Healing your heart and soul in the wake of grief by choosing healthy thoughts and behaviors is the best gift you can give to yourself, so that in turn you may be of help to others.

June 20, 2017 – Journal Entry
Today was a good day. One that has made me mindful of and grateful for all that you brought to my life while here physically, and all that you continue to bring to my life in spirit. Today I lived another precious, beautiful day. I am learning to trust more in life, and I am learning to give myself some grace when I don't always feel so amazing, which also makes me appreciate the good days so much more. I love you and I enjoy talking to you, talking to your picture on my desk. I swear you are here with me. Please keep guiding me. And yes, I hate that you were taken from me, but I feel like I have a deeper perspective and more appreciation for life,

which I recognize as the beautiful gift that it is. I hope heaven is just amazing. I promise to love hard and live well, because life is short and precious, and I thank you for teaching me that. xo

Even as I write this, I am not completely healed. I wish I could heal broken hearts and offer the grandest advice on death and grief to make the journey painless and easy for everyone. Clearly, I am unqualified for such things. The truth is, grief is messy, sad, and it plain just totally sucks. I will also tell you that I am grateful for the experience because gratitude and grace make this moving on and living thing a whole lot easier. There is sunshine after a storm, and usually, it brings with it a stunning rainbow.

I would give anything to have Randy back, but I am grateful for the depth and the perspective that came with the hardship and challenge of losing him. Each person grieves and experiences loss in very different ways, and that's where the healing begins, in being with each emotion and ache that comes with death. We all have different lessons to learn surrounding the human concept of attachment and acceptance. This was just my experience.

Yoga saved me, as it was my healthy coping method. Learning to forgive myself and others through the process was helpful. Making space to feel the tidal wave of emotions was necessary. Finding new ways of connecting to Randy was the only way I could move forward in my continued existence. Grieving Randy's death was incredibly difficult, and will probably continue to be a process, but it has made life richer, deeper, and more precious. Losing a loved one makes us realize the ever-changing nature of everything, including our own existence, so why not be overcome daily by the magic and beauty that it is to be alive? That is what I will continue to do my best to choose; I want my life to be a constant string of daily choices to love hard and live well.

There is a deep strength to be found in grief. It is to be completely

changed forever, yet to rise up with courage to continue to live, and not only live but live with the reverence and holiness that touches your soul from the journey of grief.

Kristin Schooler is a yoga instructor and co-founder of Wild Souls Yoga, a yoga workshop and retreat company dedicated to supporting women through the healing powers of yoga and sisterhood. Kristin is a wife, mother, and business owner who embraces the challenges of balancing life and love, while maintaining fierce inner peace. Kristin's free-spirited nature keeps her interested in a wide array of hobbies including reading just about anything she can get her hands on, writing, dirt biking, camping, wakeboarding, or snowmobiling. Check out WildSouls.Yoga for information on yoga workshops and retreats hosted by Kristin and Wild Souls Yoga.

The Broken Dish

by Renee Salway

We've all had it happen at one time or another. We go into the kitchen, grab a glass, or plate from the cupboard and it slips and hits the floor and shatters. Big pieces, little pieces and even slivers of glass or ceramic cover the floor. We usually just pick up the large pieces, grab a broom and sweep the floor. How many times do we sweep? Hard to tell, I know I've swept my kitchen floor after breaking a glass half a dozen times and will still see just the slightest itty, bitty piece of glass. At times I've moved the refrigerator and stove to see if there is still glass and swept there as well. And then what happens if you get one of those itty, bitty pieces of glass under your skin? It hurts like hell—or worse, it's so small you can't hardly see it. And forget trying to pull it out with tweezers… it's just not happening. But, if you get cut with a larger piece the result is much

less painful and so much easier to get the healing process in motion.

Fast forward six months or so and you're moving the living room couch to vacuum behind it and lo and behold, there's a piece of the object you broke... from months ago!!! How does this happen? Seems crazy that a piece of glass from the kitchen made its way under the couch, but we all know somehow it does! Seems a little science fiction to me, like gremlins playing tricks on us.

So, what does this have to do with working through painful trauma in one's life? I'll get there... give me a minute. Like so many of the women in this book, I have gone through quite painful and traumatic events. I dealt with parental abuse and neglect when I was very small. My parents divorced after having five children, then remarried, and my father had three more children with his second wife— who already had two children of her own. Now, to compare her to the Wicked Step-Mother in Cinderella is putting it mildly. I endured daily physical and verbal abuse, lack of food and clothing, and she had a tongue that could spit out lies quicker than water gushing from a fire hydrant. I can recall many times going to school hungry and with bruises and scratches on my body. As for my father, he was an emotionally absent alcoholic, that is, until my step-mother made him angry about something small that I did that day. Then, around one o'clock in the morning, he'd come into my room and start beating me while I was asleep... so yes, I learned to sleep with one ear open... always listening for his step. And to add insult to injury, THEIR children were treated quite differently. I wasn't "allowed" to talk to them or play with them, and we never ate meals with them either, except on Sundays, when we'd have our "family" meal together... which usually ended up with myself or my brother getting hit with the wooden "beat stick" or slapped for some insignificant behavior they didn't like—maybe I held my fork wrong, maybe I didn't pass the food correctly—but really, mostly just because I was alive and my step-mother didn't like me, let alone love me.

Then there was the hunger... I was *always* hungry. Then I learned

that foods had expiration dates and "sell by" dates. Hallelujah! During the summer months, my step-mother would typically send me out of the house around seven or eight in the morning and tell me NOT to come home until between 7-9 pm, depending on my age at that time. What's a 10-year-old to do all day? And how the heck was I supposed to feed myself? So, I'd walk to the grocery store and look at the cereal boxes to find what dates they would be tossed out. I figured cereal was a "clean" food because it was still in the box unopened. I was resourceful! I learned the grocery store routine and ate dry cereal by the handfuls, sometimes boxfuls. Occasionally, there would be over-ripe fruit that was tossed out that didn't look too bad. THAT really made my day.

Not only did I get used to growing up hungry, I was always wearing hand-me-downs. Of course, it meant that I was the kid everyone picked on, and to make it worse, I was only allowed to take a bath once a week... ONCE. A. WEEK. I was a very active "tomboy" so I'm certain I stunk pretty bad, and with such a limited wardrobe I wore my outfits three to four days at a time—plus I had oily hair... so that didn't help matters. Every day I was teased and bullied; often called "Greaseball", "Salvation Army Girl", or "Goodwill Girl". My classmates could tell my clothes were old, that they were hand-me-downs, and didn't fit well—you get the picture. Every day I was teased at school and teased at home. It made me both angry and depressed. When I was in 8th grade I had to get a job, but not so I could have money. My step-mother told me since it was HER house and I really didn't belong there I need to pay "rent". Yep, you got it. To the tune of $60 per month. Now, in the eighth grade I was making about $1.20 an hour working for a donut shop, which meant everything I made went towards my "rent", meaning my step-mother. The upside was that I learned to love donuts and even today I consider myself somewhat of a donut connoisseur. There's nothing like a warm, freshly iced donut to make you feel a little bit better.

And no, I haven't forgotten about the dish... hang on.

I was bullied, teased, hungry, working, and going to school, getting hit every day by either my drunken dad or sober step-mother—most days both. I was told from a very young age, even before I started kindergarten that I would end up working the streets because I was ugly and stupid and no one would want me. This did quite a bit of damage to my self-esteem and self-worth. In kindergarten, my step-mother started telling me I would grow up to be a whore because that's all I was good for. I didn't even know what the word meant, but I could tell by the way she said it, it wasn't a good thing. I finally looked up the word when I was in second grade in the classroom dictionary. Merriam Webster said – whore: a woman who engages in sexual acts for money; *prostitute*; also, informal + offensive: a *promiscuous* or immoral woman. Since I was only in second grade I then proceeded to look up sex, promiscuous and prostitute… after reading the definitions I felt nauseous and light headed. You can only imagine how I felt. Dirty. Worthless. Insignificant. Sick.

And there are worse things I could share, how I tried to commit suicide in third grade and again in 8th grade as well. How I learned to "pass out" at will, which I later learned is a survival technique used by prisoners. How I was raped at knife point when I was 15, walking home from working at a fast food restaurant. Which shouldn't have surprised anyone. I was typically scheduled to close the restaurant, which meant leaving around two in the morning, without a ride home. It was about a mile and a half walk, which wouldn't be too bad during the day, but at 2am, it's not so safe. After the attack, the rapist told me to go home and don't look back or he would kill me. So that's what I did. They handled rapes a lot differently back then compared to today. No forensics, no sensitivity and the mindset that the victim must have done something wrong. I was interviewed by five different police officers and asked repeatedly, "What did you do to provoke him? Were you dressed provocatively? Did you enjoy it?" It was hard to be asked those questions when I was wearing the most un-provoking of all clothing – a fast food restaurant uniform. I

thought I was going to lose my mind. Then they had the nerve to tell my parents that I most likely made the whole thing up for attention. Seriously? The officers had no clue about me or what my life was like, and the last thing I wanted was any type of "attention" from my parents. The counselor who interviewed me wanted me to attend post-rape group counseling sessions, but I couldn't bring myself to do it. I felt so much shame and embarrassment, and the thought of telling anyone else what happened seemed unbearable. I didn't attend, and later I was told that part of the reason they concluded that it didn't happen was simply because I didn't WANT to talk about it.

After that event, I really headed into a downward spiral. School meant nothing to me anymore. Thankfully I am rather bright and my grades didn't really suffer. Learning came easy to me, but I had absolutely no aspirations whatsoever; just getting through the days and weeks was an accomplishment. I started behaving very recklessly. I got in with a group that would supply me with all the pot and alcohol I wanted and for a brief while I was using uppers and downers. But deep within me, I knew what I was doing was not only wrong, but dangerous. I quit taking the pills but continued with pot and alcohol. I started sleeping around with anyone who wanted me to; I didn't care anymore. I didn't respect myself, therefore no one else respected me either. So, the lovely plate was now shattered in a million pieces, just like the dish in the kitchen.

My family believed that I made up the story of my rape, so to add insult to injury they started referring to me as "the lying whore" instead of just "whore". But deep inside, I knew the truth and I became determined not to let THEIR truth become mine, it's a funny thing though, I was living out exactly what they said. I was sleeping around and lying to them about what I was and wasn't doing on a daily basis.

My step-mother was strict. But that's an understatement. To simply use the word strict minimizes how controlling and mentally unstable she was. She would time how long it took me to get home from school and work. I would lie and say work ended at eight o'clock,

when it really ended at seven, just to give me time to get home without trouble. But then she started scrutinizing my paychecks and noticed discrepancies. She confronted me with the difference in pay compared to what I brought home (side note here—she would file my tax returns and use my refund to take HER children shopping!). When confronted one day by my step-mother about it, I didn't lie about the discrepancies, but when she asked why I did it, I didn't even bother to respond—it would have been a waste of my breath. So she said I had to move out that night. Move out where? The streets? I went to work as scheduled that night and explained my situation to a friend, who assured me it would be okay to live with her for a while. She was a senior in high school and her parents had moved a few weeks earlier into their new home while their present home was up for sale. They let my friend and her brother stay there to finish out the school year. I moved in with her, and a few months later her mother stopped in and asked me why I wasn't living at home, so I told her the story. In looking back, it probably seemed completely unbelievable to her. While I was at school she called my step-mother who (of course) said I made the whole thing up and I was the one who moved out all on my own.

My step-mother had set up a time for me to come by and pick up a few things, or so she said. What really happened was she had my friend's mom (and a few of her friends) and my friend there at my home to confront me again as to why I moved out. I was forced to lie and say it was my idea. I knew if I told the truth there would be serious consequences and it wasn't worth it. My friend's mom (to her credit) didn't believe it was my idea at all. Just from watching how the conversation evolved, she and my friend knew it definitely wasn't my idea. I then had to move back in, but I had no bed, just a foam mattress thrown on the floor and a pillow. No bed sheets, no pillow case – just a blanket as thin as paper.

Now the already fragmented pieces of the lovely plate were picked up and thrown on the floor again to shatter even more.

As I entered my senior year, my anxiety increased to monumental proportions. I would turn 18 in December and that was only halfway through the school year. I went to my school counselor and decided to tell him what was going on. I wanted to graduate, but I also knew that once I turned 18, I would have to move out permanently. I had no place to go, I had no driver's license (my step-mother refused to sign the permission slip a couple of years earlier for me to take the class) and, I had no money. After speaking with my counselor, he connected me with a place called "The Bridge", an agency that had families who took in troubled teens. Funny thing was, I'd have to say most of my trouble was my family, not me! I was introduced to a woman who had put her name on the list to accept teens into her home. It was like foster care, but for older children. After speaking with her, she and her husband agreed to allow me to move into their home. After school on my eighteenth birthday I packed up what little I owned and my new family came to the house, parked at the curb, and waited for me. And out I walked. I wasn't sure if this was going to be better or worse. I had heard stories of kids who went to these homes or were in foster care and ended up being treated worse than where they came from, so I was not immediately relieved or relaxed – just in between.

I remember that first night so clearly. We drove to the next town, got out of the car, and unloaded what I had. As we entered the home, my foster mother turned to give me a hug. I didn't know how to respond. I stood there with my arms hanging at my side as if I was frozen, and she simply wrapped her arms around my arms and body and said, "Welcome". I don't believe, up until that point, I had ever been hugged in my life. I was 18 years old and had never experienced a warm hug.

It's amazing how long-term abuse can make you feel so old and yet so ignorant at the same time. Because of the constant abuse, neglect, and always being on your guard to survive, mentally, I felt about 100 years old. Yet I didn't even have the most basic understanding

of emotional interactions. Emotionally, I had been stunted. So now what do I do? Even in my frozen emotional state, I knew there was something wrong with me, if not wrong, then not quite right. Why couldn't I hug her back? Inside I wanted to, but I couldn't move my arms. I tried to will myself to do it, but I just couldn't.

It was the result of a broken dish.

At this time in my life I also had a keen awareness of God. The night before I moved into my foster family home, I called out to Him in desperation, "Where are you? What did I do to deserve this horrible family situation? Can you hear me? Do you care?" And out of pure fear I prayed, "Please help me. Please don't let this new family harm me." I apologized for anything and everything I could possibly think of—I made a deal with Him. "If You help me out of this I will give you everything I am, all of my life and do whatever you want me to do… just help me." This wasn't just a crisis bargain, I meant it. I swear I could feel the very presence of fear and death all around me. I could not open my eyes; I was afraid of what I would see. I hugged myself in my pain and continued to cry, but silently. Not the loud screaming type of cry, but the quiet, guttural cry from the heart. As I sat there hugging myself I began to sense a bit of calming, a return to sanity, an awareness of some sort of being that was surrounding me, like a deep strong inner peace I had never felt before. It was as if a warm blanket had enveloped me and the warmth intensified until it felt as if I were sitting outside in the bright sunshine on an intensely warm summer's day. I *knew* I had been saved; that I had been delivered from whatever evil had been trying to destroy my very life. Everything would work out okay. I didn't have the slightest clue how, but I just *knew* in the very depth of my being. I felt strength, I felt hope, I felt SAFE. At the very moment I was reveling in all of these emotions, I happened to look at the clock. It read 1:05 am, December

5—the beginning of my eighteenth birthday. I remember so clearly when I was about 13 years old thinking to myself, if I can just make it to my eighteenth birthday, everything will change, everything will be different, I will be different. I just need to survive until then. So, between my thirteenth and eighteenth birthdays, when something terrible would happen—whether I was being hit, I felt hungry, or was literally passing out from being screamed at and hit at the same time, I would remind myself of how much time remained until I turned 18. As I said earlier, I learned to pass out at will. It is amazing what your mind and body do to survive.

When things got bad, my thoughts would be things like, "I can survive this—only five years left—only four years left—only three years left", and so on. My eighteenth birthday was such a significant day for me... my whole life had depended on me making it to that day!

So there I am, 1:05 am on December 5 – I'm 18!! I made it! But did I? Would this new family accept me? Would they be as abusive as my own family? I had heard such horrible stories of foster families, and "helping" families that I wasn't so sure. How do I possibly fit in to what I considered a "normal" family situation? What did that even look like? I was so emotionally scarred and scared that I had no idea. But now, I was armed with this inner peace and strength that superseded all that I knew up until this point. All I could do was take a guess and make a strong attempt at being brave and reaching out and reaching inward to make conscious decisions to become whole again.

One of the early events that helped me to begin healing was to learn about my name. "Renee". I attended a local Lutheran church for a while with my foster family during the early 80's, and I can remember it was rather important and somewhat of a fad at that time to research your name. I have no clue why my parents named me Renee, which was a very odd name compared to the rest of my family. But when I did this name research activity, I was astounded to learn my name meant Reborn, or Renew! So *very* appropriate for me! And my

middle name, Arleen, means One Who is Devoted. HE named me! Whether my parents were aware of it or not, HE had a purpose for me, He called me back to Himself. To say afterwards everything just fell into place would be a lie, because it doesn't typically work that way. As time went by, I had to work through the hurt, pain, shame, and fear of what I'd been through. I've had to reprogram my inner voice, set boundaries with myself and others to be emotionally safe. I've had to look at the very ugliness that was thrust upon me and stand against it and say NO MORE! I've had to yell at Shame and tell it to leave, I've had to nurse my wounds and, at times, peel off the bandage to cleanse the gangrenous sore, creating more pain before healing, but I have not done this alone. I have felt the full weight of being abandoned, unwanted, unloved and unlovable. I have fought against my own self telling me I am unworthy, I am unstable, I am not cherished. But I have not had to fight this fight alone. HE has been my physician, my counselor, my place of refuge when the pain is too intense, when shame runs into my heart and wants control. When Fear rears his ugly head and sneers at me that I will never have peace or comfort. HE has helped me when issues and experiences try to derail me, or throw me into darkness, or create havoc in my life—when fear shows up repeatedly, so dark and heavy and at times it is so thick I can almost touch it. But together He and I prevail!

Here is another piece of the story that never ceases to amaze me, even though it is about myself. The whole concept of reaching my eighteenth birthday became a very strong focal point to my very survival. When I was engaged to my first husband, I realized I did not have a copy of my birth certificate—which I needed to get my marriage license. I had to track down the hospital and get the necessary documents. When I received the document in the mail, I felt my throat tighten, my knees shake and my heart pound wildly. There it was, the *exact* timing of my birth—I was born at 1:05 am on December 5. Coincidence, you say? Not in the least. The obvious connection to my drive to survive and my reaching out to my Creator

during my depths of despair was not lost to me. HE knew all along. Do I think He had planned for me to have the type of family life I did? Not in the least, but we live in a broken and bruised world. And we have free will. Do I think He simply let the circumstance of my life happen without notice? Absolutely not—I DO believe He tried to reach out to my parents and whisper in their ear... "No, don't do that, you'll hurt her." I believe He tried to reach their hearts and minds. But we all have a choice and they chose not to listen. The consequences of their choices are what brought the marring of my soul. But this marring, this shattering of the lovely dish, has brought me a sense of compassion and empathy, of righteous indignation when I see wrong upon the weak. I have a determination to impact my world, the tenacity to stand strong against injustice. There have been "easy" years and there have been years of struggle to heal, to move forward to realize my value and push myself mentally, emotionally, and spiritually into wholeness and wellness. It has been hard work; it was not instantaneous.

He and I have worked together, and there are still times when a dark thought or experience will try to hinder me in my journey. It is in those moments that I push and continue to desire to be all that I am and all that I can offer this world. There are times just when I think the broken dish is almost completely put back together, and a sliver will appear and pierce me. It is at those times that I must admit I question, "Will I ever be complete? Completely whole?" But in my quest and questioning, He has told me a story.

There once was an amazingly beautiful plate created and crafted with immense care, thought, and love. This plate was glorious in design and color, and of the finest china possible. This plate was given to a woman and a man, but the woman and man did not appreciate this gift, so they broke it. The plate was so beautiful, but because they did not love themselves, it made them feel unworthy to have it and unable to love it. So, they broke it. They lifted it high in the air and let it crash to the ground. Desiring its beauty to be shattered,

to disappear. Just like when we break a dish, it shatters everywhere. When we break a plate or dish, it is amazing how many pieces it can break into and all the many sizes – large, small, very small and even microscopic slivers.

As I've gone through this journey, I've felt Him tell me I was that dish, that beautiful, exquisite plate. Broken and shattered. But He is helping me put it back together. At first you pick up the big pieces and place them together, then as you look around and sweep you find more pieces and put them back into the plate. And then the slivers, which may be tiny but are usually the pieces that hurt the most when they prick your skin. And it takes time, just like when you break one of your own dishes, you can find the large pieces quickly, and the smaller ones are usually swept up easily, but those slivers, those tiny pieces that hide under the stove, the refrigerator… it takes time to find them. Sometimes days or weeks will go by and they'll show up under a couch or in a completely different room! They take the longest to find because they are so small. They are the most difficult to remove because they are imbedded into the skin—it takes a steady hand and extreme coordination to remove them. Eventually, almost all the pieces are found, but more often than not, there are always a few very slight pieces that are never found. What to do? The plate is not complete. It's close, but not 100 percent.

I believe I need to use those tiny gaps of missing pieces as reminders; reminders to do good, to have empathy, to make a difference, to remember a small fraction of the pain and the hurt in order to propel myself to great endeavors of impact; to keep the passion of helping through healing in other's lives and in my own as well. To see a broader perspective of humanity other than the small piece of my own life. To view others beyond what I can see, to reach out, even when I'm uncomfortable to give comfort. To understand that we all suffer to some degree—hurt, pain, shame, and insecurities—it is part of our flawed humanness. To help those who do not see a way to see a way, to be an example of "yes you can" and "let me show you

how to get there." In some degree, I wear my scars as a badge of honor and humility toward my Creator and His creation. We are all a bit broken; we've all experienced pain, but we can ALL strive for completeness, not in our own strength but in HIS, and not by ourselves but with others who know how it feels to be fragmented, and to desire our original beauty to shine forth. To step forth hand in hand and say to the Universe, I MATTER! I am here on Purpose! I can share love, hope, forgiveness, kindness and brilliant ideas to create solutions to the brokenness around me. I can spread joy, humor, and understanding to lighten the world. Yes, I CAN! And so, my dear friend, can you. Reach out, reach in, reach beyond. Inhale deeply all that you are and all that you *will be*. Let us see YOU, in all your loveliness. Wear your scars bravely and go make *your* mark in the world for yourself and humanity as well.

Renee A. Salway is a Real Estate Broker in the Denver metro area with accolades as a top ten producer. Renee serves fellow real estate agents through her role as Mentor and Trainer and loves helping agents reach their full potential in an ever-changing market.

Renee's expertise in mentoring allows her to coach entrepreneurs outside the real estate industry to help them grow their business and overcome struggle, to create a life of inner peace and well-being. Renee focuses on working with people who want to move beyond any trauma or pain they have endured to live a life of fulfillment and joy.

Renee's experience with helping others work through life trauma includes being a regional speaker and representative for SAFY (Special Alternative for Fostering Youth) of Indiana, an organization that helps place older youths with caring foster families. Renee has also spread her message of hope and healing to various women's organizations, churches and faith-based associations, as well as several teen groups.

In her spare time, Renee enjoys jogging in the early morning Colorado sunshine. She is learning to play piano, and is an accomplished singer and actress. Renee is currently writing a memoir detailing more of her life and how she overcame incredible trauma, pain, and obstacles. After raising two girls on her own, Renee is now married and lives in beautiful Aurora, Colorado.

To bring Renee to your event and hear more of her inspirational story, email Chgogirl_1@msn.com.

Creating My Joy Journey

by Lynnette Adams

"There is no greater agony than bearing an untold story inside you."
– Maya Angelou

Growing Pains

We all have a chapter that we do not want to read aloud. Actually, some of us have a few. I have considered throwing the whole damn book away more than once. I have come to learn that the chapters that were the most embarrassing to read aloud were the ones that influenced me the most. It was where I gained the most growth, where I held the most pain.

Writing your own story can be hard. Even though I have been journaling most of my life, when asked to write my story, my mind became a welter of memories that I could not quite get to make coherent sense. In the struggle to develop a story I could share, I resonated with a theme in my life: accountability and authenticity. As I thought of the many stories I had to tell, they all linked back to my

not feeling comfortable with just being me.

I did not come from a traditional family. We were not two parents, two kids, a dog and a picket fence. We were a lot of love, but a lot of dysfunction. My mom was a single mom, and as an adult woman now, I have to be honest—I have no clue how she did it. My dad and mom have their own chapters that are not mine to tell. However, since it's relevant to this story, l will say that growing up in Detroit, Michigan in dysfunction wasn't always easy.

By the time I was ready for grade school my dad was in prison. I am not sure if that was supposed to be a secret, but it definitely wasn't something I wanted to tell people who didn't already know. As early as the age of six, I learned how to hide my story and create ones that sounded better. I learned how to be fake. I do not remember a specific moment I began feeling like a fraud, but even today, I struggle with letting people in. Not many people know me—the real me— they know the manufactured happy girl I pretend to be.

I do not blame my dad for not being with us, not anymore, but for a while, I did. I was angry, I felt like I was not good enough. His absence led to a lifetime of needing others to validate that I was worth it. I lacked accountability as I grew older because of this story I kept telling myself. Every time something happened, I would immediately blame the lack of my father in my life as the reason why. Nothing was ever my fault, even though deep down I knew he was not to blame for my choices.

Not to vilify my father either—I have some great memories of us together. It is amazing the memories our brain can hold. When I was a toddler, he would sing *Sugar Pie Honey Bunch* by the Four Tops, swing me around, and dance with me. He would allow me to put barrettes and rubber bands in what I would arguably say was the best afro of all time. There was never a lack of hugs, or hearing "I love you" from him. There still hasn't been, thirty plus years later, he still tells me "I love you" every time we end a phone call, and there is always a hug upon any departure. So even while my core belief was that he did not love me, his actions demonstrated the opposite.

There is much more to our story but, for now, this is about my journey of self-awareness and being accountable for holding on to stories that I never had a reason to write about in the first place. We are in a good place now, my dad and I. We have had many years to do a lot of healing. We have both found a way to meet each other where we are, even though I continue to struggle with accepting myself.

> *"Unconditional love is one of life's most beautiful gifts."*
> – Anonymous

NAVIGATING IN THE DARK

I experienced a lot at a young age, my biggest loss being the death of my brother. He committed suicide when I was just 16 years old. I guess life was just too much for him to bear. I still struggle with the guilt I had around this. Why wasn't I a better sister? Maybe if I had been a better listener he would still be alive. This tragedy fueled my belief that when people know the real me, it could actually kill them. I was saving lives by hiding my true self. It also led to a series of "why me" parties that were not healthy for a young girl to carry into adulthood.

"You talk so much." I have heard this a million times. My personality and my approach to relationships tend to leave the impression that I am extroverted, a bad listener, and maybe a little bit of an "attention hog." WHEW, that was raw! I never quite described myself that way, but I have been given the feedback. It was always hard because I knew they were mostly wrong. There were times I would want to scream, "You've got it ALL WRONG!" I DON'T want the attention, but I do need to control this connection. Not to be misunderstood, I am a little extroverted in the sense that I love to bond with others. I do sometimes get so excited just to be a part of a tribe that I can cut off a conversation before their thought is complete because I just want them to know I am listening. My ultimate desire is to be accepted and loved, and because I am too scared that no one will love the real me, I just become whatever is needed to get the validation—in the most authentic way possible, if that makes any sense at all. I have always wanted people to think I was a good person worthy of knowing; sometimes I tried a little too hard. It gave me exactly the opposite of what I was looking for, and when the results were negative, I never self-reflected. I just blamed whoever was holding the space at that moment. Additionally, I would find myself occasionally seeking out people that did view me negatively, call them friends, and when the disappointment came, I would secretly feel validated about how right I was to hate myself so passionately.

Very early on, I learned that in order to keep secrets you had to control the relationship and vice versa. Controlling the relationship also managed the secrets. Don't let anyone get too close. Learn what people want you to say and say those things. I am very academic when it comes to my relationships. I study them, and then I adapt in a way so I can control them. I have always been larger than life or an "attention hog" as some have pointed out, but only to control the narrative. I believed that controlling the relationship would allow me to show the parts I thought people would like, even if it meant I wasn't being my authentic self. I would even mislead people by bragging about how "real" I was, knowing that this didn't even come close to the truth. Even though many described me as outgoing and larger than life, I was extremely depressed and felt invisible.

Depression was a factor, but you didn't really talk about it in the black community. I was lonely, even though I was surrounded by people who loved me, though I could not imagine why they would. I needed help, but I was always told to stop being dramatic or to pray. I must have not been good at that praying thing because it never worked, and I would end up feeling like a bigger failure for not doing it right. I resorted to a series of bad decision-making and strained relationships. I didn't know how to let go—I was so scared of losing anything close to me, I didn't know how to walk away from conflict, or how to communicate effectively. I didn't know how to lose. I didn't know how to move on. I wasn't willing to hold myself accountable for anything. I stayed stuck in perpetual dysfunction. It is funny when I think back, because I don't have those kinds of conflicts now. However, I still hold the same fears. I still struggle with being authentic. I still try to hide behind a fake smile.

Through my story, I hope to be the lighthouse for those who have not realized they are in the dark, and to be vulnerable to those who have been begging to know the real me. Most importantly, I want to share my journey, and my path to finding the true, authentic Lynnette, whether people like or dislike me. This all began with my journey to Colorado, and what I learned about authenticity and accountability and the power behind taking control of my life.

> *"There will always be someone who can't see your worth.*
> *Don't let it be you."*
> – Anonymous

COLORADO: A BEAUTIFUL DISASTER

In May of 2011 at the age of 33, I moved to Colorado with my fiancé. This wasn't the first time I had tried to move out of state. Just seven years earlier in 2004, I packed my little red Ford Focus and drove cross-country from Detroit to Las Vegas, Nevada. I was a naive young woman in my 20's, and I was still blaming the world for my problems. The effort to start a new life was not successful and I walked away with a valuable realization: you cannot run away from your problems. You face them and fix them or they follow you. My feelings of unworthiness did not go away, so I took all my bad habits to Las Vegas and made all the same mistakes with people very

quickly. I had not realized that my lack of authenticity was the problem—not other people. I was in the dark and I had not yet found my lighthouse.

When I met my husband, I was stuck. I was 31 years old at this point, frustrated that the picture I painted for my life didn't resemble the one I was living. I was finishing up graduate school and in the process of ending a relationship that had run its course with someone else. I should not have been dating but the fear of being alone was terrifying. My husband was the validation I needed at the time to remind me that I was desirable. My husband and I had only been together seriously for a little over a year, when his job relocated him to Denver, Colorado. We had already been living together in Detroit, but to be honest, I contemplated ending things several times because the idea of leaving my family after my first failed move wasn't something I wanted to do. I liked our life. We had a house, we had friends, and I had a new job. Why rock the boat? Why change something that was already (in my mind) perfect, even though I knew it wasn't built on complete honesty?

This isn't a story about us, but he is how I got here. I moved here not knowing a soul except for him and his roommate, which was a good thing. This meant that I could become someone else and there would be no one who knew anything about Lynnette back in Detroit. I remember our first apartment. The sun would shine on my face every morning, waking me up. I loved how sunny it was for about a week, and then it became a nuisance, waking me earlier than I preferred. We were planning a wedding; I was in this beautiful place and I was with my best friend. Life couldn't be better... until those feelings of unworthiness crept back in.

Colorado was a struggle. I worked odd jobs—whatever I could find to make my own personal ends meet. He paid for everything else. Nevertheless, it damaged my confidence. I had never fully depended on someone before and even though he didn't complain about his role as a financial provider, I felt unworthy. I felt like a

loser. I had multiple degrees, and I was working at Old Navy.

Working at Old Navy killed my spirit. It was not because I thought I was better, but I felt I had worked hard to deserve more than a minimum wage job. I was embarrassed. I remembered the humiliation I felt being in my thirties and having to ask my 22-year-old boss for time off to go back home for the holidays. It was humbling to say the least. People back home wanted to know how I was doing, but I had left Detroit for my happily ever after and there was no way I could tell them that wasn't happening.

It took four months to find a job that would turn into a career path. Although I made several mistakes there, it became a place that gave me a sense of pride. The Non-Profit industry was the perfect fit for my bleeding heart. I was so busy telling others' stories, no one thought to ask about mine. Being a newlywed, a step mom, and a working woman was harder than the previous single woman lifestyle with no kids. I was slowly embarking on a new journey that I was not emotionally prepared to handle.

While I was working this new job, I was still making less than $40k a year. The job was extremely fulfilling, but the financial struggle and resentment around all my hard work in school to get such a low paying job left me bitter. I was also venturing into a territory I was unfamiliar with: infertility. Ever since I was a little girl, I had always painted exactly what my life would look like. It seemed like I had finally gotten it: my prince charming and my happily ever after—except it wasn't. Every person's wrong action lead to me justify why nothing was my fault. I wasn't willing to be accountable for what was happening. Even bigger, I wasn't willing to put much effort into finding the root of the problem. Having an obstacle felt much more validating than finding a solution.

I had expected to get pregnant right away, and being a mom was much more important to me than having an amazing career. We had my stepdaughter full-time, and while I was fulfilling the duties of a mom, I didn't feel like one. My need to appear perfect wouldn't let

me admit that. Thank God for Facebook. I was able to paint a picture that showed the opposite. She was just five years old and being in a new state was a lot for her, and I was not her mom. I remember feeling like such a failure most of the time because as badly as I wanted to, I felt like I was not connecting with her. Why would this child love someone who was doing so badly at parenting? I pretended I was confident, but I went to bed crying every night, wondering how I could suck at the one thing I wanted more than anything.

I began to think if I could just have my own baby, we would have this complete perfect picture. I became obsessed with my misery when it didn't happen. I remember crying every 28 days when my period would come. Not only was it confirmation that I wasn't pregnant, it was a nagging reminder that I had reached a new level of failing. Fundamentally, as a woman I was supposed to be able to bear children. That was my purpose, and I couldn't fulfill it. If I couldn't have children then I wasn't even a woman. Digesting the reality that my body didn't even trust me enough to carry a child sent me into a deep dark depression that would begin to take a dangerous toll on my marriage, and my emotional stability.

As I think back, it was always so surprising to me that I could love this little person that I cared for every day so much, but at the same time be extremely jealous that I couldn't have a baby of my own. The resentment was a lot, and, at the time, I was unable to effectively verbalize the despair behind being denied motherhood. Here was this little person I loved more than anything, but she was a constant reminder of what I would never be—a mother. Not being able to get pregnant was, to this day, one of the most devasting things I have had to come to terms with. At almost 40, I am still struggling with that chapter. To heal from this issue, I just began pretending that I didn't really want a baby anyway. I was the same six-year-old girl hiding her story because the real one was too hard to tell. I could not risk being vulnerable, and having people judge me on how inadequate I was by not being able to do the very thing a woman was

created for.

My relationship struggled. It was no one's fault—no one was to blame. We made bad decisions. I did not plan, we did not communicate and because of it, I went from good credit to bad, from depressed to suicidal. At one point, I thought this move to Colorado was possibly one of the worst decisions I had made. Not because of who I came with but because I truly believed that I didn't deserve a life where I was loved, respected, or valued. I didn't even think those things were possible for a person as worthless as me. An even greater concern was the thought that, without all the friends and distractions from back home, my husband would most certainly have more time to get to know me and realize he made a mistake in choosing me.

Here I had to unravel my first layer: accountability. I knew that in order to grow and to make it in Colorado, I had to own my circumstances. I was in full control. I began meeting more people, but I never really got too close. I controlled the narrative. I smiled often, and only a few people knew about my struggles. I lied about how happy I was and kept soundbites of positive quotes and affirmations that would lead these new friends to believe I had it all together. I almost never invited anyone to my personal space, because I didn't want to be judged. To date, I still don't invite people to my home. I feel that my space would tell more of my story than I am willing to share. The intimacy of houseguests overwhelms me.

I looked at the women out here, and they all had more than me. Better lives, more money, vacations, and happier families. I was envious—too envious to be a real friend to anyone. There were a couple people who managed to penetrate a layer or two, but as soon as I realized what was happening, I put my guard back up and built a wall. I was almost annoyed at the idea of people actually getting to know me. I felt certain if they did, they would find out I wasn't worth knowing.

I would say that the evolution of "Lynnette" definitely happened

in Colorado. I was lonely a lot even though, like in earlier years, people surrounded me. I never really believed they liked me so all attempts at constructive feedback felt like vicious attacks.

I thought about suicide more in Colorado than I ever had in my life. It was not turning out to be the fairytale I hoped for. The cost of living was rising greatly, but my salary wasn't. I was struggling but didn't fully invest in finding something else because I didn't believe I was good enough to get it.

I was running in circles around myself trying to fit in, only to not be noticed, to hold back tears in public and make my smile believable... and for the most part I succeeded, but I felt like a complete fraud. No one really knew me. I was still just the girl who talked a lot. However, I couldn't stop talking. I couldn't give a person a chance to ask any questions in fear they would dig into my past. It was a fear I walked with daily.

To top off all of my insecurities, I had another barrier I had never dealt with before: I was uncomfortable and felt displaced due to the lack of diversity. I was stuck in a world that was supposed to be home but no one looked like me. I was working and living in one of the least diverse counties, and while people were nice, I wasn't used to the micro-aggressions. As the nation was divided, I felt like the black girl eye sore in a white world left to explain or defend my culture. I hated being the only one in the room. This lead to me trying to fit in places where I couldn't help but stand out.

The big lesson in this for me was: when people don't want your authenticity, it is even more important to give it. I was stuck in "not enough" mode. I wasn't black enough for some, I was too black for others. People made assumptions based off cultural norms and I spiraled into pretend mode just to protect my sanity. This was when I should have been the most authentic. I also had to hold some of the accountability, because I chose to not be myself. It was much easier to be accepted than to be outspoken.

By 2016, I had been working two jobs, seven days a week over the

past two years. I was exhausted pretty much all the time, and one of the women I had met on my journey here invited me to her home to learn about a 12-week self-development course she was starting. The class focused on community, spirituality, and nutrition. All of these were areas I was struggling in, but I had no idea how I would fit one more thing in my schedule. I remember sitting in the initial meeting, and the first thing they asked us to do was write down the things that were important to us. I wasn't even on my list. I knew right then that I had to take this class because, although I had not put myself on my list, I also believed I didn't deserve to be on it. I am not certain where I got this belief from, but it was my core belief.

I knew the next 12 weeks would be the last chance I had, so I borrowed money to enroll. I was lost and needed this course. Life was very hard at the time, and I was desperate. The first day of the class, I walked in and saw ALL white women. I thought to myself – great, I can't be vulnerable with these women. They will judge me. I will fit any stereotypes they've been told. I am going to misrepresent my race. There is no way I can be authentic here, and I don't have the energy to fake it for 12 weeks. I went home that night wondering what I could say to get my money back. I decided not to. I'm glad I didn't try to back out. That was most cleansing 12 weeks of my life.

What did I learn in those 12 weeks?

1. Trust the process. I allowed these women I had never met to get to know me in a way people had not been able to in years. I never wondered if any of them judged me. Maybe they did, but vulnerability was freeing. I released a lot of hurt in those 12 weeks.

2. Ask for what you need. In the beginning of the program, I wrote down what I needed from the universe. Better job, new car, real friends (they were there all along) and confidence. I got all of that, and then some, almost exactly a year later. Now I have a job I love in Higher Education offering scholarships in one of the most diverse communities in Colorado. I got that job by showing up as authentically as possible.

3. It's ok to not be ok. It is ok to be yourself. Depression is not something to be ashamed of. Life doesn't have to be a continuous stream of perfection. Here I learned that I didn't have to try so hard. The wonderful thing about allowing others to get to know you, is that you don't have to be the driver all the time. Controlling the narrative can get exhausting.

4. Most importantly, I learned that I had a lot to offer the world. I grew so much over the following year. I learned how to silence the noise. I know that there are some people who won't like me, but if everyone does, I'm probably not being very authentic. I also learned to be accountable for situations I put myself in. I did not have a baby, but I also did not do everything I could to try to get pregnant. I had not bonded authentically with people, but not due to their lack of effort. It was my reluctance to let them in. Everything I wanted I did not have because I had not embraced my true authentic self, and I had not held myself accountable for any outcomes.

Colorado was where I learned you had to own your ugly. I wasn't a victim. Although for 30 plus years, I had played one unconsciously. Until this point, nothing had been my fault and I would seek out the people who would validate my pity.

"You are your own worst enemy; become your greatest ally."
– Anonymous

JOY JOURNEY

For my 39th birthday, a friend of mine asked what I wanted for my birthday. I told her in tears, "a do over. I need to do this all over." She looked at me and said, "then do it over." At that moment, my Joy Journey movement was born. I did not like the phrase "bucket list"— it sounded so final.

I decided to be intentional with my future. I would create a

bucket list, or as I call it, my Joy Journey goals. I'm not trying to knock things off the list before I die… I'm trying to add joy to my life while I live! I would like to think of myself as a working document.

Life is a journey, an incredible one, but only if you're living from the most authentic place possible. I pride myself now in being completely ridiculous when it comes to my expectations from THIS life! My favorite color is pink, my spirit animal is a unicorn, and I believe that many problems can be resolved through conversation with a good friend and dessert. It took me a minute to get there, but I'm there and it's amazing.

Even when you find your joy, your peace, life can still sometimes sneak up with chaos. Life doesn't have to perfect to be happy. I speak from a place of knowing. As I write this chapter, life hasn't magically become perfect. I am certain I will have several more stories to tell.

Sometimes, we are not even aware of where the journey is taking us, but it is important to enjoy the ride. Life is only fun if you live it! That being said, what are some of your Joy Journey goals? I am taking it a step further and sharing the experiences as well. I have already starting marking things off the list, and having fun doing it. Now go make yours!

Just remember that when things don't happen the way you want, look at the source first. Look within. The answer is usually right there.

Top Three Joy Journey Goals
1. Go to a meditation retreat somewhere fabulous. EAT PRAY LOVE style.
2. Become a published author.
3. Make a significant change in someone else's life.

"If we live for the destination we miss out on the joy we could have at every point in our journey, even when things suck."
– Nate Hilpert

Lynnette (Lynn) Adams is the Assistant Director of Donor Relations at the Community College of Aurora. Born and raised in Detroit, but relocated to Colorado, she has found a love for hiking, traveling, girls' nights and quality time with her family. Most recently, after battling depression, she created her blog JoyJourneyTravel.com. This blog chronicles her travel experiences as she shares her Joy Journey list with the world. For more information, subscribe to her blog or follow her on Facebook.com/YourJoyJourney. She can also be reached for public speaking opportunities at LynnJoyJourney@gmail.com.

See Only Love

by Andrea Rahlf

Sometimes life literally has to "hit us over the head", or in my case the heart, for us to wake up and realize that the time has come to do the "real" work we came here to do.

One evening in early February 2014, I was in my office in the clinic that I managed. I had been a healthcare administrator for almost 30 years and working 55-60 hours a week was pretty routine for me. The staff, nurses, and residents had been gone for quite a while and I was finishing up some of the work that never seemed to end. I was startled by what felt like pressure and pain in my chest. I stopped and took a couple of breaths, and the pain subsided. After a couple of minutes the chest pain returned, so I decided it was time to call it a day and head for home. On the way home, the pain came back again. I had heard many times that a heart attack felt like an elephant had

its foot on your chest. It really did feel that way. I called my husband from the car and told him I didn't feel well, that I had chest pain. He said, "Maybe you should stop at an ER on the way home". I said, "I'm not going to do that, I'll be fine". I knew that an ER visit at 7:00 pm at night would last until midnight and probably cost thousands of dollars. So I convinced myself that it would pass and I kept driving home. The next morning I got up and drove to work as usual. About halfway there, the pain in my chest came back. When I got to the clinic, I walked up to one of the residents and told him that I was having some chest pain. He said, "Well I'm not your doctor, but if I was, I'd tell you to go right to the Emergency Room".

I called my husband and then drove over to the ER at the hospital that I worked at, which was only a block away. After a long day in the ER and some imaging tests I was told that I was having a "cardiac event". This is medical jargon for a heart attack. They told me that my left main artery was 50% blocked and recommended immediate office visits to my primary care physician and a cardiologist. Since I had never been a smoker or drinker and had no family history of heart disease, my physicians decided that my heart attack was stress related. My follow-up office visits went well. I was prescribed meds that I would need to take for the rest of my life and had a nuclear stress test—I had no more chest pain. I was also referred to a psychiatric nurse practitioner to learn how to deal with stress. After several weeks, and discussions with my family and the nurse practitioner, I decided that I would retire at the end of June. I was old enough to collect Social Security and enroll in Medicare so it seemed that this would be the right thing to do. Some of my family members had retired a couple of years earlier, so I was pretty excited about a life of leisure. In April 2014, when I announced to all of my staff and colleagues that I was going to retire in two months, most of them said the predictable things you always hear like, "Oh how I envy you, not having to get up and go to work every day." "It's going to be so much fun!" "What are you going to do with all your free time?"

During the past 30 years as a professional, I was also a full-time wife and mother. I had no experience with having a lot of free time and really had no idea what to expect. I fantasized that I would make all kinds of new friends. My new friends and I would have coffee or lunch together. I also fantasized that I would spend my days taking long walks, working on creative projects around the house, and enjoying shopping for just for fun.

Fantasy and reality are two completely different things. The first problem was that I did not have any friends who were also retired. All of my friends still worked. Also, I was new to Denver having moved here for my career a little over three years prior, and making new friends was not going to happen overnight. Give me a break! I had no personal life outside of my husband, my kids and grandkids. After spending most of our lives and careers in the Midwest, my husband and I relocated to Colorado in late 2008 to be closer to two of our three children and our new grandbabies.

But, like I approached everything else in my life, I thought, "I'm up to the challenge!" I'd just go out and make new friends. I wanted to be around healthy, interesting and active people, so I started going to the local Rec center. I went to a low-impact aerobics class, yoga classes, and worked out with a personal trainer. I was sure that I would find all kinds of other healthy, active retirees who were dying to be my friend. Well that didn't work. I discovered very quickly that there were lots of active retirees at the Rec center, but they already had full lives. A few of them were friendly enough to say hello. But after nearly a year of going to the same classes, no one even remembered my name and I never really connected with anyone.

Another attempt at friendship was to start going to "Meet-ups" (groups of like-minded individuals that you can find on-line). It's easy, just Google "meet-up" and put in your zip code. I met some nice people, but in the end almost everyone I met was trying to promote their business by networking. I had no desire to promote myself because I wasn't an entrepreneur and was not about to start a business.

So there I was, home alone all day every day, reading Facebook posts from my retired relatives and friends back in the Midwest. They all seemed to be busy having fun and posting pictures of their wonderful vacations and other exciting things that you do when you don't have to work full-time. Not me. I was sitting at home reading Facebook, wondering how I would keep from going crazy until my husband could retire and we could have fun, too.

Besides having lots of hours in the day by myself, there is another aspect of retirement that I wasn't prepared for, which is living on a fixed income without tapping into my retirement savings. So I was home alone with lots of free time, no friends, and trying not to spend any money. I wondered what happened to my life and what I was going to do next. It was summer, so I busied myself with walking, gardening and projects around the house. Fall came and I volunteered at my grandson's grade school, but most days I had nothing to do.

Then, in early in September, three months after I left my job, my son, Jonathan, told me that he and his family were moving to Montana. He had moved to Denver right after college, 20 years earlier. His sister had followed him to Denver after she graduated from college. So, two of my three kids and their growing families were the reason that we had moved to Colorado. I thought that after I retired I was going to be able to focus my time on being a wife, mother, and grandmother. Now I realized that they really didn't need me. I was no longer a healthcare executive and my kids didn't need me. What was I supposed to do? I initially thought that what I felt was loneliness, but it wasn't actually loneliness because I am comfortable being alone. The feeling was loss. I had lost my identity and what I thought was my purpose for being here.

As much as I struggled to keep busy, the first year of retirement went by pretty uneventfully. Then, in the summer of 2015, I went to a workshop about finding your Life Purpose through your "Birth Path." I went to this workshop because I had always been interested in the spiritual aspects of life. I knew that I had spirit guides who

were always with me. I'm a Virgo, someone who is analytical, seeks truth and understanding, and relentlessly pursues problem solving and perfection. Surely, the birth path workshop would help me find my real purpose. That day I learned that I was a 9. There are 12 birth paths that are determined by adding the numbers in our birthdate and narrowing that number down to one cardinal number, one through nine. You can also be an 11, 22, or 33. The individuals who are 11s, 22s and 33s are said to be Master souls. Knowing our birth path can give us information about our talents and our purpose in life. My birthdate is September 8, 1945. So, 9+8+1+9+4+5 = 36; and 3+6 = 9. Someone with a birth path 9 is a humanitarian, a leader, is wise and has compassionate insight and is a writer. I also learned that in 2015, the year I went to the workshop, I was in Personal Year Seven. We can determine our personal year by using the same method. My birth date September 8, plus the current year, 9+8+2+0+1+5=25; 2+5 = 7. Our Personal Year begins every January 1 and forces us to focus on the lessons that we need to learn at that particular time. Year seven is a sabbatical or a time of quiet solitude. This period of time forces us to focus on ourselves through mystical studies, developing intuition and drawing on what's instinctively there for us to learn. Wow! This was clearly what I was doing. I was alone with no demands on a daily basis and had the time to begin to focus on myself.

Kate, who became my Life Coach and is now a dear friend, led the birth path workshop. For the next three months, she helped me by giving me some tools, and walked me through some of the hard work I needed to do to come to grips with who I really was and why I was here. Kate encouraged me to meditate and also to work with Angel cards every day. Meditation was difficult for me and I still don't like it. It was hard for me to sit still, relax, and clear my mind, especially when I had been super busy for the last 30 years. But the Angel cards really spoke to me. Angel cards are a deck of cards with beautiful pictures and messages that, if we use them to ask for our

angels' help with a particular problem or situation, can give us powerful guidance.

Little did I know that retirement would give me the space and time I needed to learn these new skills, to tap into the guiding forces in my life, and to force me to focus on my real purpose. While I can't minimize the fact that I had been a competent professional for 30 years, I had to face that I had built a career that kept me so busy that I didn't have time to think about the life that I had escaped from 35 years ago. It was time for me to confront my identity and the woman I really was. I also realized that I needed to write my story. My story isn't the one about being a healthcare executive who transitioned to retirement. It's about how I completely changed my life and became that person. It's why the loss of my career and my son's moving away threw me into the depths of despair and confusion. It was my year 7 and it was time for me to confront the loss.

The day that I started writing my story, I needed courage and guidance. So, I pulled three Angel cards from Doreen Virtue's deck, *Daily Guidance from your Angels*. My question to the Angels was, "I need help with writing my story. Where do I start?" The first card on the left was **Life Purpose**. The card on the left speaks about the immediate past with respect to the situation you inquired about. "The purpose of your life is to serve in a way that brings great joy to yourself and others. Don't worry about finding your purpose. Instead, focus upon serving a purpose, and then your purpose will serve you".

The second card, which is in the middle, was **Cupid.** The card in the middle holds messages about your question's current status and what you need to know or work on right now. "We send great waves of love into your heart and mind, awakening your love for life itself. Your clear decision to accept joy has triggered this reawakening. Allow yourself to spontaneously celebrate love in all its glorious aspects."

The third card on the right shows your immediate future if you continue on your present path and follow the guidance from

the middle card. The third card was **See Only Love**. "Look past the seeming errors, mistakes, and misunderstandings, and see only the love within each person (including yourself). Your resolute focus upon the love that underlies every situation brings about healing in undreamed-of ways."

Pulling these Angel cards was the validation I needed that it was time to write my story, the "real" story. It is the story of my identity and the total upheaval that I went through to become who I am today. Inside my story is a lot of pain, guilt, loss and shame. There was so much loss and it was all coming back because I had time to focus on myself. I knew that if I was ever going to acknowledge these things I had buried for 30 years, that I would have to tell my story from the beginning.

It was January 1, 1980 and I was 34 years old. I lived in a small town in southeast Iowa. I had been married for almost 14 years and I had three children. Looking back on it now, I was in what they call an "emotional blackout". I was functioning on autopilot in order to take care of my home and my children, but I wasn't really there mentally or emotionally. I have tried many times in the past and still do try to connect with memories specific to most of 1979, but there is nothing there. This worries me because I have a very good memory for dates, events and details. It's part of my organized Virgo nature. But, I do vividly recall New Year's Day 1980. I recall lying in the bathtub thinking how easy it would be to slip under the water and die. I was going to turn 35 on September 8, 1980 and I knew that my life had to change or I would be killed or kill myself.

Living in a small town in Iowa was both comfortable and suffocating. It was comfortable because it was easy to get around. Everyone and everything was familiar. I had wonderful friends, all of whom were young mothers with successful husbands and my days

were busy and unencumbered. My friends and I took our kids to the park, went to each other's houses for play-dates, talked about and helped each other decorate our homes. We even had a potluck group that studied Astrology. But the town was suffocating for some of the same reasons. Everyone knew everything about my husband, my family, and me. There was no anonymity and when my marriage was in trouble, everyone knew it.

I was barely 20 years old when I got married, which looking back on now is probably one of the many issues that I was dealing with. I was too young and had no experience with life on my own as a young adult. There is a learning curve in any relationship, but in those days, the husband was the head of the house, and it was the role of the wife to support him. At least that's what most women at that time did. I had lived through the 70's and pretty much watched the "women's liberation movement" from the sidelines. When we got married, I still had two years of college to finish and my husband was in veterinary medical school. After I graduated, I taught elementary school until he graduated. This is what young women did. We didn't focus on our careers, and the careers we chose were usually that of a teacher, nurse or secretary. My girlfriends and I all did the same things. We got married, supported our husbands until they could finish school, had kids, and became full-time wives and mothers.

There are lots of reasons that my marriage began to crumble. Probably the most significant was that I had five pregnancies in five years. I became pregnant for the first time in early 1970. We had been married for four years and I was a first grade teacher. I was very happy about the pregnancy but my happiness was short-lived. I had been exposed to Rubella at the elementary school where I was teaching. After a blood test showed a very high titer, which was way out of normal range, my physician recommended a therapeutic abortion because he felt that the baby would have numerous developmental problems and may not survive. I was heart-broken and depressed. I also felt a sense of guilt and shame. My doctor told me not to say the

word "abortion" out loud because abortions were illegal. He told me that he was going to admit me for a D & C (Dilation and curettage) which was an acceptable procedure. In late April 1970, just before the beginning of my second trimester, I went to the hospital, had the procedure and went home 24 hours later. I took a few days off and that was that. We didn't talk about my pregnancy with anyone. We were too busy. It was the end of the school year, my husband was graduating, and we were moving back to Illinois so that he could join a small animal practice. Shortly after we moved to Illinois that summer, I became pregnant again and my first son, Andrew, was born in April 1971.

When Andrew was five months old, we moved to a small town in the southeast part of Iowa where my husband became a partner in a growing veterinary practice. This is where I lived for the next nine years. About six weeks after our move to Iowa, I found out that I was pregnant again and our son Jonathan was born in July 1972. He was the easiest baby in the world to take care of and such a blessing. I was happy, but a little overwhelmed. I had a new home in a new community and two babies – a 14-month old and a newborn. My parents lived 200 miles away and my husband worked very long days. So, family support for a new mom was non-existent. But that was okay; it was my job to take care of the home and kids.

Just when I was becoming settled into the role of a full-time mother of two little boys, I found out I was pregnant again. Andrew was two and Jonathan was 10 months old and my third baby was due in January 1974. However, in October 1973 at the end of my second trimester, I developed a uterine infection from an IUD that had been implanted after Jon was born. I went into premature labor and my daughter Elizabeth, was born and died on October 3, 1973. Her lungs were not developed enough to support her breathing. In less than 24 hours after giving birth, I was discharged from the hospital. Elizabeth was born on a Wednesday evening, we held a small funeral on Friday and buried her in a cemetery on a hill outside of

town. I had no time to rest or to grieve because I was too busy. So I resumed the daily routine of taking care of my home, my husband and my two children.

I remember being very, very sad, but I did my best to cover it up. I wrote letters and poems to my dead daughter. Sometimes, I put the boys in the car and drove out to the cemetery just be near her. Most days I went about my daily chores, taking care of my house and my children, but I cried a lot. The grief and depression lingered under the surface on a daily basis. By this time, I had four pregnancies in three and a half years. I loved being the mom of two beautiful little boys, but the shame and guilt from the first pregnancy and the loss of my daughter was always there. I knew nothing about post-partum depression, and as I look back on it, I'm sure that's what I was dealing with. My husband didn't know what to do and I'm sure he felt helpless, so he escaped by working all of the time. He escaped from me and from the overwhelming task of being responsible for a family with two young children and a depressed wife. I also focused on having another child. I wanted to replace the daughter I had lost.

I tried to get pregnant again throughout 1974. When I didn't get pregnant, we decided that two kids were enough and we were not going to have any more children. This was in early 1975. About 6 weeks after having this discussion, I found out that I was pregnant again. I was happy, but scared. My success rate with having successful pregnancies was only 50 percent. We didn't tell anyone but my parents and a couple of my girlfriends. I stayed at home most of the time and took care of the house and the boys. Most of our acquaintances didn't know that I was pregnant again until the fall of 1975 when I was nearly seven months along.

Our daughter, Katherine, was born on December 2, 1975. By that time, my marriage was in real trouble, but I stayed busy and tried not to think about it. All I knew was that I was at home with three kids and my husband was gone. He would leave early in the morning, come home for dinner and leave again, and not come home

until late. I knew he couldn't have clients all hours of the night, but I was too overwhelmed to think about it. I would put the kids to bed at night and pace the floor wondering when he was going to come home.

During this time we stopped communicating, and it took a toll on our marriage. He was often gone at work and when he came home, he was always in a bad mood. One day when my daughter was about two, my husband's business partner called me. Apparently, he had just witnessed a scene that he felt was dangerous and he wanted to warn me about my husband's temper. I didn't know what to think. I was lonely, frustrated and scared. Shortly after this episode, I put the kids in the car drove the 200 miles to my parents' house to stay because I was afraid. I did this a couple of times during that year. At my parents' encouragement, we went to see a marriage counselor, but that didn't have any lasting effect. During the months and years between 1976 and 1979, I existed day-to-day, trying to hold things together. But I also spent a lot of time in my head planning an escape. I knew that I desperately needed something that I could do for myself. Being a housewife and mother in that small town wasn't working for my husband, the marriage, or me.

In late 1976 my husband's business partner bought a small airplane, a Piper 140. I had always wanted to learn to fly, and I guess he knew that. He offered me hours, called "dual-time," in his plane at a reduced rate and introduced me to his instructor. So, in December 1976, when my daughter was one year old, I began taking flying lessons. Oh my God! Flying was wonderful! It was exciting, exhilarating, and I felt free!

Taking flying lessons did wonders for my self-esteem. I always believed that I wasn't very smart, but my opinion about myself changed dramatically after I started flying. I soloed in January 1977. In March I went to Des Moines to take a ground school course, then studied and passed the written exam with "flying colors." Learning how to fly an airplane and getting a pilot's license was incredibly demanding. In

seven months from January to July 1977, I realized that I was smarter and more capable than I had ever thought I was. Non-pilots do not have any concept about what it takes to become a pilot. You not only have to been very intelligent but also very focused. Flying requires that you study and understand weather, navigation, aerodynamics, the mechanics of how an airplane engine works, how each instrument works, and what the instruments tell you. Then you have to put it all together simultaneously and pass two tests; a written exam and a flight exam. It takes multi-tasking to a whole new level! Only other pilots can understand the skills and mental challenges required to fly an airplane. Soon I had another small group of friends, the other private pilots in my town. In July 1977, I became only the second woman in the eastern half of the state of Iowa to get a private pilot's license.

No one in my family, except for my dad, and certainly not my husband, understood my need to fly. My dad was a glider pilot and while he didn't like the fact that I was leaving my young children with a babysitter to get in a small airplane, I knew that he understood the feeling and was proud of me. My girlfriends all thought I was crazy. Most of them were afraid of being in a small airplane. It seemed inconceivable to everyone who knew me that I wanted to become a pilot. For me, it was a huge accomplishment and most of all, it was an escape. However, flying was not the escape that was going to get me out.

Obviously, I needed money to support my flying, so I went back to work part-time. I substitute taught whenever I could at most of the elementary schools in town. I also taught two courses at the small liberal arts college in town, and I worked in a dental office. I enjoyed all of those activities, I enjoyed the independence, and I used the money that I made to pay for babysitters and support my flying habit. I was busier than ever, and I was having fun, but I knew I needed more. I still felt trapped and my husband was out of reach. He had detached a long time ago.

When my husband was home, which wasn't very often, we

argued. I wanted to go on vacations and he didn't. I wanted to buy an airplane, and of course he didn't. I wanted to redecorate the house, which he finally allowed me to do. I felt that he didn't understand me at all and he just wanted me to stay home and be a wife and mother. My marriage was a mess and it got much worse. The tension and arguments escalated and eventually led to him becoming physically abusive. This was a pattern that continued over the next two years.

In late 1979, I decided to enroll in graduate school at the University of Iowa. Iowa City was only an hour north of where I lived, which was not a bad commute. I rationalized that if I was ever going to feel less trapped and more independent, I needed a career that would support three kids and myself. I decided that a master's degree would do that and the class that I signed up for was going to start in mid-January 1980.

Using flying as a hobby and a diversion as well as enrolling in graduate school became too much for my marriage. The more independent I became, the more upset and threatened my husband was. He started to drink more and continued to work late every night. Often, after the kids were in bed, we would argue. He was pushing and shoving me, which is a behavior that started a few years earlier, but this time it was beginning to happen more often. I had bruises on my arms most of the time from his grabbing and holding me. He threatened me with knives, mostly after he'd had too much to drink. We had grown so far apart that we had become completely different people. By now I was afraid of him most of the time and I wanted out of the marriage.

One night, in the middle of the night, he put his foot on my back and kicked me out of bed. I was asleep and woke up to find myself on the floor. I was very scared and knew that I needed to get out of the house. I quickly got dressed and drove to the police station to file a complaint. I told the police about that incident and as I had thought they would, they minimized it. No one could believe that my husband would be abusive to me because he was so well-liked in

the community. But, I felt that I needed to let somebody know how scared I was. I called my girlfriend from the police station and asked if I could go over to her house and spend the rest of the night. She was kind and supportive, but I got up the next morning, drove home and tried to pretend that everything was normal. I made breakfast for the kids and we never spoke about that incident again. My graduate class started a couple of weeks later and I drove to Iowa City two nights a week leaving my husband home with the kids. I was never afraid that he would harm the kids and he never did. But worst came to worst, and I knew it was only a matter of time before I had to leave the home.

In mid-February, I went to see an attorney to get some advice about my situation and asked him how to begin the process of filing for a separation or divorce. After I told him my story, he drew up divorce papers for me. During that meeting he told me something that I didn't believe at the time, but I as I look back on it, it was spot on. He said, "If you leave your home, just remember this… whatever you take with you is all you are going to have for a very long time." At the time I thought, "That can't be right. I'll file for a divorce, which won't be a surprise to my husband. I'll get custody of my kids and a decent settlement from him and I'll start a new life." I had no idea what my new life would be, but I decided to leave. My plan wasn't very sophisticated. It was actually pretty simple, and I decided that I would figure things out as I went along. Of course, nothing is ever that simple.

One morning about a week after my visit to the attorney's office, I followed through with my plan, such as it was. I got the kids up just like I did every day, made the boys breakfast and got them off to school. Then I drove my daughter to preschool. I came home and very methodically packed a suitcase of clothes for my daughter and myself. I threw a couple of blankets and some stuffed animals in the back of the station wagon. I went to the bank and withdrew the $800 that I had saved out of my savings account. My husband was going to be served with divorce papers by the sheriff's office later

that morning. I sat down at the kitchen table and wrote the boys a note. I told them to call their dad when they got home from school and that I would see them in a few days. I didn't want to leave the boys, but I really didn't have any choice. I didn't have a clue where I was going to be living and how long the process of getting a job and getting settled in an apartment in Iowa City was going to take me. I definitely didn't want to disrupt their lives by taking them away from their home and school. I thought I was doing the only thing that was safe and secure for them. I also thought that it was just temporary and that I would be able to come and get them in a couple of weeks. I tried to act very calm, but my heart was in my throat. I was running on pure adrenalin.

I drove to my daughter's pre-school as usual, picked her up on time and then headed for Iowa City. She was confused and crying and said that she wanted to go home. I remember that we had lunch at McDonald's and I stopped in a convenience store and bought her a little monkey. She named him Montgomery. Montgomery became her closest friend for a long, long time.

It was the middle of February in Iowa. The middle of winter is not the best time of the year to escape your home and your life, but a driving force inside was propelling me. Anxiety, fear and adrenalin kept me going and kept me focused on the present moment. Later that afternoon, I called the phone number a counselor at a women's advocacy center in Iowa City had given me earlier in the week. It was the number for a shelter in Cedar Rapids for women and children who were victims of domestic abuse. The woman who answered the phone told me that they didn't give out the address of the shelter, but that someone would meet me in a Walmart parking lot the next morning and that I should follow them to the safe house. We checked into a motel for the night. I left my daughter in the motel room watching TV while I went out to park the car and get our suitcases. I remember that it was dark, cold, and sleeting. My heart was pounding. I said to myself, "God, I'm alone. Please stay with me and help me."

The next days, weeks, and months went by in a blur. I lived in the moment by putting one foot in front of the other. There was nothing else I could do. The shelter that I was living at helped me find childcare for my daughter so that I could drive to Iowa City and look for a job. I interviewed for a job at University Hospital working in the clinical lab. I was hired on the spot and started work the following Monday. Within a week, I also found an apartment in Iowa City and childcare in the same building. All of these events happened within two weeks of my leaving home. I know now that I was being guided every step of the way by God and my Angels. My prayers were being heard and answered. Nothing was the way I imagined it would be but we were safe, I had a job, and we had a place to live.

For the next year, the focus of my life became staying in school, working at the hospital, and fighting for custody of my three kids. It took fifteen months before my divorce was final in April 1981. During that time, there were lots of bitter battles over custody of the kids, days when I literally didn't have any food in the house and had constant worries about money. I also had to deal with some confrontations with my parents who just wanted me to go back home and resume my life as a wife and mother. It took an enormous amount of emotional energy to keep going, but I persevered. I had finally escaped, and I was building a new life. It wasn't the life I dreamed about, but day-by-day and month-by-month, I was becoming a new person. I was independent and I was making my own decisions. Good or bad, the decisions were mine and I was in control of my life. There were times when the emotional pain was more than I could bear. But each time I thought I couldn't go on, my guides would put something or someone in my path that would hold me up and keep me going.

I left my home in February 1980 with literally nothing but the clothes on my back and a few things in the car. Almost a year and a half later, my divorce was final. After a 14-year marriage, three children, and a lovely home, I came away with only a few material things to show for that life. I got a chair, a lamp, my daughter's bedroom

set, and a modest settlement. What I lost was overwhelming. I lost my home and most of my worldly possessions. I lost custody of my sons. I lost their childhood and the privilege of taking care of them and watching them grow up day-by-day. My daughter grew up as an only child and lost the experience of living in a home with her father and her brothers.

The guilt and shame and losses were unbearable. I had been thinking about and trying to escape for almost five years because I somehow knew at a cellular level that unless I escaped from that life, I would die. I still believe that. But through the pain, the loss, the grief, and the sadness, I became the person I was supposed to be. I carved out a new identity for myself. I graduated with my master's degree in May 1982 and my family, who had never come to visit me during those years in Iowa City, came to my graduation.

In March 1982, another amazing thing happened. About six weeks before graduation, my Angels handed me another gift, and this time it was right out of the clear blue sky. I was on an airplane, flying back to Cedar Rapids from Atlanta. I had been in Atlanta over spring break, visiting a girlfriend and interviewing for a job. The plane made a stopover in St. Louis. The person who had been sitting next to me got off and a good-looking guy with blonde hair and blue eyes sat down in the seat next to me. He told me his name was Randy and he lived in Aspen, Colorado. He was really friendly and we talked non-stop the rest of the way to Iowa. The plane landed again in Davenport, which I found out was his hometown, and as he got off the airplane, he asked me for my phone number. I thought "Sure. I'll never see you again," but gave it to him anyway. The next morning at 8:00 am my phone rang and Randy invited me to lunch. The rest is history and we were married in Davenport on the day after Christmas 1982. We have now been married for 35 years.

Through perseverance and the support of a loving husband and my family, I've had an amazing career, an amazing life, and have a large and amazing family. I have three wonderful children, a son-in-law and two daughters-in-law and eight beautiful grandchildren.

I want to fix the pain that I know my children carry for those difficult years during their childhood, but I know I can't. I believe that our souls choose our life path before we are born in order to learn the lessons we need to continue our soul's growth. I believe that it was their souls' choice to come and go through this journey with me. I can't fix their pain, I can only fix my own guilt and shame, heal my own hurt, and become strong enough to share my story with some other young mother who may be struggling like I was.

I recently watched a YouTube video of "Soul Sunday" with Oprah Winfrey whose guest was Brene Brown. They were talking about Brene's new book, *The Gifts of Imperfection*. The discussion was about showing up for others who feel shame in their lives. Her words that resonated with me most were, "You share with people who have earned the right to hear your story and with whom you are in a relationship that can bear the weight of your story."

I am now 71 years old. My blessings far outweigh my losses. None of us know what the next five, 10, or 20 years will bring. The important thing is that my soul chose the path I have walked. It was littered with sadness, loss, grief, guilt, and shame. A therapist once told me that we have to put our hip boots on and walk through our pain. I walked through it and my life has also been filled with accomplishment, spiritual growth, and an abundance of happiness and love. I will not forget to be grateful for where I've been, who I am, what I've learned, and what I still have to offer. Now, each day that I use my Angel cards, I remind myself to look past the errors, mistakes, and misunderstandings and focus on what underlies every situation, and **See Only Love.**

Andrea Rahlf was born and raised in Illinois and lived in the Chicago area for over 20 years before moving to Colorado in 2008. Most of her career was spent working in Chicago as a healthcare administrator at Northwestern University Medical School, Lurie Children's Hospital, and the University of Illinois College of Medicine. Andrea is board certified as a Medical Practice Executive through the American College of Medical Practice Executives. During her career, she managed many large physician practices in psychiatry, pediatrics, internal medicine, and general surgery. She is currently semi-retired and works part time in the Graduate Medical Education department at Saint Joseph Hospital in Denver, Colorado.

Andrea and her husband Randy have three grown children and eight grandchildren. When she's not at work she enjoys writing, volunteering and taking care of her grandkids. Andrea and Randy are both private pilots and for many years owned a Cessna 182. Over the years, the hobbies they have enjoyed together have been flying, traveling, and taking trips on their Harley Davidson. They also own a boat and love to fish.

After retiring from her full-time career, Andrea's focus has been on healthy transitions to retirement and finding her purpose. She is interested in helping others who are going through issues related to retirement and loss. Contact Andrea at AndreaR4446@gmail.com.

Shine

by Lindsey Robinson

It's funny how you think you've got everything all figured out. "By the time I'm 25, I'll be happily married and have 2.5 kids." Of course, as we let life happen to us, we often discover that the white picket fence isn't really the way things are, and possibly will never be. Better yet, we may discover that the white picket fence isn't really what we want, but are just adopting society's standards as our own. Discovering our own road to our true selves is guaranteed to be a bumpy one at times, but will always get you to your destination.

I was married for the first time at 25. My husband spent a lot of his time away due to being in the military. I still see myself standing on a runway while his plane took off over my head, carrying him off to deployment to an active war zone. I'm still pulled back to that runway every now and then. I can still see the lights on the planes as they

flew over my head. Watching the landing gear go up, and accepting that as a sign of, "You're officially on your own for the time being." The inconceivable terror was a constant force casting its shadow over my hope of his safe return. Like an uninvited guest, those thoughts and feelings would make themselves at home sans invitation or reason.

Unfortunately, he spent so much time away that we really didn't know how to communicate effectively with one another anymore, and we had both built our walls around ourselves. Too much time apart and too little experience ultimately resulted in too little and too late. We hit a point at which being around one another was actually awkward, and felt like we were completely foreign to one another. After seven years, the man I married felt more like a stranger to me than someone I had committed the rest of my life to. I remember sitting on different couches watching a movie. It was a movie where couples were getting divorced, and we kept peeking at one another with the awkward side eye as if to say, "Well, shit. How about that elephant in the room?"

We split when I was in my early thirties. The divorce process went fairly smoothly and was amicable, but it still was more painful than I ever could have imagined. I think we both learned some things, so I took it as it was. I felt like a failure at times. How could I not keep this together? That being said, it was actually not his choice to split; I ultimately used the help of our marriage counselor to tell him I wanted out. I remember thinking that there were some issues that I could never get over, like his choice to go away for extended periods of time for extra training and classes between deployments. Perhaps it was his decision to take a job on the other side of the state without including me in the decision-making process. Likely, it was everything all together, my reactions towards him, and how I perceived everything as my reality at the time. I was angry, and felt totally abandoned. Our perceptions change with experience, and I was a total rookie. As ready as I thought I was, I still broke down in

the court room while talking to the judge. He asked what happened, and I started to explain that he was in the military, and—the judge stopped me from talking, and just said, "I am so sorry," and that was it. The look of pain and compassion on that judge's face will forever be etched into my memory.

So, there I was with a clean slate. Fast forward a couple years. I did end up marrying again. I was an avid World of Warcraft player, and I ended up marring my raid leader. World of Warcraft is an on-line video game where you control a character while going on fanta-sy adventures with friends you've made through the game. Raids are especially exciting instances that you get to experience in the game. A raid leader's someone who yells at everyone for things such as, but not limited to: killing your teammates, standing in fire, not healing someone fast enough, not shooting the target fast enough, and so on. As my main character's name was "Pantsparty," it became the run-ning joke of the group to say, "That just isn't good enough, Pants." I would giggle uncontrollably as I watched everyone's characters dis-sipate in a ball of fire.

He and I were online friends for quite some time before we actu-ally met in person. I eventually moved to Virginia to start a new life with him. I had never lived far away from my family, or even outside of the state of Michigan. Yet, I seemed to be thriving, and seemingly applying learned lessons to do better. To be better. He was emotion-ally there for me, and that was something I was searching for. I tried to take the lessons I had learned from my first marriage and apply them as much as I could. I even used a discussion and listening tech-nique I learned in therapy. He felt safe and sturdy, and being with him wouldn't involve me sending care packages to the other side of the world while going to sleep alone every night. Not to say that is the reason I married him, but these were some of the things I was immensely grateful for.

And I adored his family. He and I didn't really fight. We'd have the occasional squabble over a t-shirt he insisted on wearing all the time. "No, you can't wear that shirt to dinner. It has a giant hole under the arm and I can see your left boob!" He loved that shirt, and I almost felt bad on that tragic day the shirt accidentally found its way into the garbage. He felt safe. We got married at an old civil war mansion, surrounded by all of our friends and family. It was truly a fairy tale wedding.

About 6 months after we were married, he began to change. At first, it was random anxiety, or sometimes just being crude during conversation. His demeanor seemed to change from warm and safe to unpredictable and hostile. He was cold. He was really secretive about money. I noticed underlying anger in him frequently, and he was always negative. I would pick fights about his negativity and crude remarks. He seemed double-sided, which left me utterly confused. For example, we had a conversation about waiting to have children. A day or two later, I stumbled across a text conversation between him and a friend, which consisted of his saying that I would never settle down, and that I didn't want kids. I felt so betrayed, but mostly confused about his manipulative behavior. This led to me doubting myself and my interpretation. Was he manipulative? Did I not understand our conversation? Has the English language changed at some point in the last 24 hours and was I not aware?

Red flags continued to pop up, and then became more frequent: the moodiness, anxiety attacks, crude and demeaning humor. On the surface things appeared fine. However, I had a feeling, that can only be described as heavy, that something was coming that would change everything, but had no idea what. I had no indication of what was coming, or any reason to justify why I felt that way. This was alarming to me, but even more so because I had no way to prepare, or even avoid a potential disaster. The house was tense every single day. I found myself walking on eggshells often in efforts to keep things relaxed. Our friends were noticing the changes in him as well.

However, to my surprise, their reaction was, "This is who he has always been." In other words, had he really been putting on a front this entire time? Being incredibly intuitive, I was left in a spiral of self-doubt. How the hell did I miss that?

As tough as I thought I was, I could have never prepared myself for the turn of events I was about to experience. We had come home from an outing at our friend's new house. We had gone to bed, as I was exhausted and was nearly asleep once my head hit the pillow. As he continued to make advances, I kept saying, "No. No, not tonight. I am too tired. No! Stop it." He continued on, though I continued to push him away from me. And then, I felt his hand on my arm as he pulled me over and proceeded to have sex with me anyways, all the time I was saying, "Stop!" Once it was over, I laid in silence and as still as I possibly could, with tears streaming down my face. "Did that just happen? What?" I didn't know what to do, so I just stayed as still and quiet as possible, hoping he would forget that I was still there. I was trying my best to be invisible. Being raped is a terrifying experience. Being raped by your very own husband is not only terrifying; it's also incredibly disorienting and confusing. At home. *In my safe place. He was supposed to be my safe place.* As he kissed me goodnight, I stared at the ceiling. I was so confused. Was I overreacting? Was I really saying, "Sure, go ahead," instead of repeating, "No?" I immediately doubted myself because he was so nonchalant. The more I thought about it, the more I realized what had actually happened. You may ask, "Did you call the police?" No. What would I say? "Hello officer? Yes, I think my husband just raped me but I'm not really sure because I am wondering if I am overreacting. Oh yes, yes, he's still here. He's sleeping. No, no, it wasn't 'violent,' he didn't hit me or anything. He even kissed me goodnight afterwards. Does that make it less valid?" I really wasn't interested in having that conversation, because I was unsure of myself. I talked to friends and watched their mouths fall open in disbelief. I watched their tears roll down their cheeks when I didn't know what to do with my own.

I carried on. I had to keep playing the game until I could get out. I was so afraid that I would provoke him in some way that he would do it again. I sent the blame inward on to myself. I had it all bottled in, and that cork was ready to pop. It was usually illustrated with furrowed brows and a short temper. No, it wasn't my fault, and no, I was not overreacting. I had said no, repeatedly. Who the hell did he think he was? Secretly, I made a plan to keep the status quo while I planned my exit. I wanted that dragon to stay asleep! I was like a raging ball of middle fingers ready to roll in any which direction that I felt necessary. I knew it would have to be a well-planned exit, and it would take a considerable amount of time. I made a lot less money than he did, yet I had to pay an equal amount of rent. I was struggling to pay my own bills, which made getting out on my own seem impossible. I picked up a second job without him knowing, in which I traded work for some of my expenses. I started stashing money aside and actively planning my next moves.

About a year after the rape, he asked if we could talk. He had an idea that we should do a trial separation to take a little break. I figured as long as it was his idea, it was clearly the "right way to go" in his eyes. However, the separation was simply because we weren't getting along. Not one word about that night that changed my life forever. By this time, things were incredibly distant. I was angry, and he couldn't figure out why. Since I was angry, he was angry and defensive. Though since I couldn't leave just yet, I simply moved into another room in our townhouse. It was incredibly awkward at first, but then it turned terrifying. The longer I went without crawling back into his bed, the angrier he became. He was hostile. He never laid a hand on me, but I wasn't entirely sure that he wouldn't. I wish I were kidding when I say that I slept with a hammer under my pillow. My closest friends had my address on hand, so they could call 911 for me if I texted them with a code word.

A few months of our "same house separation," we agreed to sit down and talk. Ready or not, this was my time to stand up for myself.

I was sweating and crying because I was terrified. I had people on standby in case I needed help. I had no intention of talking about the events of that particular night; I was just looking for the easiest way to exit. He began to tell me that I had changed, I was angry, and it was all because I was on prescription diet pills. Rather than quietly letting the conversation pass me by, I found myself saying loudly, "NO. I am angry because you raped me and I no longer feel safe with you." I remember thinking to myself, "Holy shit! Did that just come out of my mouth? Can I out run him if I need to?" I didn't need to. He stopped dead and just stared at me, mouth wide open. "Oh, that? I was just trying to be cute that night." It was my turn for my mouth to fall open. Cute? That was cute? How was any of that event cute? I had spent more than a year of pain and anger over a moment that he regarded as being cute?

Right about here is where something in me snapped. Not like snapped and I need to be on a television show, but snapped in that I spoke the words that were trapped in me for over a year. I popped that cork, spoke my truth, and holy shit, was it empowering! I told him that I was done, and that I was going to seek divorce. I told him that the experience with him had been traumatic, and that I hoped he sought some therapy in efforts to never treat anyone like that again. Suddenly, it was like I towered over him. I was the strong one. He was so flabbergasted that I had the gall to stand up for myself, that all he could do was literally sit down.

My financial position was meager at best, and I knew I would have a difficult time supporting myself. I found an apartment that I *technically* could afford. Mathematically speaking, it was incredibly tight. Living in northern Virginia, it was damn near impossible. I jumped on it anyway and applied for the apartment. I wish I was exaggerating when I tell you that I had a conversation with God that went something along the lines of, "Hey, I'm going to jump now. I know you have a net, and I need you to catch me. I am counting on you to catch me." With blind faith, I jumped into my new life, and moved into my very own apartment.

Looking back, I can say that I created my own way, because waiting for an opportunity to land right in my face wasn't going to happen. So, I relied on faith. Faith in myself, faith that I could do all of these adult things all by myself. After all, I *was* in my mid-thirties. This is when people are supposed to be good at "adulting," right? Adults are supposed to have their shit together, and I wedged myself in with a crow bar. Rather than retreating to a corner, I took a huge leap of faith, and told myself that everything would work out. I did in fact land in my little net. I was fine, and found myself with abundance. My bills were paid, my animals fed, and I had extra. I had done it!

Whatever "system" you believe in: God, Source, Universe, Gods and Goddesses, they are all one; a higher power that loves every single one of us and will always have a safety net ready for us if we are willing to take a leap of faith. Sure, things got tight every now and then, but I was *ok*. I was safe. My moment where I relied on my faith in God showed me to never doubt my faith again, because my safety net was right there. Soft, sturdy, and reliable. One year later, I upgraded to the largest apartment my complex had to offer. I made life happen to me! I worked on myself every single day to help myself heal and move forward. I had so much work to do, but it was, and still is, a task that I am always willing to take on. In my time of darkness, I had found my own way to shine.

Though I physically removed myself, my thoughts and sense of self-worth hadn't been so eager to come along for the relocation. I discovered that I had a habit of giving my power away by putting my sense of self-worth into how I thought others saw me. I equated my love for myself with the amount of love I thought I was receiving from others. I found myself running directly to the arms of a man who was eagerly waiting to keep me in that dark place. Perhaps it

was too soon after my divorce, but who is to say? There aren't written rules, just lessons to be learned. Of course, I didn't see that. I saw him as my knight in shining armor, who was there to rescue me, heal me, and toss in a side of happily ever after. I should have really known that the shininess of this new situation was really nothing more than tin foil. Crumply tin foil, at that; it wasn't even the fresh and crisp kind.

I am going to take this opportunity to toss out the old, "You get what you give." What you put out, you get back. Sounds familiar, right? Apparently, I forgot that I had received that memo repeatedly during the course of my life, because I decided it didn't apply here. He turned out to be a man who lied to me for nearly two years about damn near everything. He lied about being married, getting divorced, having cancer, his wife having cancer, unsuccessful court appointments, you name it—it likely came out of his mouth. You may not believe me when I tell you that I am an incredibly intuitive person. However, even the best of us have the ability to turn our "gut" off, and look the other way when we want to. I can see the moment where I turned my gut off in that situation. It would be the moment where his wife called me, and I chose to listen to him when he told me about how she was "just crazy" during the divorce process. I ignored myself for nearly two years, all the while telling myself that he made my world absolutely spin. Part of me knew, but I suppose I wasn't ready to face it. I think that I knew that I had to be in a better place to unveil the truth of the situation, or I would have been absolutely devastated. The old me would be hard on myself for doing that, and award myself a big fat "duh." However, this was a lesson for me to learn. Dwelling over it will never bring that time back, but will only drag me back into that place. Taking the hardships and looking at them for what they truly are is an incredible tool we can use to learn our lessons. Sometimes, we have to accept the hurt and experiences just for what they are, and put them in our "learned the hard way" pile. Only when we see this, can we actually start to heal ourselves and manifest a better life for ourselves. You are not broken, and there

is still hope for you. *You are not broken.* I am not broken. We are not broken. Forgive yourself, because you are worthy.

Coming out of a place of darkness, my biggest lesson was learning to not give my power away. For the longest time, I had put my power in a pretty little package, and handed it to the others in my life. "Here, this is yours. You control this now." This left me dependent on others, leaning on others, and literally crumpling when I felt any sort of rejection whatsoever. It took what little love I could have had for myself, and turned it into self-loathing and sadness. It was dark and unbelievably lonely. Who would have thought trying to attach yourself to others would be so lonely? That is a lesson learned the hard way, via constant sense of rejection. "Oh, you don't have time to talk me through my shitty day? Why do you hate me?" I was literally using the people around me as a crutch to hold myself up, while my own foundation crumbled. Once I had been a strong, confident woman. Suddenly, I was empty and unstable. Literally like an old abandoned building on the verge of collapse, all I needed was a good push to come crashing down. Worst of all, I was semi-aware of this mindset, which I punished myself for. I was so hard on myself for letting myself be in this type of position, *and* for being upset I was in this position.

When it finally came full circle, I gave up on those I was leaning on because I had decided they didn't want to be bothered by me. Meanwhile, I told myself on a daily basis that I was a failure. I had come crashing down. I was right there at the bottom, realizing that I could not feel my surroundings or people, yet I kept going. I forced myself to get up every morning. Drive to work. Do the work. Drive home. Pet the cats. Ride the horse. Do the dishes. Do the things. Adult the things. I was more robot than human being. The hardest part of being at the bottom is learning that you are the only person who can get you back up. No one is coming down there with you. You find that those you leaned on may start to fade away when you really and truly need them. This is the time that you need to learn

you are your own savior, and you alone will pull yourself out of the darkness. If you can pull yourself out of the vast emptiness, you are your very own super hero and can do absolutely anything. There will be a time where you get so tired of the dark clouds following you everywhere that you will realize that you are the only one who can bring your own light. You will shine. People may be there to give you a hand, but you have to stand up; the work is yours to do, and yours alone. Read a self-help book. Connect with the Universe. Download an app to your phone to learn how to meditate. Spend time outside with nature. Find your own healthy mechanisms that function as a ladder so you can climb out of the darkness. Spend some quality time with yourself, and learn to forgive and love yourself again. You are an infinite being of light. Shine. We all owe it to ourselves to shine as brightly as we can.

Learning to love yourself—hell, even getting reacquainted with yourself—is hard work. It's busy and constant work. It requires honesty and genuine effort. Sadly, this is the work so many of us put off because we're busy doing other things. We are chasing tails, spinning wheels, looking for the fairy tale endings that always keep their distance because the most important thing is missing: you. In today's society, we strive so hard to be selfless and put others before us. However, it starts with you. Put yourself first. *Only when you finally begin to realize your worth for the incredible being you are, can you finally start to increase your synchronization with everything you want in this lifetime.* We get what we give, remember? Give love and light, and receive love and light.

I wasn't sure exactly how to start, or even where to start. Until one morning, as I was riding the metro to work, I found myself reading a self-help book. I picked up *You Are a Badass* by Jen Sincero, thinking that in terms of self-help books, this particular one

sounded literally the most bad-assiest. I remember blogging about it, because I had become one of *those* people. Who the hell needed a book to reinforce their bad-assery? This girl. This girl right here! As I peered over the edges of the book to survey who was rolling their eyes towards me and my giant portion of self-help, I decided that it was time that I make life happen my way, rather than rolling with the punches I didn't necessarily want. I remember thinking to myself, "Behold the bad-assery you are witnessing here, ladies and gentlemen. I'm doing the things, and I'm doing them my damn way for a change!" This was my equivalent to "Hold my beer and watch this!"

What is really going on here? What is vibration, and what the hell do you mean I can "manifest" stuff? This book introduced me to some of these concepts, as I had never really heard of them before. My initial reaction was something along the lines of, "Seriously, what *is* this hippy shit?!" So I read on. I kept reading and talking to people until some of these concepts started truly making sense to me. Of course, I'd had to "feel the conversation out" with people, because I honestly figured they would think I've officially gone off the deep end. "So you're telling me that if I raise my vibration—wait... what does that even mean?" We, as beings, are energy. If we are "vibrating" at a lower frequency, we will attract lower frequency things. You know, like depleted self-worth and negativity. However, if we vibrate higher, then we attract higher vibrating things such as positivity, happiness, money, literally whatever we want. You may be saying right now, "Ok, newfound hippy girl. Says who, and would you like some coconut oil with that?" Law of Attraction says, and, yes, please bring on the coconut oil! Let's go back to what I mentioned earlier about the concept we have heard all of our lives about getting what we put out. It is exactly the same thing. We have been talking about the Law of Attraction since we were kids, and had no idea. Well, some of you may have known, but this was a pretty huge "*Aha!*" moment for me. I started working on raising my vibration with essential oils, prayer, meditation, and practicing gratitude on a daily basis. I envisioned the

love and acceptance that I had longed for, and it was returned to me. I found new friends that were supportive and loving—a new tribe.

While working on myself, I found that I was having a difficult time releasing my anger about the rape. I chose to find a way to forgive because I could see no other way to move forward. The fact that I forgave him did not excuse what he did, nor did it make it less traumatic for me. What it did do, however, is release that burden I had been carrying around on my shoulders. I told him that I was working on forgiveness, but I wasn't forgiving him for his sake. It was for mine, and I refused to carry that extra weight around any further. He thanked me. Through this process, I also learned to forgive myself. I found lots of "junk" stored from numerous experiences that was really negative. Choosing to forgive was likely the single most important decision I have made in my adult life, and I am so thankful that I was able to see it. I am also thankful that he and I became friendly again after the divorce process. Not buddies, not hanging out, but an email every now and then just to say hello was a pretty common thing. About six months after our divorce was final, he died suddenly and unexpectedly. It was a huge wakeup call for me, and served as an affirmation of my goal to not carry around all the negativity anymore. I was able to grieve his loss as a human being, as a friend, as someone that was a huge part of my life for many years, for his friends, and for his family. Our time here is never guaranteed, nor is it predictable. Finding your sense of peace is so incredibly important for moments that leave your head spinning, so you can keep yourself afloat.

I'm 38 now. My career is in full swing. People are continuously asking me when I'm going to have some babies (when I get around to it, thank you), and I continue to learn every day. I work on myself every single day. Whether it be a simple meditation, energy healing, or just taking a minute to sit still and be quiet to do some reflection. We can all do this together. I am now a Reiki Master and certified in several modalities of energy healing, and recently started my own

business where I can help people heal. A business owner, in addition to a full time RN—who *is* this girl?! Through this education came an incredible amount of self-healing. I discovered essential oils. I continue to learn new healing modalities, and am very involved in the local metaphysical community. I have watched myself morph into a lighter, more positive person over the last year. *I became my own light.* I have learned that I have the ability manifest any sort of life I want to live, and so do you. All I have to do is believe what I want is mine, and be thankful for it. All you have to do is believe it is yours, and be thankful for it. You, beautiful soul, can be your own light. Shine brightly, and never sit alone in the darkness again.

Lindsey Robinson is a Registered Nurse practicing in the Washington, DC area. In addition to her nursing career, Lindsey has recently started her own business focused on the healing and spiritual growth of others. She is a Reiki Master Teacher and is certified in several energy healing modalities, in addition to being an advocate for essential oils. She continues to strive to expand for her own personal growth, and also to provide more modalities for her clients. She is very involved in her local metaphysical community, and is always working with her colleagues to explore methods to be active in educating the local community. When not working, she is often found amongst her cats, or playing outside in the dirt with her horse. She is also an avid belly dancer and loves spending her time outdoors. To contact Lindsey, please visit her at LunaPathWellness.com.

Way of the
Warrior Princess

by Aundrea De Leon

"Life is going to push you around, beat you up and it's going to scare you. But then, one day, you realize you're not just a survivor—You're a Warrior. And you're stronger than anything life throws your way."
– Brooke Davis

I am misplaced all the time. That's how it feels when you're always the new girl in school, at church, in the neighborhood. My adoptive family moved *all* the time. Sometimes more than once in the same school year. It started when they adopted me. We moved between Nebraska, South Dakota, Colorado, and Utah before I had gone to fifth grade.

We moved so much, I stopped trying to make friends because it didn't matter. We weren't staying anyway. I loved going to school and tried so hard not to let anyone know anything about me. I made up stories about my life because it didn't matter, we were moving soon anyway, and no one would know or care. I have pictures of friends and birthday parties, but I don't know anyone's name or where we were living. I envy people who talk about their elementary years and

all the friends they still know from way back when. We had somewhere else to move to because it was always going to be better. A better job, a better house, better schools, better—better—better. At least that's the story my adoptive parents told me.

I knew I was adopted, but it wasn't allowed to be spoken of or questions asked. We didn't look alike, as I had blonde hair with blue eyes and my adoptive parents had dark hair and dark eyes. I have vague memories of a celebration and it was supposed to be exciting that my new name was Ann. I never liked my name and grew to loathe it more and more as I grew up. I was four when I was adopted, so I was aware that my life had changed and I had so many questions. Why was I adopted, who were the faces and voices in the fuzzy fog of my memories, and will I ever know those people again? Why can't I talk to them if they're my family? Am I adopted because they don't love me anymore? Did I do something wrong to make them not want me?

I learned it wasn't okay to ask. Asking meant bringing on the darkest anger and resentment that visibly washed over my adopted mother's face and in her eyes. I only saw darkness and deep, seething, pure hatred towards me. The heat of her fury and anger would scare me to my core and I would retreat quietly inside myself and make myself as small as possible. I tried not to be *me* so much and be more like who she wanted me to be.

Deeply I knew I didn't belong. I was misplaced.

She doesn't like me. That is confusing because she says she's my mom and moms exist to love their kids. I know she doesn't like me because when we are alone her true feelings come out through her actions and words. Her words to me are mean, hateful, full of spite. Her actions hurt me and leave bruises. I'm afraid all the time and I try really hard to be on her good side. Sometimes when she looks at me I see into her soul the deep dark hatred that no one else sees. It's my fault, I shouldn't be here. I try to be a good girl so she'll like me and even maybe one day, love me. This isn't my family and these aren't my parents. I'm an outsider borrowing someone else's family.

My parents were too young and too troubled to be parents. My birth father took his own life when I was only two months old and my birth mom was overwhelmed by the stress of a newborn, loss of a husband, and pressure to find her own way in life, so she left. My real family sent me away and that is all I ever knew. But something in my heart told me there was more. I always felt there was more to the story and that there was more to *my* family. I prayed that someday my family would want me.

As we moved again and again. I grew taller, older, and uglier. Life was constantly getting worse. From the outside, we looked like a normal family with Dad, Mom, and three daughters. I was the oldest by six years with two younger sisters who weren't adopted. My adoptive parents had two biological daughters of their own, and I could tell Mom loved them. The way she looked at them with love, the way she sang to them was warm, and was far different than how she treated me. It wasn't obvious to me when I was younger, but as I grew older it became more obvious that her expectations of my behavior and how she treated me was very different than the expectations and treatment of my sisters. If they did anything wrong, I was blamed and told I was setting a poor example for them. If they got in trouble it was always trouble for me since they said I was the cause and the reason for their wrongdoing.

My adoptive father worked all the time. I couldn't keep up with all of his jobs, but usually it involved being a salesman or store manager for grocery stores. I remember he worked late nights, busy days, weekends, whenever he was needed. Which meant he was needed all the time. He would promise the family trips or time for fun on the weekends, but then work would need him and promises were broken. He broke promises to the family all the time. Just like promises of no more moving.

We girls were home with my adoptive mother. Sometimes she

worked outside the home, but mostly she ran the house and took care of us kids. We went to church, I babysat, and she was skilled in homemaking, so we were constantly busy. From the outside, we all looked normal and all of us girls were so admired and received countless compliments. When he was home my adoptive father doted on us and told us how we were his beautiful girls. But there were dark secrets inside the walls of our house.

In our house, the expectation was that we would cook, clean, sew, look presentable at all times, be polite, go to church, be useful, be smart (but don't let people know you're smart), and be seen but not heard. We were told we had to learn homemaking skills so we could take care of our families when we grew up. Our future would be to graduate high school, fulfill our church obligations, and start a family.

I loved cooking, but tolerated sewing. Cleaning was constant and never complete, and I always seemed to fail miserably at my adoptive mothers' expectations. I didn't move fast enough to complete chores, clean dishes or the house perfectly, I didn't get all the laundry done to her expectations and overall—I didn't do anything to her expectations. I remember feeling deflated that there was nothing more in life for me aspire to. I watched Miss America and Miss Universe pageants and dreamed of traveling the world to see the states and countries where these beautiful women lived. I wanted to do makeup and hair, and I wanted to play sports—I was a tomboy. Even worse, I struggled with our religious beliefs and teachings. I didn't fit in. I didn't fit in at home, or church, or school.

I hated watching Cinderella when I was young because I felt like it was partially based on my life. Cook the breakfast, scrub the dishes, wash the laundry, sweep the steps, and wear the ugly clothes. I was the Princess, only there was no glass slipper or Prince Charming to save my life.

When my adoptive father came home from work I would sit in my room with the deepest, darkest sinking feeling in the pit of my

stomach listening to my adoptive mother lament about all the egregious behaviors I displayed that day. It was the same story over and over. It usually ended with a whipping on top of the beatings I had already endured from my adoptive mother. The beatings were never shared with him. He would rack his knuckles on top of my head and tell me to "use it or lose it".

So much confusion when you're told to use your head and be smart, while being ridiculed for everything you do and how imperfect you are. Parent-Teacher conferences were the worst. Anything to do with school was the worst. I didn't write well enough, I was too bossy, I wasn't perfect and even though my report cards showed academic excellence, I was a disgrace and an embarrassment. I learned to sit at home with the suspense of her return tormenting me.

The raging storms of violent outbursts directed at me were fierce and unexpected, which added to their intensity. Pots, pan, dishes, kicking me, hitting me across the head and face, fly swatters, belts, hangers, pounding my head into walls and floors, holding my face under running water in the kitchen sink until I couldn't breathe, sitting on me and holding me down for what felt like an eternity to beat my naked body, throwing me down the stairs, bashing my head against walls and windows until they broke. Spiteful, fuming, hostile beatings that left me petrified to be at home.

The physical violence was only part of my torment. Her words and the way she would say them and how she would glare at me when she spoke them, left emotional scars that lasted long after the physical abuse ended. I'd break records for physical fitness challenges at school, I'd do well academically, but there were never words of encouragement or support from my adoptive mother. The response was always a comparison of how my cousins were doing better, or I didn't do my best and could have done better. Or threats of not showing up for events because I was no one that was worth showing up for. Always some snide remark or final reminder of my constant disappointment to her life.

Hell felt safer and nicer than home, and I wanted to go there. I prayed to God at night to please kill me and take me off the face of the planet. I begged for death, to run away and never be found, for my family to change their minds and want me back. I prayed for help on how to be more perfect and how to be better so she would like me. I knew she would never love me, but if I could make her like me, maybe life would be ok.

And then it happened. She finally broke me...

Life had gotten very stressful at home and our last few moves were horrible. My adoptive father was gone more than before, even though I wasn't sure how that was possible. We didn't live in great neighborhoods and I was constantly in trouble at school. Being the tallest person in class wasn't the issue—being the tallest, whitest, blonde girl in schools with higher minority ratios was the worst. I wasn't at the same place in school work as everyone else, and I was harassed mercilessly daily for the way I looked, dressed, talked, and walked. And I was naïve and not street smart. Everyone at school hated me, everyone at home hated me, and even I hated me. I was an outsider, I was misplaced.

I had just turned 12 in October. My adoptive father happened to be home when one of her episodes of emotional outrage occurred. There had been tension in the house that lingered like floating fog. It was December and the day of our school holiday performance. As usual I picked the wrong attire for the day and was sent to the store to purchase pantyhose to wear under a skirt. This situation then put us behind and I didn't have enough time to finish breakfast, take care of dishes, and complete all my other responsibilities in order to leave for school on schedule.

I had false hope that the presence of a school friend riding with us that day would deter her vengeful actions, but that proved futile. She sent my friend and the girls to the car ahead of us, waited for me to walk in front her, then waged her vengeance on me. As she dropped us at school she made sure to share her final remarks reminding me

of her spite towards me and the disdain which she held for me. Since I was such an embarrassment to society, she wouldn't be showing up for our performance.

On any other day after any other episode I would move on. But something inside me broke that day. I was embarrassed to be seen, I couldn't mentally focus on school, and I ran into the bathroom to hide in the farthest corner stall I could find, and sobbed. My body ached from the beating, but my soul ached worse. I was done and could take no more. She was right. I was a loathsome human with no place in the world.

School officials contacted authorities when they finally coaxed me out of my corner and heard my story of the morning's events. Of course, then more stories of previous episodes were shared and the entire day and my life were turned upside down. I was taken away and placed in temporary care and eventually placed in a foster home.

After finishing the school year at the foster home, I did return to live with my adoptive family, but it was only for a short time. Aside from the fact that I wasn't harmed physically, it was miserable. I slept on the floor in a sleeping bag and my clothes were in boxes in the basement, which was also a garage. I was treated like an outsider and barely acknowledged unless my adoptive father was home. As usual, he worked a million hours a week and was rarely around. I was miserable at school, under constant duress of being bullied and beaten by gangs of girls, but I had no one to tell. My adoptive parents ridiculed and raged at me verbally for not making friends with kids at church and inviting them over. That was our religious tradition, to host friends and win them over with our hospitality. I didn't even have a bedroom, my family clearly despised me, so making friends and inviting them into our home was the furthest thing from my mind.

I was driven away one night and sent to foster care. Vague stories of my mental health, and safety for my needs, a better situation to support me were all I remember. It would be the last time I was in their home.

For a girl, the 12-14 year age range is an extremely delicate imbalance of self-esteem and emotions from a hormone change perspective. Add on top of that my adoptive family convincing everyone I was mentally ill, twisting day-to-day events into half-truths that all pointed to me being a problem child who was out of control. This phase of my life was cold blackness. I had no self-worth or self-respect remaining. At one of the temporary foster homes, I walked with a group of kids to Target and stole a box of diet pills. They told me the pills were like speed and would make me super hyper and I'd have fun. I swallowed the whole box (it might have been two) hoping it would kill me. The last thing I remember was standing looking out the glass door—then blackness. For several days I was violently ill, throwing up, passing out as soon as I sat up, fog, sleeping for hours. I was never taken to a doctor or the hospital.

I was shipped around to foster homes and group homes. The group home was an okay place and I felt like I could fit in there. But for unknown reasons my adoptive parents continued to wage war against me and sent me to live at Denver Children's Home (DCH). What little childhood innocence I had left was stripped from me there. I was thrown into life with kids much older, far more street smart, kids that had committed crimes I had never imagined or heard of, and I was clearly an outsider amongst outsiders. If you can imagine being an outcast in a home full of misfits, then you might begin to imagine the depth and rawness of the wounds to my heart and my soul. I was raped and drugged, and just like my adoptive parents, the counselors and team of people whom I was told were there to help me, all placed the blame on me and wanted to know why I would make those choices.

I ran away. I would live on the streets wherever and with whomever I could find shelter. I would get picked up or I'd eventually call my adoptive father and ask for help. They'd take me back to DCH,

and I ran away again, and again, and again. I was homeless, desperate, deflated, demoralized, confused, and misplaced. I was exposed to alcohol, drugs, stealing, breaking into homes to find shelter, and more horrifying experiences that a 13-year-old girl should not have to live through. The last time that I ran away and was picked up by authorities I demanded to be sent anywhere else but DCH and I promised them I would find a way to run away again and we would repeat the cycle if they sent me there. So, I was sent to a locked psychiatric unit at a hospital.

Because of the continual treatment of being thrown away, condemned, ridiculed, beaten down, and outcast, I was a very ugly person at this point. I hated everyone and refused to participate in counseling discussions. I was tired of people talking at me and trying to get me to discuss my anger issues. No one cared about me. I would sit in front of every counselor and psychiatrist with a cold blank stare, then tell them they were nothing more than a paid professional required to sit in front of me and I hated them. Hate isn't even a strong enough word. I despised everyone in the world. Including me.

While I was in the hospital, my adoptive father continued his emotional abuse by constantly promising to visit, promising to get me home... promising... promising... promising. Always promising and never showing up. That was his specialty in my life. He'd say, "The next house and job are going to be better... I promise." He taught me promises are empty words said to make someone feel better with no intent to actually deliver. And this scenario was no different. He never showed up and like a dog waiting for its owner to show up at the end of the day, I'd get excited and happy and wait... and wait... and wait. No phone call, nothing. More broken promises.

Since all my counseling sessions and conversations were about taking responsibility for my actions, I was beginning to believe the lies and false stories made up about me. After living on the streets and in Denver Children's Home, I figured going home would be a better alternative. I was desperate to get out of the hospital. I figured the only way to get out of the hospital and return home was to take accountability for my actions and apologize to my family for being a terrible daughter and sister. I wrote letters to them. I wrote a letter to my adoptive mother apologizing for being a horrible child, accepting that I wasn't perfect and didn't respect her, and that I would have better actions and behavior and become a better daughter because I loved her.

Her response was something I should have expected. She wrote me back telling me what a horrible person I was, that no one in the world would ever love me, and that I didn't deserve to be part of a family, nor would I ever amount to anything. Words like prostitute, scum, sick... so many more lies.

I can't remember all the words in her letter to me, but what I do remember is how it made me feel. I went through phases of emotion, beginning with pure, raw, unfiltered anger. My counselors let me take my mattress and pillows and beat them for what seemed like hours. I kicked and screamed and pounded my head and fists until I was so exhausted I could do no more than cry. Not just a sad cry, but a deep hurt sob from the center of my soul. I had no idea that from far away where I couldn't even be seen, her hate and resentment towards me could cut so deep. In my anger, I shredded the letter. Then I burned it. I didn't want to be constantly reminded how hateful words have so much power.

After anger, I remember feeling hollow. I remember asking other kids and counselors how it was possible that a parent could write that type of letter. I was a 13-year-old girl, who had never been taught to stand up for herself, or the details of how my body and life would change with puberty, how to handle boys, or anything that I needed to keep myself safe. I was never taught to speak up for myself, or how to have boundaries to tell people no when they hurt me. I was taught how to be useful, how to clean, how to cook for an army of 20, how to fold laundry, and how to shut the hell up when someone hurt me and take it. No one wanted me, no one loved me, and I had no home or family.

Shortly thereafter, my personal belongings were delivered to me at the hospital and my adoptive family left the state. More moving, but this time I wasn't going with them and I would never see them again. I had asked to see my personal belongings and a counselor sat with me in her office looking through my life (in two boxes) in pictures and scrapbooks.

For the first time in my life, someone asked me to tell them my story. And as we looked through my pictures, birthday cards, report cards, and memorabilia, I shared my life story from my perspective. And she listened to me without judgement and heard me. And when I was done sharing and we were discussing the most current events of recent years, that counselor hugged me and told me I was beautiful. Then she held me in her arms like I imagined a mother who loved her child would do, and allowed me to cry. For a very long time.

The simple act of listening to someone and giving them a genuine and caring hug provides an amazing amount of healing power. I normally didn't like people hugging me, but after years of being hit, yelled at, despised, hated, cast away, belittled, and shunned in my own home and school and church—I felt like I would melt. I felt like a warrior who had been on the battlefield fighting a non-stop barrage of enemies for an eternity, who finally found a quiet spot where battle had not touched, and I rested. I cried, and slept, and slept, and cried. The questions from my counselors and doctors changed, which changed our conversations. And the winds of change swept in to move my life in a new direction.

I was allowed to go back to the group home I enjoyed before DCH, and I began working through the devastation of my life. My adoptive parents paid me a brief visit at the group home, and my adoptive mother did all the talking and my adoptive father sat there doing and saying nothing. They wanted to tell me in person they were relinquishing their parental rights and that the State of Colorado would be taking care of me. Shortly after my 14th birthday, I received official word from my social worker that the paperwork was complete and I was officially a ward of The State of Colorado. My former adoptive family sent me a parting gift of a dozen yellow roses with a belated Happy Birthday note. I didn't have any emotions left for them or for the situation. I hate yellow roses.

All that existed of my previous life were pictures and memories.

Now I am not just misplaced, I am lost and alone in the world. I will no longer be a princess trapped and bound out of obligation. I am now a warrior and I will *not* be hurt by anyone.

I tried to be normal at school, but how normal can you be in eighth grade when you've been through the crap I had just experienced? I didn't fit in before all this happened, and it wasn't any better. I was still ugly, my clothes were disgusting, my hair and makeup were vile, and I was a foster kid. All the kids at school knew us girls from "the home". However, I kept trying to be something better. I participated in sports, cared about my classes, for the most part, and usually tried to get along.

My temper definitely had more control over me and when I was angry or feeling like something wasn't going my way or someone wasn't treating me fairly, I'd rage and lash out. I spent many days in the in-school suspension room and learning on my own in isolation. Sometimes I enjoyed the silence and not having to be around hundreds of other students and teachers. I had a part-time job as a receptionist at a nursing home, I got involved in our church youth group, and I even mustered the courage to try out for the Miss Teen Colorado pageant. Up and down, up and down, I'd keep trying to be something better even though I had lots of crashes and failures.

Towards the end of eighth grade, the group home parents announced their retirement and we would all have to be moved to new homes. Not great news. I was hell bent on finding a way to emancipate because I was tired of being told where to live and having

no control over my life. However, the universe had better plans in mind for me. My junior high counselor had become a trusted advisor and friend. She often took me home on weekends and let me babysit her kids and spend time with her family. They were kind and caring people and I was always so excited to spend time with them. After I plopped myself down in her office and asked—in my usual sarcasm—if she knew anyone who wanted a 15-year old because I needed a new home, my counselor and her husband worked with my case-worker to obtain a foster parent license that would allow me to move in with them.

These amazing people took me into their home and loved me. I didn't make it easy on them. I was hurt and a little on the wild teen side, but they didn't send me away. They loved me like I was their own, allowed me to play sports and be involved in activities that I enjoyed, taught me how to be a good person to others, shared their family vacations and experiences with me, and gave me a home to be a kid and grow. They nurtured the good in my heart and supported me. They saved my life. They became my bonus family.

My name is now not Ann or Andrea—*my name is Aundrea*. One of the best gifts my newfound bonus family gave me was the gift of self-identity. I hated my name. I always hated my name and now that my adoptive parents had no legal influence in my life, I started to take control. I changed my name to Aundrea, took back my last name at birth, and began the process of finding myself.

I am Aundrea, Warrior Princess.

By definition, a warrior princess is a female with a dark past on a journey to redeem herself. It fit me perfectly.

I finally started making friends, found positive experiences, and started finding self-confidence. However, I was always guarded. I'd let people get close to me, but only close enough and not too close. My

heart was shielded and I would shut down and turn people away at the drop of a hat. I was gifted at shutting off all emotion and caring at any moment. I could change from a kind, happy, easy going, caring person to a cold, distant, unreachable shell of a person in a snap. For all the good choices I'd make in life, I'd follow up with some whopping choices that would create a reminder of my imperfections and faults. Always behind the good lay dormant an undertone of insecure, dejected, inadequate feelings that found their way to the surface.

I did exactly that in my junior year of high school. I had been playing on the varsity basketball team since my sophomore year and continued to play club basketball in the off season thanks to the kindness and generosity of my bonus family. I had friends, I was well liked in school, and in general life was going great. But my dark side was always active, reminding me how I didn't deserve this life and that deep down, I was an imposter. I was flawed, less than everyone else, undeserving of the good life being given to me. I had a dark, wild side that required feeding. I had learned at age 13 about the fabulous feeling of numbness that alcohol brings, and how to find older guys to flirt with who would buy it for me. I would seek adventures and situations to feed the darkness. I knew the more guys thought I liked them, the more I could have fun and be wild and free without failing people's expectations of me.

Good girl by day, bad girl by night. Warrior Princess at heart. One side light and looking toward the future, one side dark and hiding secrets from the past.

And in all my wildness and partying, I became pregnant at 16. I easily hid my pregnancy from family and friends for close to six months before I had to reveal the truth. It ate at my insides and added more weight to the dark, black pit that lived constantly in the center of my body. I knew I was pregnant and that all the good things in my life would come crashing to an end. I was scared my bonus family would finally reject me and send me away. I was afraid my new girlfriends would judge me and turn their backs on me.

On the surface, my bonus family thought I was doing great and that I was moving forward in a positive direction. My bonus dad even told me how proud he was of me for being so loving and kind to the family. I wanted to die. I was so angry at myself for sabotaging a wonderful life that was given to me, and I didn't know what to do or who to tell. I eventually had to tell a friend, and, of course, all the appropriate adults in my life were informed, exposing my new secret to the world.

Everyone asked me what I wanted to do. Adoption was my first choice, but I was afraid that my adoptive experience would influence the future of this child and I was stuck. I said adoption because it was what I believed was the right choice and I knew that recently turning 17, I had no capability to be responsible for a child. I hadn't even lived a life of my own, and I was not prepared to be a parent. I was ashamed and I was truly stuck.

By this time in my life I had spent a good amount of effort evaluating my beliefs both religiously and spiritually. I had grasped and held onto the belief that we all have the power to influence our life by the thoughts and words we use. I let go of the belief that I previously held when I was younger that there was a master puppeteer in the sky pulling the strings on all of our day-to-day events in life. I refused to believe that a God, touted in scriptures to love us all so much, would purposely make bad things happen to us. And I believed there were guardians watching over my life helping me in dire situations, to find a way through.

There had been situations, when I lived on the streets, where I would sense some kind of power around me, giving me strength to fight. In fact, there were times when I was on the run, and in situations that were going down a dangerous, volatile path, when I would hear someone yell my name or something would brush against my arms and tell me to leave. I could never actually see them, but I felt their presence and I knew they were for me and I should listen. I believed there was a higher power helping our lives.

I also believed in the power of choice. I believed that inside there is a strength to live through and survive any situation in life, that I can choose the direction of my destiny. I didn't know how this worked, I just believed in my heart and soul that it was possible.

I prayed. I didn't pray to God, but I prayed to the power I felt inside me and around me. I prayed every night and every morning that I would receive the help I needed to find my way through this situation. I wanted to kill myself, but my morals and values prevented me from taking that thought too seriously to act upon. Besides, I had a child that was depending on my life to begin their own. I vowed that if I had the help I needed, I would aspire to a better life. That I would become a positive member of society, I would make good choices and stop being reckless, I would make myself a better person, and if I received help that I would do the right thing for this child.

Then, one day, a miracle was given to me.

By pure accident, I met the woman who had let go of me as an infant. The woman who had handed me over to a family in hopes of a better life for me showed up front and center in my life. My biological mother. When she walked into the room I remember thinking how beautiful she looked. I really didn't know how to feel, and the reunion was rather calm, considering the circumstances.

I believe the universe put my birth mother in my life at exactly that moment, because she knew how to help me. I believe the higher power I prayed to knew I needed at that moment to know how much my own mother loved me, and what her hopes and dreams had been for my life. I needed to know her heart broke into a million pieces when she heard the details of my time with my adoptive family, and the journey to finding her. I believe this was the message I needed to know so that I could make the right choice for me and for the child I carried. I needed to know love, so I could make a decision based on love for my own child. I needed to know I wasn't a disappointment to my own mother.

My bonus mother and my biological mother stood beside me.

They supported me and took care of me during the final months of my pregnancy and helped me find strength to keep moving forward. I went from having no family and no one to love me, to having two moms.

Everything was a little crazy in life as I literally met my own mother at seven months pregnant. My bonus family had two younger children of their own and my situation definitely caused some confusion and stress for them. My bonus family never turned me away, and they worked together with my biological mother with grace to support this new relationship in my life. My biological mother was there the day I delivered a baby boy, and she stuck with me through a few tumultuous months of indecision and fear.

I was so sure about adoption until my son arrived. Then I was confused and scared, and not so willing to let this beautiful bundle of joy just walk away. It took a few months of indecision and utter chaos for the decision to become clear. With so much help from both my moms, I picked an adoptive family, met them in person, and handed over my son. I wasn't afraid for his life or his future, even though my adoption had been a horrible disaster. I knew that I had done everything in my power to pick a family that was beyond my expectations for unconditional love, caring, and kindness. And I knew they would raise him and provide for him in ways that I was not capable of, given my youth and lack of life preparation. The adoption agency was amazing, and the adoptive family was gracious in their commitment of open communication with me. They would send pictures and letters to provide glimpses into their life in the future. I was reassured that *my* story would *not* be my son's story.

It would be easy to say this is the end of my struggle and life magically moved forward with ease and grace. Of course, that is not reality, but I started to find peace and love for myself.

I did graduate from high school. That was step one after all the mayhem of my life. And I took time to live on my own and find myself. I took a break from family expectations and spent a few years in a phase of life that I call rebellion. It's the description I use to describe the time I was 18 and moved out of my foster home until my mid-twenties. I moved away from the bonus family who continued to care for me and love me as their own for the four short years I lived with them.

During this time of rebellion, I lived on my own. I lived with a horrible man, lived on my own again, drank too much, partied too often, worked multiple jobs earning meager wages to barely pay my bills, slept with too many men, made new friends, and just lived one day at a time. I can only describe it as a time of running wild and free, refusing to be told what to do, and finding my own likes and dislikes in life. Learning more about myself and deciding who I wanted to be when I grew up. I never had that chance as a child.

I truly stepped fully into my Warrior Princess persona in my mid-20's. I had enough with struggle, trying to change people's perceptions of me, and their constant expectations of what I should do with my life. I was ready to embark on a journey for me and for me alone, to redeem myself from my past and create the person I wanted to be.

I was ready to go to school and get an education so I could have a career actually making money and living instead of surviving. I decided on the school, picked the location, filled out all my paperwork, and told no one until just a few months before I needed to leave. I wanted a clean slate and fresh start with no one around to interject their opinions and expectations into my decisions.

I was turning 25 and I felt it was time to put my past behind me and create a future. There were too many skeletons in my life all around me. They didn't need to hide in the closet because they were already exposed and all over my life in broad daylight. People from high school knew me as the girl who got pregnant, after high school

I was mostly known for partying and the fun-time girl. Employers knew me as the girl who couldn't show up to work on time and made stupid mistakes. My friends and family knew me as the girl with so much potential, who wasn't doing anything with it. There was boyfriend after boyfriend, and dysfunctional relationships that wouldn't end. I could walk through the grocery store and run into someone and see it in their eyes. I could show up at the movie theatre alone and hear the whispers. Judgement, judgement, judgement.

Away I went. I left the only stability I'd ever known in my life. A town and a state that I loved with all my heart. I put on my armor, grabbed my shield, and drove my butt to Arizona.

There is liberation in embarking on an adventure alone. And there is beauty in anonymity. I decided where to live, where to work, who to talk to. It was amazing. No one knew me unless I wanted them to know me. And if I met someone who said or did anything that didn't sit right with me, I slashed them out of my life with no hesitation. I was fiercely dedicated to school and focused only on my goal: success. There was no other option.

I found myself. I truly was Aundrea, Warrior Princess. A dark past filled with pain, suffering, torment, triumphs, tribulations, wins, losses, ups, and downs. But now a life of redemption. A successful career, a loving husband, a family, a home, a positive outlook on life.

I've spent a lot of years constantly working to be better. Better at my job, better as a mother, better as a wife, just better at everything. I constantly pursued growth and advancement in my career, because I was never satisfied with my results. I would reach a goal, and still feel unsatisfied. I'd make new friends, and still feel inadequate. I've built an amazing life. I put myself through college, enjoyed a successful IT career, married an amazing man who loves me unconditionally, have four beautiful children, live a quality life, have the love of my bonus

family and my biological family, and the list of blessings goes on and on. Yet, I've constantly struggled with self-doubt, insecurity, feelings of inadequacy, and stuck without self-love.

I'd start a project feeling inspired and excited to be doing something new and adventurous. Then I'd quit or start believing it didn't matter because I'd probably fail or screw it up anyway. I judge myself harshly for the mistakes I make in life. Believe me when I say no one can judge me any harsher than I've judged myself. I found myself as a parent falling into the same trap of never being proud of what my kids achieved and telling them they could have done better. I still felt out of place at work and in the community. I wasn't happy with myself and still felt I needed to achieve more, make more money, have a better house, or accomplish something amazing for people to like me or love me. I lived in fear that if people knew all my mistakes in life and how imperfect I am, they wouldn't like or love me anymore.

And then I stopped. I stopped all the noise in my head and decided that it all had to end. I have to love the person I am before I can truly embrace the love that graces my life in abundance.

I read books. I stopped trying to please everyone. I worked with a life coach to explore my life purpose and why I was placed on this earth with these experiences. I started meditating. I searched my soul for every ache, pain, fear, and sadness and replaced it with love, light, beauty, and most importantly… forgiveness.

I believe in power. I believe in the power that lives inside each of us that is pure and comes from the higher power that some call God, Universe, or Spirit. I believe we all have it and we are free to choose how to use it. I believe we all have choices. Our power is choice and no one can take that away.

As I look back on how I chose to move forward in my life after battling through my first 18 years, I see that I chose to use my power for good. For good to create a life of abundance and joy, for helping other people achieve their goals and dreams, for conscious decisions to make everyday a better day than the one before. I chose to

find strength from my experiences. I chose to love who I am and all that I am.

After all, I am a Warrior Princess.

Aundrea lives in Colorado and enjoys life with her husband, four children, two dogs, and a cat. Her tenacity to live a life of love, joy, and fun is contagious to anyone who spends time with her. When she's not working, or managing a busy family life, Aundrea is a life-long learner and considers herself a professional life changer. Aundrea is a certified Reiki Practitioner who works with people to find their deep wounds from traumatic life experiences, and empowers them to harness the power of energy healing in order to free their hearts and truly experience self-love. She is pragmatic about life in general and uses her ability to break down complex concepts into simple and relatable lessons in her career, personal life, and community. You can find more of her short stories and life lessons online at WayOfTheWarriorPrincess.com or Facebook.com/AundreaDWarriorPrincess.

Forgive and Flourish

by Jennifer Knoble

After three years of being together, one night in 2011, my husband suddenly began smacking me in the face, punching me in the face, grabbing me by the hair, and pulling me around the room. I had no time to really react, it all happened quite fast. It was a bit of an out of body experience for me. It was as though my brain went into flight or fight mode—I knew I was going through it but I shut down to protect myself. Maybe if I had reacted, it would have made it worse and he wouldn't have stopped. What prompted such violent and unpredictable behavior?

A few weeks prior, I was in his home country, visiting his family with the purpose of also bringing his sister back with me to live with us, while he was still in Colorado. During that time, he would keep me up all night talking… seeking out very private and personal

details about me, which I thought was normal for spouses to share, so I did. You see, though, there was a seven hour time difference, so while he was keeping me up until five or six in the morning, causing me to be utterly exhausted, he would be able to go to sleep around 10 pm and sleep a whole night. On one occasion, he asked me for my email password. I hesitated. Then he insisted, and that turned into demanding it. So after about two hours of arguing with him about it, I caved in and gave him my password. Determined to find incriminating evidence, he began to methodically go through my emails written as far back as when we were casually dating. In the process, he discovered messages exchanged between me and other men I had casually dated when we weren't exclusive. When I returned home with his sister, it was only a matter of time before he would confront me...

It only took him three days. Moments before he started hitting me, he came into our room right before 10 pm, grabbed his laptop, and began showing me the emails and pictures that he had saved from the previous weeks while he was searching through my email. As I admitted hesitantly to the emails and pictures, my body began to tense up. I can remember seeing his eyes go from relaxed to tightly squinted and his face turned red. He was filled with anger. After nearly 30 minutes of the physical abuse, he suddenly stopped and started to wipe the blood from my lips and the tears from my face. My brain couldn't process all of this. I was in shock. He made it clear that it was my fault, I caused him to hurt me, and he only did it because he loved me. In turn, I blamed myself—I truly felt like it was my fault for getting him so upset. By now it was probably one in the morning and I was mentally, emotionally, and physically exhausted. While I lay on the floor outside our bedroom on the stair landing (as that is where he allowed me to sleep after he was done), I wept trying to understand why this happened. The pieces slowly started coming together as I thought of all the subtle things he had done or said to me between when we met and that night.

We met online using plentyoffish.com. I was 26 and his profile said he was 33. We talked for a while before meeting and about two weeks later, we went on our first date; he took me to a pool hall. He stated that he wasn't looking for a relationship and that we could be just friends with benefits. I should have realized then not to continue seeing him. During the first six months together, we had a mutual understanding that we were not exclusive and free to date (and presumably sleep with) others. I honestly can't explain why I continued to see him, or what drew me to him. I could make up a fabulous story as to why, but there isn't one. He was good looking, a bit of a charmer, he was from another country (but already a US citizen), and from his profile I believed he had a steady job.

This is where my nightmare began…

I fell in love, and two years later we verbally declared that we were common law married. It was around this time that I learned he was not the age he said he was—instead of being seven years older, there was a 16-year gap, which meant that he was 42 years old when I met him. I also learned that he had been married in his home country and had two children from that marriage. Even after finding out about these withholdings on his part, I was still madly in love with him.

Little did I know, there was more verbal, mental, emotional, financial and physical abuse that I had endured leading up to this night in 2011. From the beginning of our relationship, he would belittle me by making me feel like I was stupid, saying I didn't know what I was talking about, even in my own job. He would make fun of me by making comments like, "You look like a clown face with makeup on," and smack me across the face. He told me to stop shaving my legs because he preferred all natural. After the hair grew out, he would rub my legs and make disgusted sounds and say, "I didn't

know I was with a man," and then he would say he preferred smooth legs. He was good at playing mind games. I remember the man I was so in love with would call me "big mama." I believe some of the abuse was so subtle that I didn't even know it was happening. Over time, he had convinced me that my friends were controlling me and that I should discontinue those friendships. I somewhat believed him, but not fully. I created a secret Facebook profile so I could keep in touch with those friends that he so subtly forced me to drop.

Despite all of this, I was in denial and made excuses for him. My gut told me something was wrong, but I ignored it. After all, I was in love with him. To me, he was amazing. We had explored Colorado together, we traveled to his home country, we would go dancing and have fun together. If I was sick, he would take care of me by taking me to the hospital, watching over me, and making me soup. His kind acts that I mistook for love canceled out the negative. In my head, I had created an alternate reality with him and justified his behavior.

This went on for years, until that night in 2011 that forced me to face reality. While I was on the landing, I sent a text message to my best friend back home in Missouri and told her about what had happened. I was in complete disbelief of what had just happened. I was still shaking, and I couldn't really sleep even though I needed to. My mind was going in circles trying to process everything.

The next morning, he wanted to take his sister sightseeing and demanded that I accompany them. Deep inside I was certain he thought I might run away and wanted to make sure that I was within his sight. To explain my busted lip and swollen face, he told his sister that I had fallen in the shower. My friend was texting me, scared for me, but unfortunately, I was afraid to respond to her messages in front of him. When we were eating lunch, I stepped away and went to the bathroom so I could secretly respond to her. She ended up calling our local police to try and protect me. Throughout that day, while riding in his car, I would stare out the window praying for God to help me. I couldn't understand why the man I loved would abuse me the way he did.

When we returned to our home after taking his sister around the city, the police were there waiting to arrest him. That moment was so intense. I felt my stomach drop as I saw the police cars parked at our townhouse. I knew what was about to occur. Part of me wanted it to happen and part of me didn't want it to happen. Inexplicably, I actually felt bad for him.

The police took pictures of my face and filmed a video interview of what happened. They arrested him and took him to jail. I was trembling and my voice shaking as I answered their questions. I wanted to cry, but his sister was with me and was confused about what had just taken place. My heart broke for her. This was her first time to ever leave her country, and just three days after she arrived, she witnessed her brother being arrested. At the time, she didn't speak English, so I pulled myself together and used Google Translate to communicate from English to French about what had happened, and then from French to English so I could understand her questions and responses. I explained to her that I had not fallen in the shower, but that her brother had beaten me the night before. She was in shock as well. She said her brother had changed so much since he moved to the USA. She thought it was her fault; that her coming to live with us caused the fight. This conversation seemed to go on for hours, I was completely drained. I somehow managed to organize and recruit some friends to help me pack my stuff and put it in a storage unit. It was around 11 pm before I went to bed, and I knew the next day was going to be a long one. My father was driving from Missouri to come help me and take me back home.

The next morning, I went to the courthouse and filed a restraining order against my husband. I can remember sitting there shaking from nervousness. The judge granted the restraining order. It was saddening that it had come to this, but it was also such a relief. After spending only one night in jail, he was released, and instructed to take domestic violence classes, pay a fine, and have no contact with me. As my dad and I drove out of Colorado to Missouri, I got a

text message from a mutual friend saying that he had been released. I wasn't concerned about him but more concerned about his sister. I relayed a message to our mutual friend, that my husband should go back to our home to be with his sister and that I was returning to my hometown for a while. I can remember talking to my dad as we were driving through flat Kansas about how betrayed I felt, and how hard it would be on my husband now to get his own place. I wanted him to suffer; I wanted his life to be more difficult. My body would be overcome with anger and then just as quickly filled with sadness.

I was confused and heart broken. I wanted so badly to be with him, but I was torn because I couldn't believe that he would have such disregard for my wellbeing and hurt me by hitting, punching, and pulling me around. This was the man I loved, the man I wanted to have children with, the man I wanted to spend my life with. How did this happen?

As I sifted through memories of that terrible night, I made the connection between the "incriminating" emails and the day he had forced me to provide him with my email password. This is what set him off. Leading up to that night, I along with his family had been begging him to drop it. That what I had done prior to becoming Muslim should no longer matter. I was no longer the same person he had met. I was humiliated and embarrassed by the things I had done when I first met him. I did not respect myself nor anyone else. The day I became Muslim my attitude towards myself and those around me changed. I started showing more respect and had more appreciation for life. Unfortunately, he didn't see who I had become but only focused on who I was. And in that moment, he lost control of his anger.

"A moment of patience in the moment of anger prevents a thousand moments of regret."
– 'Ali Ibn Abi Talib

I continued to replay memories of our relationship, and all of the abuse I had endured. Another haunting memory surfaced. What I am about to share only a couple of people know. When I was 27, and we were still casually dating, we went to a club – we were dancing and drinking. I was heavily intoxicated. He drove us to my place and helped me inside. As I was nearly passed out, lying face down on my bed, he started to have anal sex with me. I blocked that out for several years until I sought out counseling. After recalling this night, it still infuriates me.

In addition to this behavior, he would always try to come up with a reason why I shouldn't go back home to Missouri to visit my family. At the end of 2009, at 27 years old, I went back to college as a full-time student and was working as a nanny for two separate families, and doing child care at a church. He refused to work during this time. I was responsible for paying nearly all of our bills. He did manage to pay his half of the rent using a workers' compensation settlement he had received, but I had to take out student loans to make ends meet.

As a new Muslim, I had become active in the local mosque attending regular service every week. When I would bring up things that I found him doing wrong from the teachings that I had learned at the mosque, he would get so upset and try to convince me that I was wrong. Ultimately, through manipulation he convinced me to stop going to the mosque! I want to take a moment here to express that his behavior and treatment towards me is not at all what Islam teaches. And I don't let my experience with him change my view or my belief in Islam. I chose to become Muslim and I love my faith and I love God.

Somehow, he had managed to make me so dependent on him; I had to have his approval, his opinion, his permission to do anything. He wanted to know where I was going, who would be there, start time and end time, and would text me while I was gone as well. I became a compulsive liar. I would lie and tell him I was babysitting

just so I could go to dinner with friends. I began hating who I was becoming—heck, I didn't even recognize who I was.

But even after experiencing and realizing all of that abuse, I still ended up going back to him about four weeks after going with my dad back to Missouri. He bought his sister a phone and through his sister we spoke. He knew exactly what to say—he convinced me that he was going to change and be a better man. When I returned to Colorado, he moved out of the house and in with a friend so that I could stay with his sister, as we weren't allowed to see each other with the restraining order in place.

When I would leave and go to work, he would visit his sister at the house and leave me sweet notes. This was the first time ever that he was actually loveable and kind, and it made my heart melt. Everything I had been wanting, hoping for, praying for was what appeared to be happening. He even opened a joint bank account and started paying for everything. I could use money from this account to buy groceries and pay bills without having to seek his permission. I felt like things were coming together and finally my marriage was as I had hoped it would be. He convinced me to write a letter to the judge to have the restraining order lifted so we could be back together.

Four months after going to the courthouse to seek protection from him, the judge dropped the restraining order at my request. My husband and I had been making plans for once the restraining order was removed, and agreed that we should officially get married instead of simply being common law married. We got a marriage license and went to the mosque and became officially married both in the State of Colorado and Islamically. For both, it requires signing a piece of paper that states we are married in the presence of witnesses. During our discussions of officially becoming husband and wife, we talked about the traditions that are usually done in Islamic weddings: henna parties for the bride and her female family members and friends, the dresses the bride wears, the food, and the music. When the time came, none of that happened. On the day, we went to

the mosque to get married, I asked him to wear a traditional Islamic outfit as I was. And he threw it on the floor and refused to wear it. I broke down in tears. I got that gut feeling again telling me I shouldn't go through with it. Yet, I got in the vehicle with him and went to the mosque to get married. The entire 20 minutes it took, I was in tears. I knew I was making a mistake and yet I couldn't find the courage within me to say how I felt and stop from proceeding. Unfortunately, I foolishly and officially locked myself with him by law. Looking back now, I know that if we had just stayed common law married, I could have denied we were married and been able to leave him and not have to worry about going through court divorce proceedings to officially be disconnected from him. Despite these disappointments, I was still convinced our relationship would work.

Over the next four years, I left approximately 30 times.

Every time I left and came back, our relationship would be good for a while and then turn around again, and I'd find myself right back to the same reasons I had previously left. I would usually end up at a friend's place, but sometimes I wouldn't get far before he would call and convince me to return. Each time, he would convince me to return either by saying exactly what I wanted to hear, or by manipulation and coercion. I left on so many occasions, because of our fighting and his bringing up the past, or for getting angry and acting like he was going to hit me again, or for his constant name calling. It was always something. Each time I left, I would try to figure out a better way to leave, and work to cut different strings of attachment or dependence on him. He had bought a laptop for me while I was in college. One of the times I left, he demanded that I give him back the laptop, and that it belonged to him. So, the next time I left after that, I bought my own laptop so he couldn't use the one he bought as a way to pull me back in.

A little over a year after his arrest, I moved out and put all of my belongings in storage. Even though I eventually went back to him, I still kept my things in storage as a way to ensure I would at some point leave for good.

I continued to try different tactics. I tried explaining that it wasn't going to work, that we didn't trust each other, and that we had tried numerous times to reunite and it just wasn't going to work. I tried leaving without his knowing; I tried telling him that I was leaving. It just didn't seem like anything worked. It took two more years for me to move out and rent my own apartment with a great roommate. I felt safe and happy for the first time in a long time.

Even with these new living arrangements, not much changed about the situation, unfortunately. He was calling and texting me non-stop, begging me to see him. I can't explain why I somehow couldn't cut off the communication with him. It was like some sick, twisted dilemma in my head. He wore me down with his constant calling and texting. He convinced me again and again to come back to him, and six months after moving out, I moved back in with him. It was good for about a month and then it increasingly became worse. Again. I was increasingly getting tired of living in fear; fear that he would lose his temper and hurt me physically again, fear of him tracking me, fear that he would catch me lying to him.

During our relationship, there were many frustrating situations for me, outside of the abuse. I'm going to point out two specific situations. First, I have long wanted to be a mother. I thought for sure by now I would be a mother. We tried to get pregnant numerous times, yet I was always disappointed when my period came. He declared that it was a problem with me, not him because he has two kids already. I wanted to find out if it was me or not. I started seeing a fertility doctor in January 2015. I went through all the testing and probing, and even had to have a procedure done to remove a polyp from my uterus. These tests are some of the most uncomfortable and painful tests I've ever gone through and he refused to go with me. Come to find out, there is absolutely no reason why I haven't gotten

pregnant. The next step was for him to be tested. He was insulted and refused to have anything to do with this process. I became bitter and was filling up with anger towards him. I was willing to do what was necessary to become a mom, and he made it clear he didn't care.

Second, it bothered me that he would never go with me to visit my family, who was just a two-hour flight or eight-hour drive away. This was a constant issue for me. Every time I went back home, I felt like I was alone and single, not married. When my family would ask why he didn't come with me, I'd have to make an excuse for him. I became even better at lying. Lying to him, lying to my family, lying to friends, and lying to myself.

Finally, in 2015, he said he would go with me to visit my grandmother in Ohio. I was so thrilled and bought tickets for both of us to go. Just a few days before we were supposed to leave, he informed me that he couldn't take time off work and was unable to go. I was furious. That was truly my last straw. I was sick of him never being willing to do anything for me or with me—it was always about him and what he wanted – he never took me into consideration. I was done with his selfish behavior and being unimportant to him.

So, within days after he canceled on our trip to visit my grandmother, I made another plan to leave him. I bought a new vehicle so I didn't have to rely on him to fix my current one. I found a family that was willing to take me in and give me a safe place to live, in a stable environment. I needed that more than I knew. I spent seven years of my life devoted to trying to be with him, yet it was so unstable and abusive.

I once again packed up all of my belongings and put them in storage. It was the best decision I made. I sought out counseling, and forgave myself for not listening to my gut, for not standing up for myself, for internally beating myself up and blaming myself for what I had gone through, for allowing him to have my power, and for returning over and over again. I also forgave my husband. Not because he deserved forgiveness, but because I needed to heal. And I knew I couldn't heal without forgiving him.

I proclaimed 2016 was my year, and I made it my year. I worked on my own self-development, discovering who I was and who I wanted to be. In doing that, I had to start focusing on taking better care of myself. I began reading books about self-care, life after an abusive relationship, and more. I also joined a six-month course that met twice monthly called Flourish. This course was life changing and exactly what I needed at the right time in my life. I broke through the limiting beliefs he had instilled upon me. I was able to forgive him and find healing. For the first time that I can remember, I was able to be authentic and stop lying to myself and those around me.

Never before had I focused on myself in my life. I was amazed at how transformed I became through the program. By focusing on myself, I became stronger and built more confidence. I was truly amazed. I was surrounded by amazing people who were encouraging, uplifting, empowering, loving, caring, and above all, supportive. Through all the support that has been given to me, I'm trying to give back by telling my story. Everyone needs a second chance in life.

There were red flags and my gut instincts were warning me, but I didn't listen. I lived in denial. I defended him. And I stayed with him. Until you have experienced domestic violence either personally or through a friend or family member, it is hard to understand why a victim stays in an abusive relationship. I had countless people ask me repeatedly, "Why don't you leave?" "What is wrong with you?" "Why did you go back?" The truth is, I couldn't answer those people. I don't know why I went back. I wanted out so badly, and every time I went back I hated myself more and more. The physical abuse had stopped after that awful night, but the verbal, mental and emotional abuse escalated. I got depressed and even had suicidal thoughts; I prayed for someone to hit me while I was driving and kill me. I could never kill myself, but wanted someone else to kill me so I didn't feel the pain. I now realize that I can choose to no longer tolerate disrespecting, abusing, controlling and manipulating treatment. This is a big change for me.

Now that I am a survivor, I can recognize when others are going through this same struggle. Through my experiences, I was able to see the warning signs with a friend of mine who I met through work. She was in an abusive relationship. Her boyfriend was controlling and extremely jealous, among other things. One particular moment I won't forget. In 2015, I had just left my husband for the last time and that same weekend I got a text message from her with a picture of her face. Her eye was swollen, black and blue and purple, and the blood vessel in her eye busted. Her boyfriend didn't physically do it, but he took her to his sister's house and had his sister give the brutal beating. I instantly broke down to the point where I was hyperventilating. I was determined that I would do whatever it took to help her get out safely.

I want to acknowledge that her story isn't mine to fully share, but it is relevant to where I am now. I saw the signs and began talking to her about my own experience. At one time, I had mentioned to her a book I was reading, *Why Does He Do That?*, and how some of the things she said her boyfriend would say or do were exactly what I was reading about at that time. She wasn't ready to hear it and told me so. I told her that I would be here when she was ready. Over the course of several months, she opened up more to me. I remember taking her to a basketball game and on the way home she shared how she wanted out of her relationship but felt stuck. She didn't see a way out. I then shared that if she wanted out and was done, all she had to do was call me and I would have a crew and truck there, and would have her out and in a safe place within three hours. That was the first time she realized she had an option. I also helped her in other areas of her life, providing guidance with starting college, and finding a new apartment. I also helped her with her taxes, and when she had concerns about her job. I started inviting her to activities with my friends and she began calling me her "Fairy Godmother."

Stirring deep within me, I felt like I needed to do something more around helping victims of domestic violence. After some consideration and conversations with family and friends, I decided to establish a non-profit called the "Fairy Godmother Project". The organization's purpose is to help victims of domestic violence leave the situation safely and thrive. We will connect victims with the resources they need (i.e. moving companies, storage facilities, attorneys, shelter or other housing, safety planning, and more) along with a focus on providing self-care services (i.e. self-defense training, nutritional coaching, fitness coaching, support groups, massages, makeovers, and more) to help with their transformation from victim to survivor. Through staying true to myself, helping others and continuing my counseling, I believe this will ensure that I also remain a survivor and never end up back in an abusive relationship.

Domestic violence affects one in four women in the United States. Only about 10-15 percent of abuse is actually reported. As I have mentioned, abuse comes in many different forms: physical, emotional, mental, verbal, financial, spiritual, sexual, and more. The non-physical abuse is harder to prove and so is typically not reported. If you or someone you know is in an abusive relationship and don't know what to do, please don't hesitate to reach out to the Fairy Godmother Project for support and resources. If it is an emergency, please immediately call 9-1-1 or the National Domestic Violence Hotline number at 1-800-799-7233.

Jennifer Knoble is the Founder and President of the Fairy Godmother Project, a non-profit organization that helps victims of domestic violence transform, survive, and flourish. Jennifer currently works in Human Resources and Operations, and is the administrator for a local church. She is a graduate from the University of Colorado Denver with Bachelor Degrees in Human Resources and Business Management. She enjoys hiking, photography, traveling, butterflies, and focusing on her own self-care and self-development. She also enjoys giving back to the community by volunteering with Extreme Community Makeover, Ambassadors of Compassion, and the Alumni Student Mentoring Program at her alma mater. To learn more about the Fairy Godmother Project, contact Admin@MyFairyGodmotherProject.org, 720-609-1771, or visit MyFairyGodmotherProject.org.

The Sound
of Truth

by Crystal Blue

"If you are falling... dive. We're in a freefall into the future. We don't know where we're going. Things are changing so fast, and always when you're going through a long tunnel, anxiety comes along. And all you have to do to transform your hell into a paradise is turn your fall into a voluntary act. It's a very interesting shift of perspective and that's all it is... joyful participation in the sorrows... and everything changes."
– Joseph Campbell

In Buddhism, there are Four Noble Truths. First, in life there exists suffering, pain, and misery. Second, this suffering is caused by attachments (often subconscious) to negative thoughts, behaviors, and personal desires. Third, we have the ability to transcend suffering and attachments. Finally, freedom from suffering can be achieved through the Eightfold Path, which consists of the right view, intention, speech, action, livelihood, effort, mindfulness, and concentration.

Throughout my journey, I have experienced tremendous suffering and agonizing pain. At times, I was convinced that my entire life was going to be a series of traumatic and overwhelming events that would continue to push me beyond my limits, burying me in a deep, dark pit of loneliness, rage, and fear. I was convinced that I would never be able to break free, to release myself from this endless cycle, to rise above the ferocious storms that always surrounded me.

After many years of questioning and searching, I am now able to reflect on this journey and see the higher purpose and experience life from a different perspective. From this, I have developed my own personal truths grounded in acceptance, surrender, mindfulness, and love. Yes, there is suffering, and we can experience this all throughout our lifetime. However, this suffering can be linked to our attachments. Attachment to possessions. Attachment to expectations. Attachment to control. Attachment to outcome. We often fear the outcome, the endless possibilities, and the unknown. We want to feel like we are in control. These attachments and fears can prevent us from being free and experiencing the joys of life.

What if we could be free from attachments and fear? What if we could accept our past as a blessing and release it? How would it feel to surrender to the flow of life and just *be*? What would we be able to receive and achieve when we are not standing in our own way? What would our world look like? Who would we become?

I believe we have the potential to be free, to live free. Free from attachments and fear. Free to experience joy and happiness. Free to become who we are meant to be. To become our Truth.

While I am able to realize and share my truths, mastering them is an ongoing process. I am still learning to live from this space. I live to become my truth.

WOUNDED WARRIOR

Shortly after my 18th birthday, I packed my things and started to float and roam between spaces, working several jobs, and having no real "home." Even though I didn't know where I would be staying the next week or the following month, it was still better than what was behind me. I was living like a gypsy and loving it.

In my wild and reckless years to come, I didn't care or think too much about *how* I was living. As long as I had a job and somewhere safe to sleep, I was doing just fine. I didn't have a long-term plan. I didn't really see the point. I enjoyed the feeling of freedom, but with this lifestyle I avoided getting close or attached to anyone or anything. This included rejecting even the healthiest of relationships. This was my first experience with "detachment." I was coming from a wounded place, but instead of feeling like a victim, I felt like a warrior. I had survived a battle—an emotional, physical, and mental battle, scarred by those who were closest to me. With the exception of my devoted grandparents, the people I had expected to care for me and nurture me only abused, neglected, and rejected me. I was not safe. I was not loved. I did not belong.

On the inside, my heart was broken, my ego bruised, and my inner light dim. I learned to protect myself by defending myself, throwing glares like swords and words like daggers. No one fucks with *me*.

I didn't have high expectations for myself or anyone else, and I didn't care. I didn't want to care. Caring led to disappointment… disappointment and rejection. So why bother trying? Why would it matter? Does any of it matter… ?

Live like there's no tomorrow. Carpe diem.

Through these dark times, there was one thing that did seem to matter—music. Growing up, my favorite subjects were math and music. They made sense to me. Math was logical and explained in proofs—facts as numbers. Music was its voice. When I played the

piano, I could see the numbers coming together to sing and dance, forming patterns into rhythm and harmony. Every sound could be translated into numbers and formulas. I couldn't explain why it made me feel so whole and connected, but I could definitely feel it. Math was real. Sound was truth.

As I ventured out into the world, I found even more truth in music. For every feeling of angst, heartache, joy, and passion there was a sound. No matter where I was, or what I was feeling, I could express myself through music. I could scream and thrash with the drums. I could feel sorrow and weep with the violins. I could escape into the rhythm and get lost in the bass. Through music, I was free to be me.

In the midst of working, partying, dancing, getting high, and not caring, I slowly started to open up. I started to explore and discover hidden pieces of myself. I embraced my love of photography and started working in a local shop developing film and processing orders. I revealed my passion for reading and accepted a job at a local bookstore. To my surprise, I started to meet more like-minded people who shared my interests and values. I took more pictures. I read more books. I discovered new music. I created more meaningful friendships. Who knew I could actually start to enjoy life?!

I branched out even further and enrolled in a few classes at a community college. I enjoyed drawing, graphic design, color theory, philosophy, and physics. I read about different religions and learned enough about Transcendentalism and Buddhism to know that they spoke to my heart. I took long walks through my favorite park and sketched my favorite spots. Other times, I would bring my camera and capture everything from the smallest blooming buds to the tallest towering trees. One of my new friends introduced me to night hiking, and we secretly made our way through parks and trails after dark. There was something so calming about being outdoors, especially under the stars. I found peace in nature. I loved every minute.

To feed my constantly questioning mind, I began reading about various philosophers and theories, the edge of time and space,

parallel universes, alternate realities, worm holes and black holes...
and then my heart caught fire when I discovered cognitive science.

I started pulling titles like *The Undiscovered Mind, Phantoms in
the Brain,* and (literally) *The Brain Book,* followed by *How the Mind
Works* and *The Blank Slate* by my new idol Steven Pinker. I started
reading about neuroplasticity and cognitive reframing: *Change Your
Brain, Change Your Life. The Emerging Mind. The Brain that Changes
Itself. Use Both Sides of Your Brain.* I devoured it all. I went out of my
way to attend lectures downtown, and went to a brain exhibit that
was hosted in the sketchiest part of the city. After finishing my basic psychology classes, I went on to study abnormal psychology and
case studies. I had never been interested in something so intensely
and completely. I felt like I was seeing people in a different light, discovering hidden secrets about the how's and why's of human behavior. We have so much potential. Everything started to make more
sense. Outside of math and music, this became my leading truth.

Life seemed to take on a whole new meaning. I felt my mind expanding. New realities started to appear. I could see so far beyond
myself. I felt small and insignificant, yet I was impressed and in awe
of our mere existence. What a gift. I then realized that all of this information and knowledge only led to more questions. What is the
point of it all? Why are we here? Why am *I* here... ? I continued my
search for more truth.

Through my studies and exploration, I decided that my dream
was to become a brain surgeon. Through this work, I could continue
to study human behavior, and I would learn how to "fix" significant
psychological issues, injuries, and traumas. I could help ease suffering. I could help people feel better and live a healthier, happier life. I
could help others heal. I finally felt like I had a purpose.

On the other hand, the more I researched this path, the more
it seemed out of reach. It would be a long road ahead, and I had so
much self-doubt. After all, I hadn't been given much encouragement
when I needed it the most. When I shared my intentions with friends

and family, my doubts were only confirmed by the surprise on their faces and echoed through the confusion in their voices. "How and where would you start?" "Isn't that going to be hard? Why do you want to do that?" These questions lead me to consider, *"How could I possibly be smart enough and capable enough to take this on? Who am I kidding... How will I ever become a brain surgeon?!"*

During this time of deep reflection, pondering, and wandering, I wanted to settle down in one place, yet remain independent, but I could not afford my own space. A new opportunity presented itself. Through a cousin, I met a man who was previously married to her dad's sister... or something like that. Joe was goofy and fun, had a room to rent, and the three of us shared good times. To support my desire for stability and independence, I accepted the invitation to move in and felt like I was finally getting somewhere. And because the stability, independence, and acceptance felt so good, I put on blinders and normalized the alcoholism that surrounded me. I downplayed dangerous situations and relationships. I didn't want to see what was happening all around me. "Nothing that bad can happen to me. I can handle it. Bring it on!" I thought. I may have been wounded, but now I felt like an invincible warrior.

PTSD: PARALYSIS. TERROR. SHAME. DESPAIR.

After my cousin moved out and it was just me and Joe living together, I continued to work two, sometimes three jobs, enroll in more classes, and "find myself." I felt like I had "evolved" and moved on from my past. I felt like I was creating a new identity. I decided to start getting more serious about life; studying more, partying less... I even considered making some long-term plans and establishing realistic life goals. As I ventured out, I became frustrated with all of the rules and regulations of the "grown up life," but I had support and encouragement along the way. In addition to a handful of very

special people in my life, Joe recognized that I was exploring and discovering my true self. He would encourage me to keep going, and said that I was a "shining star."

During this time, I was casually dating several men. One relationship in particular turned out to be extremely abusive. The more time I spent with him, the more I realized that I was reluctantly, often out of guilt and lack of boundaries, pushing aside my priorities, my focus, and my other relationships to be with him. At first, I saw that he was damaged and I took pity on him. I felt like I could help him. But after countless insults, public arguments, physical violence, and a loss of self-esteem, my sympathy came to an end.

When I told Joe about this situation, he was upset. I later discovered that he had decided to purchase a gun. I rationalized that, in his own twisted version of reality, this was his way of protecting me. He wanted me to feel safe. We went to the shooting range together so I could learn how to fire the gun. I wasn't scared or intimidated, but I didn't feel empowered either. I realized that this gun was just a tool. It was just a piece of metal that some people used as a weapon. I knew that the *real* power was inside of me.

One night, as we were finishing dinner at home, I was setting up our regular chess game when Joe came stumbling down the hall with his gun. He showed me that it wasn't loaded and started singing and goofing around as usual. I wasn't afraid of him or the gun and didn't even give it a second thought. "Put that thing away, you idiot," was pretty much all I said before I went back to setting up the chess board. He then started talking nonsense about a game called Russian Roulette. I looked at him as if he was speaking a foreign language. I rolled my eyes, dismissed what he was saying and told him again to put the gun away. By this time, he was probably on his fifth—or tenth—drink. He ignored me and went on to explain the rules of the game. "… then… you hold the gun… up to your head… and pull the trigger…" As I turned my head to tell him yet again to shut up and put the gun away, I saw him pull the trigger. He forgot to check the chamber.

He dropped to the floor. Blood went everywhere. I called 9-1-1.

When the first responders arrived, I was eerily calm. Shock is a strange process. My brain had started to shut down parts of itself and I went into a happy place. Part of me disappeared deep within myself and my autopilot protocols kicked in. I became completely present with what was going on around me. Everything seemed to be happening in slow motion. I was fascinated by the gun powder test. I even asked questions about how it worked. I expressed my gratitude to the rescue team who came to help. Out of the corner of my eye, I saw a large, black bag being carried out on a stretcher. A man's voice reassured me that Joe would be flown to the nearest hospital, but I had already overheard another voice say, "DOA." It wasn't a surprise. I knew he was dead. When I was on the phone with the emergency dispatcher, she told me to grab some kitchen towels and apply pressure to his wound. She didn't know that he had specifically purchased hollow point bullets, which expand on impact. There was a massive hole in his temple. The towels weren't going to help. I did it anyway.

Time stops and everything blurs together. Someone comes to pick me up. I don't know what to do. I can't think. I can't sleep. I try to process what happened. Nothing seems real. I start doing shots of hard liquor to calm my nerves… I stop keeping track of how many and just keep pouring until the alcohol starts to do its thing. When I am finally able to sleep, I wake up in a panic, screaming. I only see loud, twisted, blood-filled memories. The sun is up. I'm moving towards my car. I can't feel my body. I don't know what or how to tell my family. Somehow, I find myself staying with my dad and his family. My 22nd birthday comes and goes. I am lost. I am numb. Nothing is real.

Someone takes me to a counselor who specializes in grief. She seems nice, but I'm hesitant and confused. I'm not sure how to start. I know I need to be here, but I don't know what to say. I've never done anything like this before. Eventually, I start talking. I tell her

what happened in a very blunt, direct, and graphic way. I don't feel anything. The words don't register. It's like I'm just reading a script, repeating a story that I heard from someone else, a long, long time ago. I am convinced that it didn't actually happen. Maybe I'm dreaming. Maybe I'm going crazy and I made it all up. Maybe I'm dead and this is some kind of purgatory. Or maybe this is Hell.

I am referred to a psychiatrist who asks me several probing questions. No, I can't sleep. No, I don't have an appetite. No, I am not depressed. No, I do not think about taking my own life. On a scale from one to ten my anxiety level is a four, maybe five (*but that's normal, right?*). I don't really feel anything, but I'm fine… really (*seriously, why am I even here?*). He prescribes me some pills to help me sleep. Instead of two hours, I can now sleep for four hours at a time. The graphic images are still terrifying, and the panic still returns, followed by confusion and numbness. *"It's nothing I can't handle."* I keep telling myself this…

Time passes by and I slowly start to feel more comfortable with the counselor. One day, as I'm talking about Joe, I feel an overwhelming sense of panic. My adrenaline kicks in and I feel like I'm right back in the living room with him. My body starts shaking, my heart starts pounding, and I can't breathe. I am paralyzed. I don't understand what's happening. Suddenly, I see the moment just before he pulled the trigger and the pause seems to go on for eternity. There was time… I could have done something… I could have stopped him… it's all my fault.

It's all my fault.

I break down. I cry. *I finally feel something.*

Shortly after this breakthrough, my brain starts to unravel. I try to process how everything fits together, but it doesn't make sense. I can't seem to remember much beyond the event, before or after. The emotions rage through my body like violent tornados. I go through cycles of extreme anxiety, panic, and fear… then everything goes numb. I am exhausted but see no way out. I am a slave to these

storms. I am dead inside.

I continue to meet with the psychiatrist and finally give a voice to my struggles. I still can't eat or sleep through the night. My anxiety now extends beyond his scale. I don't want to end my life, but I sure as hell don't want to be in it, either. He prescribes some antidepressants and anti-anxiety medications. Nothing seems to change. He increases the dosage. Again. And again. After more time passes, I start to notice a small change. The highs and lows are not as extreme, but the cycles continue. Paralysis. Terror. Shame. Despair.

I find that I don't want to be alone. I feel better when someone else is with me, or at least where I can see or hear them. When other people are around, the world feels slightly more real. I can focus on something outside of myself. My mind is not a safe place to be. I'm able to hold my shit together long enough to interact with the outside world, but only in small doses. Loud and sudden noises send me into an uncontrollable internal spiral, as I am flooded with graphic images and intense emotions from the event… reality starts to fade, everything around me starts to disappear, and I find myself back in the living room with Joe, witnessing and reliving the tragedy over and over again.

Even without immediate triggers, the flashbacks continue to occur several times throughout the day and night. I get lost in the memories. Part of me feels like I'm stuck in the room with him. Years seem to pass and the medications start having more of a stabilizing effect. I start writing in a journal and am impressed with how poetic the tragedy becomes. The panic attacks don't happen as often, but I find myself becoming more numb, more often. I start to wonder, and then just assume, that this is what my life will be like from now on.

When someone mentions going back to work, I don't think twice. I welcome the thought of something more "normal." Someone helps me with my résumé and I start applying for office jobs in the area. As I start shopping for professional work clothes, I realize that I have lost over 30 pounds. People who haven't seen me in a while notice

the dramatic change and say I look great. On the outside, they see me smile and say, "… thanks…" On the inside, I am a hurricane of vengeful emotions screaming, "fuck off!" *If they only knew…*

Underneath the projected image of myself, I am a million pieces of shame and despair. I wear a mask of happiness from Maybelline and a cloak of normality from Banana Republic. I figure out what other people want to see and hear and become that person. I disguise my fears and insecurities as confidence and not giving a shit. I create a version of myself that allows other people to smile, laugh, and feel comfortable. Out of necessity, I become a vacant shell of my real self. Inside, I feel like a smaller, distant version of me is just pulling the strings on the larger puppet that interacts with the outside world.

I somehow manage a few interviews and receive a job offer from a non-profit organization that supports and promotes music education. I recognize a sense of gratitude, and feel a placeholder for excitement. I look forward to reconnecting with music, my long-lost friend. When I sign the paperwork, I see the date and experience a very odd sense of reality: It has only been one month since Joe shot himself…

FINDING TRUTH

I continue to take my daily dose of "Serotonin Soup" to help prevent the day and night terrors from returning, to help me function like a "normal" human being. Through my daily therapy sessions, I learn coping strategies and techniques to help me compartmentalize the trauma and help manage the episodes of panic and terror. In the beginning, the visualizations seem to help, but other times I have to rely on instinct. I find myself creating simple "affirmations" that I say to myself in the bathroom, rocking back and forth, hugging myself tight, trying to breathe normally. *"I am OK. Everything is going to be OK… I am OK. Everything is going to be OK…"*

Days, weeks, and months drone on. I continue taking medication and attending individual and group therapy sessions. Everything feels the same, day after day. I try to care about my job. I wonder what a "normal" person might do, and decide to allow myself to make friends. The relationships seem fake and shallow, even though most people are genuinely nice. They don't know the "real" me... but I'm sure they wouldn't like that person. I couldn't possibly tell anyone what had happened. No one could possibly understand what I've been through. It's too much. No one else can handle it. I continue to carry the burden and keep the dark secret hidden, buried deep inside, along with all the pieces of my old shattered self.

One day, a colleague offers to teach a yoga class in the conference room after work. I randomly attend out of curiosity. I am introduced to Kundalini Yoga, with no prior knowledge or experience. It's all a bit strange, but I welcome the concept of something new. I hear my heartbeat and focus on my breath. An odd yet familiar sensation arises. I feel... calm... and... peace... and... love. I don't realize what the yoga is doing for me or how powerful it really is, but I know I feel good after the classes.

Over time, I naturally start to develop deeper relationships with some of the people around me. I allow myself to feel closer to a select few and am finally able to open up to them. I brace myself for inevitable rejection and horror as I tell my story. The reactions are not what I imagined. Not only are they completely sympathetic and supportive, but they are also impressed by how "normal" I seem on the outside (my disguises were working well). I feel an extreme sense of relief and connection as I am finally able to share this deep, dark secret with someone in the "outside world." These friends would not only support me emotionally, but they would continue to allow me to build trust and continue my path of self-discovery. My path to finding truth. I am forever grateful for these amazing souls.

The days go on, and a friend from the office organizes Tai Chi in the mornings. The outdoor class begins at sunrise, which is tough

for me at first, but after a few days I grow to love it. I start to appreciate the soft morning glow. I start to remember just how beautiful nature can be. The sweet songbirds, the fragrant flowers, the leaves letting go… something beautiful happens to my brain. I slowly start to wake up…

After a period of time that feels like ages, I am finally able to sleep.

When I am able to step outside of myself for brief moments, I find this whole process of trauma fascinating, and I take a vested interest in learning as much as I can about what is happening to my brain. In the years prior, when I was reading and learning about cognitive science, I was unknowingly preparing myself for the trauma ahead. Now I can use some of my research and education to put myself back together. I casually glance through my books and continue to be fascinated and inspired by articles about neuroplasticity. My grandfather introduces me to the works of Deepak Chopra and tells me about doshas and a different way of looking at overall health. He starts practicing Transcendental Meditation and gives me copies of tapes to listen to and books to read. I find it all intriguing, but I'm not quite ready to absorb it. I can only process and retain small pieces of the information, but somewhere deep within my subconscious, there is a part of me that still believes in healing my brain and achieving my dreams. There is a small seed of hope, planted long ago, just waiting to blossom and grow.

I begin to notice that my triggers are farther apart and less intense. They are normally limited to violent movies or specific words and phrases. In these cases, I can usually remove myself from the trigger or situation at hand. When I experience an intense flashback, my heart and mind still race, and extreme panic still courses through my body, but it doesn't take me as long to come back to reality. I breathe deeply and return to my affirmations or "Safety Mantras" until my internal systems are convinced that there is no actual threat. At least there has been some progress.

When I start to recognize this stability, I am motivated to keep moving forward. I am determined to regain my independence and get my life back. I gently test the waters as I move into a shared apartment with coworkers. Over time, and with great encouragement and support from a small group of friends, family, and counselors, I slowly wean myself off of talk therapy and medication. At this point, I have gained the 30 pounds back, plus an additional 30 – the heaviest I have ever been. While the medication helped my systems normalize so that I could sleep and eat, the side effects, in addition to my body holding the stress, threw everything else out of balance. I didn't know what to do. The doctors never offered a long-term plan or any alternatives to medication. There was never any education or information provided on stress or trauma, how it affects the body, or what to do next.

I decide that I have put enough time and energy into healing and need to start focusing on *living*. I feel like I have to play catch up. I feel like I have missed out on the last three years of my life. I push myself and work quickly to put my life back together. Nothing can stop me now.

I spend the next several years finishing my college degree through online courses while working full-time. I have a few serious relationships, continue to establish healthy boundaries, and act quickly when my needs aren't being met. Every so often, I refer back to my "brain books," reading an article about a new breakthrough in cognitive science, and daydream about what might have been. After I receive my degree in IT Management at age 26, I save enough money to take my bucket-list trip to Italy. When I return, I focus on stepping up my career. I take a job supporting web-based software, and from there I move on to contracting work for the Federal Government. I feel a sense of pride and accomplishment when I apply for

and receive my first top-secret clearance. I continue to make travel a priority, as this brings me a renewed sense of adventure and purpose.

Years later, my grandfather passes away and I am heartbroken. I feel like a part of me has died. I feel empty and lost without him. I find solace in the botanical gardens, sitting there for hours, allowing the flowers and birds to comfort me with their sweet songs and harmonious dance.

Shortly after this tragic loss, a new relationship began transforming from friendship into romance. Just as we started to get serious and were in the "meet the parents" stage, I was hit by another car while driving to work and sustained several injuries that left me unable to drive or sit at a computer. In my stubbornness, I still tried to do everything on my own. Even at age 33, it was extremely difficult for me to allow someone else to take care of me, and trust that they were capable of doing so. To my surprise, the man I was dating not only stayed with me through the rough times, he also supported me physically, financially, and emotionally. This was a life-changing lesson for me and, to this day, I am tremendously grateful for this challenge.

Deep down, I began to wonder how long this relationship was going to last, expecting him to leave at any point. Not only did he stay, but he confirmed his commitment and asked me to marry him. Despite all that I had been through, this person still loved me and wanted to be with me. Imagine that!

After the wedding, we moved across the country to start a new adventure together. I welcomed this change with open arms. It was a chance for a fresh start. While I was leaving some of my best friends and memories behind, I was also putting distance between me and my dark past.

Colorado is beautiful. The sky, the mountains, the air... I am

home. I establish a new business as a consultant providing website design and marketing services for small businesses. I am able to set my own hours and choose my clientele. Life is good. A few years after we settle into our new home, I had a haunting realization. It became clear to me that my PTSD issues were still present after having several relapses and panic attacks. I thought I was done with this shit! By now, I learned to instinctively close my eyes and take deep breaths. I would notice the change in my body, and try my best to keep it under control. In my mind, I silently repeated my Safety Mantra, *"I am OK... Everything is going to be OK..."* But I definitely did not *feel* OK. I learned that while I may have physically moved away from my past, it was still very present within me. I met with a local counselor, and I immediately felt the panic return simply by referring the old trauma.

I am not ready to deal with this.

Instead, I am inspired to revisit yoga and incorporate it back into my routine as part of my physical healing process. As soon as I hit the mat, I am reconnected with a feeling of love and inner peace, just as I had experienced years ago. I remember how good it feels to take time out for myself. I open my mind to other opportunities for healing.

I visit a naturopath, a massage therapist, an acupuncturist, and a chiropractor. I learn about herbs and various natural remedies that can help balance my body and mind. The excess weight starts to melt off, and I am reminded of my grandfather's daily doses of vitamins, supplements, and sage advice on natural remedies. I tell myself that he would be proud.

My favorite yoga studio offers several other classes and workshops, and it is here where I experience my first gong bath. I am transported through time and space. I see multiple lifetimes flash before me. Something beautiful happens to my brain...

"Curiouser and curiouser..." I explore further down the rabbit hole. I learn about mantras and mudras. I attend classes on Ayurveda and reconnect with Deepak Chopra. I remember all of the wisdom

that my grandfather tried to share with me years ago. I somehow feel like he is still with me, guiding me through this journey. I discover that gong baths are just one of many healing modalities in **Sound Healing**. What? That's a thing? Where has this been all my life? I am in awe and in love. I seek out other sound healing experiences – I want to do it all.

I buy books and read articles on sound healing and vibrational therapy. I can't believe I have not heard of this before! I attend classes on the chakra system and learn how it is used in Ayurveda and yoga. Something clicks for me and so many pieces start to come together. During a chakra meditation, I visit a deep part of myself that has been hidden inside of a temple. When I come back to the room, I feel like a door has opened inside of my mind. A few days later, it hits me: Sound Healing is it. This is what I was meant to do. All things have led me to this point and I am confident that this is my life purpose.

Soon after, I attend my first crystal bowl sound bath. My intention was simply "love." Not only did I experience love, but I felt a significant shift that changed my outlook on life. This was the most significant release I had ever felt. It was like a really good cry, but something was different. It was as if it had moved on its own. I didn't have to focus on it, and I didn't even need to know what it was. I just knew that it was gone. I also felt something different within my body. It felt like warm, radiant light in my chest. The next day I tried to process everything. I could not find the words to explain it. As soon as I opened my mouth, I would start to cry. It was the most unusual and beautiful feeling I had ever experienced. It was unconditional love. Divine Love. A truly incredible gift that still cannot be touched by words.

From here, I am launched into an unbelievable state of transformation. Everything happens so fast—I feel like I'm flying. I see the beauty all around me and more opportunities present themselves. I am truly grateful for everything that is coming my way.

I stumble upon an ad for a free film screening of *ACRONYM*, a

movie about Veterans with PTSD and how each of them had survived their own storms. The intention of the film is to promote PTSD awareness and to help prevent PTSD-related suicides. The screening takes place at a local country club just a few miles away from my house. Something deep within my body trembles, but I push through it as I register for the event. This will be the first time that I openly acknowledge in a public setting that I have a personal connection to PTSD.

I'm not sure what to expect—a supportive friend comes with me to the screening. I want to tell her why I am going and why it is important, but I feel my throat close up and my heart start to race. I breathe through the anxiety and tell her my story– the first time I have repeated it in years, and the first time since moving across the country. Talk about being vulnerable… I feel totally exposed and start to regret my actions… but just like the others, she is sympathetic and supportive and thanks me for trusting her. At the movie screening, we both cry as we hear numerous stories of brave men and women tormented by PTSD. Even though I was not in a combat zone, I could relate to their stories: the same feelings of panic and terror; the cycles of shame, despair, and numbness; the alcohol and drugs; the medications and hopelessness.

Finally, someone was giving a voice to what had been buried in my heart for so many years. These brave soldiers were speaking out about their PTSD, and bringing an awareness to the reality of the illness, trying to make a difference for others. Their methods of healing included a myriad of treatments, from meditation and equestrian therapy, to yoga and *sound healing*! In that moment, I am inspired to share my story and help others with PTSD. I am humbled by this community and it is an honor to connect with them. I feel a strong urge to rekindle my passion for cognitive science, to finish what I had started so long ago. I don't know how, but I pledge to follow my dream of helping others heal.

Shortly after the film screening, I see an ad for *Neurosculpting*.

Intrigued by the name, I dig deeper and discover that it is a new process that can help with all types of psychological issues, including depression, anxiety… and PTSD. When looking up locations, I see that the Neurosculpting Institute is based right down the road in Denver. Thank you, Universe!

The first class I take is amazing. As I walk into the room, I spot a poster showing the anatomy of the brain – the exact same poster that I had purchased more than ten years ago. I feel right at home. In this class, I learn that through Neurosculpting, we activate both sides of our brain so that we can process old emotions and traumas, release old patterns, and ultimately create new patterns and behaviors. I am fascinated and eager to learn more.

With all of this information and tons of new ideas, I start feeling overwhelmed by the possibilities. A new friend encourages me to "ask The Universe for clarity." I am very skeptical but put it out there anyway. "OK, Universe—show me my next step." The answer is clear when I am presented with a trip to India the very next day. Every fiber of my being is telling me to blindly trust and go. I sign up with conviction and start packing.

While in India, I visit several ancient temples nestled in the Himalayas, many of them thousands of years old. Something about the land brings me peace. I feel like I have been here before. I feel like I have come home. During an early morning meditation, I learn the story of Hanuman and his unwavering love and devotion. I feel this in my heart as it expands. I see him opening his chest, exposing his heart that beats for Ram. My heart becomes a radiant light, and as it grows it cannot be contained. It explodes through my chest and love beams in all directions. Something beautiful happens to my brain…

I am awake…

I am infinite. I am timeless.

I am love. I am light.

Upon returning from India, I feel out of place. Something has changed. While I have a loving husband, a beautiful home, a

successful business, and amazing friends, I still feel like something is missing. I feel like part of me is still in India. So how do I integrate such a soulful experience into this life? I soon learn that it is not possible. I have found my truth. The old life is no longer. A new life must begin.

BECOMING TRUTH

Over the next few months, my journey of truth continues as I dive deeper and deeper into the mysteries of sound healing. During the winter solstice following my trip to India, I am in deep meditation when I feel inspired to rearrange my home office. *Take out the desk, and the chair. You don't need them.* I am very confused about how I was supposed to do my job without them. Regardless, I listen to my inner guidance and start moving furniture. Soon the room is empty. Now what? *This is your new healing space.* OK... ? What does that even mean?

I was very excited about the idea of starting a healing practice, but I didn't know where to begin. I was intrigued by Neurosculpting but wasn't sure if that was enough. I had looked into toning and vibrational therapy, but didn't have any equipment. I had purchased a few singing bowls in India, but had no idea how to play them. I began researching online and found sound healing classes about an hour away. When I read about the instructor, the name sounded familiar. I searched my library and realized that I had randomly purchased a book about singing bowls by the same man just a year before. I must be on the right path.

I started offering free intuitive sound healing sessions so I could "practice my practice." I didn't have any official training or experience at this point, but I knew that I wanted to help people feel better. I had witnessed the benefits first-hand, and wanted to share this with others. While working with one of my early clients, I felt a bubble of

energy that filled the room with warmth as we focused on expanding her inner light. I decided that it was time to add Reiki to my toolbox.

During my Reiki training, I did more research on energy healing and kept seeing "Shamanism" pop up. I had heard of this in various texts but always associated it with ancient cultures and assumed it was outdated. A friend invited me to a "healing expo" where there would be several talks on different healing modalities, including nutrition, sound healing, Neurosculpting, and Shamanism. I was still trying to get comfortable with the idea of working in this space, but I was open to learning more. During these talks, I was hit with a message loud and clear: *These are my people. This is something I feel called to do.*

When talking to a friend about my recent experiences and trying to piece them together with my newfound path, she suggested that I visit a local Shaman. This led me to more research and ultimately more questions. And then I found it. A Shamanic Training intensive in Sedona, Arizona. My body started tingling and I knew this was my next step.

During my training, I was reunited with old souls. I was reminded of the beauty and importance of connecting with and honoring nature. We can learn so much from the elements and cycles all around us. I learned about spirit guides and totems. I learned and practiced different healing modalities, using drums, rattles, singing bowls, fans, Shamanic breath, and guided visualizations. I practiced quantum meditation and experienced the void. I learned how to hold space for a ceremony to honor all transitions in life, including death. I was reminded of how to respect boundaries – mine as well as others'. I learned to trust and honor my intuition.

Through this training, I not only learned of even more healing modalities to help others, I received deep healing for myself. I found the dead weight and was ready to let it go.

During my drive home from Sedona, I had a few days to absorb and integrate all that I had learned. Physics, philosophy, music,

psychology, neuroplasticity, cognitive reframing… yoga, Ayurveda, chakras, meditation… Neurosculpting, sound therapy, Reiki… and now Shamanic healing. I began to see a common thread. So much of what we consider "alternative" healing has deep roots in other cultures. For example, Neurosculpting and NLP (Neurolinguistics Programming) both use what I call "release and replace." Releasing negative thoughts, feelings, beliefs, and patterns and replacing them with positive thoughts, feelings, beliefs and actions. The same can be said for Reiki and Shamanic healing. There is *truth* to the ancient methods – they used the resources that were available to them at the time. When we compare these old modalities with modern day tools, I can see how we are all working towards the same goal: Healing the past so we can enjoy the present and embrace the future. We are showing people that they can get better, that *they have the power* to end their suffering and find inner peace. All it takes is a little guidance. It is truly up to the individual to do the work. The teachers and practitioners are merely facilitators.

So, I decided to step in and do my part. *I am here to serve.* I am here to guide people on their path to healing. To help others discover their truth. Shortly before my 38th birthday, I officially launched *Sound Balance Healing*. Now I know it is possible. I am living my dream. I am becoming my truth.

MY PERSONAL TRUTHS

1. **Acceptance is the First Step**

Suffering is Part of My Path. While I did experience some horrendous shit that most people will never even dream about, this is my suffering and my trauma to work through and learn from. This suffering is part of *my* path. Just as each person has their own mountain to climb, their own path to walk.

This has been difficult for me because I am an empathetic person. I used to find purpose in taking on other people's problems. I carried so many of them. But now I have learned that just because others are suffering does not mean that I also have to suffer. This includes our families, our country, and all beings on the planet. How can we be happy when others are suffering? How is it fair for some to suffer but not all? We all have our own stories to tell, our own lives to experience. We all have our own battles to fight and our lessons to learn. We all have our own path to healing.

The events of my life have made me who I am. When I was finally able to start loving myself and others, rather than blaming myself and others, I was able to feel gratitude for each experience. The events of my past shaped me into a warrior—one who can understand what it's like to experience trauma, and then rise above it. To show others that it can be done. To have compassion for those who are just beginning their journey. To offer counsel to those who seek it. To understand that place of suffering. To become the Wounded Warrior.

Just when I thought life couldn't get worse, it did. And then worse again. But slowly and surely, I got myself out of that hole and kept going. When I feel intense fear, grief or defeat, I remember the warrior within. I see her pulling me up, lifting me up, with her words and her actions. She tells me her story of suffering, strength, and courage, and how she survived every battle. I admire her and want to be her... and then I realize I *AM* HER.

2. Surrendering is Healing

...And healing is a process. After we accept and come to terms with our past, when we let go of negative thoughts and feelings, we make room for positive change. It's all about letting go and detaching from old patterns, stories, projected fears, feelings, and beliefs. When we believe that life is happening TO us, we acknowledge the lack of control, but still live in fear. When we shift this perception

and release our fears by surrendering, we can start to make room for peace and healing. We still do not have complete control, instead we *do* have will to make choices and take action. We can *then* surrender to the outcome.

For me personally, I had a huge fear of sharing my story because of my fear of judgment. As I was writing these words, I still felt the trauma in my body. The adrenaline, the anxiety, the fear… but this time, I let it come. I sat with it, acknowledged it, and gave it space. I breathed deep and let the emotions flow through me. I surrendered. I listened to my body. *"There is still so much pain, loss, and grief. This wound has not yet healed."* I heard the pain and felt compassion. I'm writing this story so that I can heal my body, mind, and soul… so I can release the trauma, in hopes that others may find healing in these words. I am ready to let this go. I surrender these words to the world so that my trauma will no longer have power over me.

You can do this for yourself as well. Notice what emotions are coming up and be gentle with them. Allow them to surface and give them space. You can see them, say hello, and then invite them to flow through you. You don't have to shame them or dismiss them, and you don't have to hold or carry them. They are part of your healing process and should be honored; however, they do not have to rule your life.

3. I Can Mindfully Create My Reality

We all create, perceive, and project our reality. We are a product of our thoughts, feelings, and actions. When we are mindful of this connection and focus on our intentions, we all have the power to manifest our dreams and live our truth. We can overcome struggle, challenge, trauma, and suffering and create a new identity, a new reality. We are not limited by our history or diagnosis.

What is your truth? Who are you? What do you want to create in your life? Who do you want to be? These answers determine your own personal truth and how you want to live from that space. With

this personal power, why not choose to create and experience a life of joy? Even when our world seems to be falling apart, it is possible. See this as an opportunity to learn and reflect.

In life, we survive and thrive not just through hope, but also by willing ourselves to take action. We can be given all of the tools to succeed, but they are useless until we begin to use them. When we take action, we manifest our reality. We cannot expect everything in life to happen through wishful thinking. We cannot move forward if we are controlled by self-doubt and fear. We must take command of our perceptions in order to release negative thoughts and emotions. When we disarm and liberate these fears, we can make room for a new reality. From here, it is up to us to decide how we want to see the world. In any moment you have a choice: you can choose pain and suffering, or you can choose acceptance, surrender, and joy.

Our truth cannot be shown to us, we must find it for ourselves and strive to become it. Then we can truly live it. Then we can truly be free.

4. Love is Strength

We are not meant to walk alone. As much as I value my independence and strength, I have learned that life is a little easier and brighter when someone has our back. Through the darkness, my small sense of hope came from the love and support I received from my grandparents. My grandmother was a nurturer and was excited to teach me about nature. Everything from growing corn and planting trees to birdwatching, hiking, and how to admire and appreciate the beauty in life. She gently shared with me the basics of eastern philosophies and religions. She supported my creativity by singing and dancing with me, and making sure I didn't miss a piano lesson. She fostered my inner child as we invented new games and names for things. She encouraged me to see the patterns and cycles among plants, animals, people, and seasons... and how we are all truly connected. My grandfather was the logical one, always teaching me the facts, unraveling the mysteries of everything around us. He taught

me how to play chess, encouraged me to solve puzzles and think critically. He fed my curious mind and was famous for his unsolicited lectures on anything from the engineering behind telephones, televisions, and cameras to how to fly an airplane, how to build a computer, and how our eyes work with our brains to process images. He was always encouraging me to analyze, explore, and learn about everything. Including myself. The most important question he ever asked me was, "Who is Crystal Blue?"

My grandparents and I frequently traveled and explored together and we shared countless adventures that I will always remember and cherish. Their involvement, support and influence has had a tremendous impact on who I have become. Even after their passing, I still appreciate the many lessons I have learned, and continue to learn from them. They taught me everything from crafting and gardening to science and meditation... but most importantly, they taught me how to love.

Embrace your journey and invite someone along. There are people out there who want to support us and lift us up. To see us succeed. We can create a system of love and support, even if we are not born into one. When we allow others to love and support us, they can show us how to love ourselves. They may or may not be the people who gave us life, or the ones who raised us, but they are family. They are the people we *choose* to call brothers and sisters. They are the friends and mentors we look to for advice and guidance. They encourage us to be the best version of ourselves. They nurture us and hold us when we need comfort. They reflect back to us all of the positivity and good that we have put out into the world. They see in us what we see in them. They love us for who we are, despite who we may have been, and look forward to who we will become.

I truly believe that love will always win. It is so easy to slip into fear, anger, and disappointment when things aren't going the way we expect. It is easy to let the shadow take over when we can't see the light. But to love... that takes real strength and power. To love your enemy. To love yourself.

When we exist from a place of love, we can detach from fear, expectations and suffering. We can make space for compassion and forgiveness. We can see all as one. You are me, and I am you. We can all exist together.

FINAL THOUGHTS AND BLESSING

The journey continues. As I started to write this chapter, I was flooded with the same feelings of grief and anxiety that lay dormant for so long. While writing specifically about the trauma, I found myself experiencing the same old triggers and changes in my body. Knowing that these words would be published in a book, I could feel the tightness in my chest and the dark pit in my stomach. I felt nauseous and anxious and wanted to give up several times. I began feeling physically ill. However, I knew that I wanted and needed to share my story to release my past. I was determined to disarm my PTSD and take back the power it had stolen from me. I was determined to follow through with my commitment to share my story, to help and heal others.

I had recently started reading several books on somatic psychology and therapy. In "*The Body Keeps the Score*," Bessel Van der Kolk talks about how the body stores trauma. I found it fascinating. He explains different types of trauma and PTSD, and goes on to reference different types of therapies, including yoga, meditation, Thought-Field-Therapy, and EMDR. Through the last two methods, trauma is located in the body, then both sides of the brain are engaged so that the trauma can be processed and released (sound familiar?). Out of curiosity and impatience with the constant inconvenience of PTSD symptoms, I searched for a recommendation and found a few professionals who could provide TFT and EMDR sessions. At this point, I was willing to try anything. I was ready for this to be over.

After a few sessions, I immediately noticed a difference. Time

seemed to slow down, and my body felt more relaxed. I recognized this feeling from past vacations. I didn't realize how much anxiety I was living with until it was gone. There was no worry, no urgency, no panic. Could it really be this easy? I was skeptical, but hopeful. As the weeks progressed, I was able to revisit my story and write with more ease. I was able to make it through the chapter without having a panic attack. Soon after, I was even able to talk to people about my story without feeling the symptoms return. I experienced a sense of freedom as I finalized my story and prepared for publishing. I was ready to share my truth. Even though I have made it this far, I know that the journey will continue. I know that there will be more opportunities for me to learn and grow.

I used to see my life divided into pieces, before and after traumatic events. I felt like I had to completely disconnect from those parts of my life in order to live a "normal" life. Through this work, I was able to see and accept everything as one whole and continuous life experience. I am the little girl who was neglected, the individual who witnessed a tragedy, and the grown woman who has had to reinvent herself again and again. My life is not a fragmented cycle of never-ending disasters, but a stage for opportunities and lessons. I am not a victim of circumstance, but a wounded warrior with the strength to endure, to rise above the storms and battles to help those who are still fighting. *I am OK... Everything is OK.* This time, I truly believe it. I am no longer living in darkness. I *am* the light.

I began my story with Joseph Campbell's quote, *"If you are falling... dive..."* and I would like to offer my version as a blessing and hope for all:

If you are falling… fly. Shift your perception into a voluntary flight. All throughout this unpredictable journey, you can choose to suffer or soar. In any moment you can choose to look beyond the challenge of the climb to experience the majesty of the mountain. Seek your path and then gently surrender to the guidance of the wind. When you are ready to live a life of joy, to become your truth and set yourself free… you are ready to fly.

About the Author

Crystal Blue is originally from the Washington, DC area where she studied Philosophy, Psychology, and IT Management. After moving to Colorado, she created *Sound Balance Healing*, a sanctuary for deep healing and transformational experiences. She has extensive experience and training in various practices including Counseling, NLP, Sound Therapy, and Shamanic Healing. She is a member of the Sound Healers Association and currently shares her offerings as a Certified Vibrational Sound Therapy Practitioner.

Her mission is to help others liberate their past, enjoy the present, and embrace the future with a clear mind and open heart. She supports the process of releasing negative and limiting beliefs in order to create and nurture a deep connection to one's inner strengths. She provides personalized sessions and programs, and will be hosting and facilitating retreats centered around establishing your personal power and becoming your personal truth.

Crystal has created her own unique belief systems and practices that pull from New Thought, Mysticism, Shamanism, Hinduism, Buddhism, Taoism, and *The Four Agreements*. She enjoys visiting and observing both modern and ancient places of worship for meditation, connection, and deep reflection. She remains passionate about exploring cognitive science and studying the human experience. She aspires to travel the world while learning from and experiencing different cultures and ways of life. During her personal time, she appreciates photography, astronomy, discovering and listening to all types of music, deepening her yoga practice, sitting with nature, and all things Zen.

What does your truth sound like? She is ready to listen. Connect with Crystal through ReadyToFlyBook.com.

Acknowledgments

We are strong. We are brave. We are women.

To my dear soul sisters who have taken this leap of faith...I honor you. These 15 courageous women agreed to join me on this wild and crazy ride called writing a book. I am extremely grateful for each beautiful soul, and every learning opportunity that presented itself through this process. Not only is this an amazing group of writers and storytellers, but some of these women also volunteered to help edit and review for their peers. We truly did this as a team. We laughed together, we cried together, and now we will fly together.

Deep gratitude for all of the editors in the house, and all those who helped with the publishing process. Janice O'Kane, Kerrie Lee Brown, Kyra Storojev, Polly Letofsky, Chris Williams, Victoria Wolf, Susie Schaefer, Andrea Costantine, and the entire team at My Word Publishing. You rock.

To my amazing husband. The Yang to my Yin. The peanut butter to my jelly. I see you... My warrior. My champion. My mountain. My home. You have truly helped me find my wings. I am forever grateful for your unconditional love and unwavering support.

To my grandparents, my heroes. You have given me so much in so many forms. Timeless Love and Support, Encouragement and Guidance. Freedom to be curious and explore. Freedom to create and feel safe. Freedom to love and be loved. I cherish our many adventures and memories together. Your light lives in my heart.

To all of my guides and teachers along the way. I honor you each day and express my gratitude for all of the lessons you have shown me, and all that I may receive on the path moving forward.

Om Manipadme Hum.

56059142R00162

Made in the USA
Columbia, SC
19 April 2019

CONTENTS

09. ALL ALONE — 3

10. IMPACT — 75

11. A GIRL IN THE SNOW — 139

3

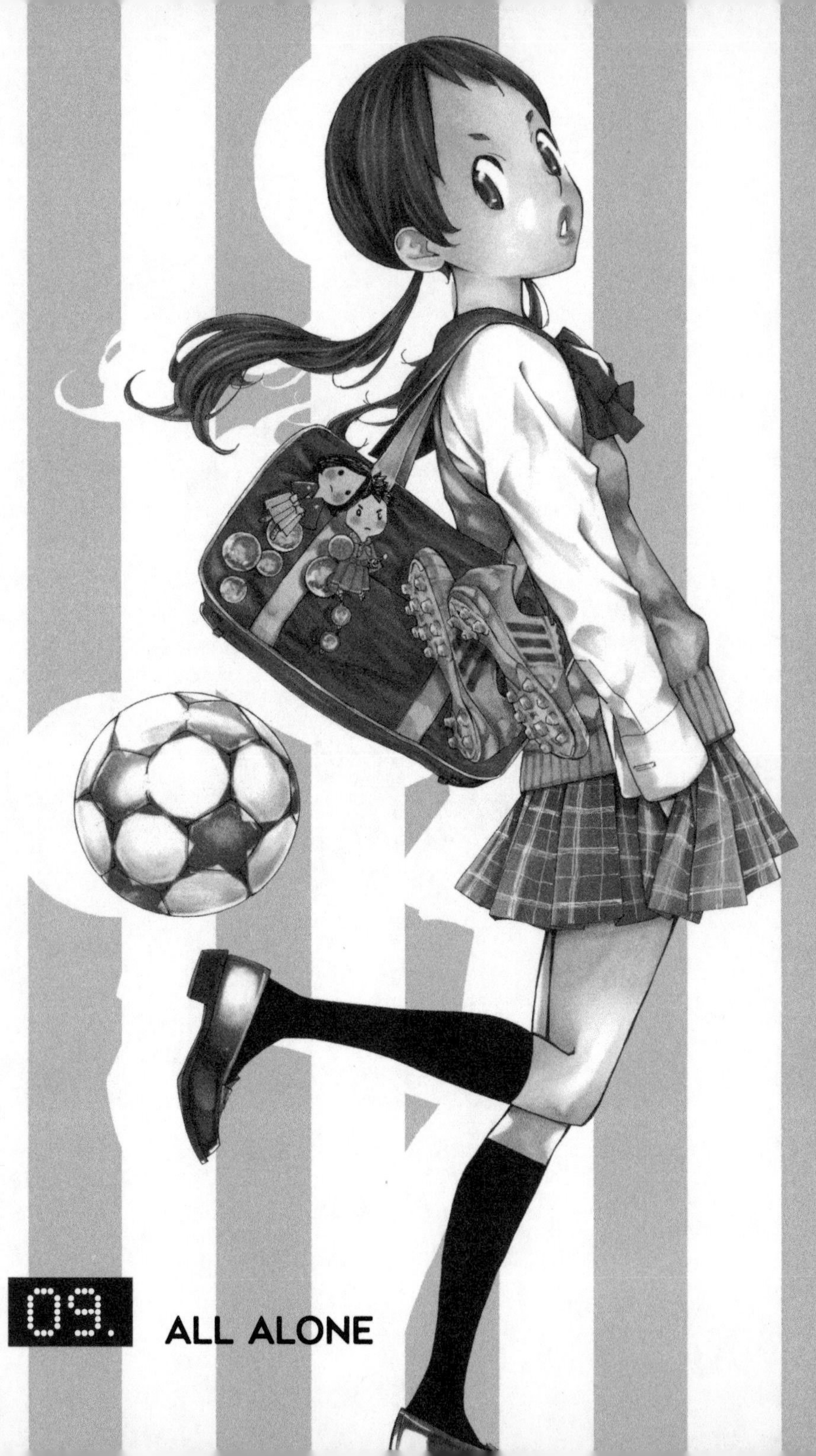

09. ALL ALONE

Farewell, My Dear Cramer

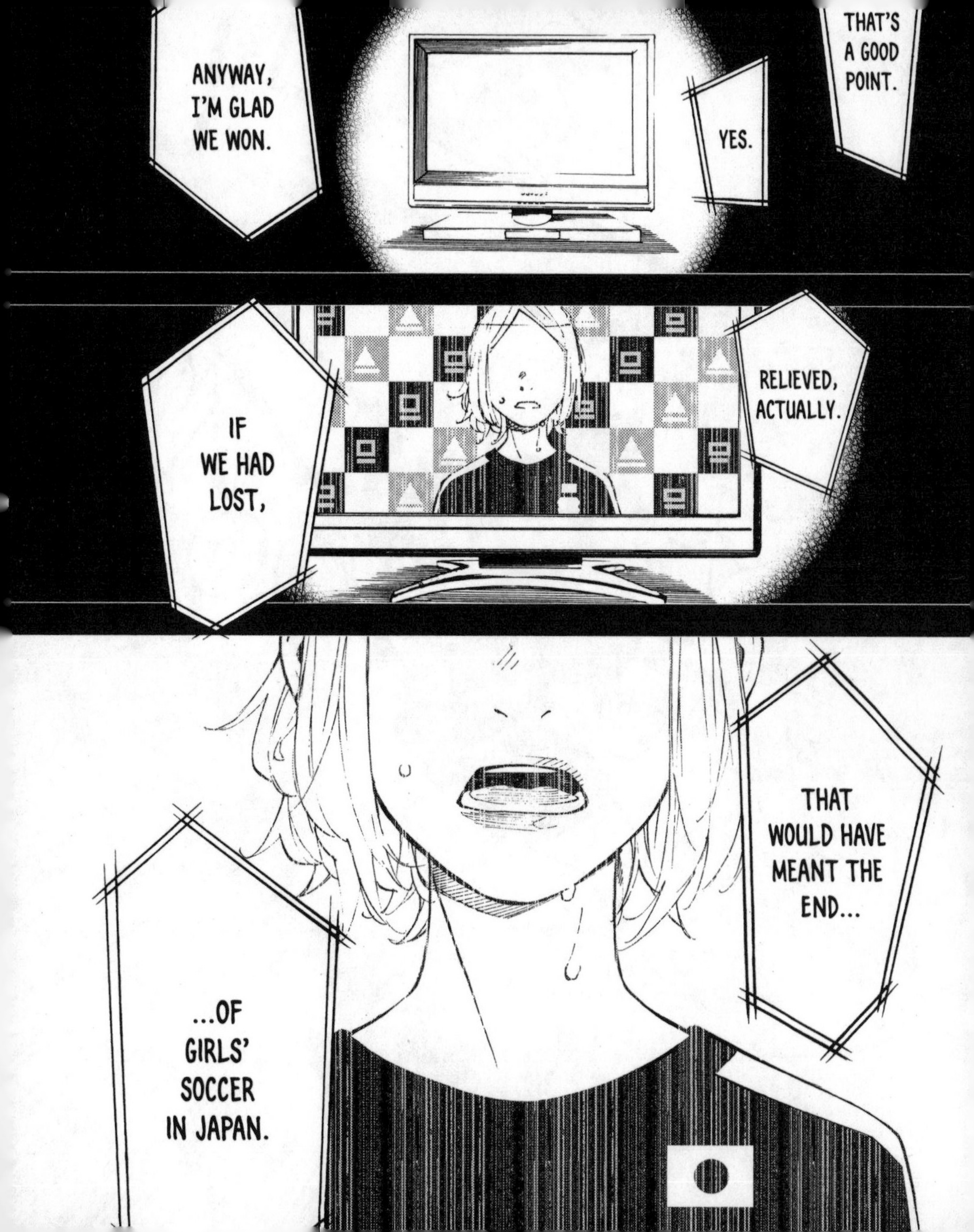
THAT'S A GOOD POINT.
YES.
ANYWAY, I'M GLAD WE WON.
RELIEVED, ACTUALLY.
IF WE HAD LOST,
THAT WOULD HAVE MEANT THE END...
...OF GIRLS' SOCCER IN JAPAN.

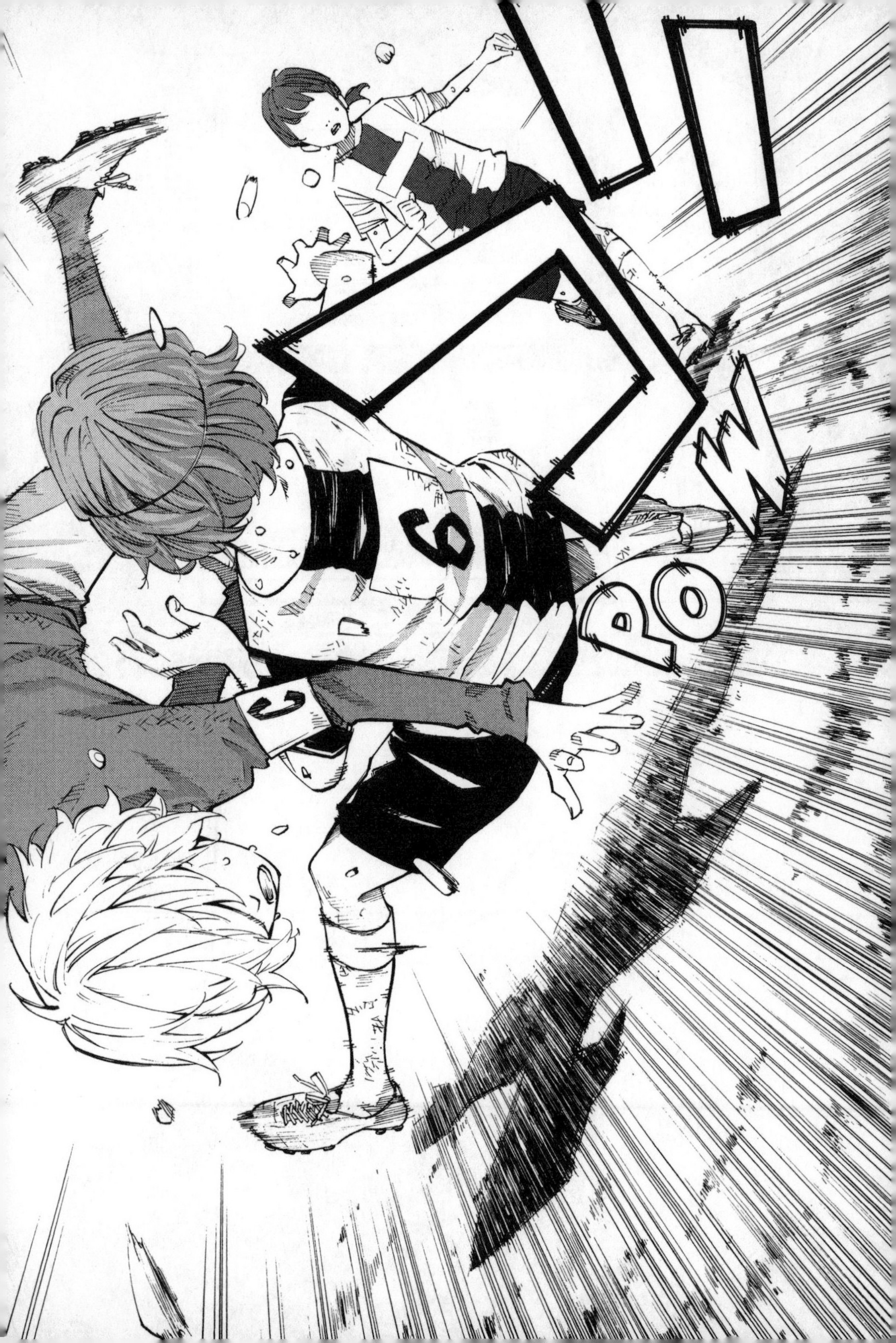
POW

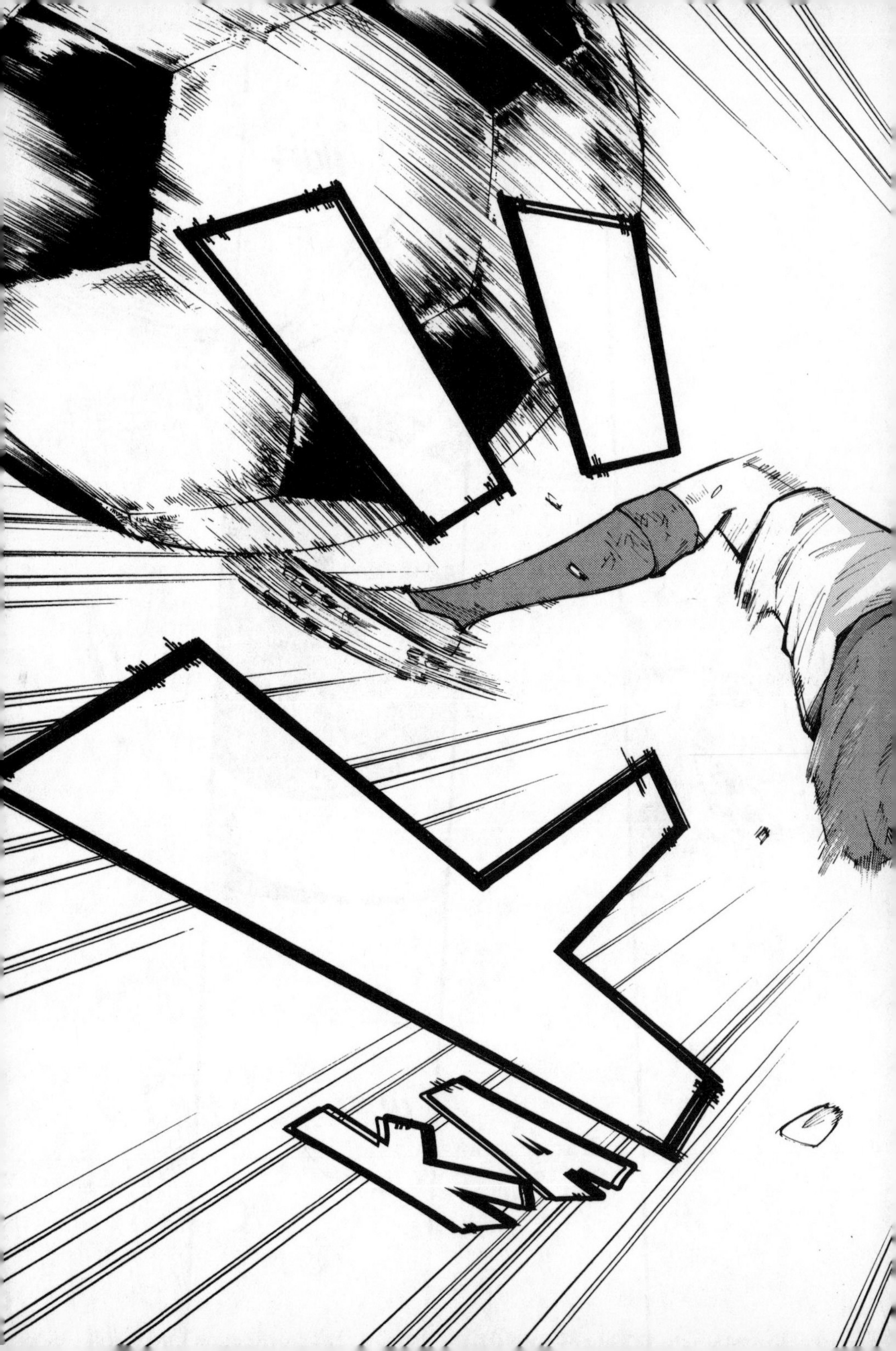

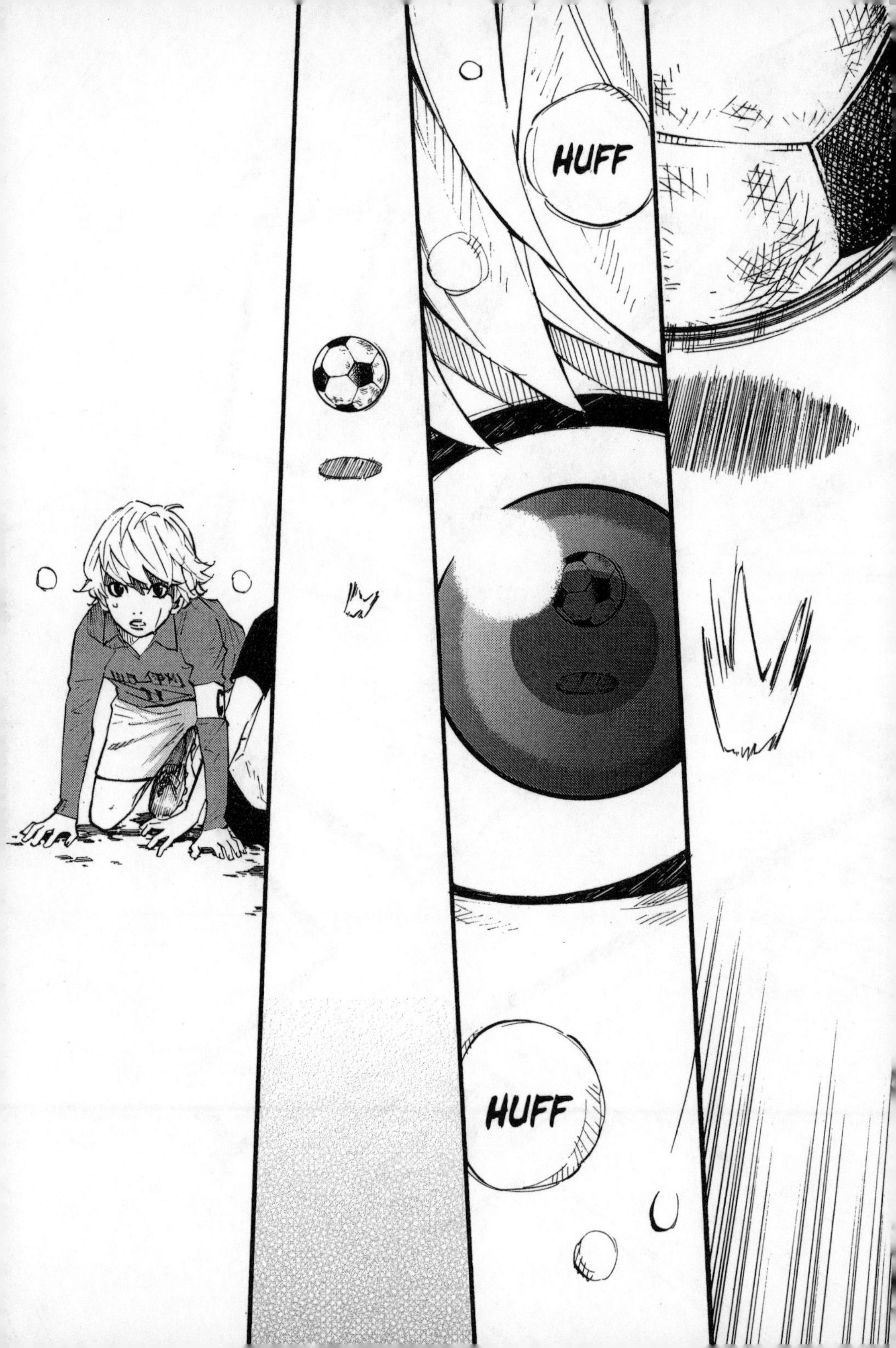
HUFF
HUFF

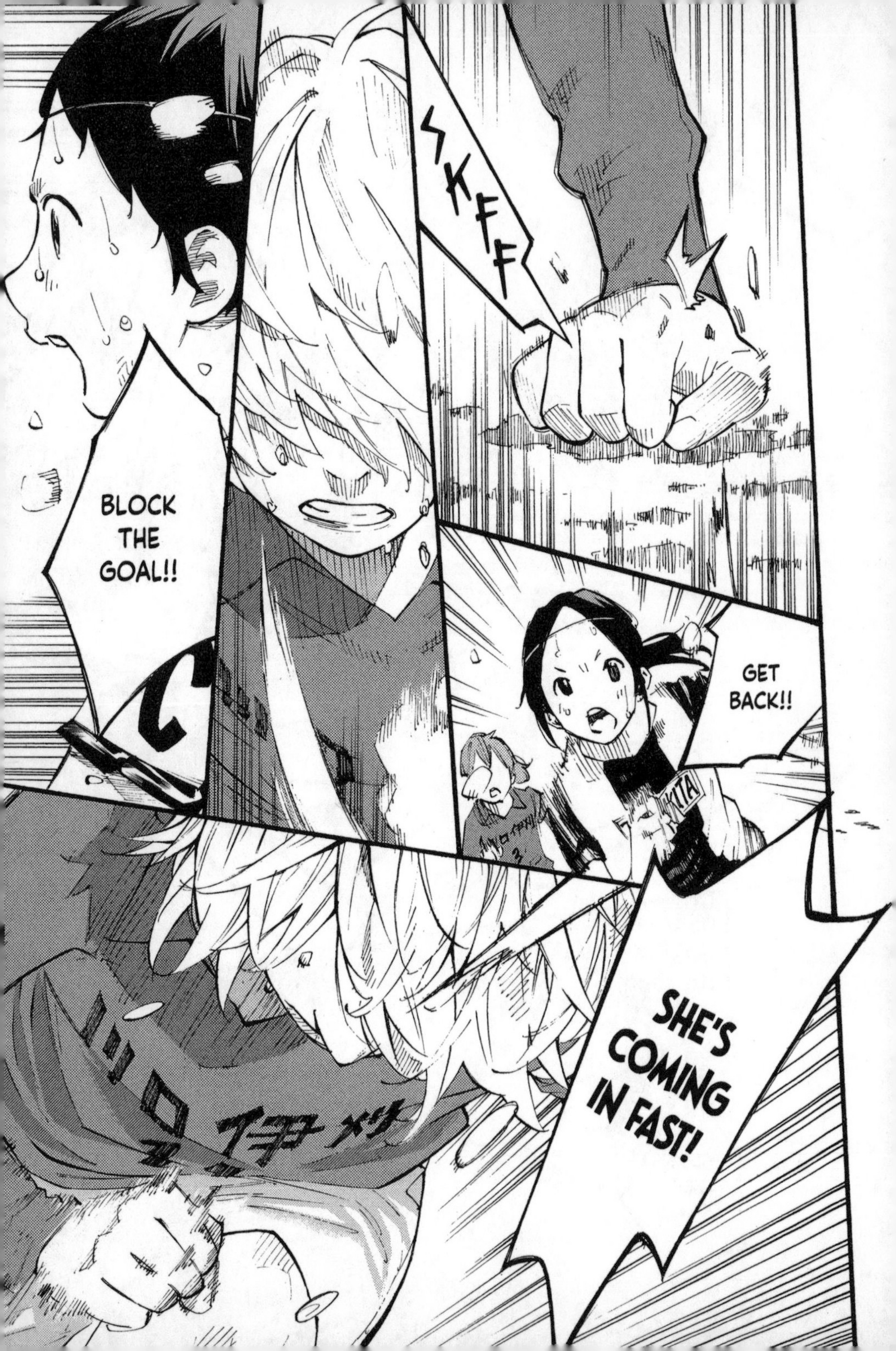
SKFF
GET BACK!!
KITA
BLOCK THE GOAL!!
SHE'S COMING IN FAST!

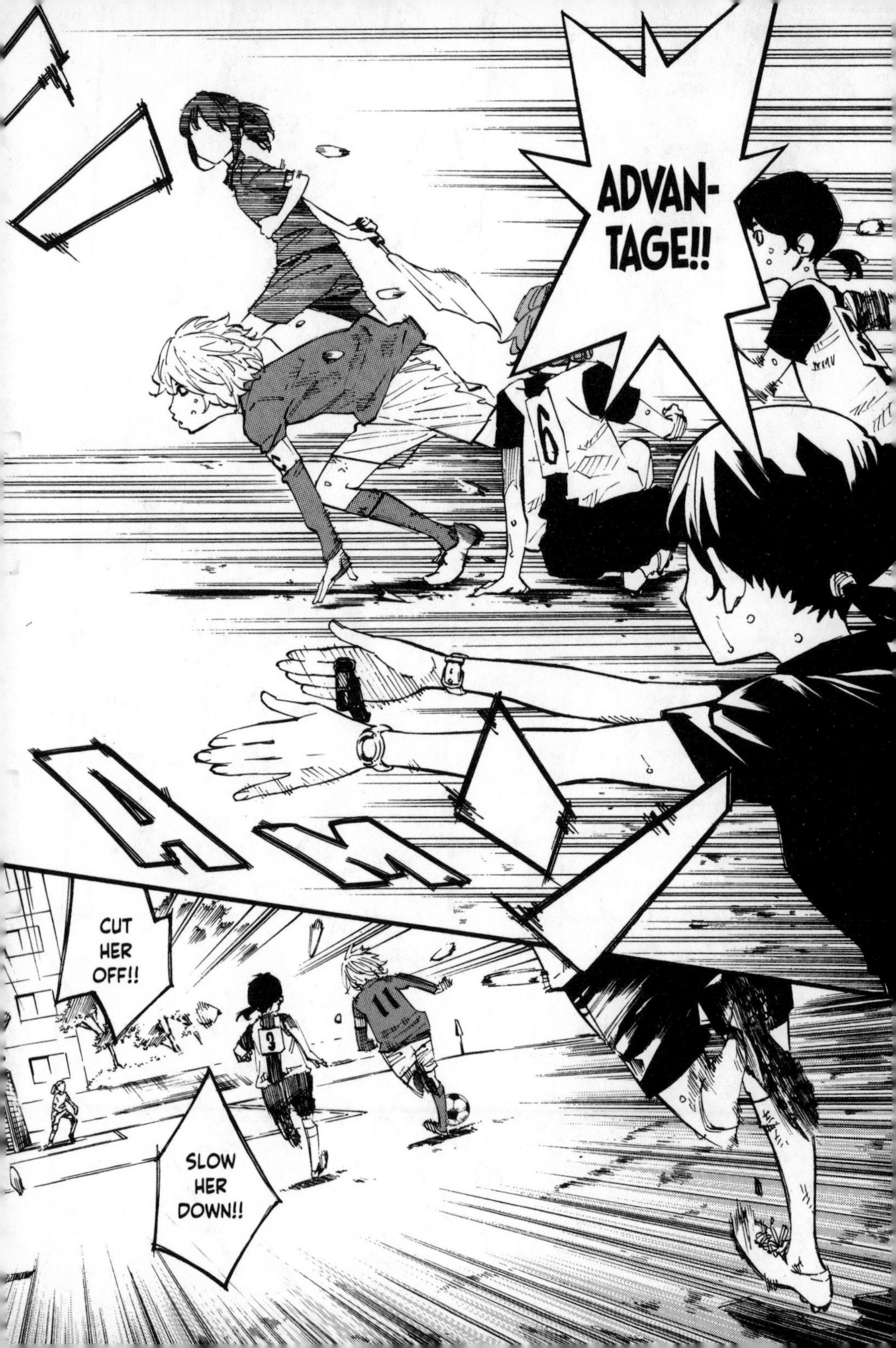
ADVAN-TAGE!!
CUT HER OFF!!
SLOW HER DOWN!!

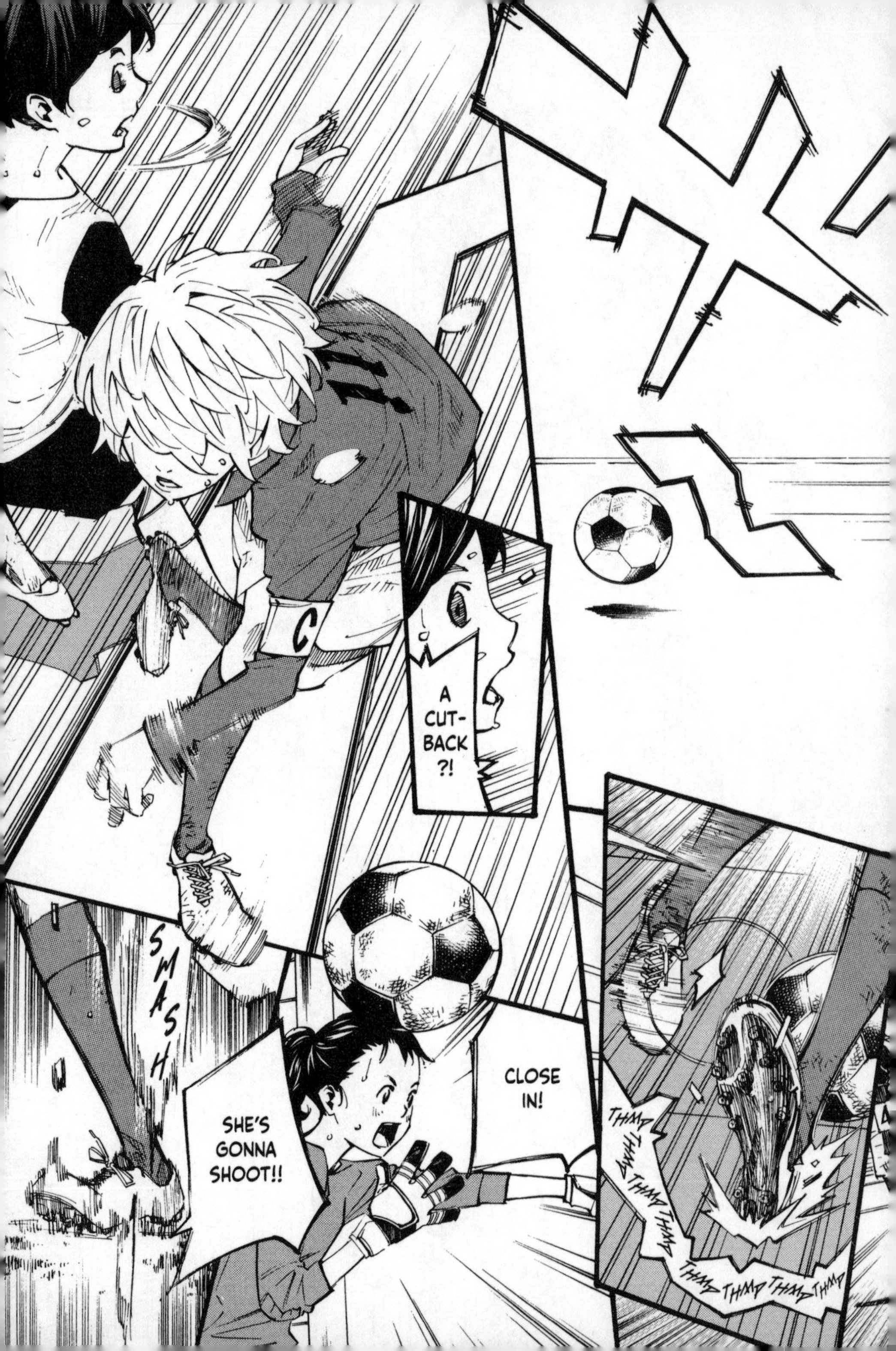
A CUT-BACK?!
THMP THMP THMP THMP THMP THMP THMP THMP
CLOSE IN!
SHE'S GONNA SHOOT!!
SMASH

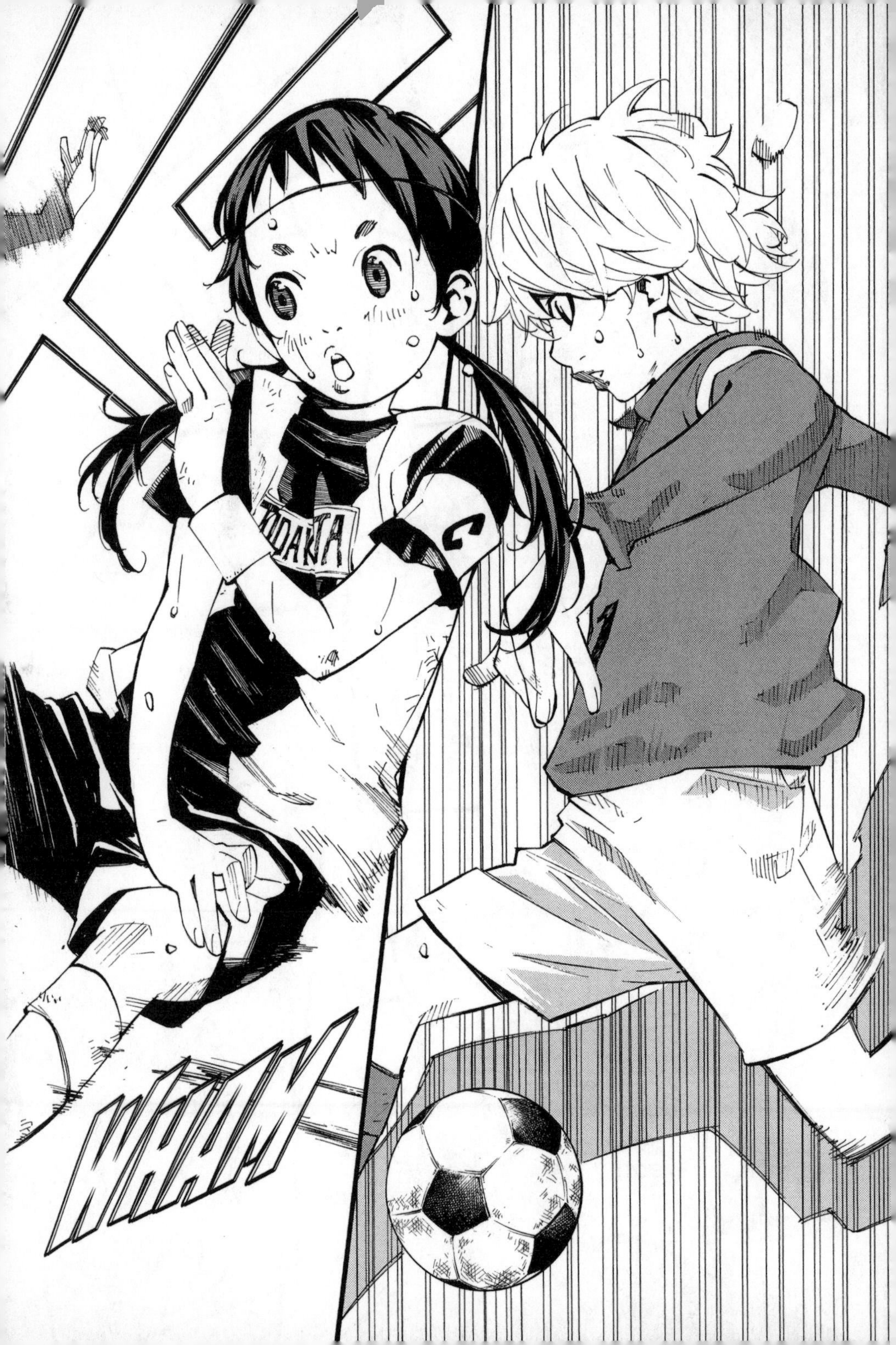
WHAM

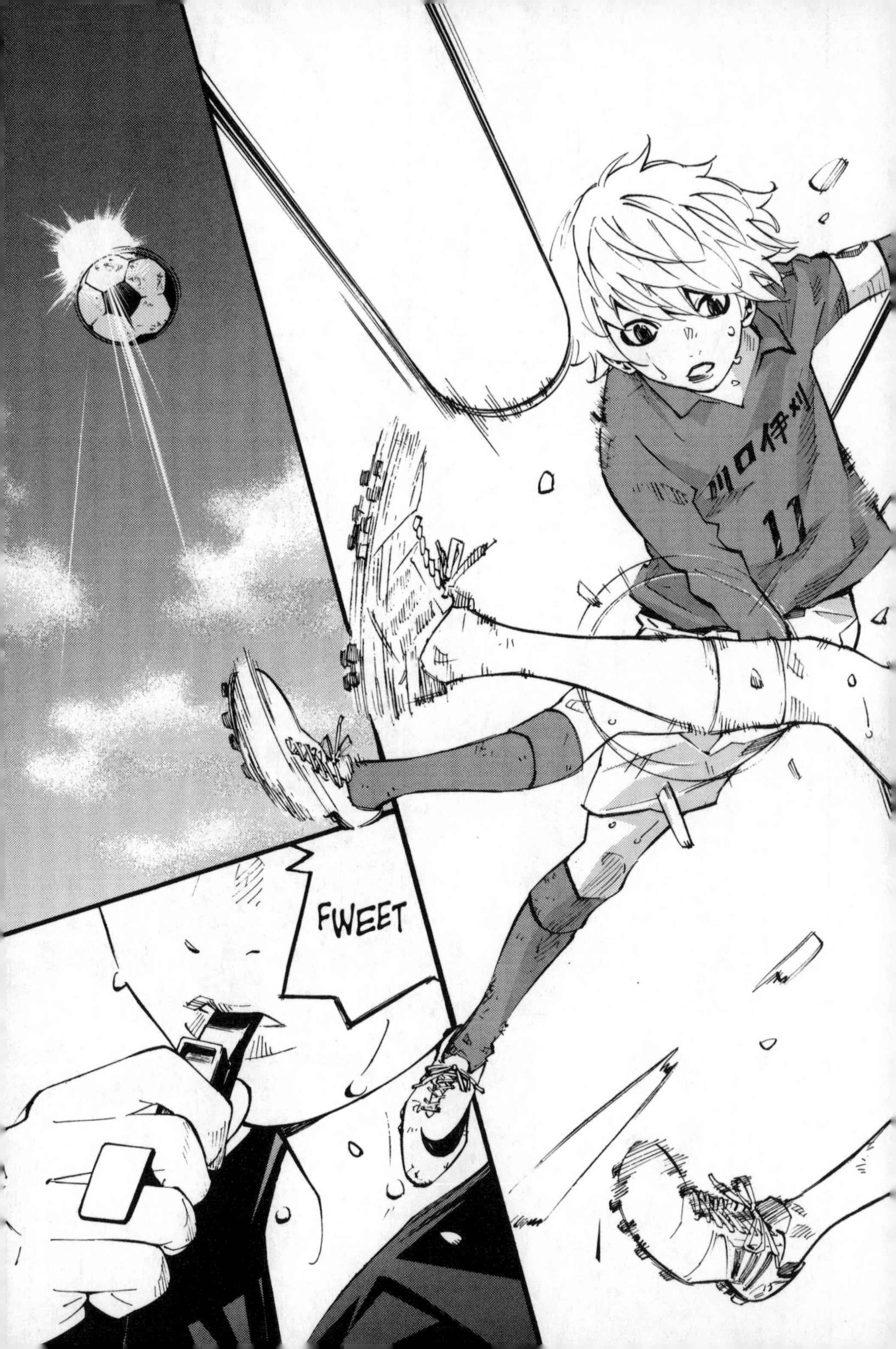
FWEET

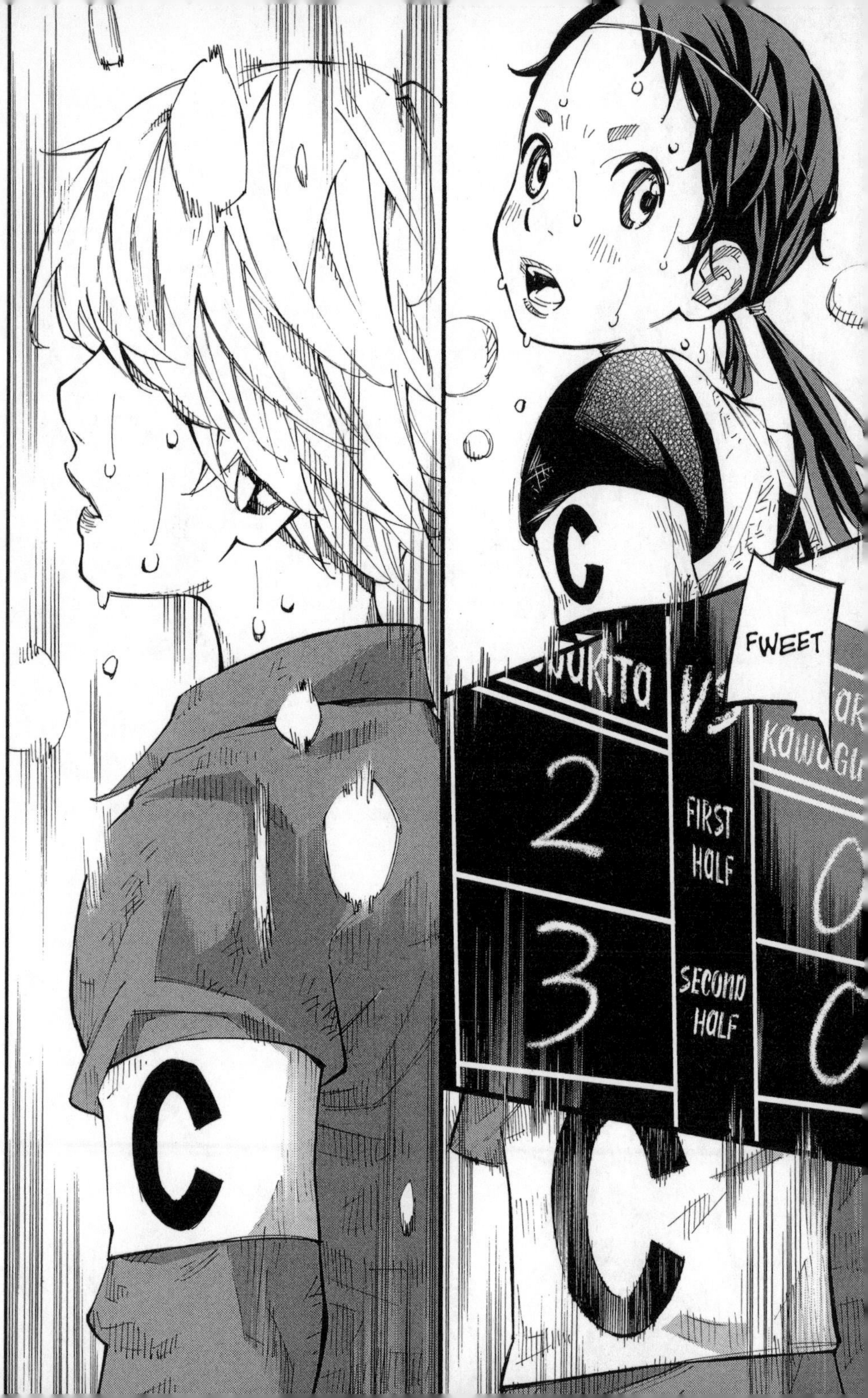
FWEET
2
FIRST HALF
3
SECOND HALF

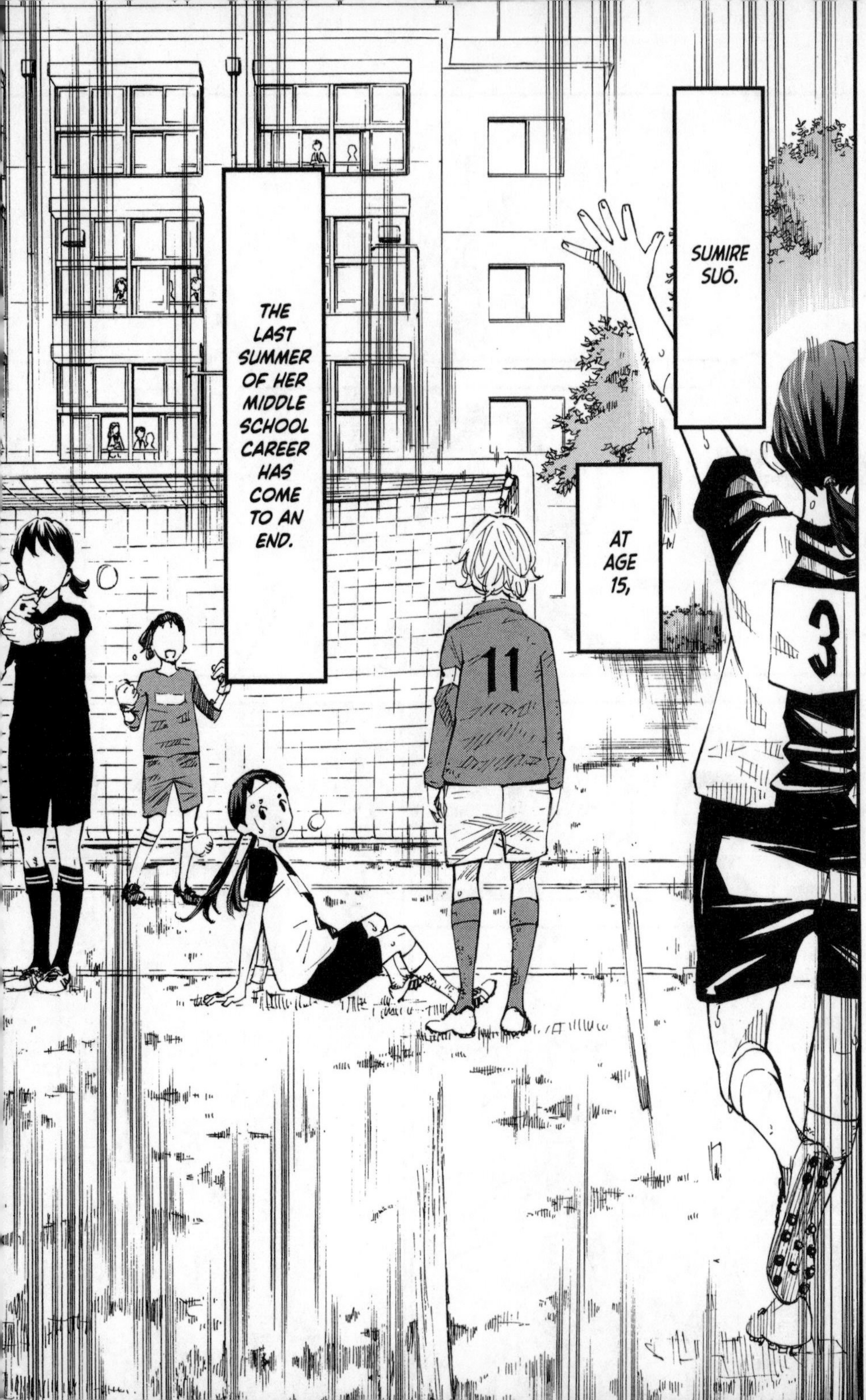
SUMIRE SUŌ.
AT AGE 15,
THE LAST SUMMER OF HER MIDDLE SCHOOL CAREER HAS COME TO AN END.

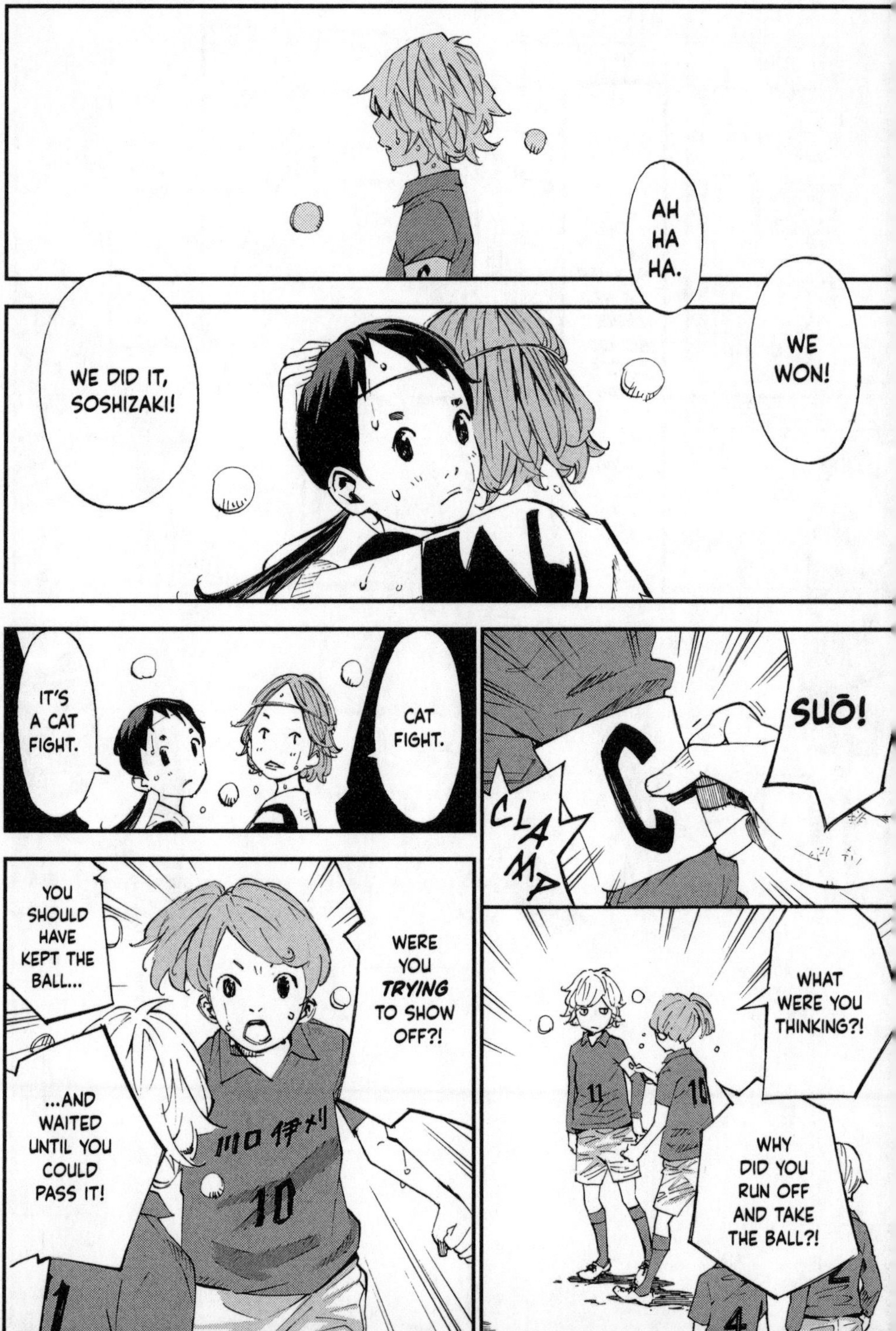
AH HA HA.
WE WON!
WE DID IT, SOSHIZAKI!
SUŌ!
CLAMP
CAT FIGHT.
IT'S A CAT FIGHT.
WHAT WERE YOU THINKING?!
WHY DID YOU RUN OFF AND TAKE THE BALL?!
WERE YOU *TRYING* TO SHOW OFF?!
YOU SHOULD HAVE KEPT THE BALL...
...AND WAITED UNTIL YOU COULD PASS IT!
川口伊刈

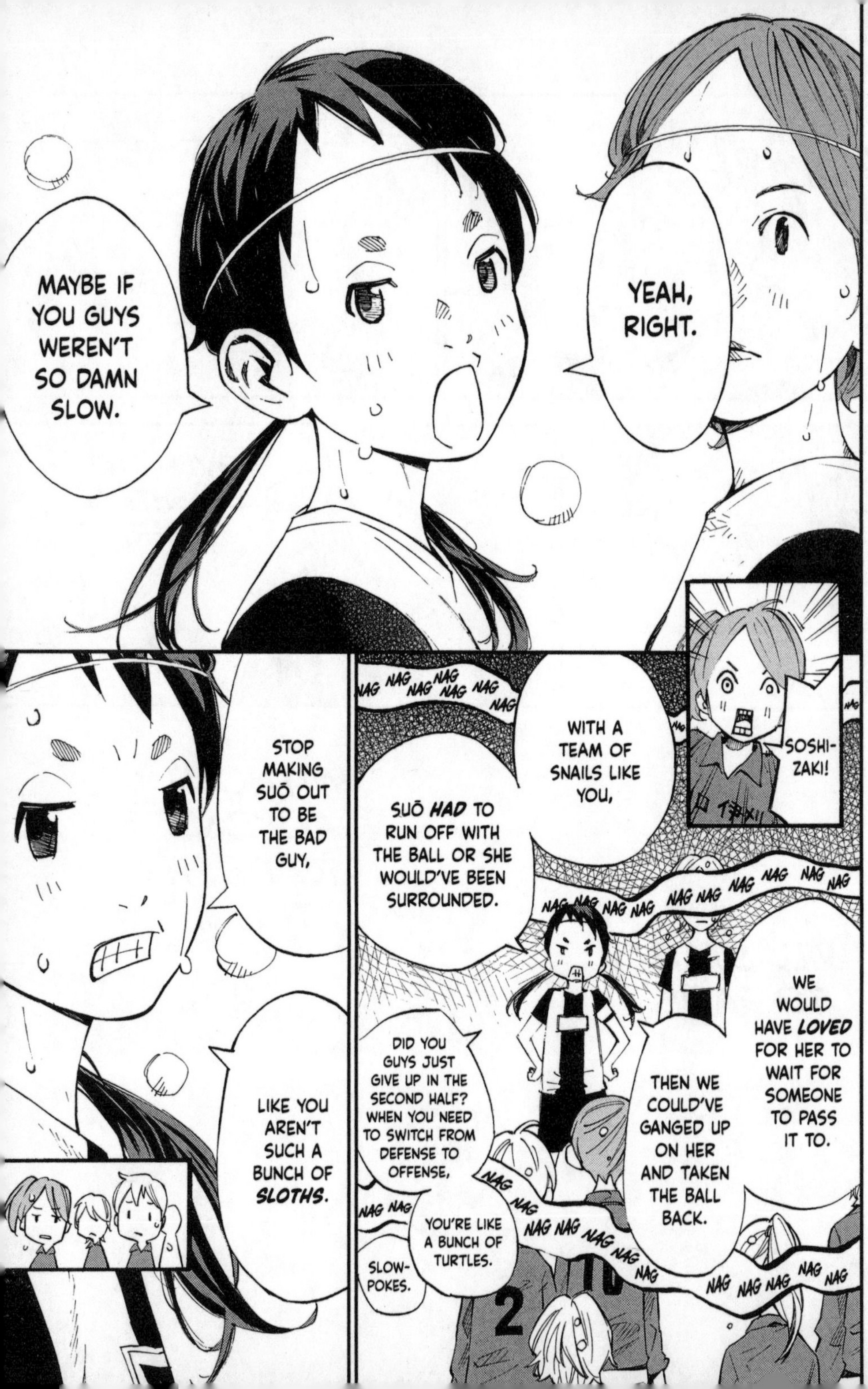

YEAH, RIGHT.
MAYBE IF YOU GUYS WEREN'T SO DAMN SLOW.
SOSHI-ZAKI!
NAG NAG NAG NAG NAG NAG NAG
WITH A TEAM OF SNAILS LIKE YOU,
SUŌ HAD TO RUN OFF WITH THE BALL OR SHE WOULD'VE BEEN SURROUNDED.
NAG NAG NAG NAG NAG NAG NAG NAG NAG NAG
WE WOULD HAVE LOVED FOR HER TO WAIT FOR SOMEONE TO PASS IT TO.
THEN WE COULD'VE GANGED UP ON HER AND TAKEN THE BALL BACK.
DID YOU GUYS JUST GIVE UP IN THE SECOND HALF? WHEN YOU NEED TO SWITCH FROM DEFENSE TO OFFENSE,
YOU'RE LIKE A BUNCH OF TURTLES.
SLOW-POKES.
NAG NAG NAG NAG NAG NAG NAG NAG NAG NAG NAG NAG NAG
STOP MAKING SUŌ OUT TO BE THE BAD GUY,
LIKE YOU AREN'T SUCH A BUNCH OF SLOTHS.

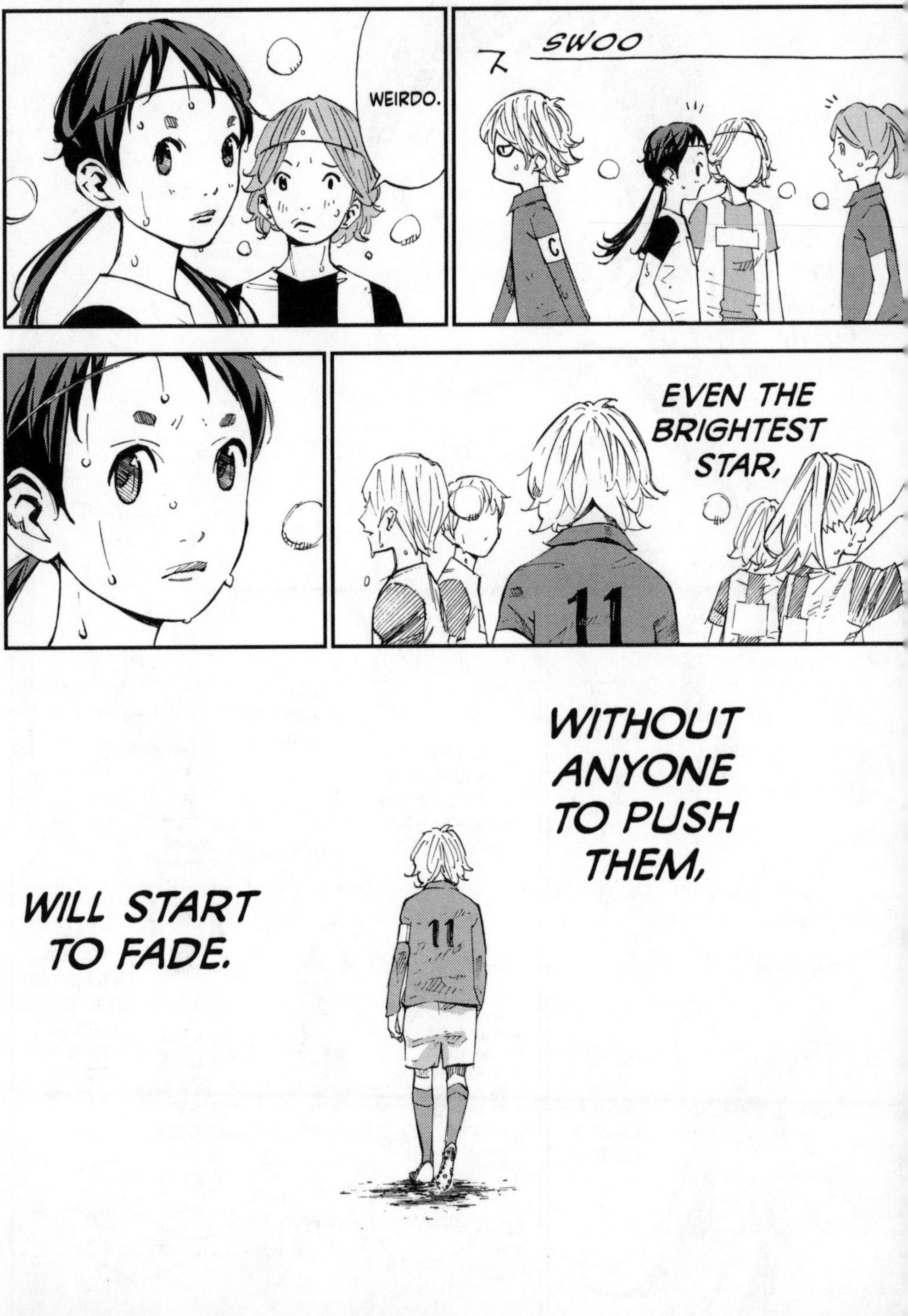
SWOO
ス
WEIRDO.
EVEN THE BRIGHTEST STAR,
WITHOUT ANYONE TO PUSH THEM,
WILL START TO FADE.

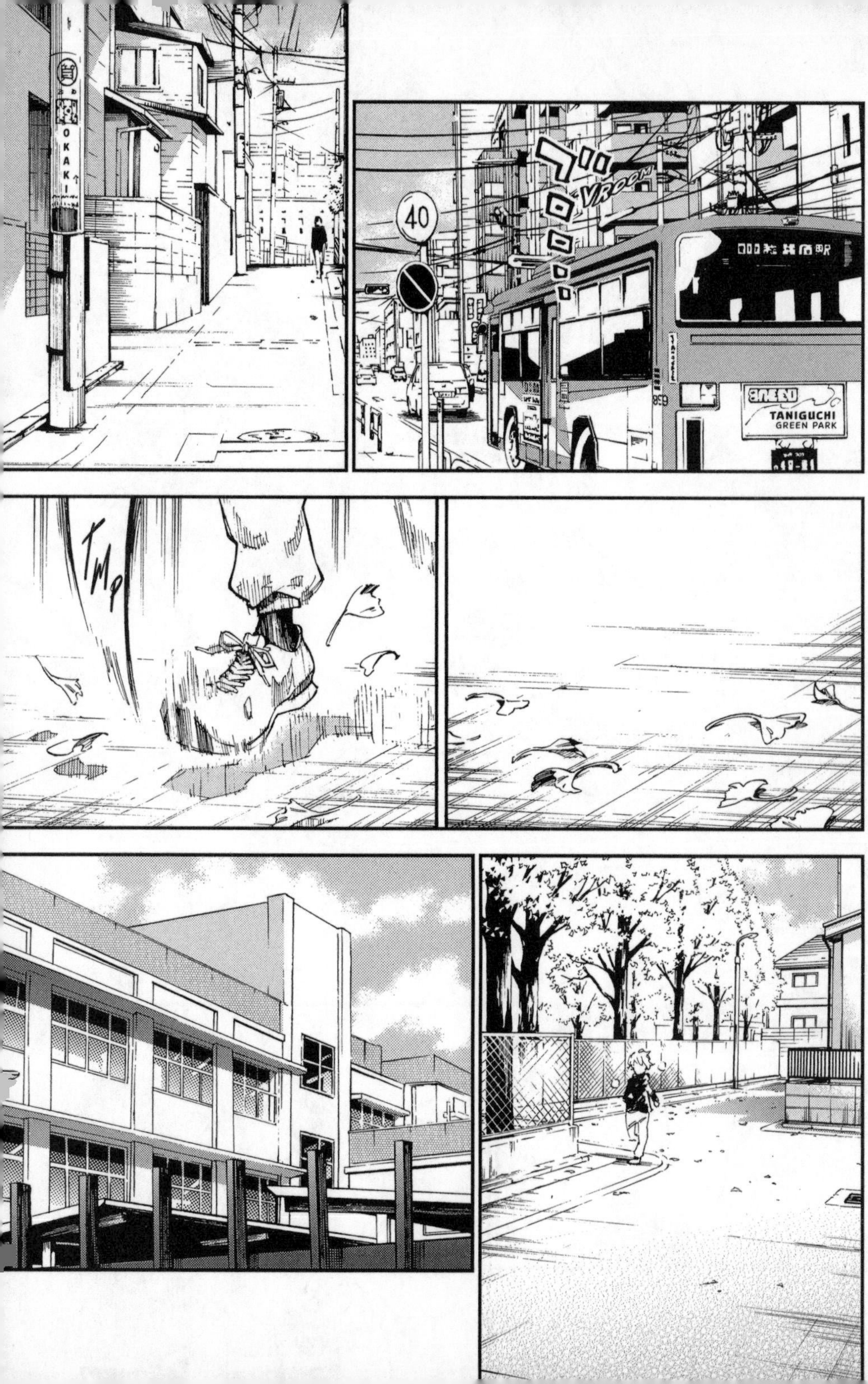
VROOM
40
TANIGUCHI
GREEN PARK
OKAKI
TMP

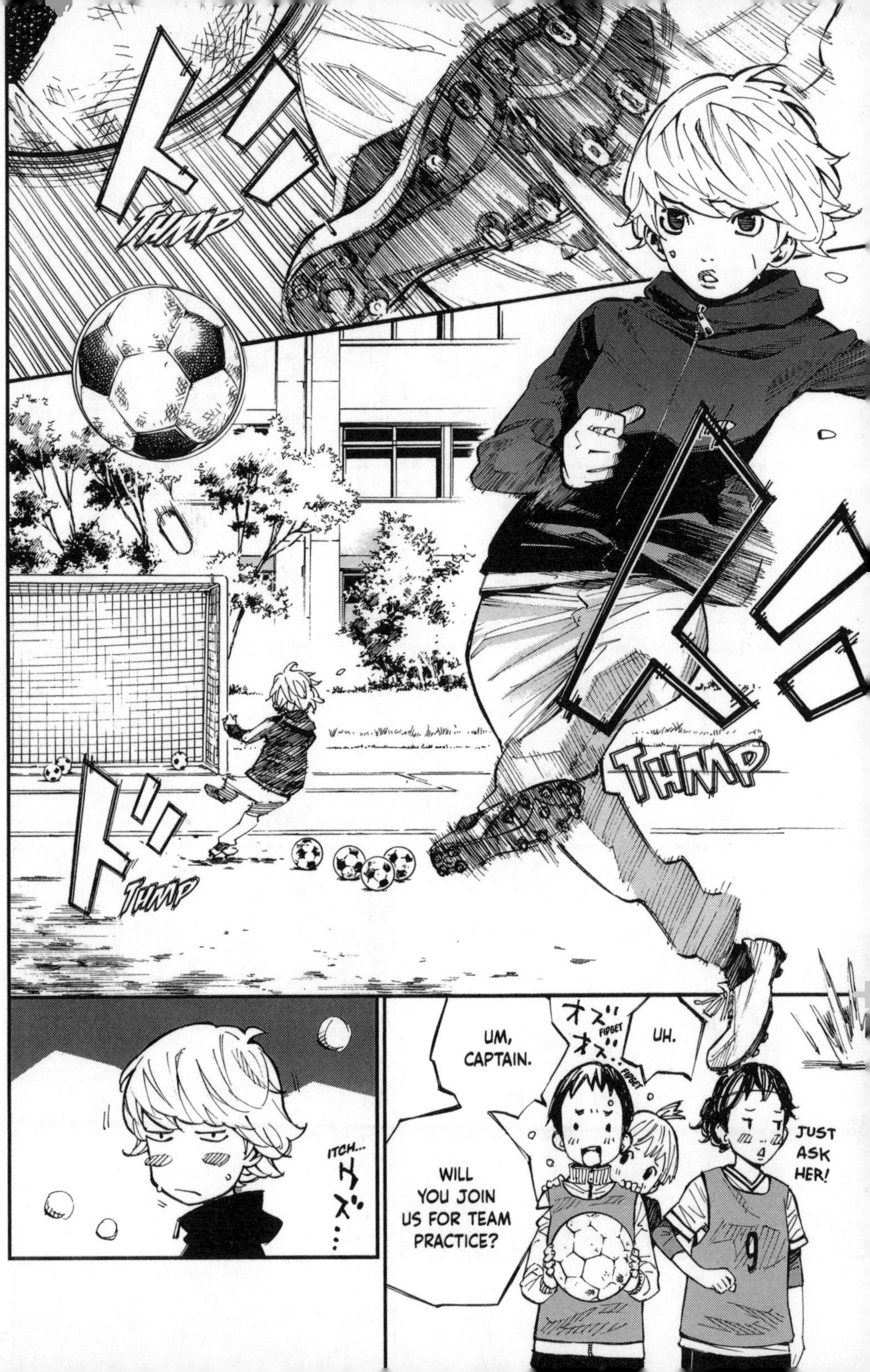

THMP
THMP
THMP
UM, CAPTAIN.
FIDGET
FIDGET
UH.
WILL YOU JOIN US FOR TEAM PRACTICE?
JUST ASK HER!
ITCH...

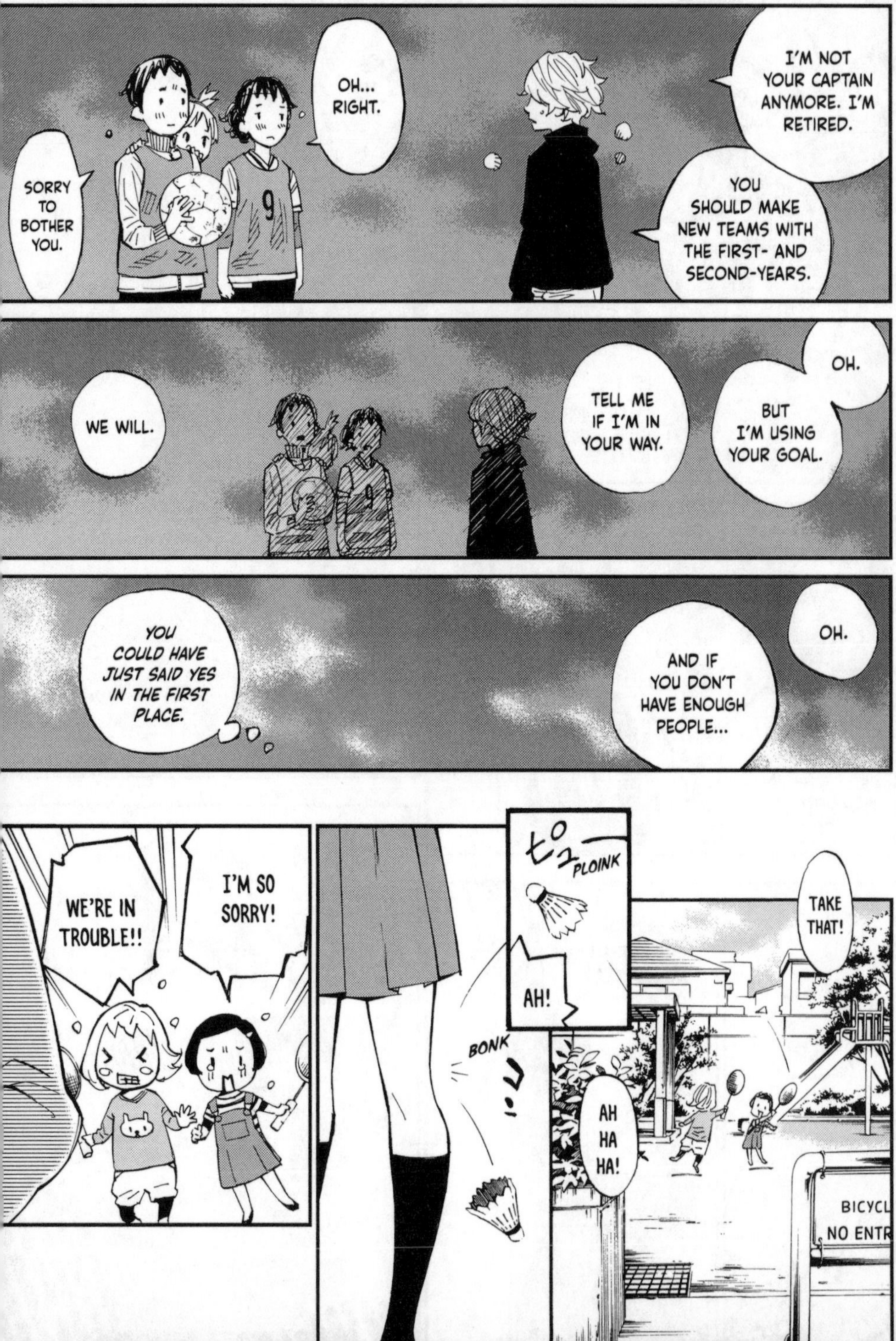
I'M NOT YOUR CAPTAIN ANYMORE. I'M RETIRED.
YOU SHOULD MAKE NEW TEAMS WITH THE FIRST- AND SECOND-YEARS.
OH... RIGHT.
SORRY TO BOTHER YOU.
OH.
BUT I'M USING YOUR GOAL.
TELL ME IF I'M IN YOUR WAY.
WE WILL.
OH.
AND IF YOU DON'T HAVE ENOUGH PEOPLE...
YOU COULD HAVE JUST SAID YES IN THE FIRST PLACE.
TAKE THAT!
AH HA HA!
BICYCL
NO ENTR
PLOINK
AH!
BONK
I'M SO SORRY!
WE'RE IN TROUBLE!!

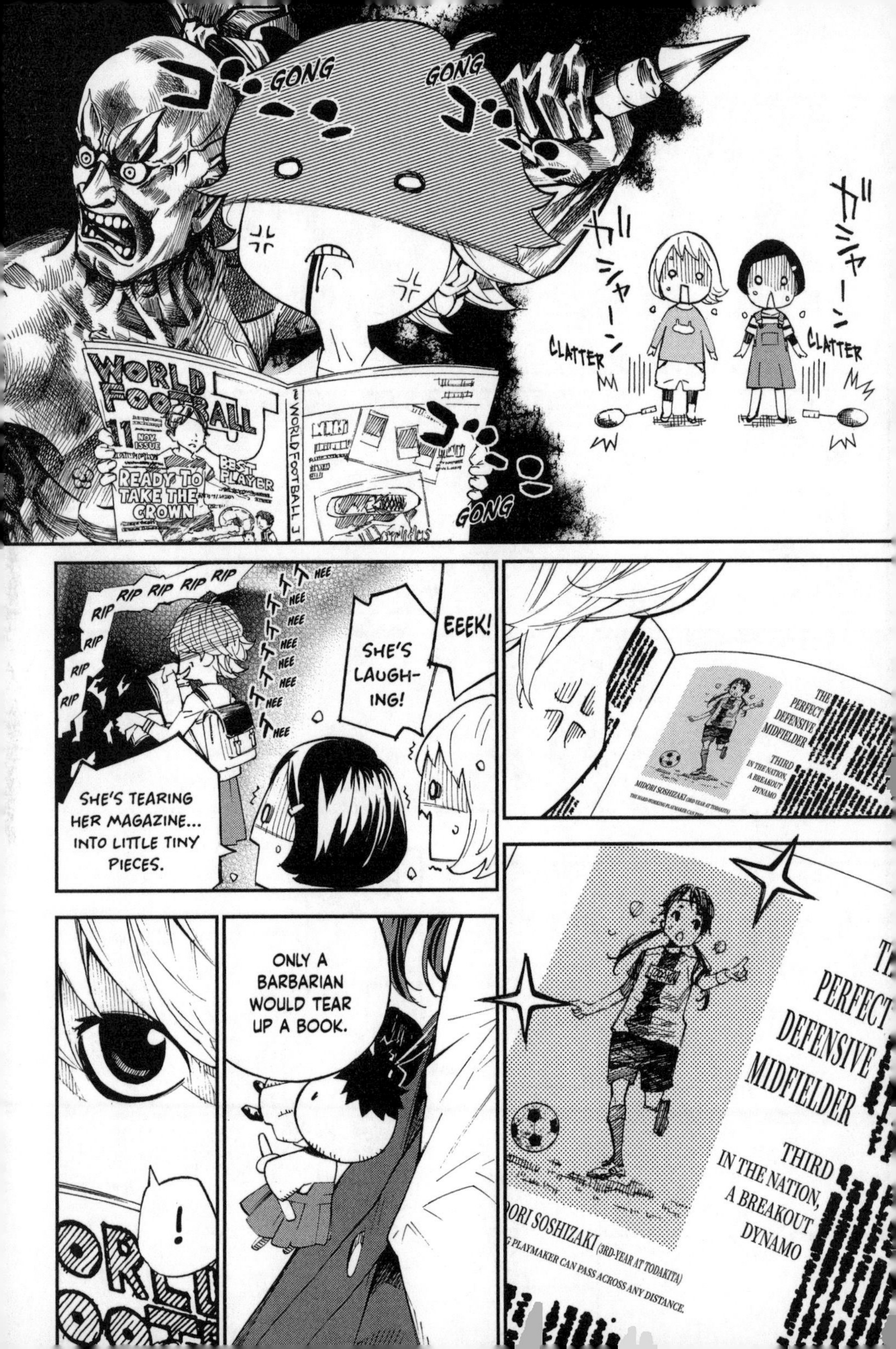
ガシャーン
CLATTER
ガシャーン
CLATTER
GONG
GONG
WORLD FOOTBALL J
11 NOV. ISSUE
BEST PLAYER
READY TO TAKE THE CROWN
WORLD FOOTBALL J
GONG
THE PERFECT DEFENSIVE MIDFIELDER
THIRD IN THE NATION, A BREAKOUT DYNAMO
MIDORI SOSHIZAKI (3RD-YEAR AT TODAKITA)
THE HARD-WORKING PLAYMAKER CAN PASS ACROSS ANY DISTANCE.
EEEK!
SHE'S LAUGHING!
HEE HEE HEE HEE HEE HEE HEE HEE
RIP RIP RIP RIP RIP RIP RIP RIP
SHE'S TEARING HER MAGAZINE... INTO LITTLE TINY PIECES.
THE PERFECT DEFENSIVE MIDFIELDER
THIRD IN THE NATION, A BREAKOUT DYNAMO
DORI SOSHIZAKI (3RD-YEAR AT TODAKITA)
G PLAYMAKER CAN PASS ACROSS ANY DISTANCE.
ONLY A BARBARIAN WOULD TEAR UP A BOOK.
!

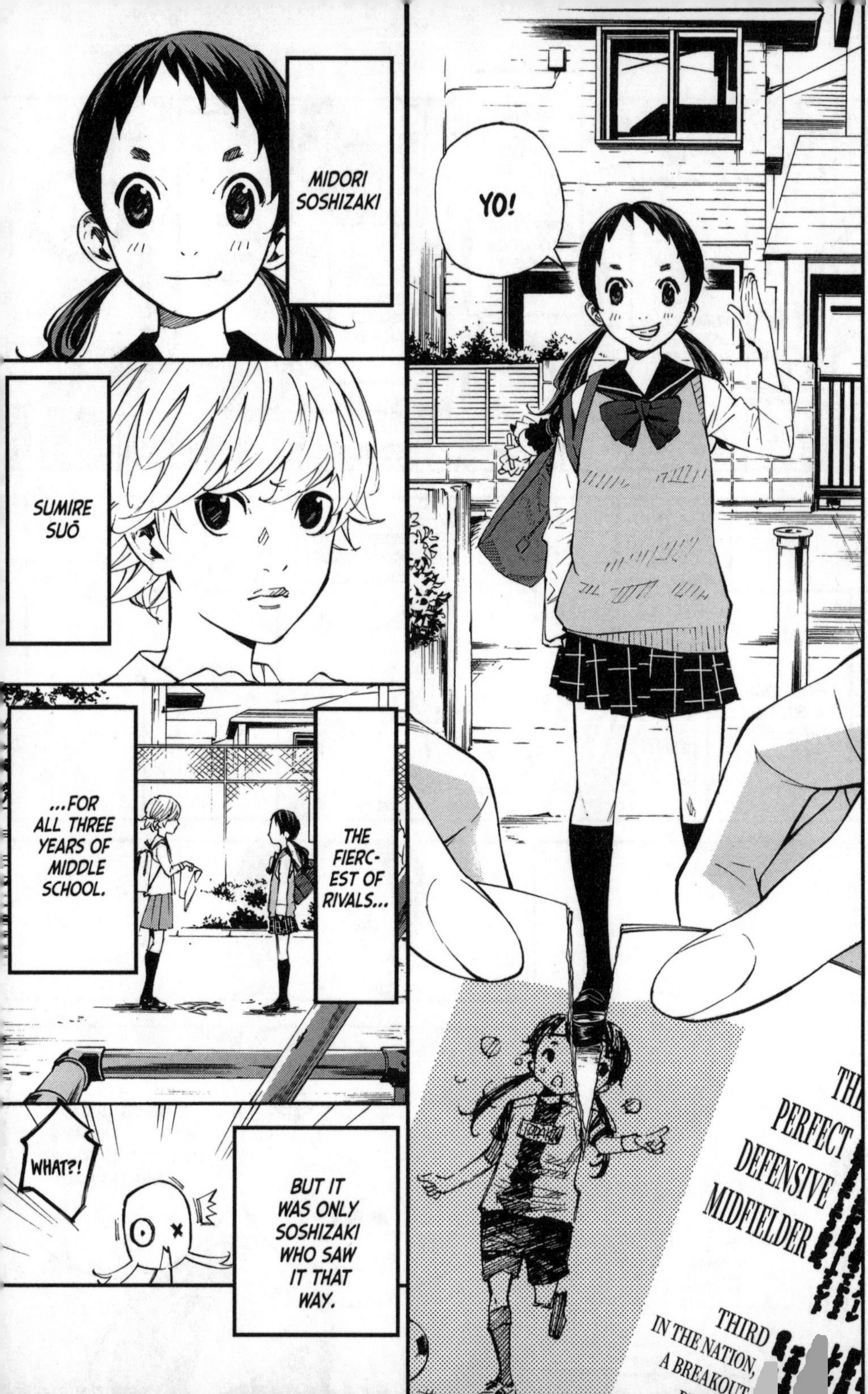
YO!
THE PERFECT DEFENSIVE MIDFIELDER
THIRD IN THE NATION, A BREAKOUT
MIDORI SOSHIZAKI
SUMIRE SUŌ
THE FIERC-EST OF RIVALS...
...FOR ALL THREE YEARS OF MIDDLE SCHOOL.
BUT IT WAS ONLY SOSHIZAKI WHO SAW IT THAT WAY.
WHAT?!

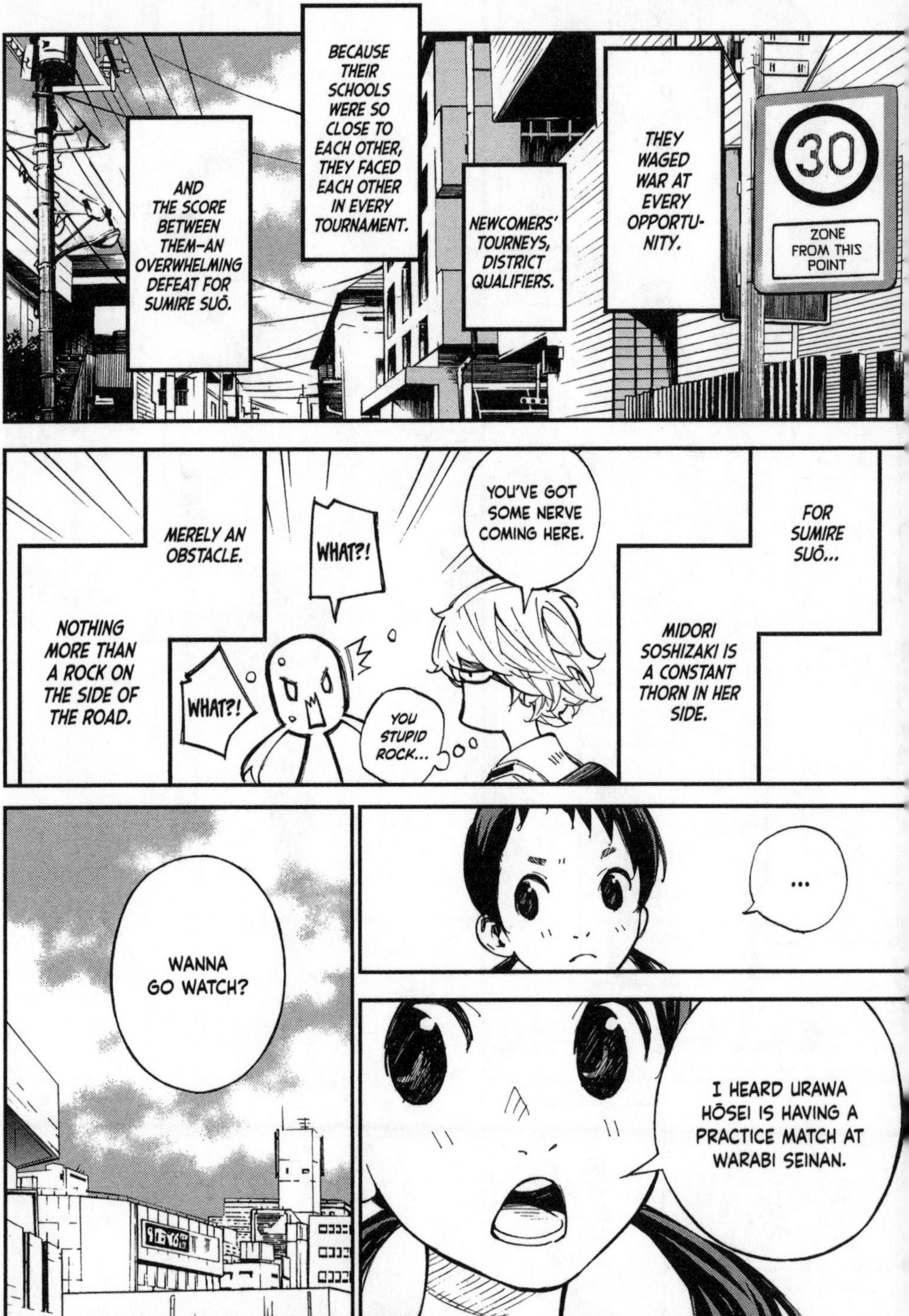

30
ZONE FROM THIS POINT
THEY WAGED WAR AT EVERY OPPORTUNITY.
NEWCOMERS' TOURNEYS, DISTRICT QUALIFIERS.
BECAUSE THEIR SCHOOLS WERE SO CLOSE TO EACH OTHER, THEY FACED EACH OTHER IN EVERY TOURNAMENT.
AND THE SCORE BETWEEN THEM—AN OVERWHELMING DEFEAT FOR SUMIRE SUŌ.
FOR SUMIRE SUŌ...
MIDORI SOSHIZAKI IS A CONSTANT THORN IN HER SIDE.
YOU'VE GOT SOME NERVE COMING HERE.
WHAT?!
WHAT?!
YOU STUPID ROCK...
MERELY AN OBSTACLE.
NOTHING MORE THAN A ROCK ON THE SIDE OF THE ROAD.
...
I HEARD URAWA HŌSEI IS HAVING A PRACTICE MATCH AT WARABI SEINAN.
WANNA GO WATCH?

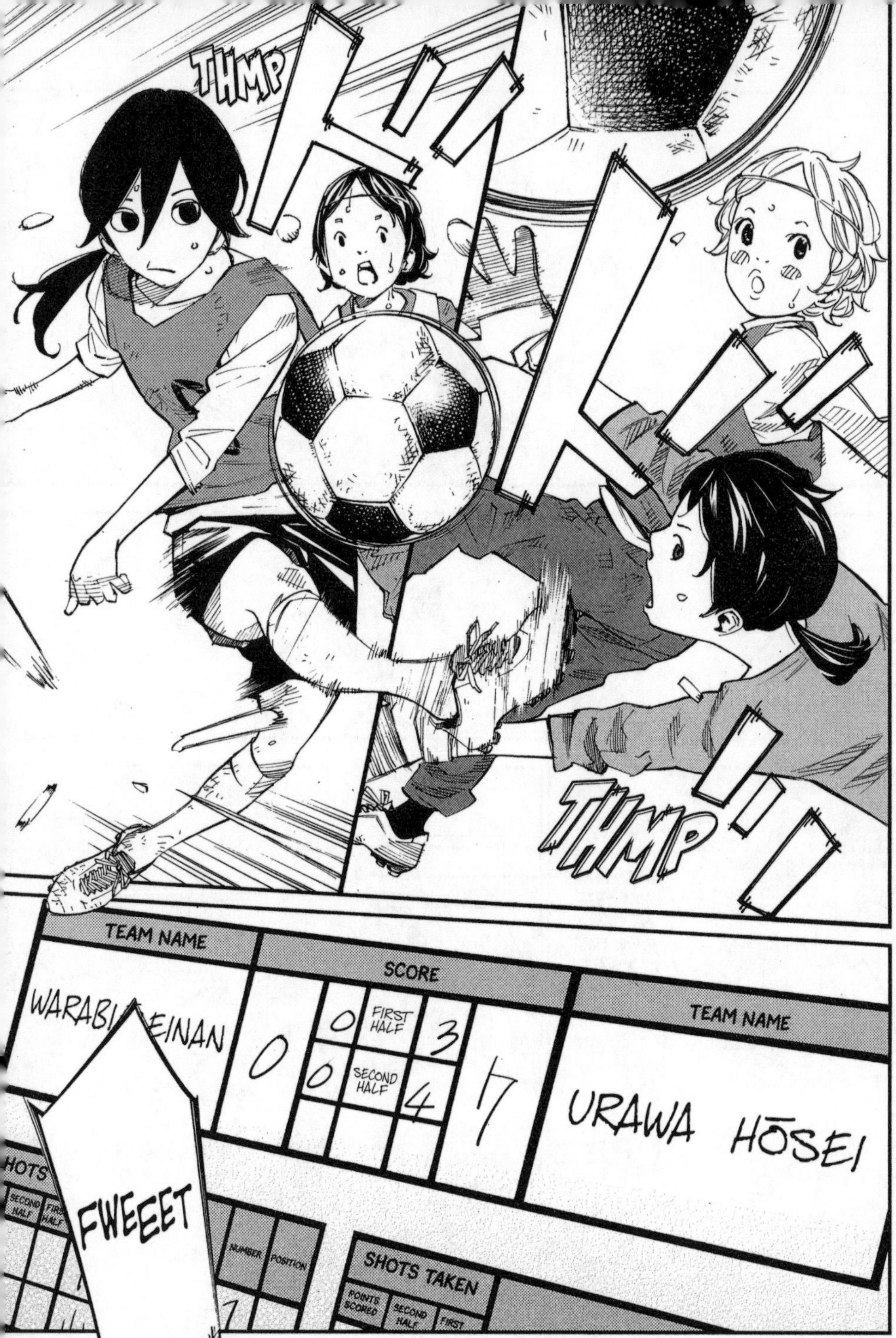
THMP
THMP
TEAM NAME
URAWA HŌSEI
SCORE
7
3
FIRST HALF
4
SECOND HALF
0
0
0
TEAM NAME
WARABI
EINAN
SHOTS TAKEN
POINTS SCORED
SECOND HALF
FIRST
NUMBER
POSITION
HOTS
SECOND HALF
FIRST HALF
FWEEET

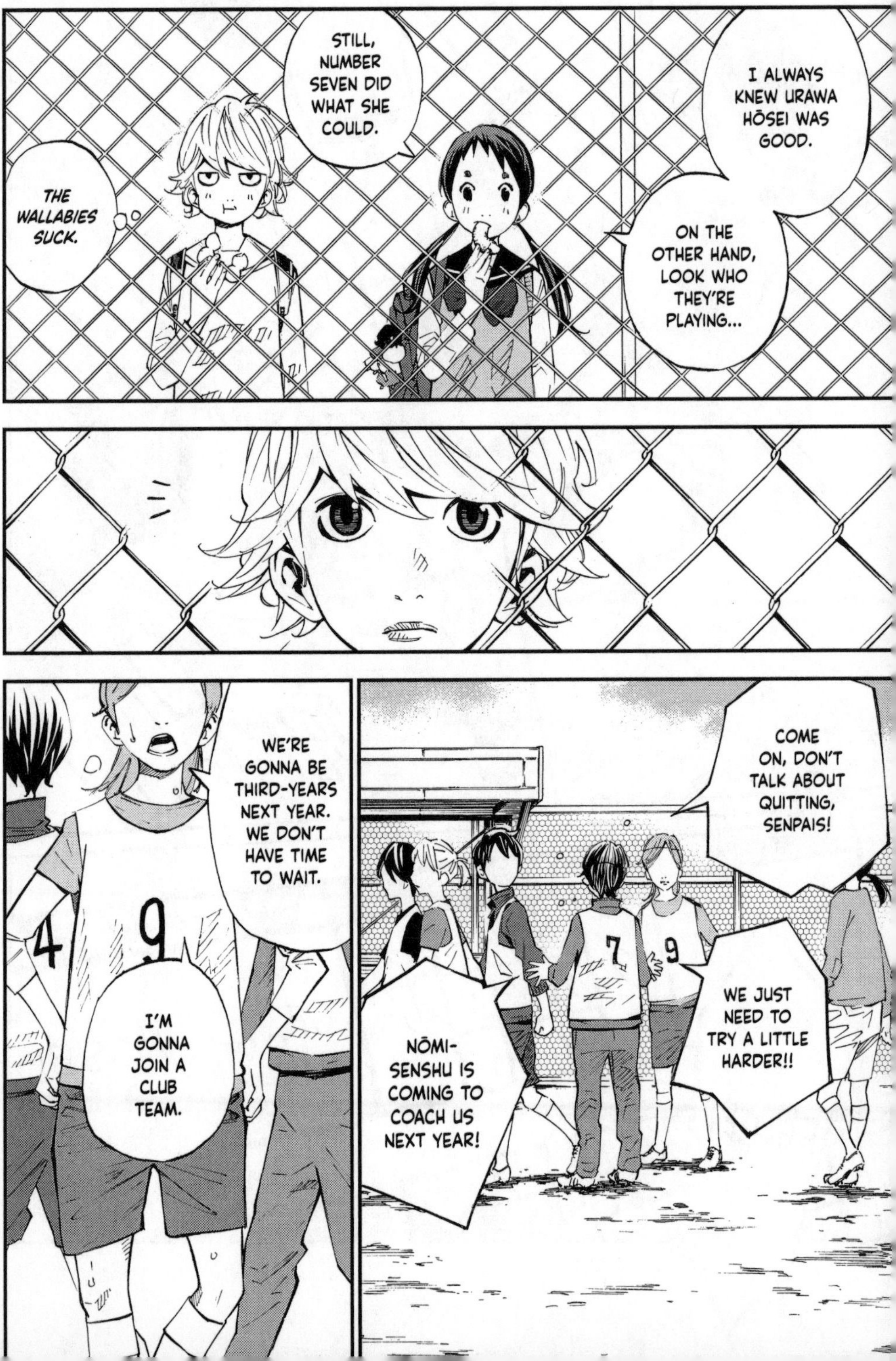
I ALWAYS KNEW URAWA HŌSEI WAS GOOD.
ON THE OTHER HAND, LOOK WHO THEY'RE PLAYING...
STILL, NUMBER SEVEN DID WHAT SHE COULD.
THE WALLABIES SUCK.
COME ON, DON'T TALK ABOUT QUITTING, SENPAIS!
WE JUST NEED TO TRY A LITTLE HARDER!!
NŌMI-SENSHU IS COMING TO COACH US NEXT YEAR!
WE'RE GONNA BE THIRD-YEARS NEXT YEAR. WE DON'T HAVE TIME TO WAIT.
I'M GONNA JOIN A CLUB TEAM.

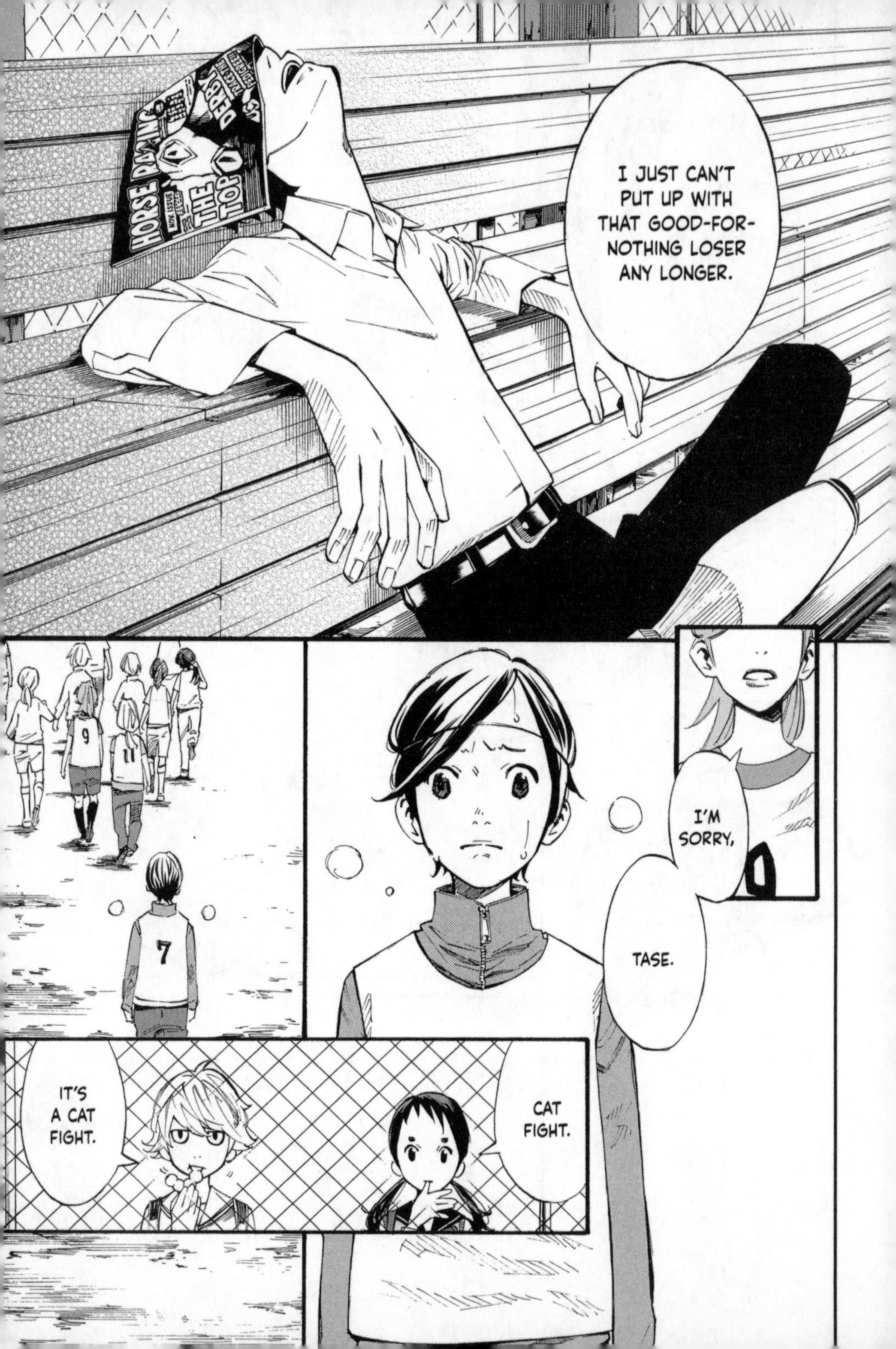
I JUST CAN'T PUT UP WITH THAT GOOD-FOR-NOTHING LOSER ANY LONGER.
I'M SORRY,
TASE.
CAT FIGHT.
IT'S A CAT FIGHT.

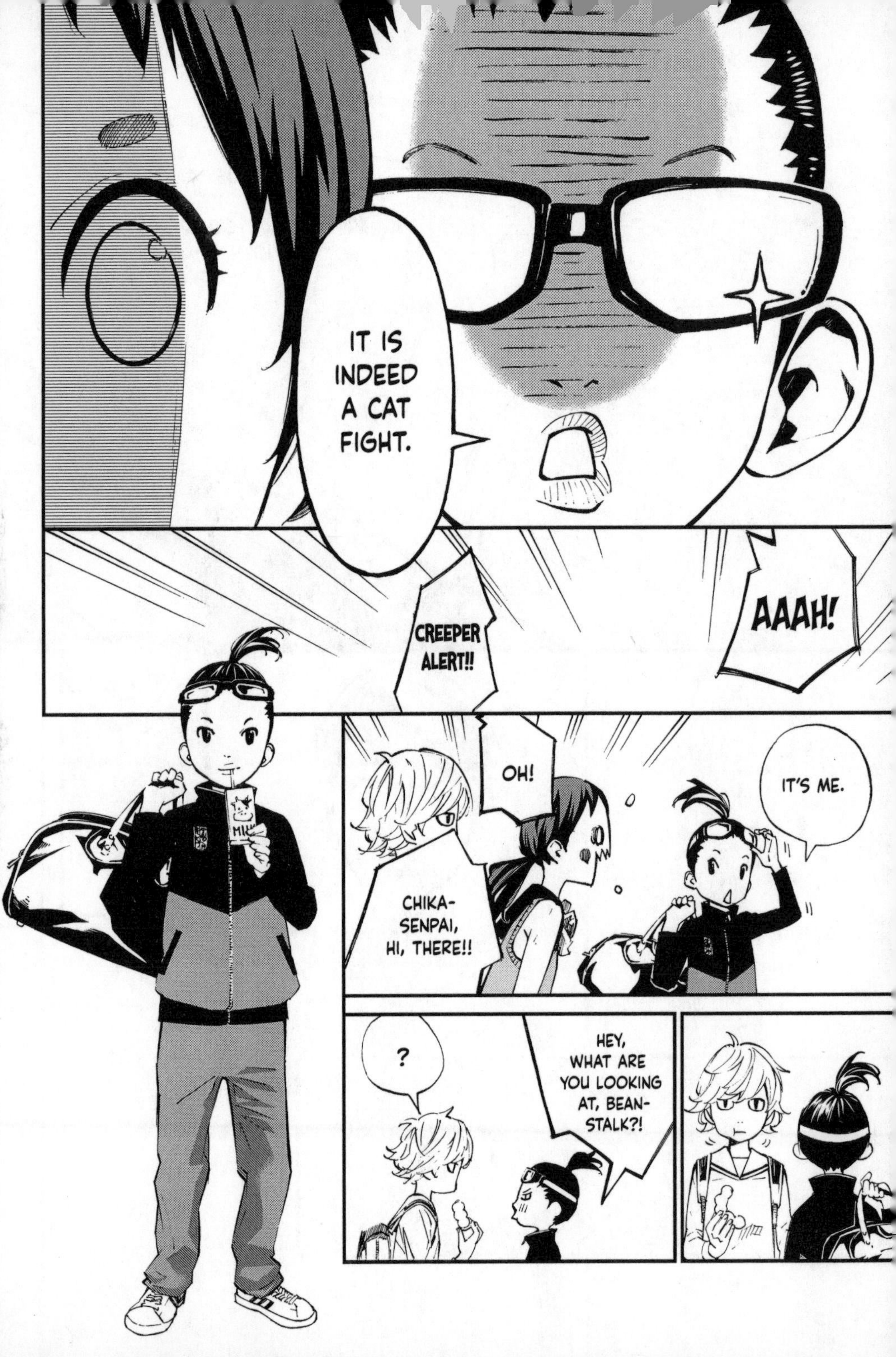
IT IS INDEED A CAT FIGHT.
AAAH!
CREEPER ALERT!!
IT'S ME.
OH!
CHIKA-SENPAI, HI, THERE!!
HEY, WHAT ARE YOU LOOKING AT, BEAN-STALK?!
?

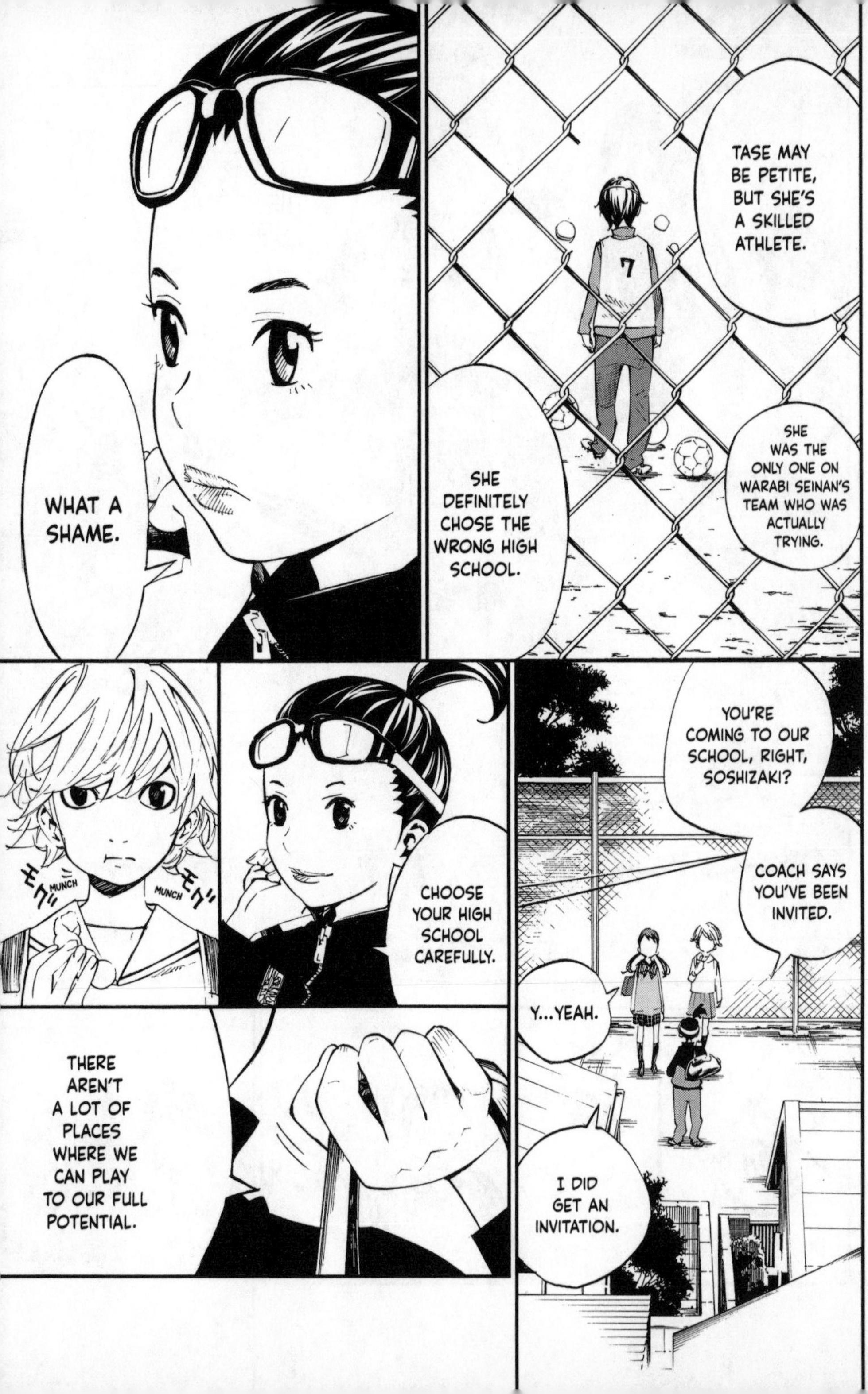
TASE MAY BE PETITE, BUT SHE'S A SKILLED ATHLETE.
SHE WAS THE ONLY ONE ON WARABI SEINAN'S TEAM WHO WAS ACTUALLY TRYING.
SHE DEFINITELY CHOSE THE WRONG HIGH SCHOOL.
WHAT A SHAME.
YOU'RE COMING TO OUR SCHOOL, RIGHT, SOSHIZAKI?
COACH SAYS YOU'VE BEEN INVITED.
Y...YEAH.
I DID GET AN INVITATION.
CHOOSE YOUR HIGH SCHOOL CAREFULLY.
モグ MUNCH
モグ MUNCH
THERE AREN'T A LOT OF PLACES WHERE WE CAN PLAY TO OUR FULL POTENTIAL.

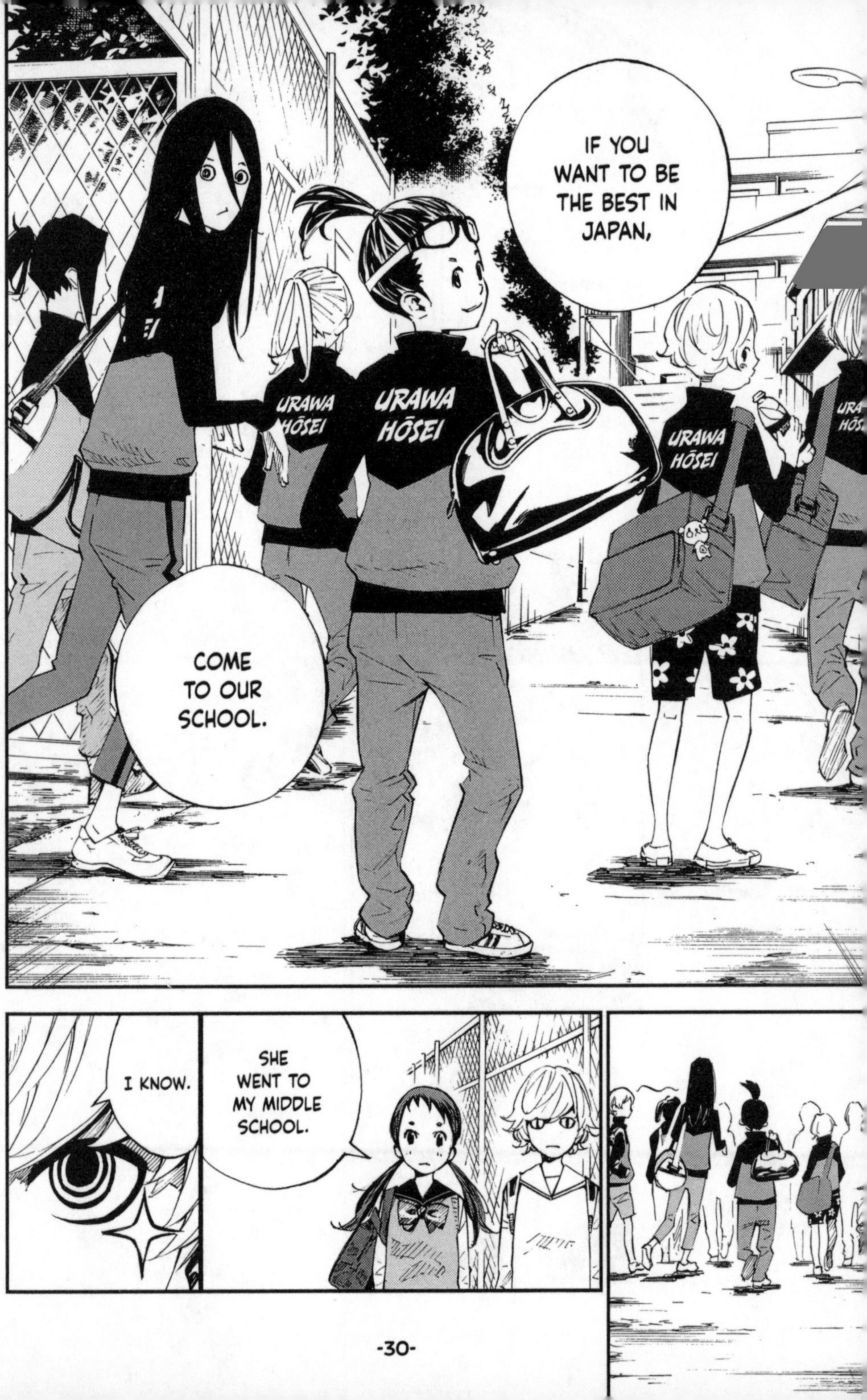
IF YOU WANT TO BE THE BEST IN JAPAN,
URAWA HŌSEI
URAWA HŌSEI
URAWA HŌSEI
URA HŌS
COME TO OUR SCHOOL.
SHE WENT TO MY MIDDLE SCHOOL.
I KNOW.

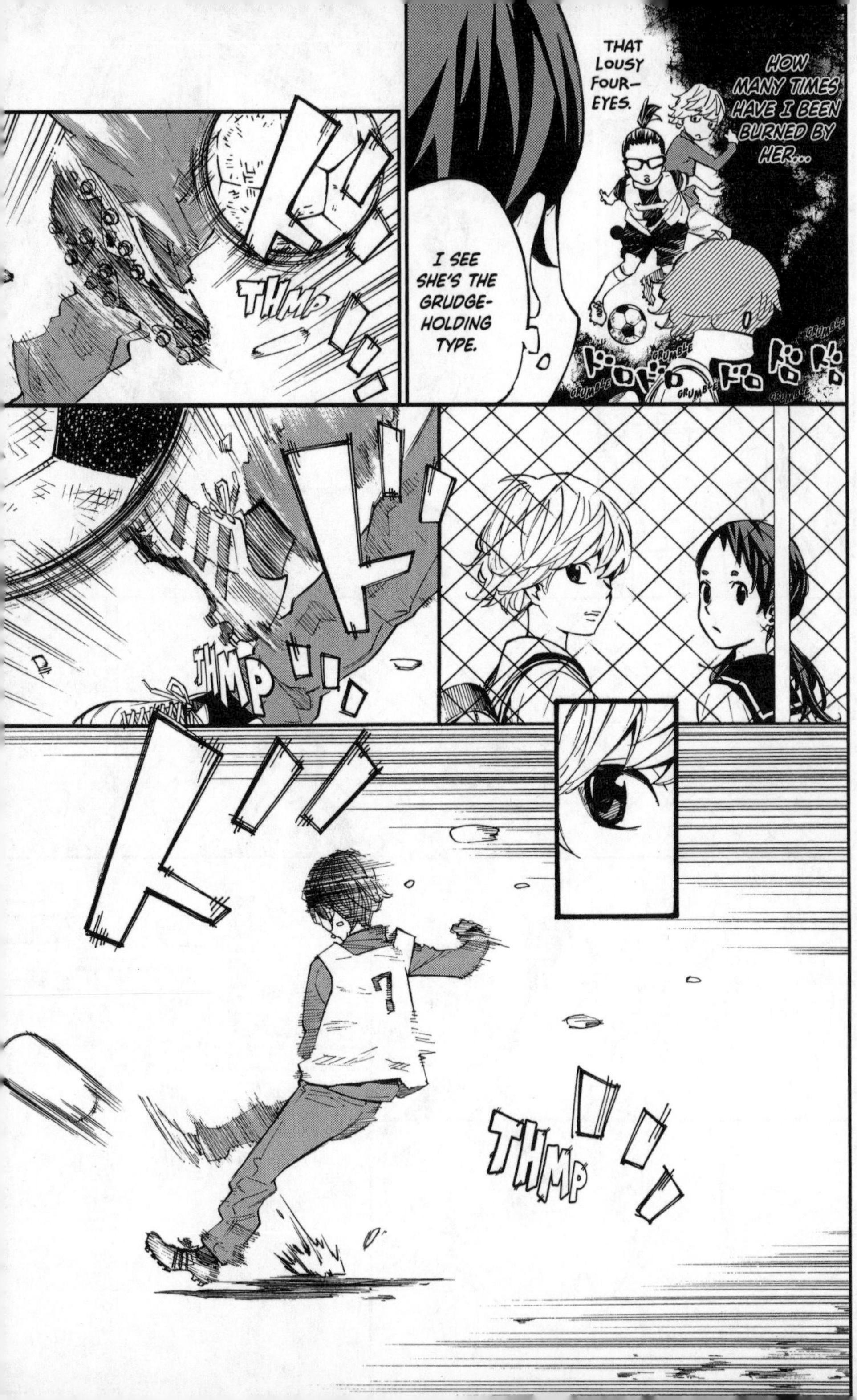
HOW MANY TIMES HAVE I BEEN BURNED BY HER...
THAT LOUSY FOUR-EYES.
I SEE SHE'S THE GRUDGE-HOLDING TYPE.
GRUMBLE GRUMBLE GRUMBLE GRUMBLE GRUMBLE
THMP
THMP
THMP

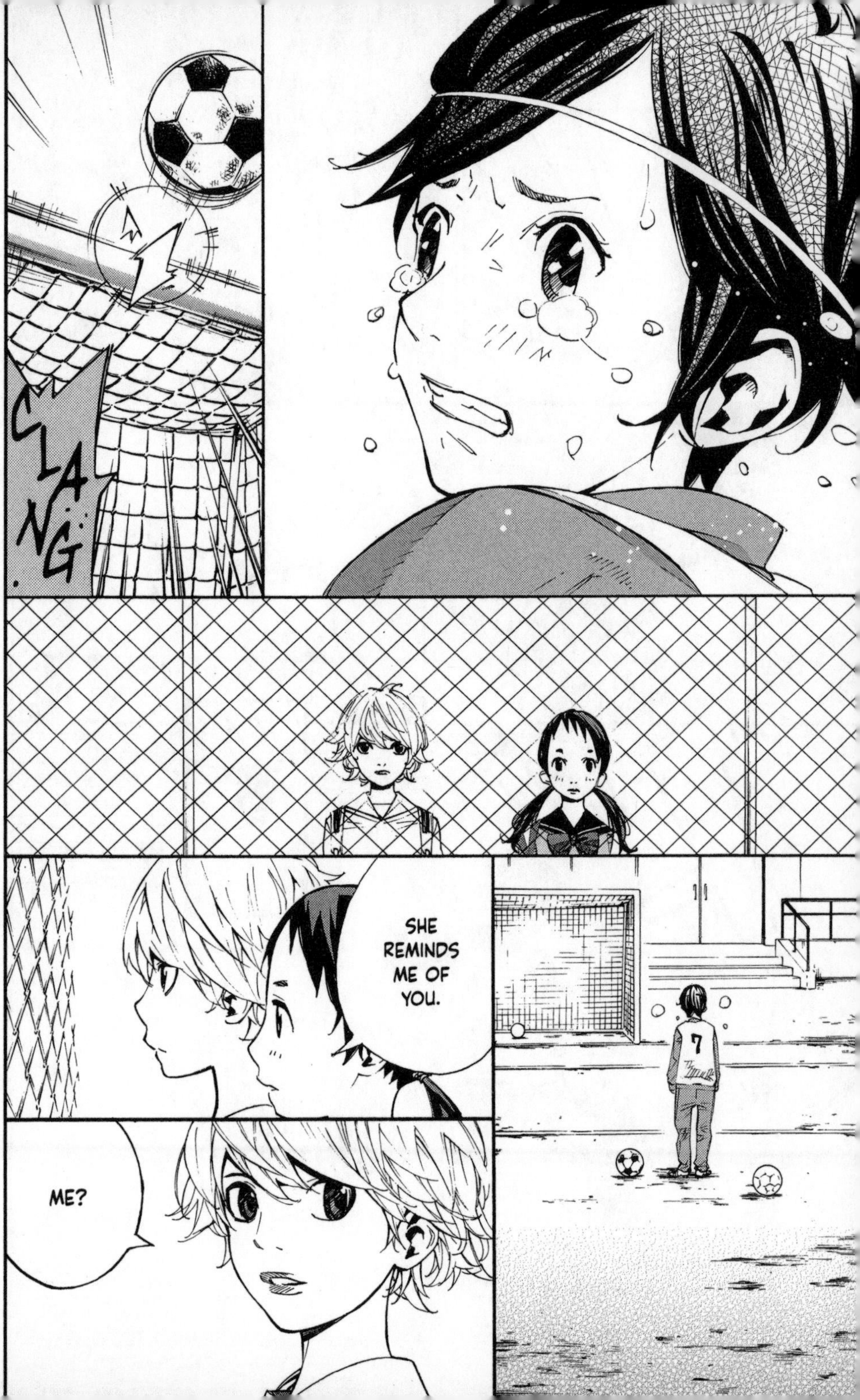
CLANG
SHE REMINDS ME OF YOU.
ME?

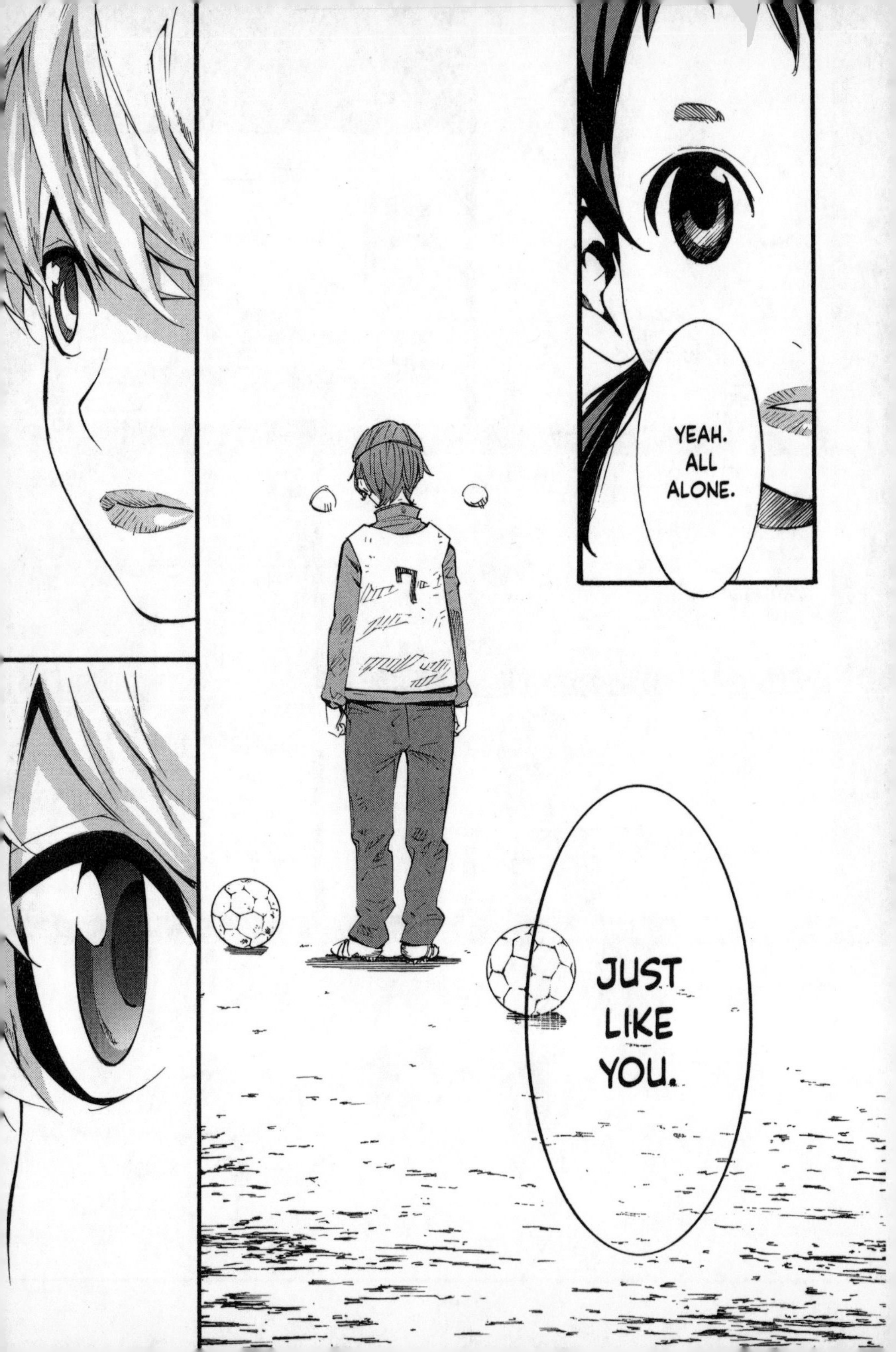
YEAH. ALL ALONE.
JUST LIKE YOU.

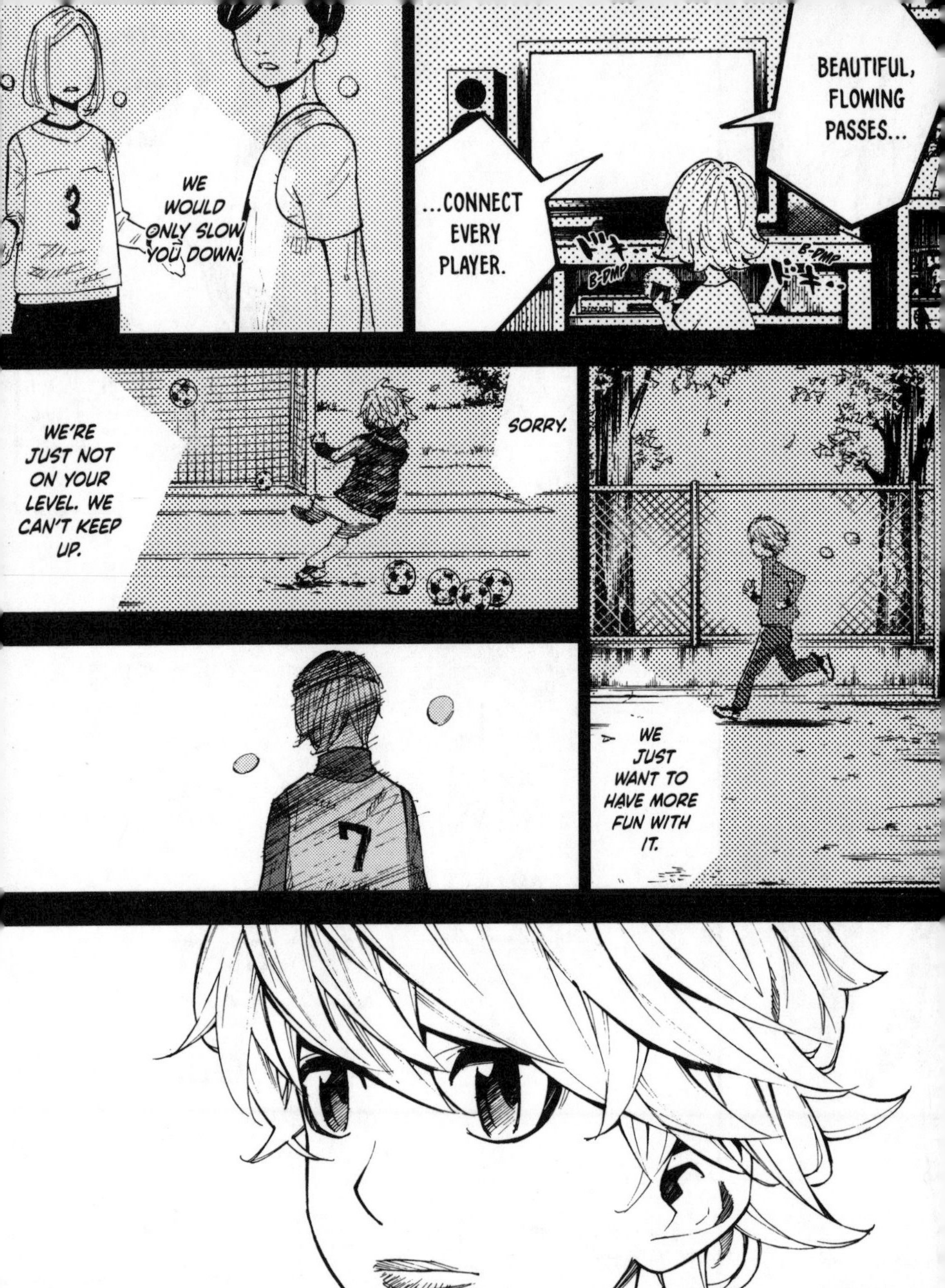
BEAUTIFUL, FLOWING PASSES...
...CONNECT EVERY PLAYER.
B-DMP
B-DMP
WE WOULD ONLY SLOW YOU DOWN!
WE JUST WANT TO HAVE MORE FUN WITH IT.
SORRY.
WE'RE JUST NOT ON YOUR LEVEL. WE CAN'T KEEP UP.

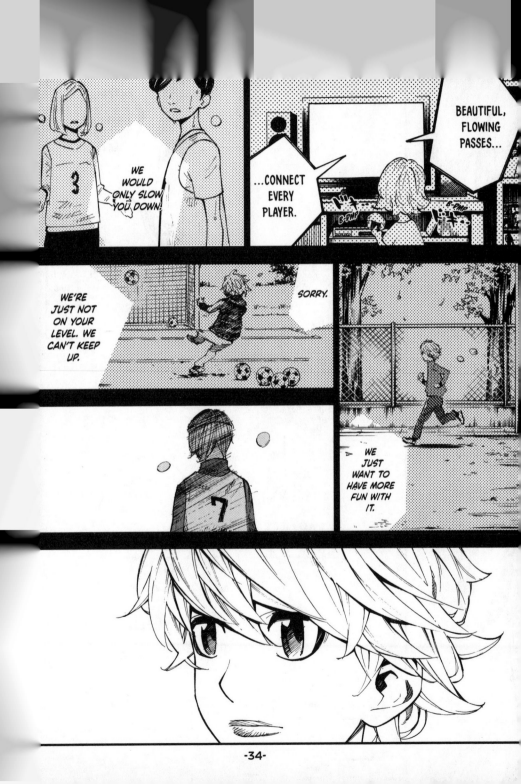

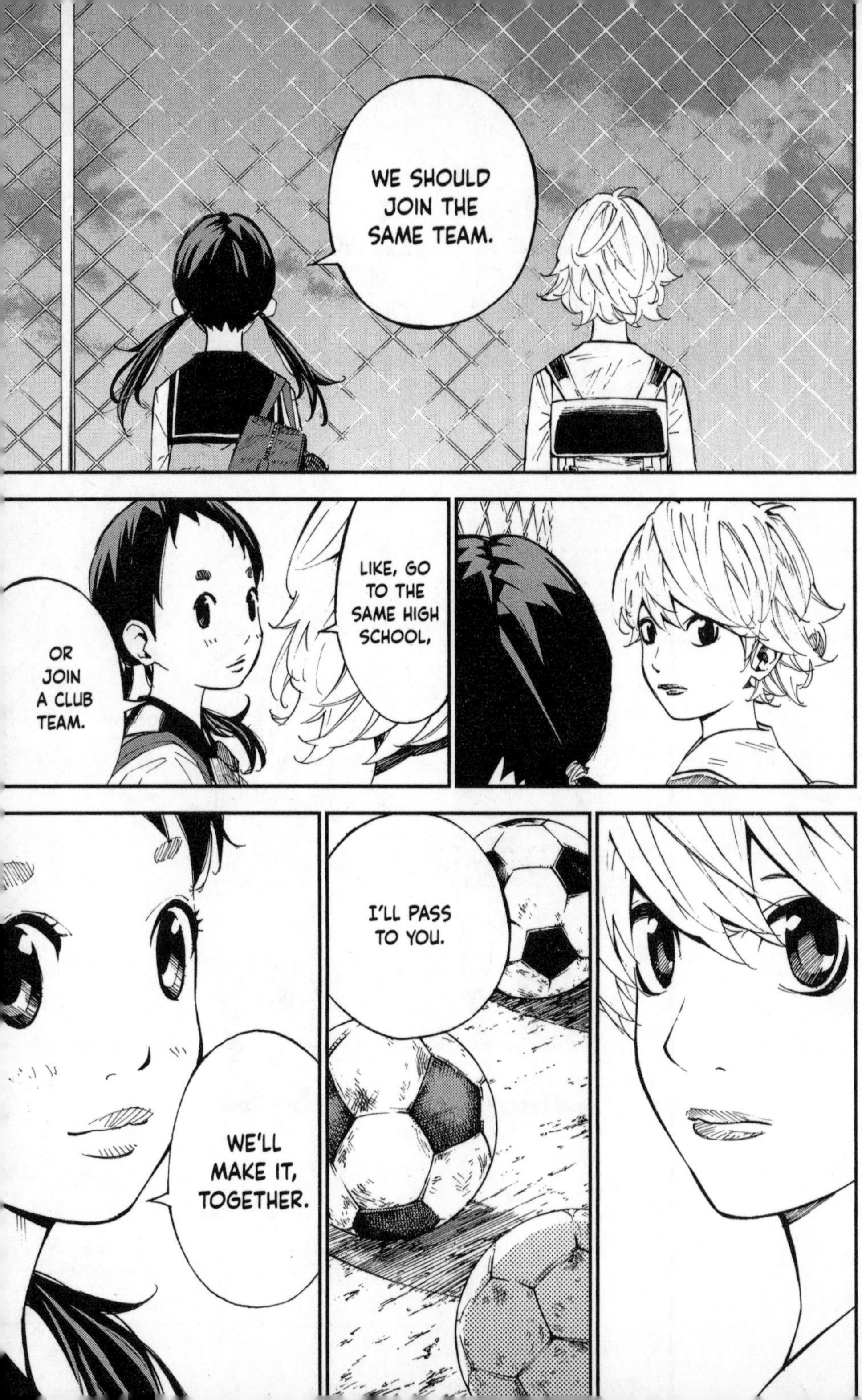
WE SHOULD JOIN THE SAME TEAM.
LIKE, GO TO THE SAME HIGH SCHOOL,
OR JOIN A CLUB TEAM.
I'LL PASS TO YOU.
WE'LL MAKE IT, TOGETHER.

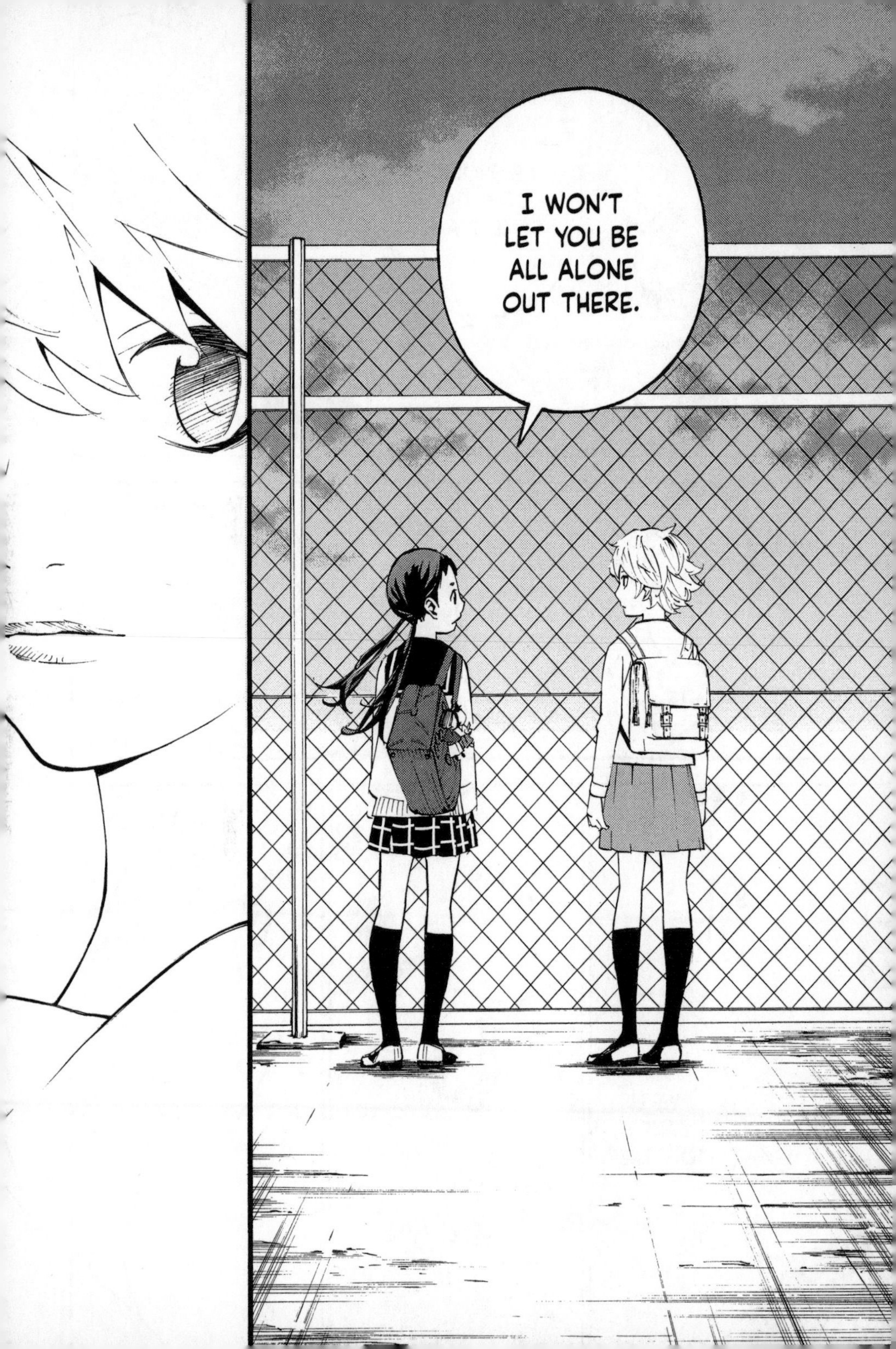
I WON'T LET YOU BE ALL ALONE OUT THERE.

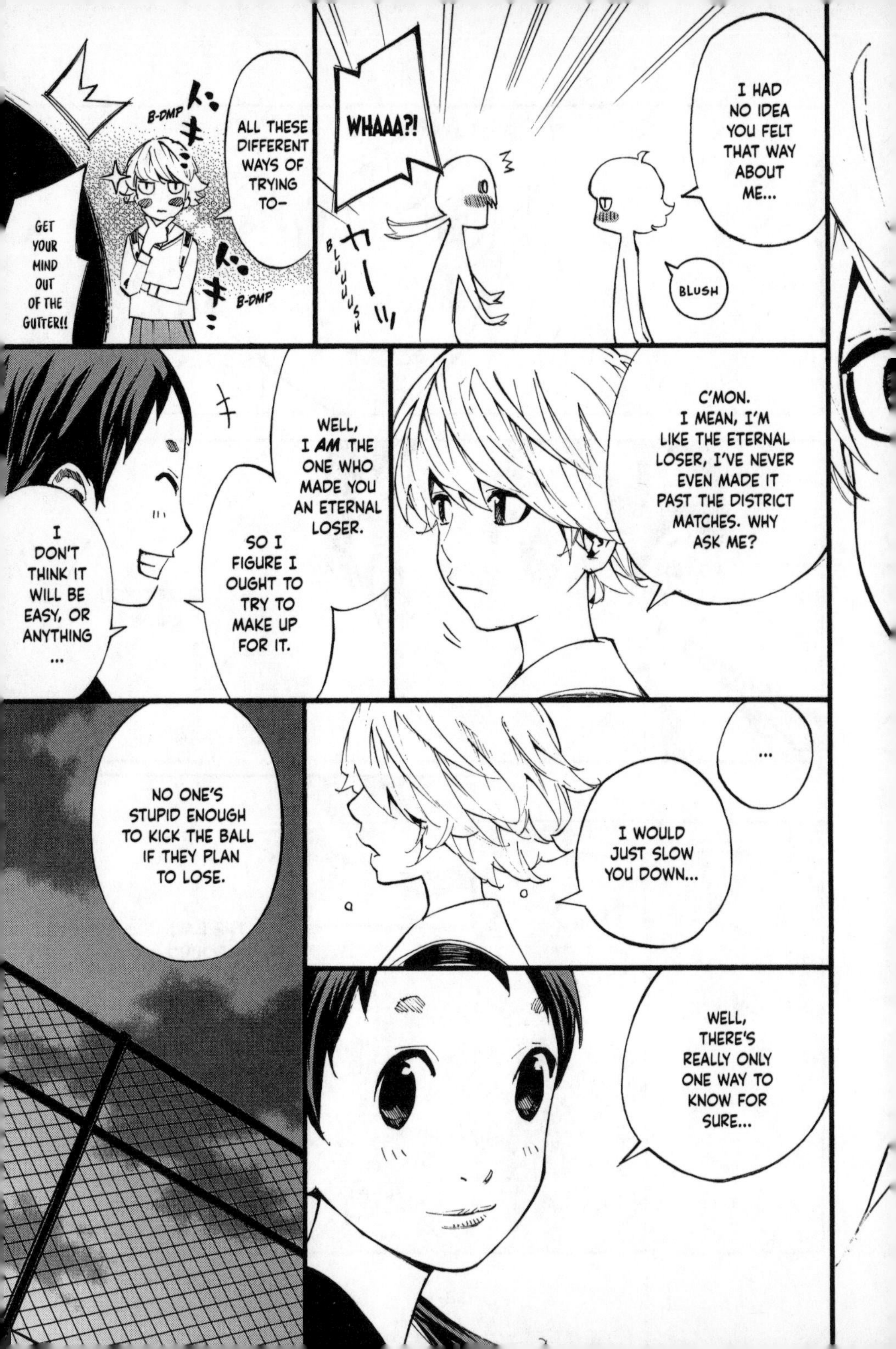
I HAD NO IDEA YOU FELT THAT WAY ABOUT ME...
BLUSH
WHAAA?!
BLUUUUUSH
ALL THESE DIFFERENT WAYS OF TRYING TO–
B-DMP
B-DMP
GET YOUR MIND OUT OF THE GUTTER!!
C'MON. I MEAN, I'M LIKE THE ETERNAL LOSER, I'VE NEVER EVEN MADE IT PAST THE DISTRICT MATCHES. WHY ASK ME?
WELL, I *AM* THE ONE WHO MADE YOU AN ETERNAL LOSER.
SO I FIGURE I OUGHT TO TRY TO MAKE UP FOR IT.
I DON'T THINK IT WILL BE EASY, OR ANYTHING ...
...
I WOULD JUST SLOW YOU DOWN...
WELL, THERE'S REALLY ONLY ONE WAY TO KNOW FOR SURE...
NO ONE'S STUPID ENOUGH TO KICK THE BALL IF THEY PLAN TO LOSE.

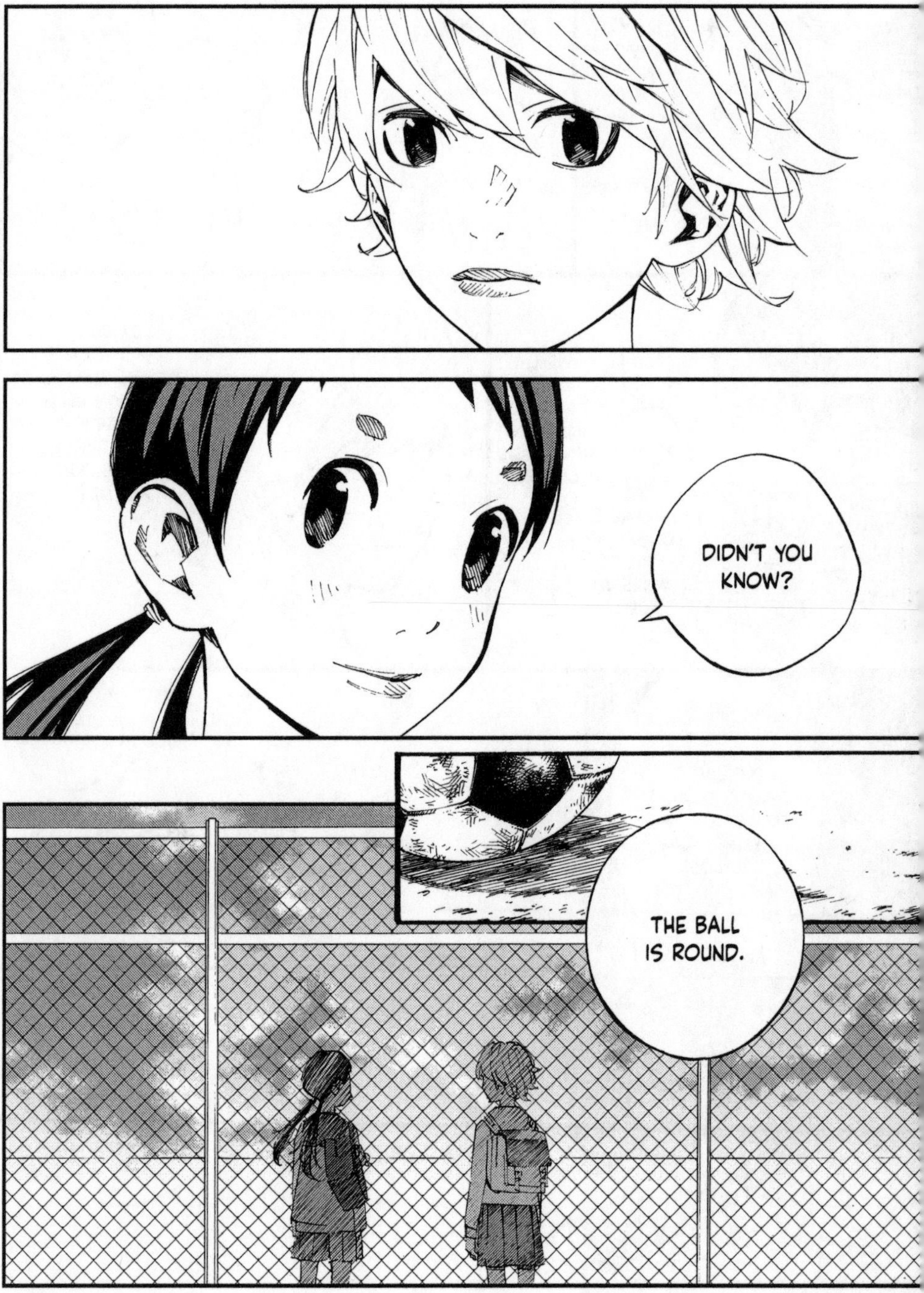
DIDN'T YOU KNOW?
THE BALL IS ROUND.

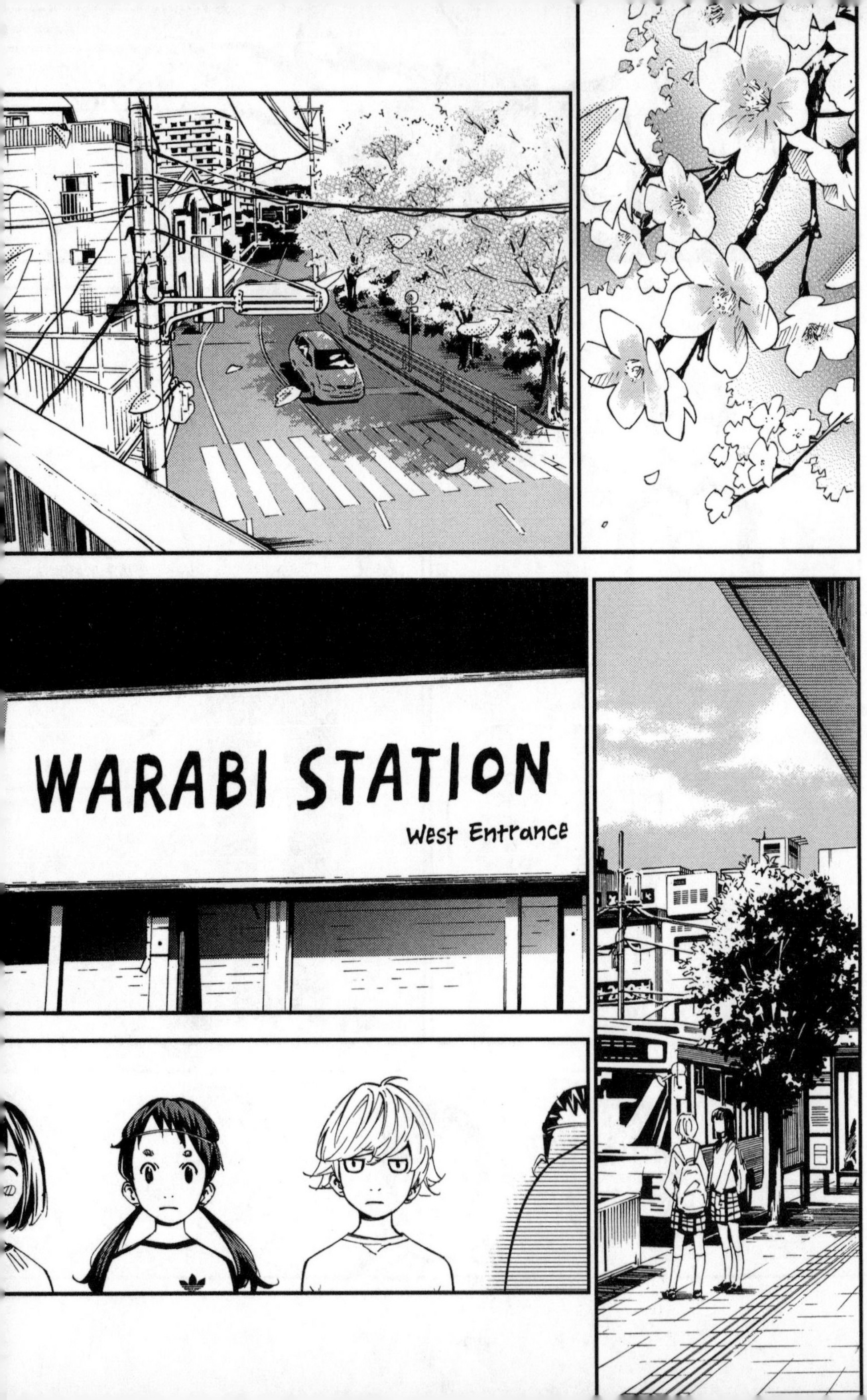
WARABI STATION
West Entrance

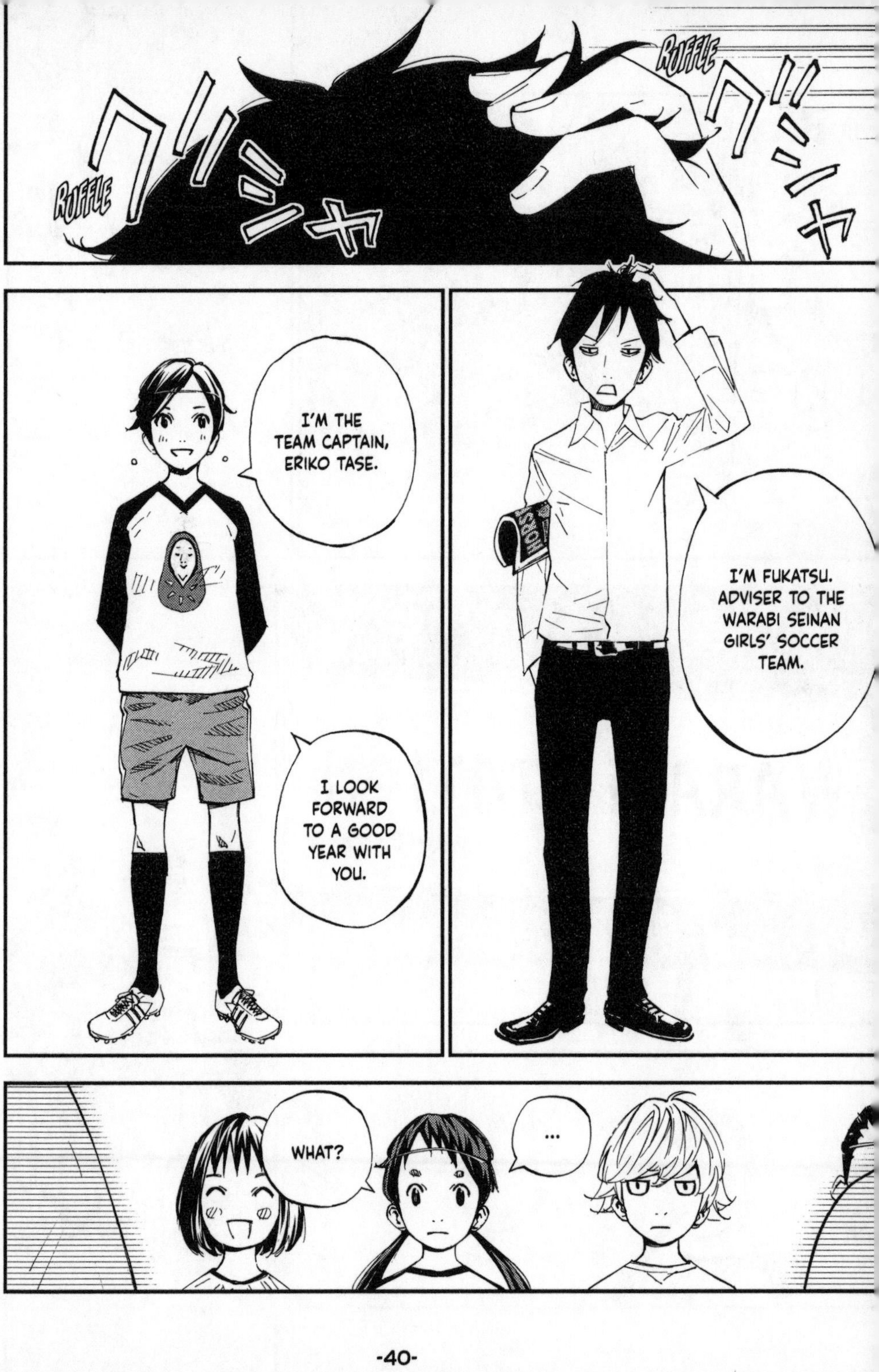
RUFFLE
RUFFLE
I'M FUKATSU. ADVISER TO THE WARABI SEINAN GIRLS' SOCCER TEAM.
I'M THE TEAM CAPTAIN, ERIKO TASE.
I LOOK FORWARD TO A GOOD YEAR WITH YOU.
...
WHAT?

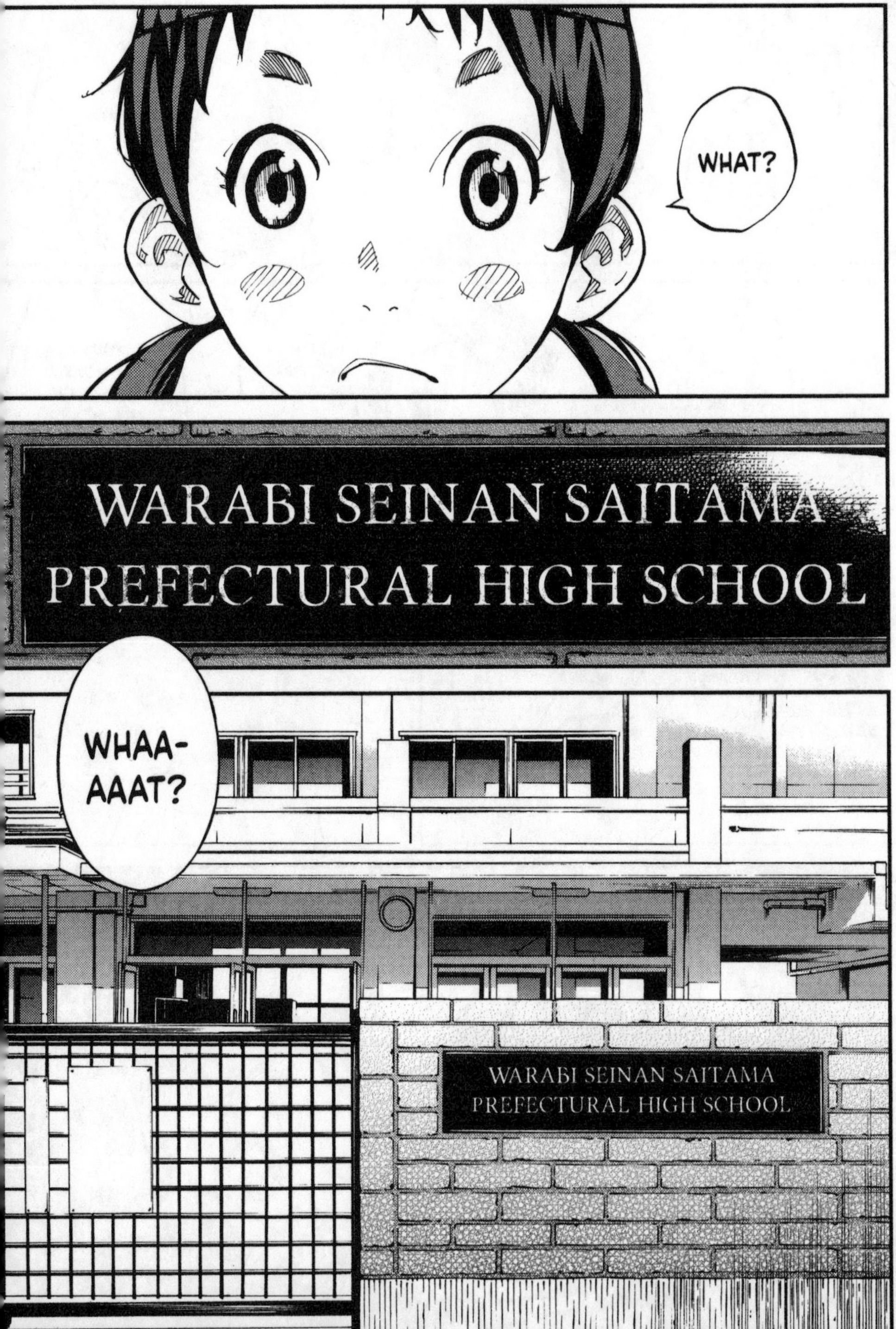
WHAT?
WARABI SEINAN SAITAMA PREFECTURAL HIGH SCHOOL
WHAA-AAAT?
WARABI SEINAN SAITAMA PREFECTURAL HIGH SCHOOL

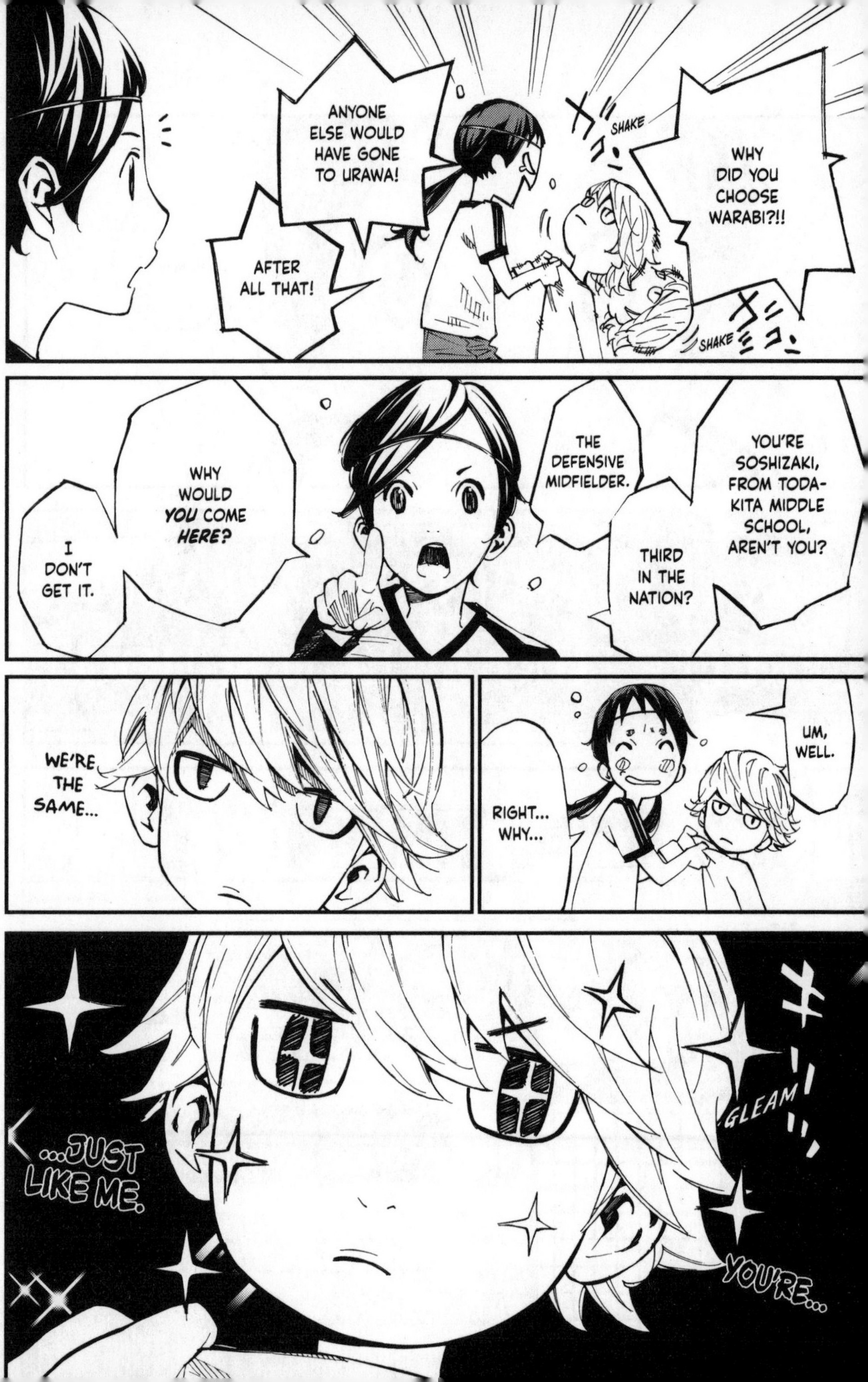
WHY DID YOU CHOOSE WARABI?!!
SHAKE
SHAKE
ANYONE ELSE WOULD HAVE GONE TO URAWA!
AFTER ALL THAT!
YOU'RE SOSHIZAKI, FROM TODA-KITA MIDDLE SCHOOL, AREN'T YOU?
THIRD IN THE NATION?
THE DEFENSIVE MIDFIELDER.
WHY WOULD *YOU* COME *HERE*?
I DON'T GET IT.
UM, WELL.
RIGHT... WHY...
WE'RE THE SAME...
GLEAM
YOU'RE...
...JUST LIKE ME.

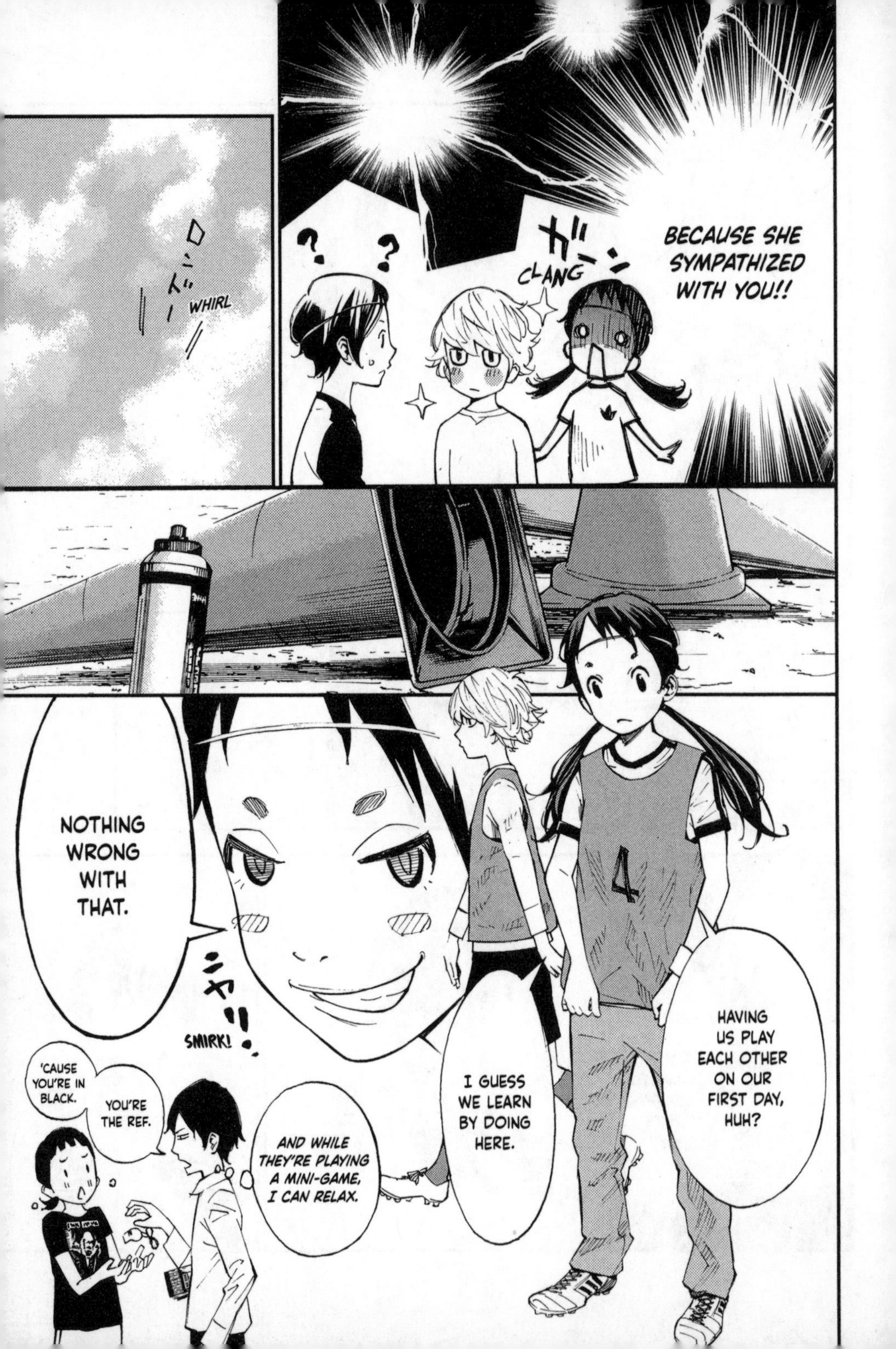
? ?
ガーン
CLANG
BECAUSE SHE SYMPATHIZED WITH YOU!!
WHIRL
HAVING US PLAY EACH OTHER ON OUR FIRST DAY, HUH?
I GUESS WE LEARN BY DOING HERE.
NOTHING WRONG WITH THAT.
ニヤ!!
SMIRK!
AND WHILE THEY'RE PLAYING A MINI-GAME, I CAN RELAX.
YOU'RE THE REF.
'CAUSE YOU'RE IN BLACK.

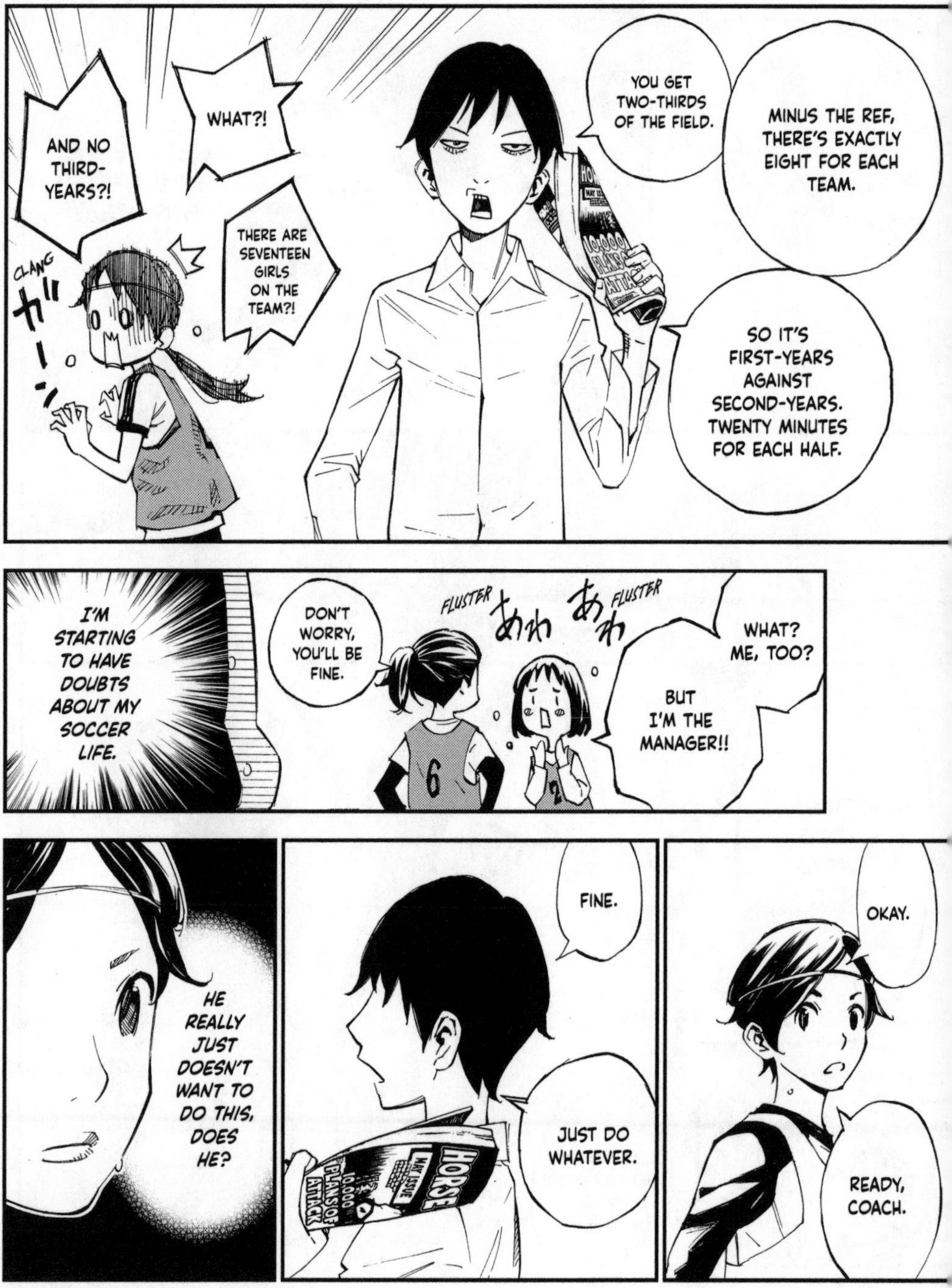
MINUS THE REF, THERE'S EXACTLY EIGHT FOR EACH TEAM.
YOU GET TWO-THIRDS OF THE FIELD.
SO IT'S FIRST-YEARS AGAINST SECOND-YEARS. TWENTY MINUTES FOR EACH HALF.
WHAT?!
THERE ARE SEVENTEEN GIRLS ON THE TEAM?!
AND NO THIRD-YEARS?!
CLANG
WHAT? ME, TOO?
BUT I'M THE MANAGER!!
FLUSTER
FLUSTER
DON'T WORRY, YOU'LL BE FINE.
I'M STARTING TO HAVE DOUBTS ABOUT MY SOCCER LIFE.
OKAY.
READY, COACH.
FINE.
JUST DO WHATEVER.
HE REALLY JUST DOESN'T WANT TO DO THIS, DOES HE?

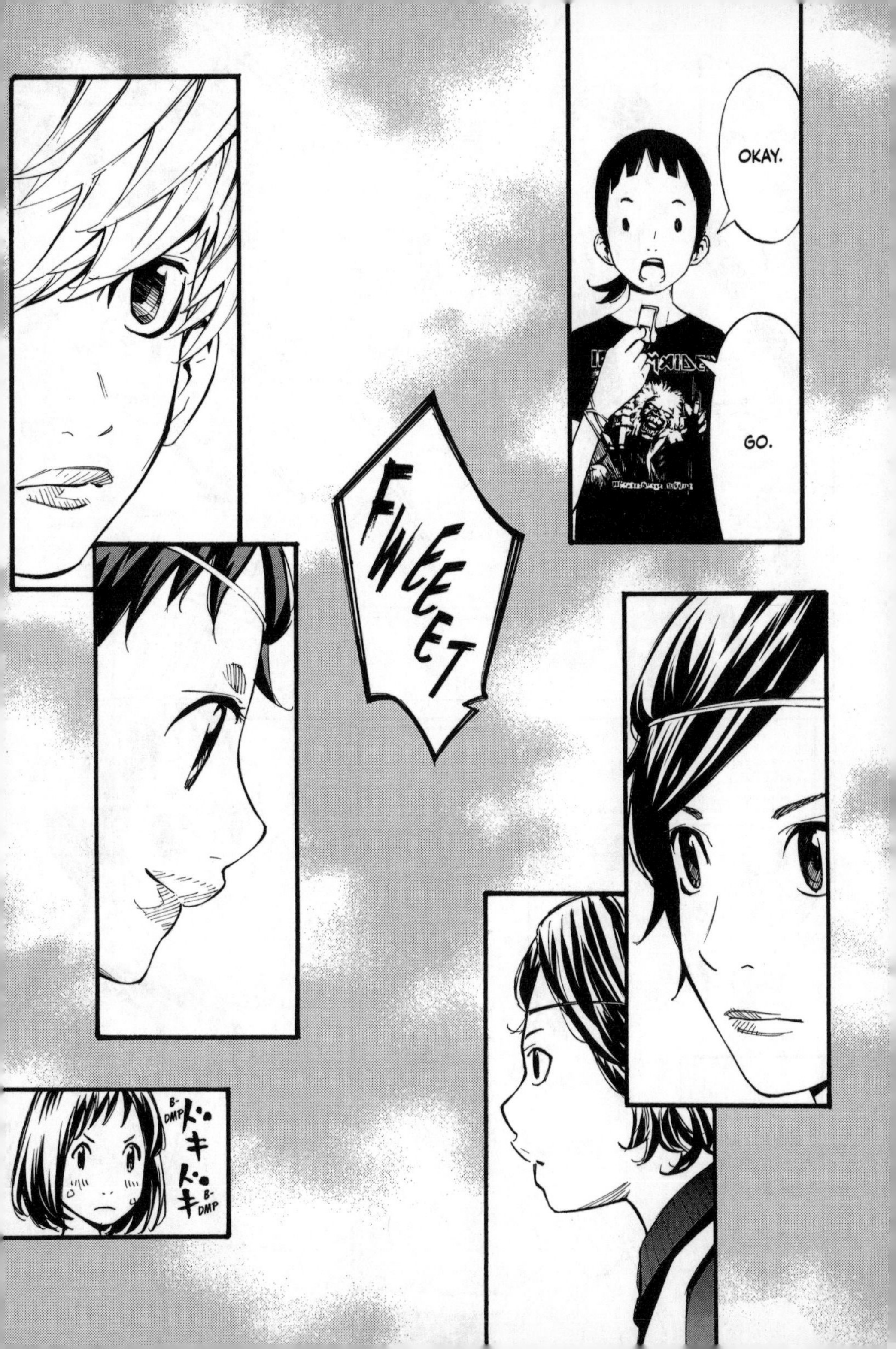
OKAY.
GO.
FWEEET
B-DMP
ドキドキ
B-DMP

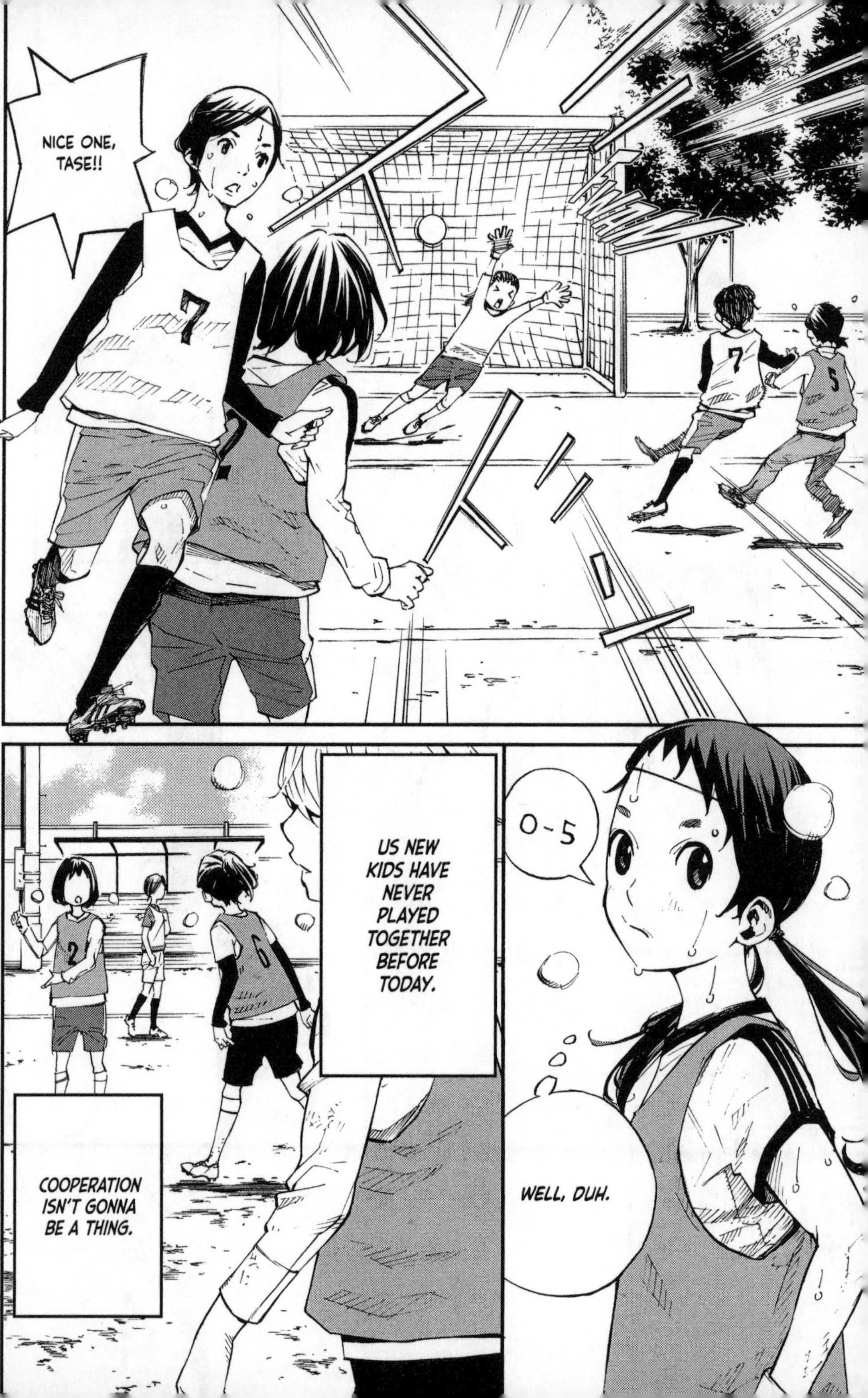
NICE ONE, TASE!!
0-5
WELL, DUH.
US NEW KIDS HAVE NEVER PLAYED TOGETHER BEFORE TODAY.
COOPERATION ISN'T GONNA BE A THING.

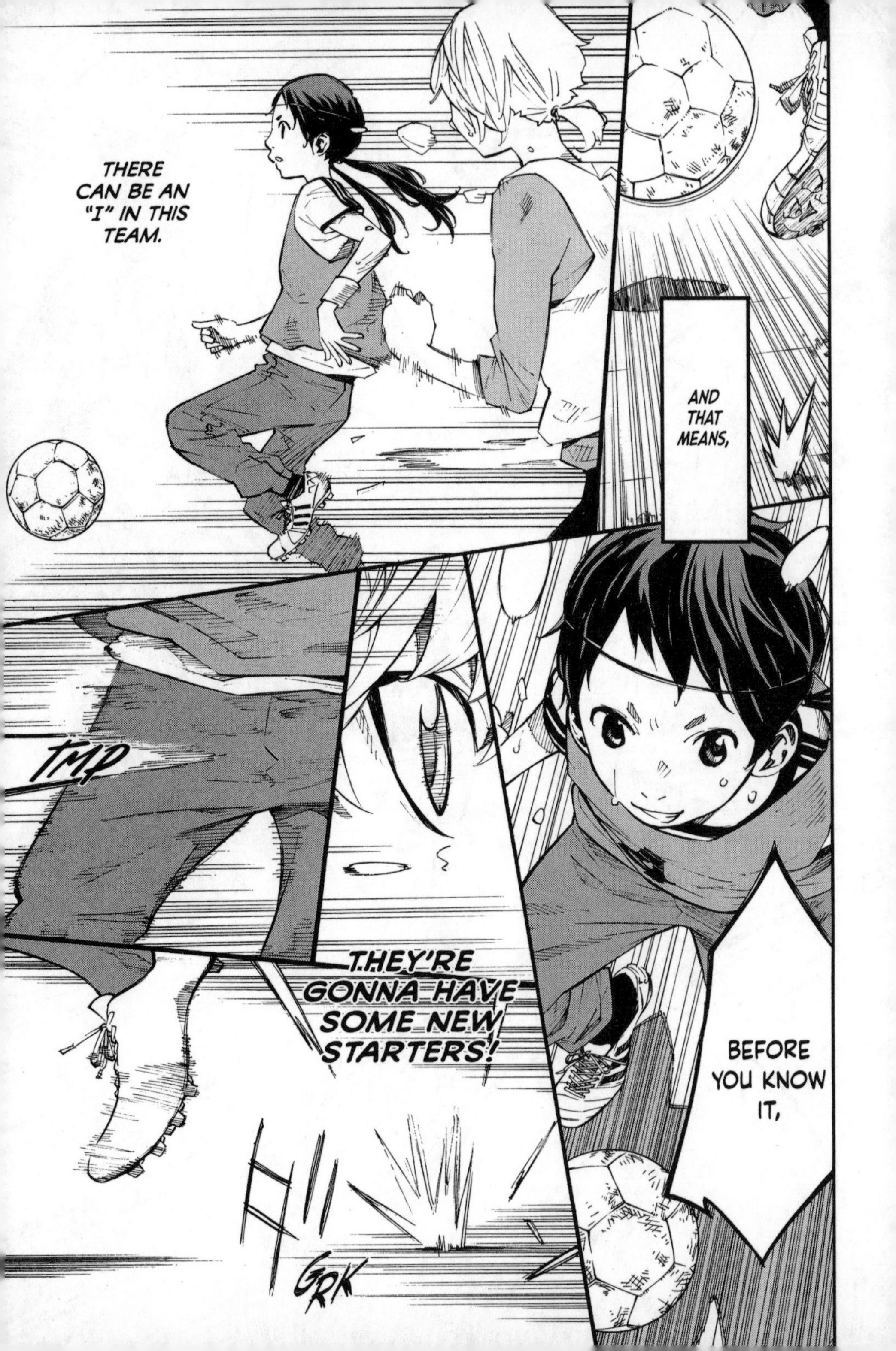
THERE CAN BE AN "I" IN THIS TEAM.
AND THAT MEANS,
BEFORE YOU KNOW IT,
THEY'RE GONNA HAVE SOME NEW STARTERS!
TMP
GRK

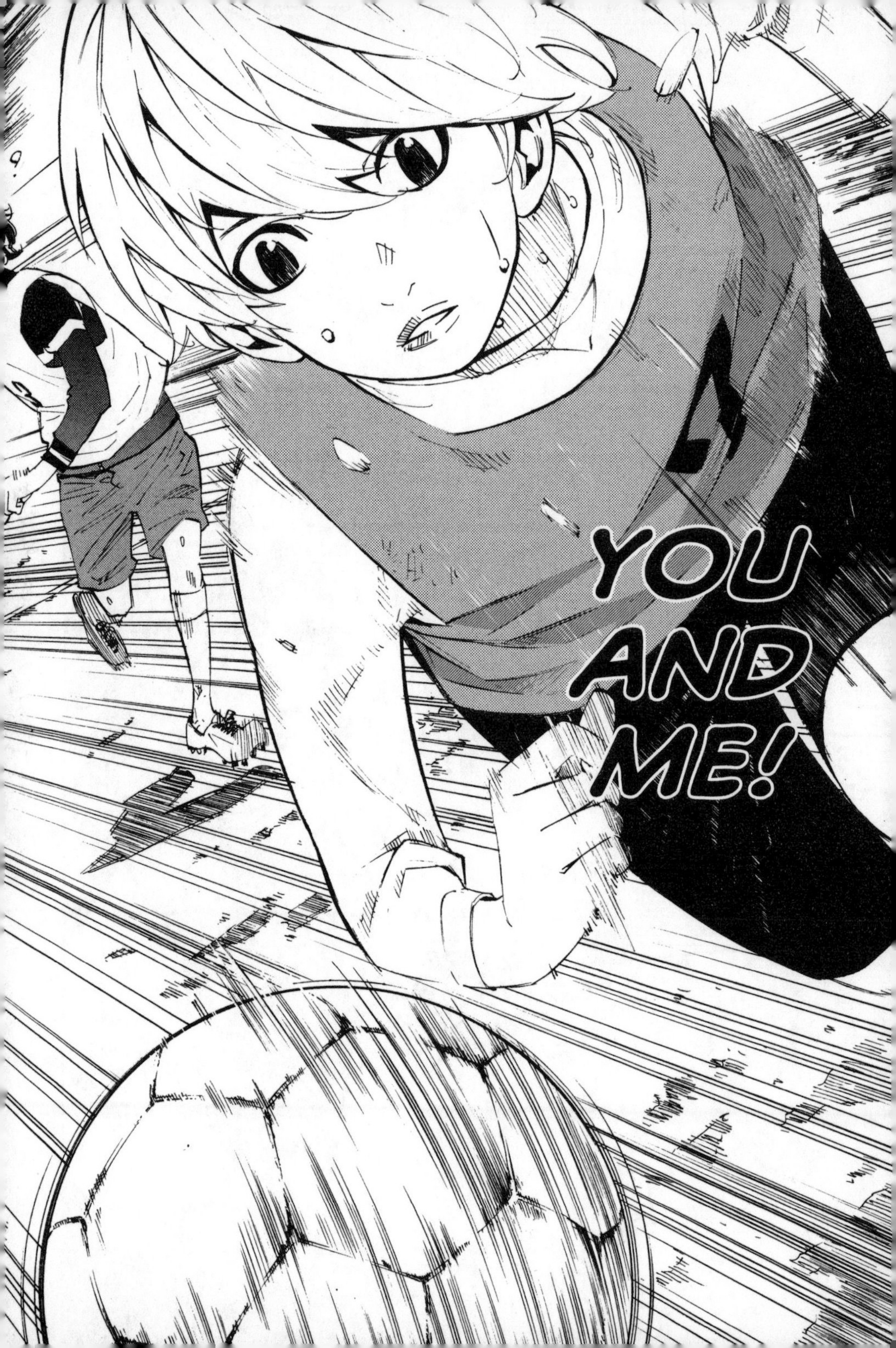
YOU AND ME!

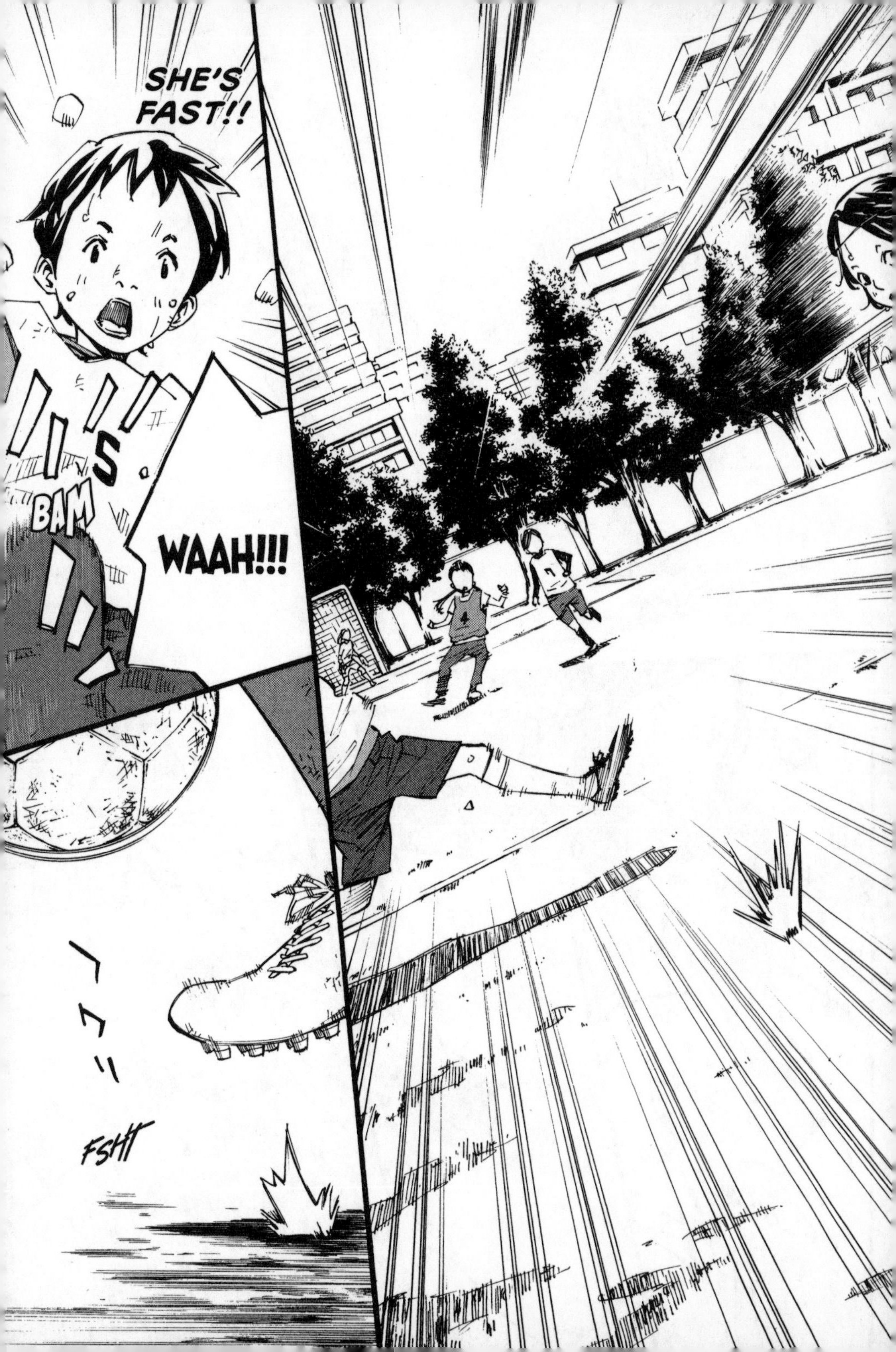
SHE'S FAST!!
WAAH!!!
BAM
FSHT

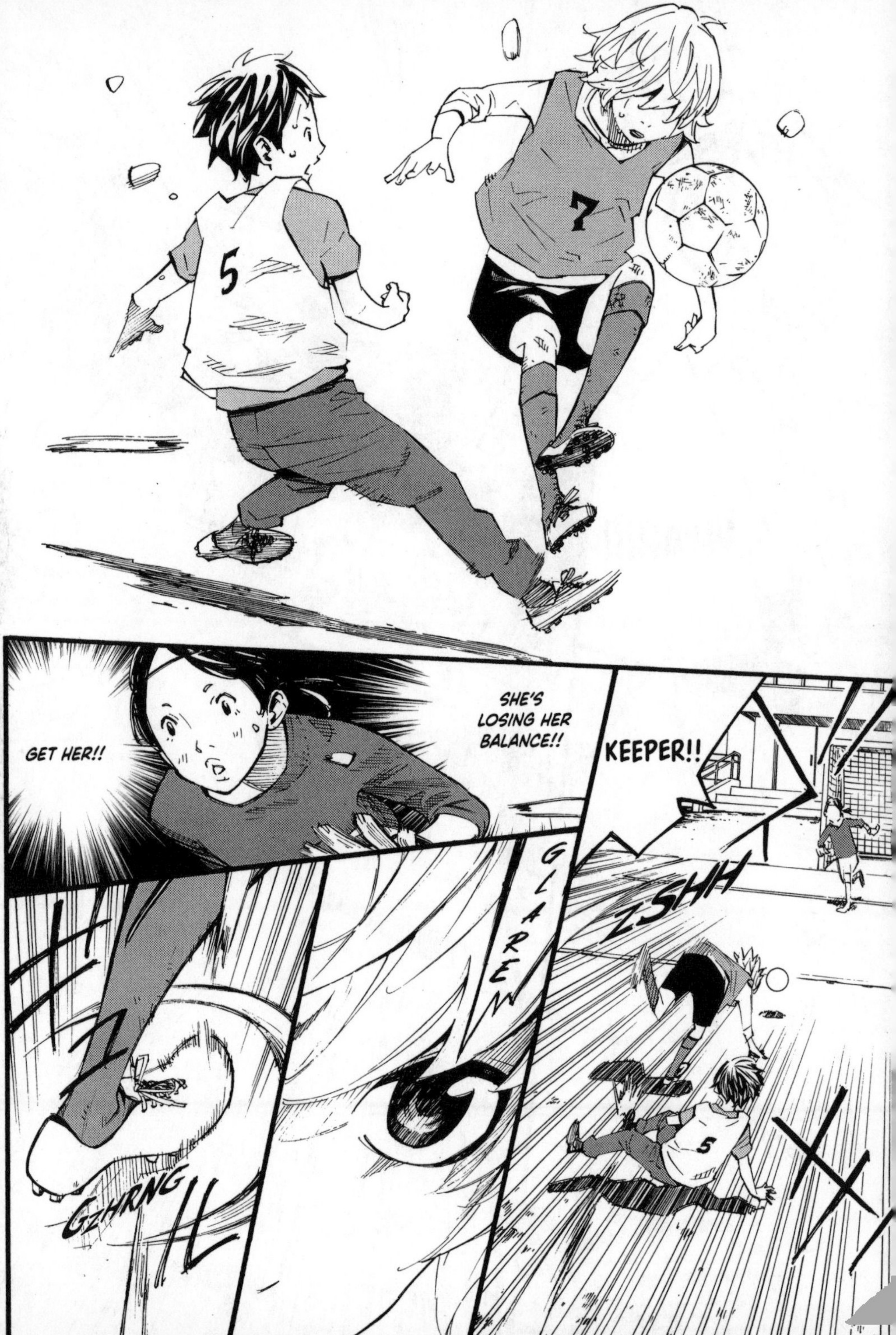
KEEPER!!
SHE'S LOSING HER BALANCE!!
GET HER!!
ZSHH
GLARE
GZHRNG

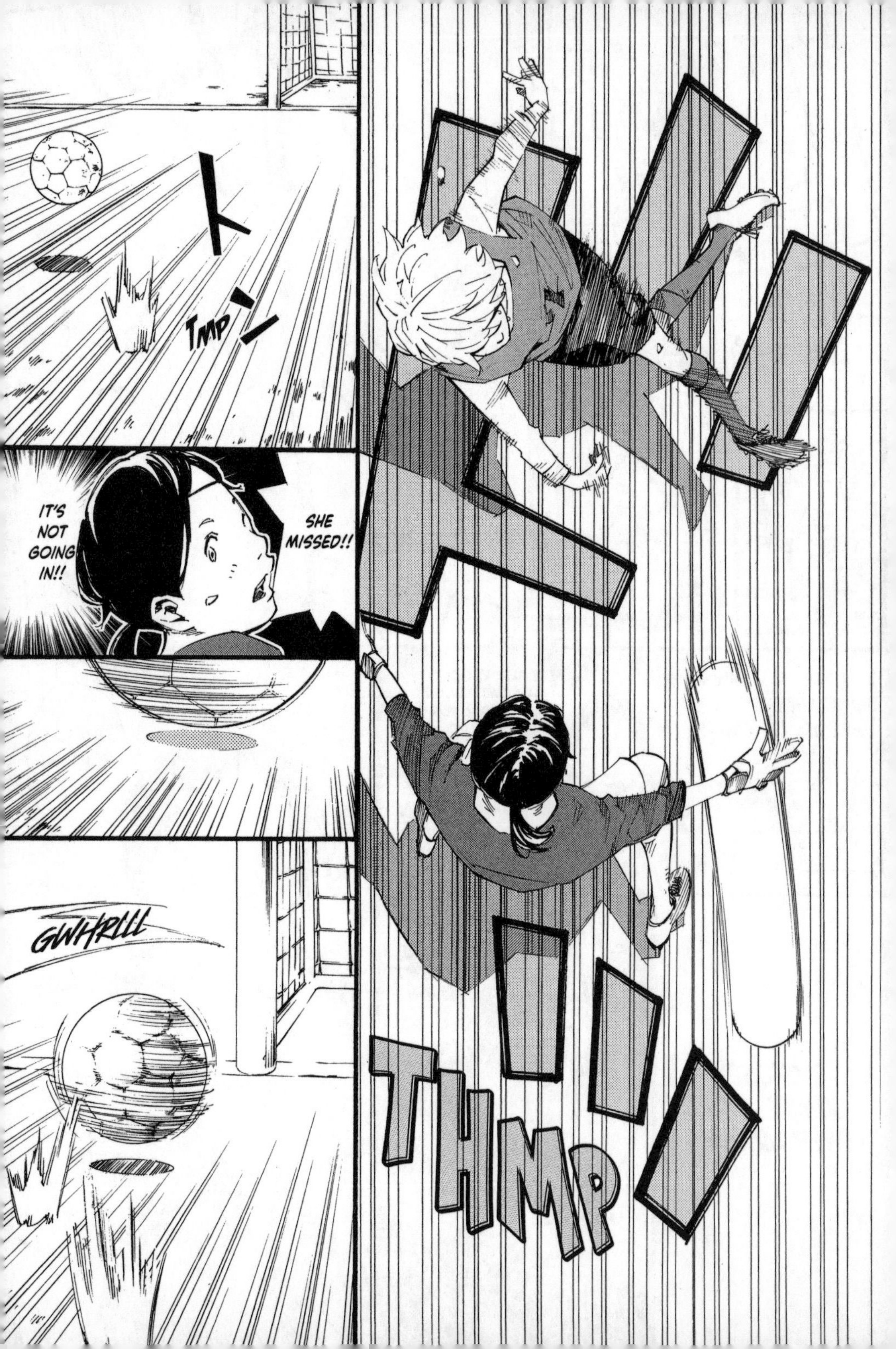
THMP
TMP
SHE MISSED!!
IT'S NOT GOING IN!!
GWHRLLL

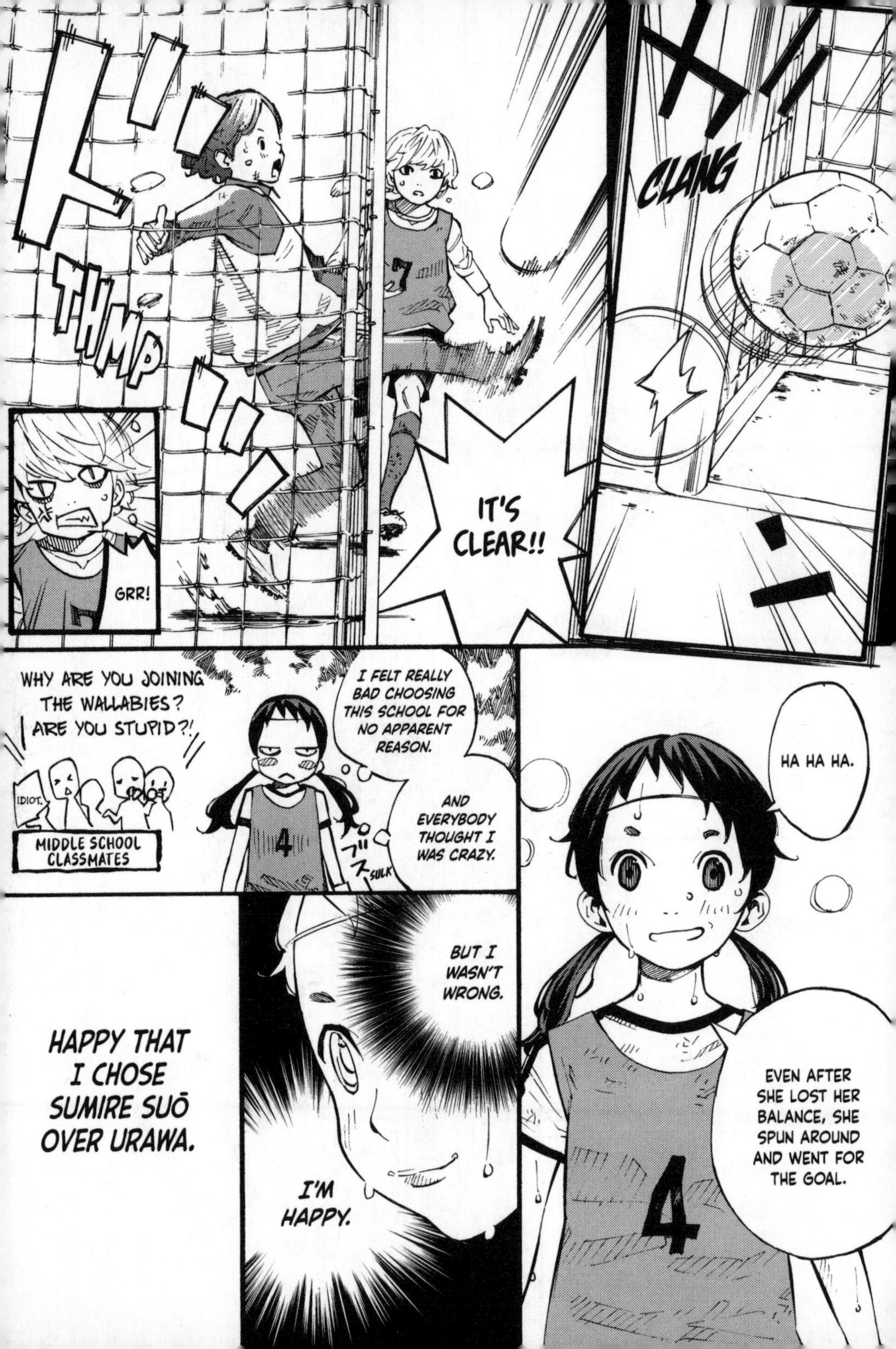
CLANG
IT'S CLEAR!!
THMP
GRR!
HA HA HA.
EVEN AFTER SHE LOST HER BALANCE, SHE SPUN AROUND AND WENT FOR THE GOAL.
I FELT REALLY BAD CHOOSING THIS SCHOOL FOR NO APPARENT REASON.
AND EVERYBODY THOUGHT I WAS CRAZY.
SULK
WHY ARE YOU JOINING THE WALLABIES? ARE YOU STUPID?!
IDIOT.
IDIOT
MIDDLE SCHOOL CLASSMATES
BUT I WASN'T WRONG.
I'M HAPPY.
HAPPY THAT I CHOSE SUMIRE SUŌ OVER URAWA.

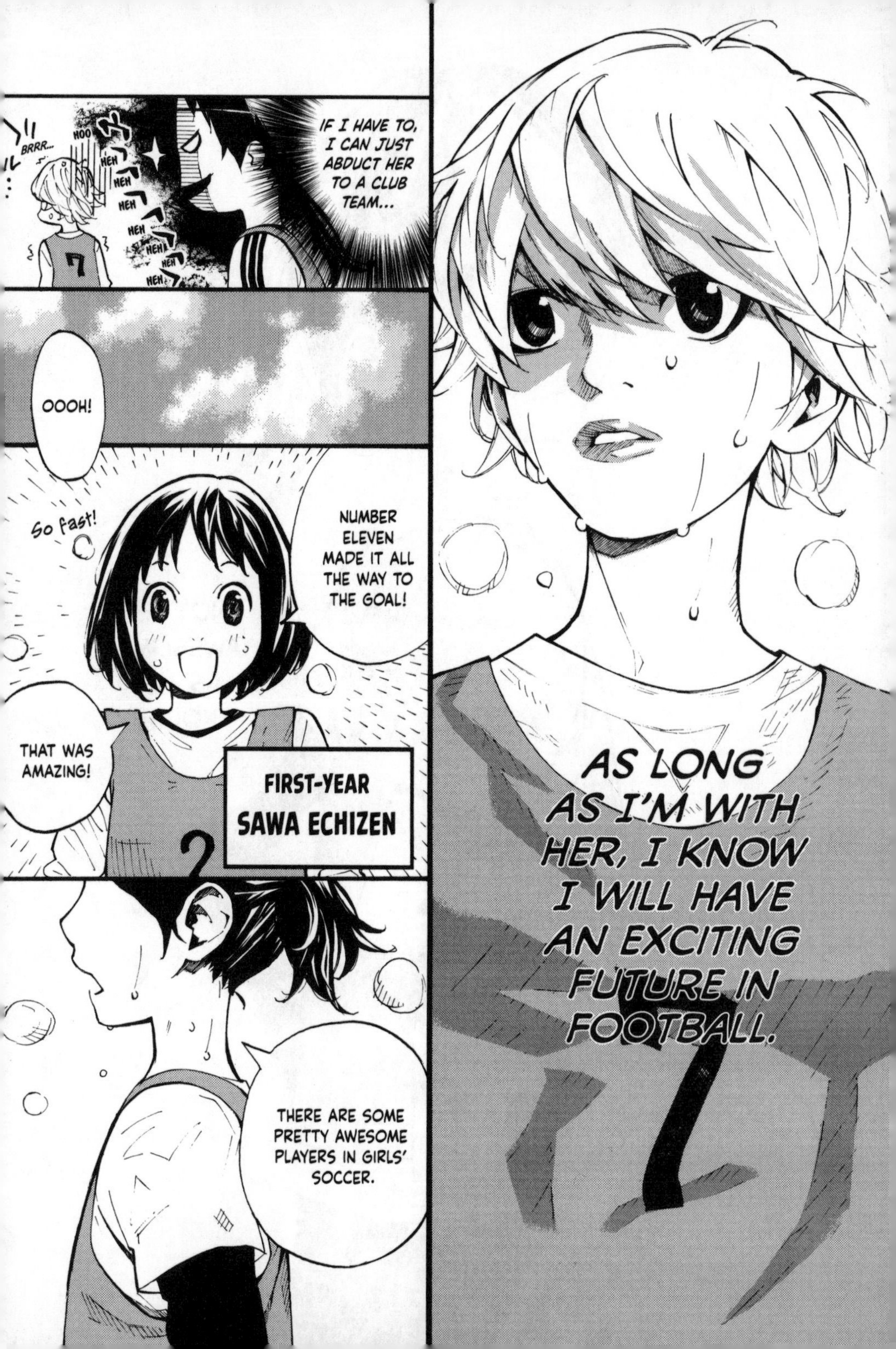
AS LONG AS I'M WITH HER, I KNOW I WILL HAVE AN EXCITING FUTURE IN FOOTBALL.
IF I HAVE TO, I CAN JUST ABDUCT HER TO A CLUB TEAM...
HOO
HEH HEH HEH HEH HEH HEH HEH
BRRR..
OOOH!
NUMBER ELEVEN MADE IT ALL THE WAY TO THE GOAL!
So fast!
THAT WAS AMAZING!
FIRST-YEAR SAWA ECHIZEN
THERE ARE SOME PRETTY AWESOME PLAYERS IN GIRLS' SOCCER.

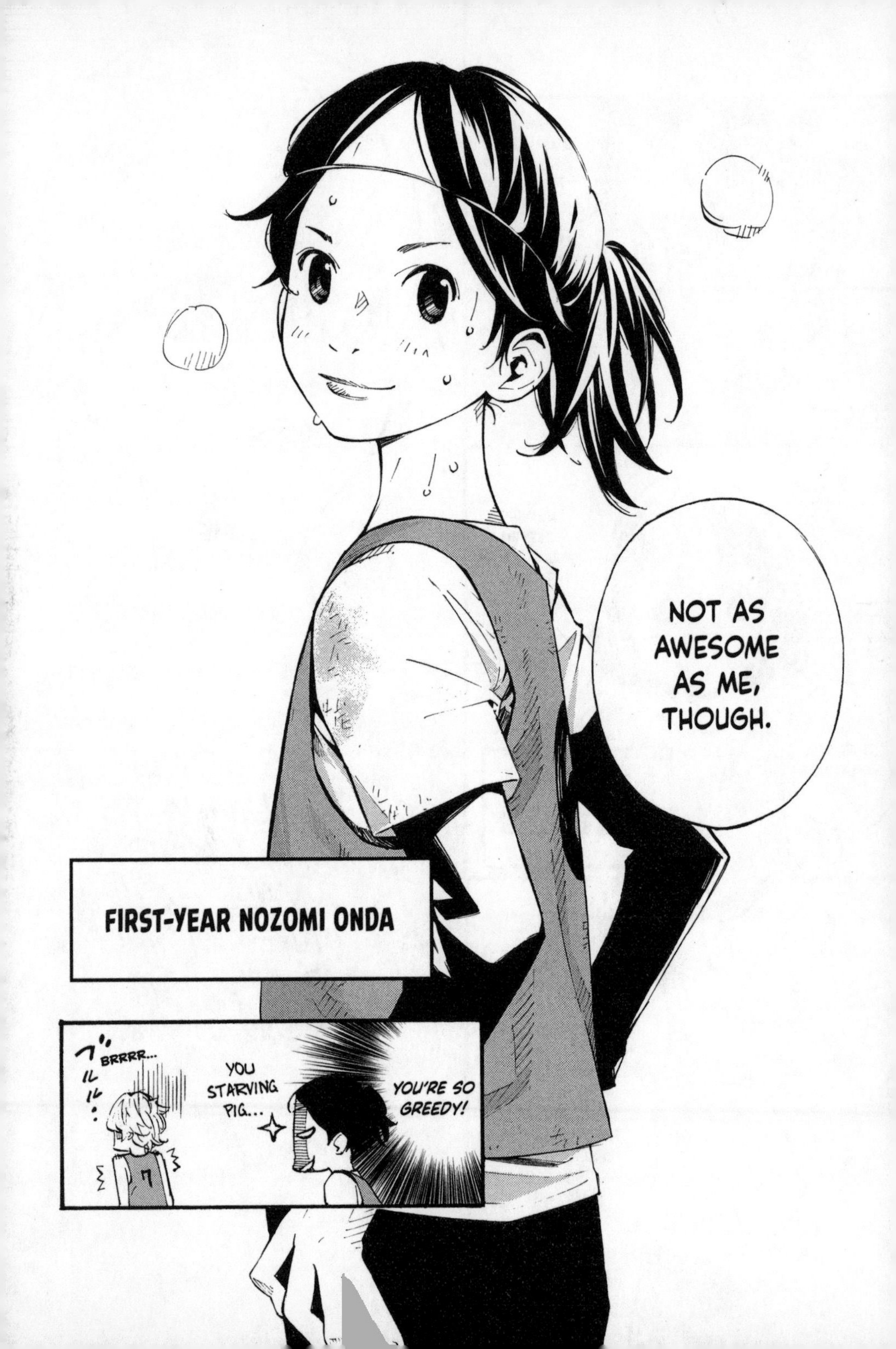
NOT AS AWESOME AS ME, THOUGH.
FIRST-YEAR NOZOMI ONDA
YOU'RE SO GREEDY!
YOU STARVING PIG...
ブルル‥
BRRRR...

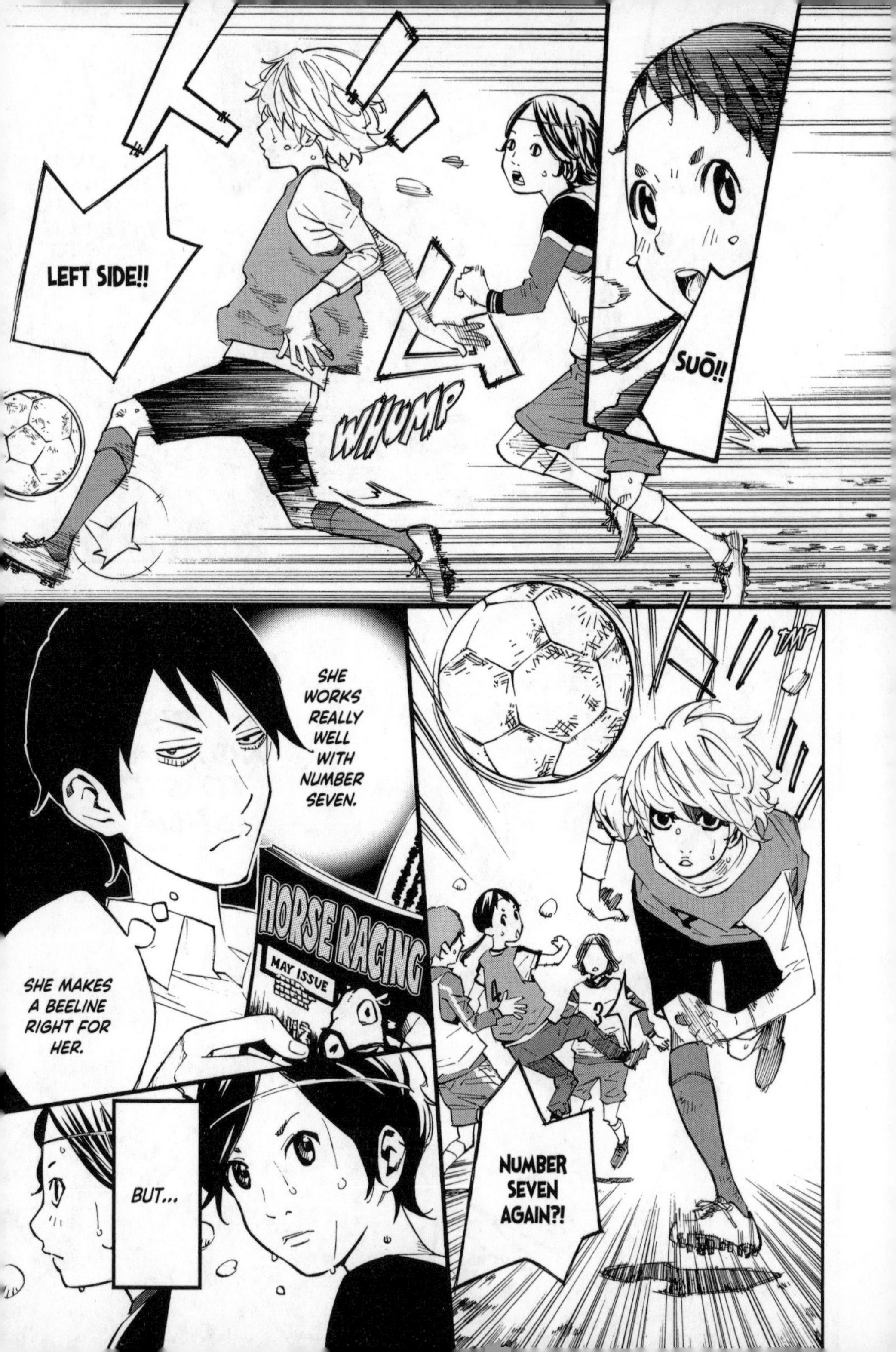
SUŌ!!
LEFT SIDE!!
WHUMP
TMP
NUMBER SEVEN AGAIN?!
SHE WORKS REALLY WELL WITH NUMBER SEVEN.
SHE MAKES A BEELINE RIGHT FOR HER.
HORSE RACING
MAY ISSUE
BUT...

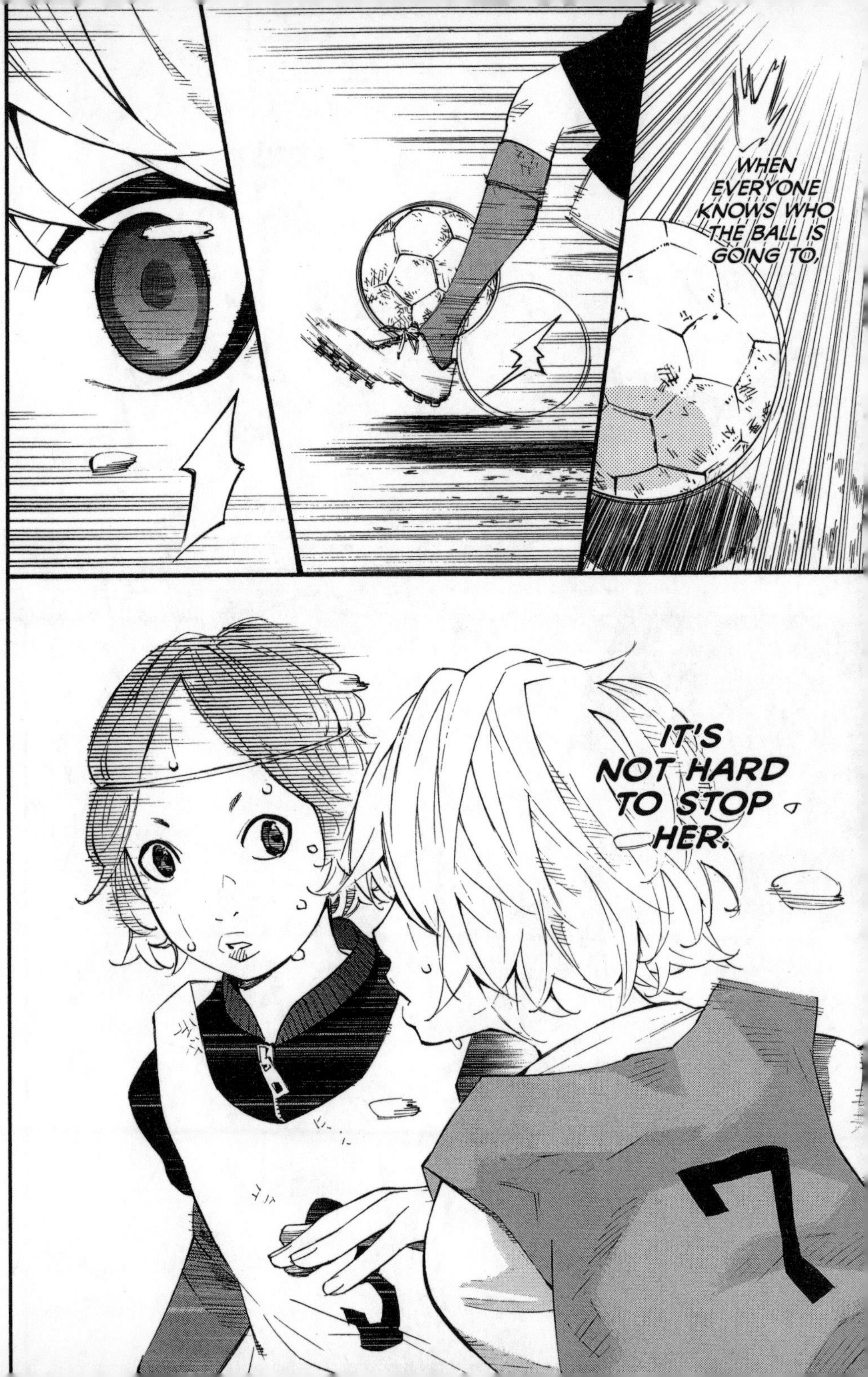
WHEN EVERYONE KNOWS WHO THE BALL IS GOING TO,
IT'S NOT HARD TO STOP HER.

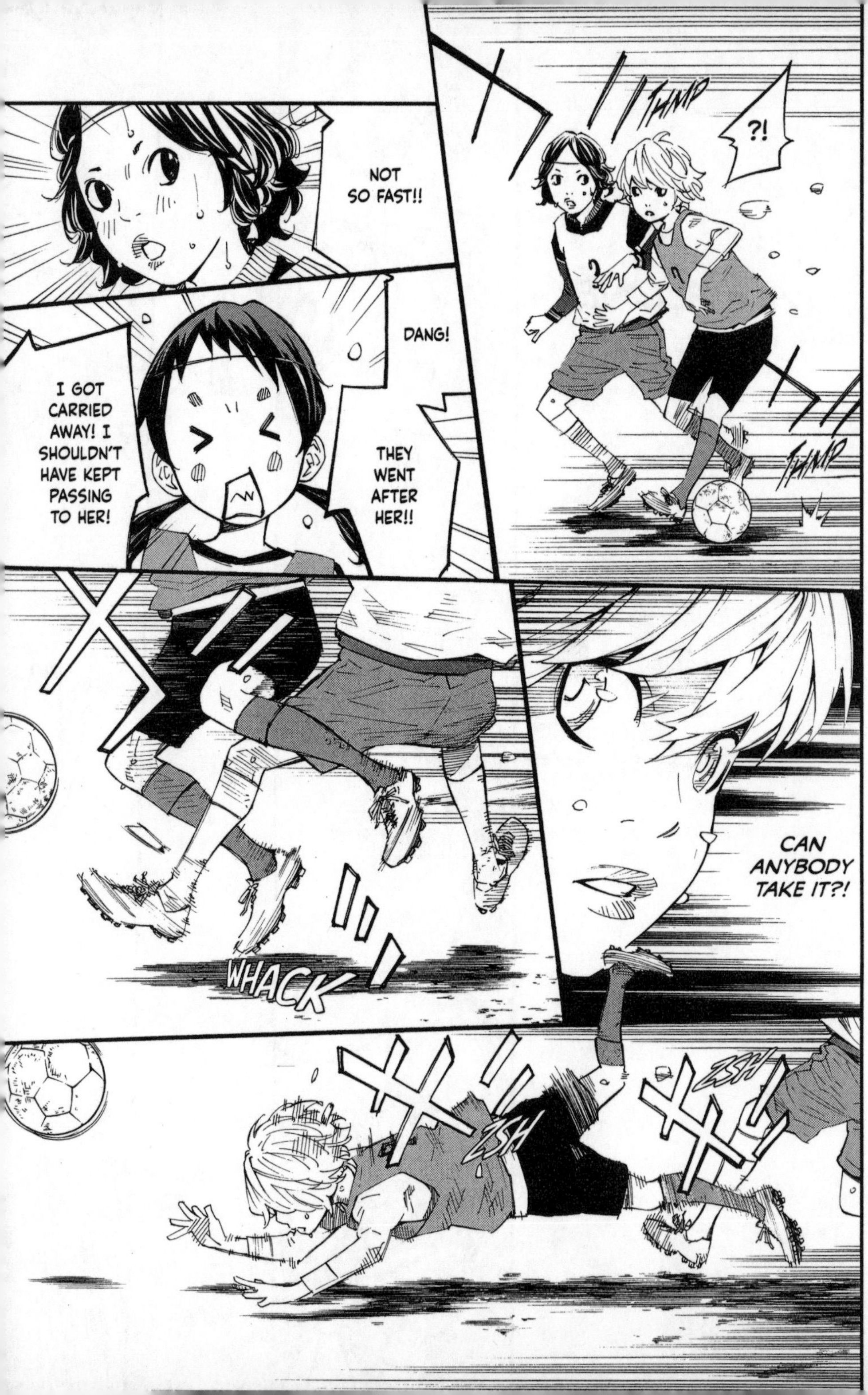
THMP
?!
THMP
NOT SO FAST!!
DANG!
THEY WENT AFTER HER!!
I GOT CARRIED AWAY! I SHOULDN'T HAVE KEPT PASSING TO HER!
CAN ANYBODY TAKE IT?!
WHACK
FSH
FSH

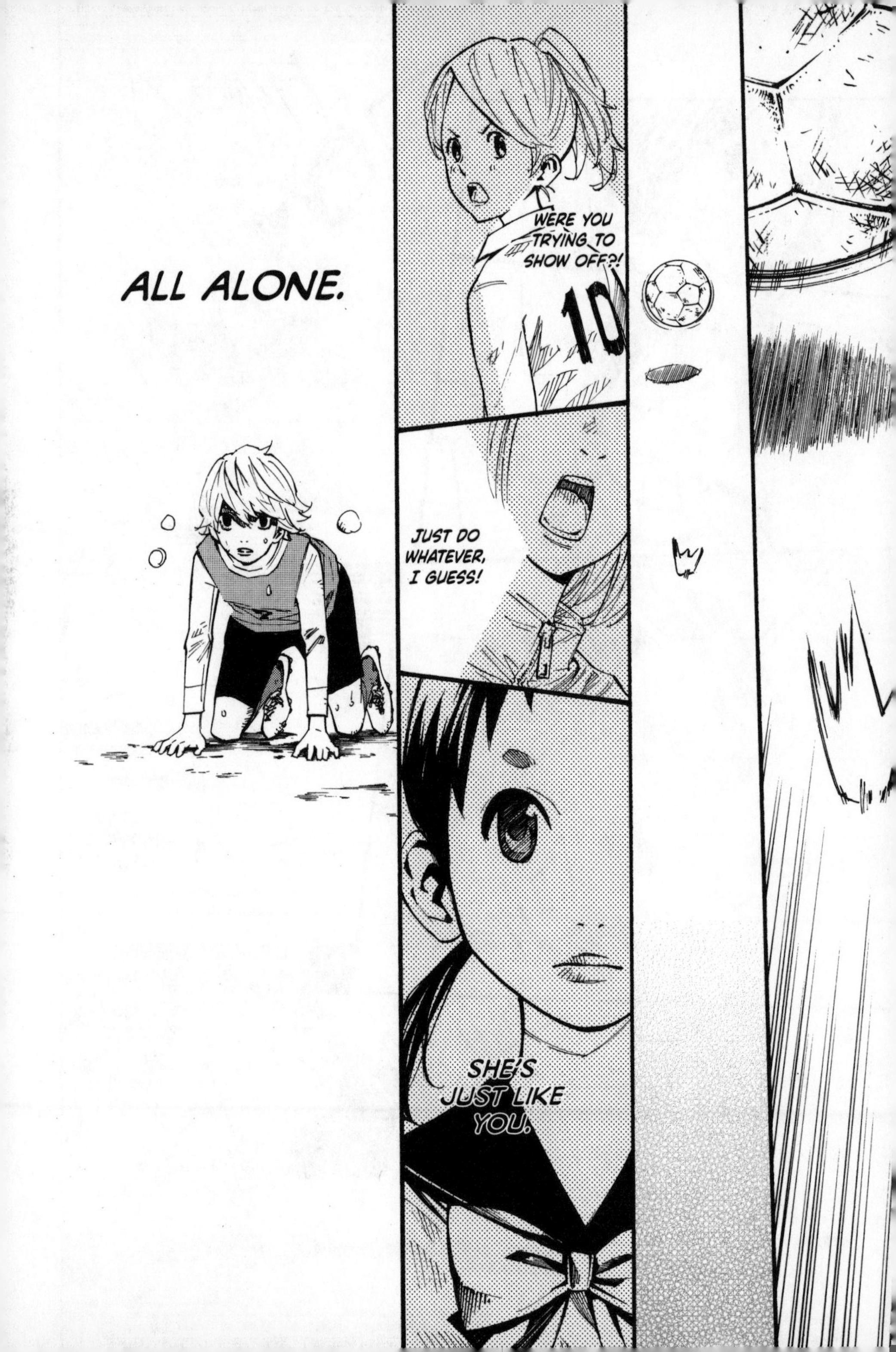
WERE YOU TRYING TO SHOW OFF?!
JUST DO WHATEVER, I GUESS!
SHE'S JUST LIKE YOU.
ALL ALONE.

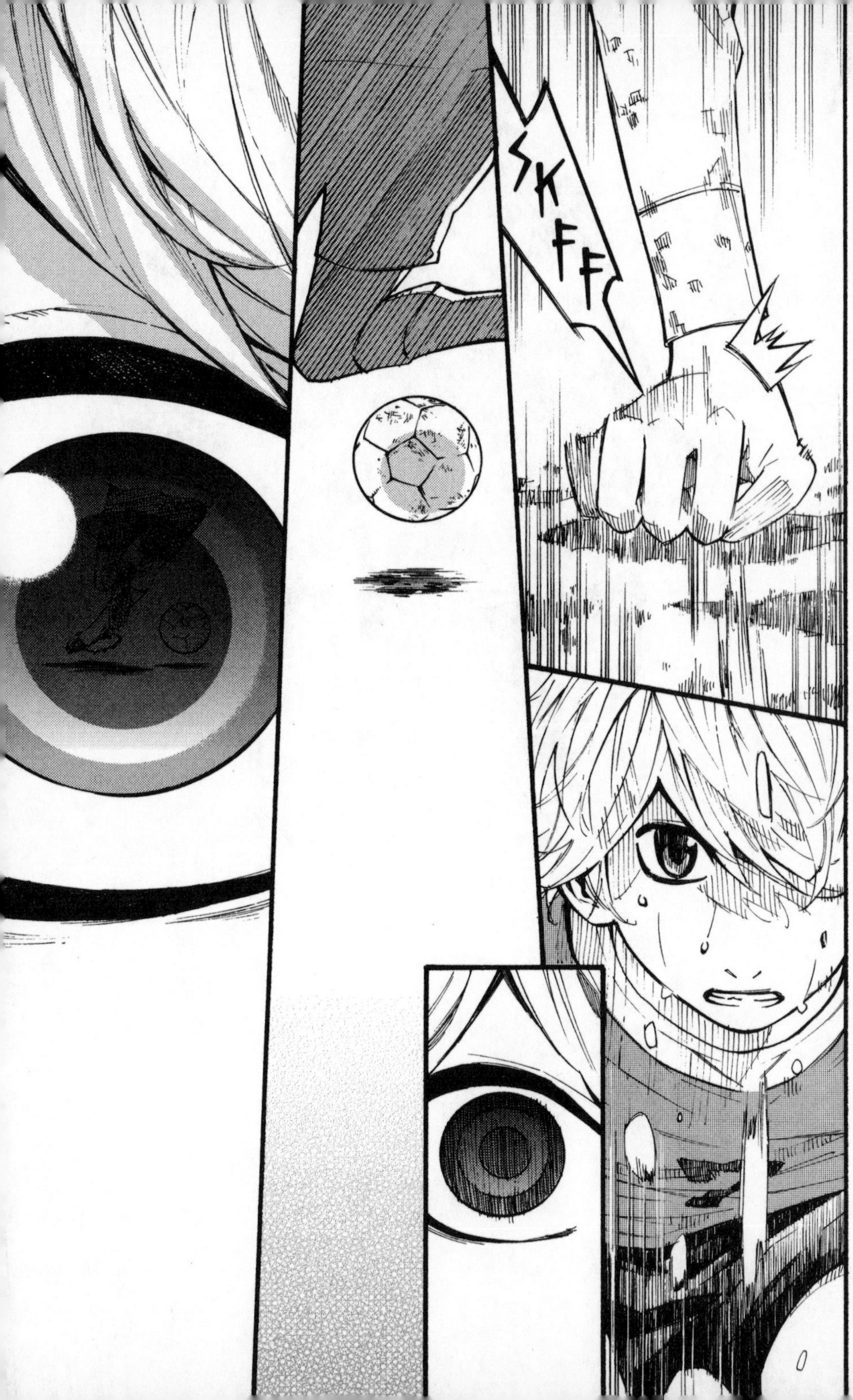
SKFF

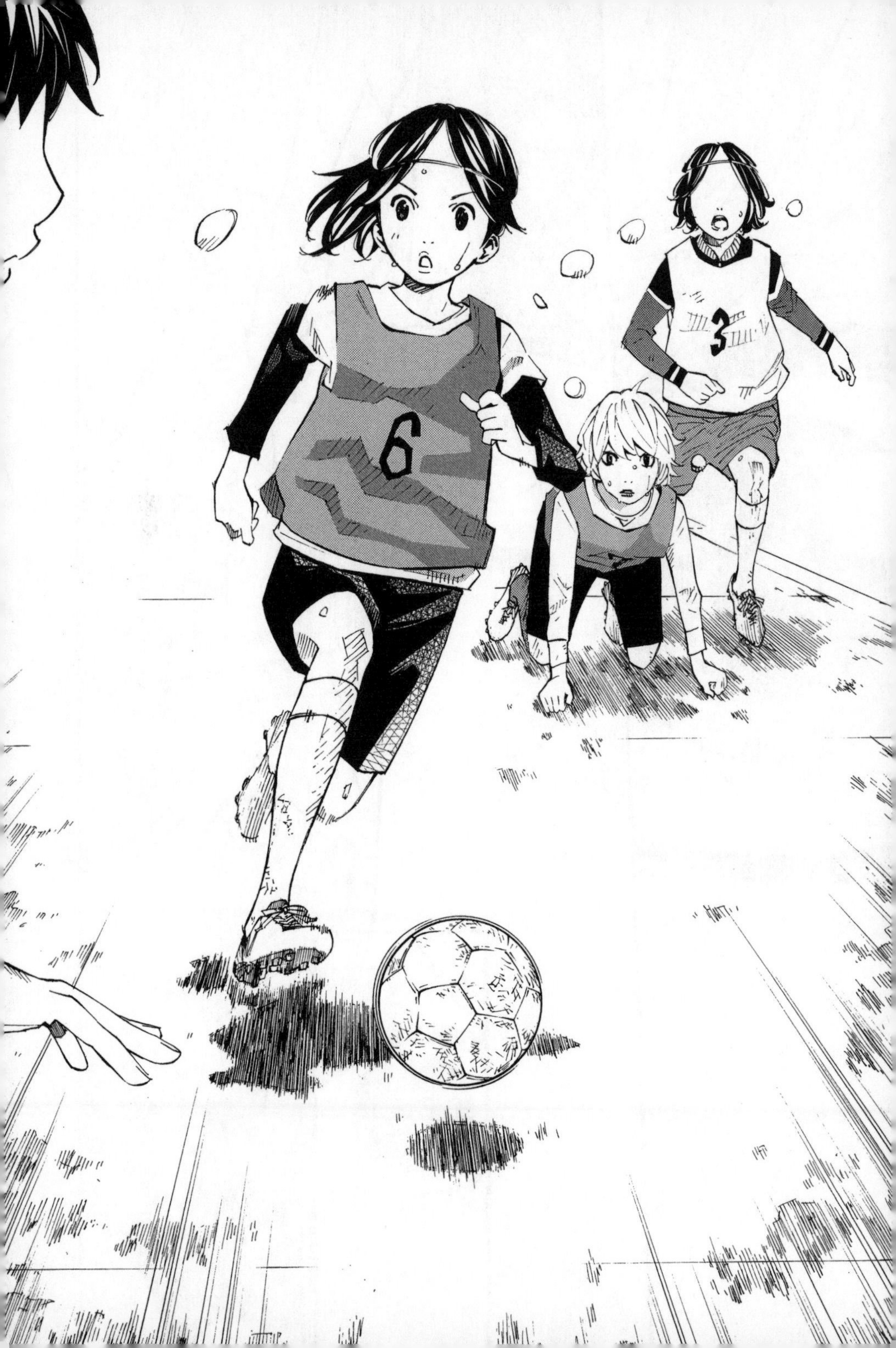

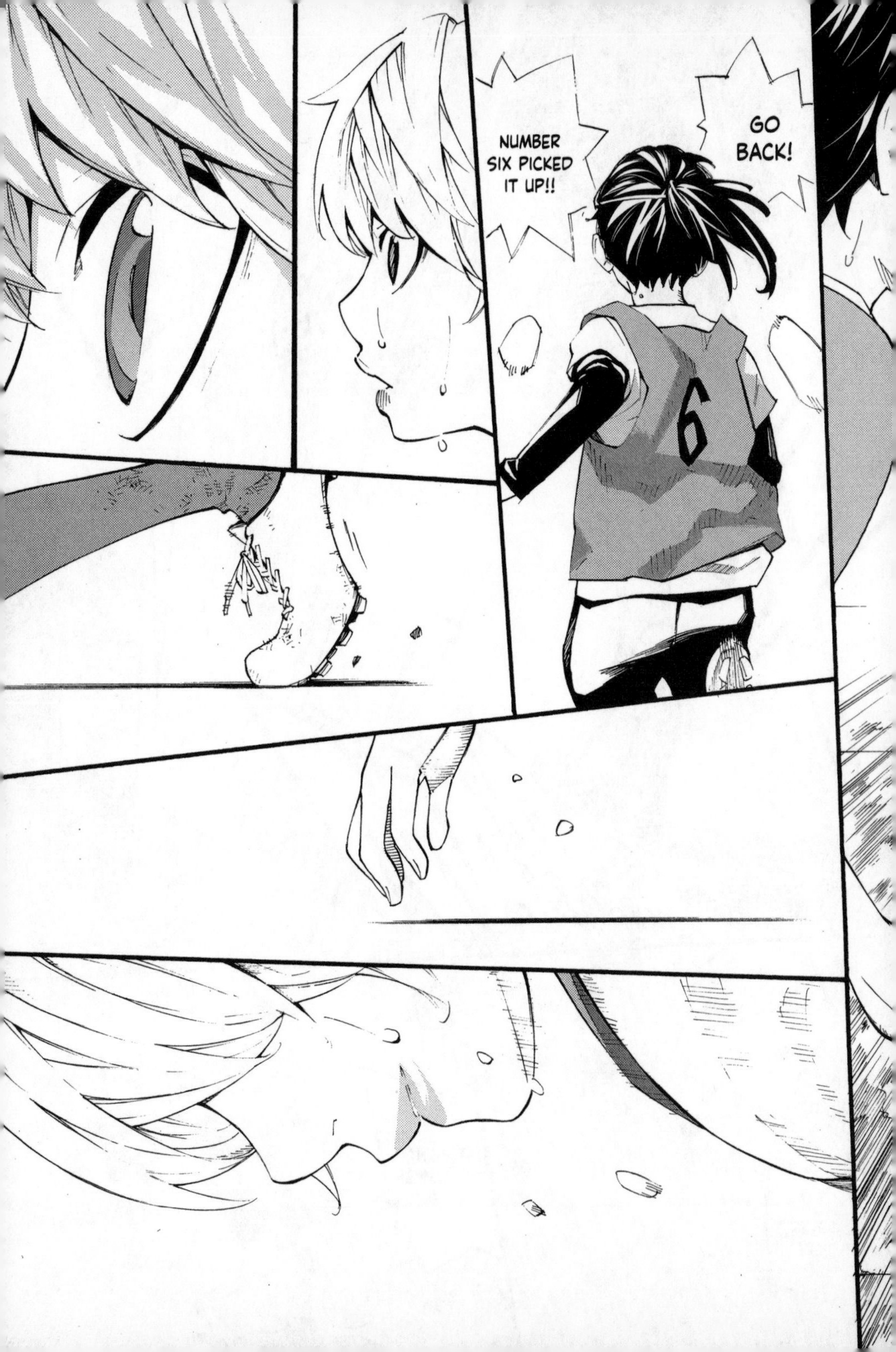
GO BACK!
NUMBER SIX PICKED IT UP!!

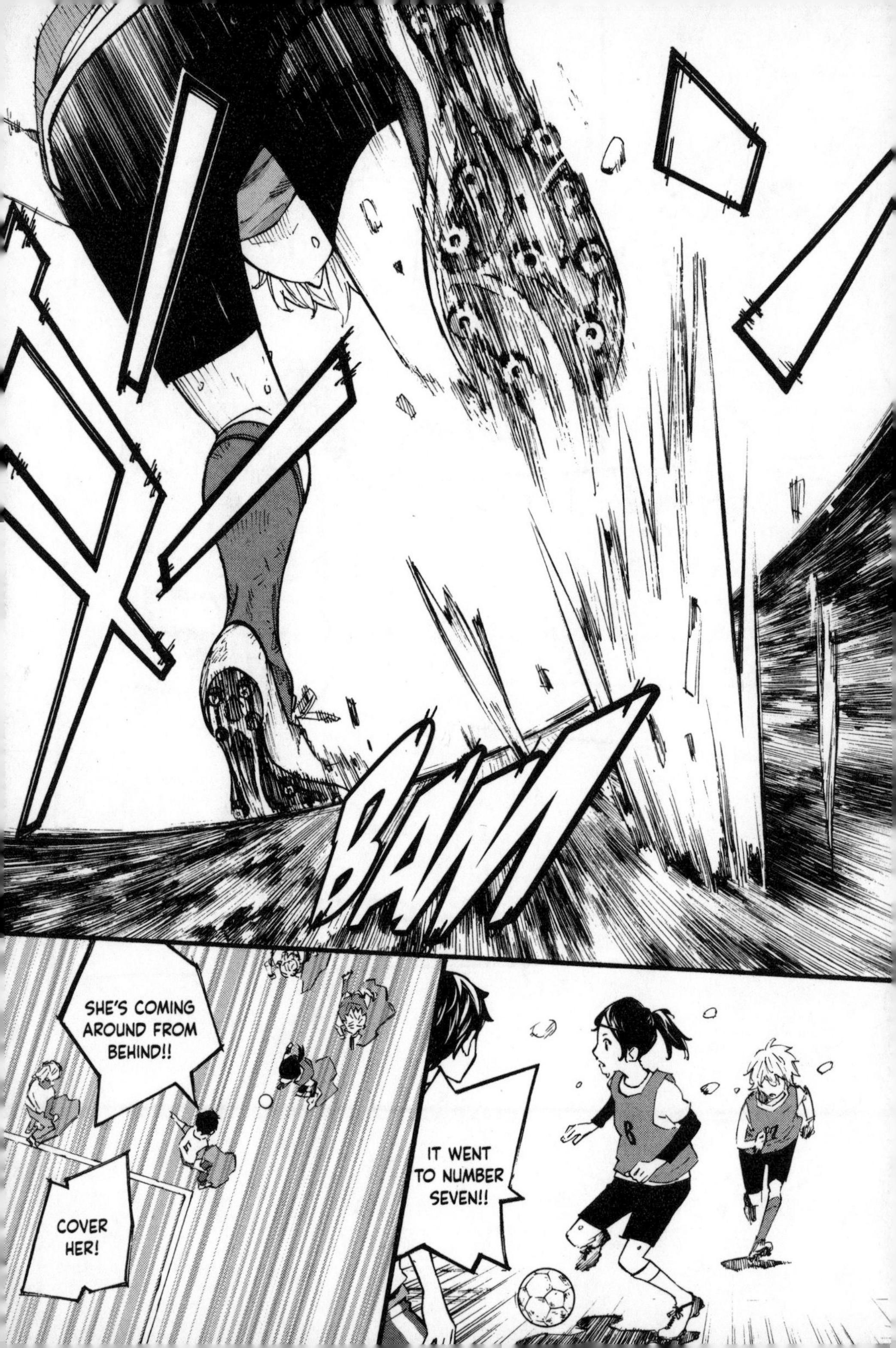
BAM
IT WENT TO NUMBER SEVEN!!
SHE'S COMING AROUND FROM BEHIND!!
COVER HER!

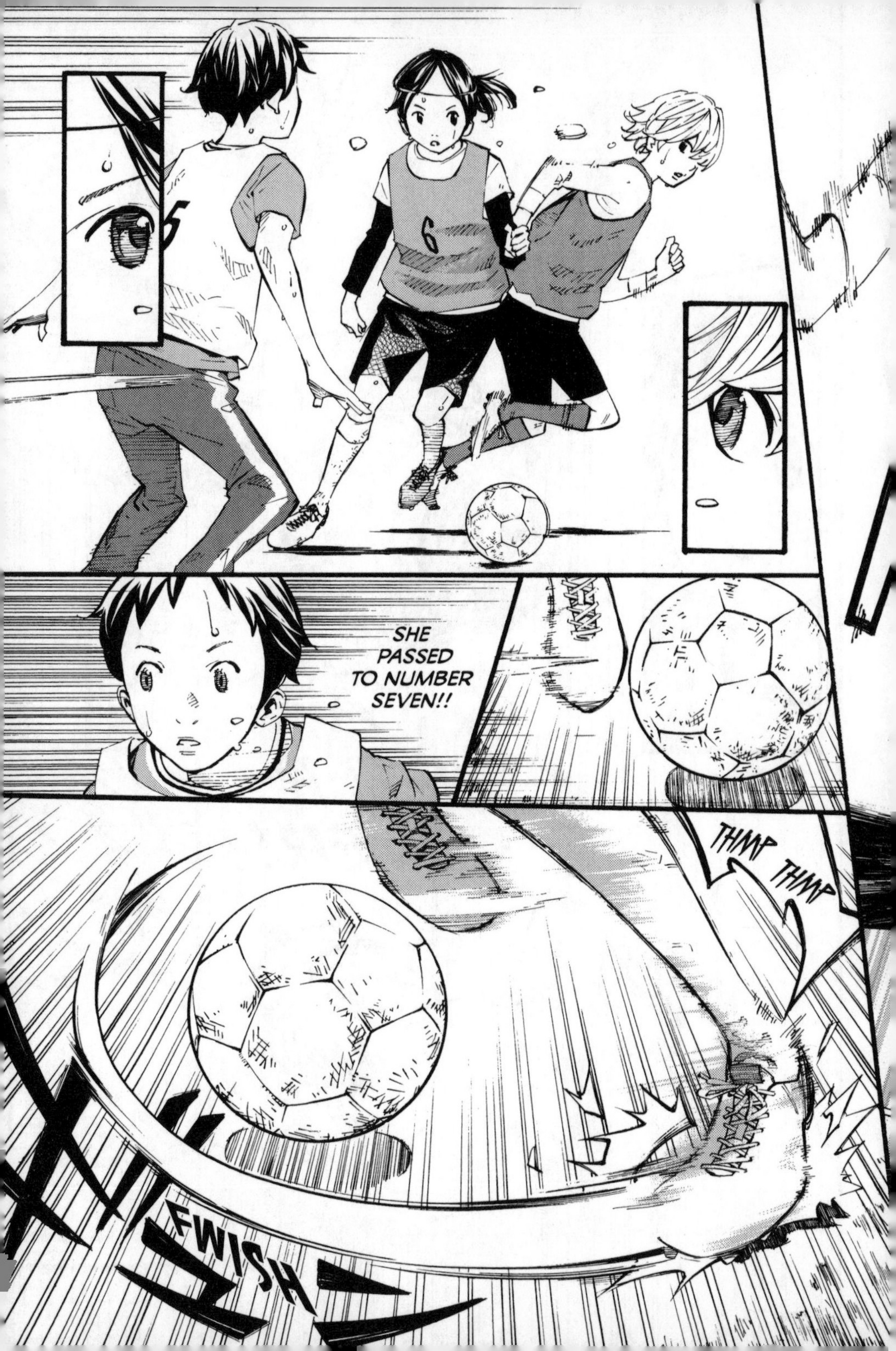
SHE PASSED TO NUMBER SEVEN!!
THMP THMP
FWISH

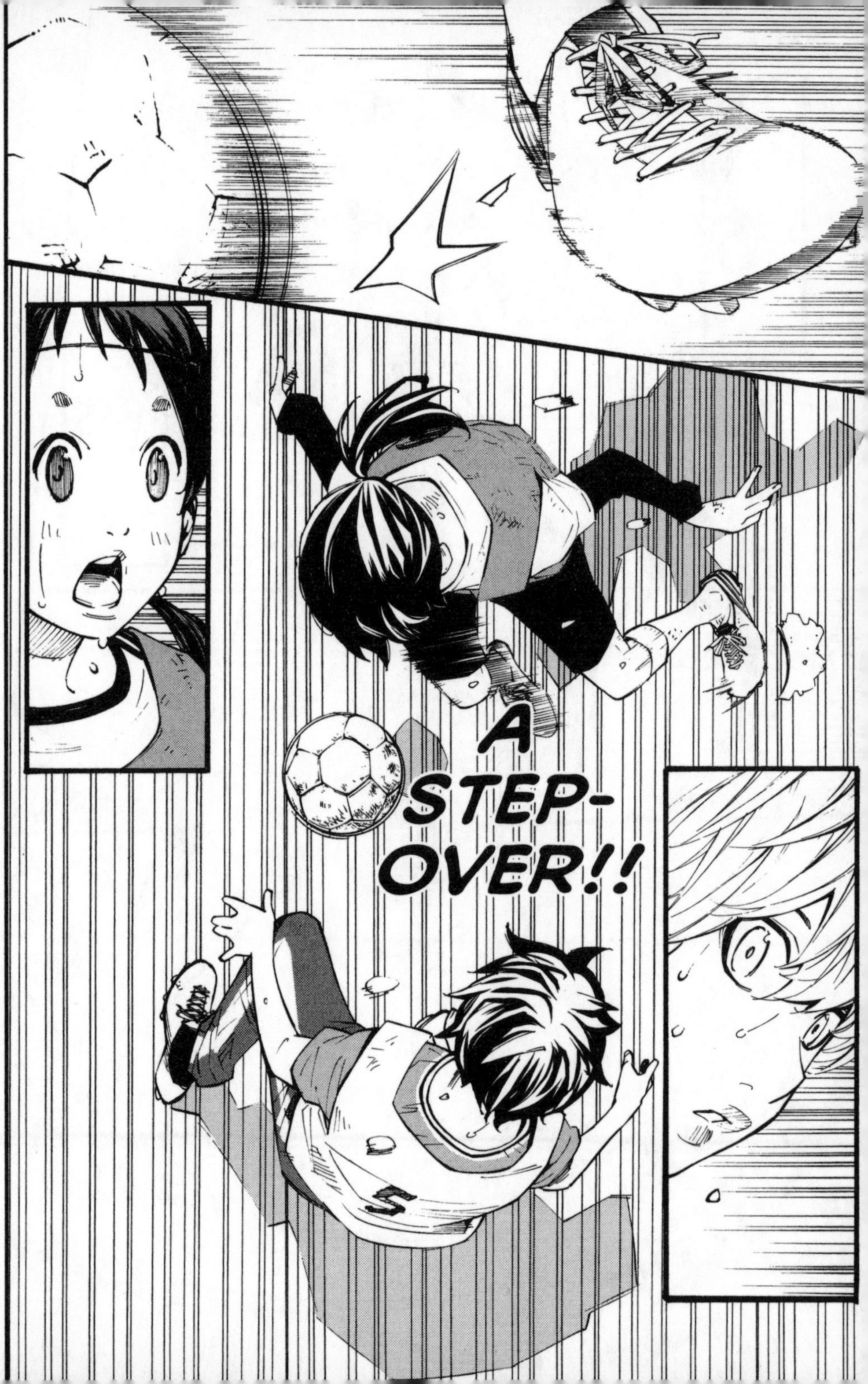
A STEP-OVER!!

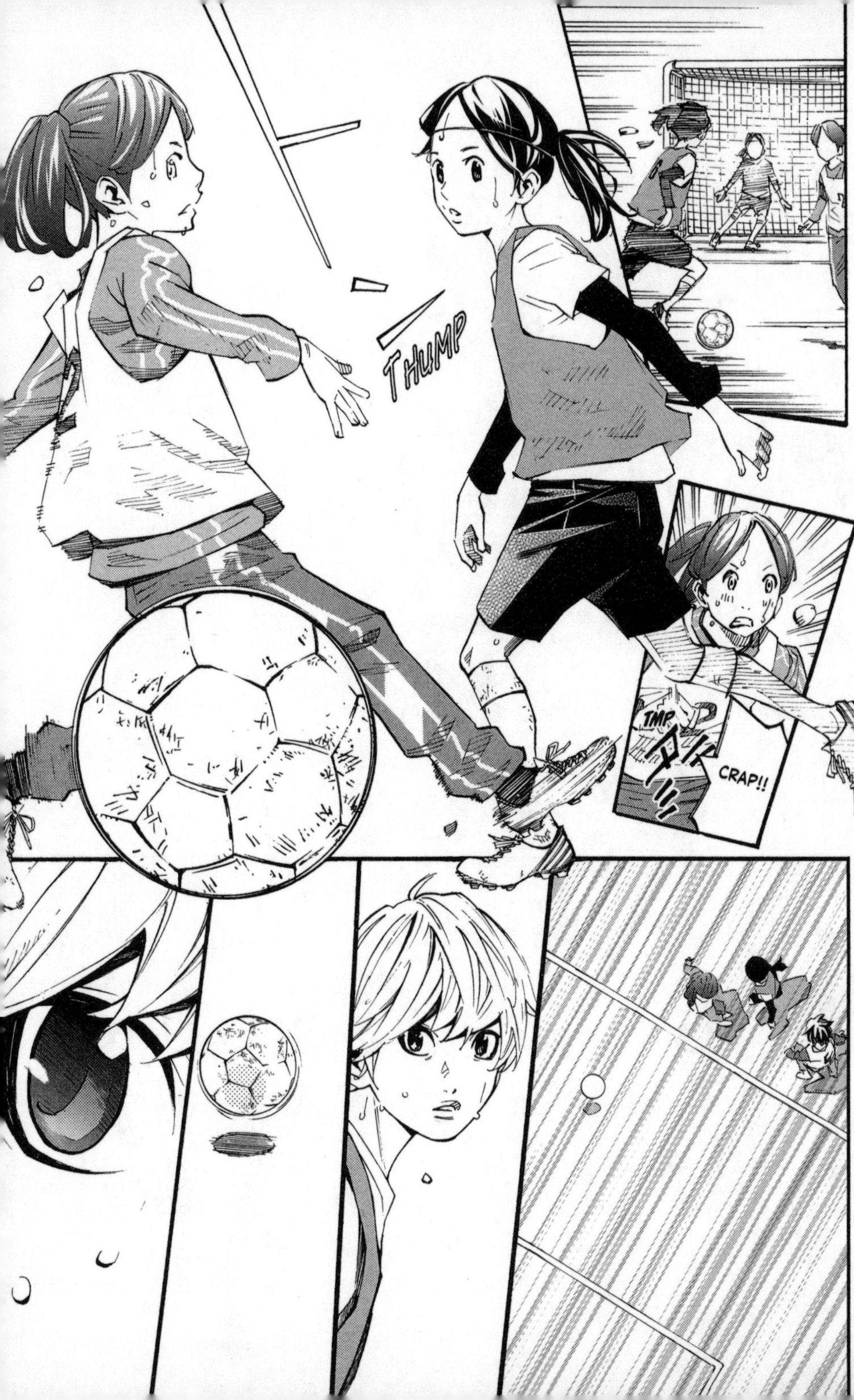
THUMP
TMP
CRAP!!

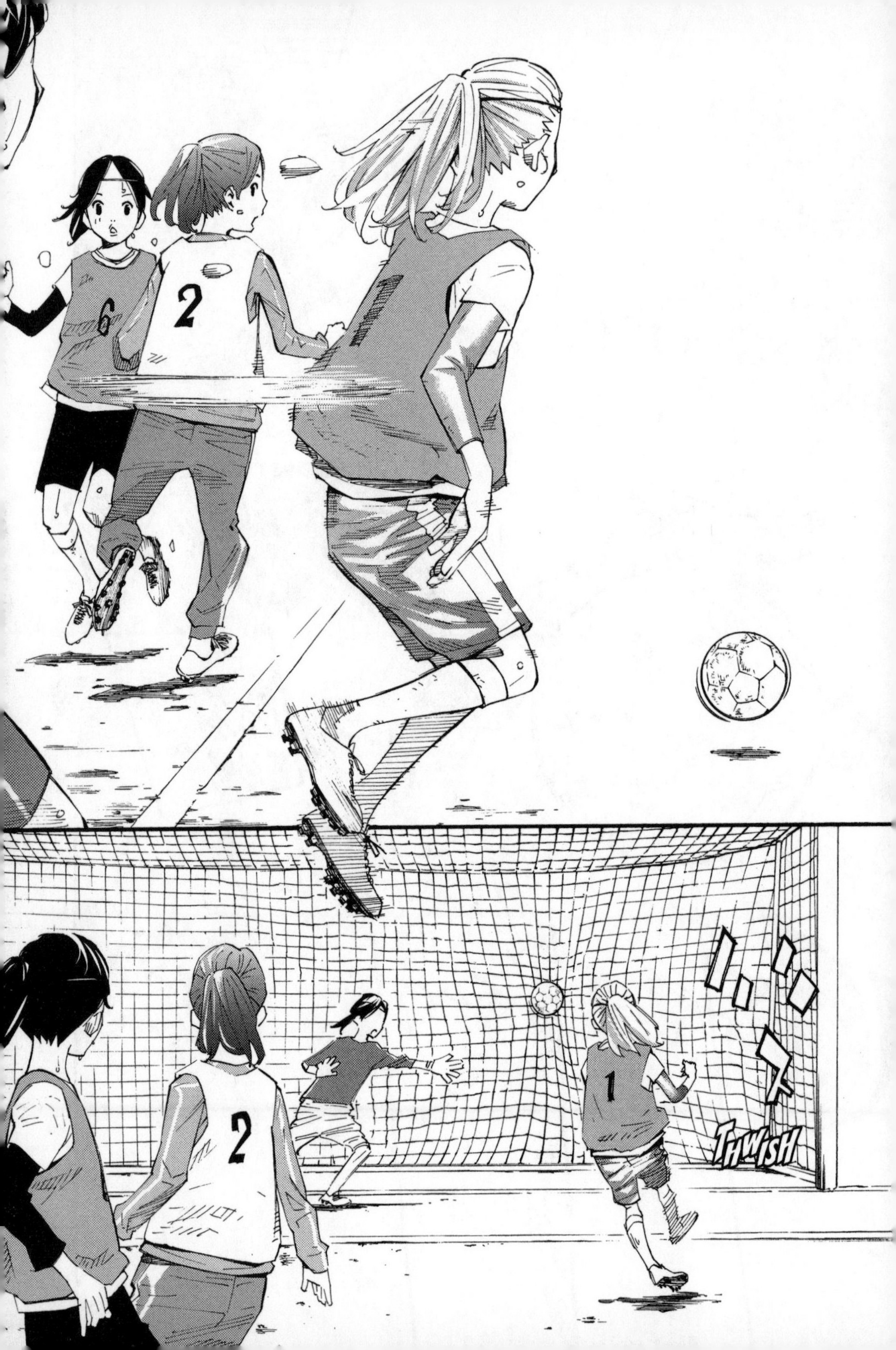
THWISH

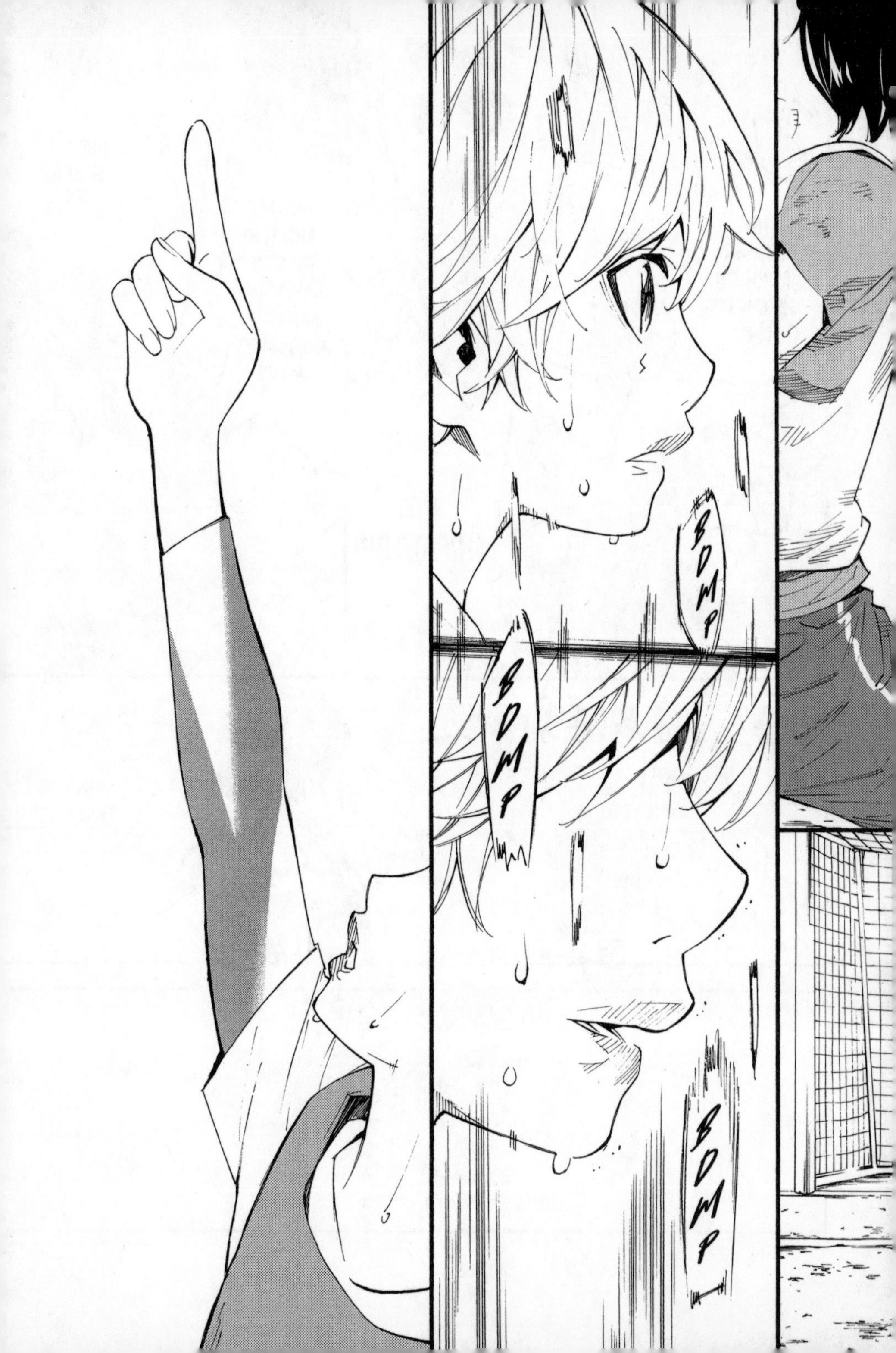
BDMP
BDMP
BDMP

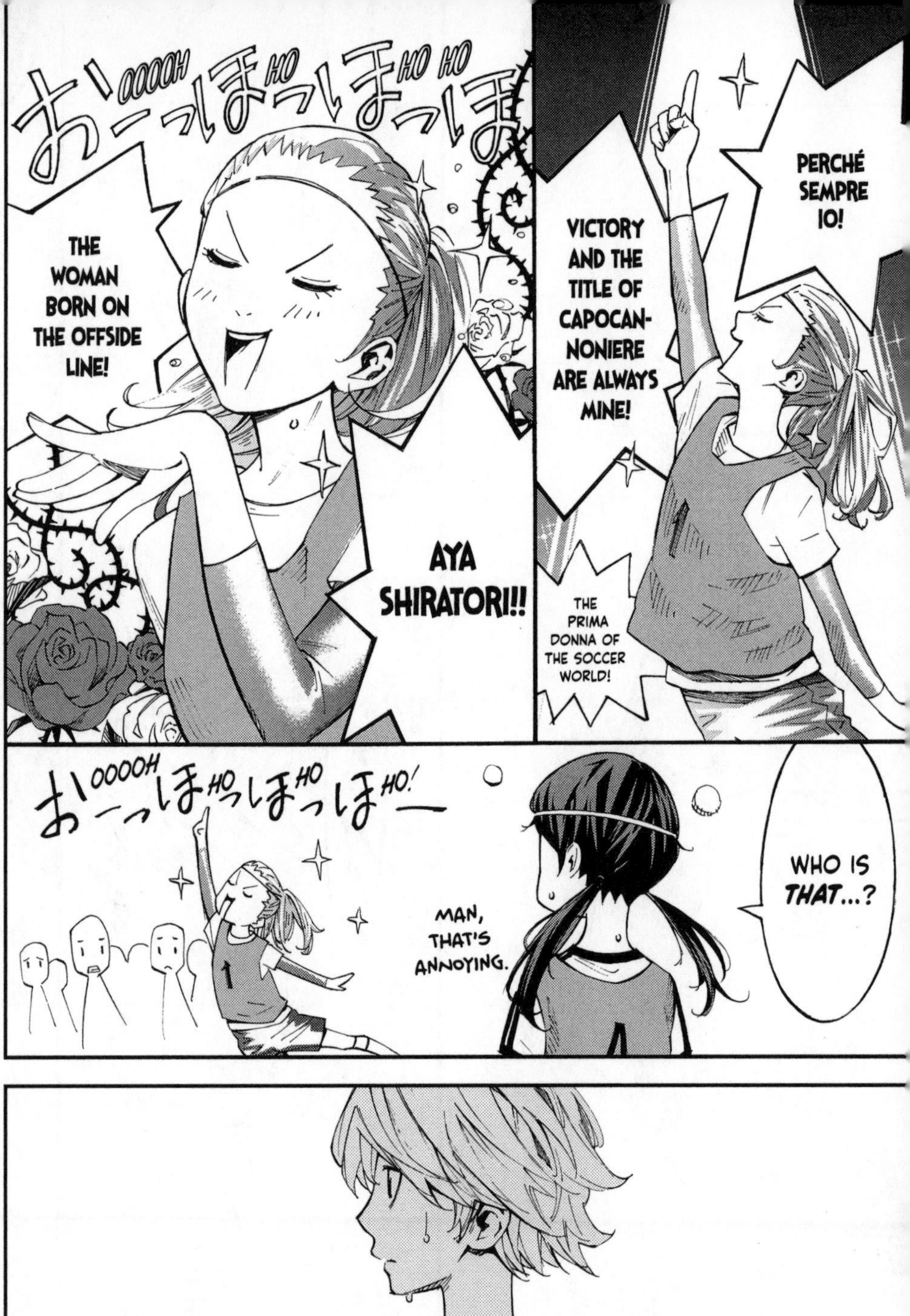
PERCHÉ SEMPRE IO!
VICTORY AND THE TITLE OF CAPOCAN-NONIERE ARE ALWAYS MINE!
THE PRIMA DONNA OF THE SOCCER WORLD!
おーっほっほっほ
OOOOH HO HO HO
THE WOMAN BORN ON THE OFFSIDE LINE!
AYA SHIRATORI!!
WHO IS *THAT*...?
MAN, THAT'S ANNOYING.
おーっほっほっほー
OOOOH HO HO HO!

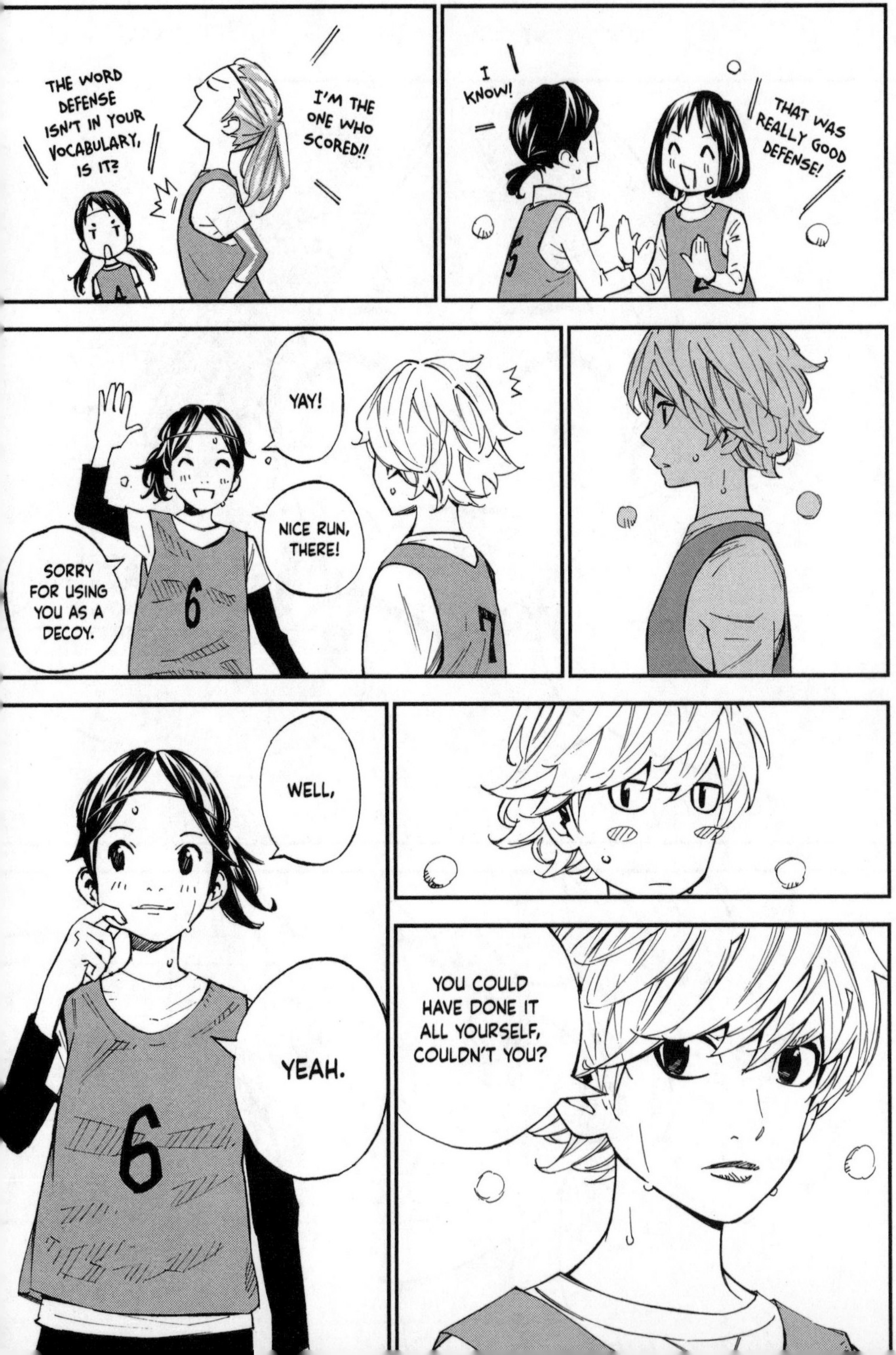
THAT WAS REALLY GOOD DEFENSE!
I KNOW!
I'M THE ONE WHO SCORED!!
THE WORD DEFENSE ISN'T IN YOUR VOCABULARY, IS IT?
YAY!
NICE RUN, THERE!
SORRY FOR USING YOU AS A DECOY.
YOU COULD HAVE DONE IT ALL YOURSELF, COULDN'T YOU?
WELL,
YEAH.

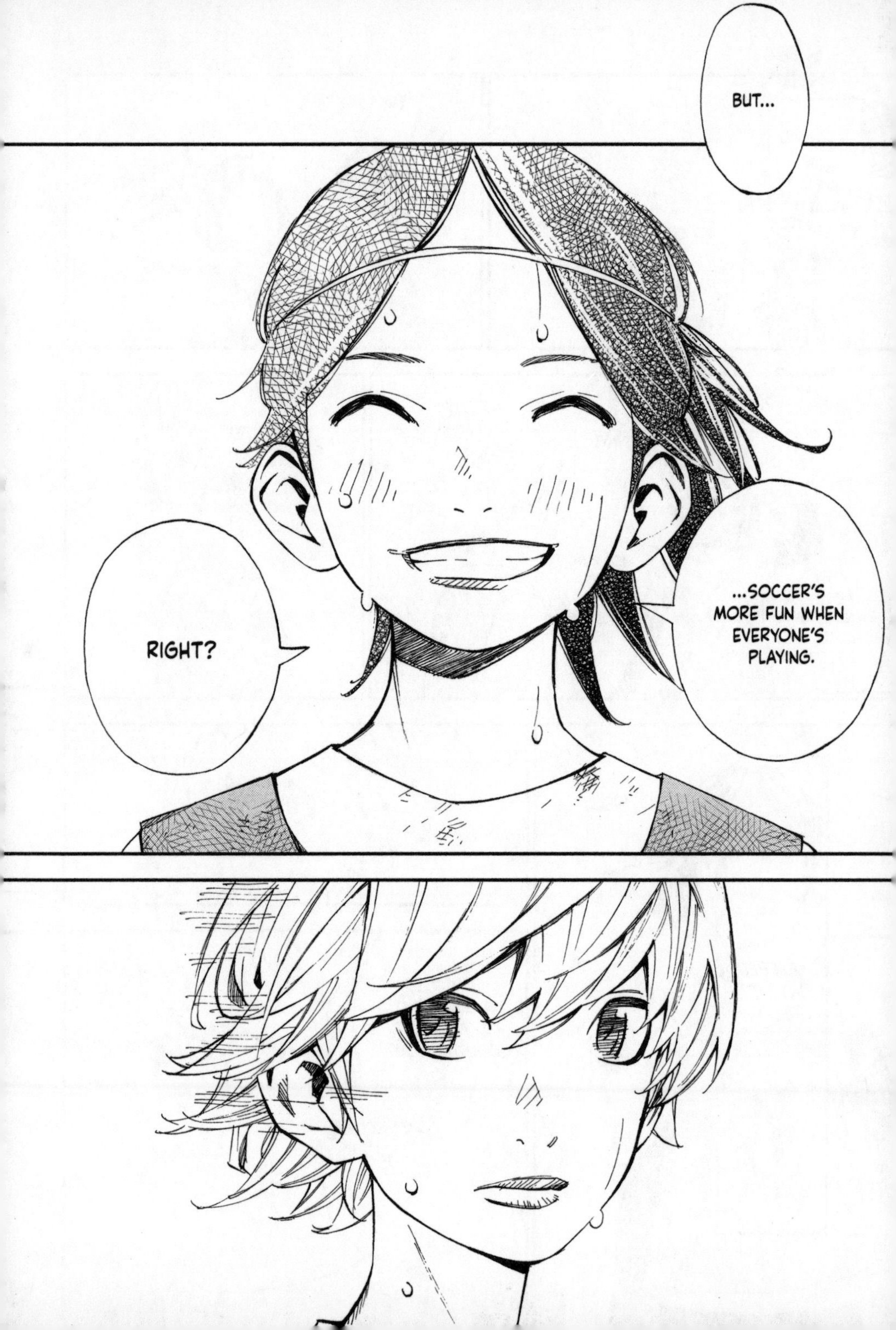
BUT...
...SOCCER'S MORE FUN WHEN EVERYONE'S PLAYING.
RIGHT?

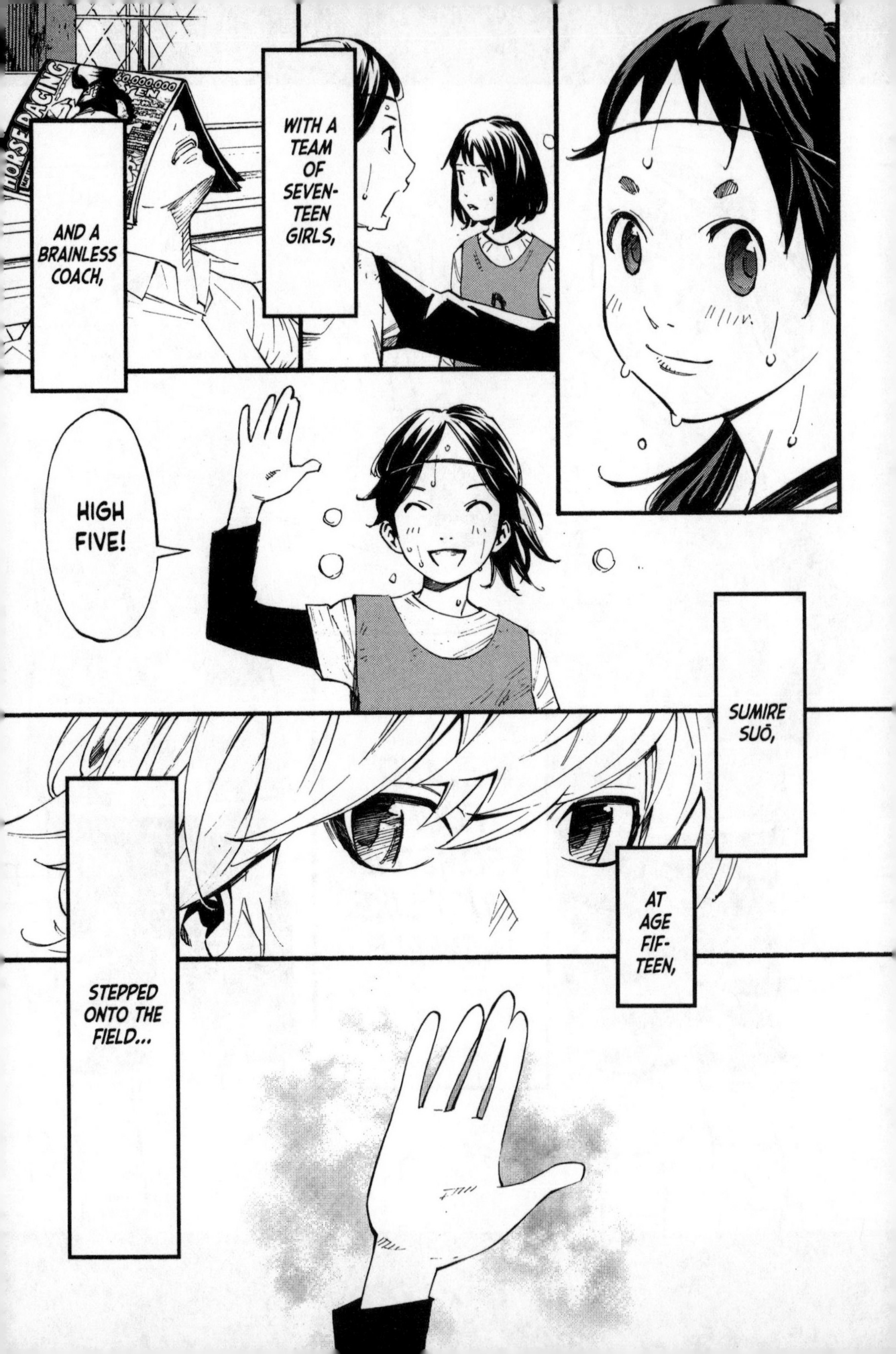
WITH A TEAM OF SEVEN-TEEN GIRLS,
AND A BRAINLESS COACH,
HIGH FIVE!
SUMIRE SUŌ,
AT AGE FIF-TEEN,
STEPPED ONTO THE FIELD...

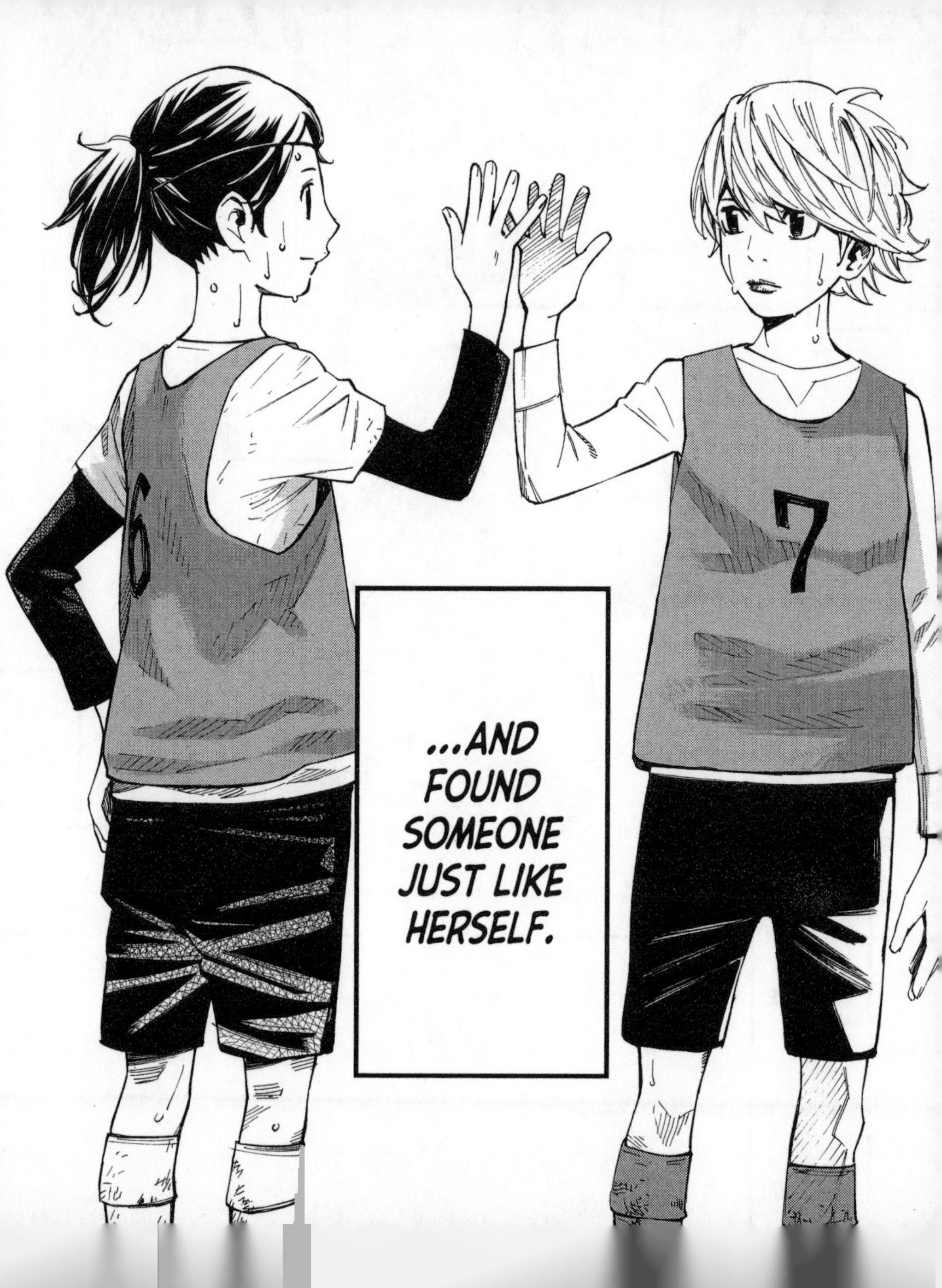
...AND FOUND SOMEONE JUST LIKE HERSELF.

Farewell,
My Dear
Cramer

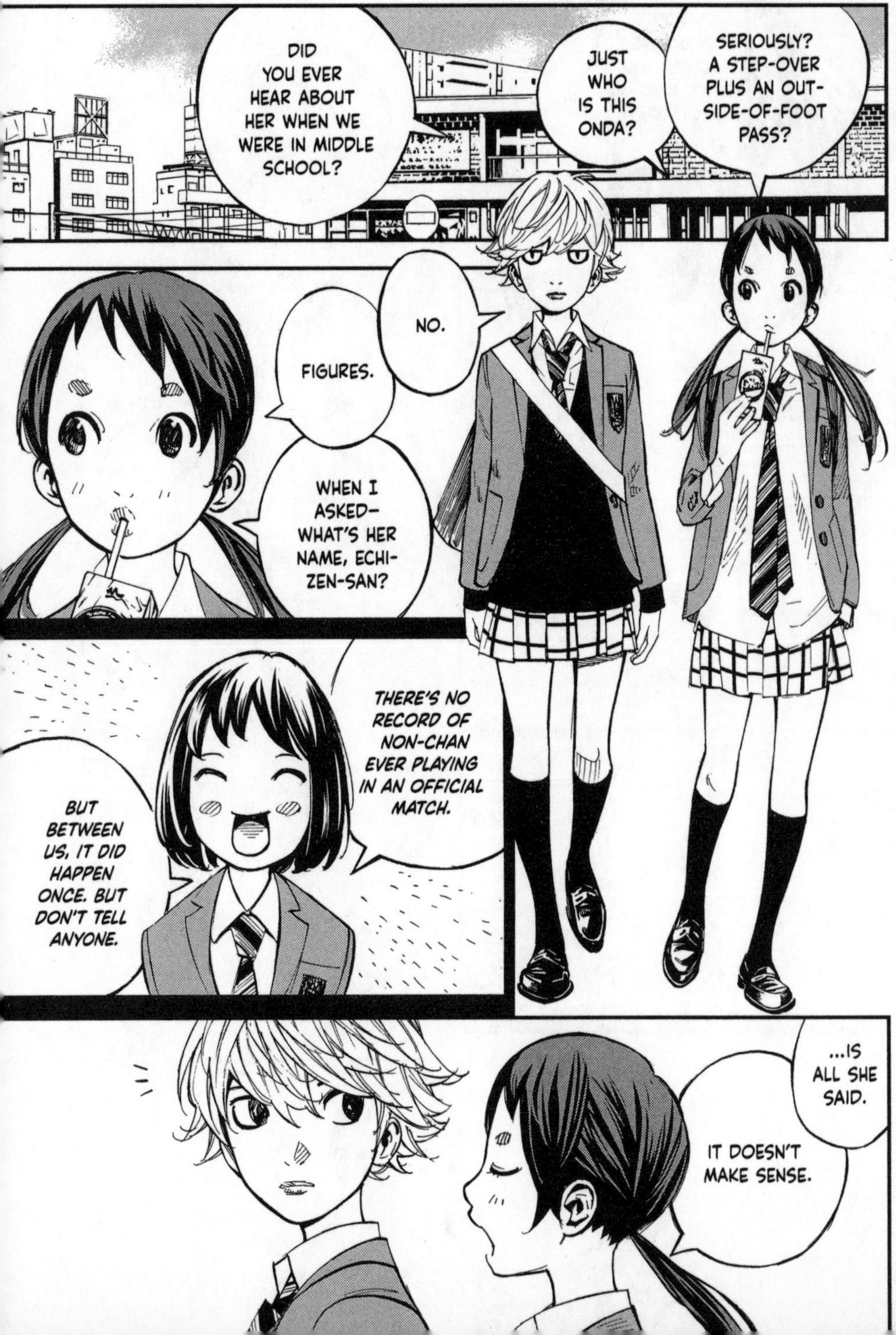
SERIOUSLY? A STEP-OVER PLUS AN OUT-SIDE-OF-FOOT PASS?
JUST WHO IS THIS ONDA?
DID YOU EVER HEAR ABOUT HER WHEN WE WERE IN MIDDLE SCHOOL?
NO.
FIGURES.
WHEN I ASKED—WHAT'S HER NAME, ECHIZEN-SAN?
THERE'S NO RECORD OF NON-CHAN EVER PLAYING IN AN OFFICIAL MATCH.
BUT BETWEEN US, IT DID HAPPEN ONCE. BUT DON'T TELL ANYONE.
...IS ALL SHE SAID.
IT DOESN'T MAKE SENSE.

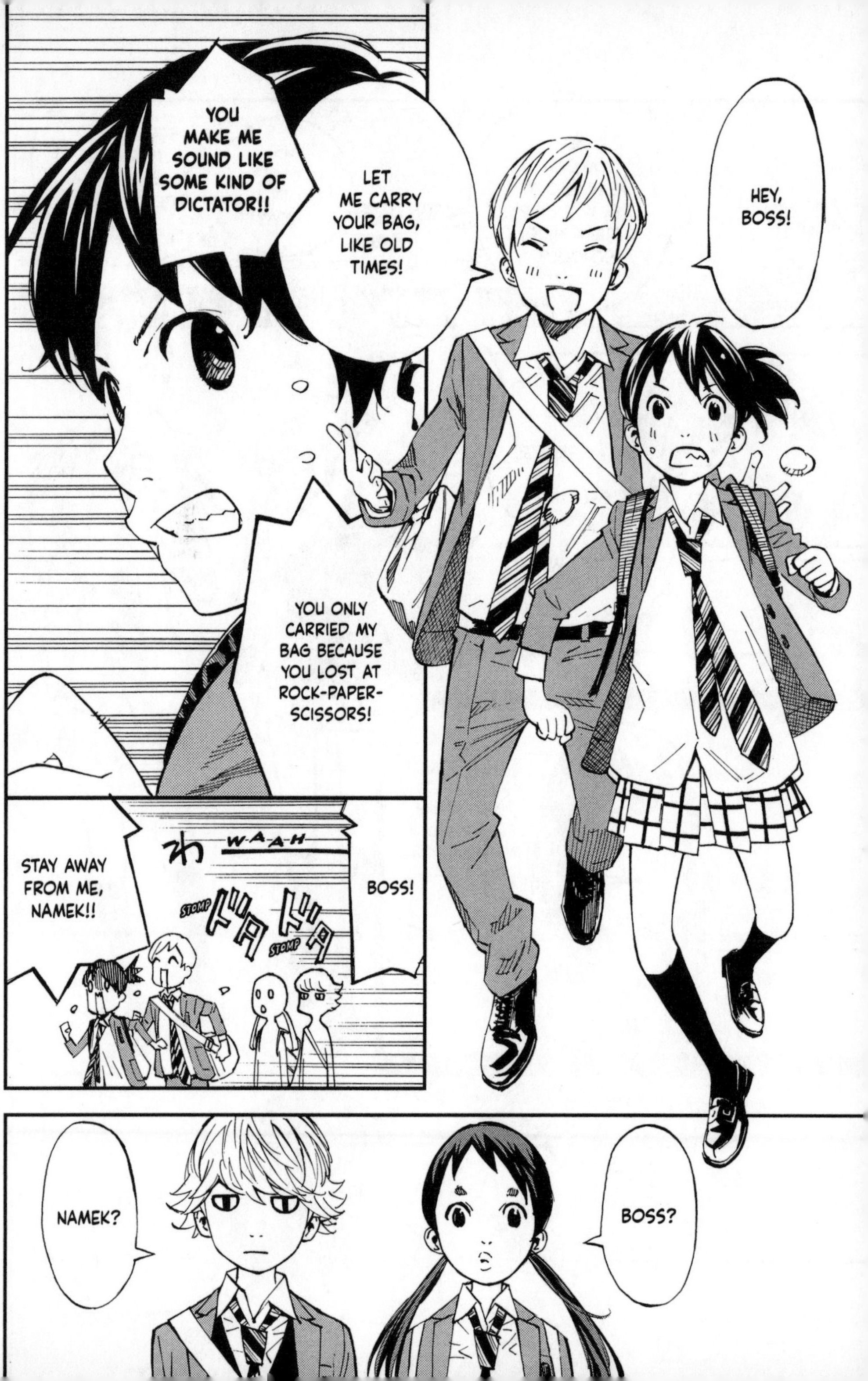
HEY, BOSS!
LET ME CARRY YOUR BAG, LIKE OLD TIMES!
YOU MAKE ME SOUND LIKE SOME KIND OF DICTATOR!!
YOU ONLY CARRIED MY BAG BECAUSE YOU LOST AT ROCK-PAPER-SCISSORS!
BOSS!
わ W-A-A-H
STOMP ドタ
STOMP ドタ
STAY AWAY FROM ME, NAMEK!!
BOSS?
NAMEK?

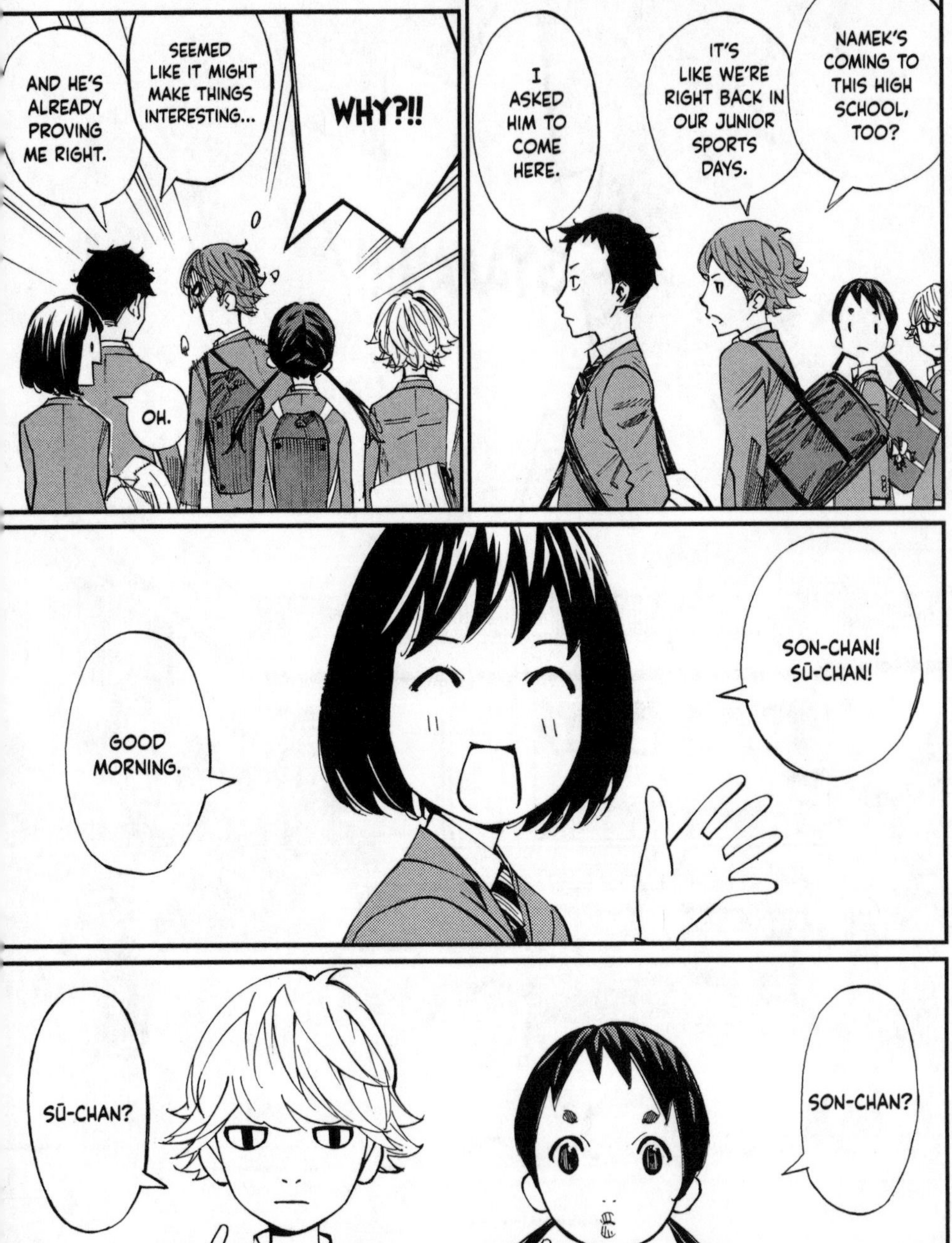
NAMEK'S COMING TO THIS HIGH SCHOOL, TOO?
IT'S LIKE WE'RE RIGHT BACK IN OUR JUNIOR SPORTS DAYS.
I ASKED HIM TO COME HERE.
WHY?!!
SEEMED LIKE IT MIGHT MAKE THINGS INTERESTING...
AND HE'S ALREADY PROVING ME RIGHT.
OH.
SON-CHAN! SŪ-CHAN!
GOOD MORNING.
SON-CHAN?
SŪ-CHAN?

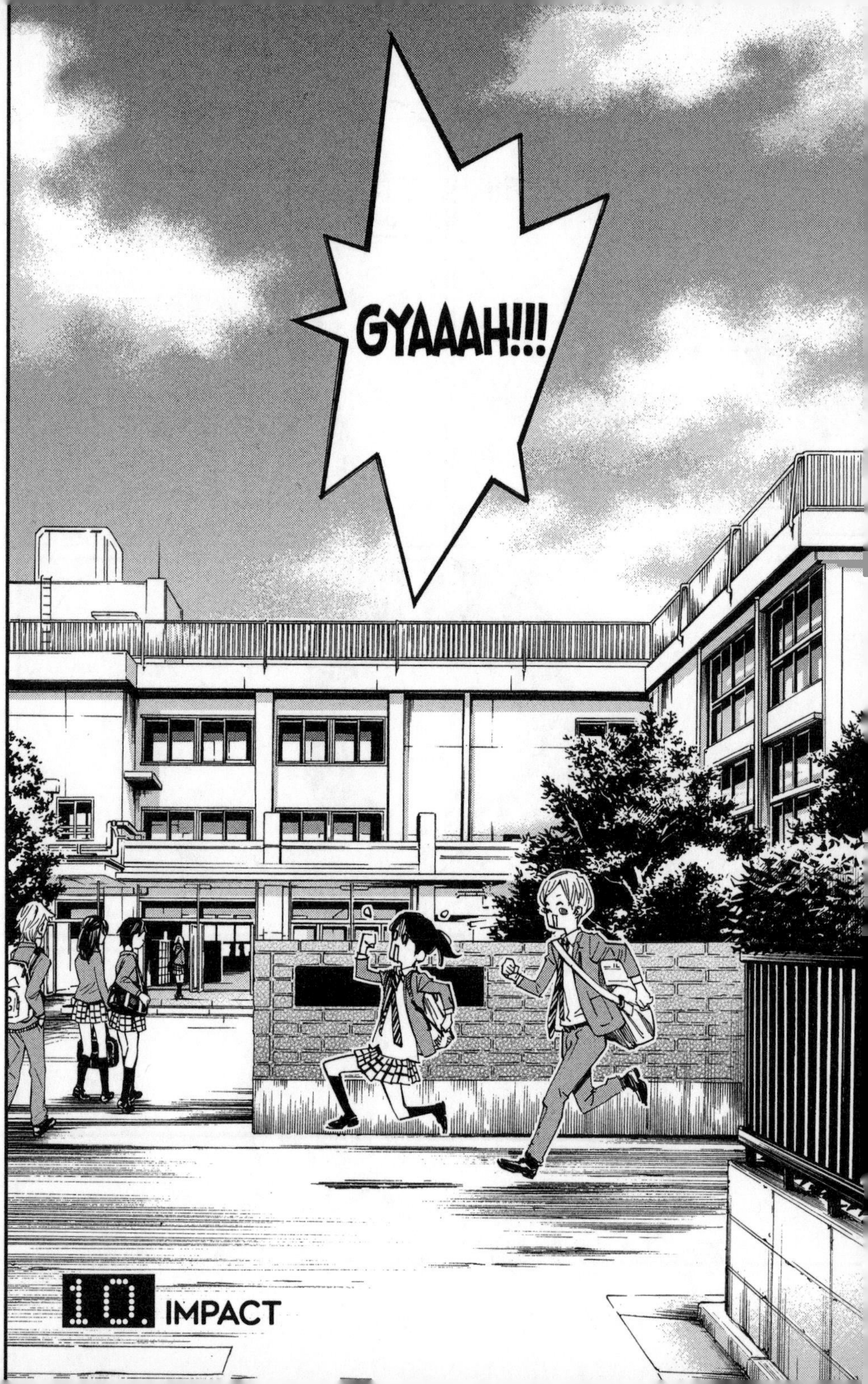
GYAAAH!!!
10. IMPACT

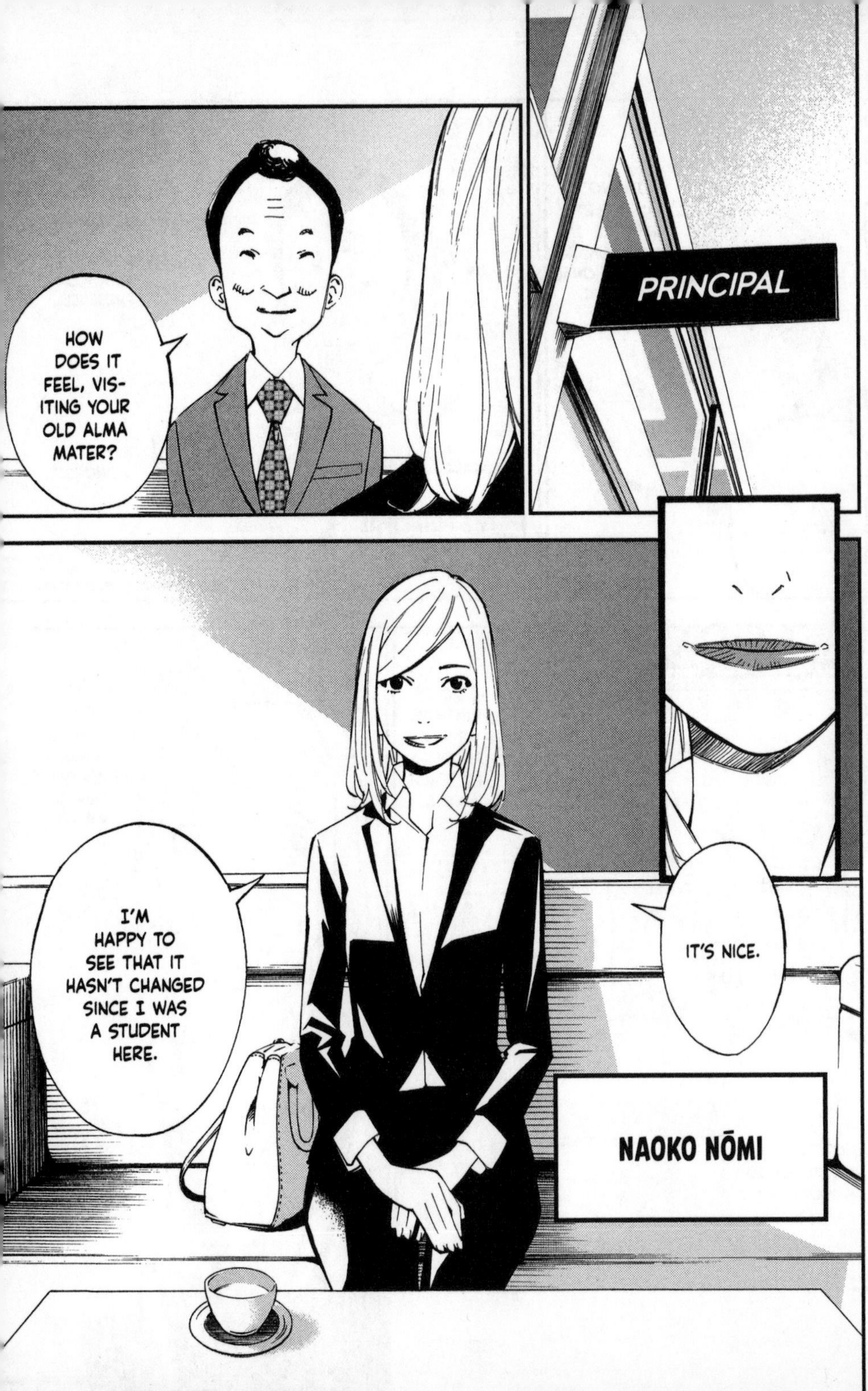
PRINCIPAL
HOW DOES IT FEEL, VIS-ITING YOUR OLD ALMA MATER?
IT'S NICE.
I'M HAPPY TO SEE THAT IT HASN'T CHANGED SINCE I WAS A STUDENT HERE.
NAOKO NŌMI

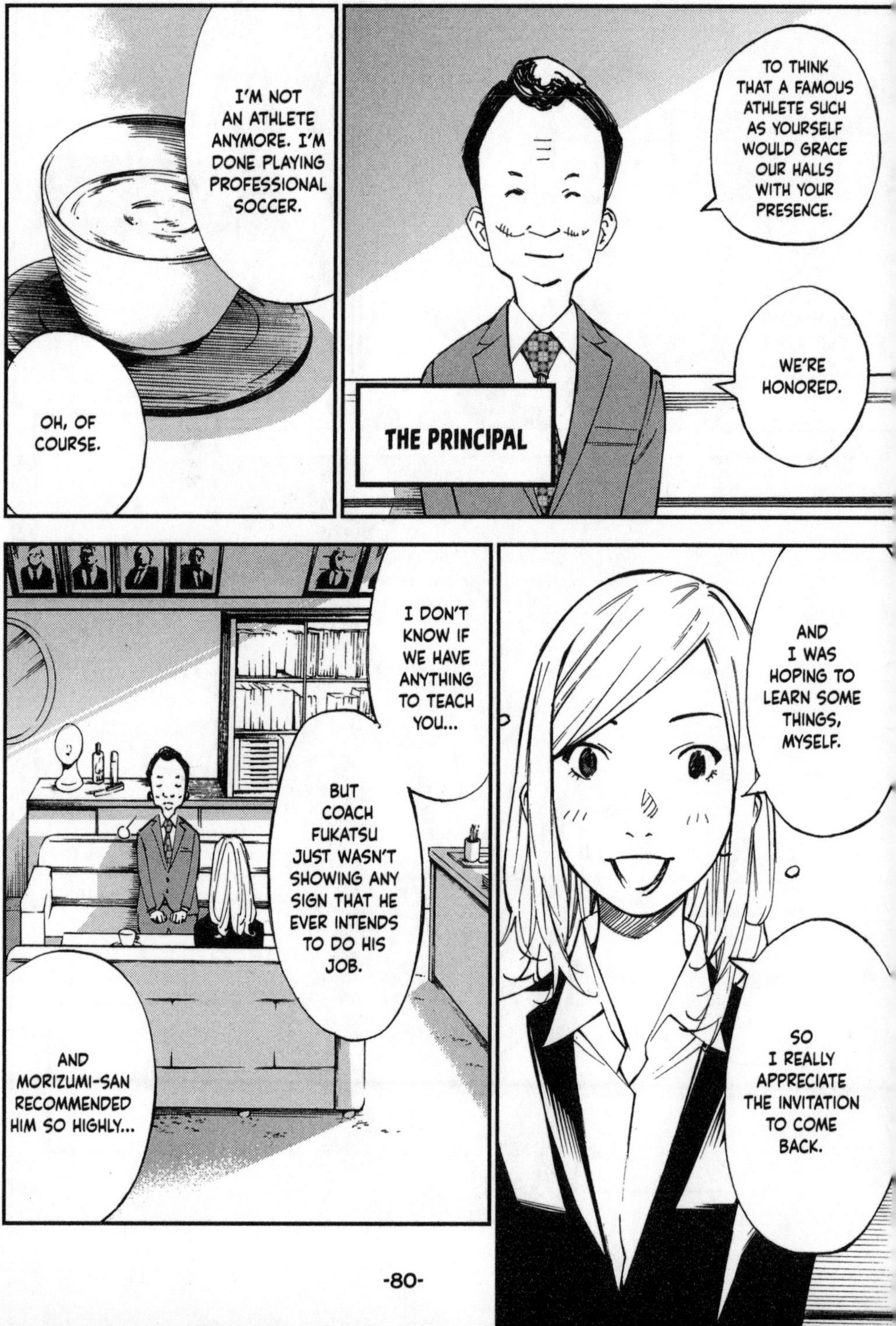
TO THINK THAT A FAMOUS ATHLETE SUCH AS YOURSELF WOULD GRACE OUR HALLS WITH YOUR PRESENCE.
WE'RE HONORED.
THE PRINCIPAL
I'M NOT AN ATHLETE ANYMORE. I'M DONE PLAYING PROFESSIONAL SOCCER.
OH, OF COURSE.
AND I WAS HOPING TO LEARN SOME THINGS, MYSELF.
SO I REALLY APPRECIATE THE INVITATION TO COME BACK.
I DON'T KNOW IF WE HAVE ANYTHING TO TEACH YOU...
BUT COACH FUKATSU JUST WASN'T SHOWING ANY SIGN THAT HE EVER INTENDS TO DO HIS JOB.
AND MORIZUMI-SAN RECOMMENDED HIM SO HIGHLY...

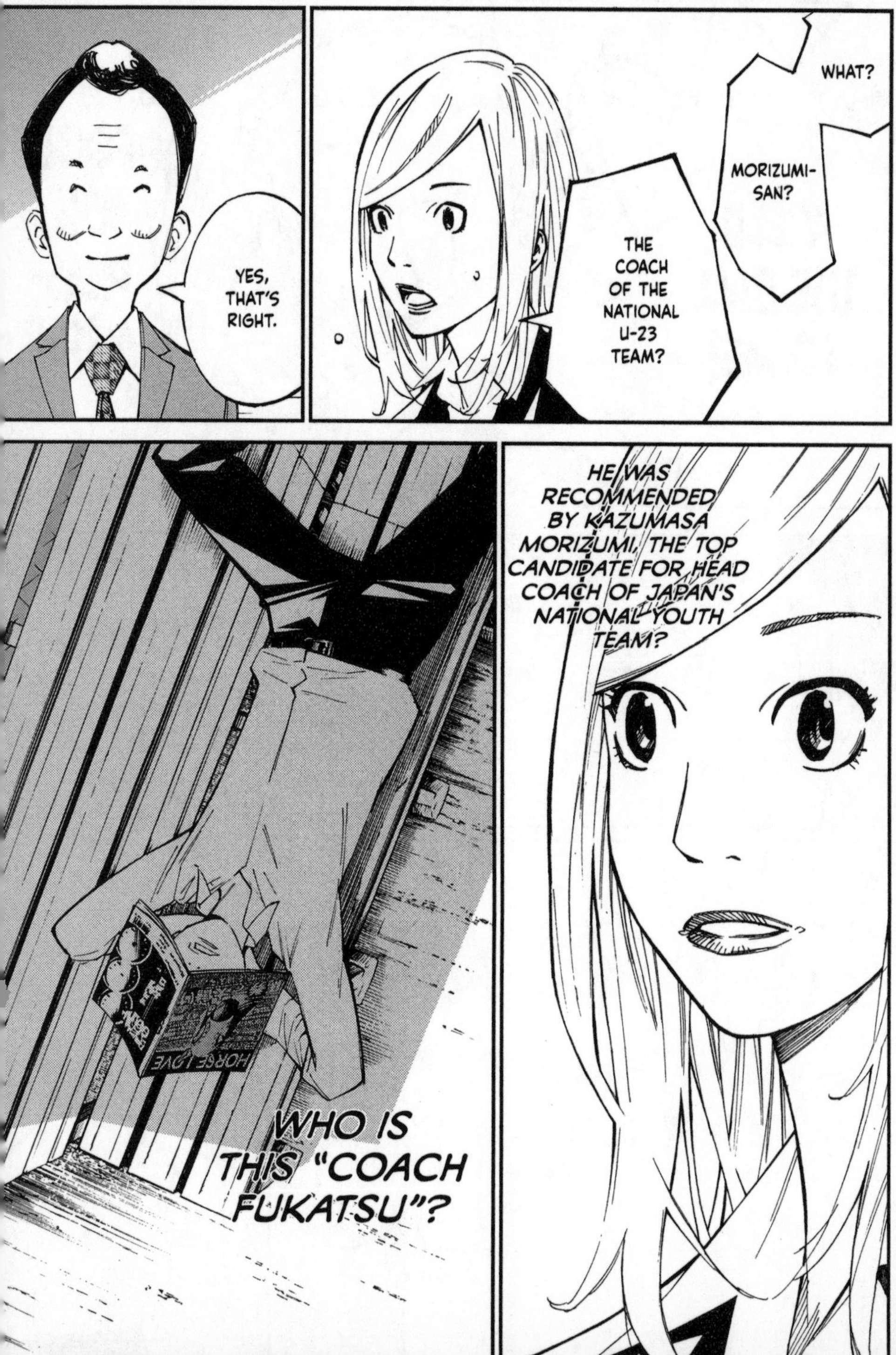
WHAT?
MORIZUMI-SAN?
THE COACH OF THE NATIONAL U-23 TEAM?
YES, THAT'S RIGHT.
HE WAS RECOMMENDED BY KAZUMASA MORIZUMI, THE TOP CANDIDATE FOR HEAD COACH OF JAPAN'S NATIONAL YOUTH TEAM?
HORSE LOVE
WHO IS THIS "COACH FUKATSU"?

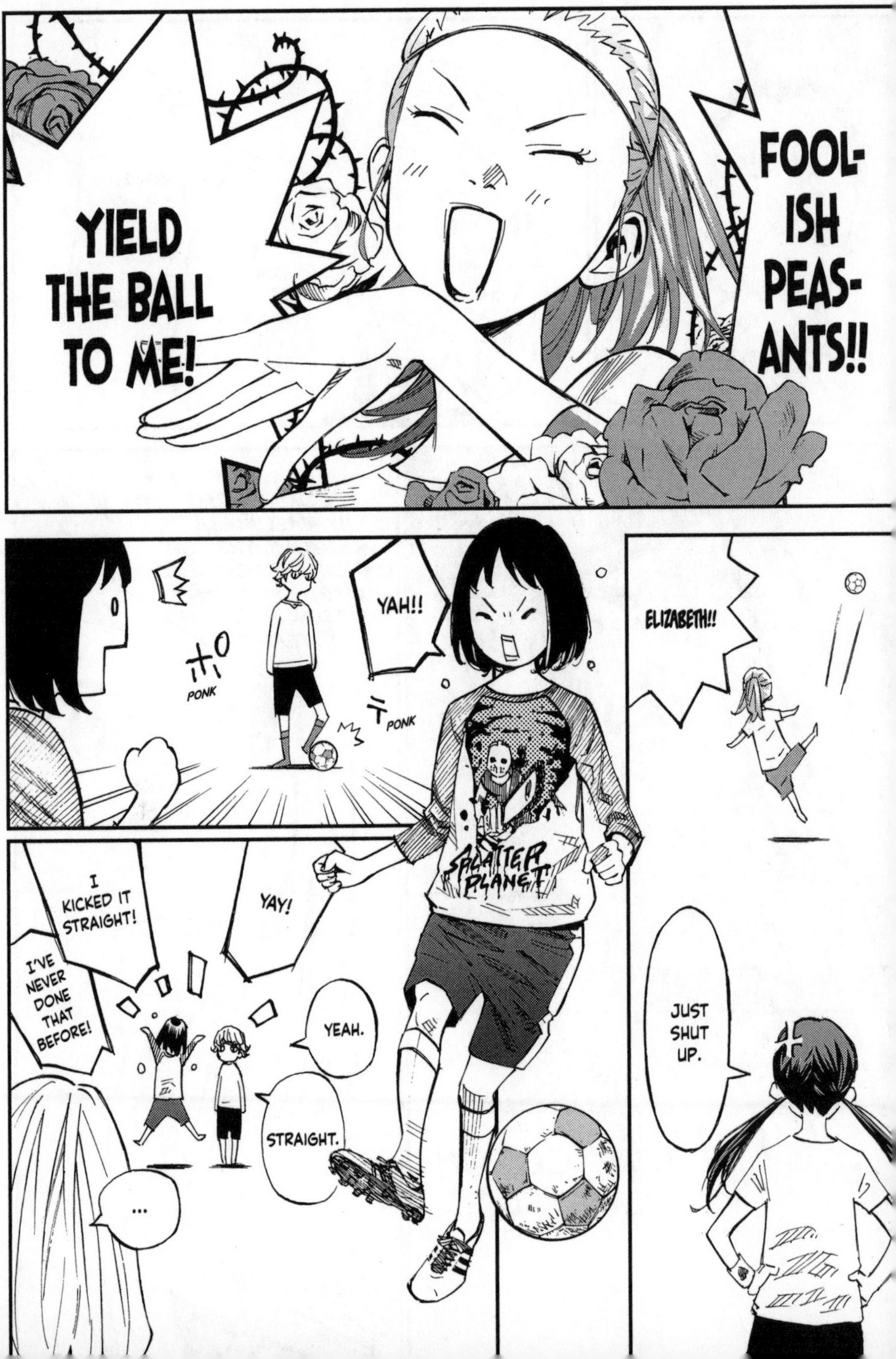

FOOL-ISH PEAS-ANTS!!
YIELD THE BALL TO ME!
ELIZABETH!!
YAH!!
PONK
PONK
JUST SHUT UP.
YAY!
I KICKED IT STRAIGHT!
I'VE NEVER DONE THAT BEFORE!
YEAH.
STRAIGHT.
...

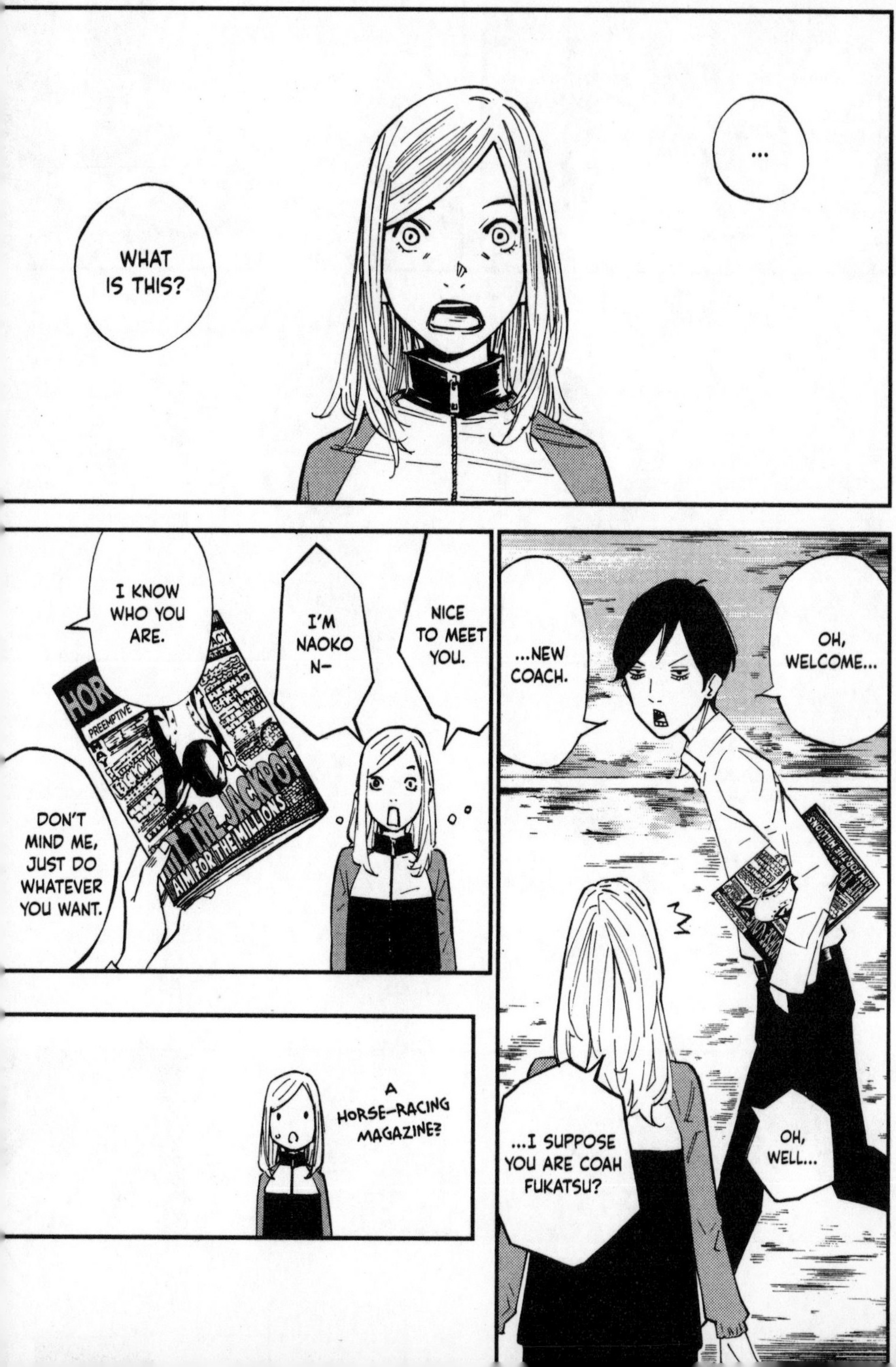
...
WHAT IS THIS?
OH, WELCOME...
...NEW COACH.
OH, WELL...
...I SUPPOSE YOU ARE COAH FUKATSU?
AIM FOR THE MILLIONS
NICE TO MEET YOU.
I'M NAOKO N–
I KNOW WHO YOU ARE.
HOR
PREEMPTIVE
AIM FOR THE MILLIONS
DON'T MIND ME, JUST DO WHATEVER YOU WANT.
A HORSE-RACING MAGAZINE?

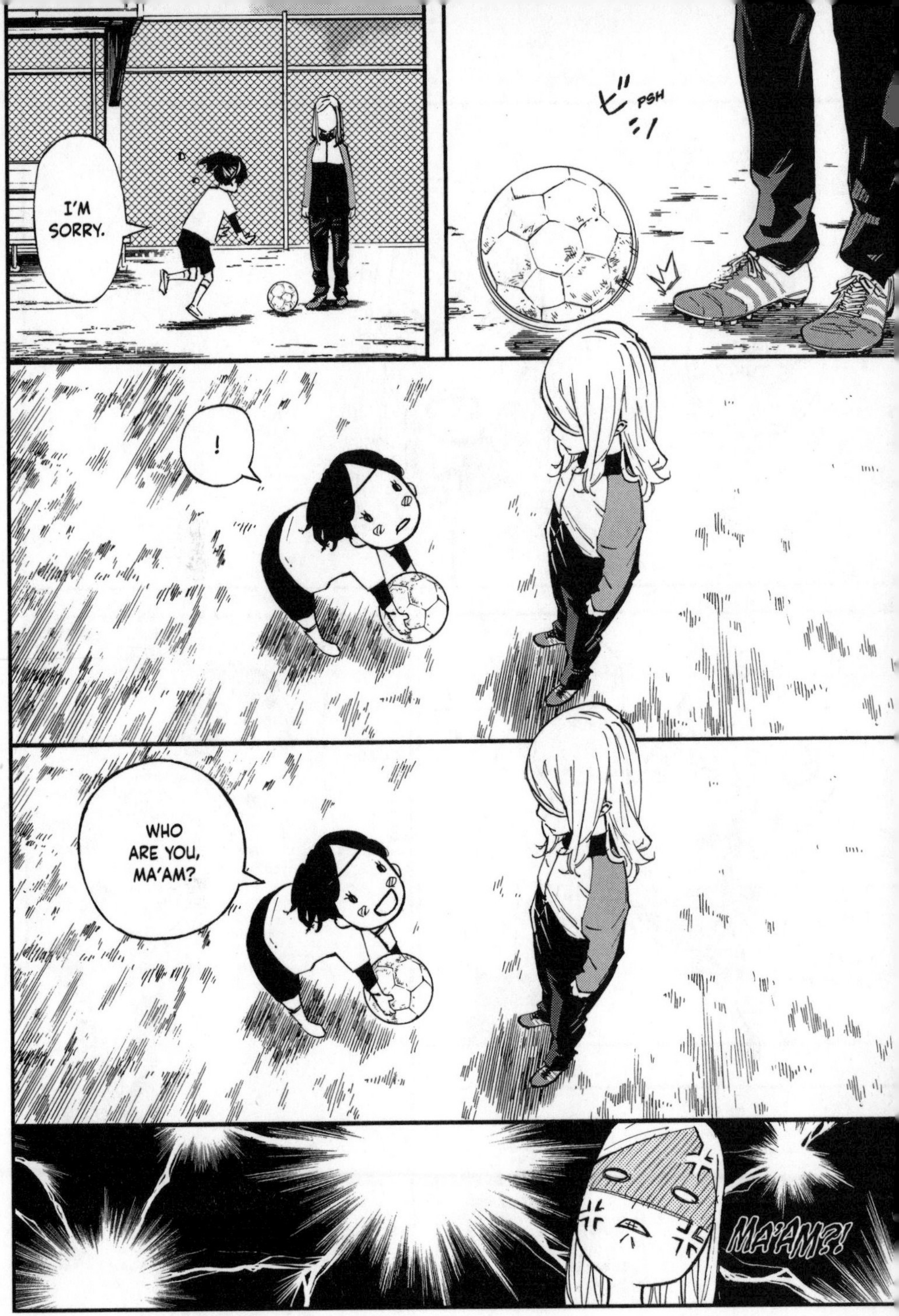
PSH
I'M SORRY.
!
WHO ARE YOU, MA'AM?
MA'AM?!

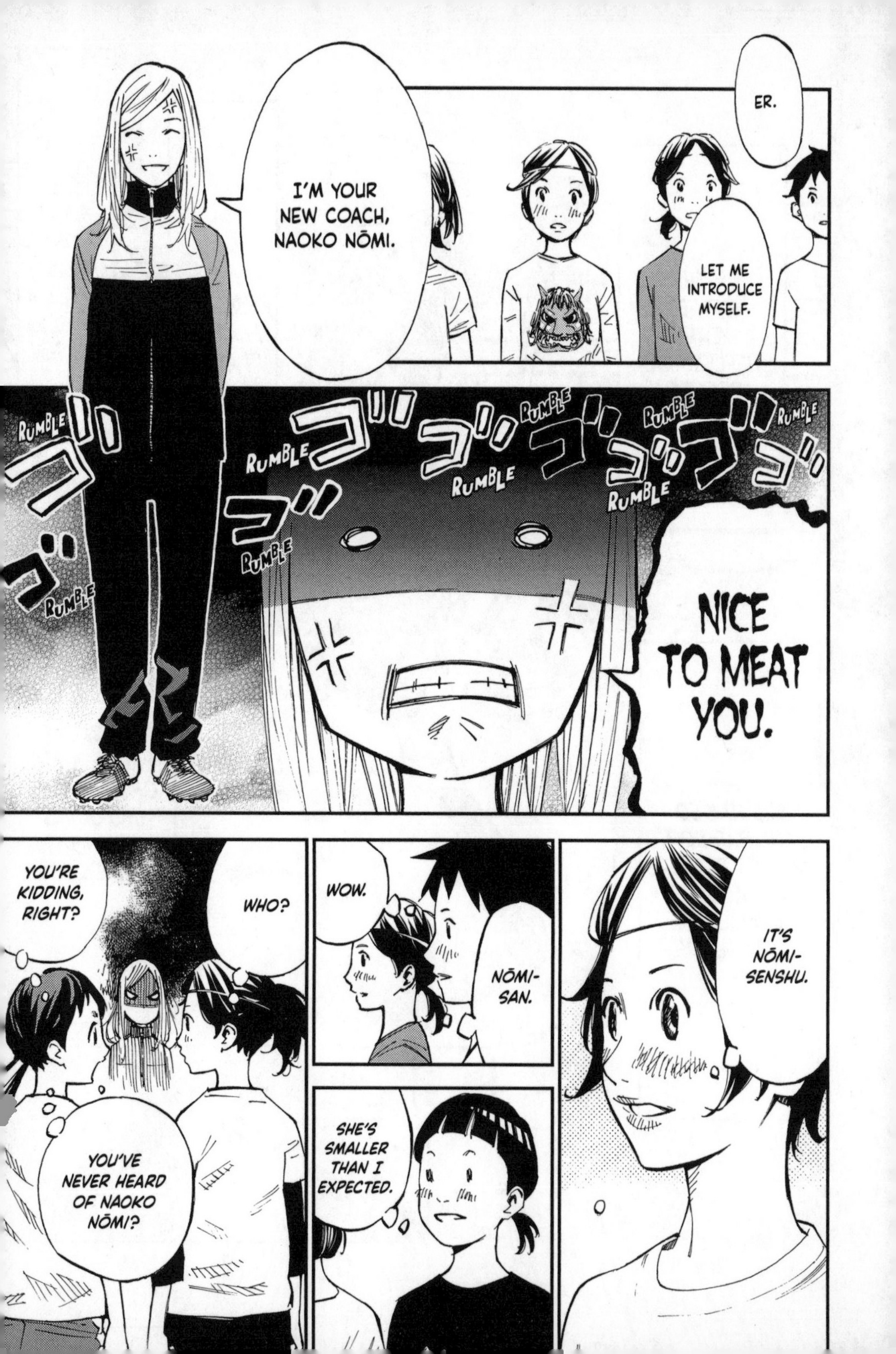
ER.
LET ME INTRODUCE MYSELF.
I'M YOUR NEW COACH, NAOKO NŌMI.
RUMBLE
RUMBLE
RUMBLE
RUMBLE
RUMBLE
RUMBLE
RUMBLE
RUMBLE
RUMBLE
NICE TO MEAT YOU.
IT'S NŌMI-SENSHU.
NŌMI-SAN.
WOW.
SHE'S SMALLER THAN I EXPECTED.
WHO?
YOU'RE KIDDING, RIGHT?
YOU'VE NEVER HEARD OF NAOKO NŌMI?

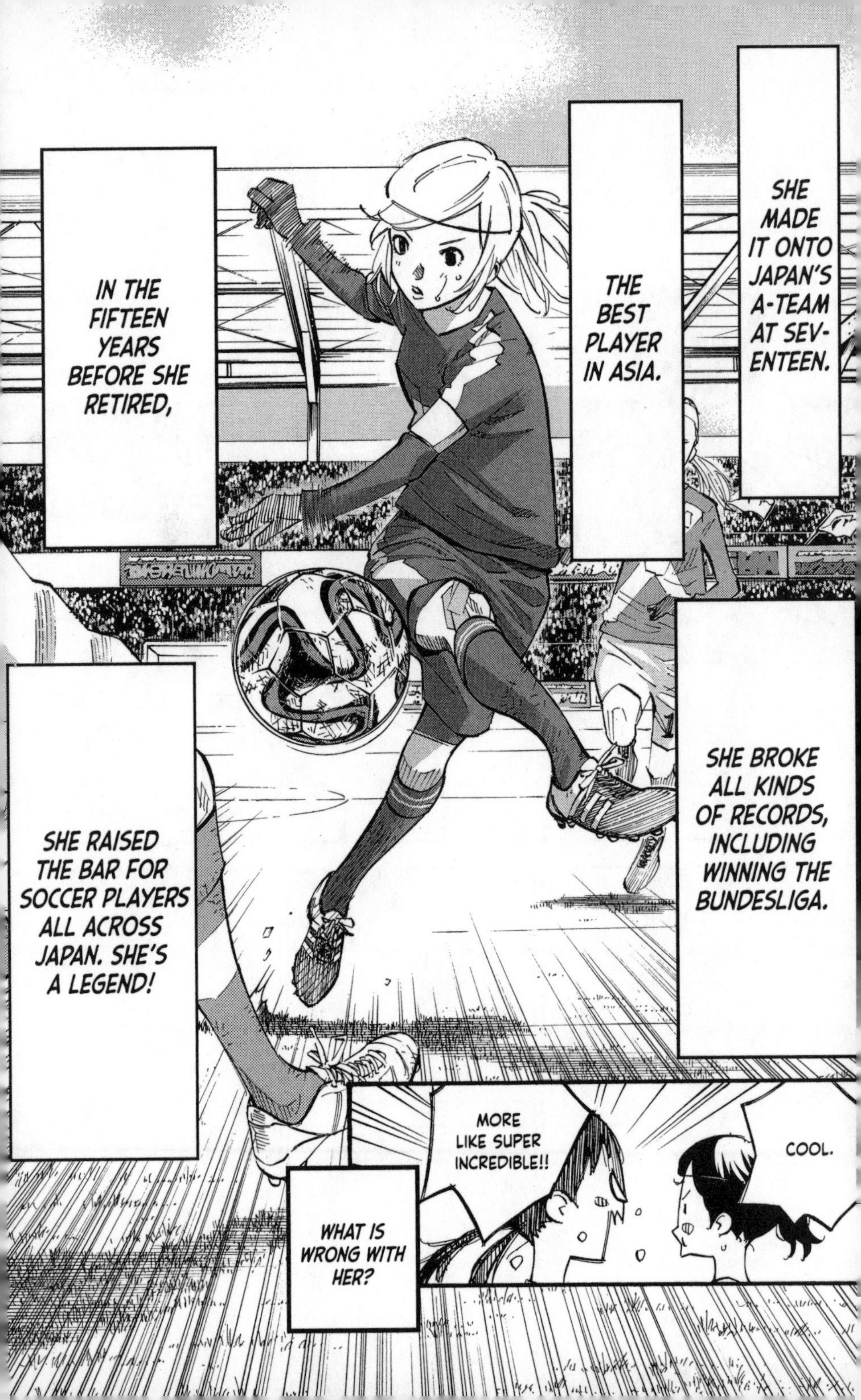
SHE MADE IT ONTO JAPAN'S A-TEAM AT SEV-ENTEEN.
THE BEST PLAYER IN ASIA.
IN THE FIFTEEN YEARS BEFORE SHE RETIRED,
SHE BROKE ALL KINDS OF RECORDS, INCLUDING WINNING THE BUNDESLIGA.
SHE RAISED THE BAR FOR SOCCER PLAYERS ALL ACROSS JAPAN. SHE'S A LEGEND!
COOL.
MORE LIKE SUPER INCREDIBLE!!
WHAT IS WRONG WITH HER?

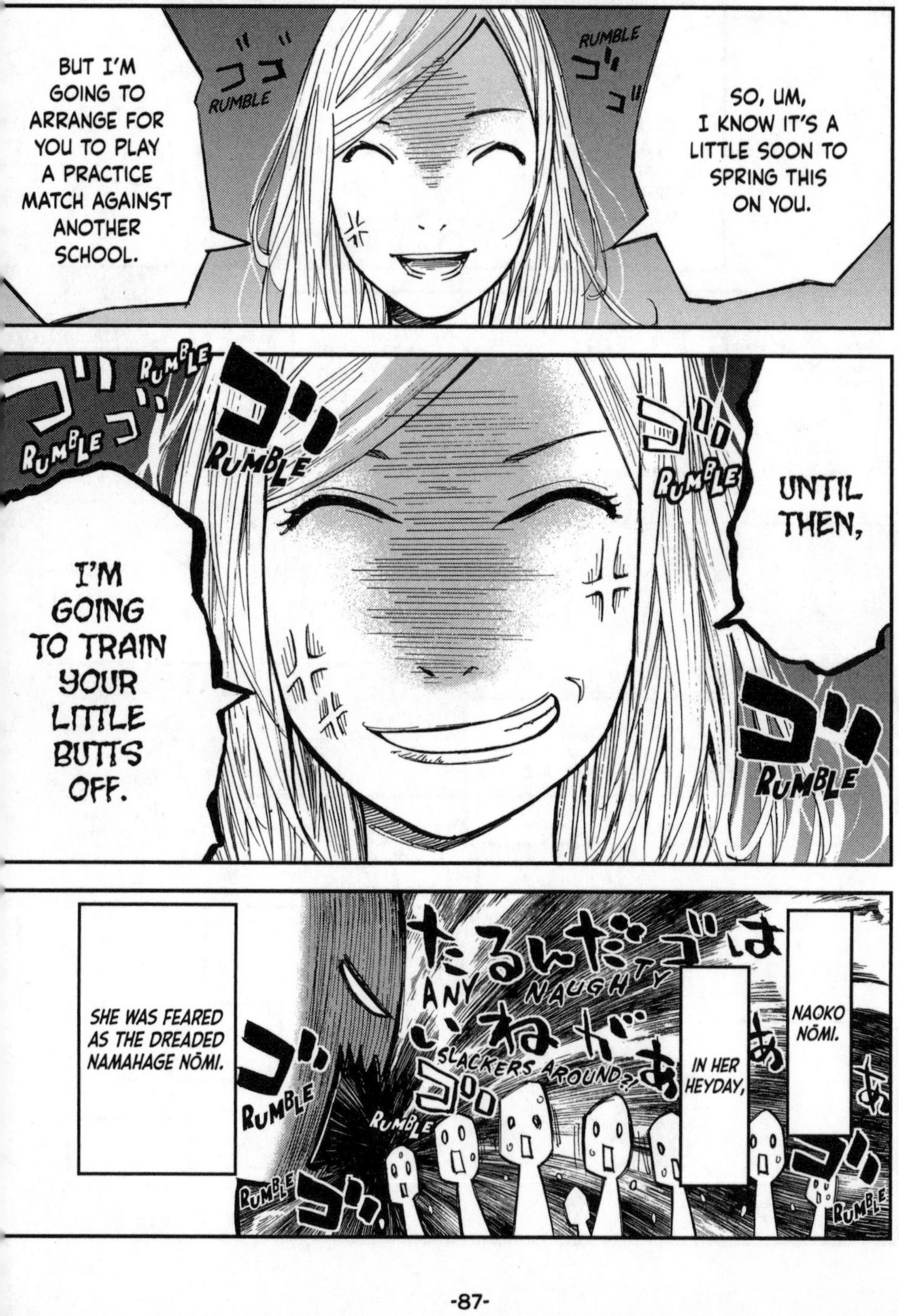
RUMBLE
SO, UM, I KNOW IT'S A LITTLE SOON TO SPRING THIS ON YOU.
RUMBLE
BUT I'M GOING TO ARRANGE FOR YOU TO PLAY A PRACTICE MATCH AGAINST ANOTHER SCHOOL.
UNTIL THEN,
RUMBLE
RUMBLE
RUMBLE
RUMBLE
RUMBLE
I'M GOING TO TRAIN YOUR LITTLE BUTTS OFF.
NAOKO NŌMI.
IN HER HEYDAY,
ANY NAUGHTY SLACKERS AROUND?
RUMBLE
RUMBLE
RUMBLE
RUMBLE
SHE WAS FEARED AS THE DREADED NAMAHAGE NŌMI.

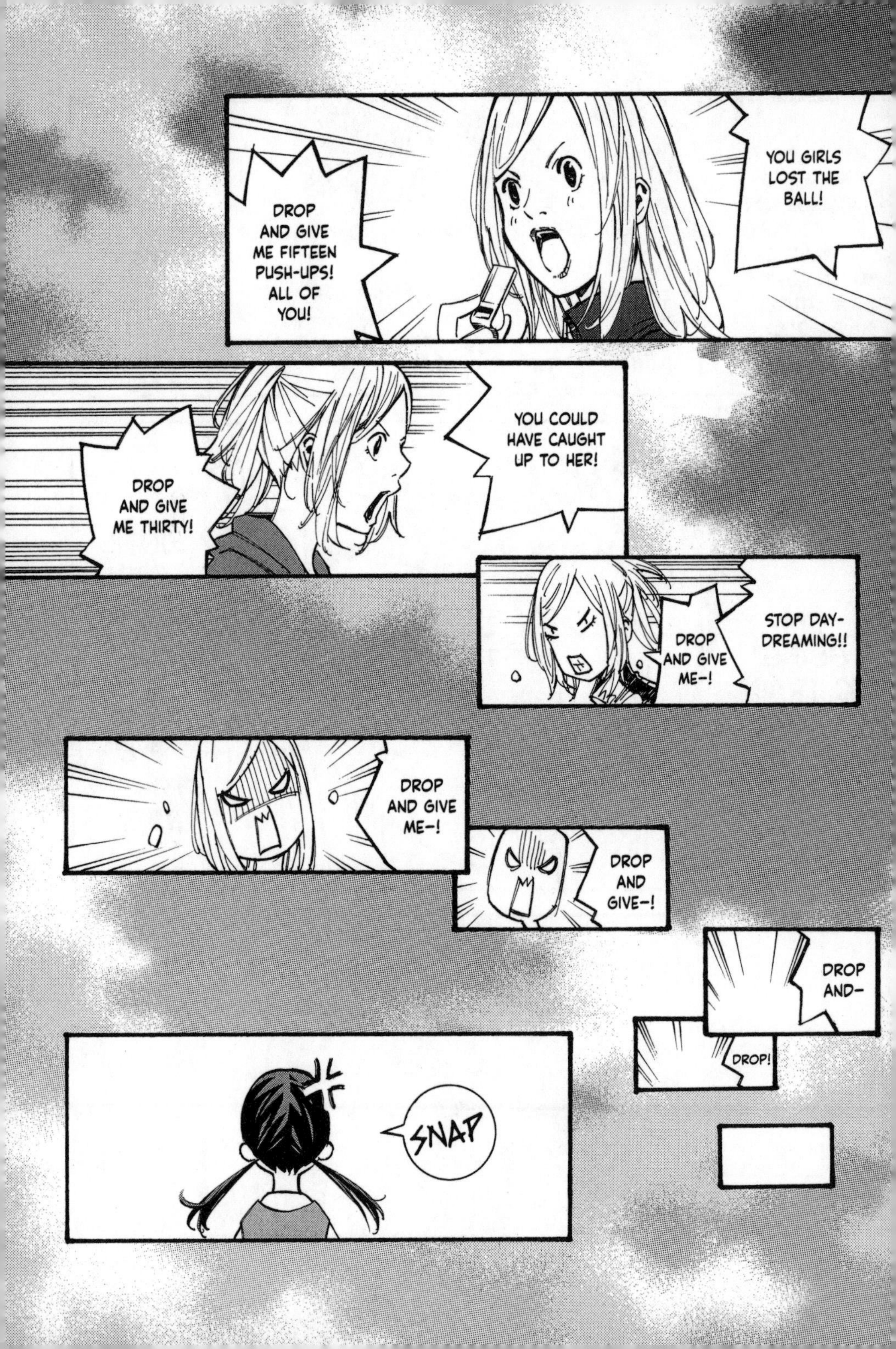
YOU GIRLS LOST THE BALL!
DROP AND GIVE ME FIFTEEN PUSH-UPS! ALL OF YOU!
YOU COULD HAVE CAUGHT UP TO HER!
DROP AND GIVE ME THIRTY!
STOP DAY-DREAMING!!
DROP AND GIVE ME-!
DROP AND GIVE ME-!
DROP AND GIVE-!
DROP AND-
DROP!
SNAP

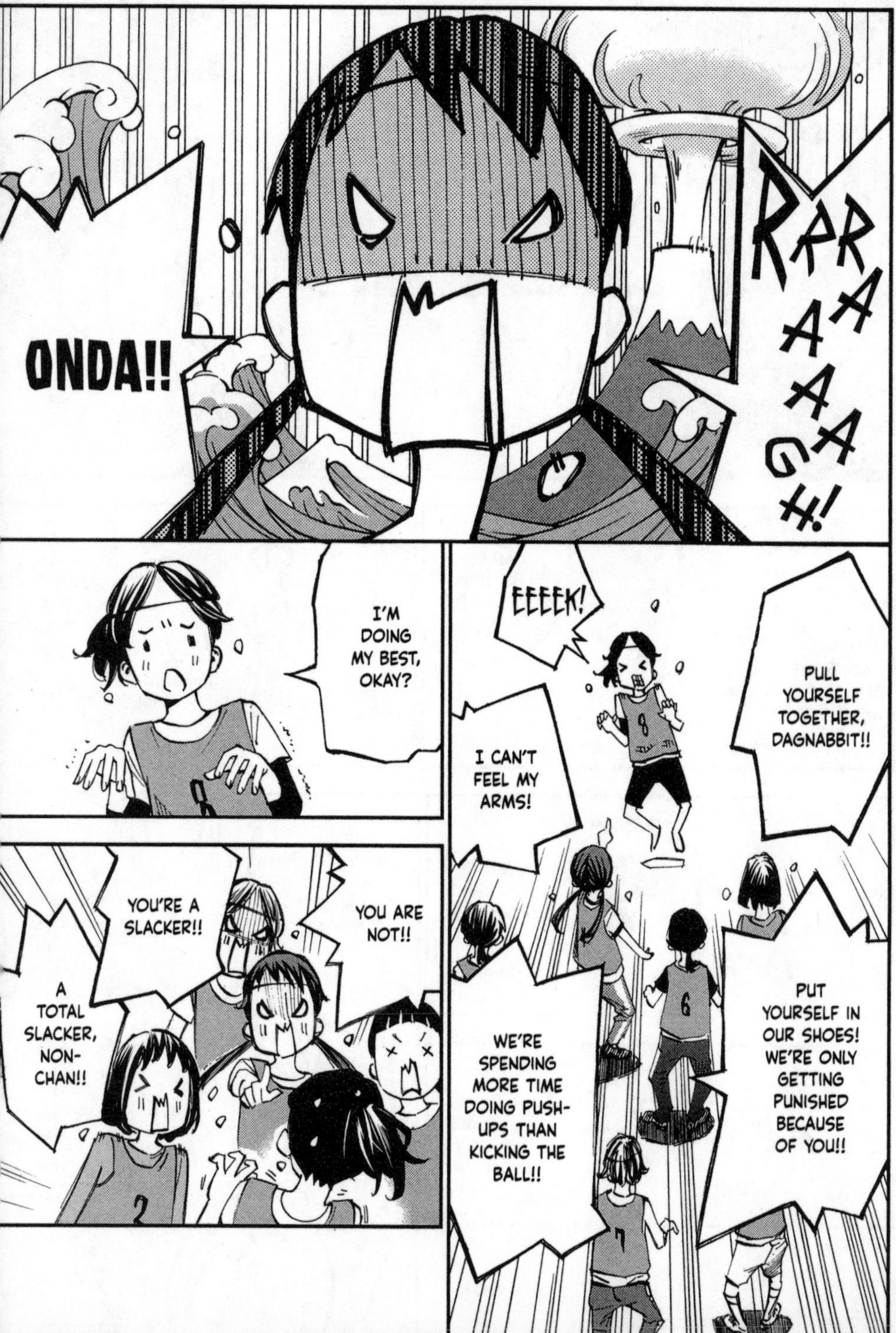
RRRAAAAAGH!
ONDA!!
PULL YOURSELF TOGETHER, DAGNABBIT!!
EEEEK!
I CAN'T FEEL MY ARMS!
PUT YOURSELF IN OUR SHOES! WE'RE ONLY GETTING PUNISHED BECAUSE OF YOU!!
WE'RE SPENDING MORE TIME DOING PUSH-UPS THAN KICKING THE BALL!!
I'M DOING MY BEST, OKAY?
YOU ARE NOT!!
YOU'RE A SLACKER!!
A TOTAL SLACKER, NON-CHAN!!

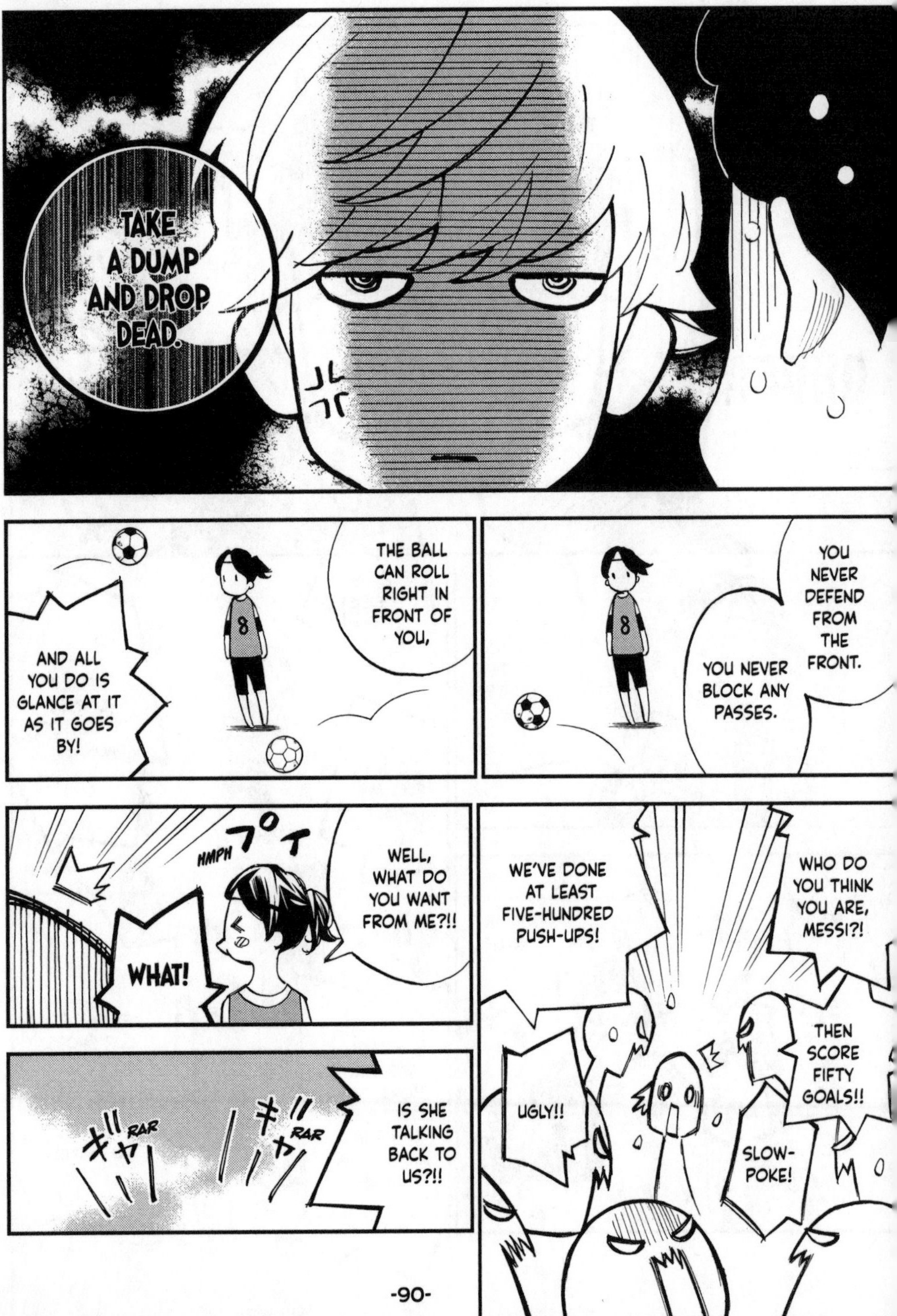
TAKE A DUMP AND DROP DEAD.
YOU NEVER DEFEND FROM THE FRONT.
YOU NEVER BLOCK ANY PASSES.
THE BALL CAN ROLL RIGHT IN FRONT OF YOU,
AND ALL YOU DO IS GLANCE AT IT AS IT GOES BY!
WHO DO YOU THINK YOU ARE, MESSI?!
WE'VE DONE AT LEAST FIVE-HUNDRED PUSH-UPS!
THEN SCORE FIFTY GOALS!!
UGLY!!
SLOW-POKE!
WELL, WHAT DO YOU WANT FROM ME?!!
プイ HMPH
WHAT!
IS SHE TALKING BACK TO US?!!
ギャ RAR
ギャ RAR

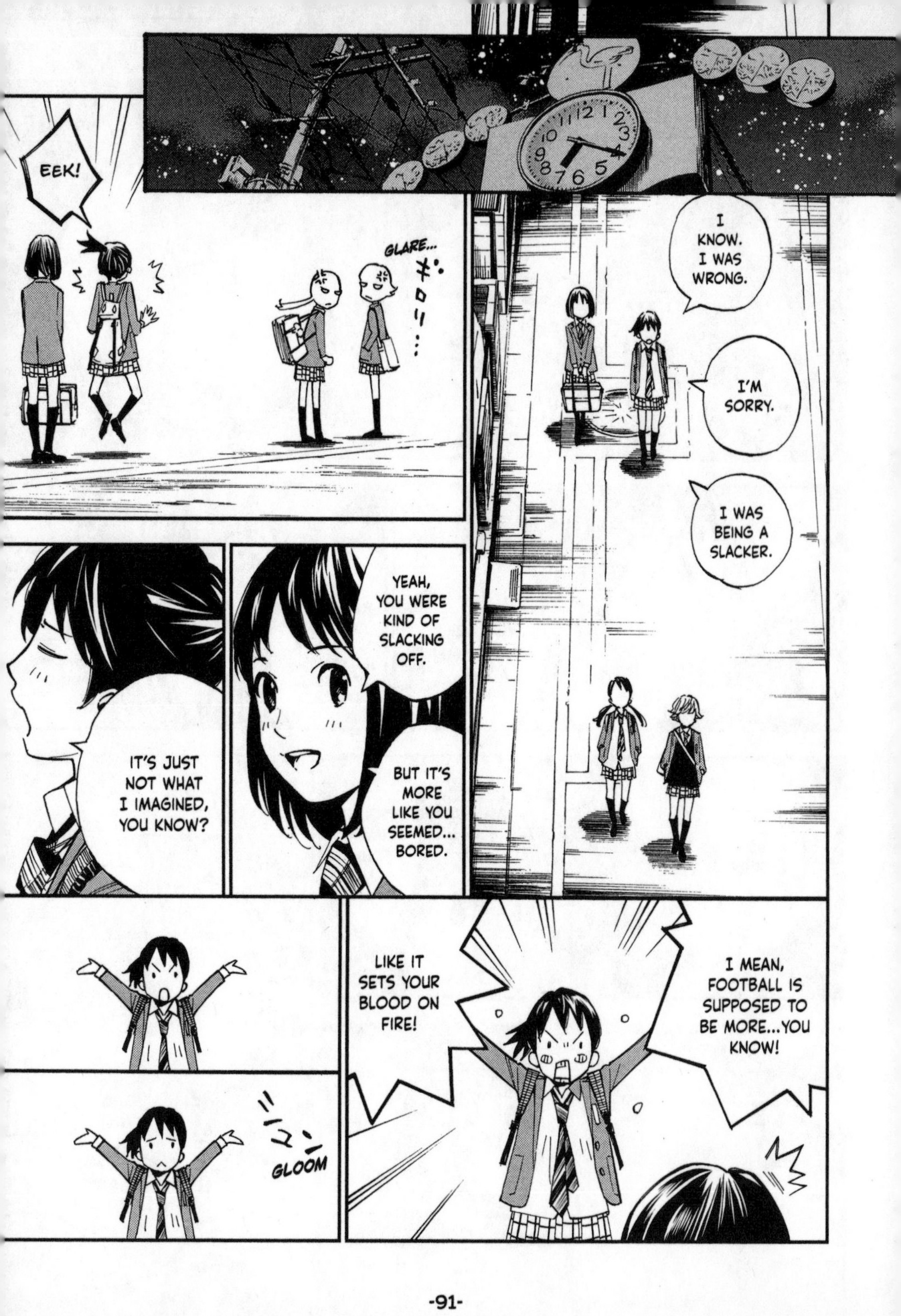
I KNOW. I WAS WRONG.
I'M SORRY.
I WAS BEING A SLACKER.
EEK!
GLARE...
ギロリ…
YEAH, YOU WERE KIND OF SLACKING OFF.
BUT IT'S MORE LIKE YOU SEEMED... BORED.
IT'S JUST NOT WHAT I IMAGINED, YOU KNOW?
I MEAN, FOOTBALL IS SUPPOSED TO BE MORE...YOU KNOW!
LIKE IT SETS YOUR BLOOD ON FIRE!
シュン
GLOOM

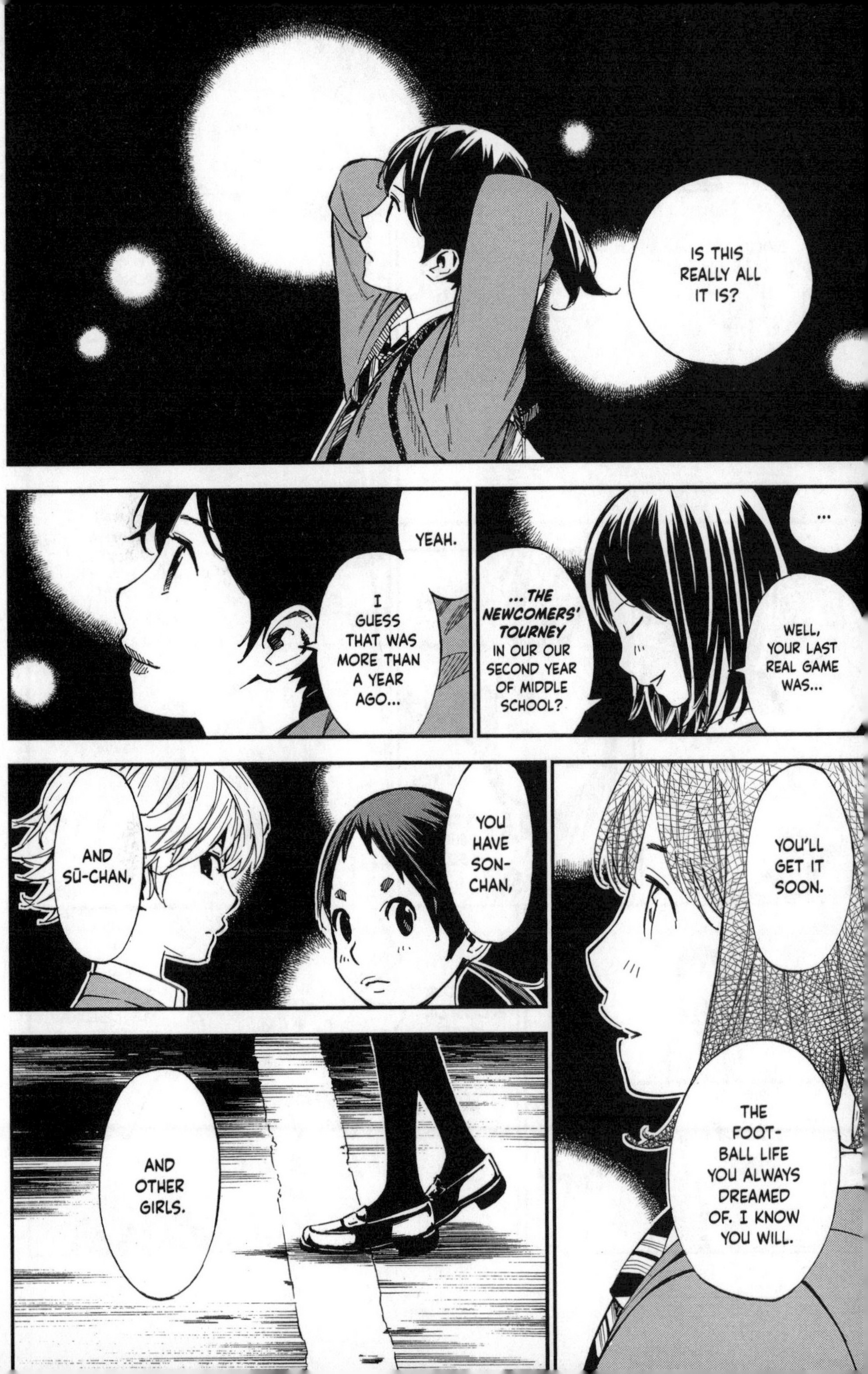
IS THIS REALLY ALL IT IS?
...
WELL, YOUR LAST REAL GAME WAS...
...THE NEWCOMERS' TOURNEY IN OUR OUR SECOND YEAR OF MIDDLE SCHOOL?
YEAH.
I GUESS THAT WAS MORE THAN A YEAR AGO...
YOU'LL GET IT SOON.
THE FOOT-BALL LIFE YOU ALWAYS DREAMED OF. I KNOW YOU WILL.
YOU HAVE SON-CHAN,
AND SŪ-CHAN,
AND OTHER GIRLS.

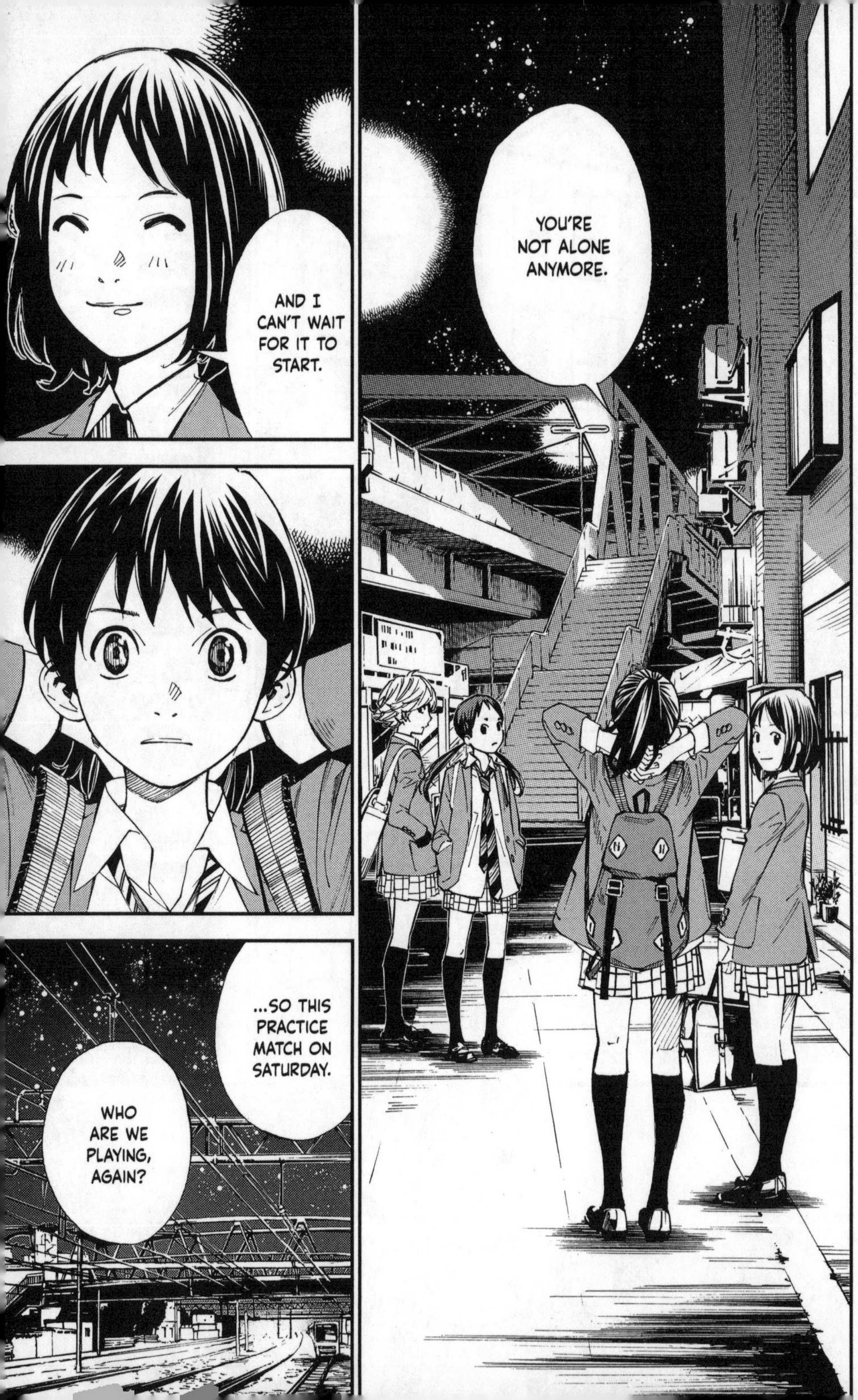
YOU'RE NOT ALONE ANYMORE.
AND I CAN'T WAIT FOR IT TO START.
...SO THIS PRACTICE MATCH ON SATURDAY.
WHO ARE WE PLAYING, AGAIN?

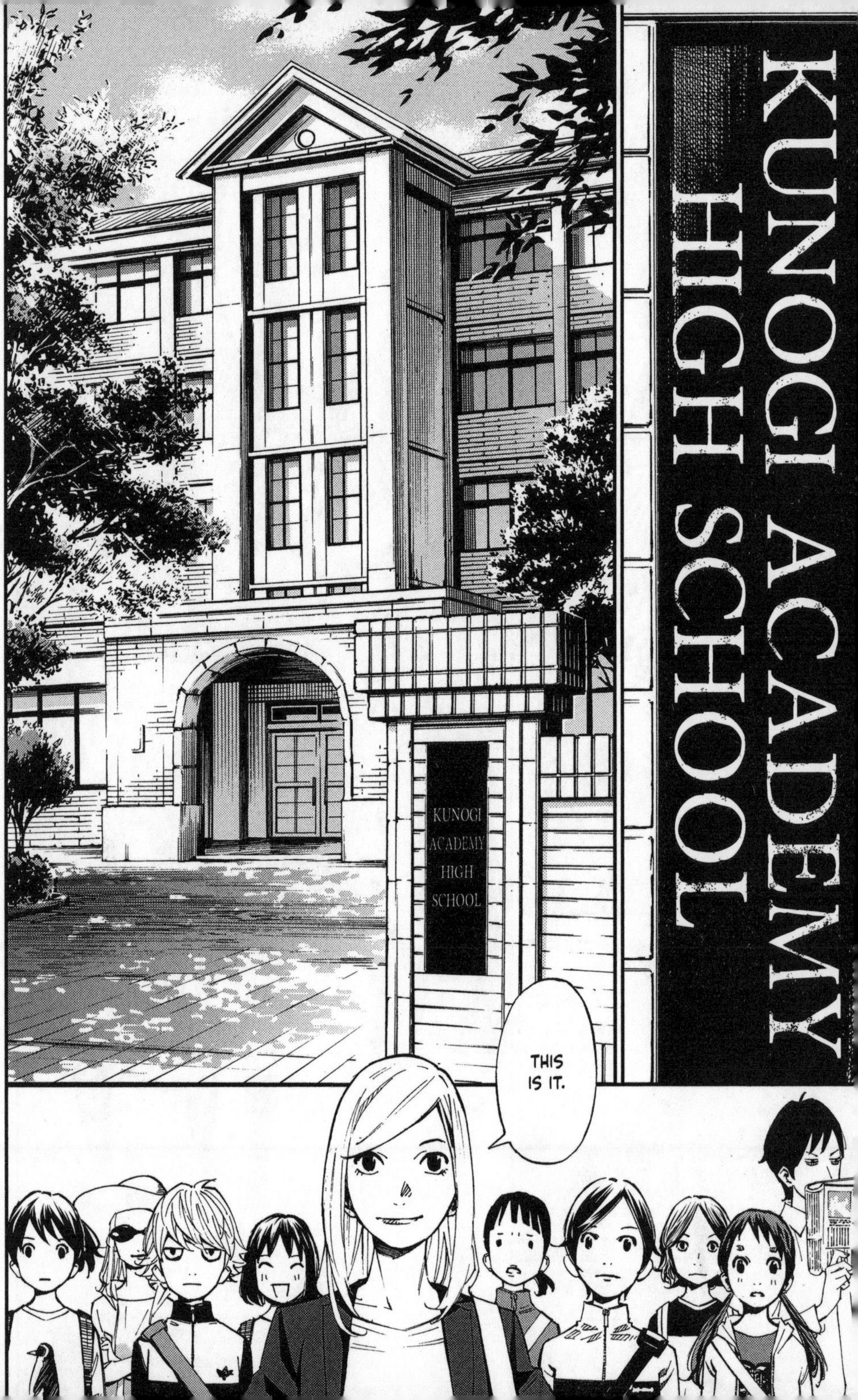
KUNOGI ACADEMY HIGH SCHOOL
KUNOGI ACADEMY HIGH SCHOOL
THIS IS IT.

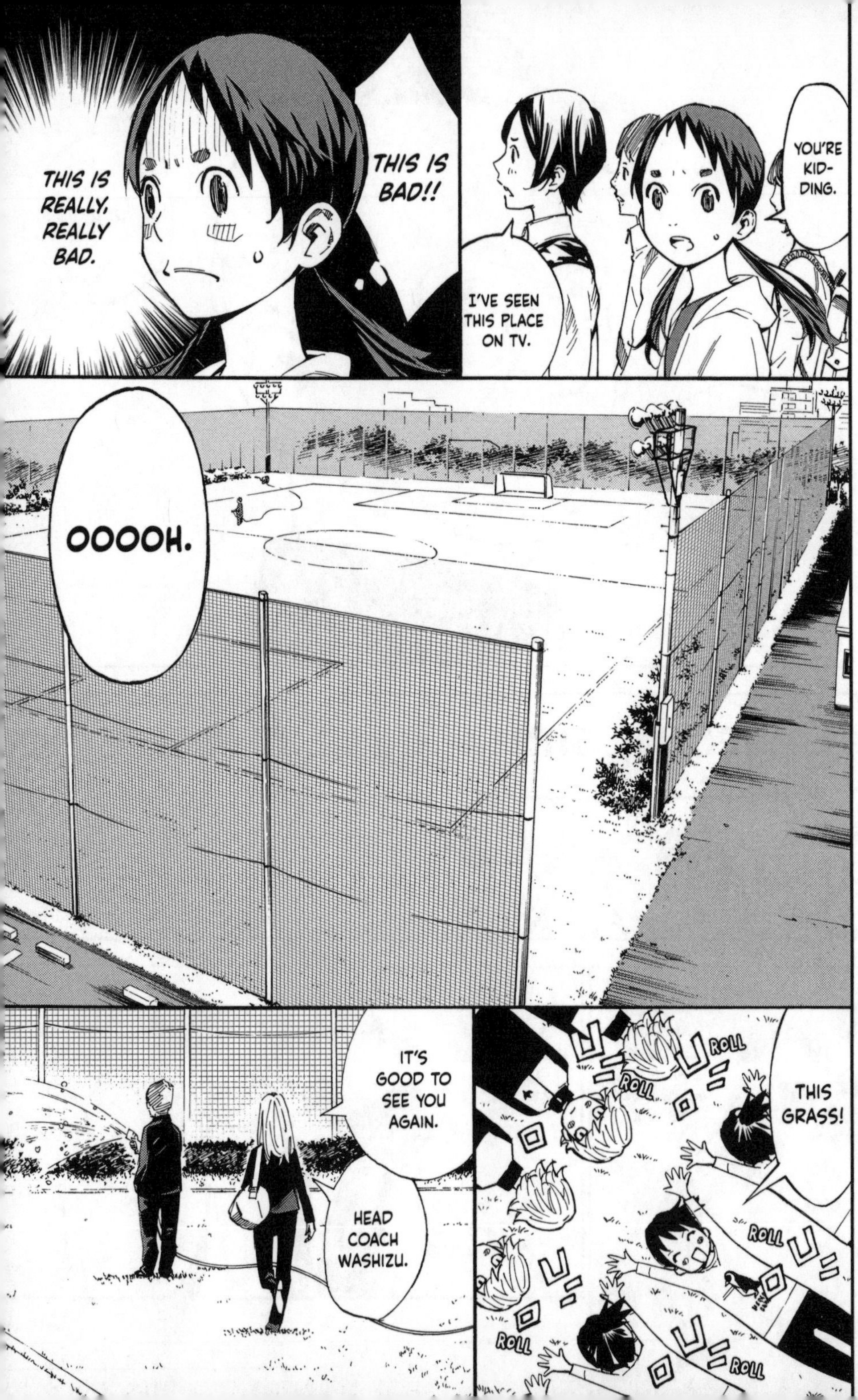
YOU'RE KID-DING.
I'VE SEEN THIS PLACE ON TV.
THIS IS BAD!!
THIS IS REALLY, REALLY BAD.
OOOOH.
THIS GRASS!
ROLL
ROLL
ROLL
ROLL
ROLL
IT'S GOOD TO SEE YOU AGAIN.
HEAD COACH WASHIZU.

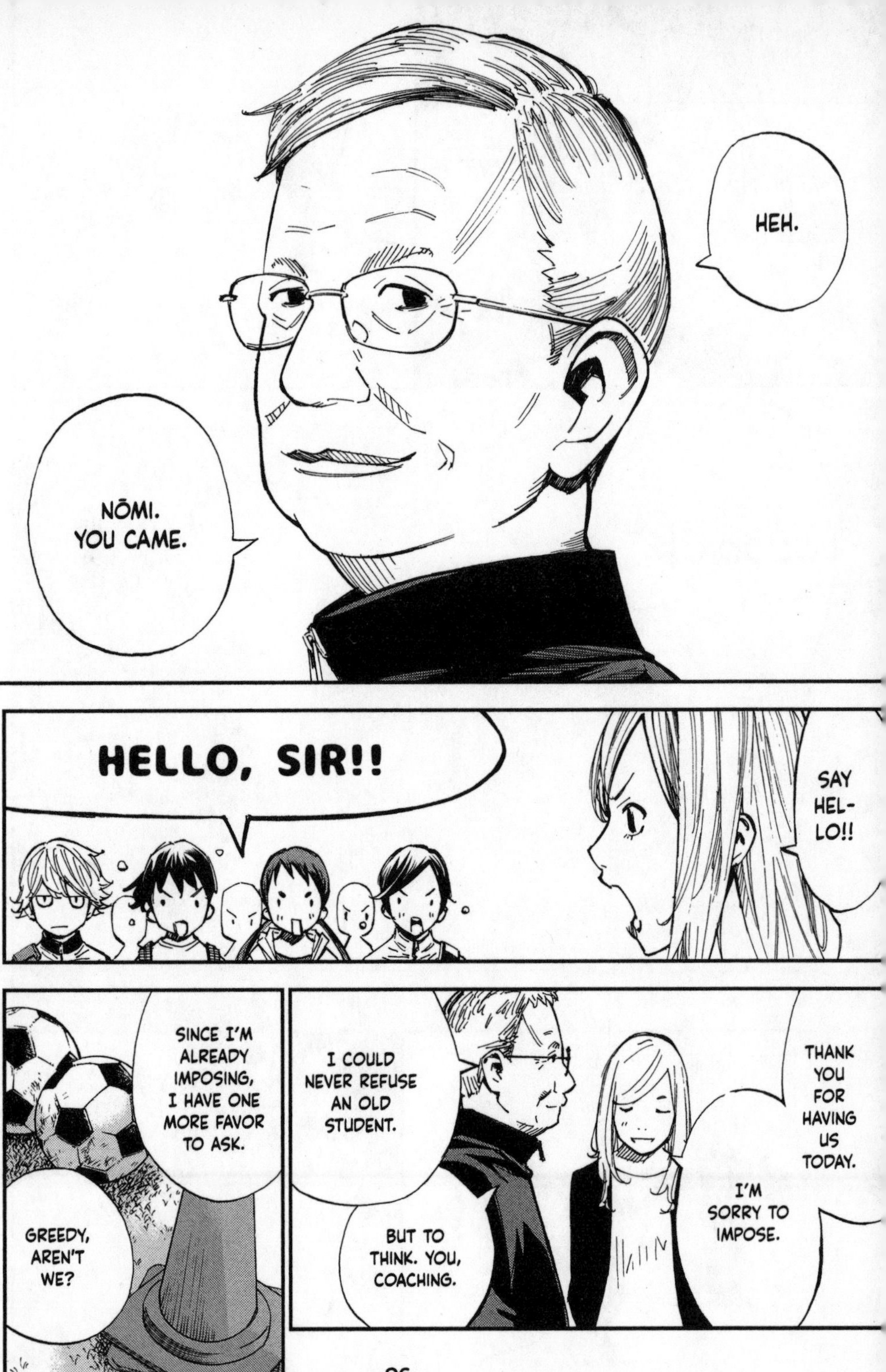
HEH.
NŌMI. YOU CAME.
SAY HEL-LO!!
HELLO, SIR!!
THANK YOU FOR HAVING US TODAY.
I'M SORRY TO IMPOSE.
I COULD NEVER REFUSE AN OLD STUDENT.
BUT TO THINK. YOU, COACHING.
SINCE I'M ALREADY IMPOSING, I HAVE ONE MORE FAVOR TO ASK.
GREEDY, AREN'T WE?

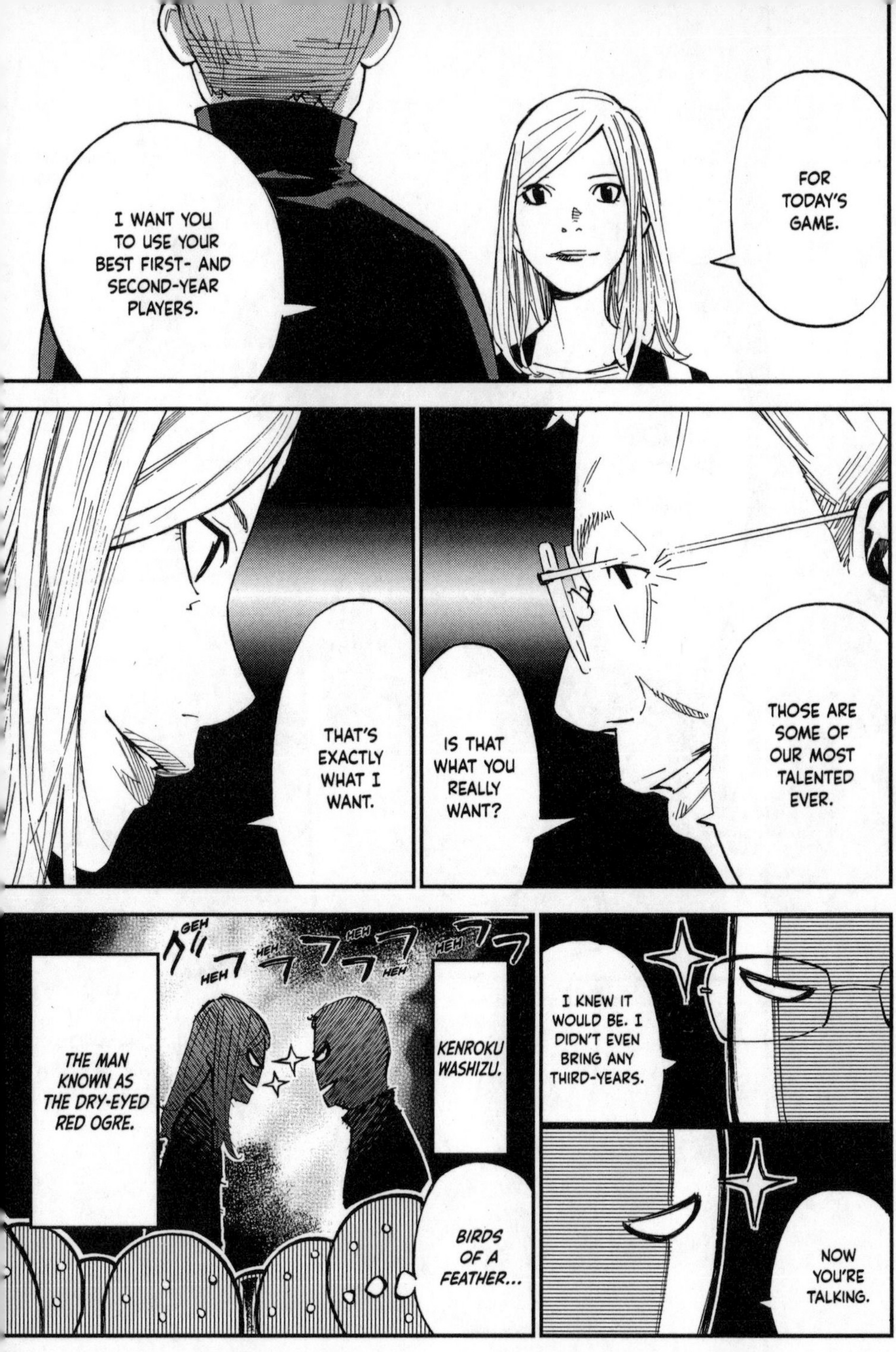
FOR TODAY'S GAME.
I WANT YOU TO USE YOUR BEST FIRST- AND SECOND-YEAR PLAYERS.
THOSE ARE SOME OF OUR MOST TALENTED EVER.
IS THAT WHAT YOU REALLY WANT?
THAT'S EXACTLY WHAT I WANT.
I KNEW IT WOULD BE. I DIDN'T EVEN BRING ANY THIRD-YEARS.
NOW YOU'RE TALKING.
GEH HEH HEH HEH HEH HEH
KENROKU WASHIZU.
THE MAN KNOWN AS THE DRY-EYED RED OGRE.
BIRDS OF A FEATHER...

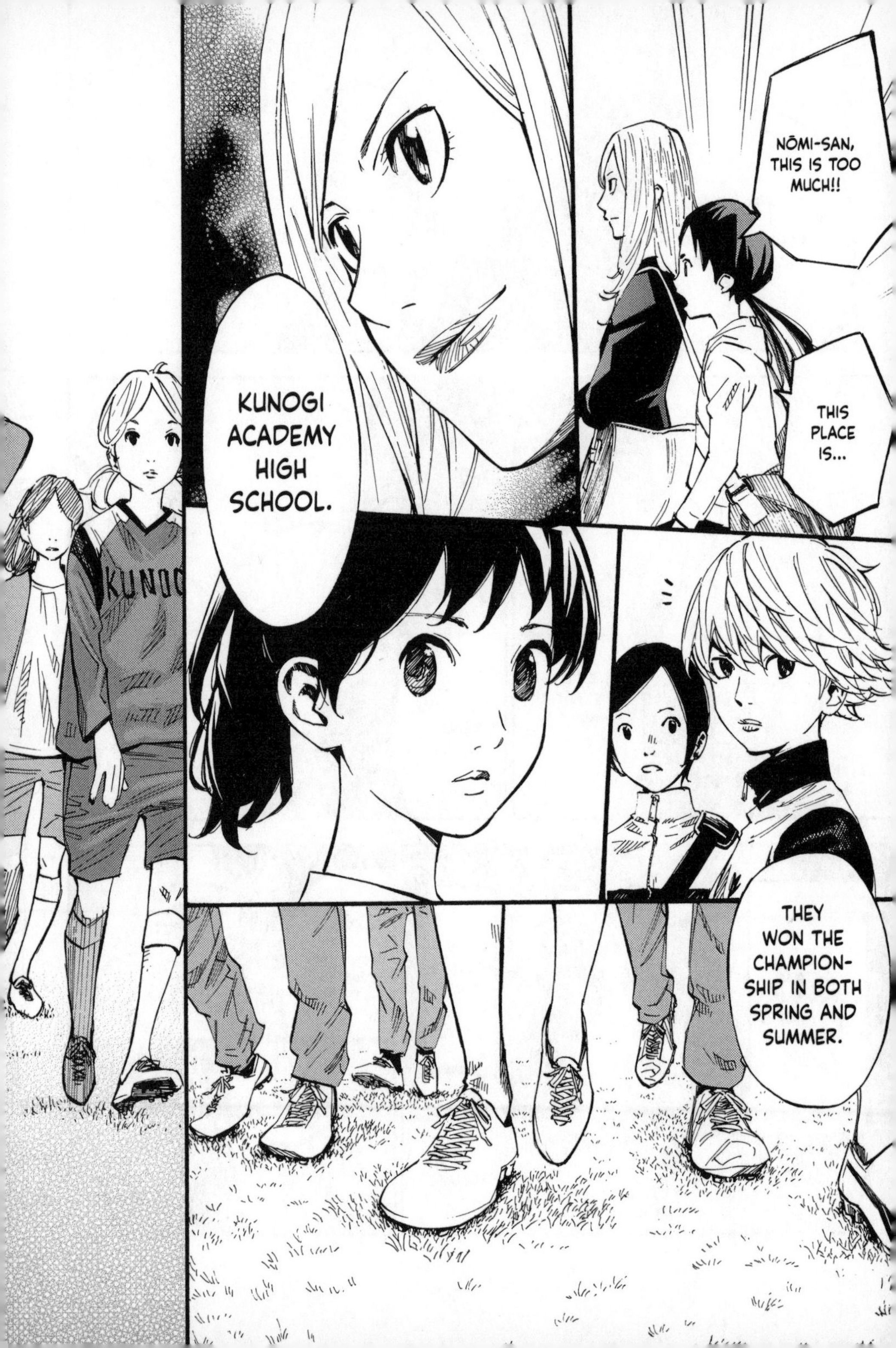
NŌMI-SAN, THIS IS TOO MUCH!!
THIS PLACE IS...
KUNOGI ACADEMY HIGH SCHOOL.
THEY WON THE CHAMPION-SHIP IN BOTH SPRING AND SUMMER.

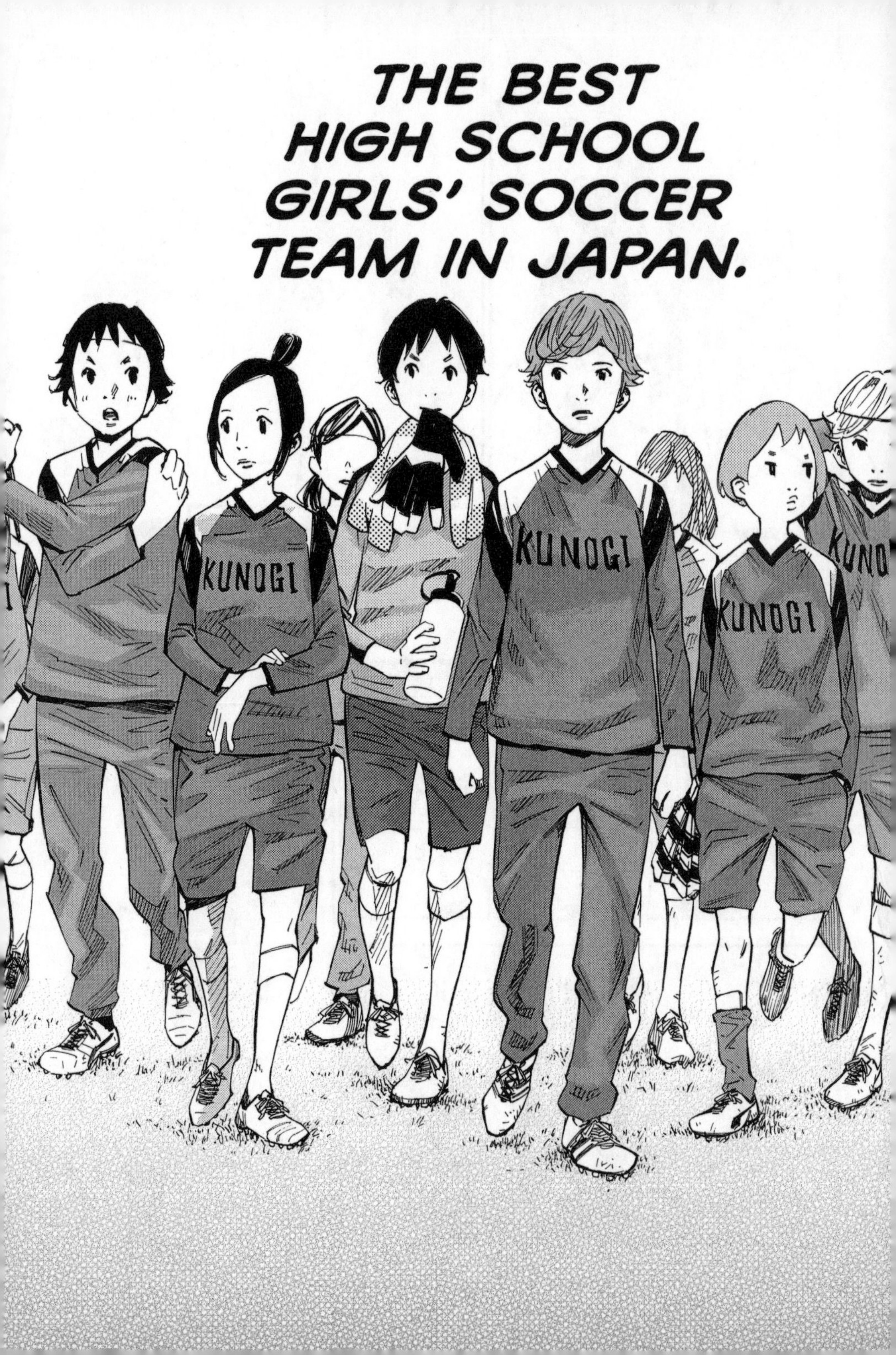
THE BEST HIGH SCHOOL GIRLS' SOCCER TEAM IN JAPAN.
KUNOGI
KUNOGI
KUNOGI
KUNO

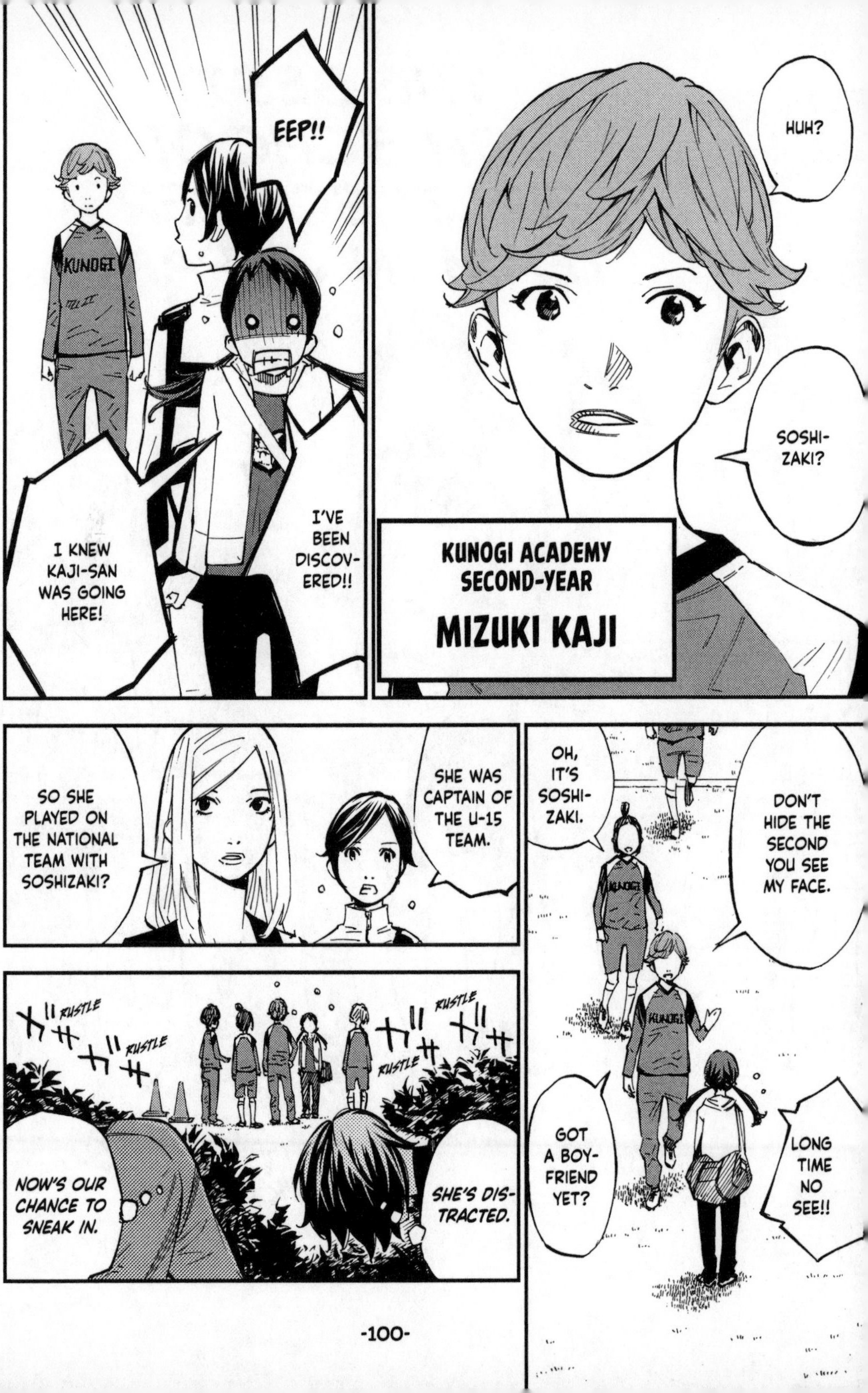
HUH?
SOSHI-ZAKI?
KUNOGI ACADEMY SECOND-YEAR
MIZUKI KAJI
EEP!!
I'VE BEEN DISCOVER-ED!!
I KNEW KAJI-SAN WAS GOING HERE!
DON'T HIDE THE SECOND YOU SEE MY FACE.
OH, IT'S SOSHI-ZAKI.
LONG TIME NO SEE!!
GOT A BOY-FRIEND YET?
SHE WAS CAPTAIN OF THE U-15 TEAM.
SO SHE PLAYED ON THE NATIONAL TEAM WITH SOSHIZAKI?
RUSTLE
RUSTLE
RUSTLE
RUSTLE
SHE'S DIS-TRACTED.
NOW'S OUR CHANCE TO SNEAK IN.

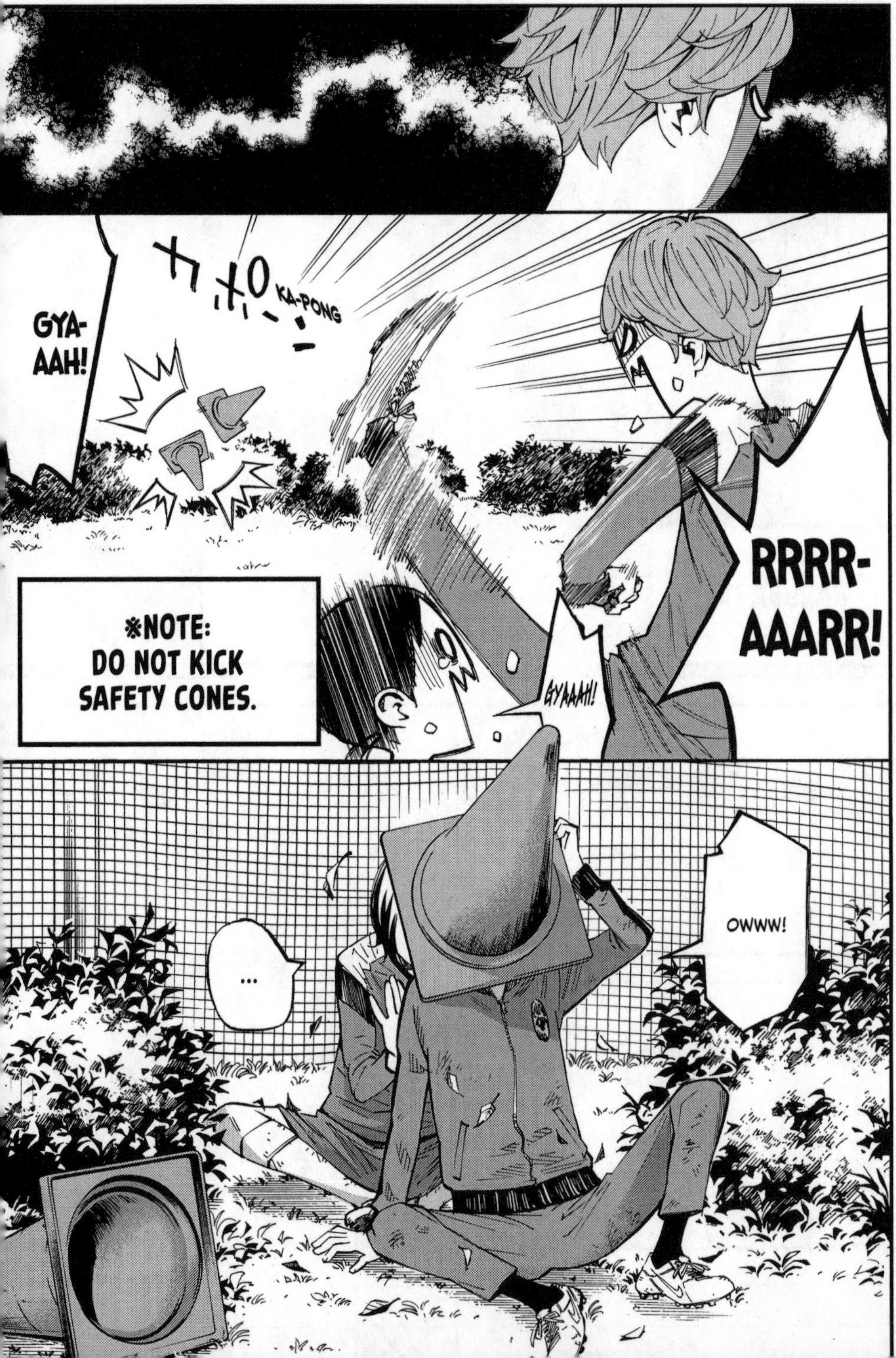
KA-PONG
GYA-AAH!
RRRR-AAARR!
GYAAAH!
※NOTE: DO NOT KICK SAFETY CONES.
OWWW!
...

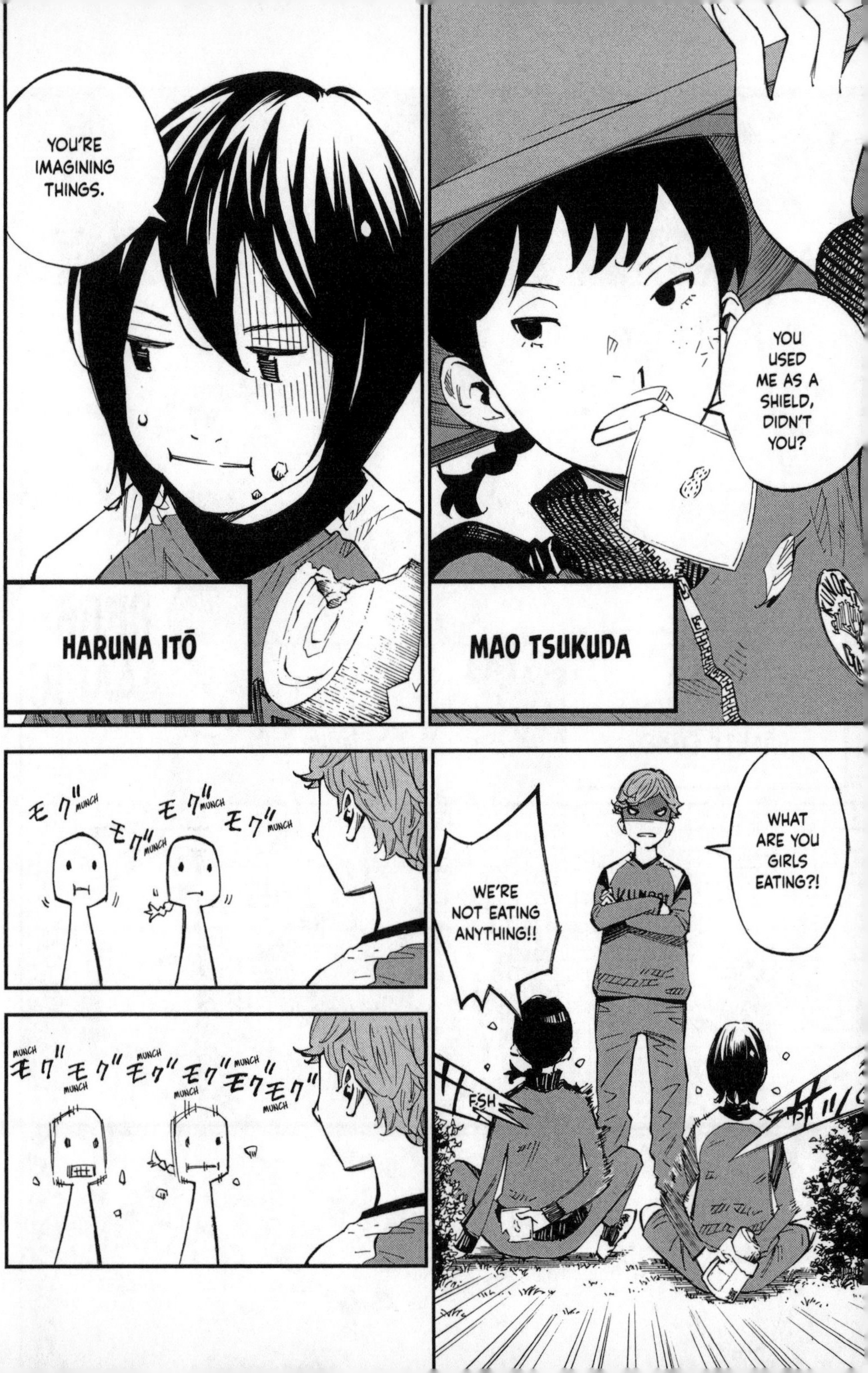
YOU USED ME AS A SHIELD, DIDN'T YOU?
MAO TSUKUDA
YOU'RE IMAGINING THINGS.
HARUNA ITŌ
WHAT ARE YOU GIRLS EATING?!
WE'RE NOT EATING ANYTHING!!
FSH
FSH
モグ MUNCH モグ MUNCH モグ MUNCH モグ MUNCH
モグ MUNCH モグ MUNCH モグ MUNCH モグ MUNCH モグ MUNCH モグ MUNCH

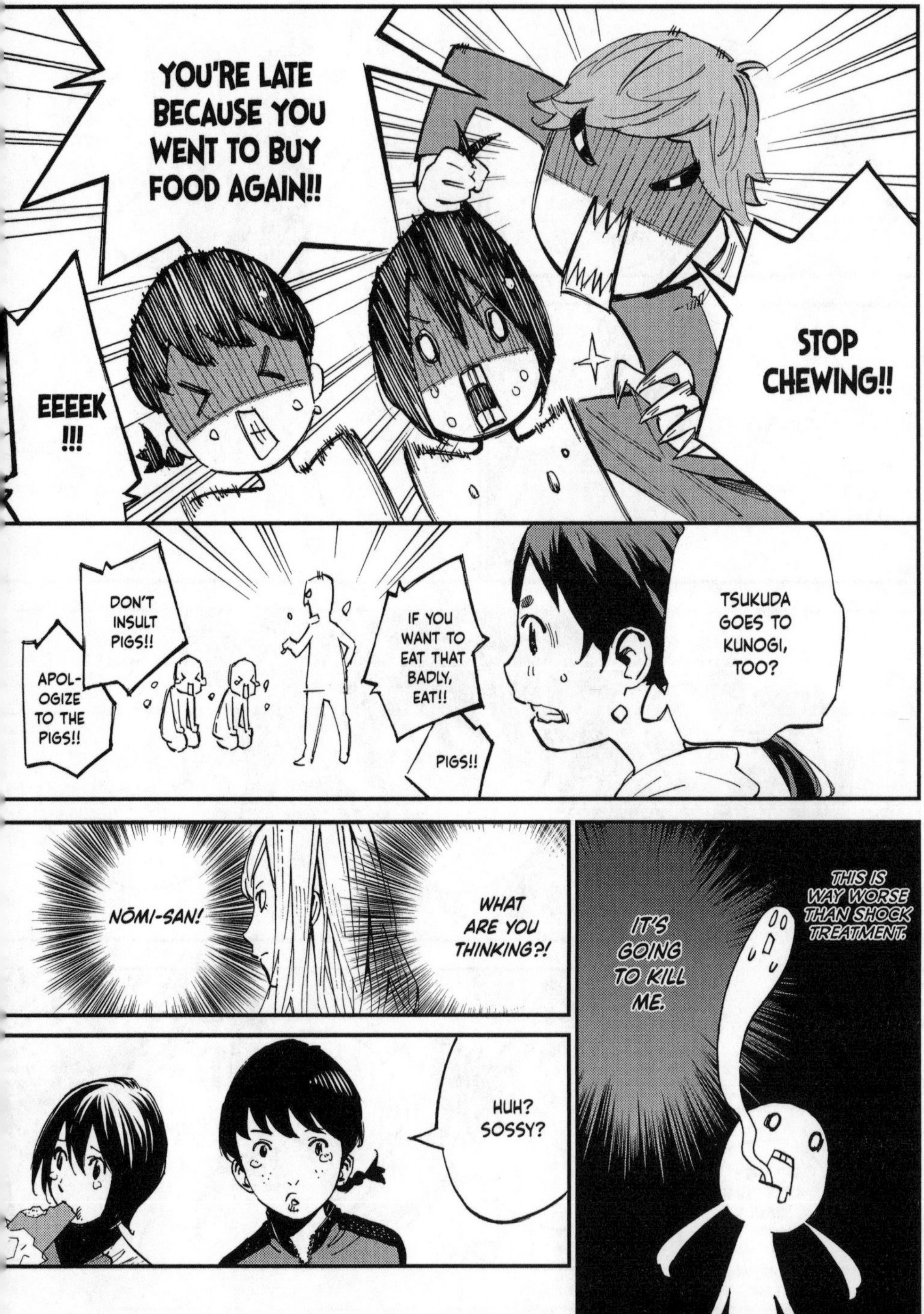
YOU'RE LATE BECAUSE YOU WENT TO BUY FOOD AGAIN!!
STOP CHEWING!!
EEEEK!!!
TSUKUDA GOES TO KUNOGI, TOO?
IF YOU WANT TO EAT THAT BADLY, EAT!!
PIGS!!
DON'T INSULT PIGS!!
APOLOGIZE TO THE PIGS!!
THIS IS WAY WORSE THAN SHOCK TREATMENT.
IT'S GOING TO KILL ME.
WHAT ARE YOU THINKING?!
NŌMI-SAN!
HUH? SOSSY?

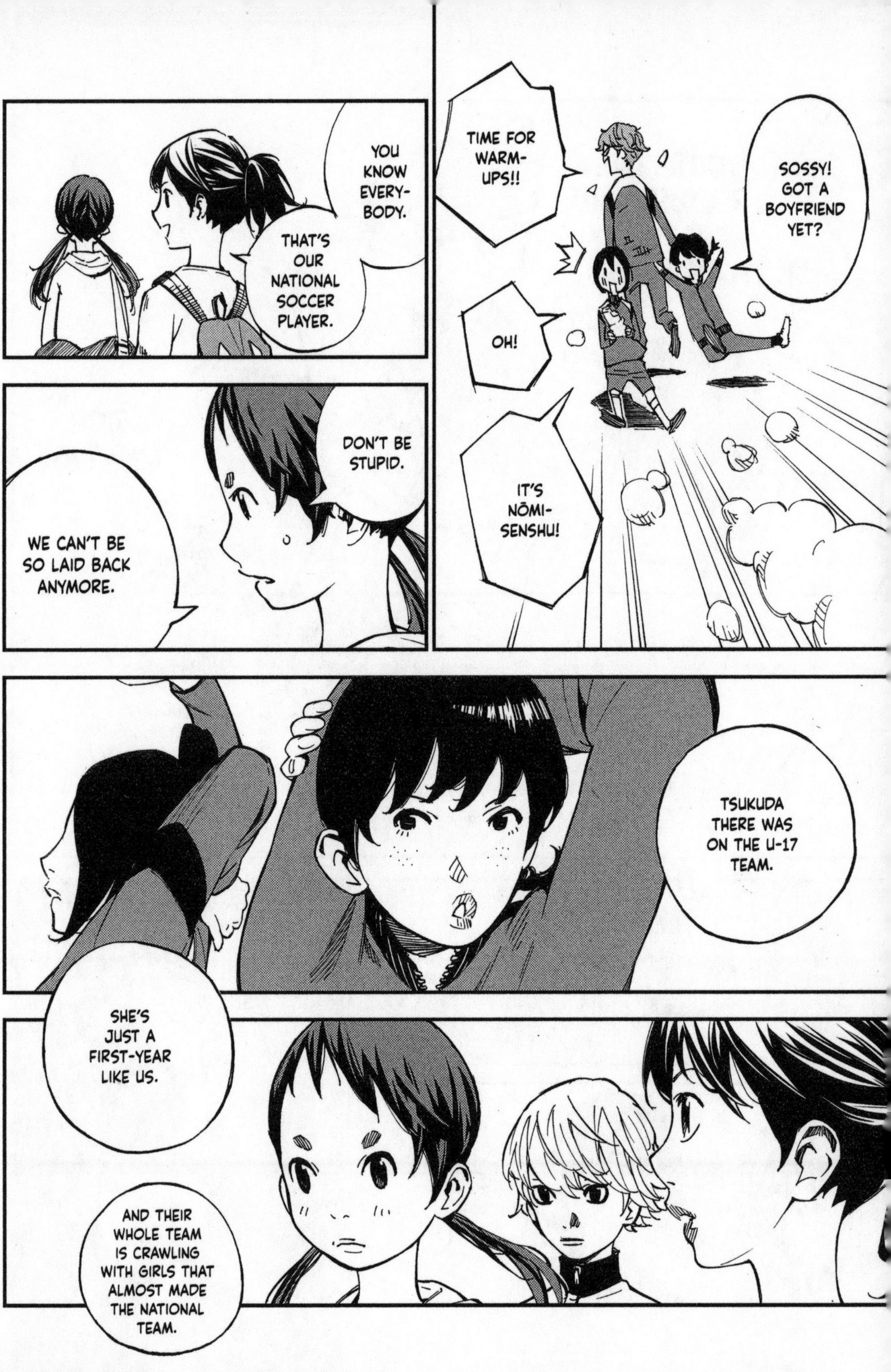
SOSSY! GOT A BOYFRIEND YET?
TIME FOR WARM-UPS!!
OH!
IT'S NŌMI-SENSHU!
YOU KNOW EVERY-BODY.
THAT'S OUR NATIONAL SOCCER PLAYER.
DON'T BE STUPID.
WE CAN'T BE SO LAID BACK ANYMORE.
TSUKUDA THERE WAS ON THE U-17 TEAM.
SHE'S JUST A FIRST-YEAR LIKE US.
AND THEIR WHOLE TEAM IS CRAWLING WITH GIRLS THAT ALMOST MADE THE NATIONAL TEAM.

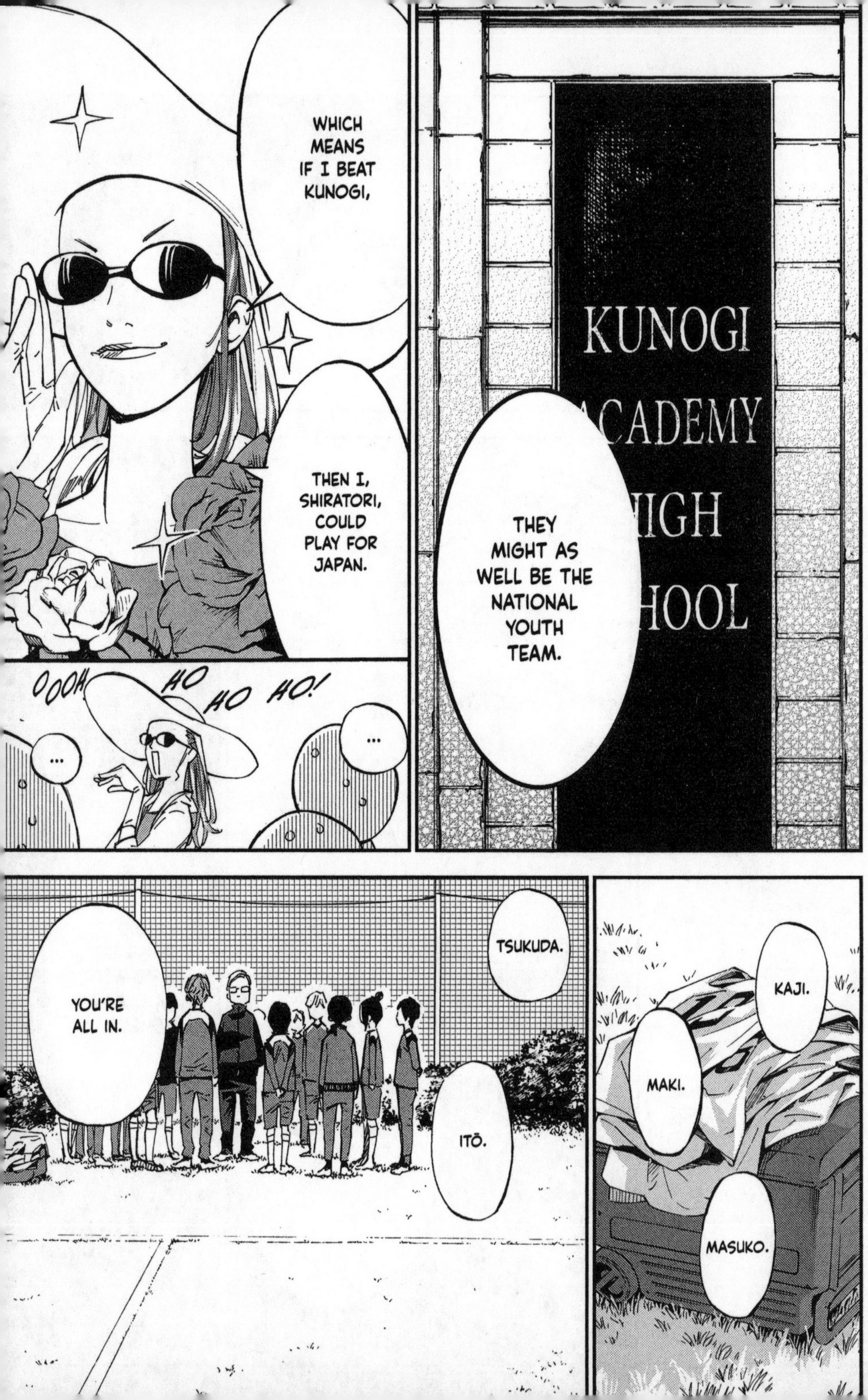
KUNOGI
ACADEMY
IGH
HOOL
THEY MIGHT AS WELL BE THE NATIONAL YOUTH TEAM.
WHICH MEANS IF I BEAT KUNOGI,
THEN I, SHIRATORI, COULD PLAY FOR JAPAN.
OOOH HO HO HO!
...
...
KAJI.
MAKI.
MASUKO.
TSUKUDA.
ITŌ.
YOU'RE ALL IN.

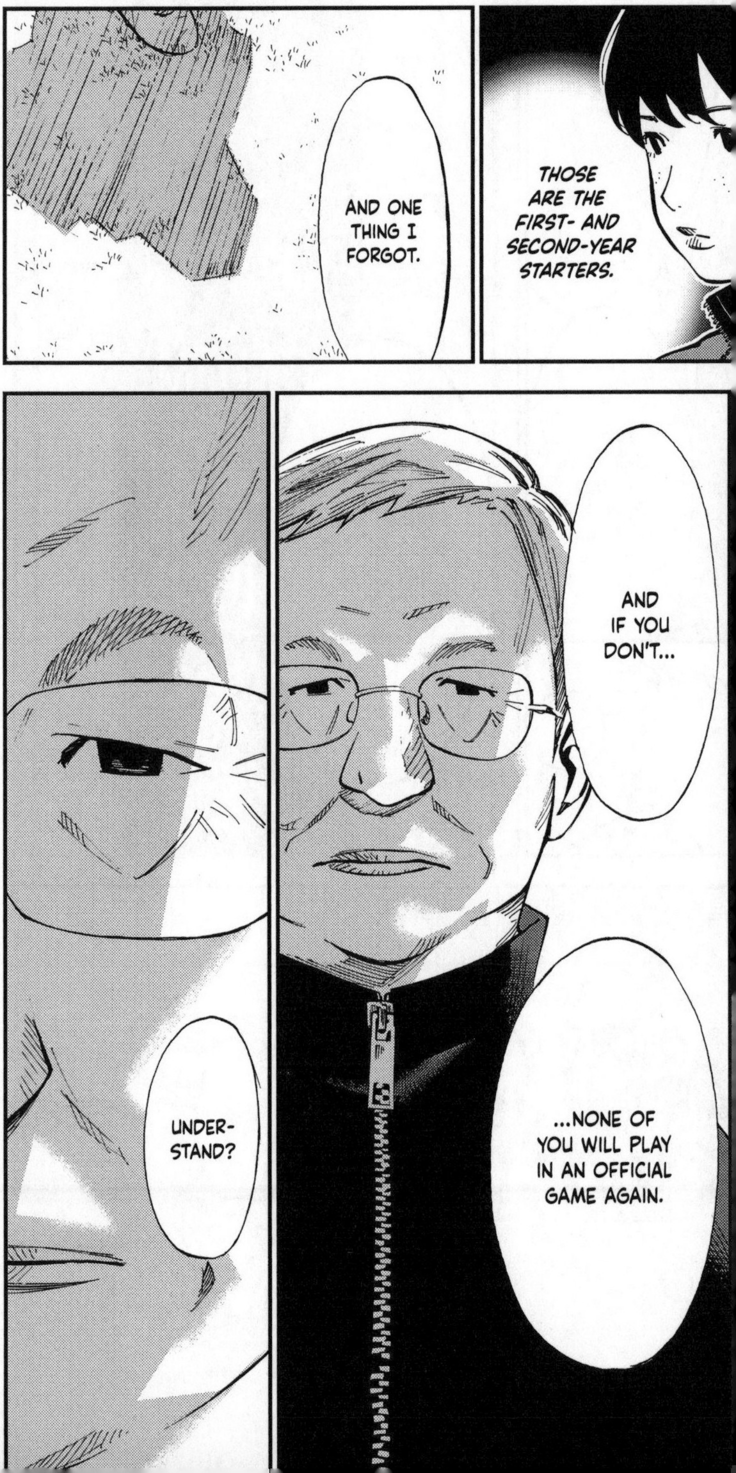
THOSE ARE THE FIRST- AND SECOND-YEAR STARTERS.
AND ONE THING I FORGOT.
AND IF YOU DON'T...
...NONE OF YOU WILL PLAY IN AN OFFICIAL GAME AGAIN.
UNDER-STAND?

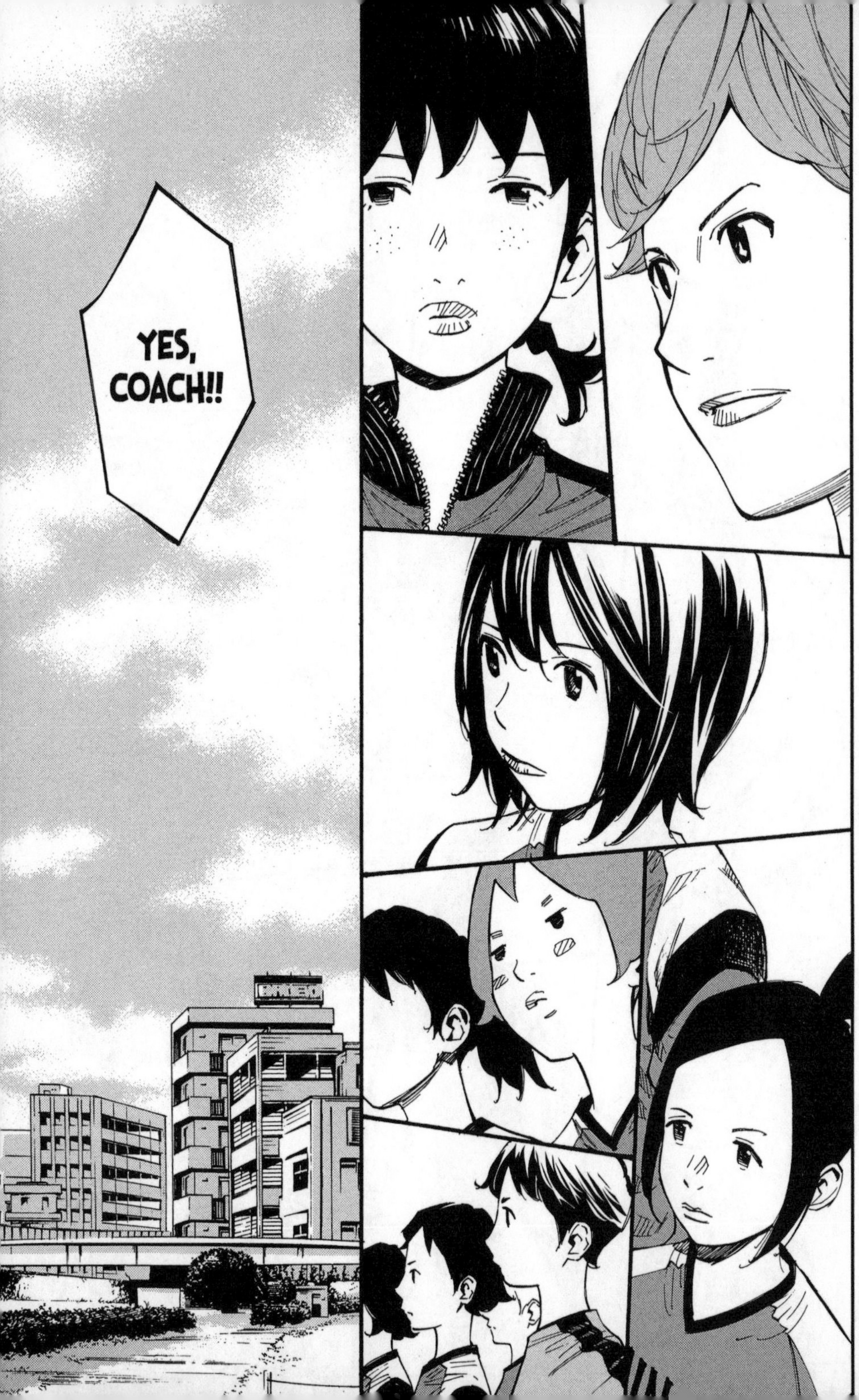
YES, COACH!!

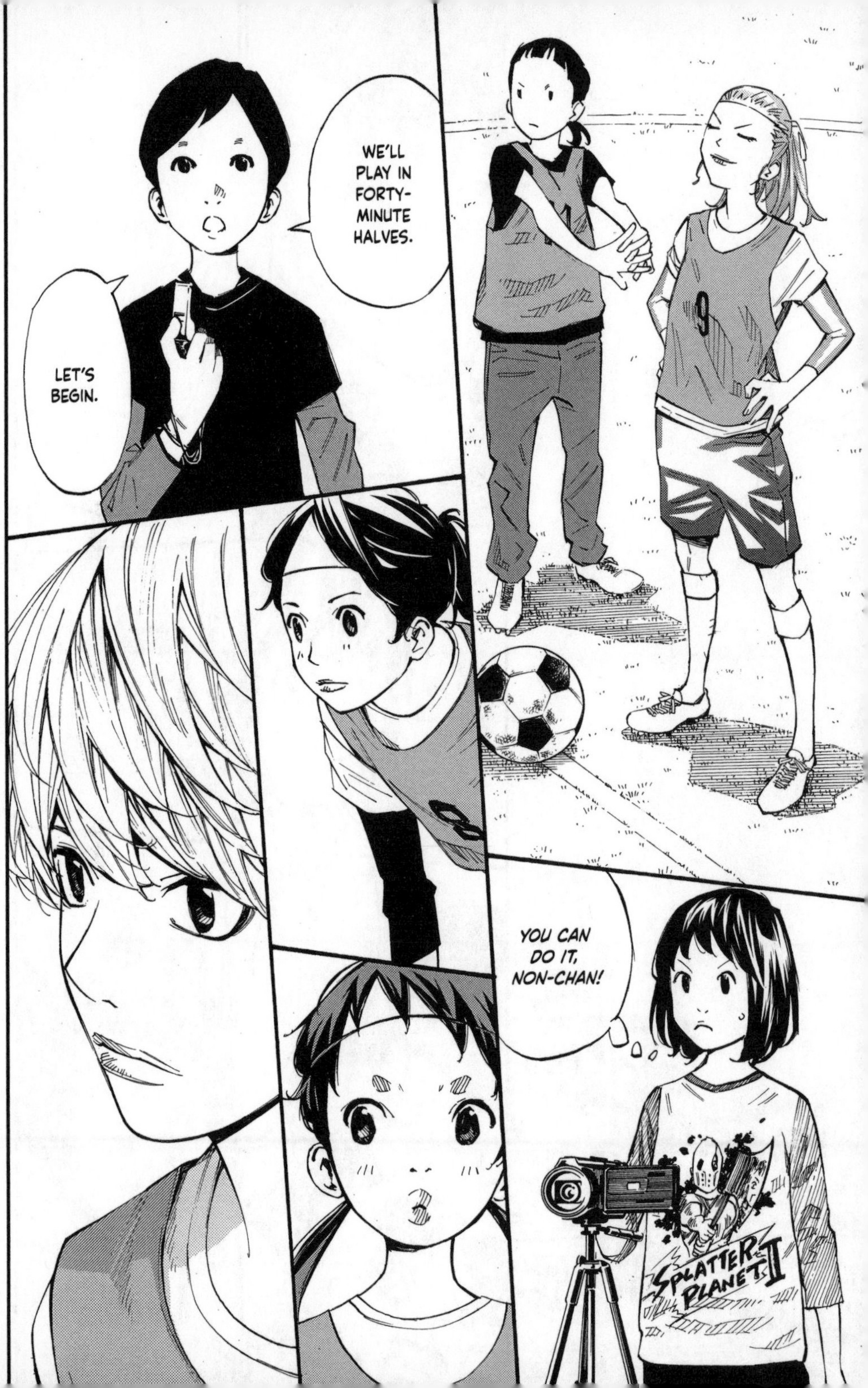
WE'LL PLAY IN FORTY-MINUTE HALVES.
LET'S BEGIN.
YOU CAN DO IT, NON-CHAN!
SPLATTER PLANET II

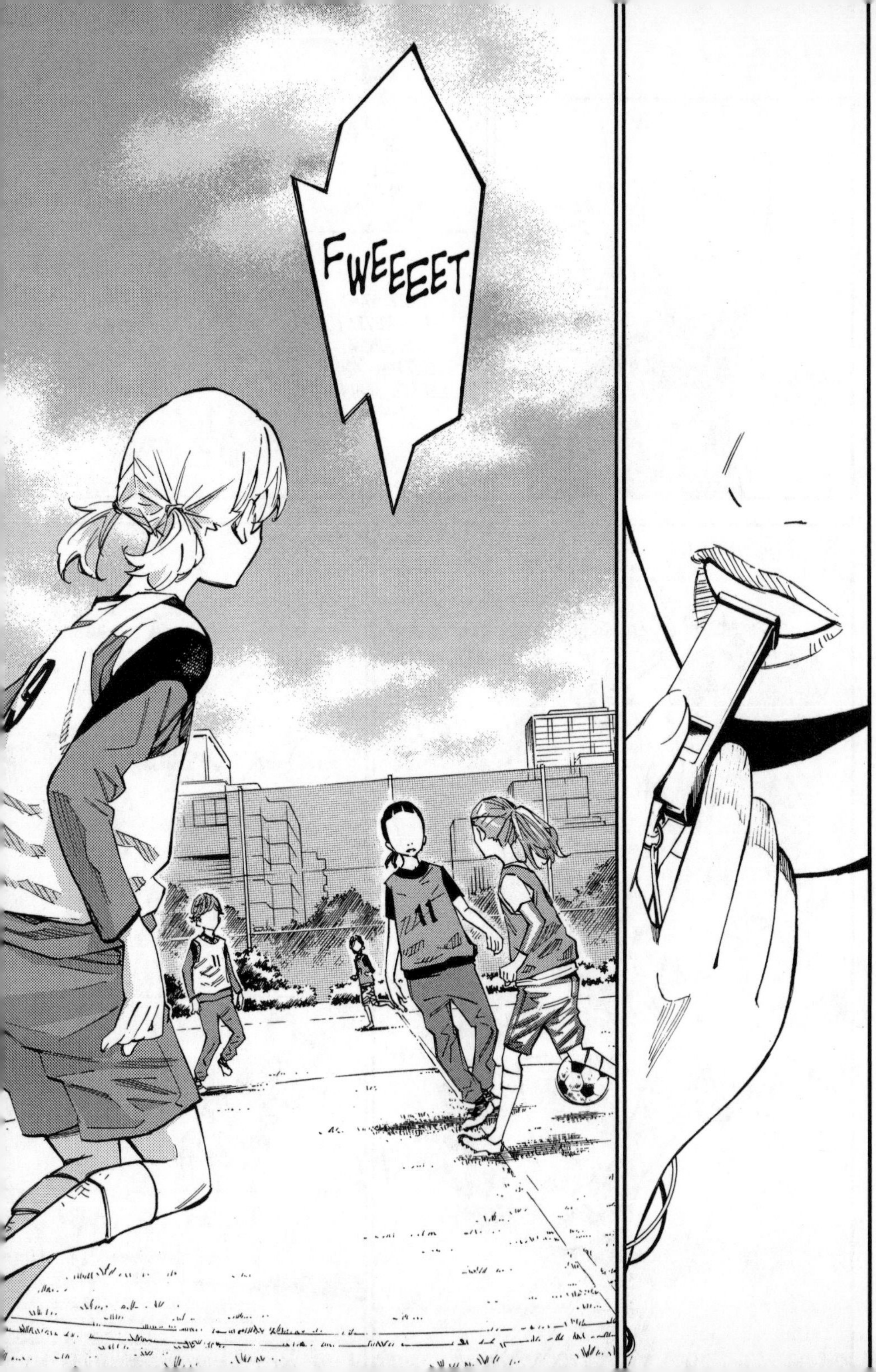
FWEEEET

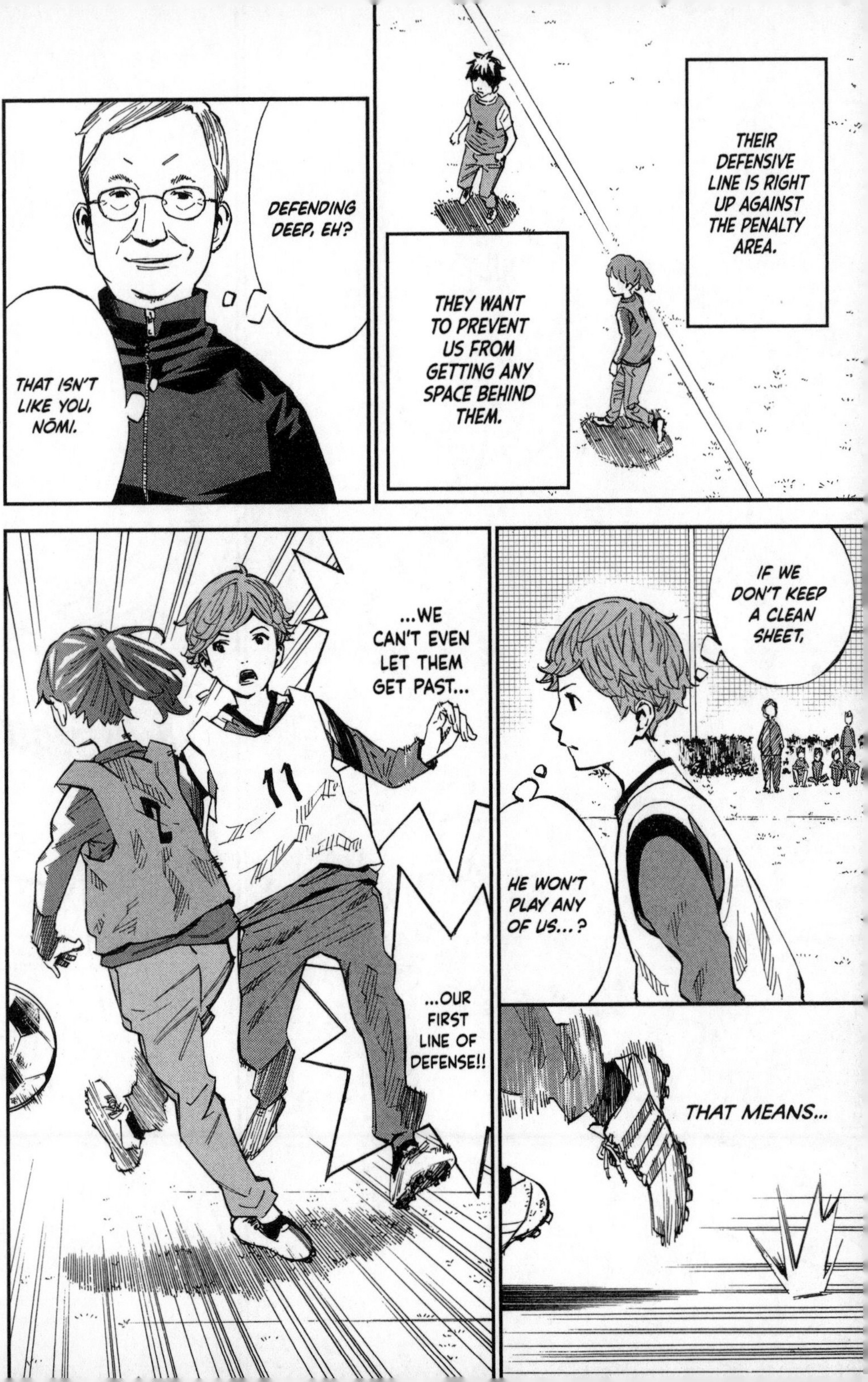
THEIR DEFENSIVE LINE IS RIGHT UP AGAINST THE PENALTY AREA.
THEY WANT TO PREVENT US FROM GETTING ANY SPACE BEHIND THEM.
DEFENDING DEEP, EH?
THAT ISN'T LIKE YOU, NŌMI.
IF WE DON'T KEEP A CLEAN SHEET,
HE WON'T PLAY ANY OF US...?
THAT MEANS...
...WE CAN'T EVEN LET THEM GET PAST...
...OUR FIRST LINE OF DEFENSE!!

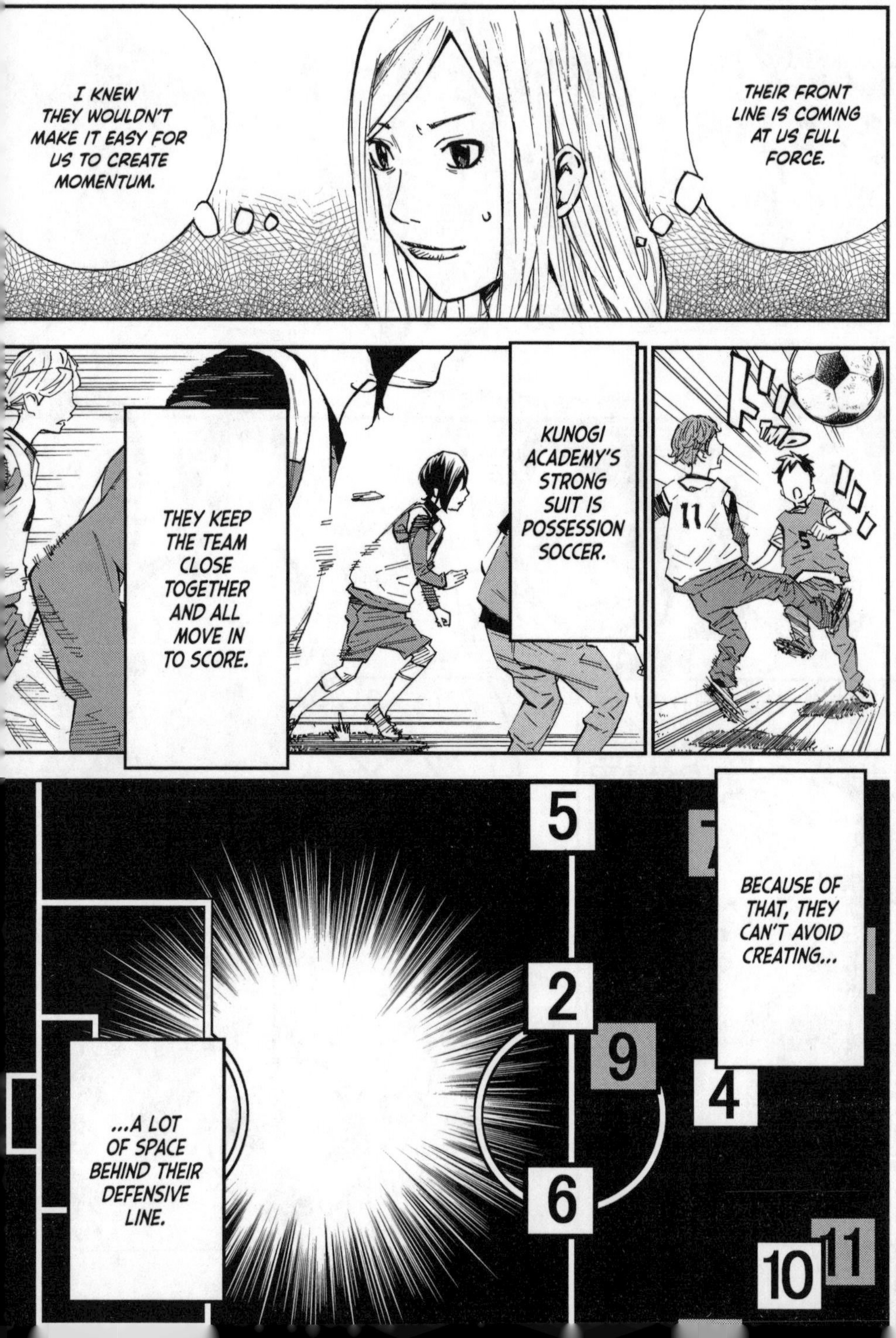
THEIR FRONT LINE IS COMING AT US FULL FORCE.
I KNEW THEY WOULDN'T MAKE IT EASY FOR US TO CREATE MOMENTUM.
ドッ
THMP
KUNOGI ACADEMY'S STRONG SUIT IS POSSESSION SOCCER.
THEY KEEP THE TEAM CLOSE TOGETHER AND ALL MOVE IN TO SCORE.
BECAUSE OF THAT, THEY CAN'T AVOID CREATING...
5
2
9
4
6
10
11
...A LOT OF SPACE BEHIND THEIR DEFENSIVE LINE.

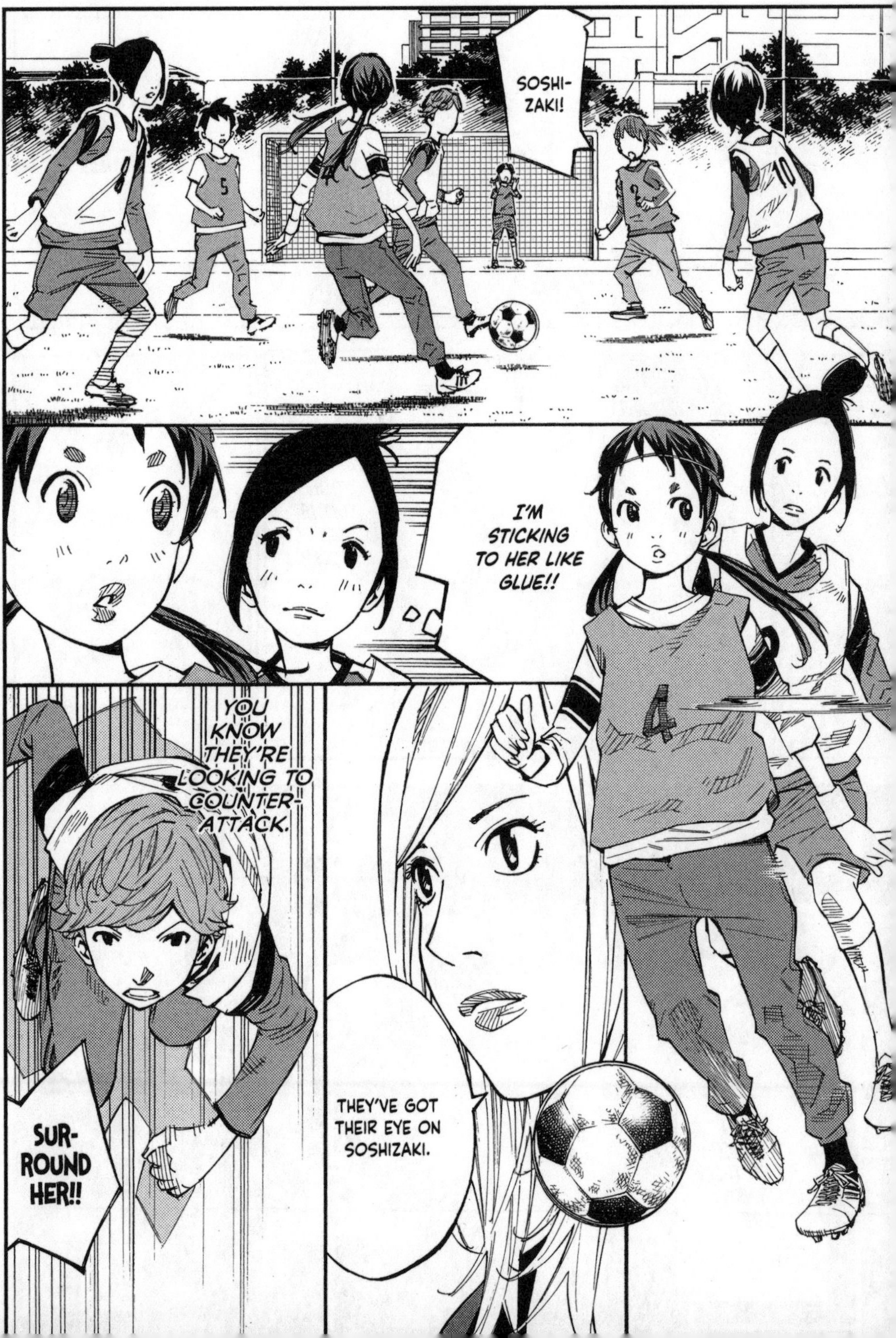
SOSHI-ZAKI!
I'M STICKING TO HER LIKE GLUE!!
THEY'VE GOT THEIR EYE ON SOSHIZAKI.
YOU KNOW THEY'RE LOOKING TO COUNTER-ATTACK.
SUR-ROUND HER!!

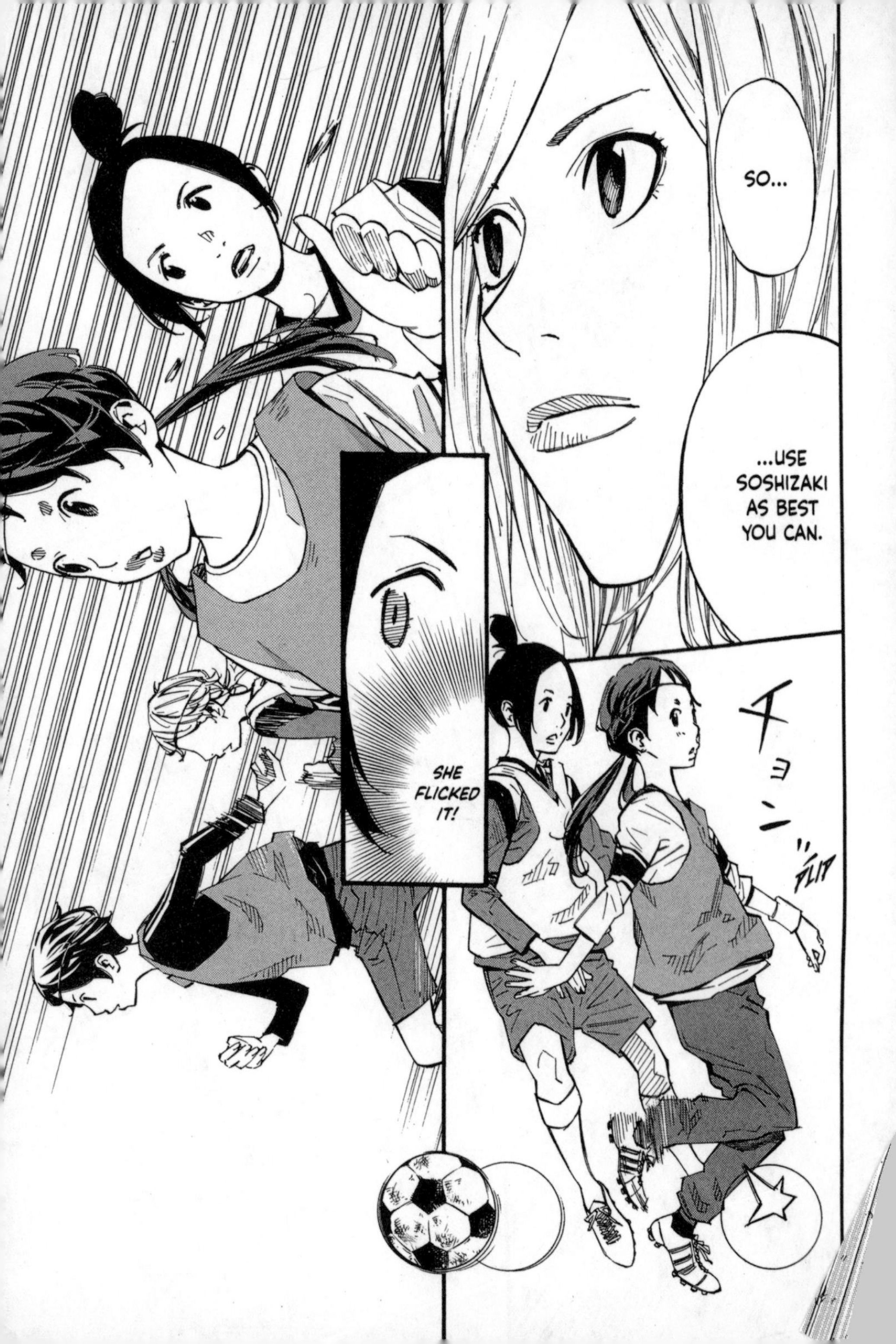
SO...
...USE SOSHIZAKI AS BEST YOU CAN.
チョンッ
FLIP
SHE FLICKED IT!

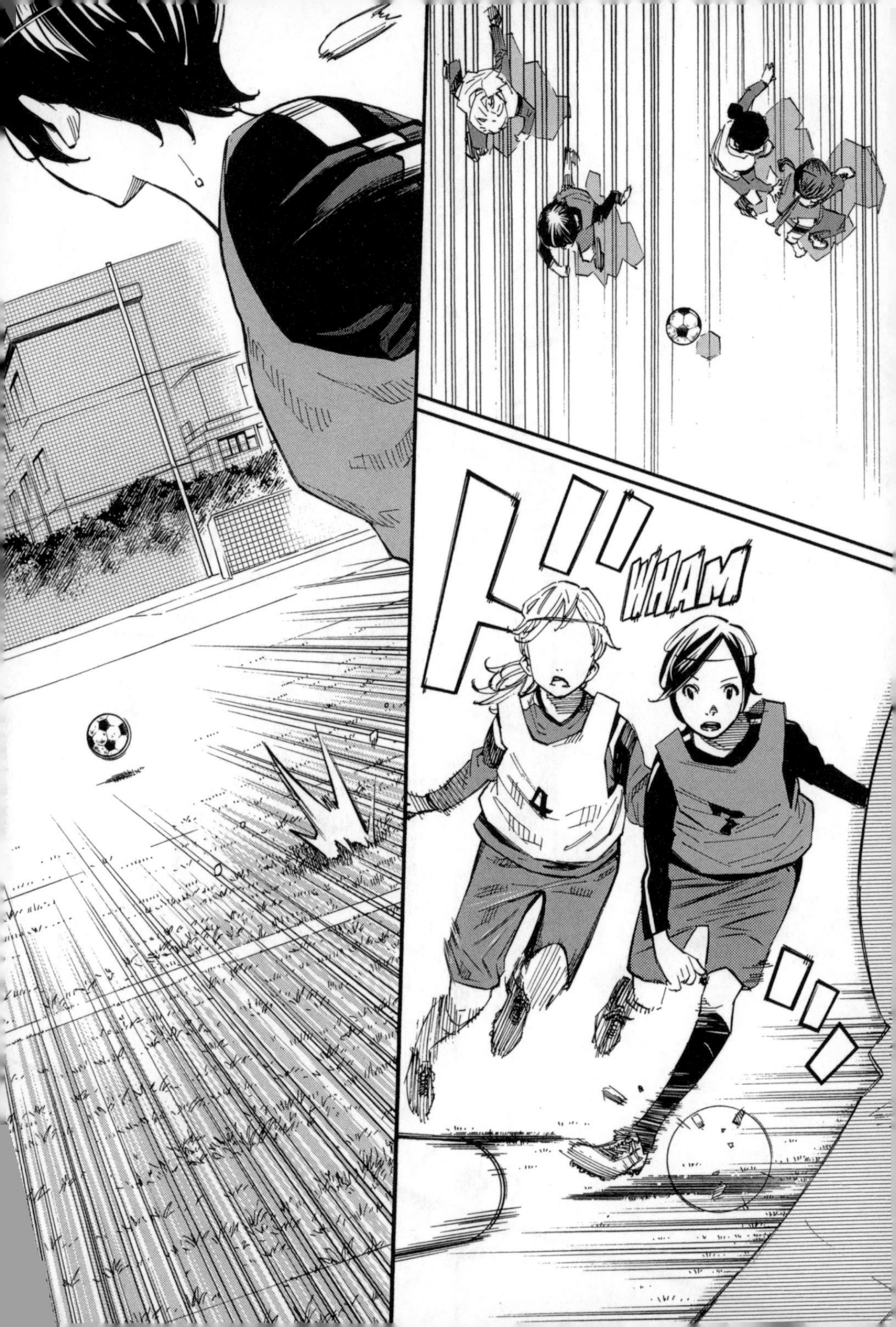
WHAM

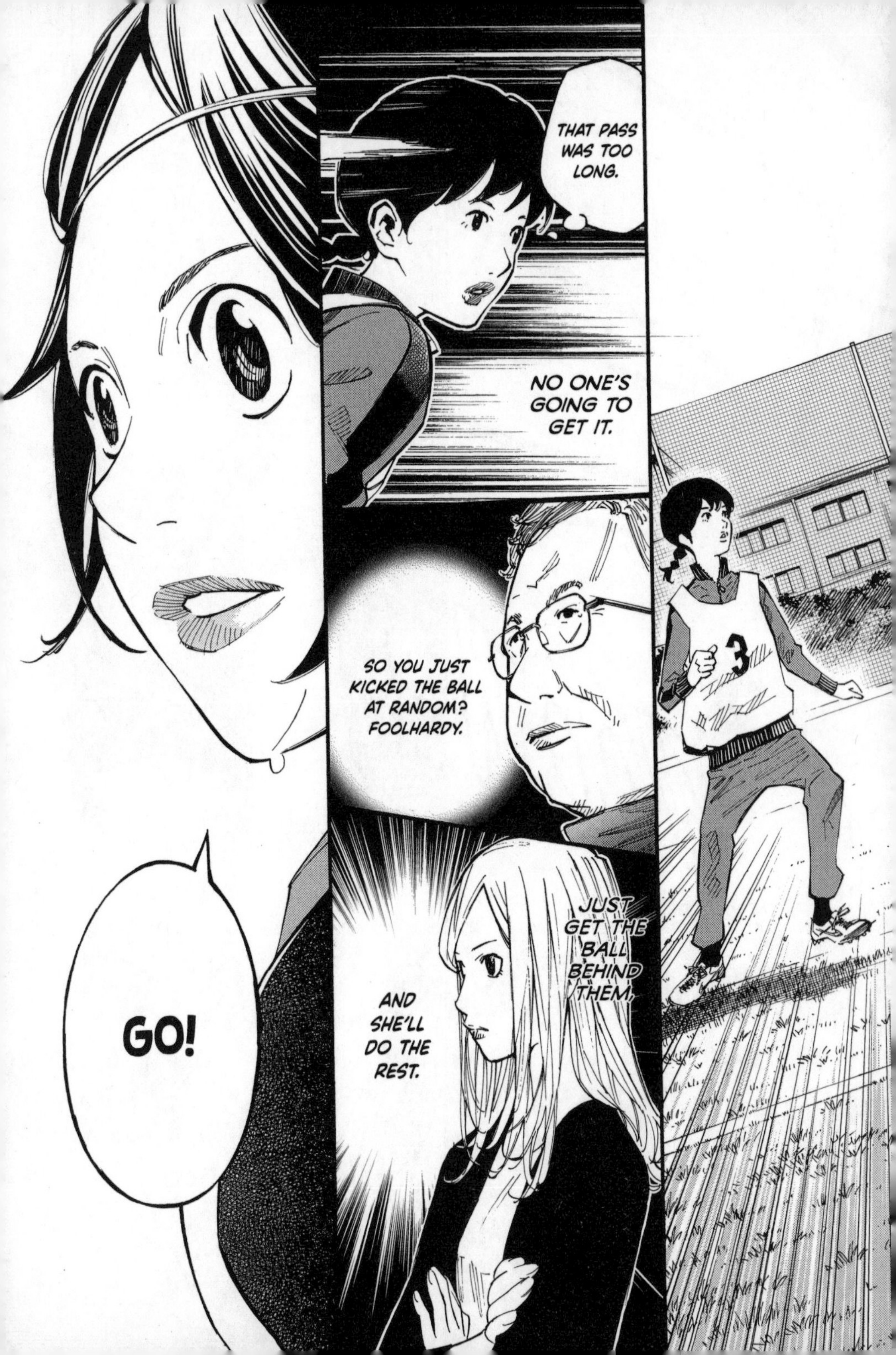
THAT PASS WAS TOO LONG.
NO ONE'S GOING TO GET IT.
SO YOU JUST KICKED THE BALL AT RANDOM? FOOLHARDY.
JUST GET THE BALL BEHIND THEM.
AND SHE'LL DO THE REST.
GO!

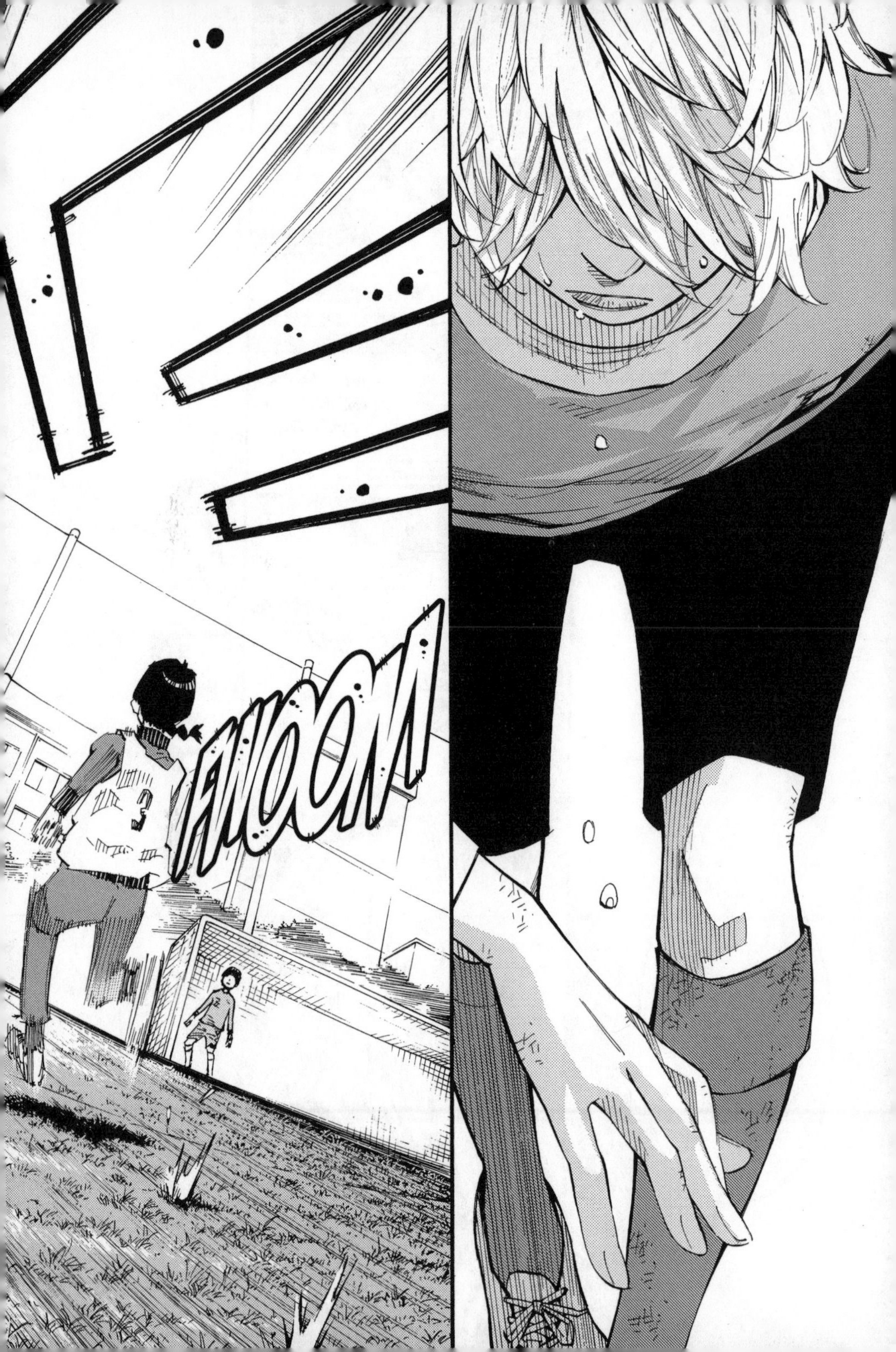
FWOOM

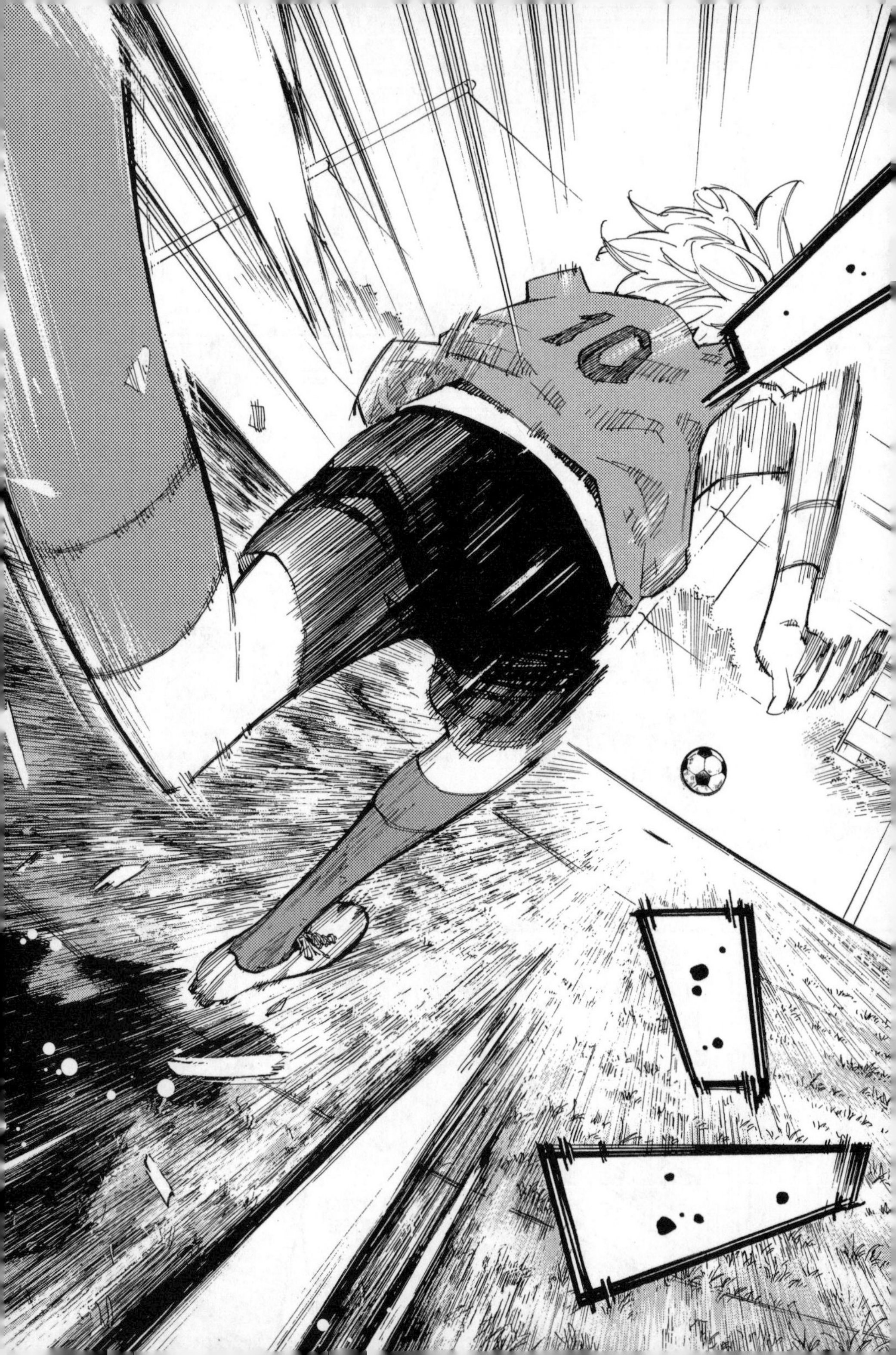

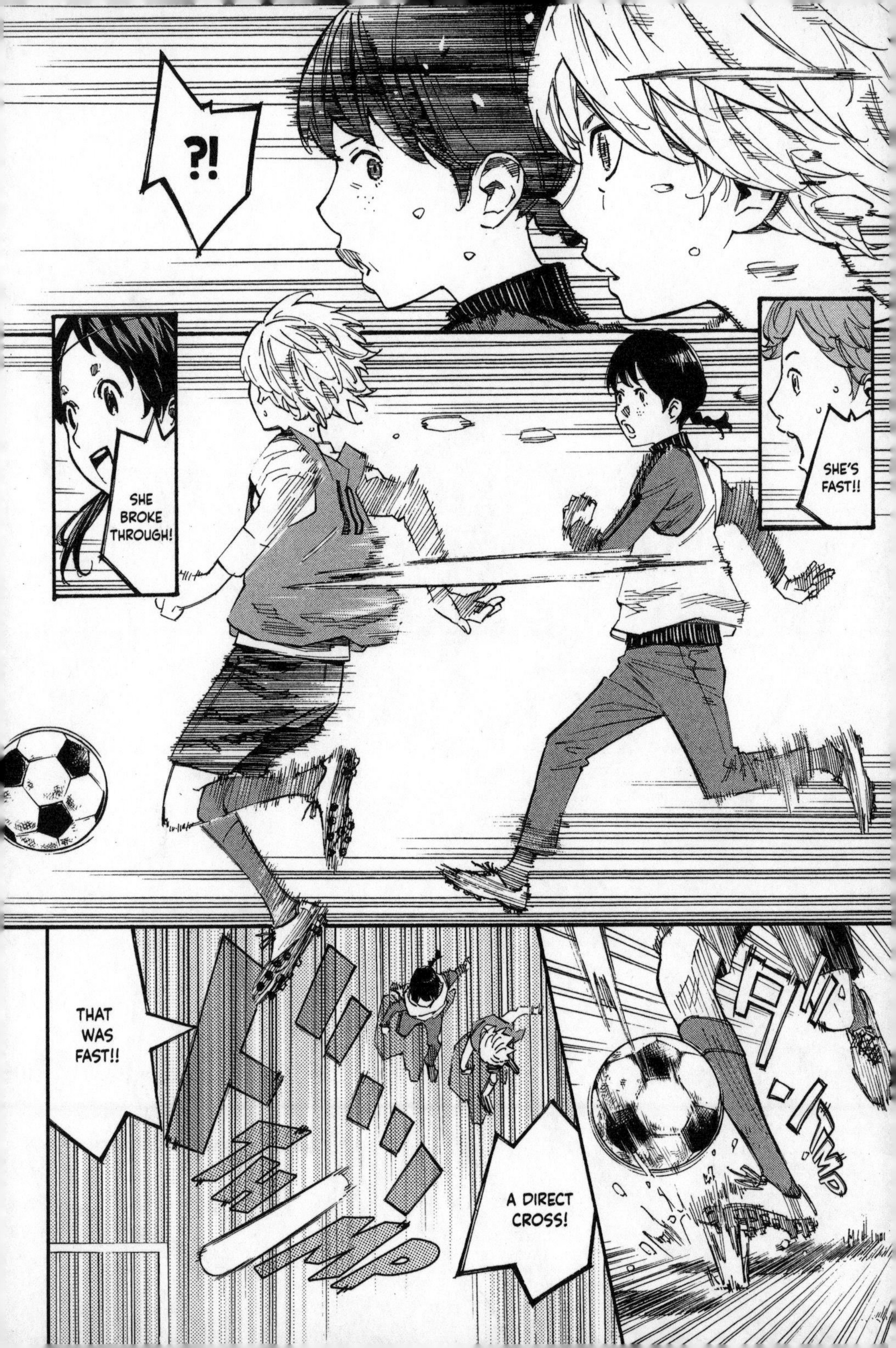
?!
SHE'S FAST!!
SHE BROKE THROUGH!
A DIRECT CROSS!
THAT WAS FAST!!

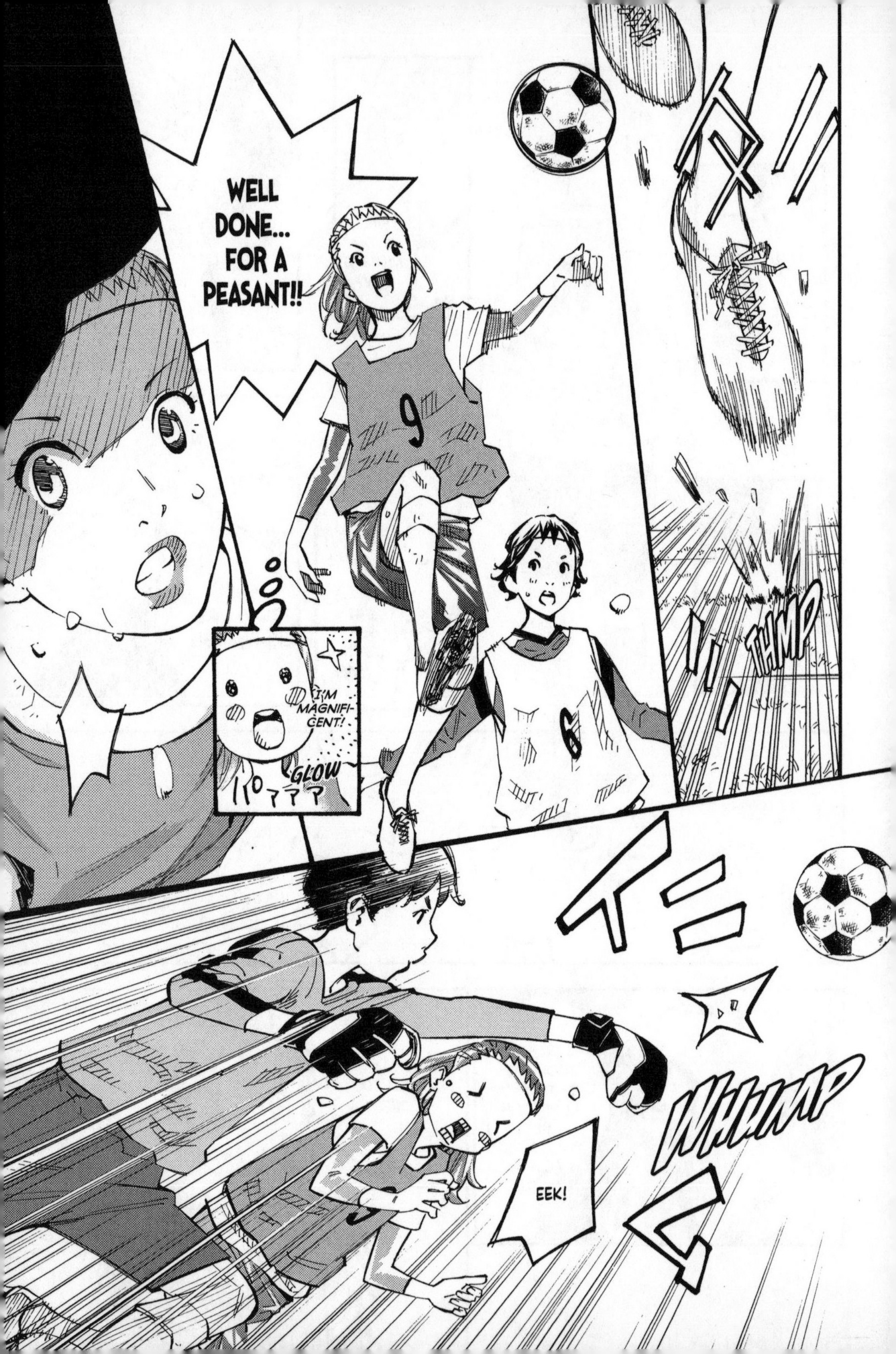
THMP
WELL DONE... FOR A PEASANT!!
I'M MAGNIFI-CENT!
GLOW
WHUMP
EEK!

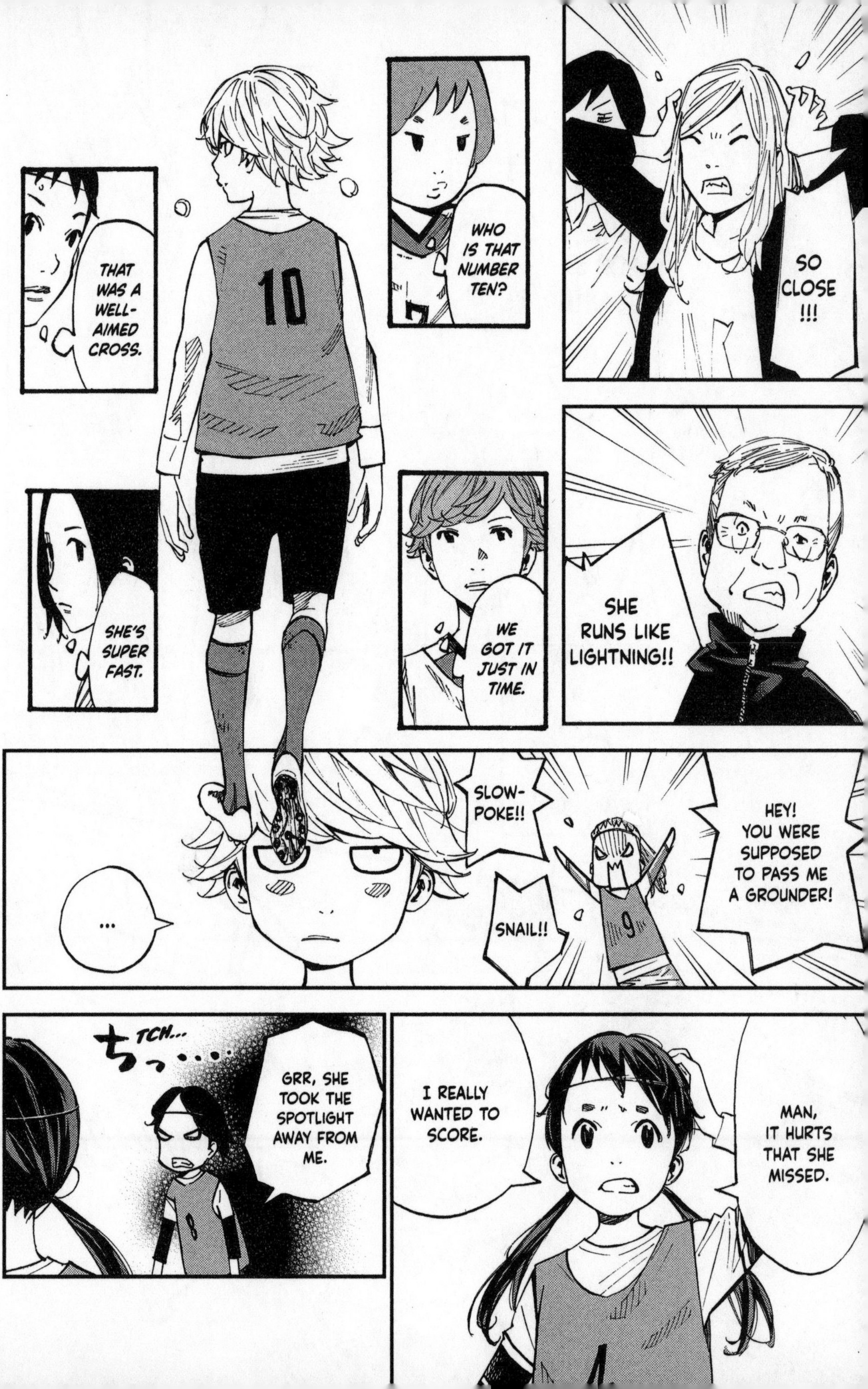
SO CLOSE !!!
WHO IS THAT NUMBER TEN?
THAT WAS A WELL-AIMED CROSS.
SHE RUNS LIKE LIGHTNING!!
WE GOT IT JUST IN TIME.
SHE'S SUPER FAST.
HEY! YOU WERE SUPPOSED TO PASS ME A GROUNDER!
SLOW-POKE!!
SNAIL!!
...
MAN, IT HURTS THAT SHE MISSED.
I REALLY WANTED TO SCORE.
TCH...
GRR, SHE TOOK THE SPOTLIGHT AWAY FROM ME.

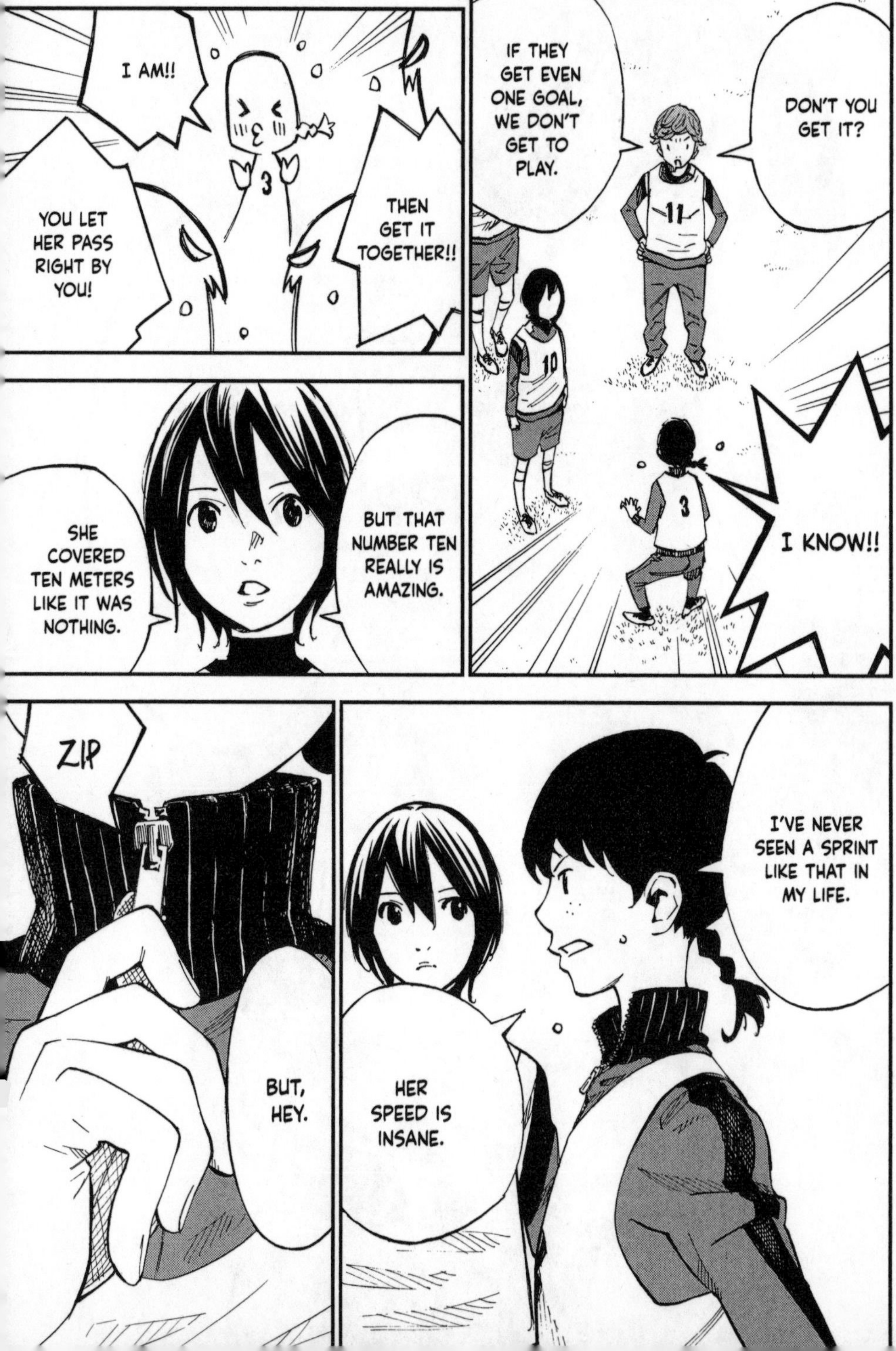
DON'T YOU GET IT?
IF THEY GET EVEN ONE GOAL, WE DON'T GET TO PLAY.
I KNOW!!
I AM!!
THEN GET IT TOGETHER!!
YOU LET HER PASS RIGHT BY YOU!
BUT THAT NUMBER TEN REALLY IS AMAZING.
SHE COVERED TEN METERS LIKE IT WAS NOTHING.
I'VE NEVER SEEN A SPRINT LIKE THAT IN MY LIFE.
HER SPEED IS INSANE.
ZIP
BUT, HEY.

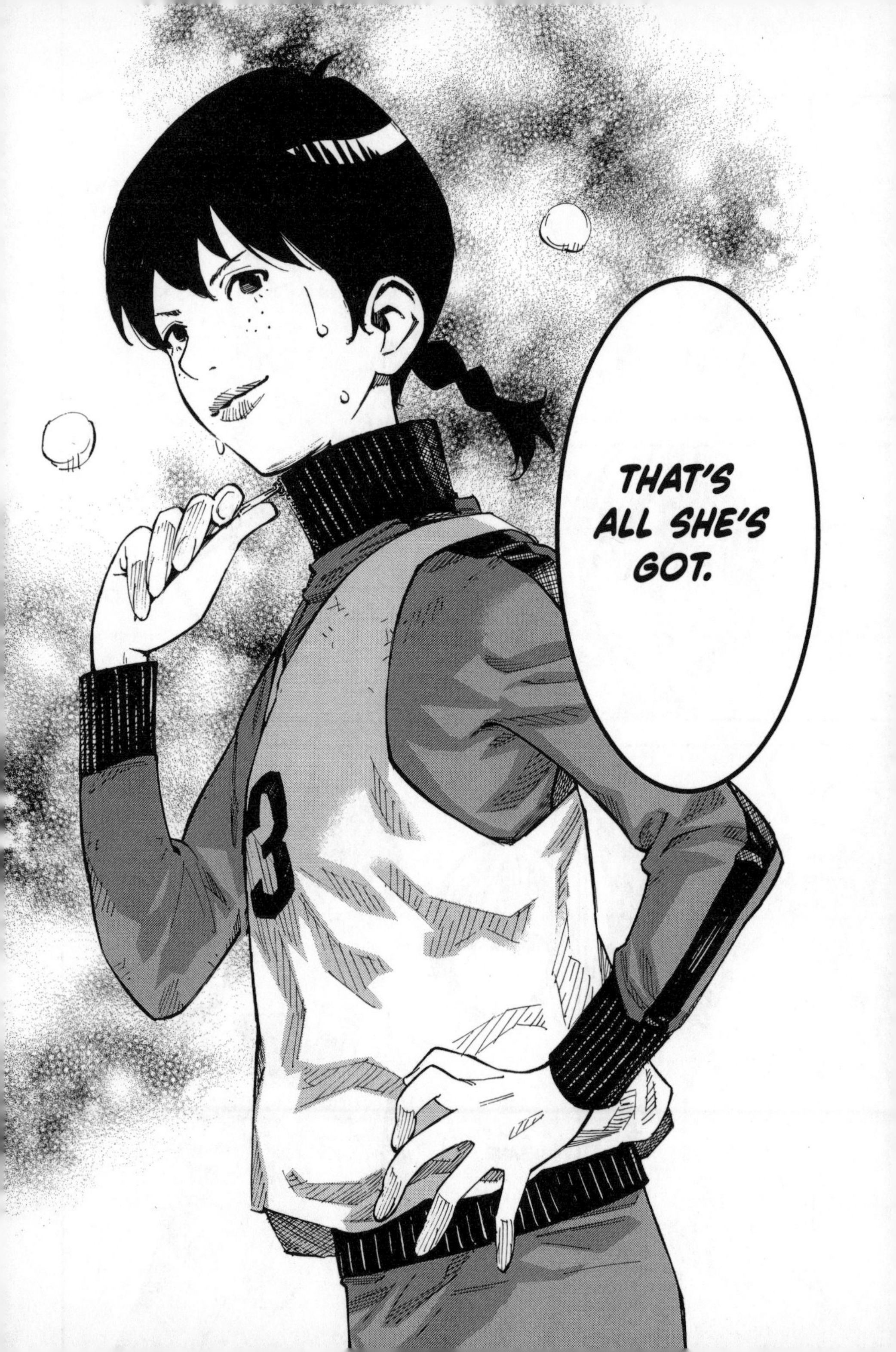
THAT'S ALL SHE'S GOT.

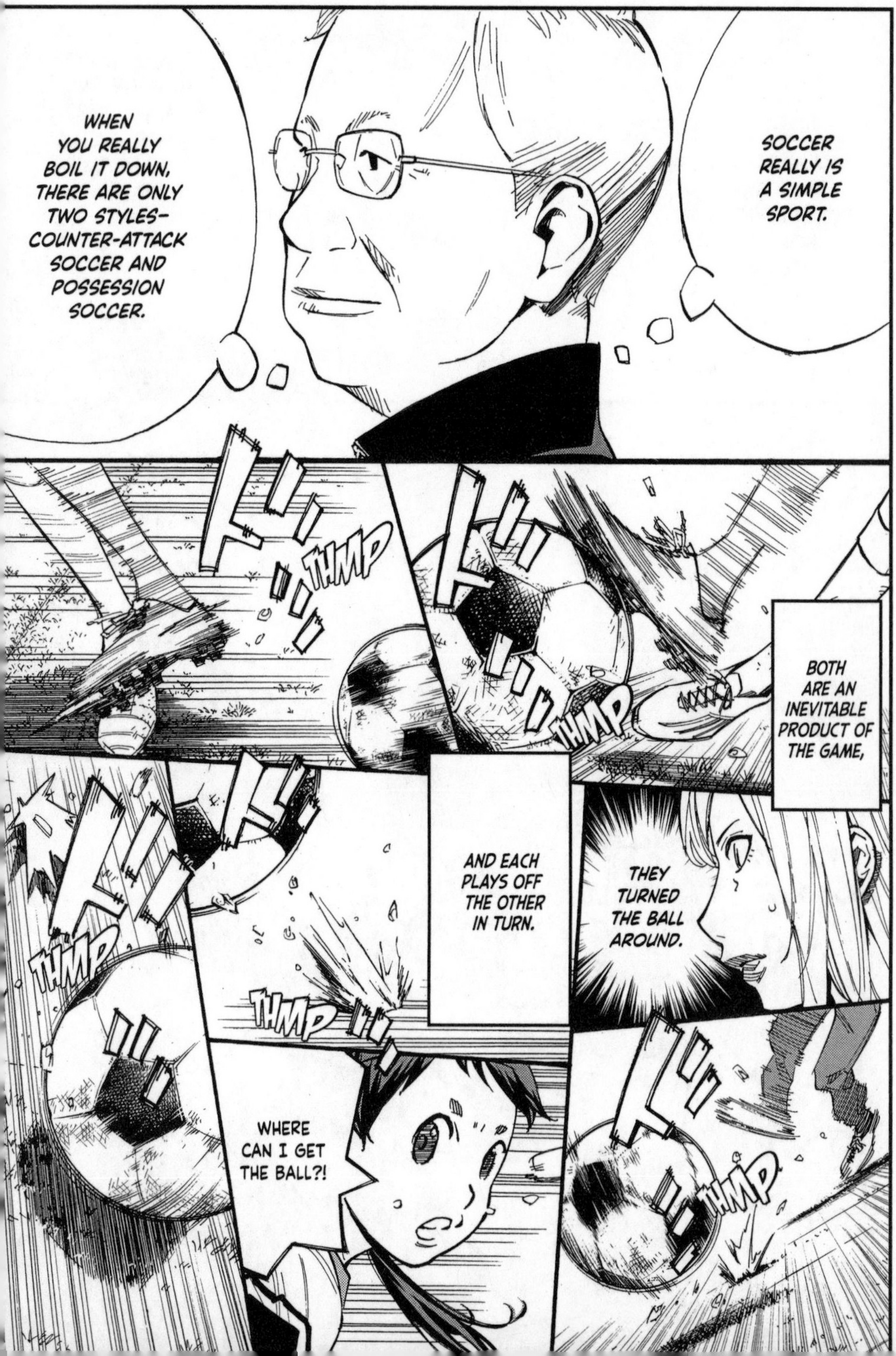
SOCCER REALLY IS A SIMPLE SPORT.
WHEN YOU REALLY BOIL IT DOWN, THERE ARE ONLY TWO STYLES— COUNTER-ATTACK SOCCER AND POSSESSION SOCCER.
BOTH ARE AN INEVITABLE PRODUCT OF THE GAME,
THMP
THMP
AND EACH PLAYS OFF THE OTHER IN TURN.
THEY TURNED THE BALL AROUND.
THMP
THMP
THMP
WHERE CAN I GET THE BALL?!

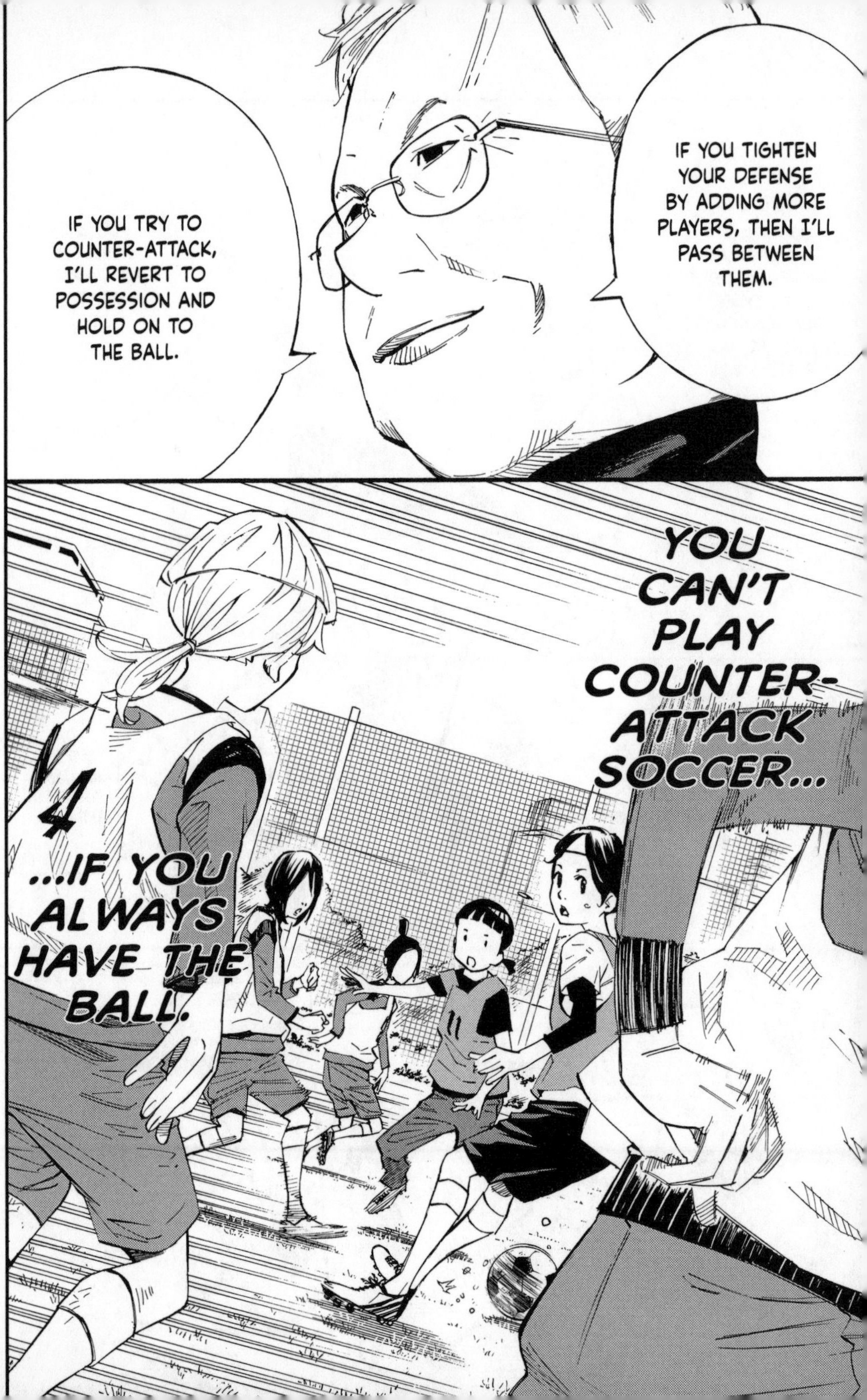
IF YOU TIGHTEN YOUR DEFENSE BY ADDING MORE PLAYERS, THEN I'LL PASS BETWEEN THEM.
IF YOU TRY TO COUNTER-ATTACK, I'LL REVERT TO POSSESSION AND HOLD ON TO THE BALL.
YOU CAN'T PLAY COUNTER-ATTACK SOCCER...
...IF YOU ALWAYS HAVE THE BALL.

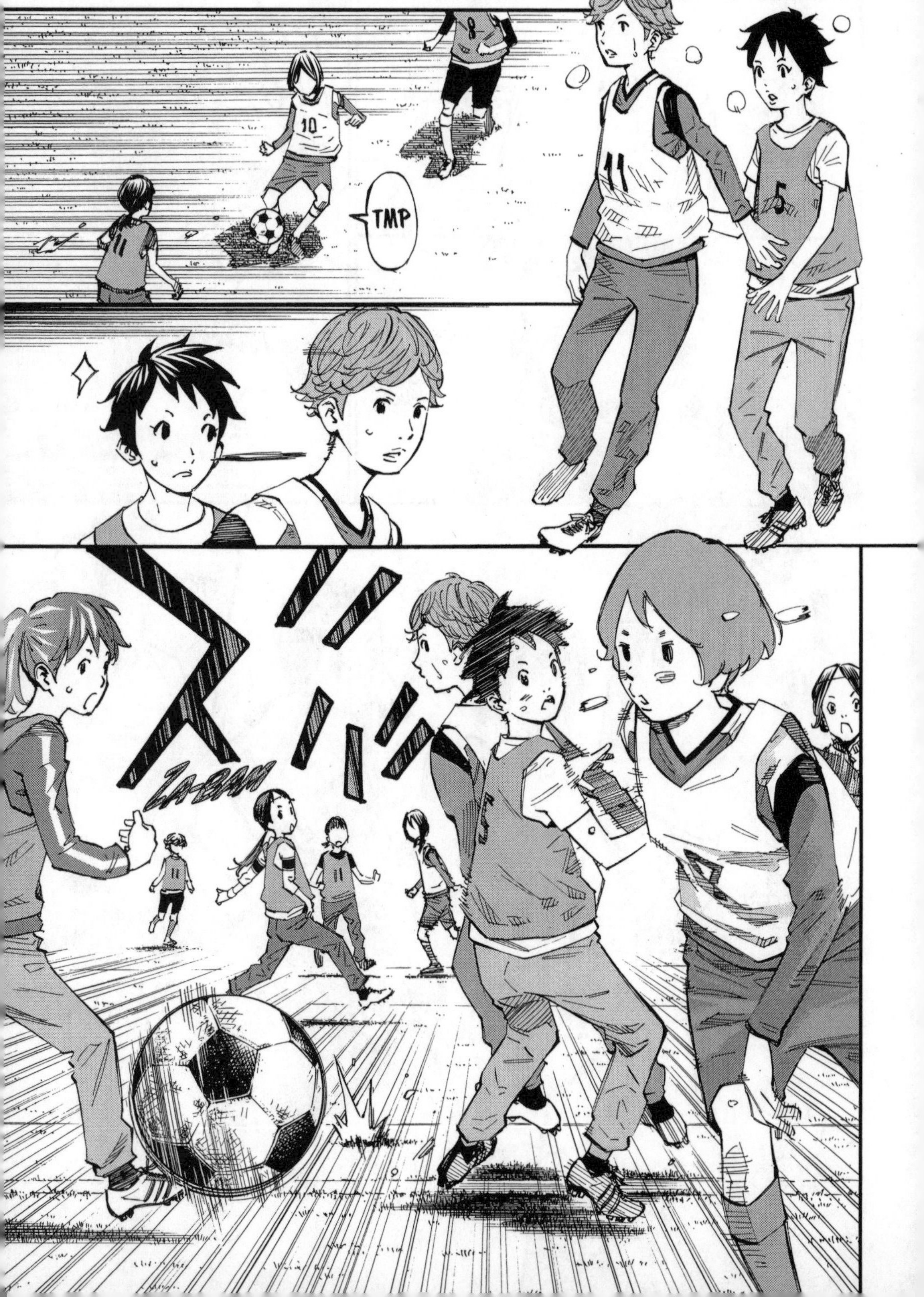
TMP
ZA-BAAN

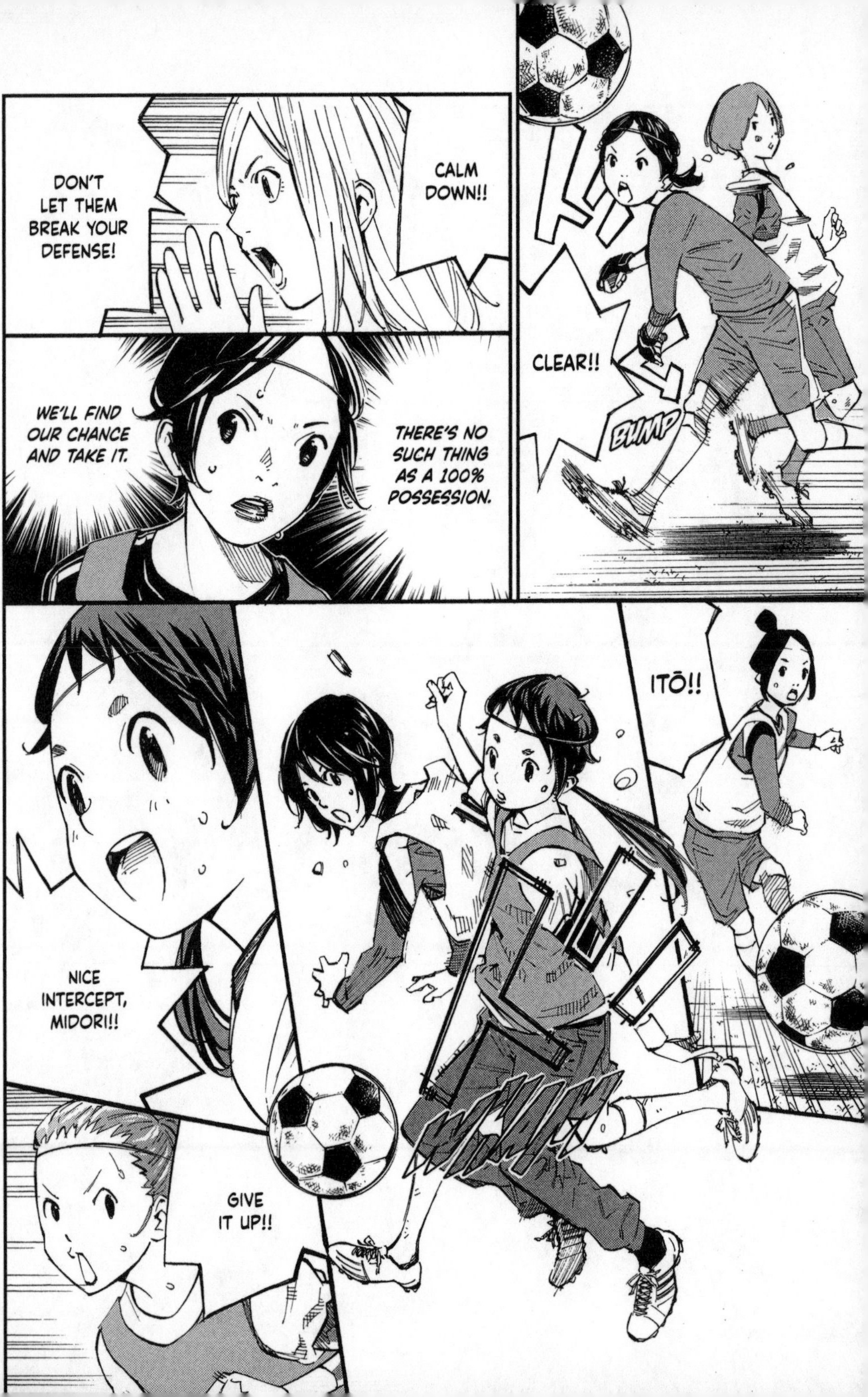
CLEAR!!
BUMP
CALM DOWN!!
DON'T LET THEM BREAK YOUR DEFENSE!
THERE'S NO SUCH THING AS A 100% POSSESSION.
WE'LL FIND OUR CHANCE AND TAKE IT.
ITŌ!!
NICE INTERCEPT, MIDORI!!
GIVE IT UP!!

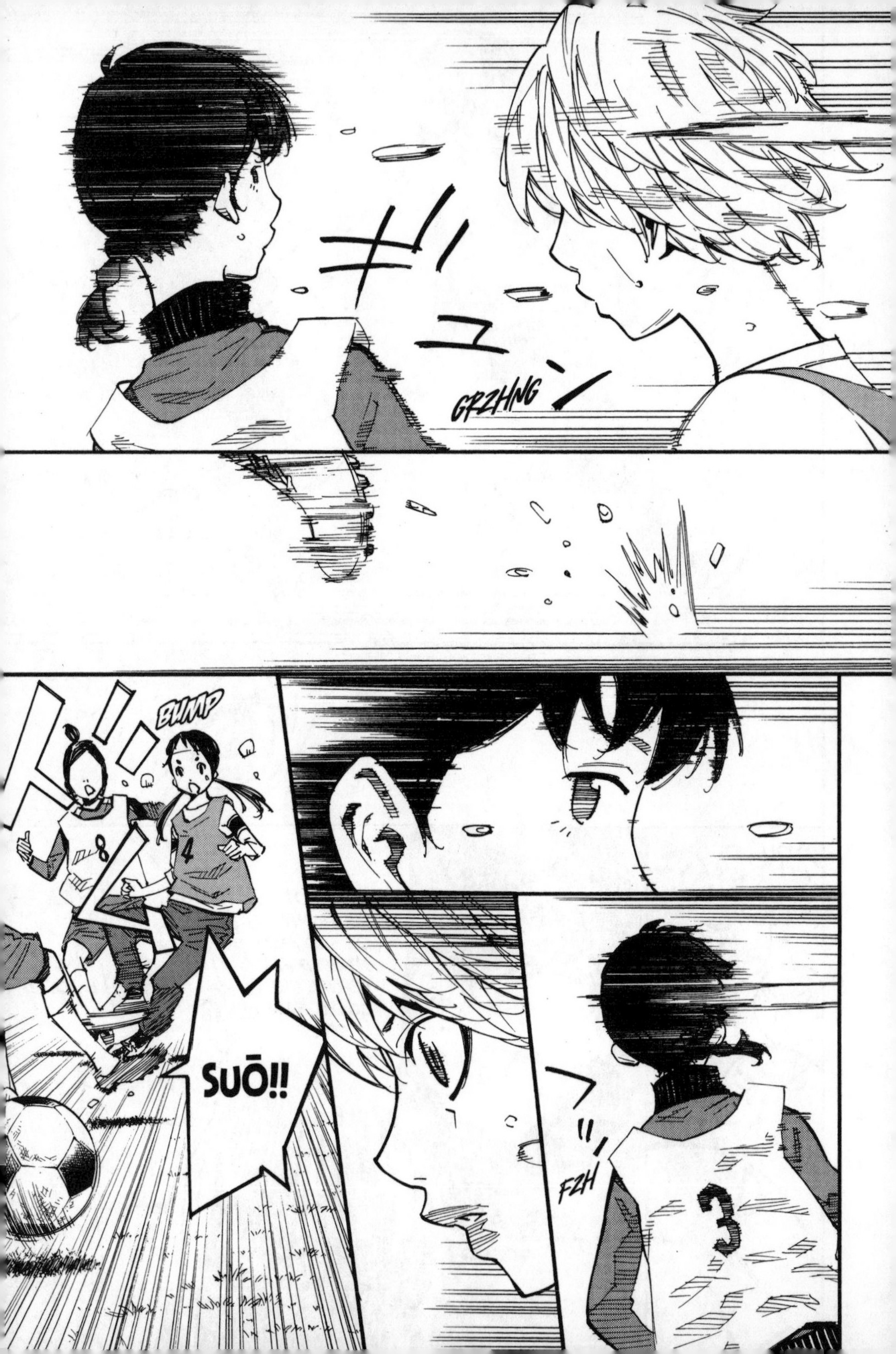
GRZHNG
FZH
BUMP
SUŌ!!

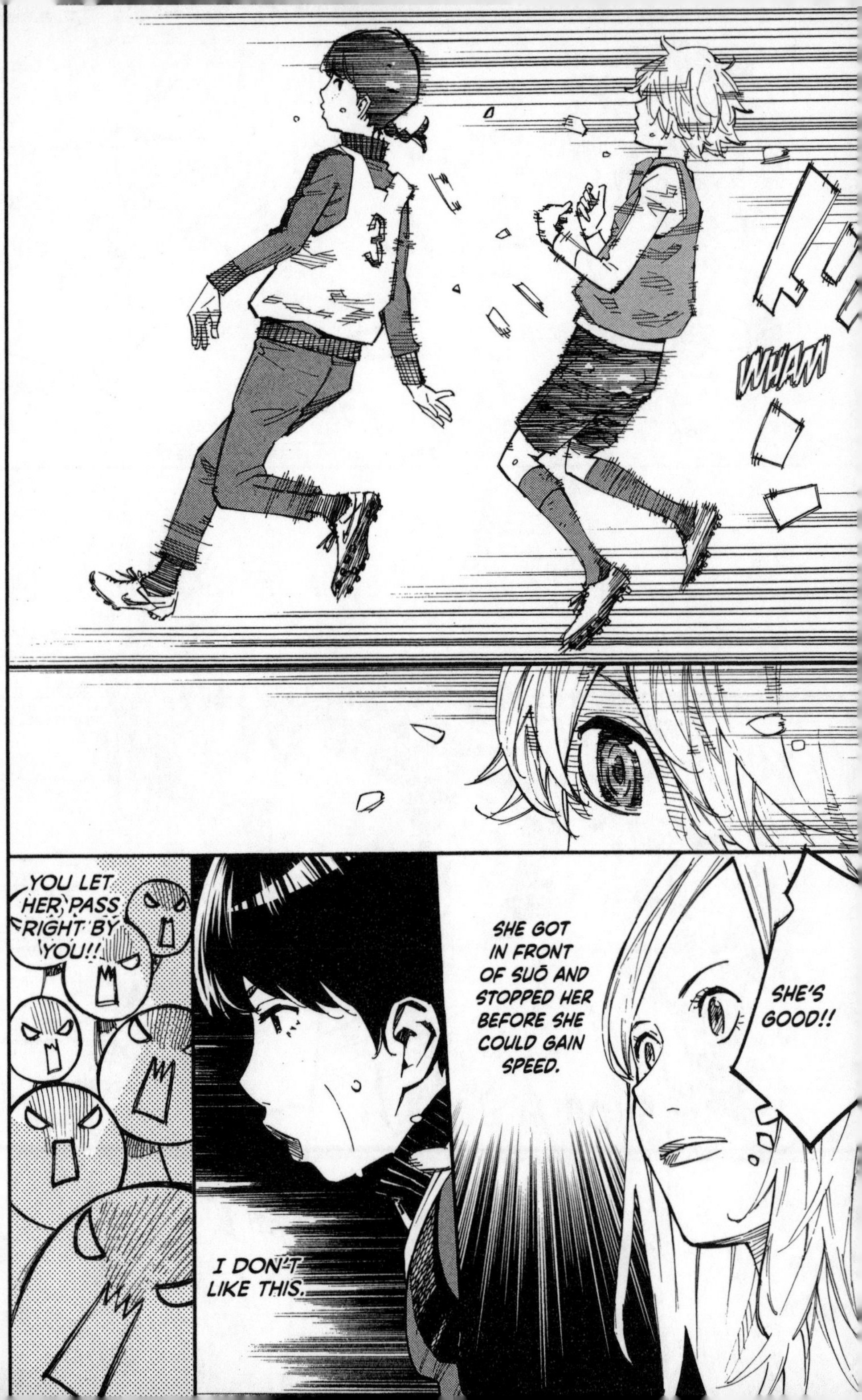
WHAM
SHE GOT IN FRONT OF SUŌ AND STOPPED HER BEFORE SHE COULD GAIN SPEED.
SHE'S GOOD!!
I DON'T LIKE THIS.
YOU LET HER PASS RIGHT BY YOU!!

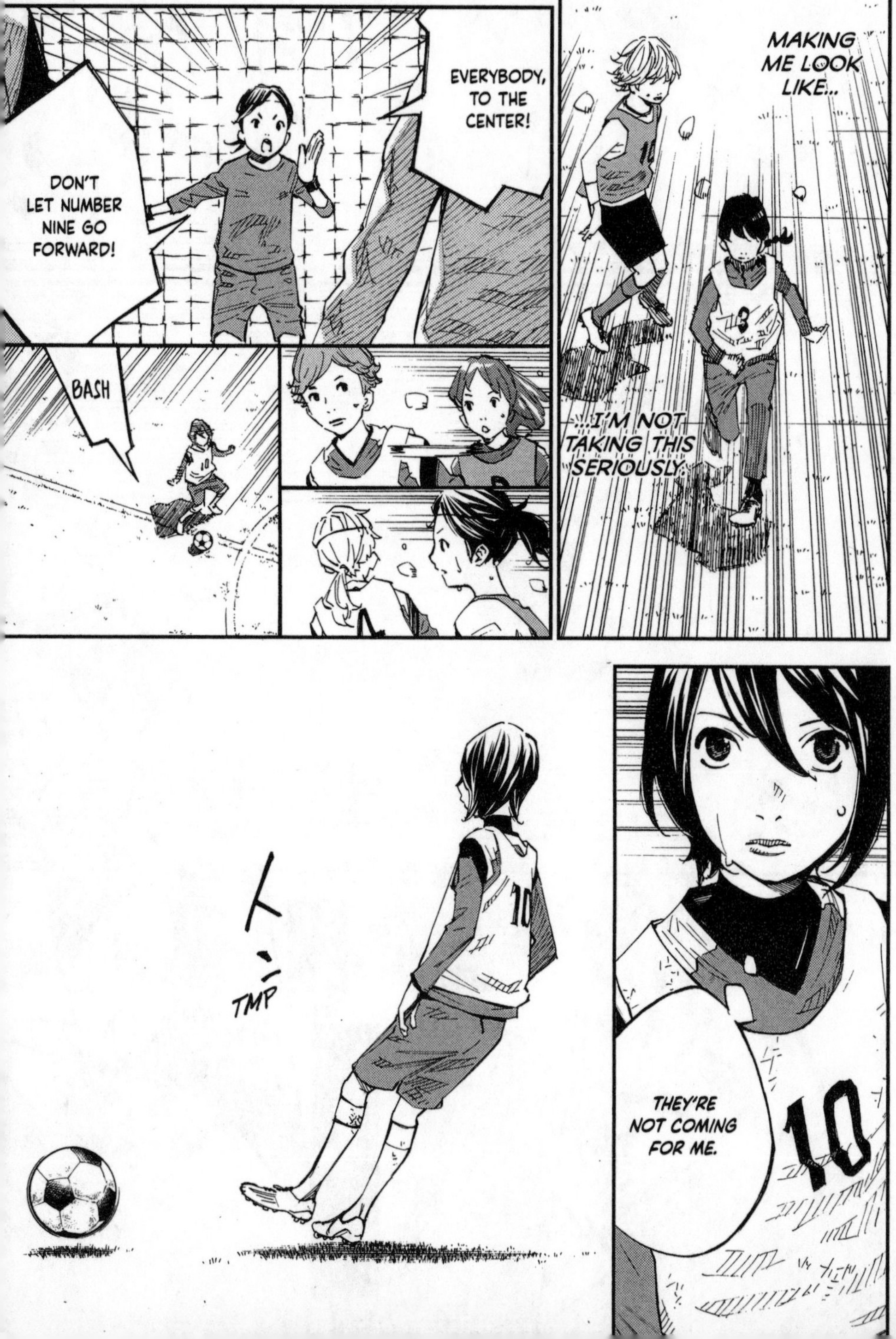
MAKING ME LOOK LIKE...
...I'M NOT TAKING THIS SERIOUSLY.
EVERYBODY, TO THE CENTER!
DON'T LET NUMBER NINE GO FORWARD!
BASH
THEY'RE NOT COMING FOR ME.
TMP

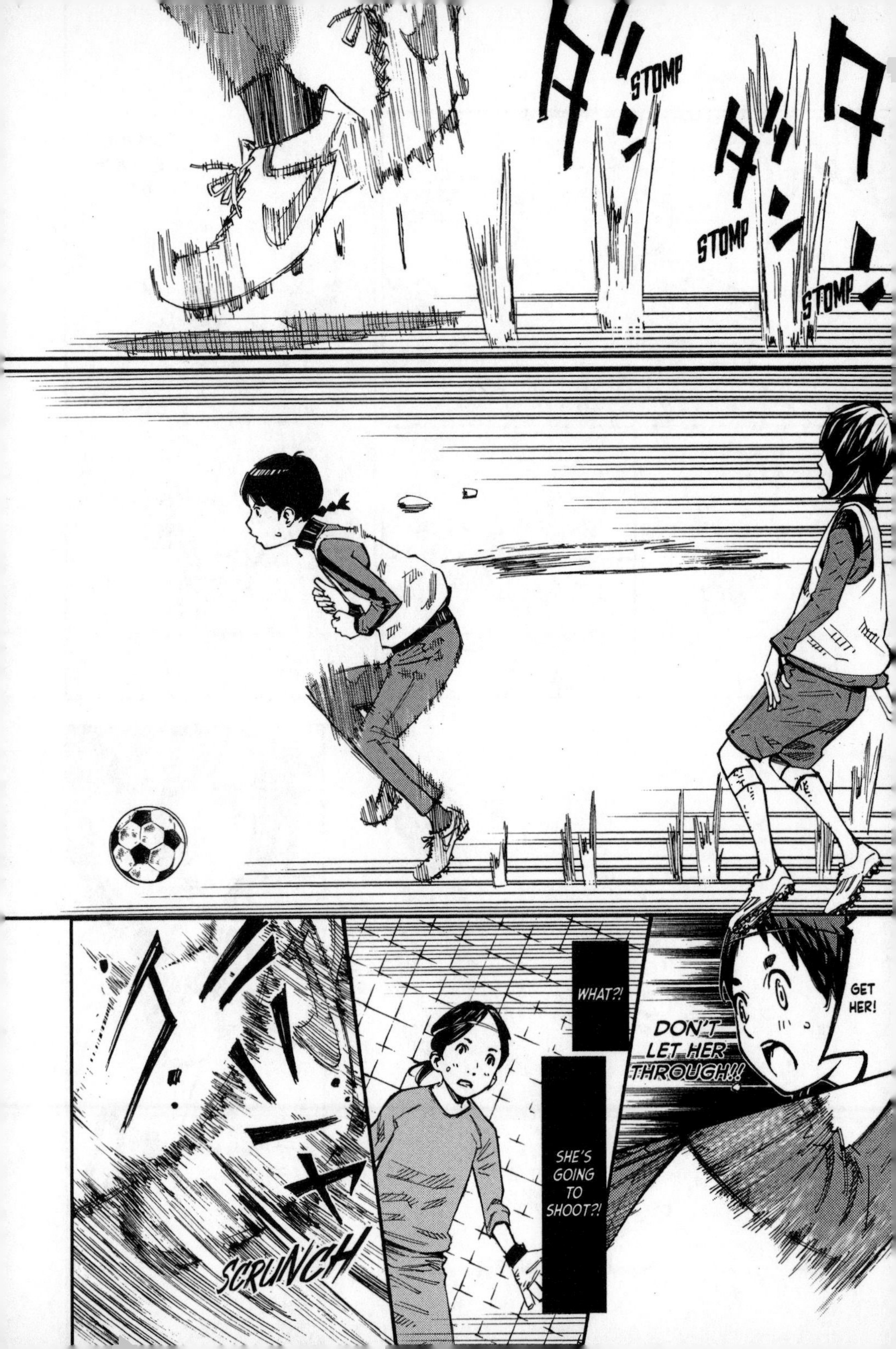
STOMP
STOMP
STOMP
GET HER!
DON'T LET HER THROUGH!!
WHAT?!
SHE'S GOING TO SHOOT?!
SCRUNCH

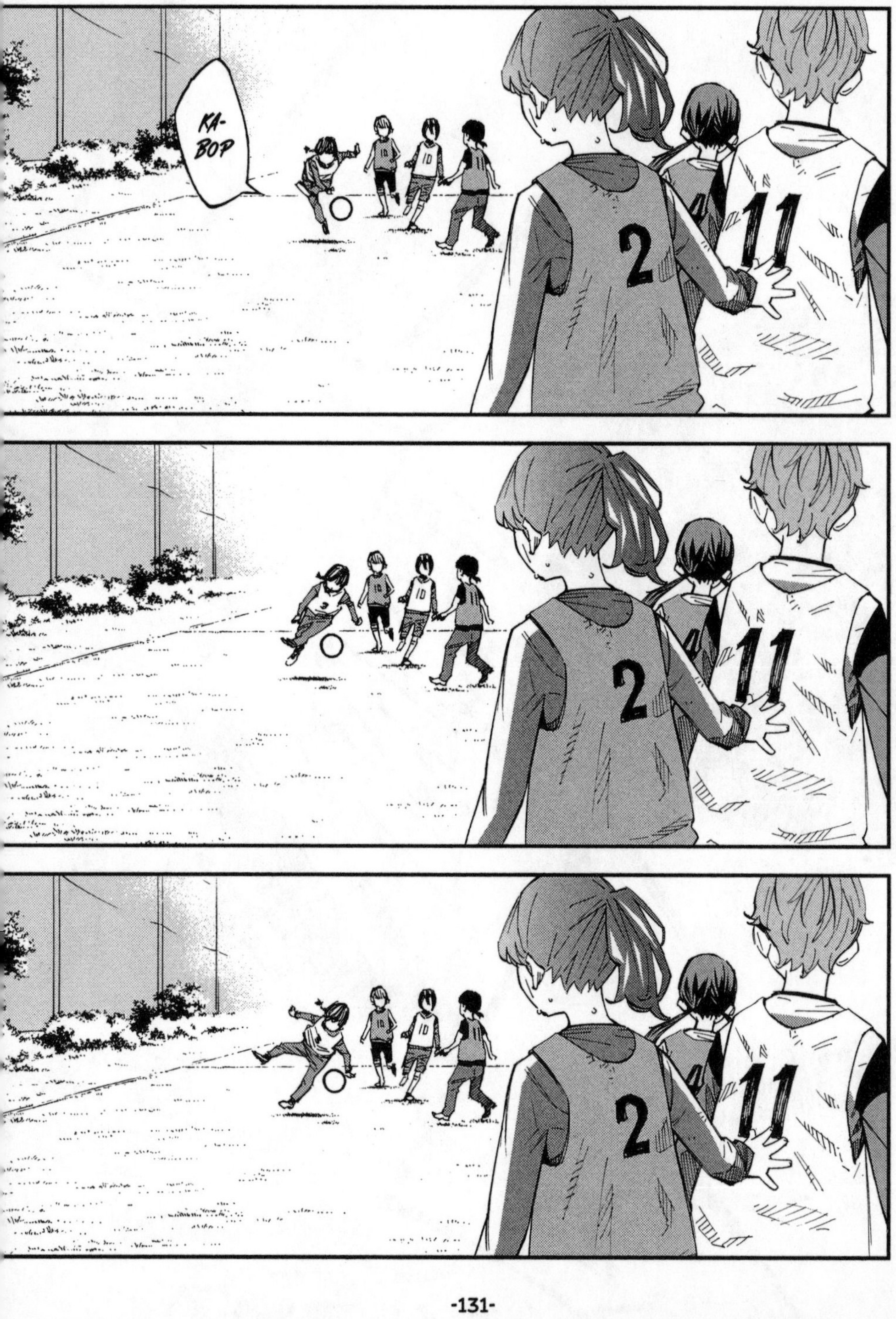
KA-BOP

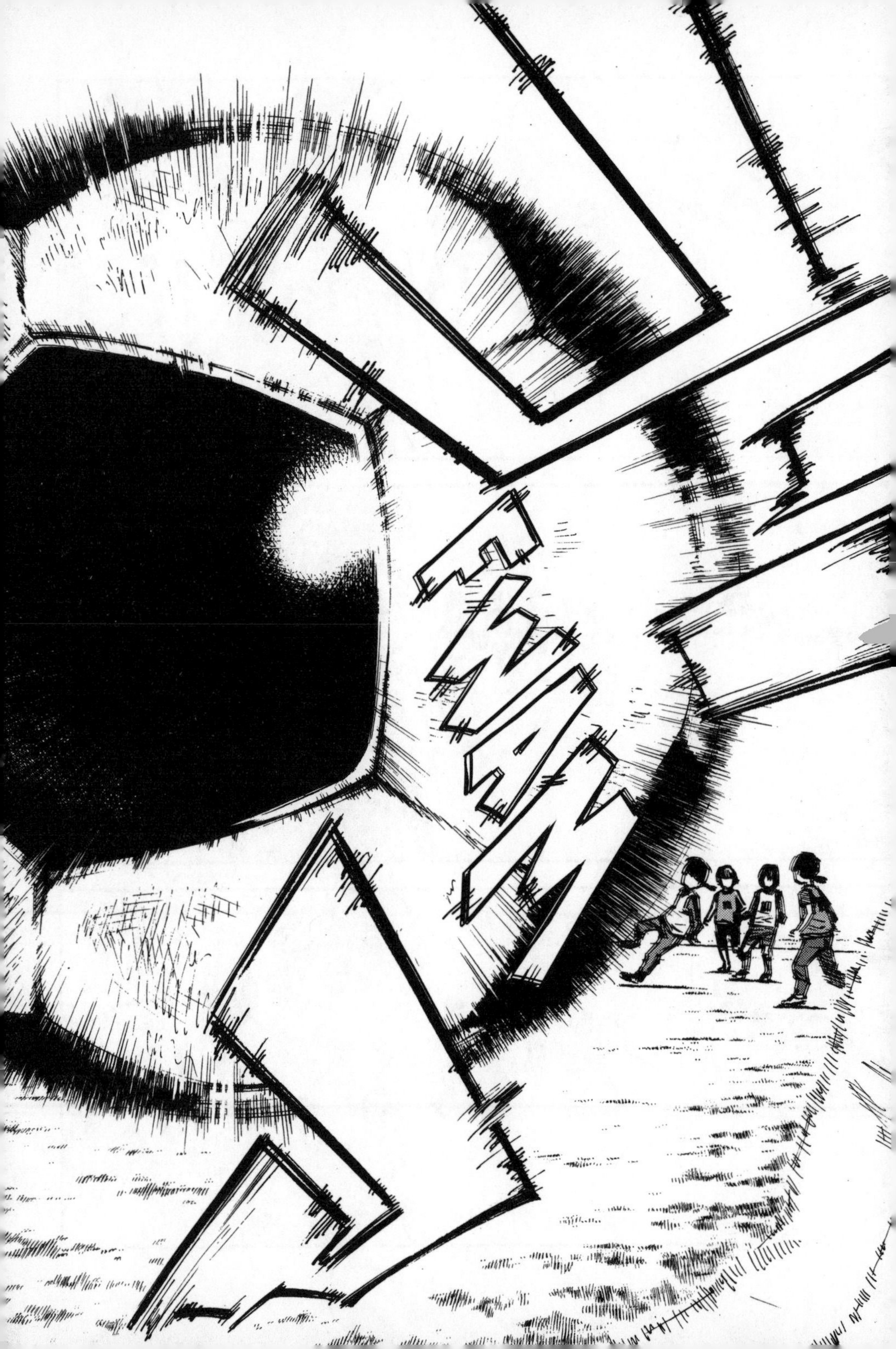

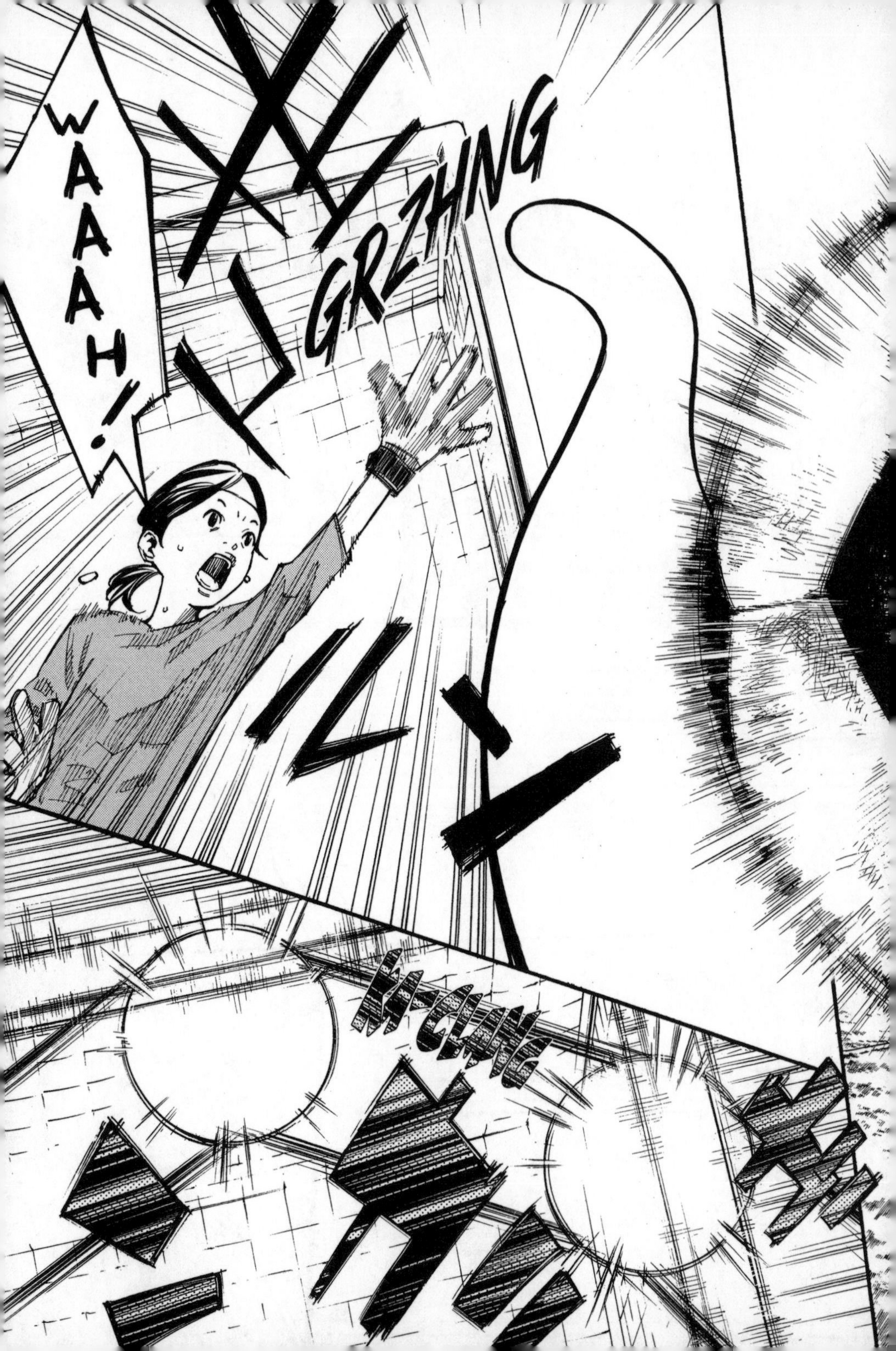
GRZHING
WAAAH!!
KA-CLING

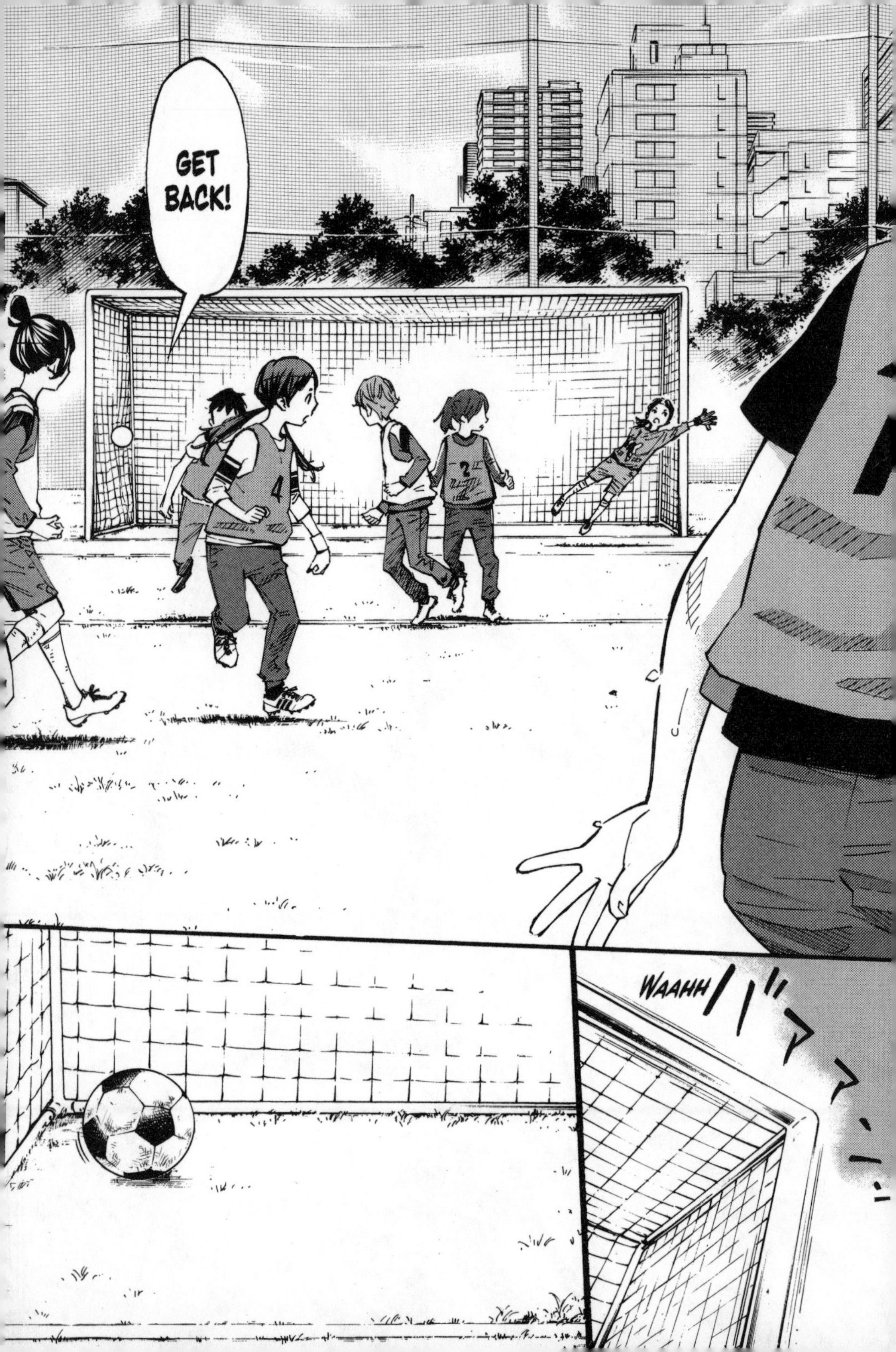
GET BACK!
WAAHH

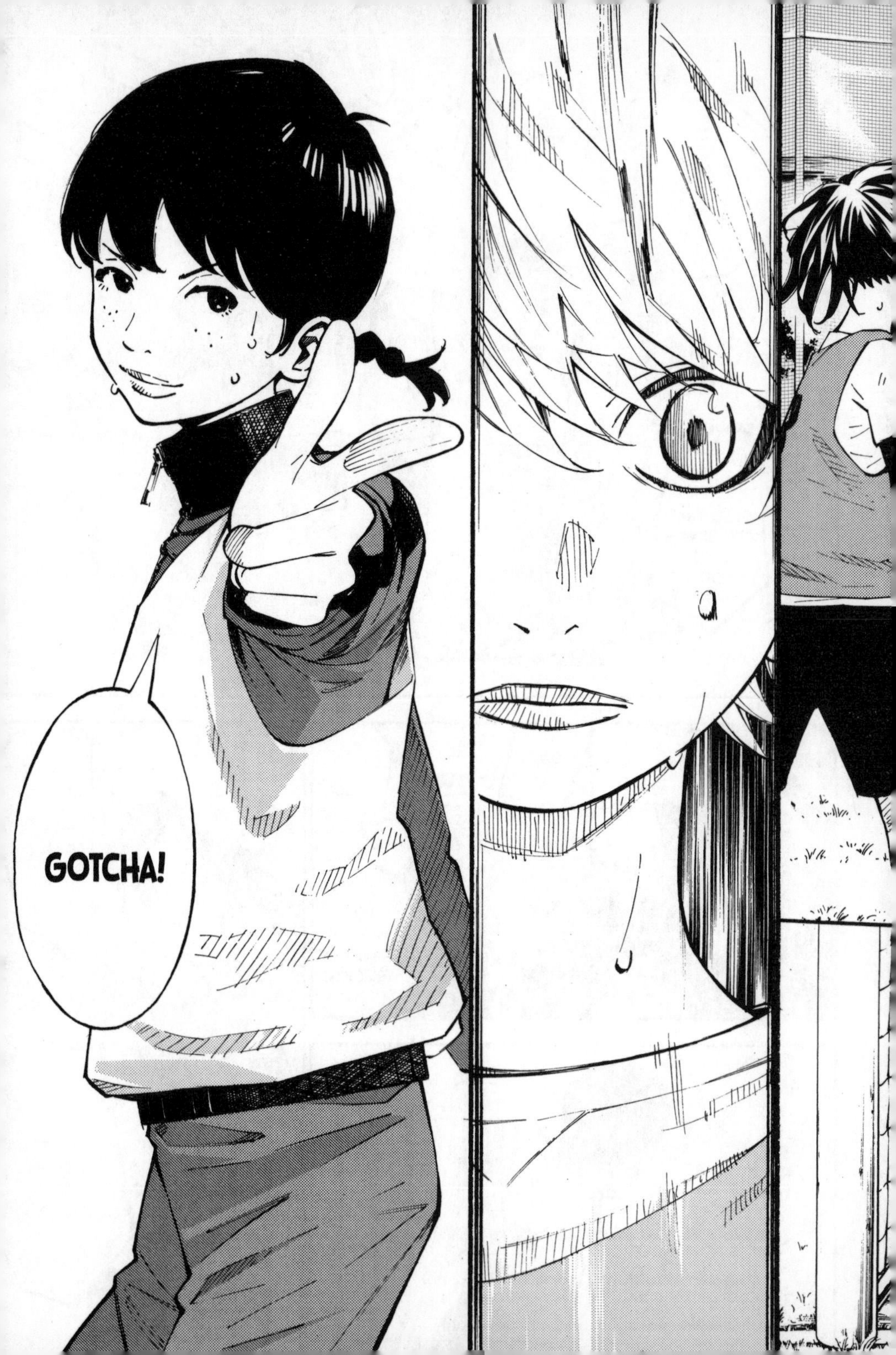
GOTCHA!

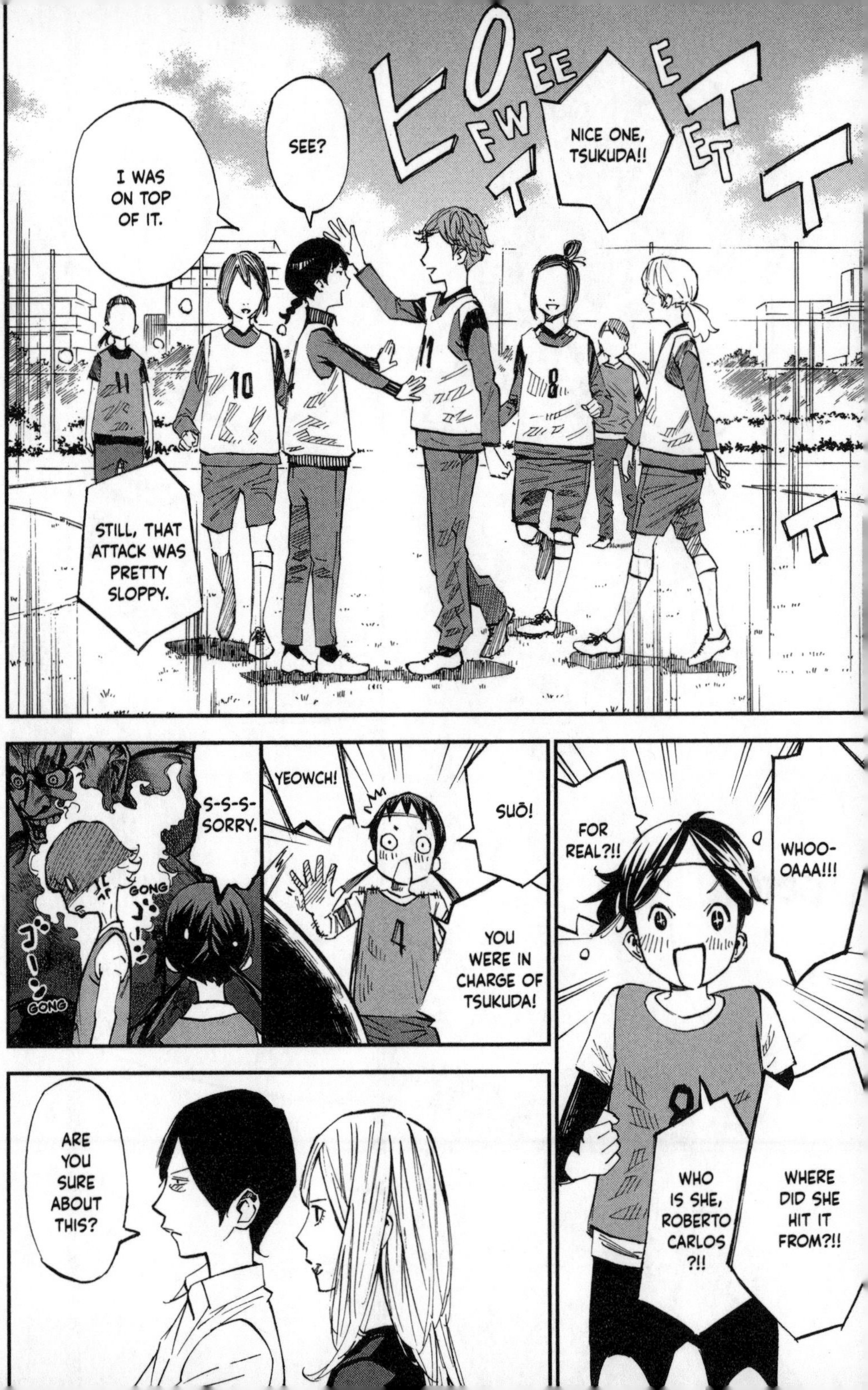
NICE ONE, TSUKUDA!!
FWEEEET
SEE?
I WAS ON TOP OF IT.
STILL, THAT ATTACK WAS PRETTY SLOPPY.
WHOO-OAAA!!!
FOR REAL?!!
WHERE DID SHE HIT IT FROM?!!
WHO IS SHE, ROBERTO CARLOS?!!
SUŌ!
YOU WERE IN CHARGE OF TSUKUDA!
YEOWCH!
S-S-S-SORRY.
GONG
GONG
ARE YOU SURE ABOUT THIS?

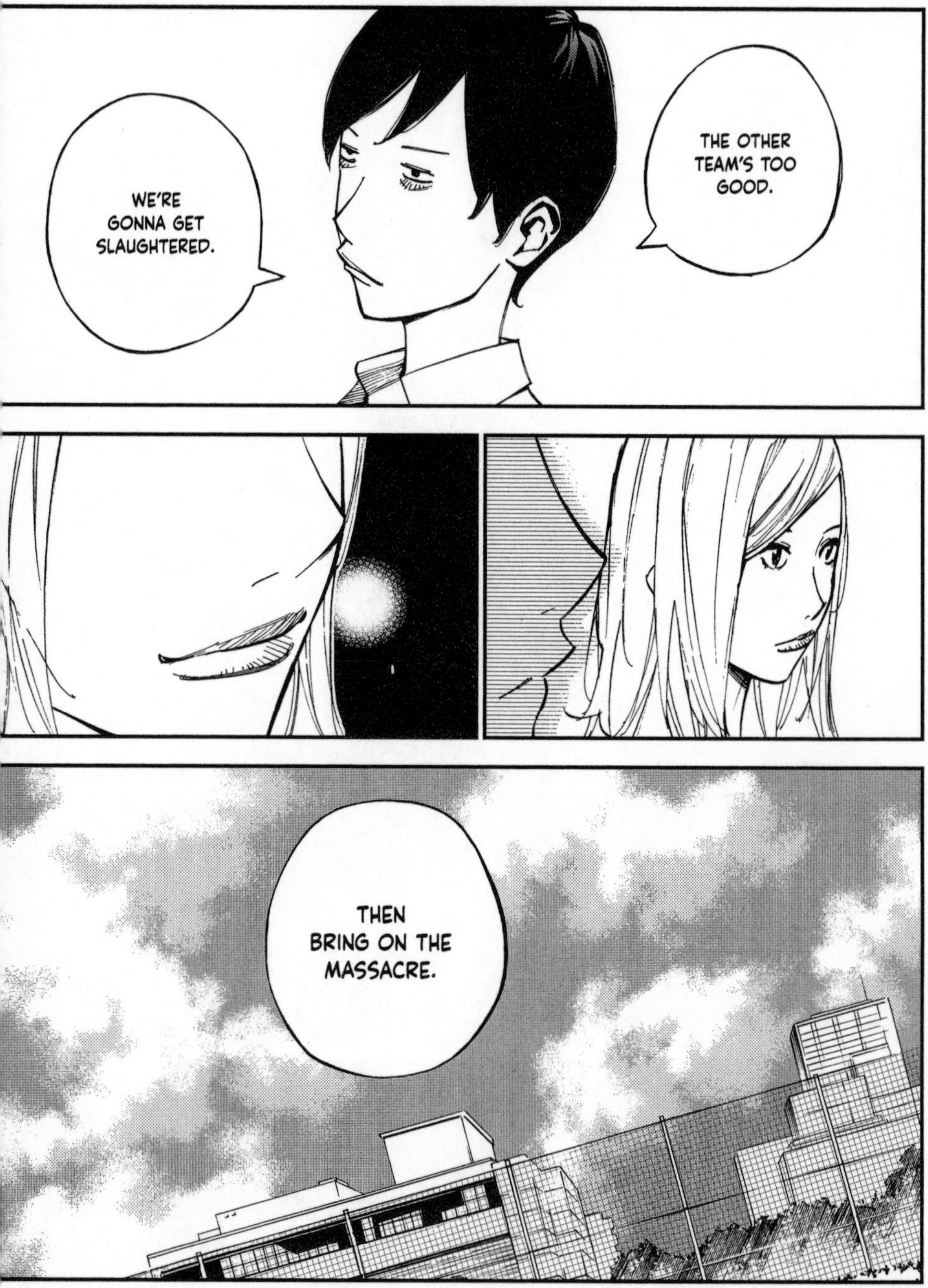
THE OTHER TEAM'S TOO GOOD.
WE'RE GONNA GET SLAUGHTERED.
THEN BRING ON THE MASSACRE.

Farewell, My Dear Cramer

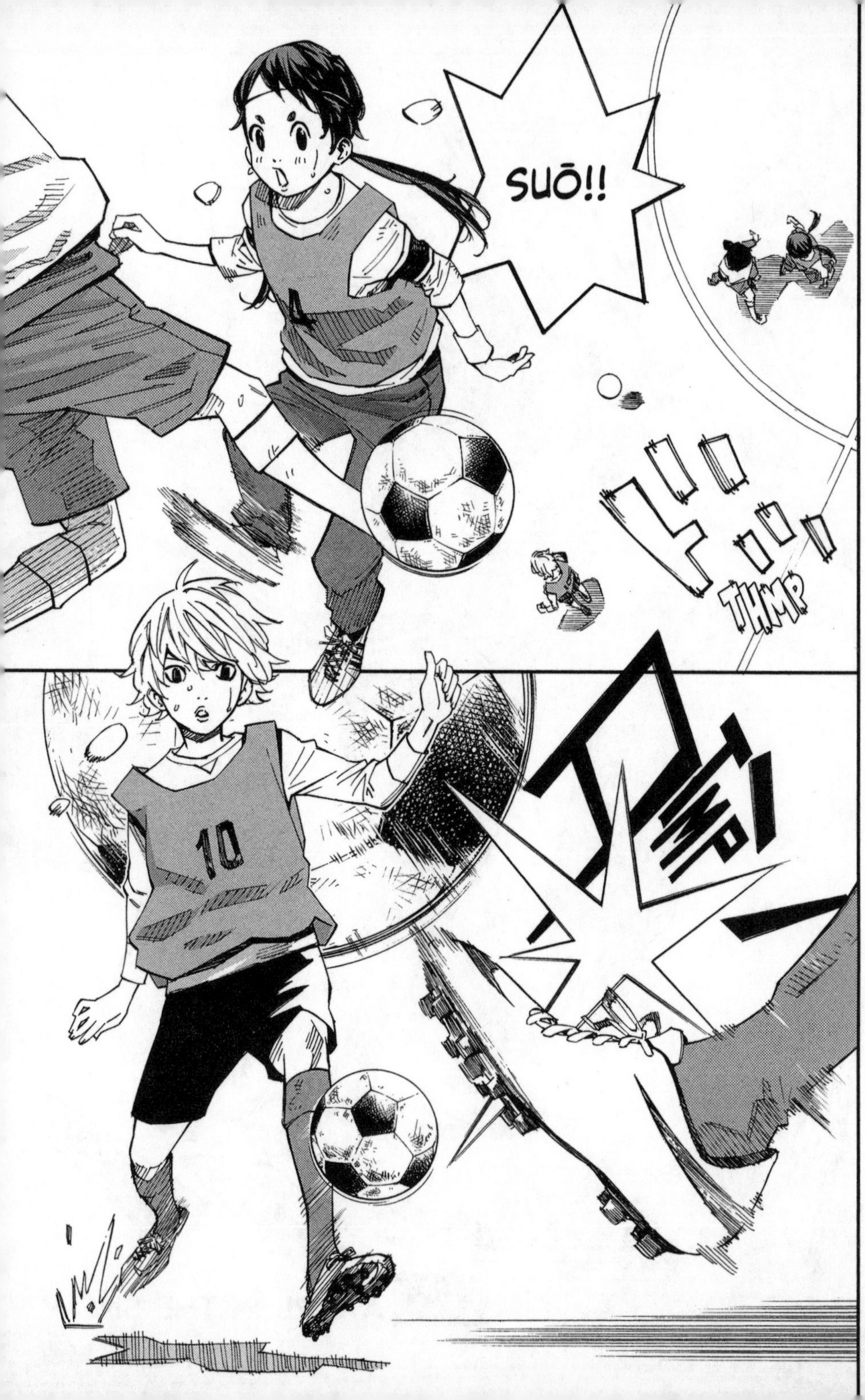
SUŌ!!
THMP
THMP!

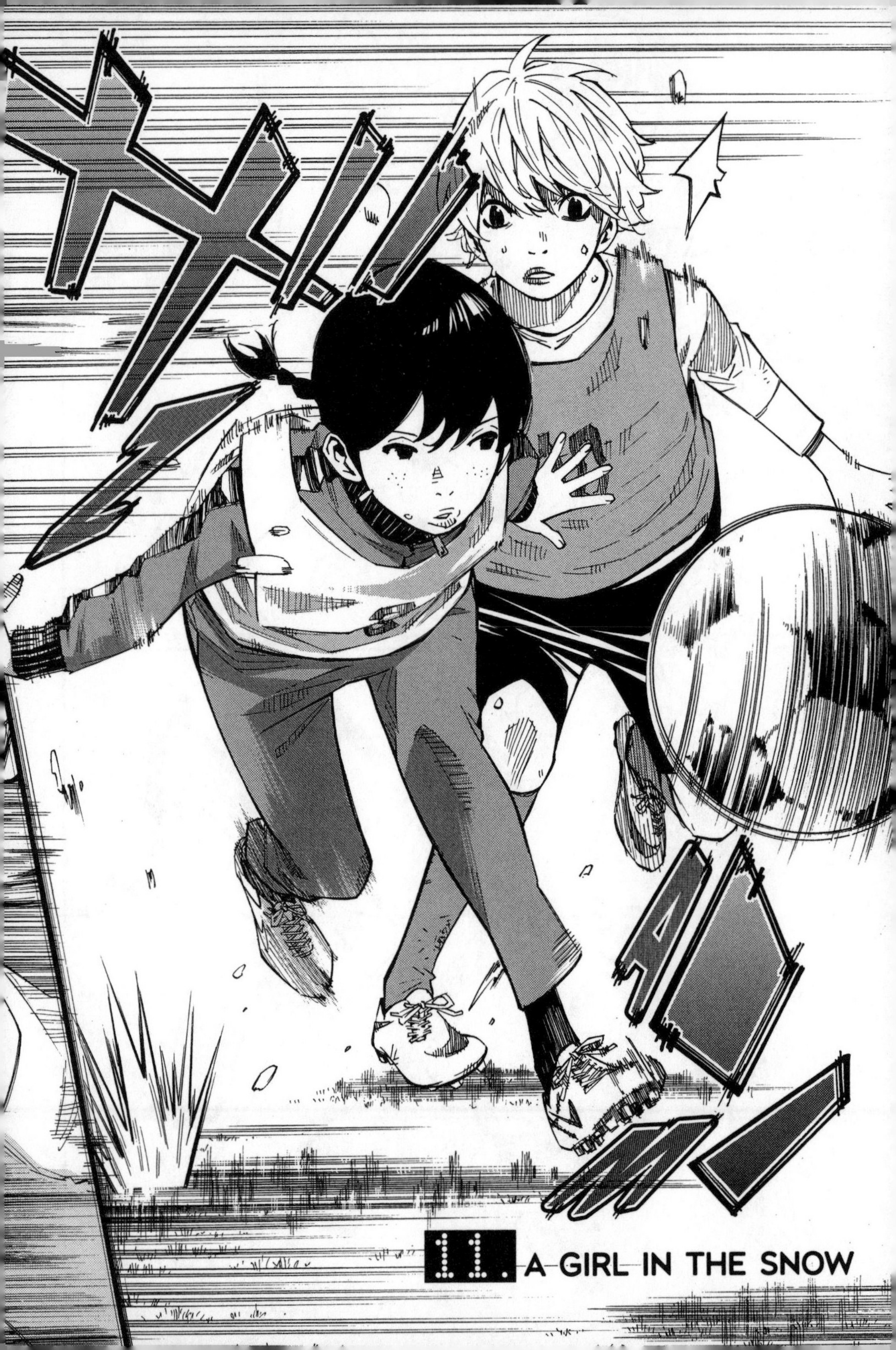

11. A GIRL IN THE SNOW

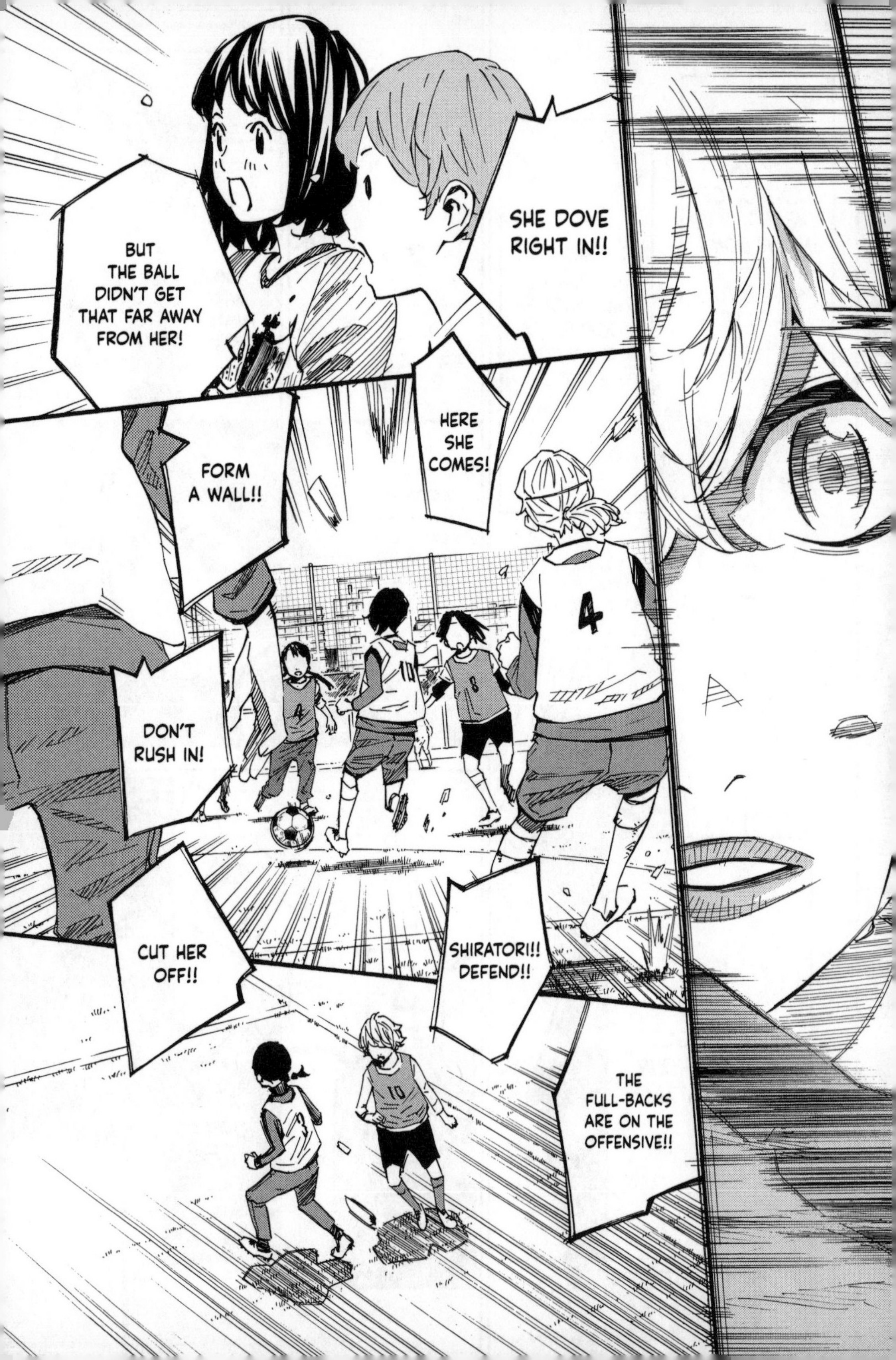
SHE DOVE RIGHT IN!!
BUT THE BALL DIDN'T GET THAT FAR AWAY FROM HER!
HERE SHE COMES!
FORM A WALL!!
DON'T RUSH IN!
SHIRATORI!!! DEFEND!!
CUT HER OFF!!
THE FULL-BACKS ARE ON THE OFFENSIVE!!

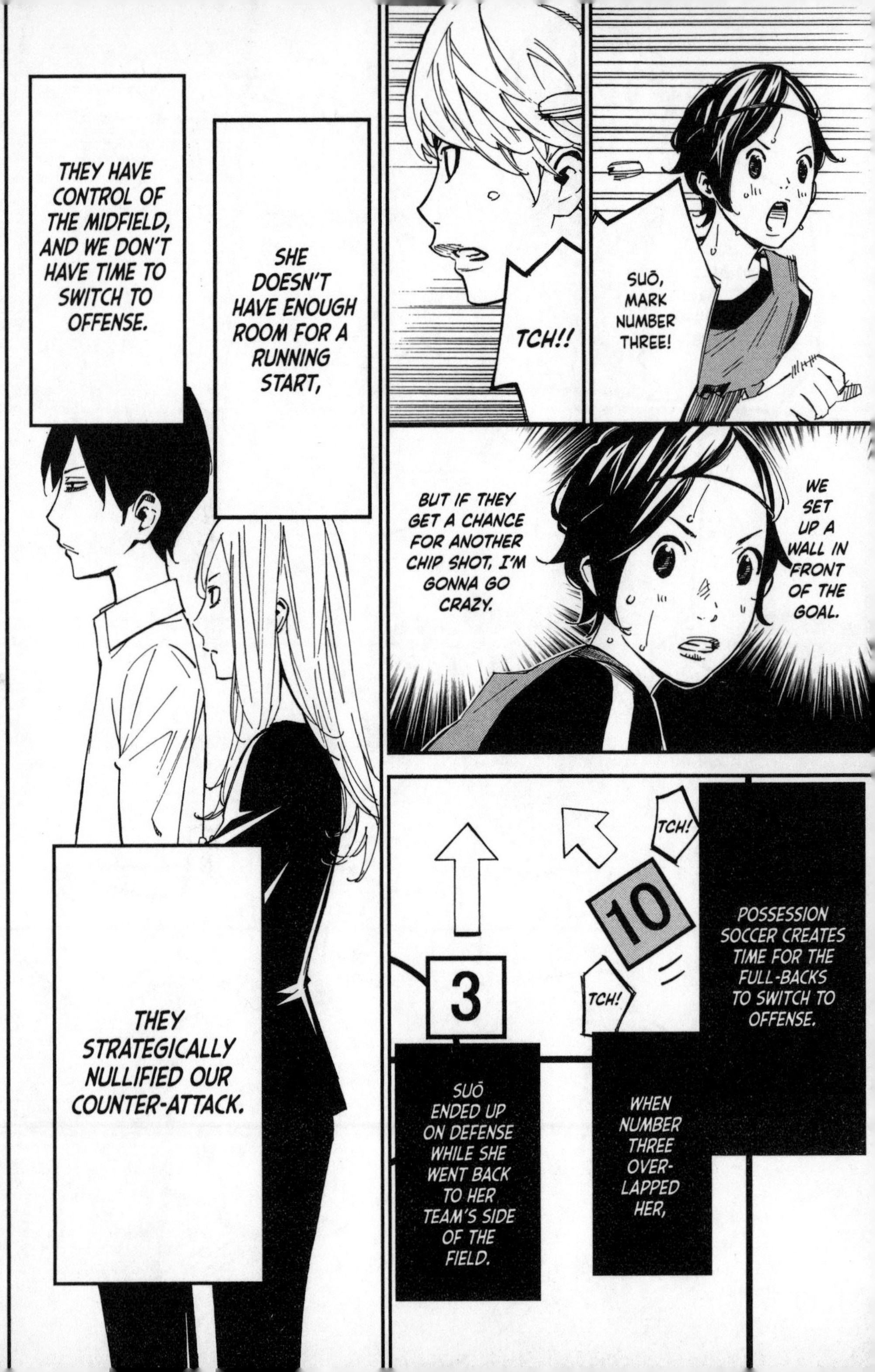
SUŌ, MARK NUMBER THREE!
TCH!!
WE SET UP A WALL IN FRONT OF THE GOAL.
BUT IF THEY GET A CHANCE FOR ANOTHER CHIP SHOT, I'M GONNA GO CRAZY.
POSSESSION SOCCER CREATES TIME FOR THE FULL-BACKS TO SWITCH TO OFFENSE.
TCH!
10
TCH!
3
WHEN NUMBER THREE OVER-LAPPED HER,
SUŌ ENDED UP ON DEFENSE WHILE SHE WENT BACK TO HER TEAM'S SIDE OF THE FIELD.
SHE DOESN'T HAVE ENOUGH ROOM FOR A RUNNING START,
THEY HAVE CONTROL OF THE MIDFIELD, AND WE DON'T HAVE TIME TO SWITCH TO OFFENSE.
THEY STRATEGICALLY NULLIFIED OUR COUNTER-ATTACK.

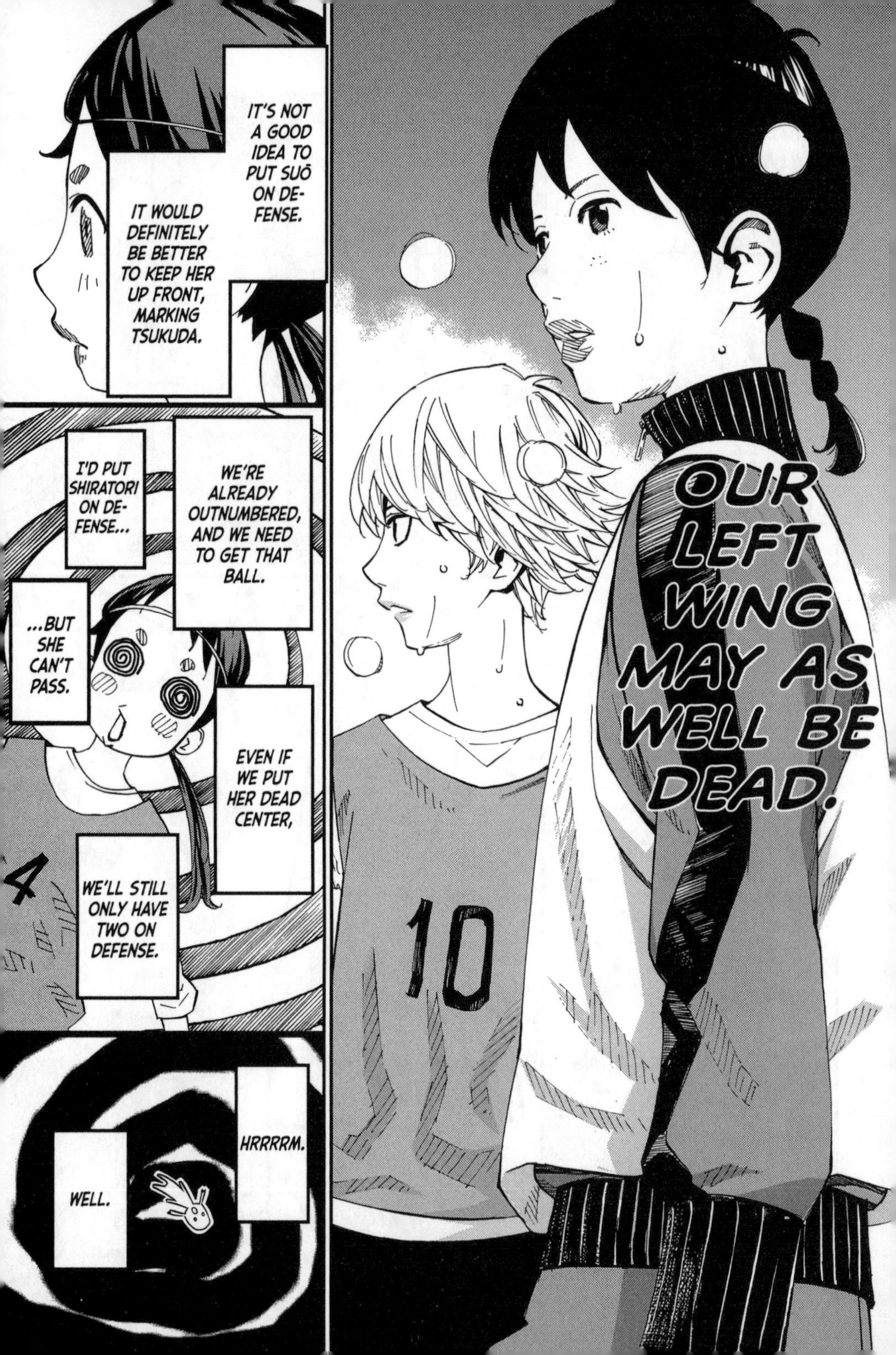
OUR LEFT WING MAY AS WELL BE DEAD.
IT'S NOT A GOOD IDEA TO PUT SUŌ ON DE-FENSE.
IT WOULD DEFINITELY BE BETTER TO KEEP HER UP FRONT, MARKING TSUKUDA.
WE'RE ALREADY OUTNUMBERED, AND WE NEED TO GET THAT BALL.
I'D PUT SHIRATORI ON DE-FENSE...
...BUT SHE CAN'T PASS.
EVEN IF WE PUT HER DEAD CENTER,
WE'LL STILL ONLY HAVE TWO ON DEFENSE.
HRRRRM.
WELL.

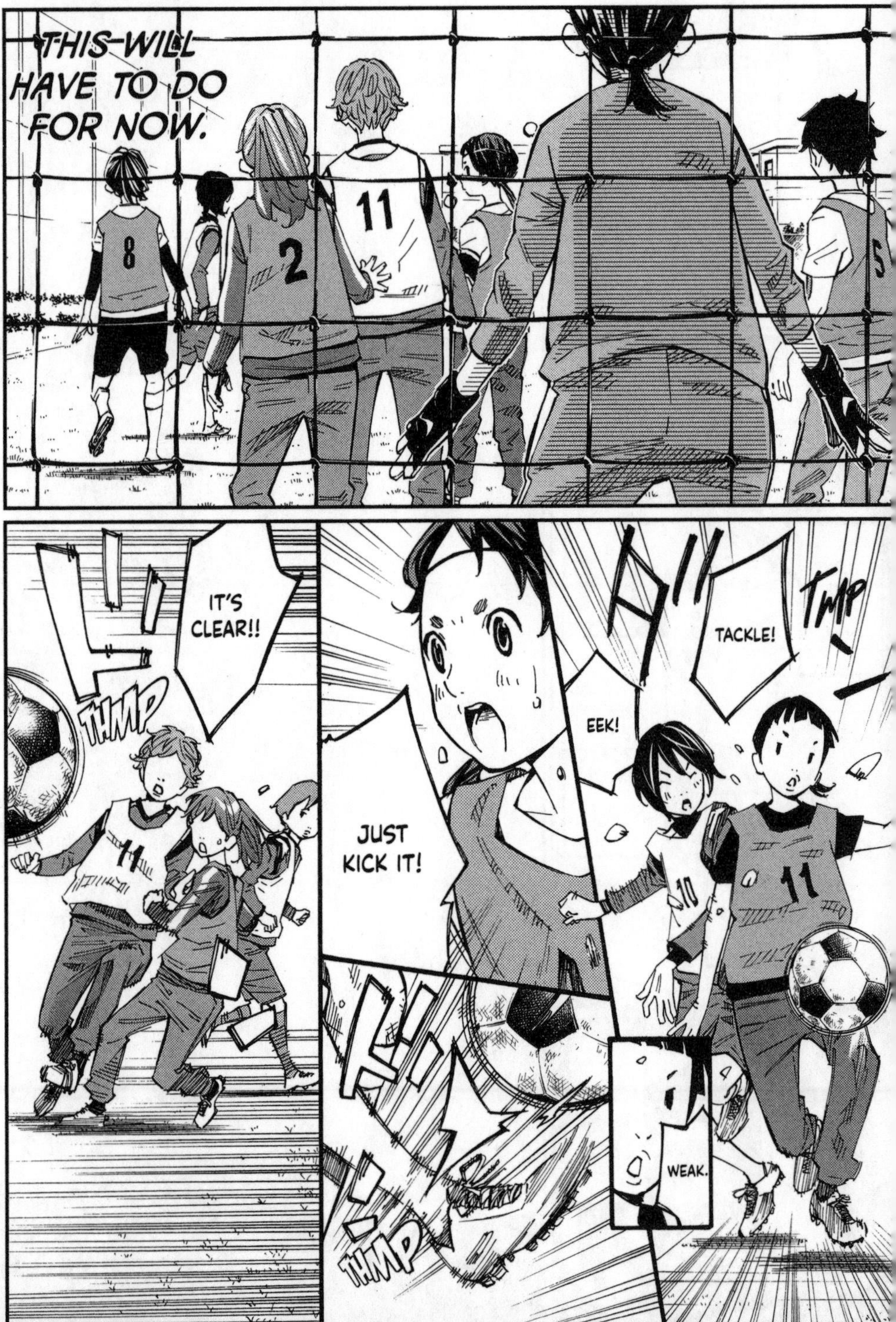
THIS WILL HAVE TO DO FOR NOW.
TMP
TACKLE!
EEK!
JUST KICK IT!
WEAK.
THMP
IT'S CLEAR!!
THMP

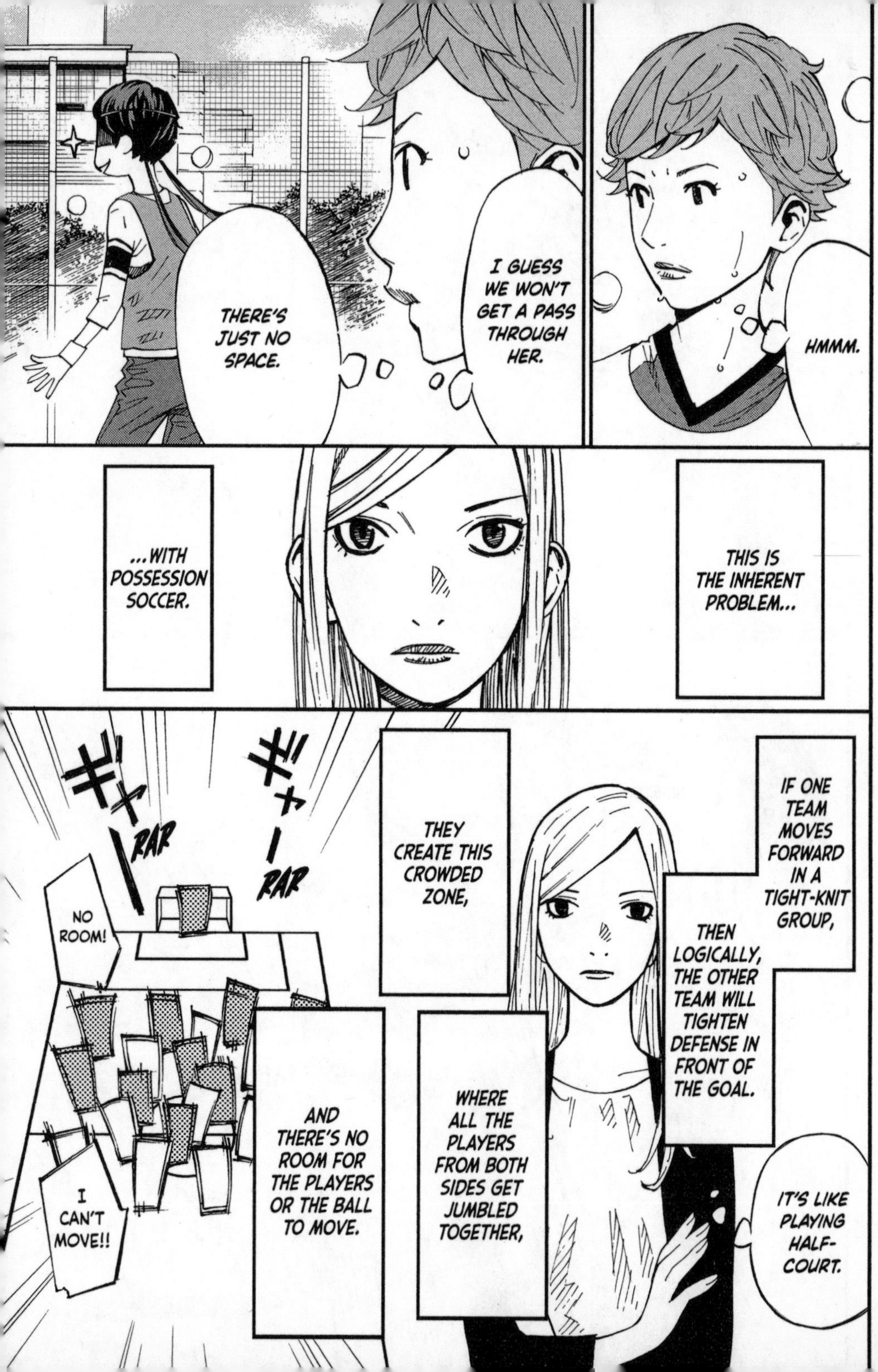
HMMM.
I GUESS WE WON'T GET A PASS THROUGH HER.
THERE'S JUST NO SPACE.
THIS IS THE INHERENT PROBLEM...
...WITH POSSESSION SOCCER.
IF ONE TEAM MOVES FORWARD IN A TIGHT-KNIT GROUP,
THEN LOGICALLY, THE OTHER TEAM WILL TIGHTEN DEFENSE IN FRONT OF THE GOAL.
THEY CREATE THIS CROWDED ZONE,
WHERE ALL THE PLAYERS FROM BOTH SIDES GET JUMBLED TOGETHER,
AND THERE'S NO ROOM FOR THE PLAYERS OR THE BALL TO MOVE.
IT'S LIKE PLAYING HALF-COURT.
RAR
RAR
NO ROOM!
I CAN'T MOVE!!

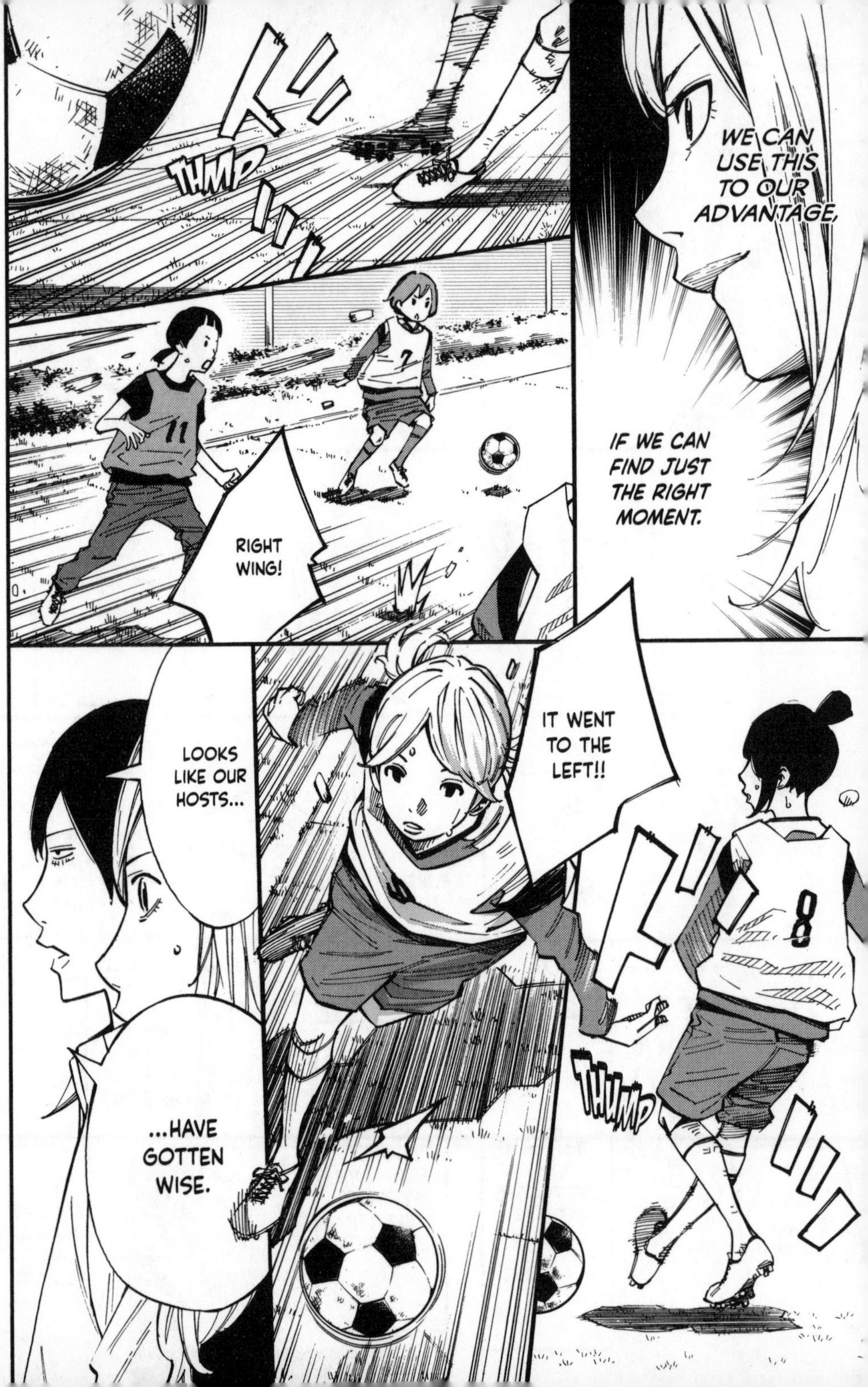

WE CAN USE THIS TO OUR ADVANTAGE,
IF WE CAN FIND JUST THE RIGHT MOMENT.
THMP
RIGHT WING!
IT WENT TO THE LEFT!!
THUMP
LOOKS LIKE OUR HOSTS...
...HAVE GOTTEN WISE.

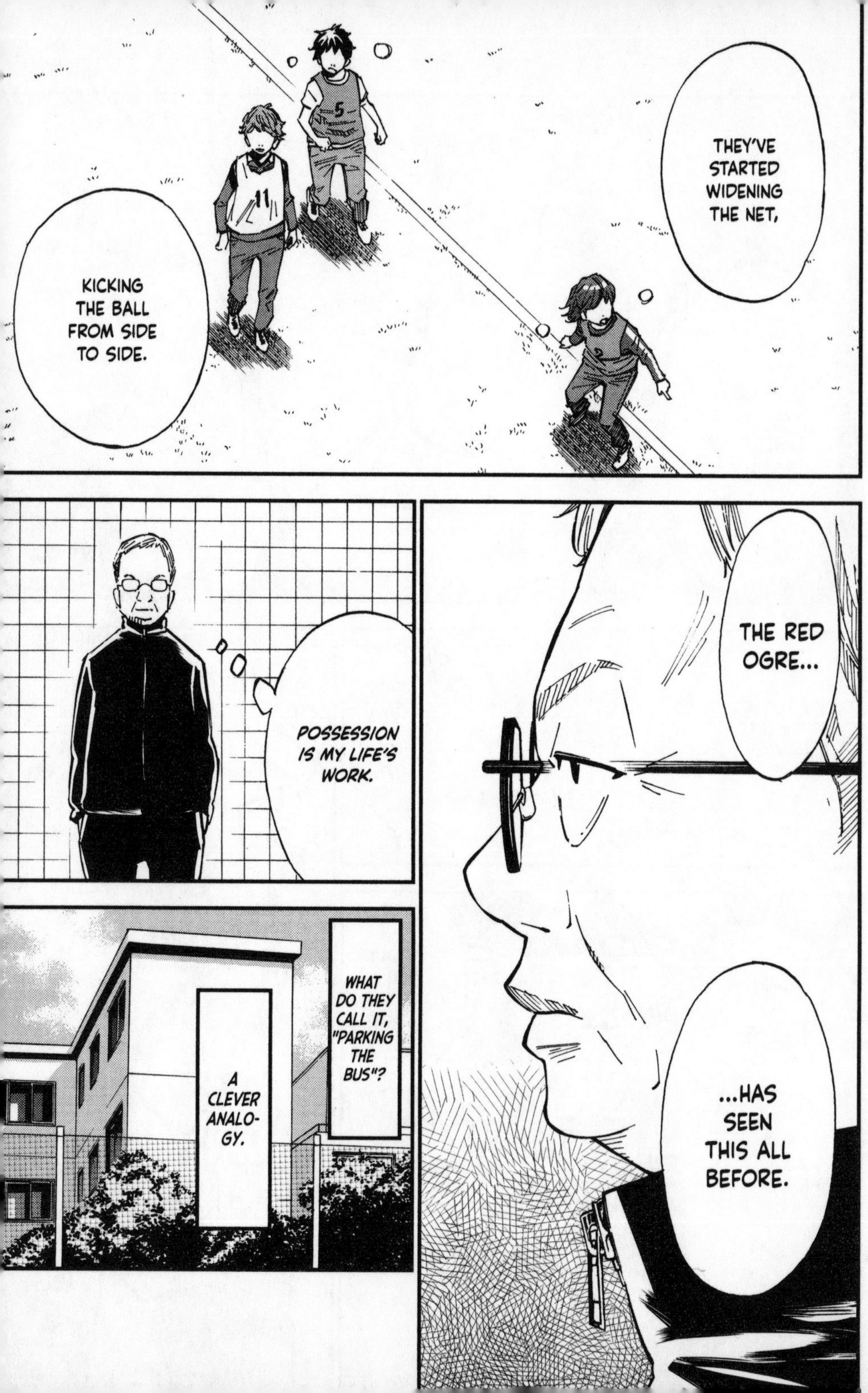
THEY'VE STARTED WIDENING THE NET,
KICKING THE BALL FROM SIDE TO SIDE.
THE RED OGRE...
...HAS SEEN THIS ALL BEFORE.
POSSESSION IS MY LIFE'S WORK.
WHAT DO THEY CALL IT, "PARKING THE BUS"?
A CLEVER ANALOGY.

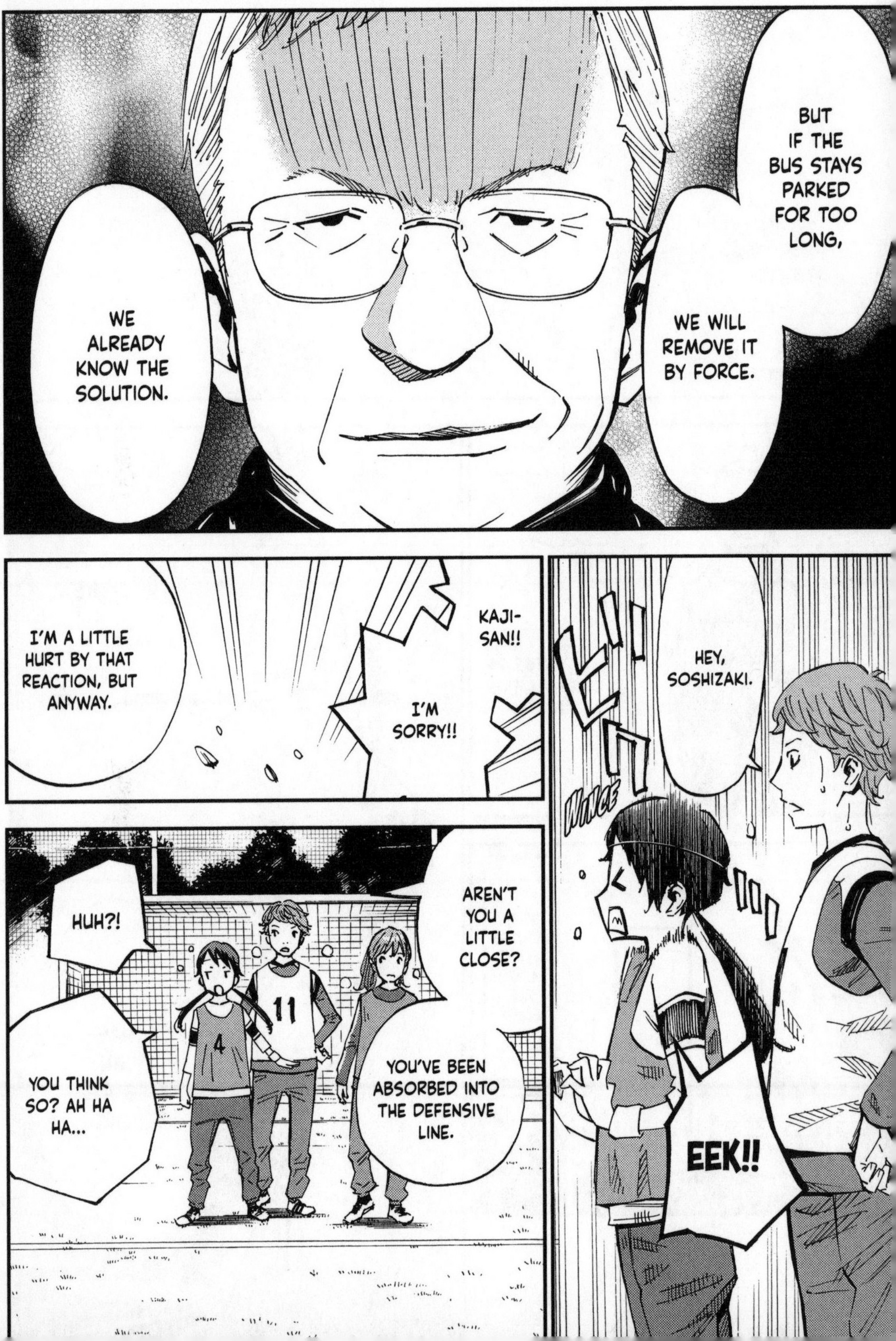
BUT IF THE BUS STAYS PARKED FOR TOO LONG,
WE WILL REMOVE IT BY FORCE.
WE ALREADY KNOW THE SOLUTION.
HEY, SOSHIZAKI.
WINCE
EEK!!
KAJI-SAN!!
I'M SORRY!!
I'M A LITTLE HURT BY THAT REACTION, BUT ANYWAY.
AREN'T YOU A LITTLE CLOSE?
YOU'VE BEEN ABSORBED INTO THE DEFENSIVE LINE.
HUH?!
YOU THINK SO? AH HA HA...

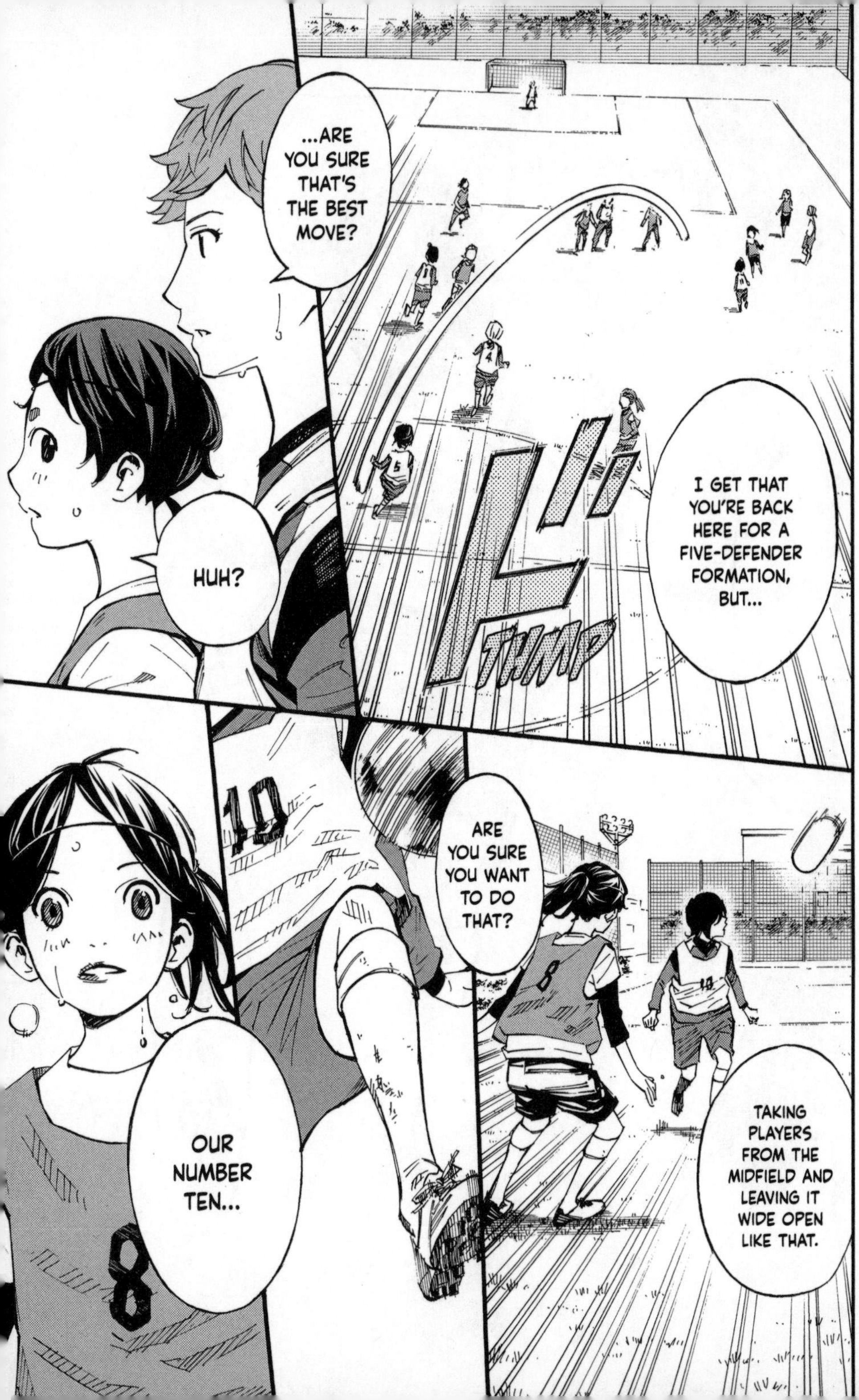

I GET THAT YOU'RE BACK HERE FOR A FIVE-DEFENDER FORMATION, BUT...
THMP
...ARE YOU SURE THAT'S THE BEST MOVE?
HUH?
TAKING PLAYERS FROM THE MIDFIELD AND LEAVING IT WIDE OPEN LIKE THAT.
ARE YOU SURE YOU WANT TO DO THAT?
OUR NUMBER TEN...

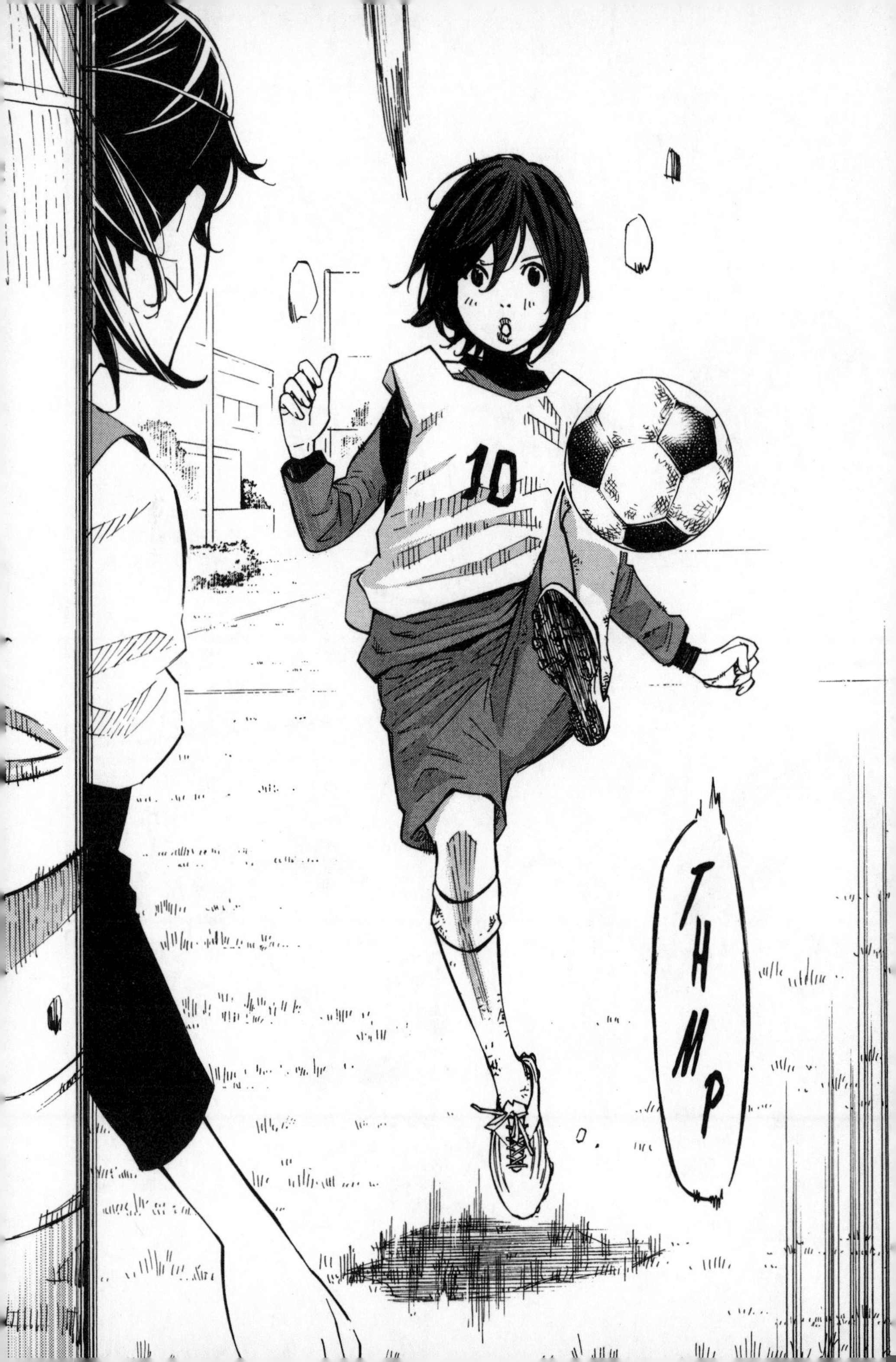
10
THMP

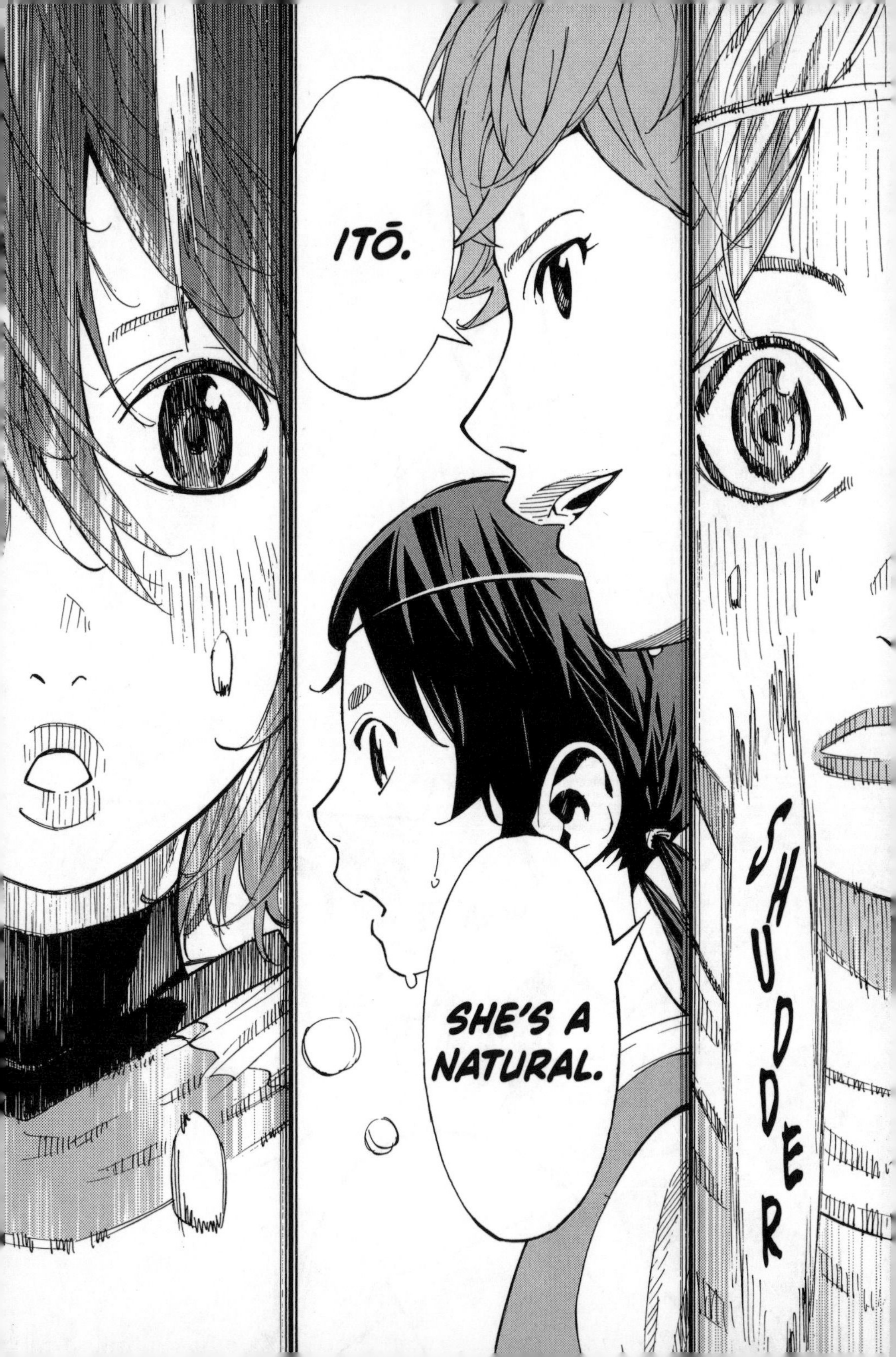
SHUDDER
ITŌ.
SHE'S A NATURAL.

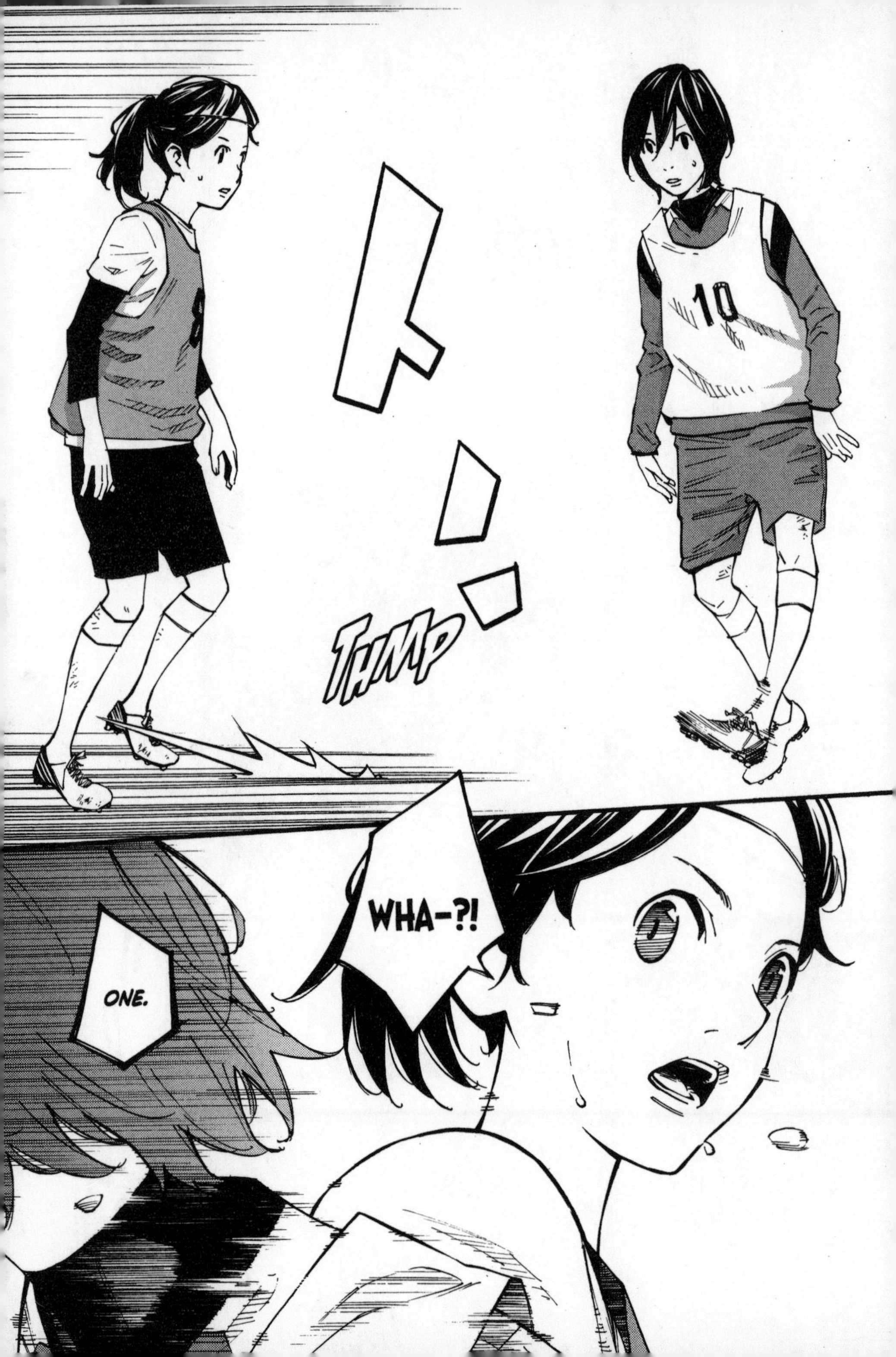
THMP
WHA-?!
ONE.

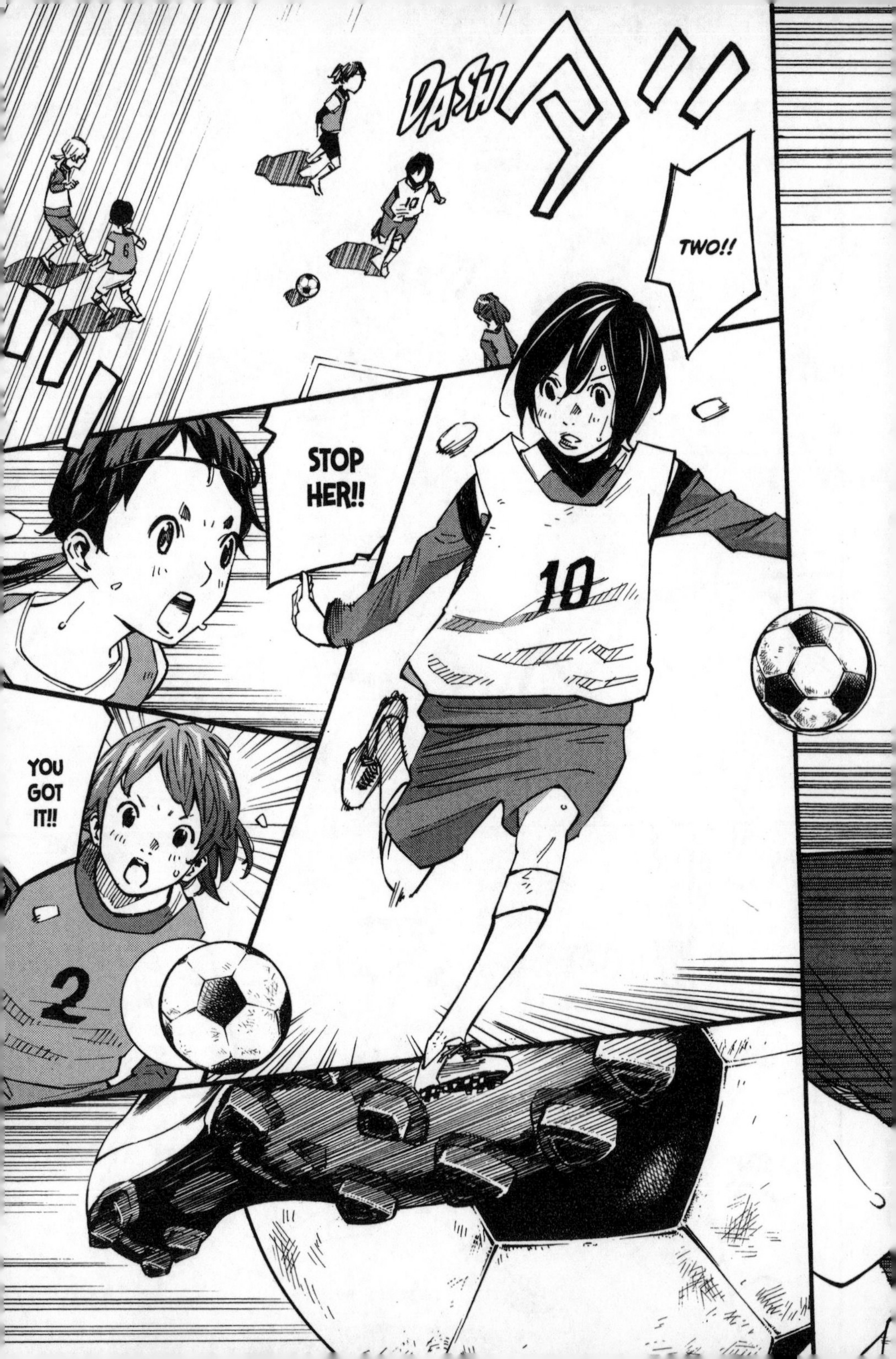
DASH
ダッ
TWO!!
STOP HER!!
YOU GOT IT!!

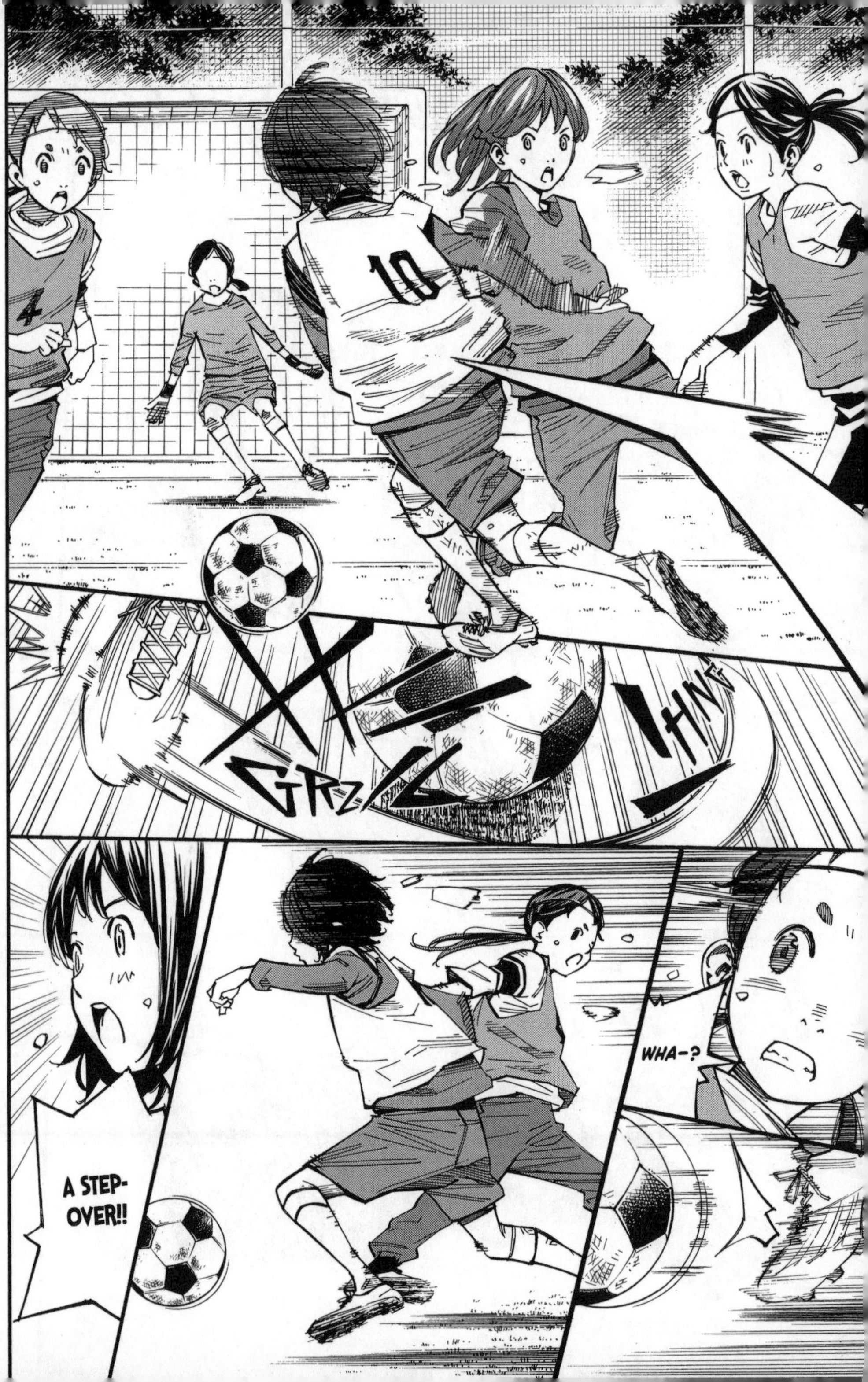
WHA-?
A STEP-OVER!!

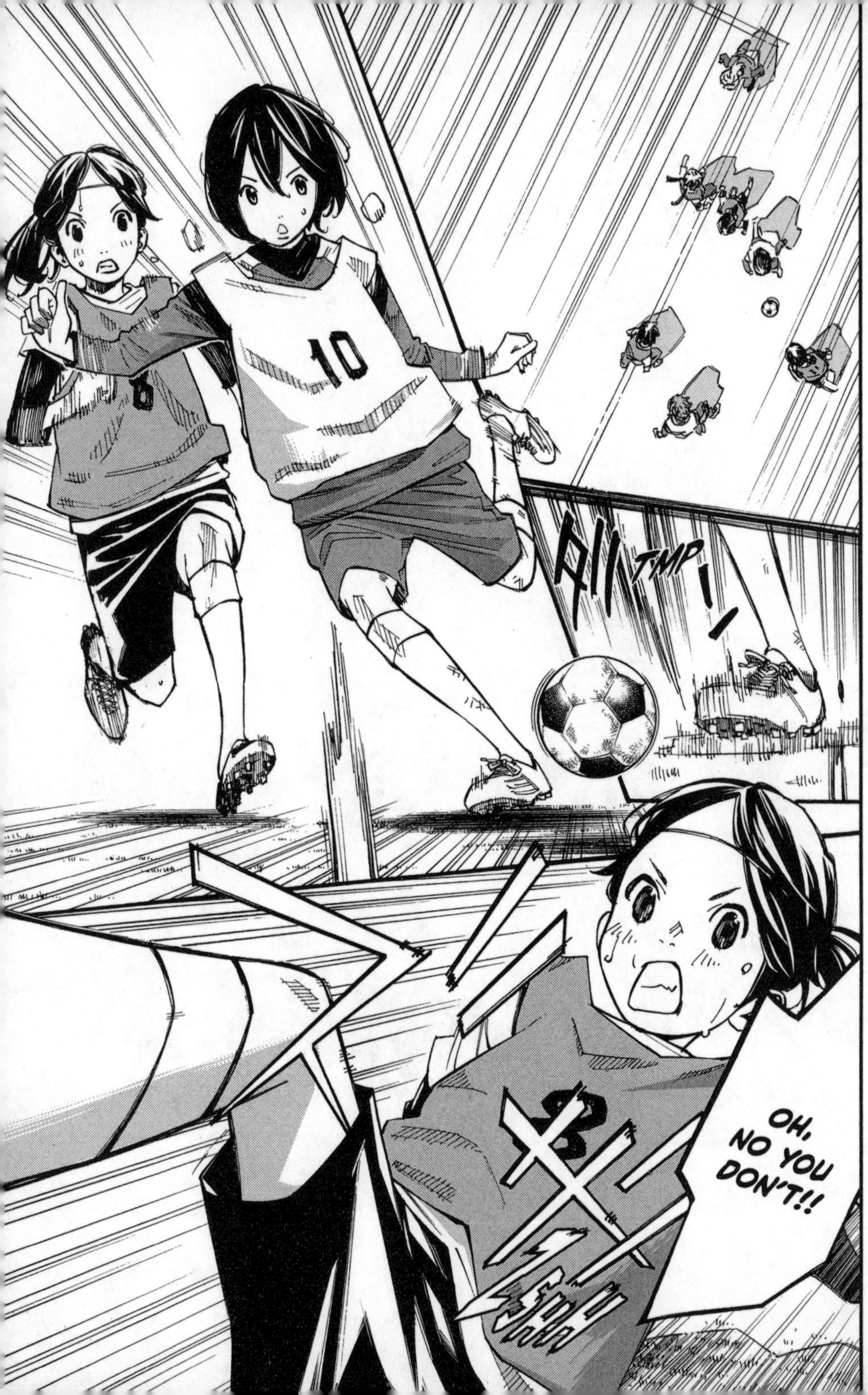
TMP
OH, NO YOU DON'T!!

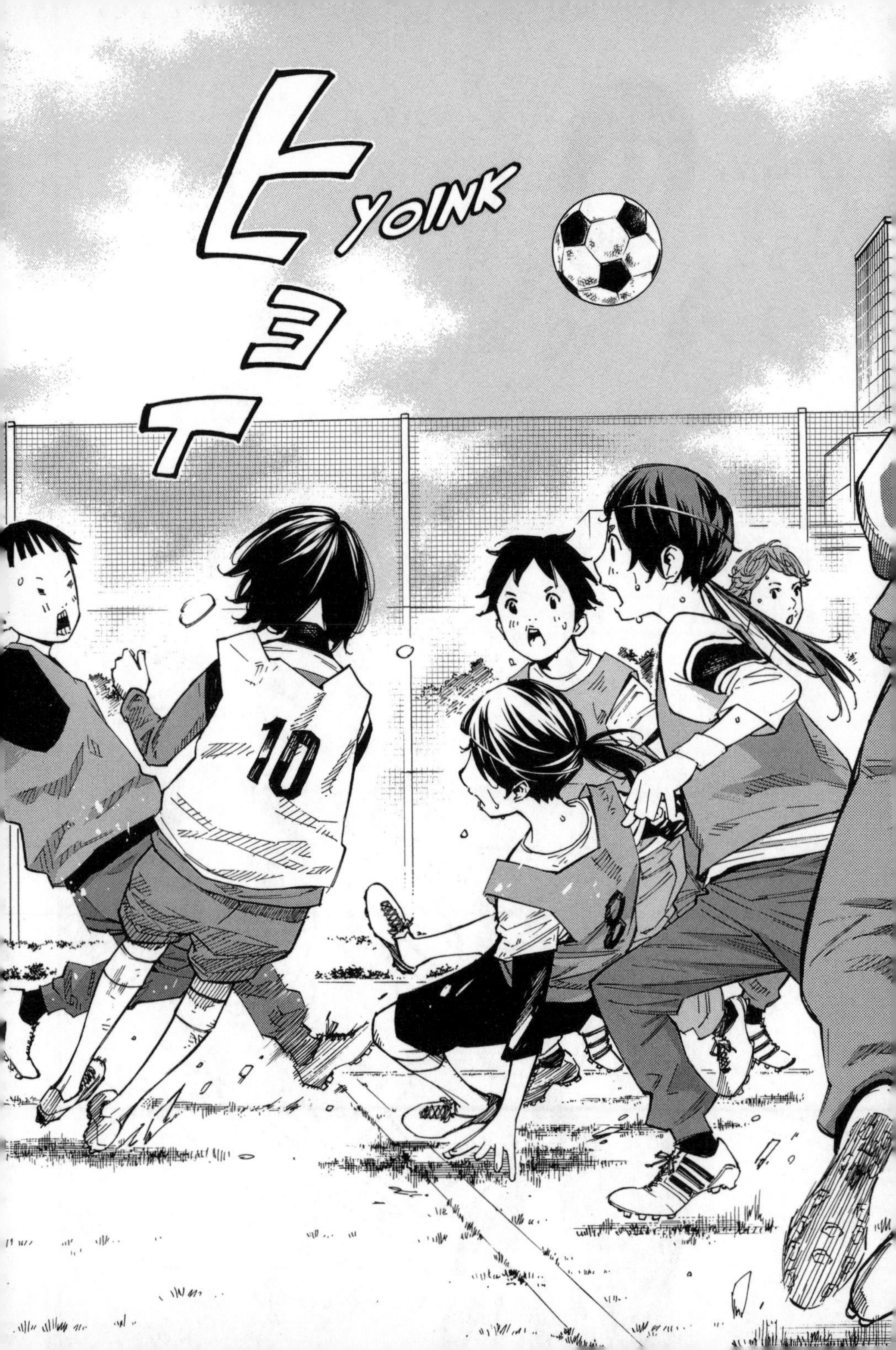
ヒョイ
YOINK

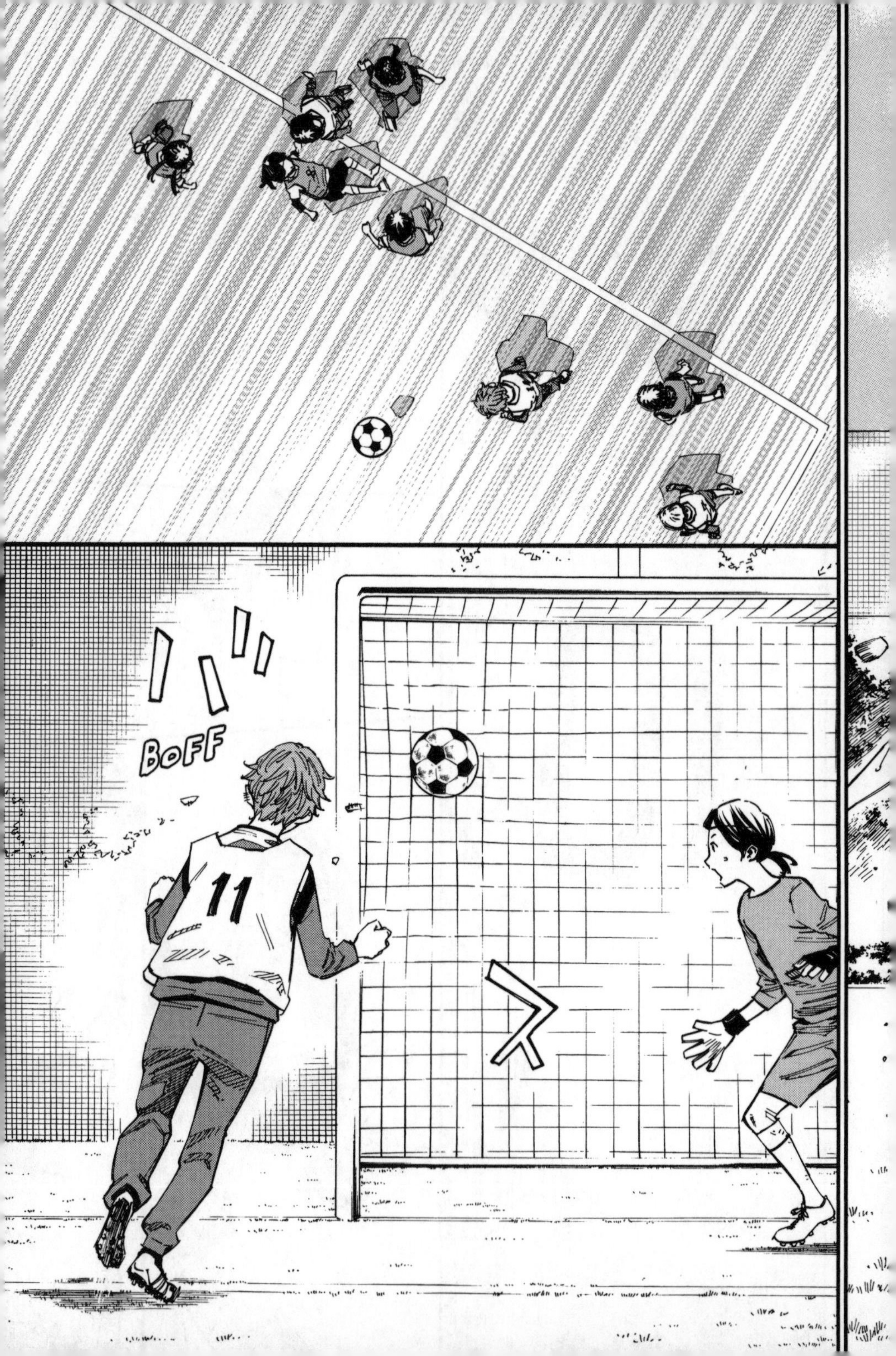
BoFF

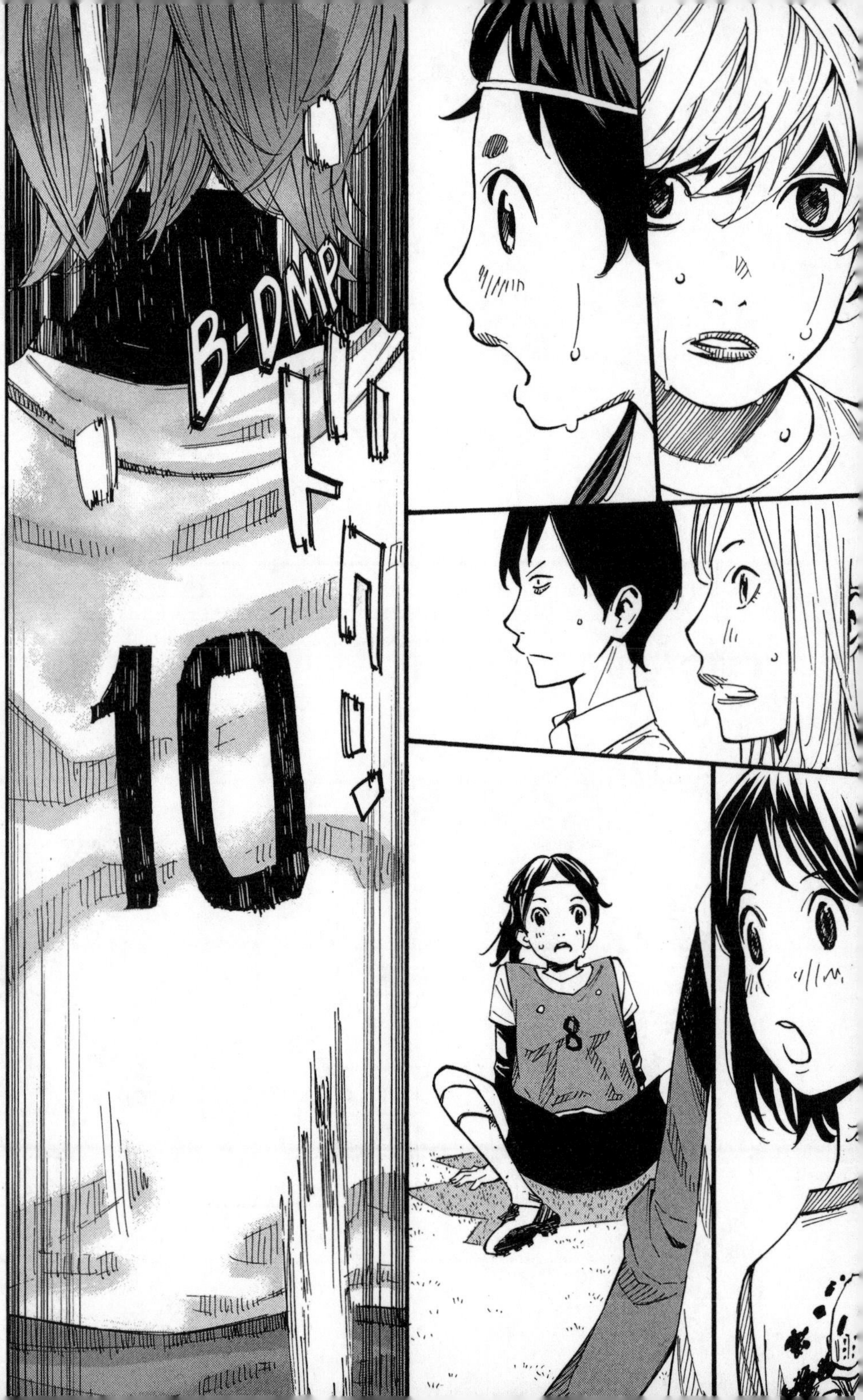
B-DMP

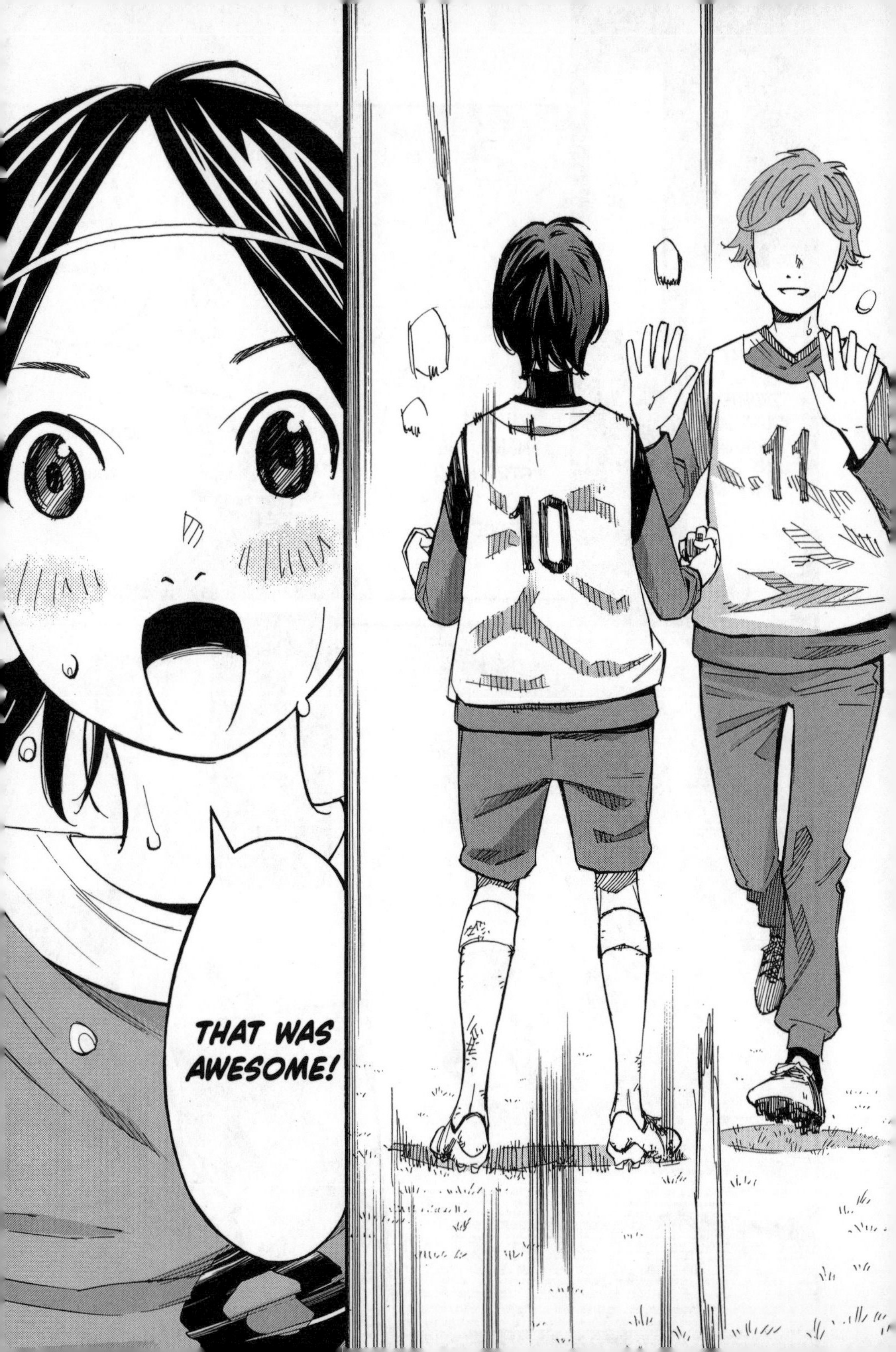
THAT WAS AWESOME!

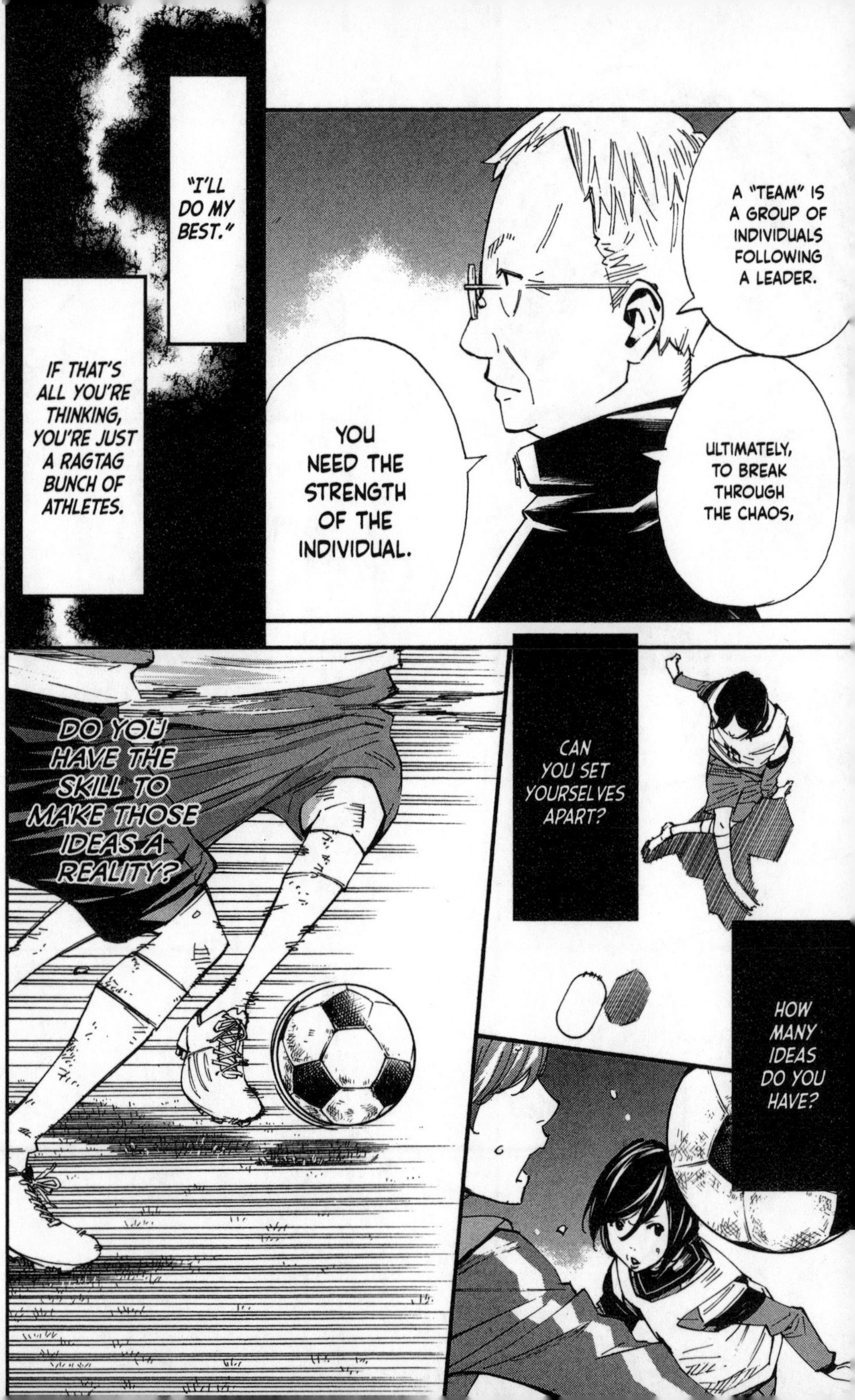
A "TEAM" IS A GROUP OF INDIVIDUALS FOLLOWING A LEADER.
ULTIMATELY, TO BREAK THROUGH THE CHAOS,
YOU NEED THE STRENGTH OF THE INDIVIDUAL.
"I'LL DO MY BEST."
IF THAT'S ALL YOU'RE THINKING, YOU'RE JUST A RAGTAG BUNCH OF ATHLETES.
CAN YOU SET YOURSELVES APART?
HOW MANY IDEAS DO YOU HAVE?
DO YOU HAVE THE SKILL TO MAKE THOSE IDEAS A REALITY?

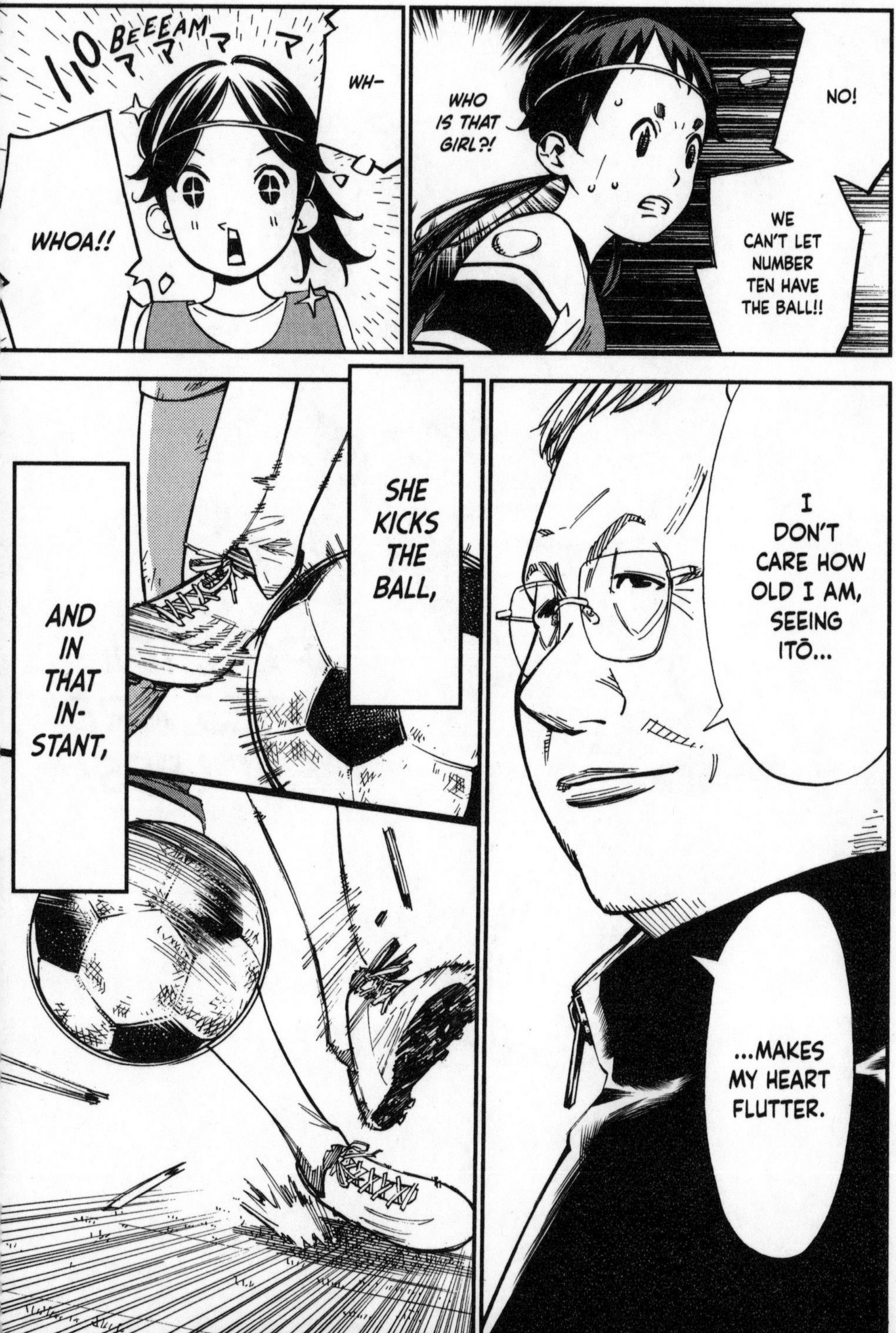
NO!
WE CAN'T LET NUMBER TEN HAVE THE BALL!!
WHO IS THAT GIRL?!
BEEEAM
WH-
WHOA!!
I DON'T CARE HOW OLD I AM, SEEING ITŌ...
...MAKES MY HEART FLUTTER.
SHE KICKS THE BALL,
AND IN THAT IN-STANT,

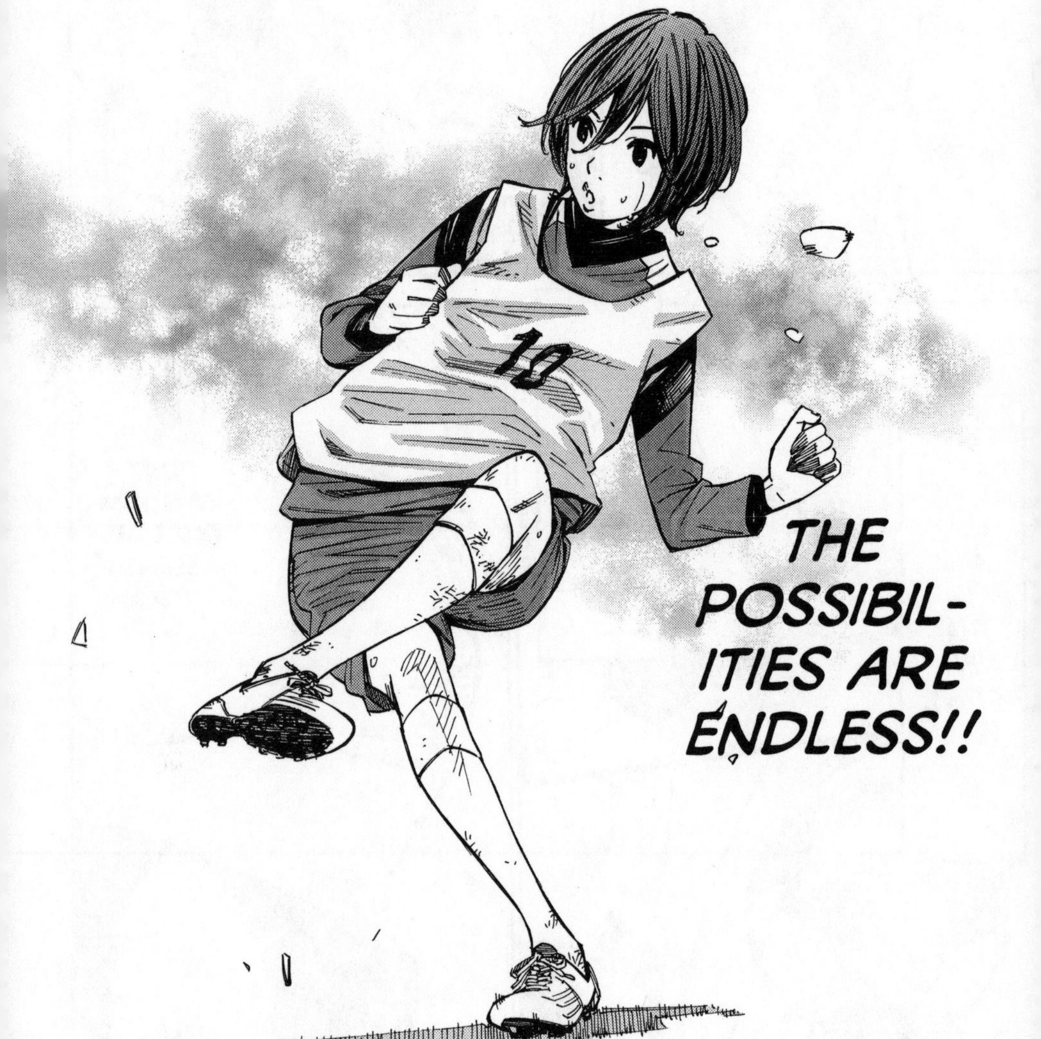
THE POSSIBILITIES ARE ENDLESS!!

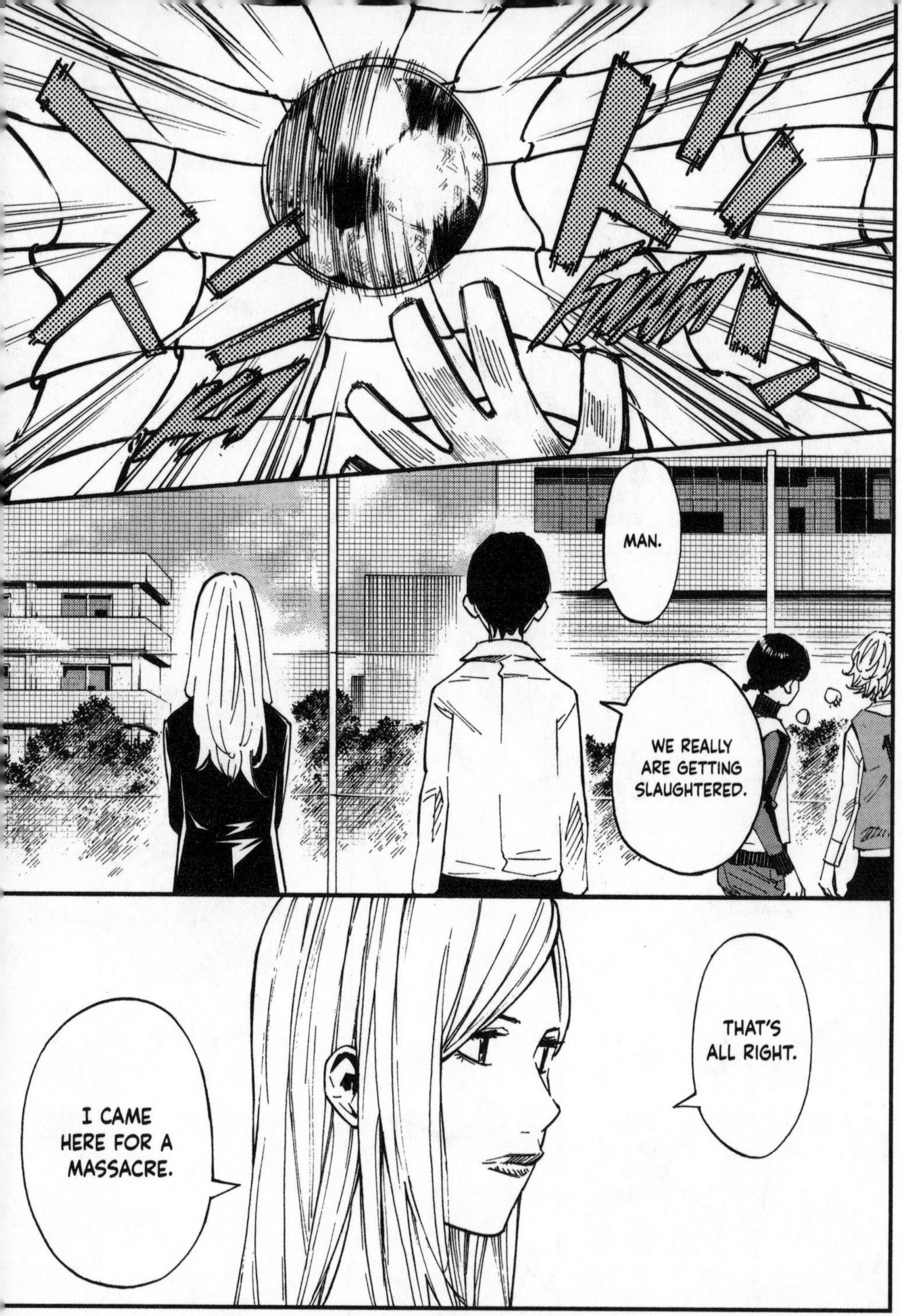
MAN.
WE REALLY ARE GETTING SLAUGHTERED.
THAT'S ALL RIGHT.
I CAME HERE FOR A MASSACRE.

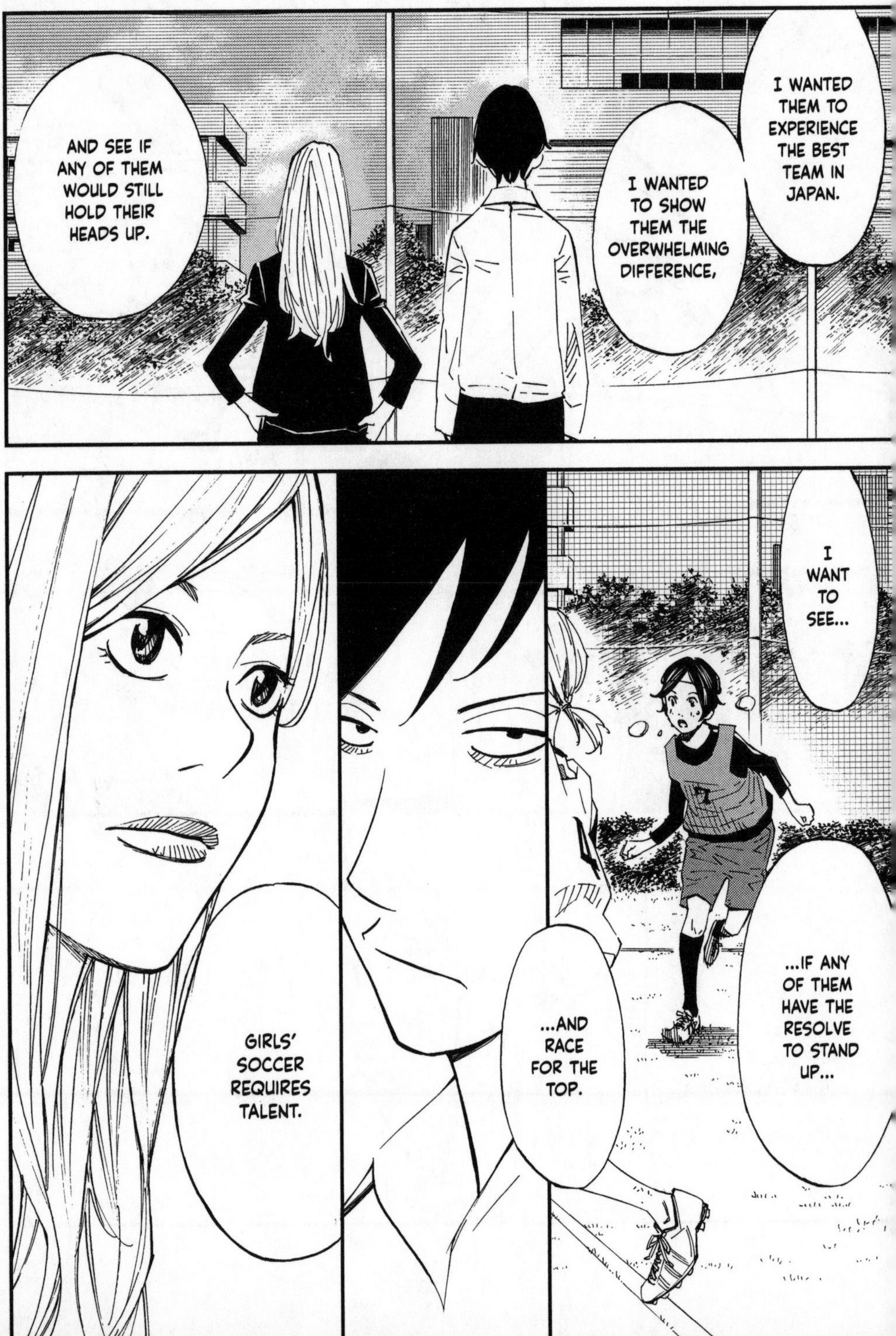
I WANTED THEM TO EXPERIENCE THE BEST TEAM IN JAPAN.
I WANTED TO SHOW THEM THE OVERWHELMING DIFFERENCE,
AND SEE IF ANY OF THEM WOULD STILL HOLD THEIR HEADS UP.
I WANT TO SEE...
...IF ANY OF THEM HAVE THE RESOLVE TO STAND UP...
...AND RACE FOR THE TOP.
GIRLS' SOCCER REQUIRES TALENT.

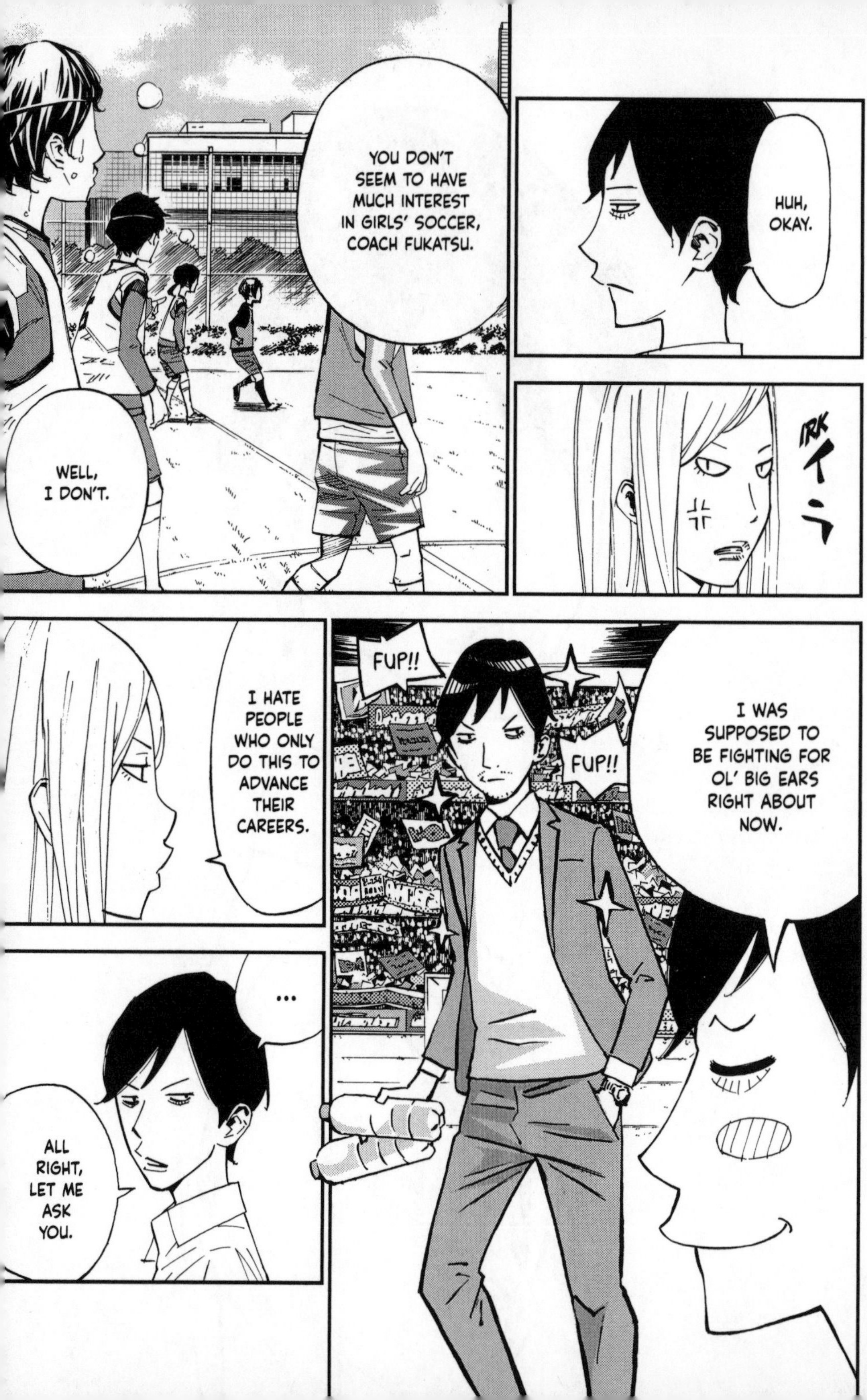
HUH, OKAY.
IRK
イラ
YOU DON'T SEEM TO HAVE MUCH INTEREST IN GIRLS' SOCCER, COACH FUKATSU.
WELL, I DON'T.
I WAS SUPPOSED TO BE FIGHTING FOR OL' BIG EARS RIGHT ABOUT NOW.
FUP!!
FUP!!
I HATE PEOPLE WHO ONLY DO THIS TO ADVANCE THEIR CAREERS.
...
ALL RIGHT, LET ME ASK YOU.

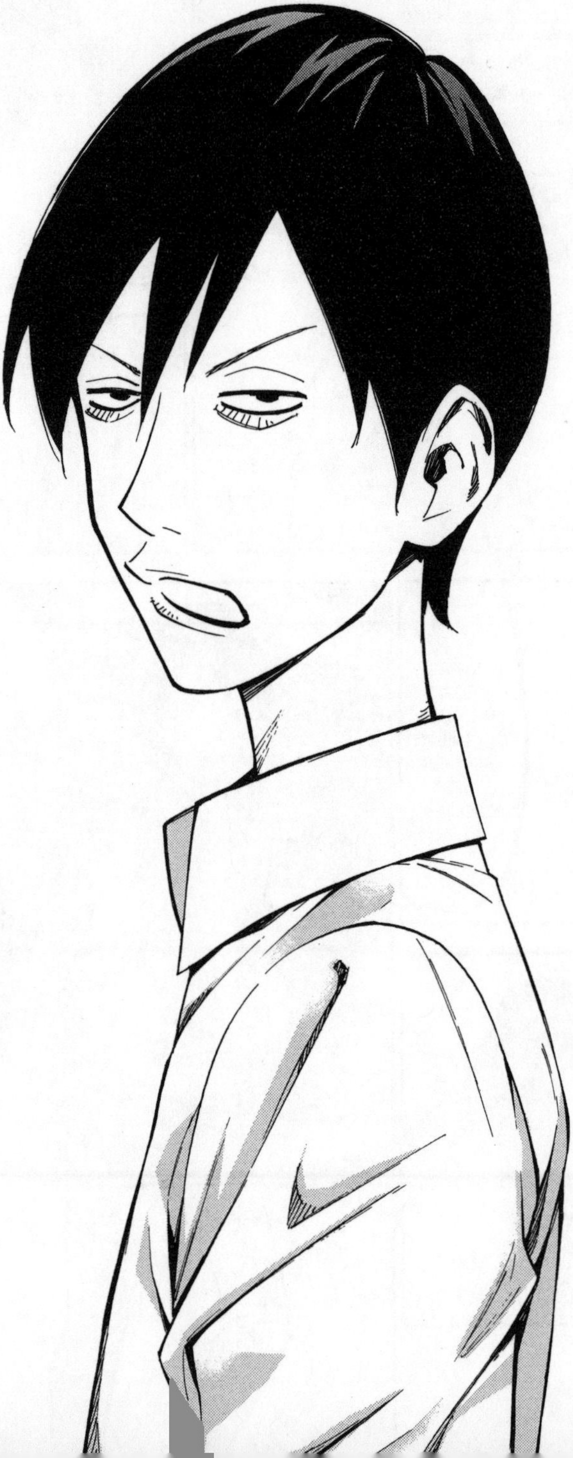

IS THERE
ANY FUTURE
IN GIRLS'
SOCCER?

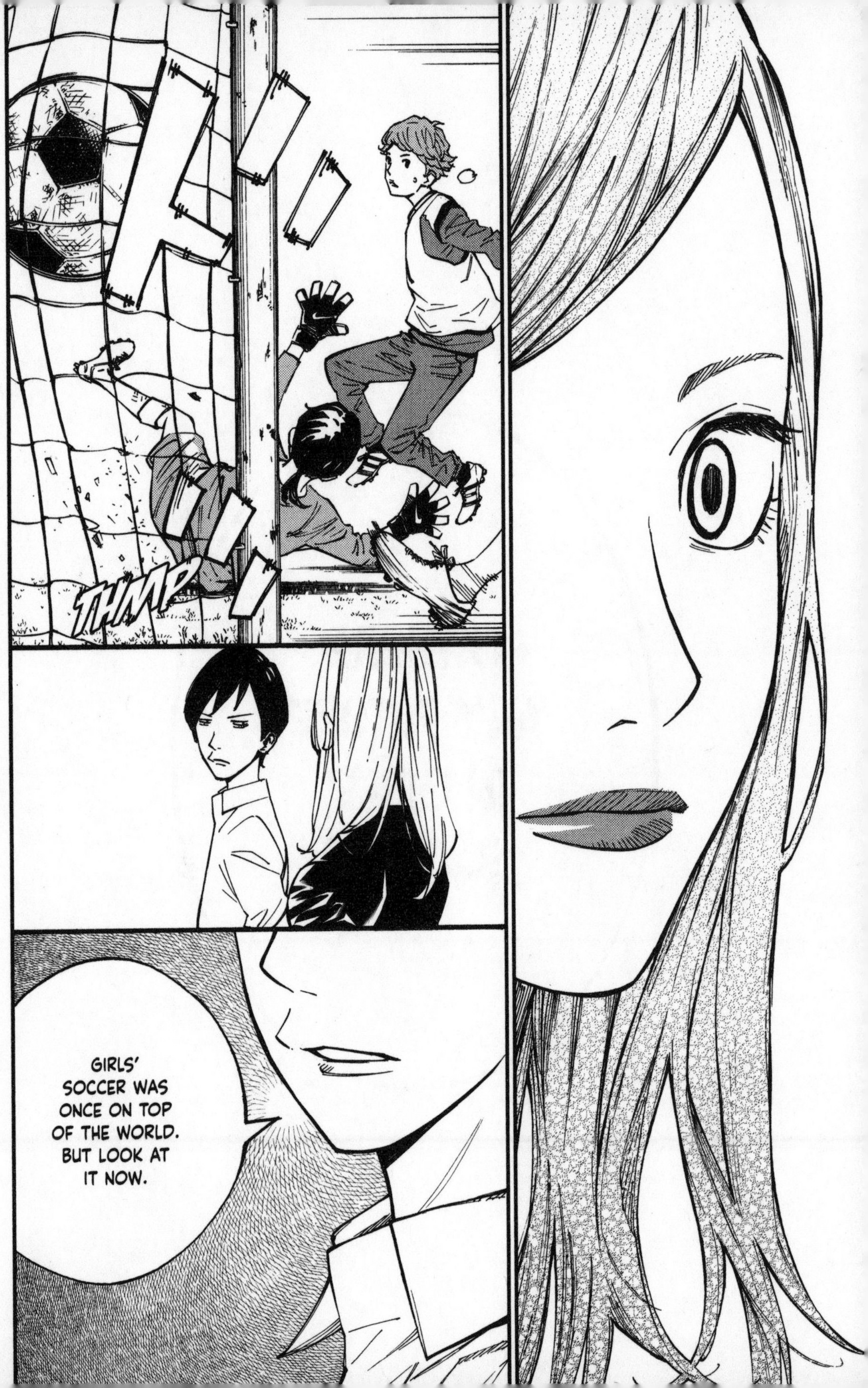
THMP
GIRLS' SOCCER WAS ONCE ON TOP OF THE WORLD. BUT LOOK AT IT NOW.

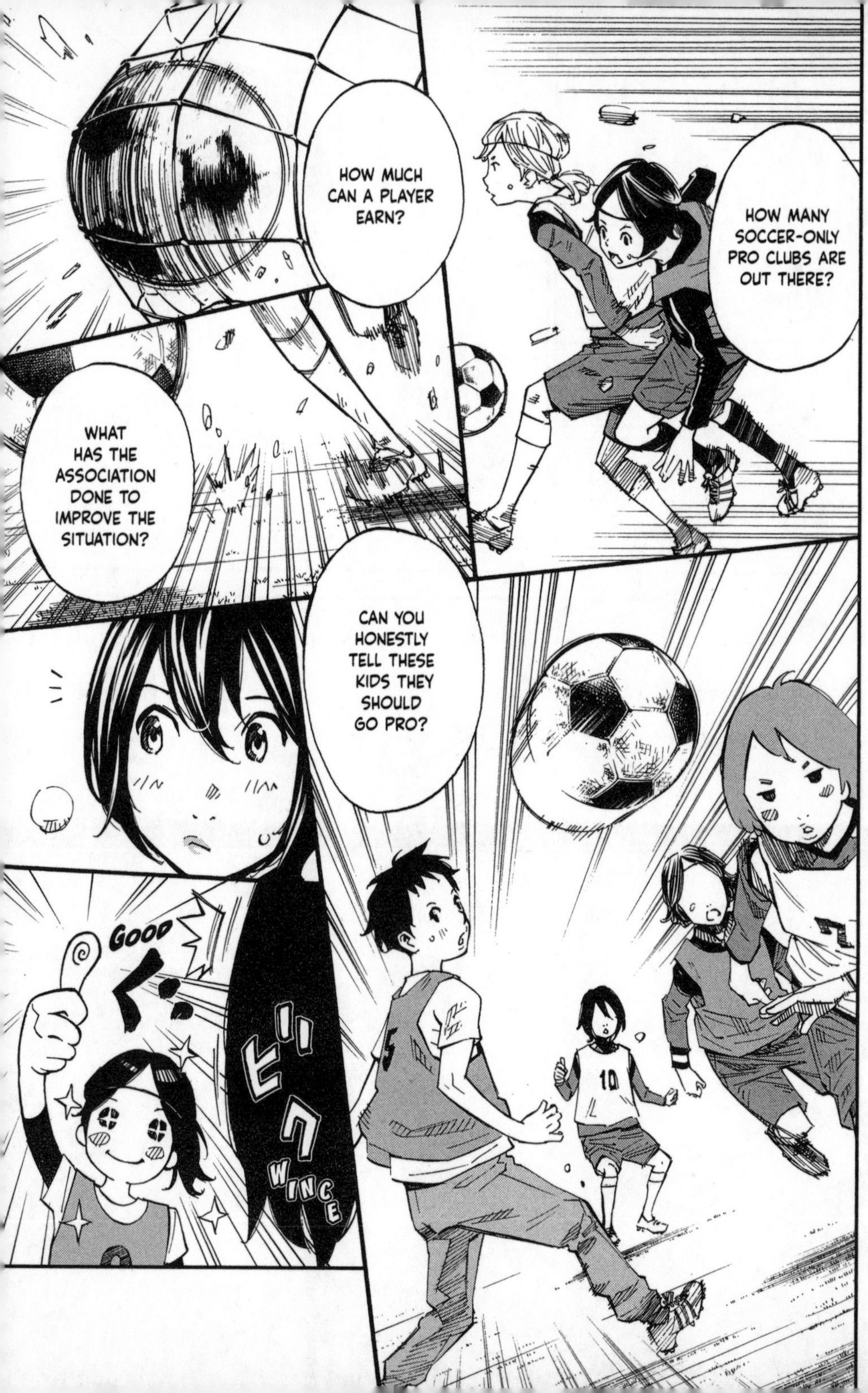
HOW MANY SOCCER-ONLY PRO CLUBS ARE OUT THERE?
HOW MUCH CAN A PLAYER EARN?
WHAT HAS THE ASSOCIATION DONE TO IMPROVE THE SITUATION?
CAN YOU HONESTLY TELL THESE KIDS THEY SHOULD GO PRO?
WINCE
GOOD

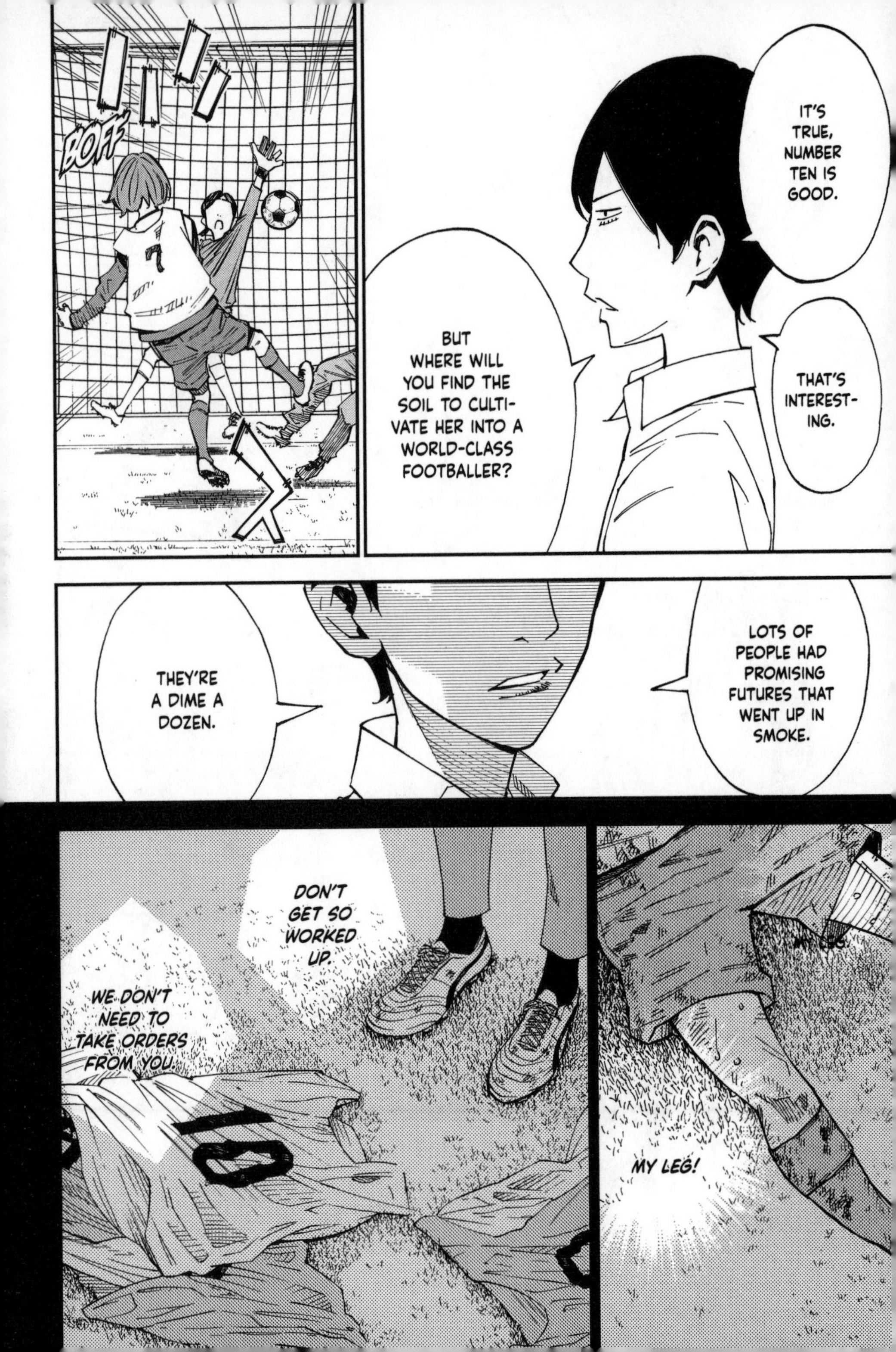
IT'S TRUE, NUMBER TEN IS GOOD.
THAT'S INTEREST-ING.
BUT WHERE WILL YOU FIND THE SOIL TO CULTI-VATE HER INTO A WORLD-CLASS FOOTBALLER?
BOFF
LOTS OF PEOPLE HAD PROMISING FUTURES THAT WENT UP IN SMOKE.
THEY'RE A DIME A DOZEN.
MY LEG!
DON'T GET SO WORKED UP.
WE DON'T NEED TO TAKE ORDERS FROM YOU.

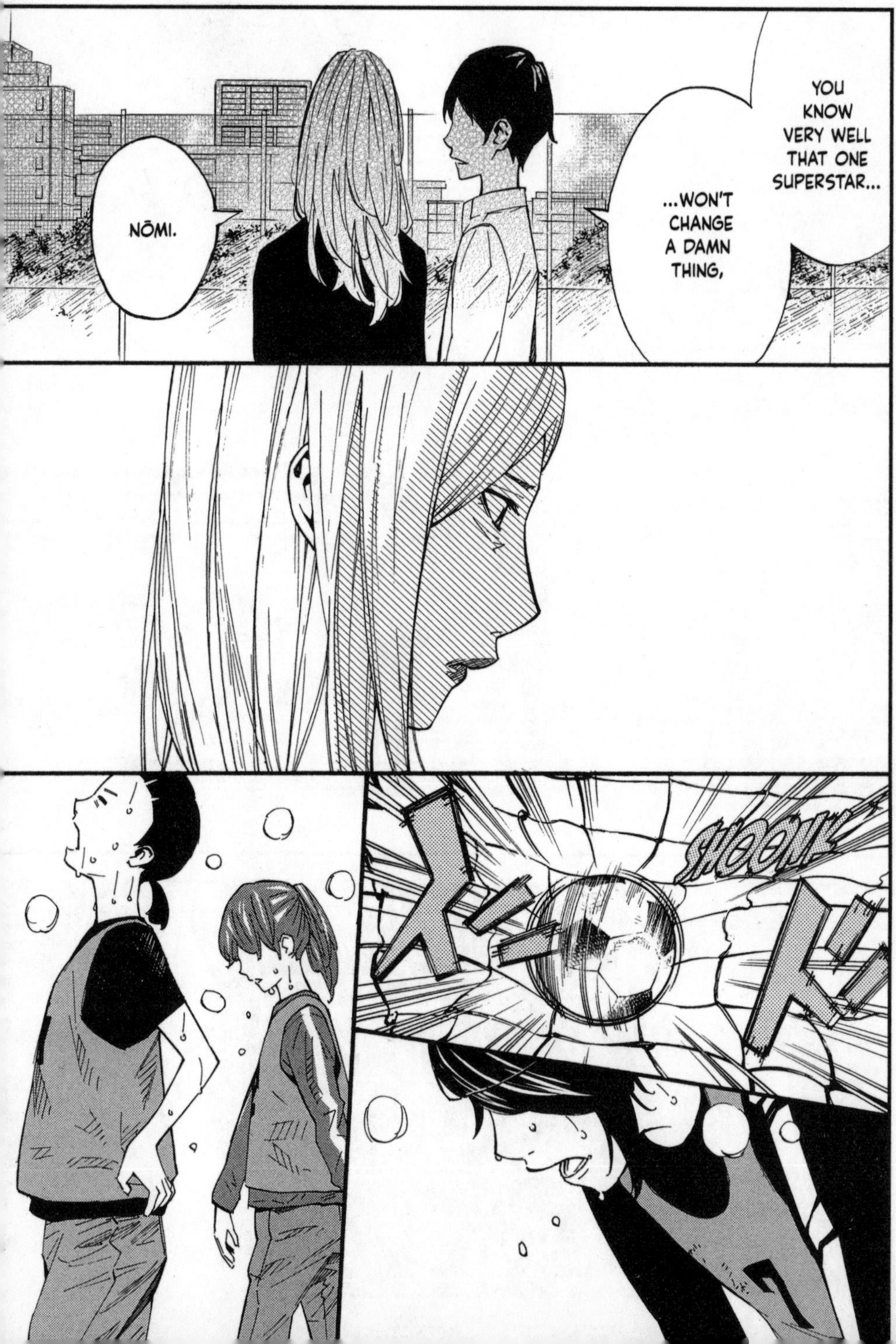
YOU KNOW VERY WELL THAT ONE SUPERSTAR...
...WON'T CHANGE A DAMN THING,
NŌMI.
SHOOM!

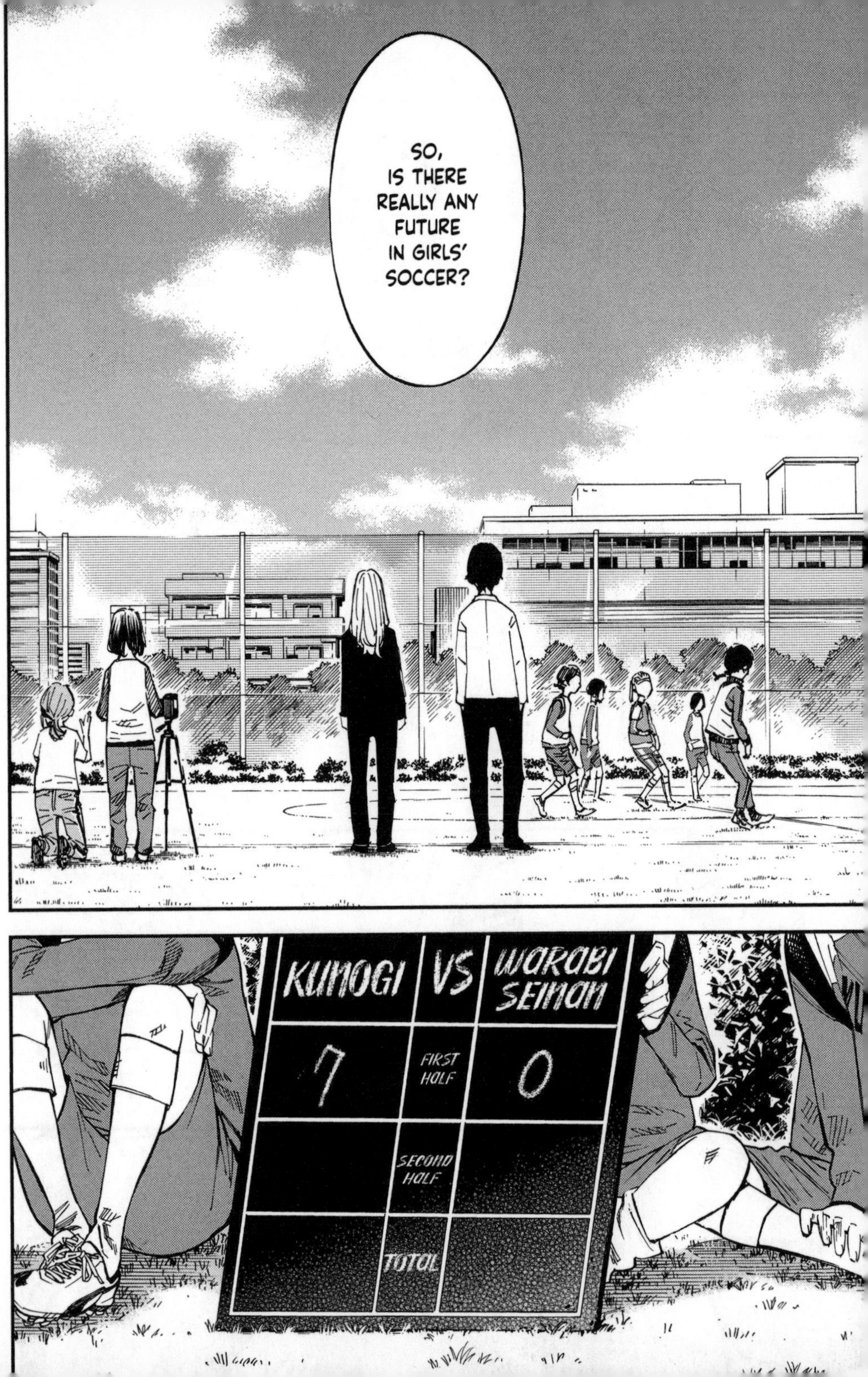
SO, IS THERE REALLY ANY FUTURE IN GIRLS' SOCCER?
KUMOGI
VS
WARABI SEINAN
7
FIRST HALF
0
SECOND HALF
TOTAL

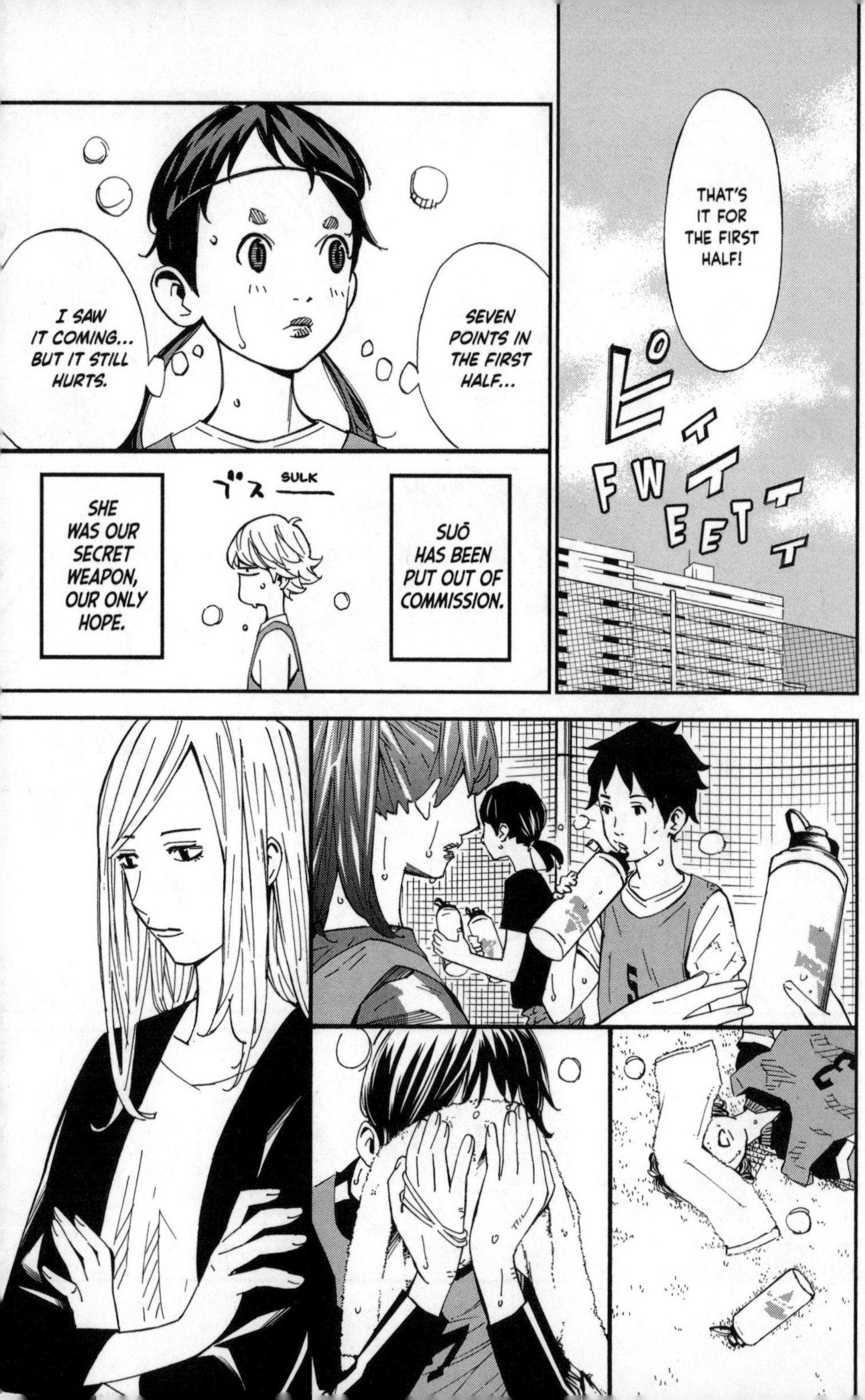
THAT'S IT FOR THE FIRST HALF!
ピー
FWEETTT
SEVEN POINTS IN THE FIRST HALF...
I SAW IT COMING... BUT IT STILL HURTS.
SUŌ HAS BEEN PUT OUT OF COMMISSION.
ブス
SULK
SHE WAS OUR SECRET WEAPON, OUR ONLY HOPE.

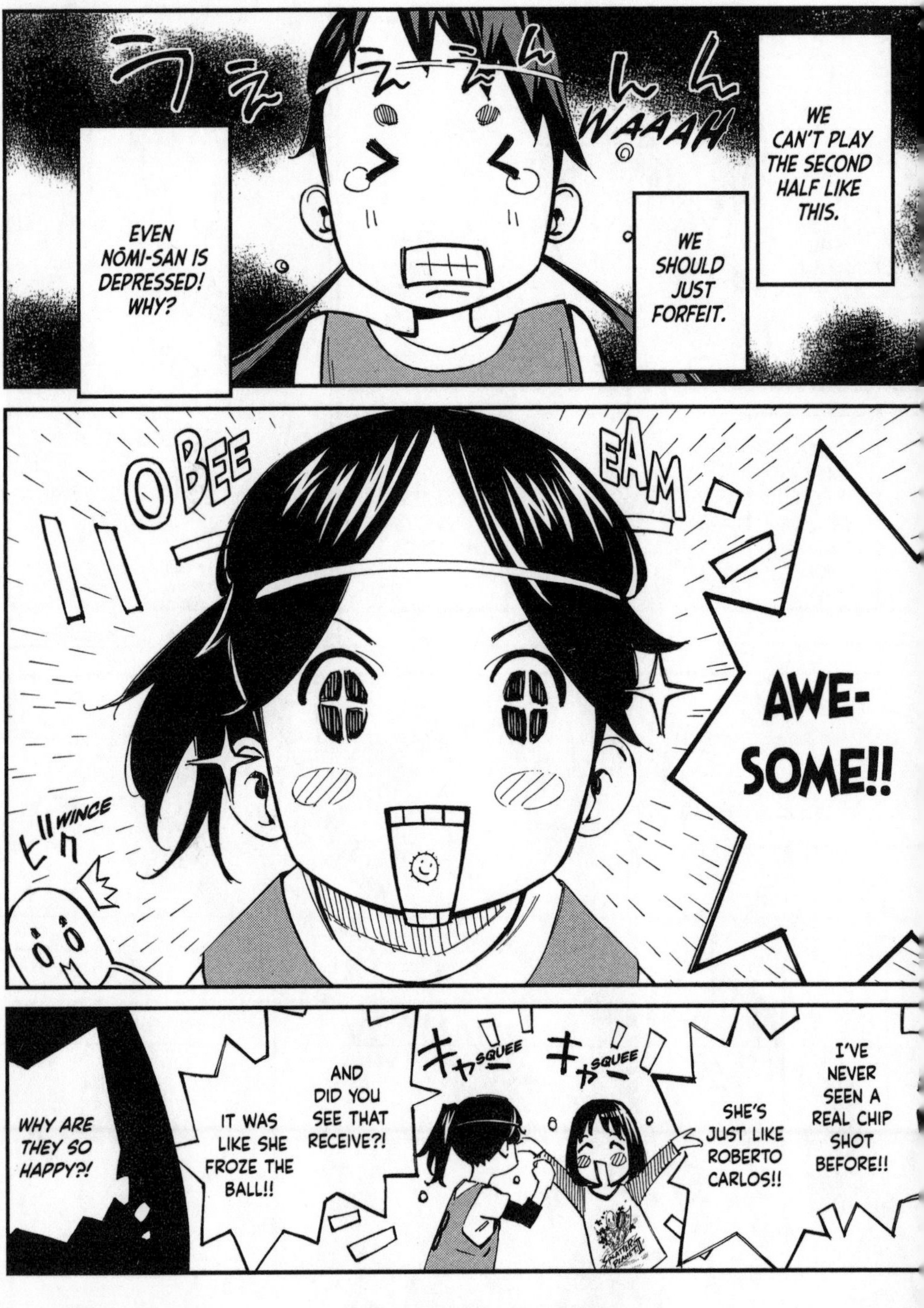
WE CAN'T PLAY THE SECOND HALF LIKE THIS.
WE SHOULD JUST FORFEIT.
WAAAH
EVEN NŌMI-SAN IS DEPRESSED! WHY?
AWE-SOME!!
WINCE
I'VE NEVER SEEN A REAL CHIP SHOT BEFORE!!
SHE'S JUST LIKE ROBERTO CARLOS!!
SQUEE
SQUEE
AND DID YOU SEE THAT RECEIVE?!
IT WAS LIKE SHE FROZE THE BALL!!
WHY ARE THEY SO HAPPY?!

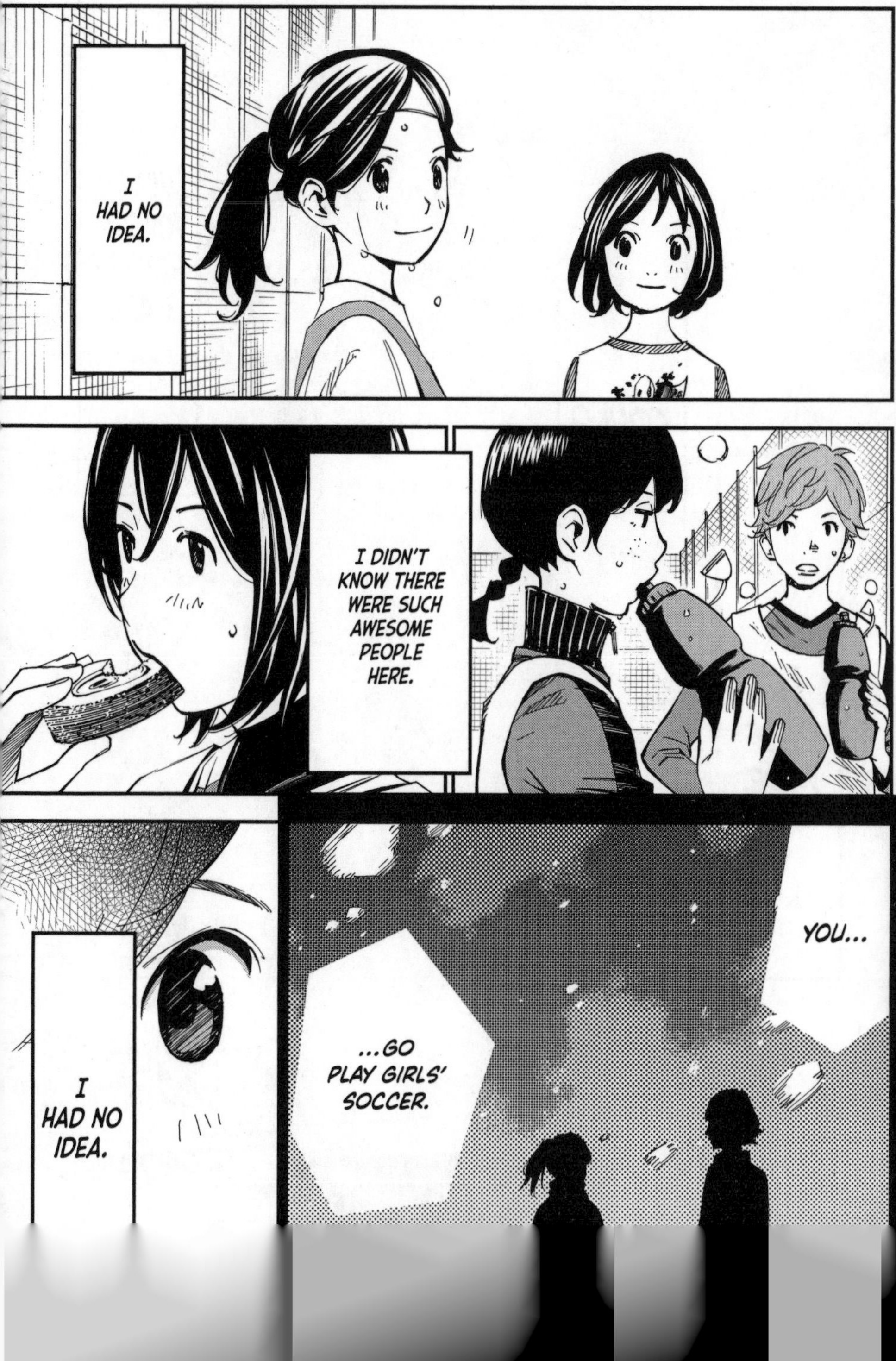
I HAD NO IDEA.
I DIDN'T KNOW THERE WERE SUCH AWESOME PEOPLE HERE.
YOU...
...GO PLAY GIRLS' SOCCER.
I HAD NO IDEA.

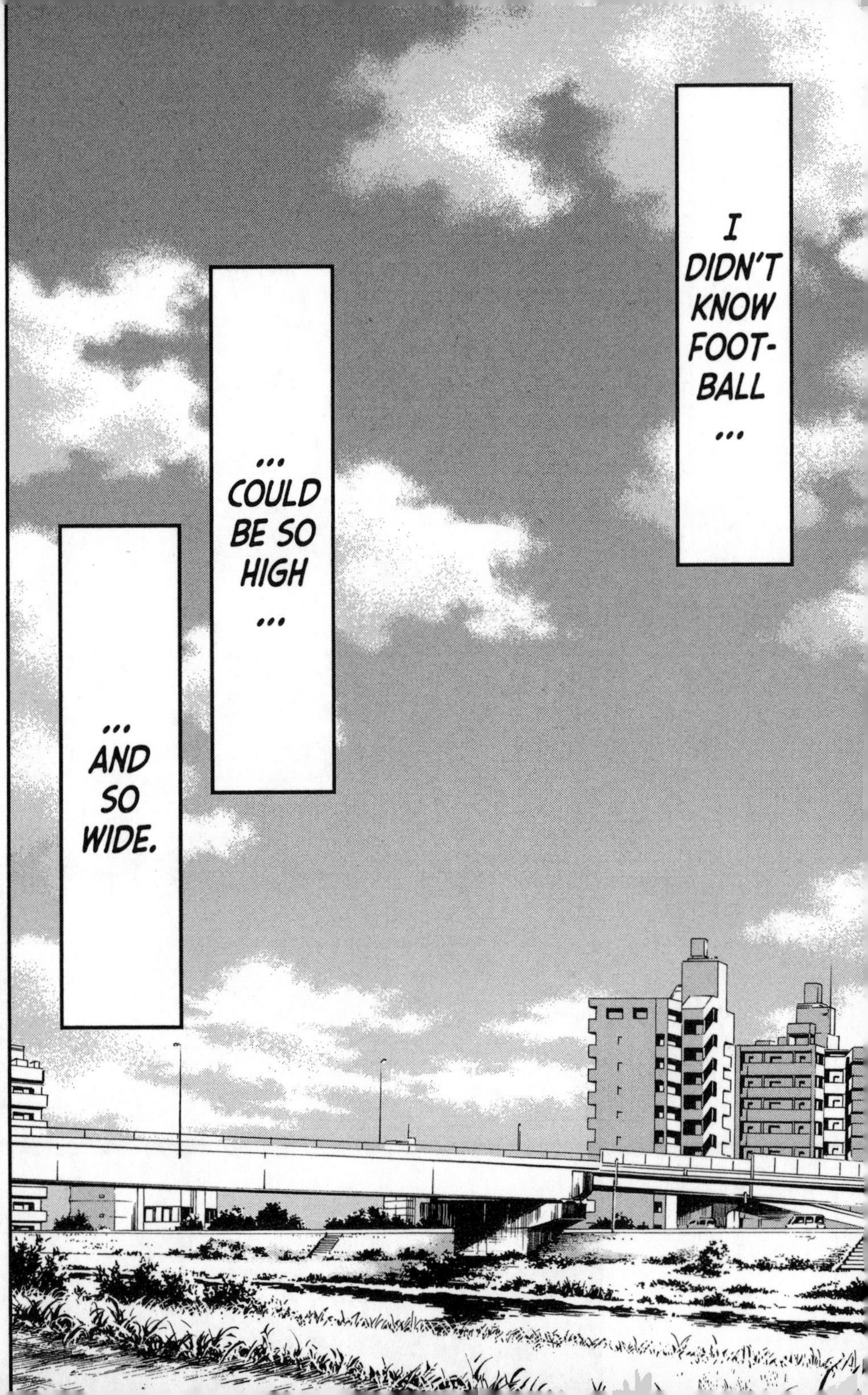
I DIDN'T KNOW FOOT-BALL ...
... COULD BE SO HIGH ...
... AND SO WIDE.

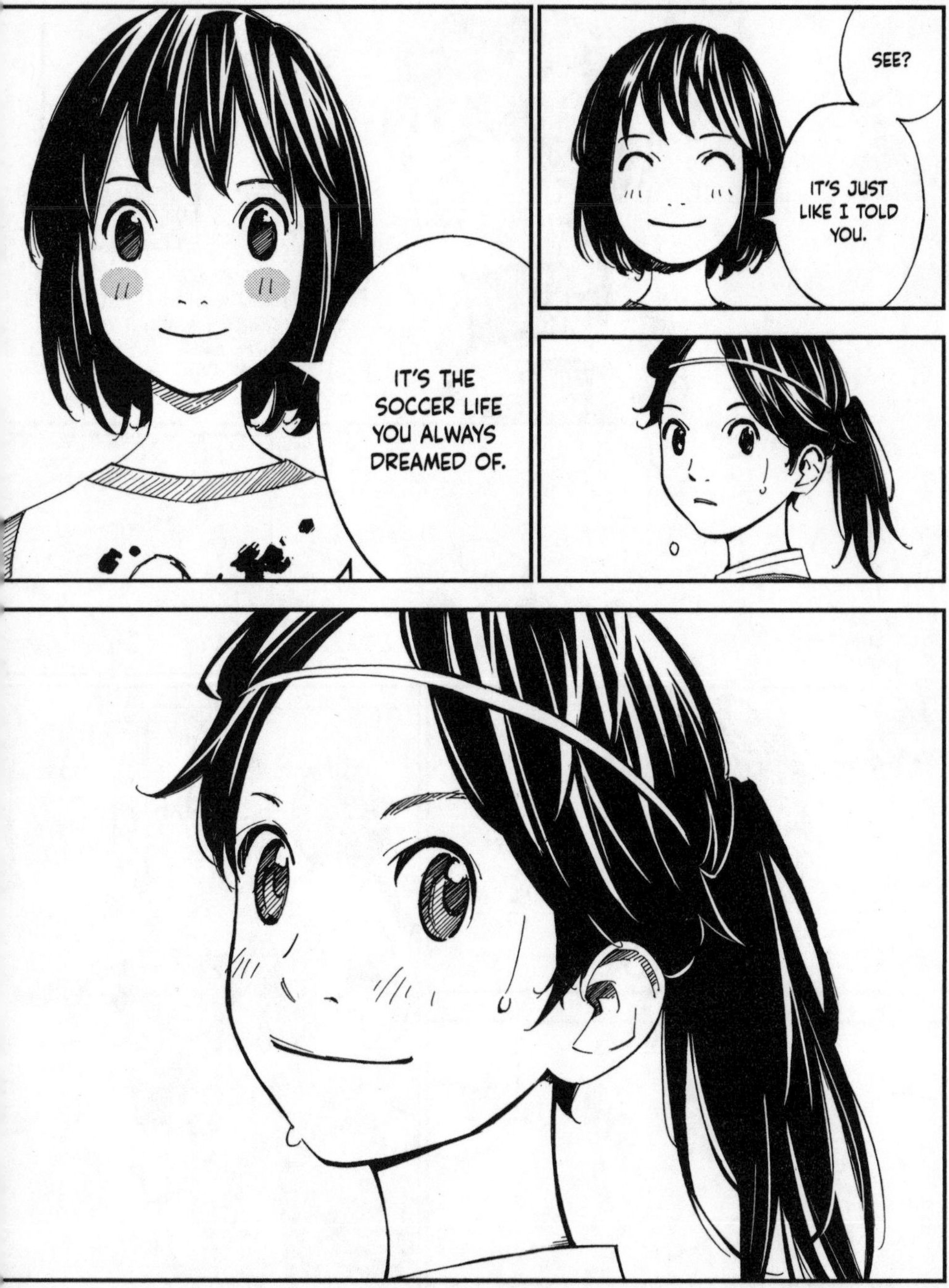
SEE?
IT'S JUST LIKE I TOLD YOU.
IT'S THE SOCCER LIFE YOU ALWAYS DREAMED OF.

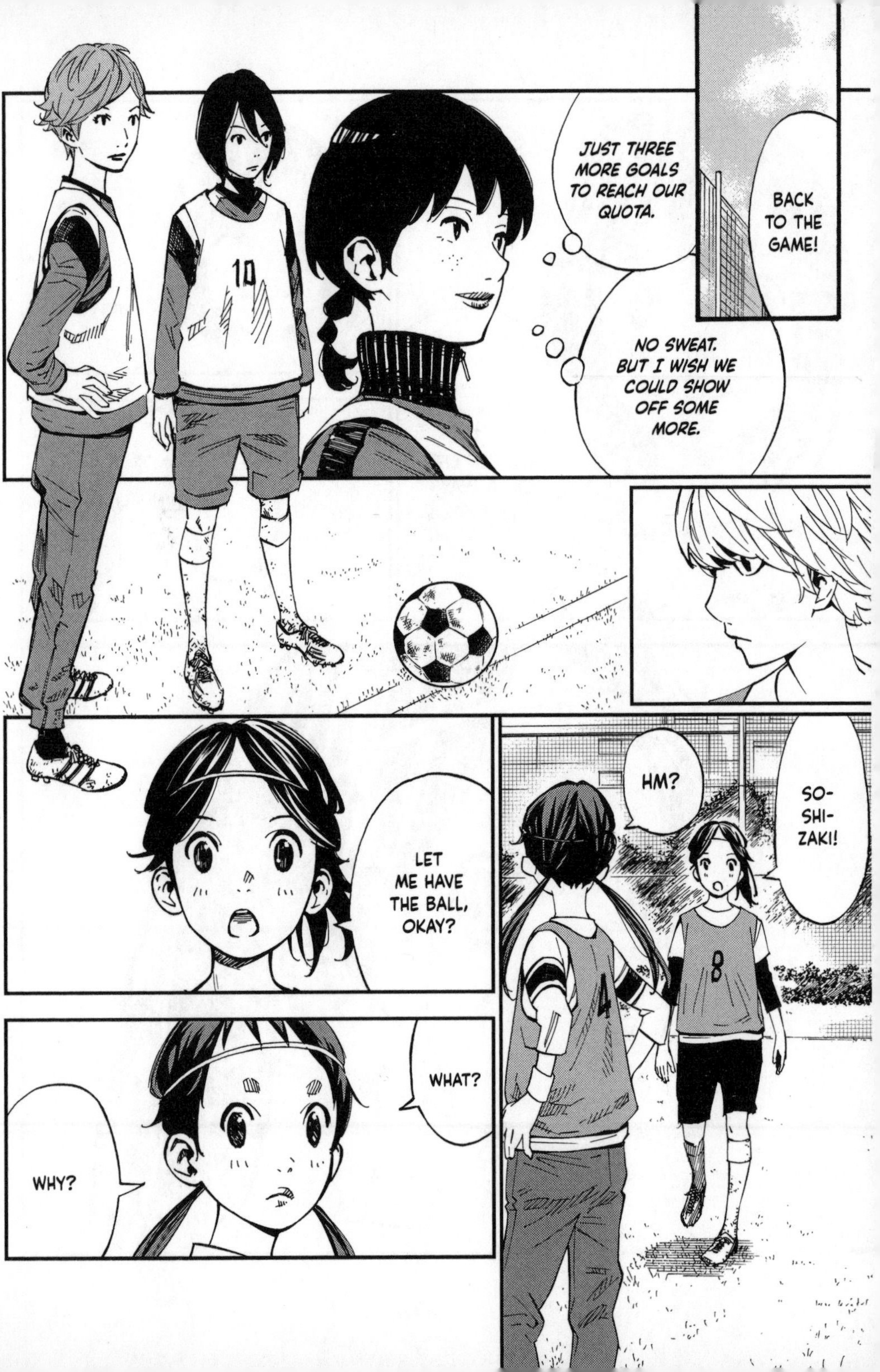
BACK TO THE GAME!
JUST THREE MORE GOALS TO REACH OUR QUOTA.
NO SWEAT. BUT I WISH WE COULD SHOW OFF SOME MORE.
SO-SHI-ZAKI!
HM?
LET ME HAVE THE BALL, OKAY?
WHAT?
WHY?

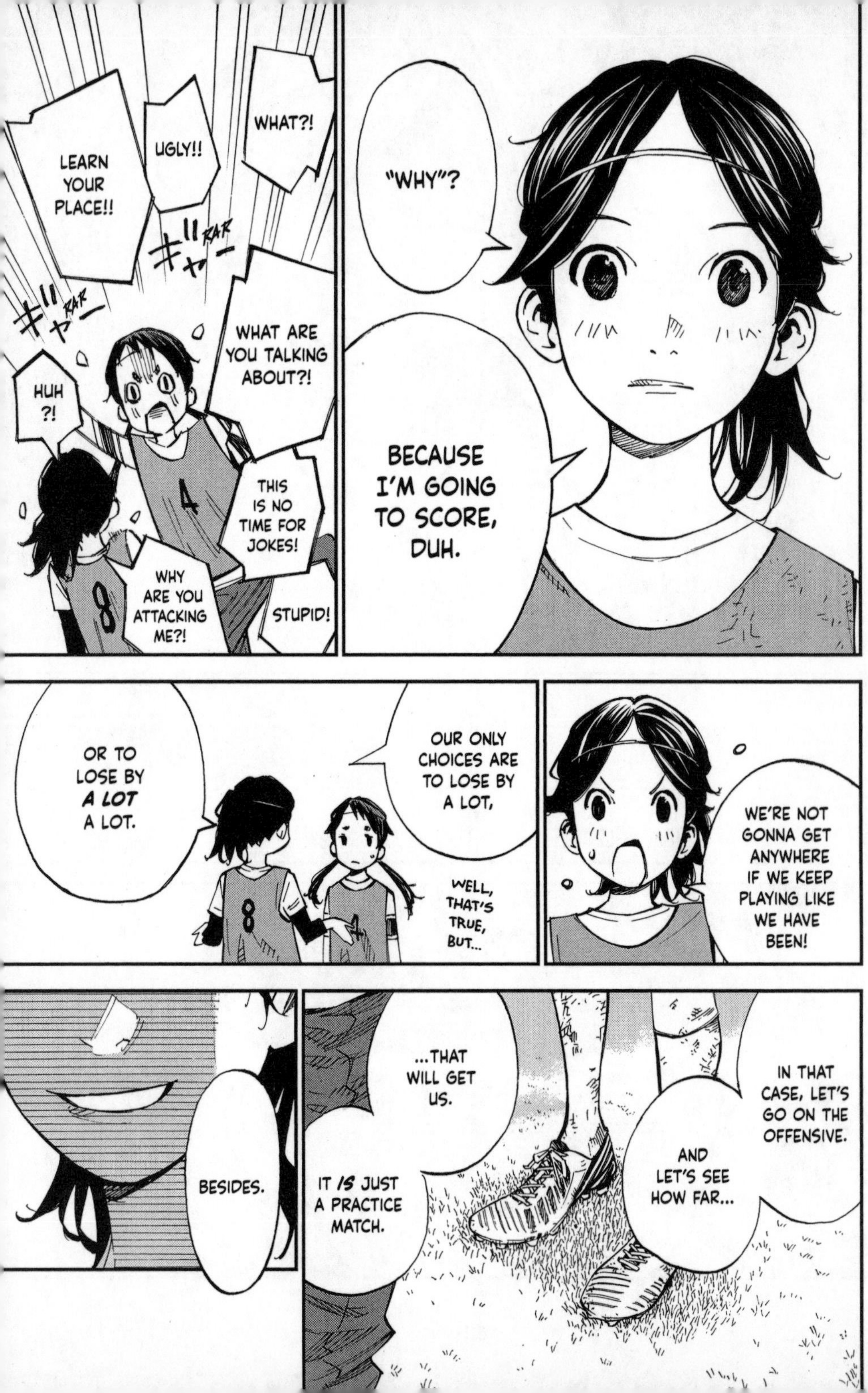
"WHY"?
BECAUSE I'M GOING TO SCORE, DUH.
WHAT?!
UGLY!!
LEARN YOUR PLACE!!
RAR
RAR
WHAT ARE YOU TALKING ABOUT?!
HUH?!
THIS IS NO TIME FOR JOKES!
STUPID!
WHY ARE YOU ATTACKING ME?!
WE'RE NOT GONNA GET ANYWHERE IF WE KEEP PLAYING LIKE WE HAVE BEEN!
OUR ONLY CHOICES ARE TO LOSE BY A LOT,
WELL, THAT'S TRUE, BUT...
OR TO LOSE BY *A LOT* A LOT.
IN THAT CASE, LET'S GO ON THE OFFENSIVE.
AND LET'S SEE HOW FAR...
...THAT WILL GET US.
IT *IS* JUST A PRACTICE MATCH.
BESIDES.

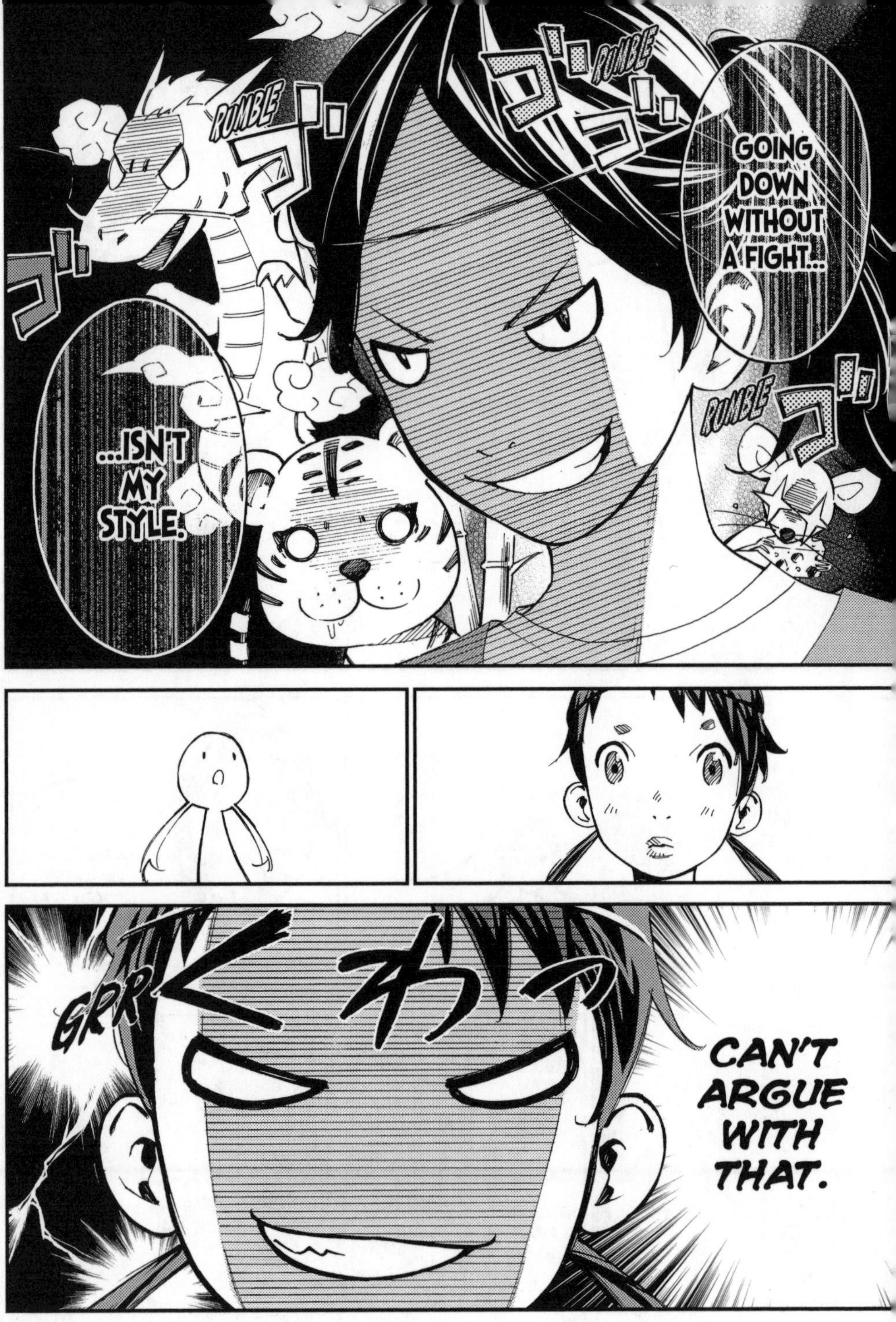
RUMBLE
GOING DOWN WITHOUT A FIGHT...
RUMBLE
RUMBLE
...ISN'T MY STYLE.
CAN'T ARGUE WITH THAT.
GRR

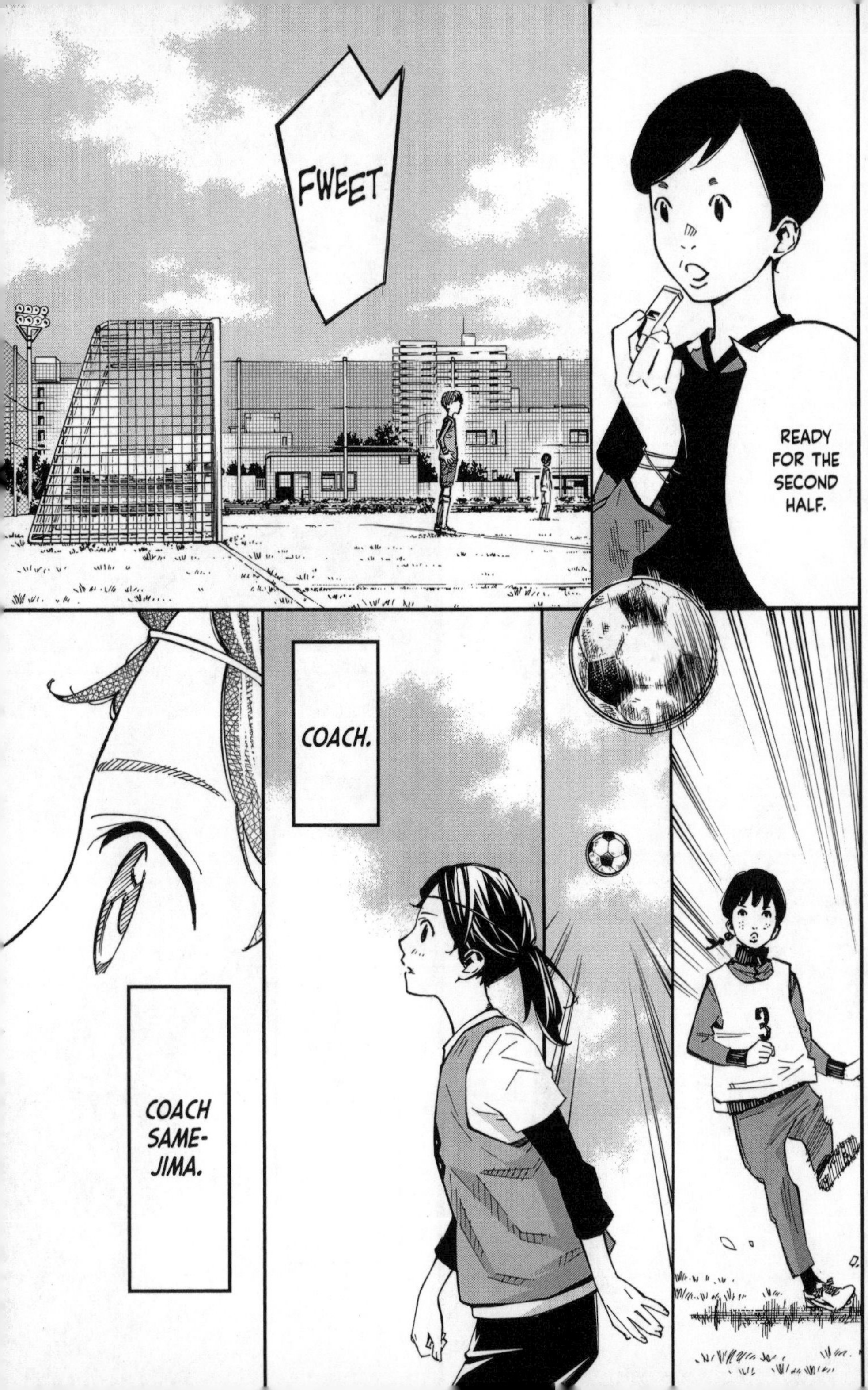
READY FOR THE SECOND HALF.
FWEET
COACH.
COACH SAME-JIMA.

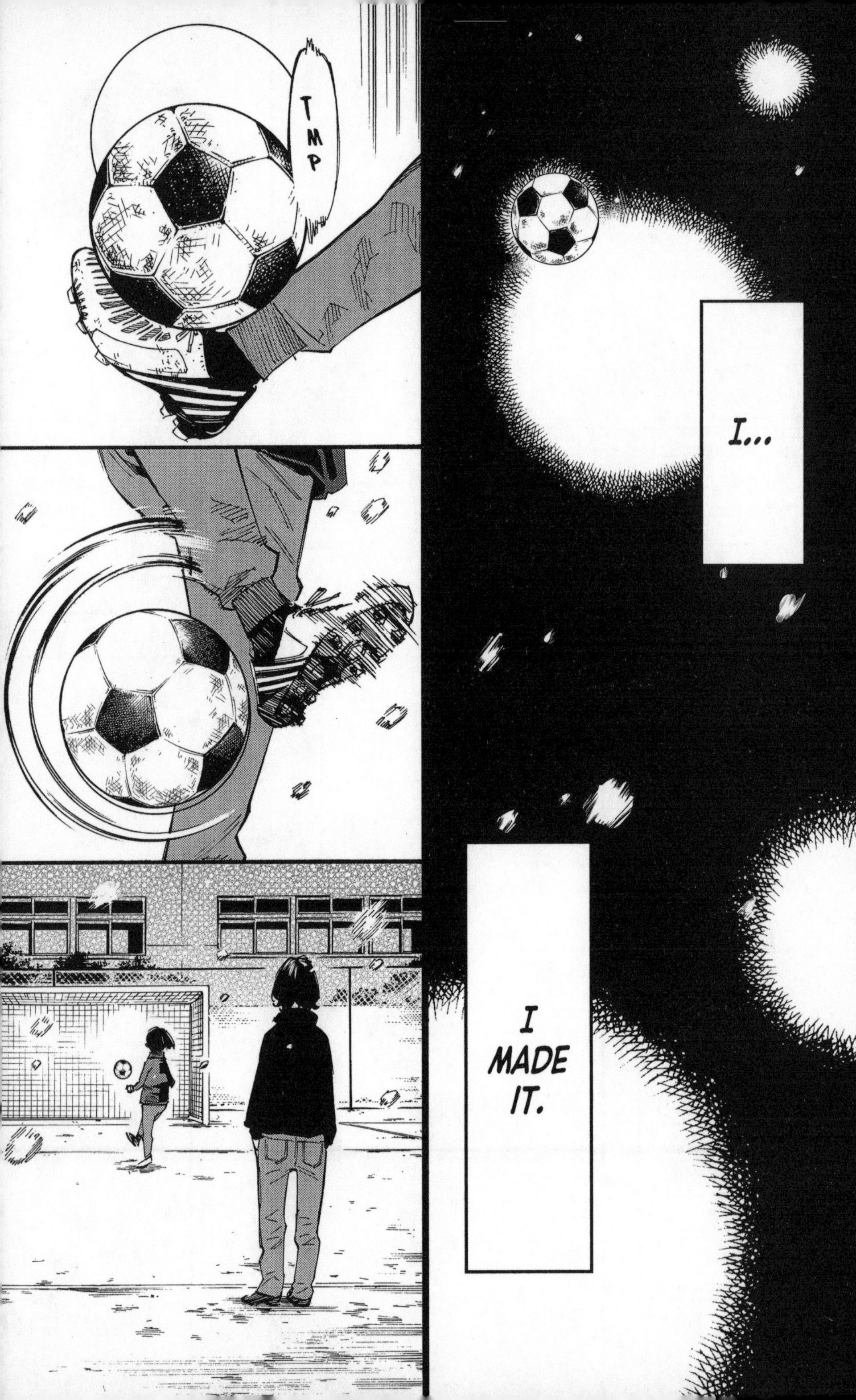
I...
I MADE IT.
TMP

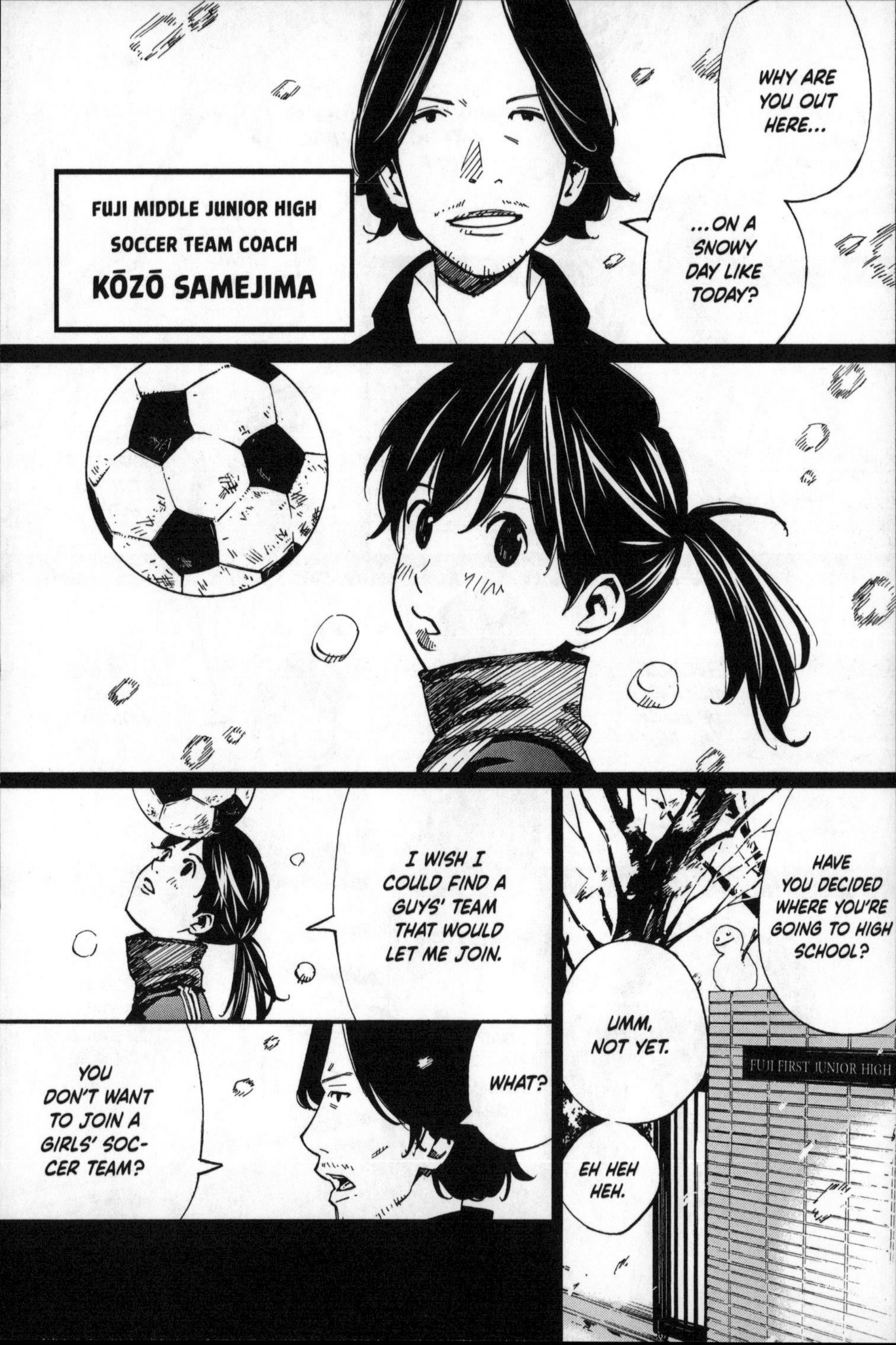
WHY ARE YOU OUT HERE...
...ON A SNOWY DAY LIKE TODAY?
FUJI MIDDLE JUNIOR HIGH SOCCER TEAM COACH
KŌZŌ SAMEJIMA
HAVE YOU DECIDED WHERE YOU'RE GOING TO HIGH SCHOOL?
UMM, NOT YET.
FUJI FIRST JUNIOR HIGH
EH HEH HEH.
I WISH I COULD FIND A GUYS' TEAM THAT WOULD LET ME JOIN.
WHAT?
YOU DON'T WANT TO JOIN A GIRLS' SOC-CER TEAM?

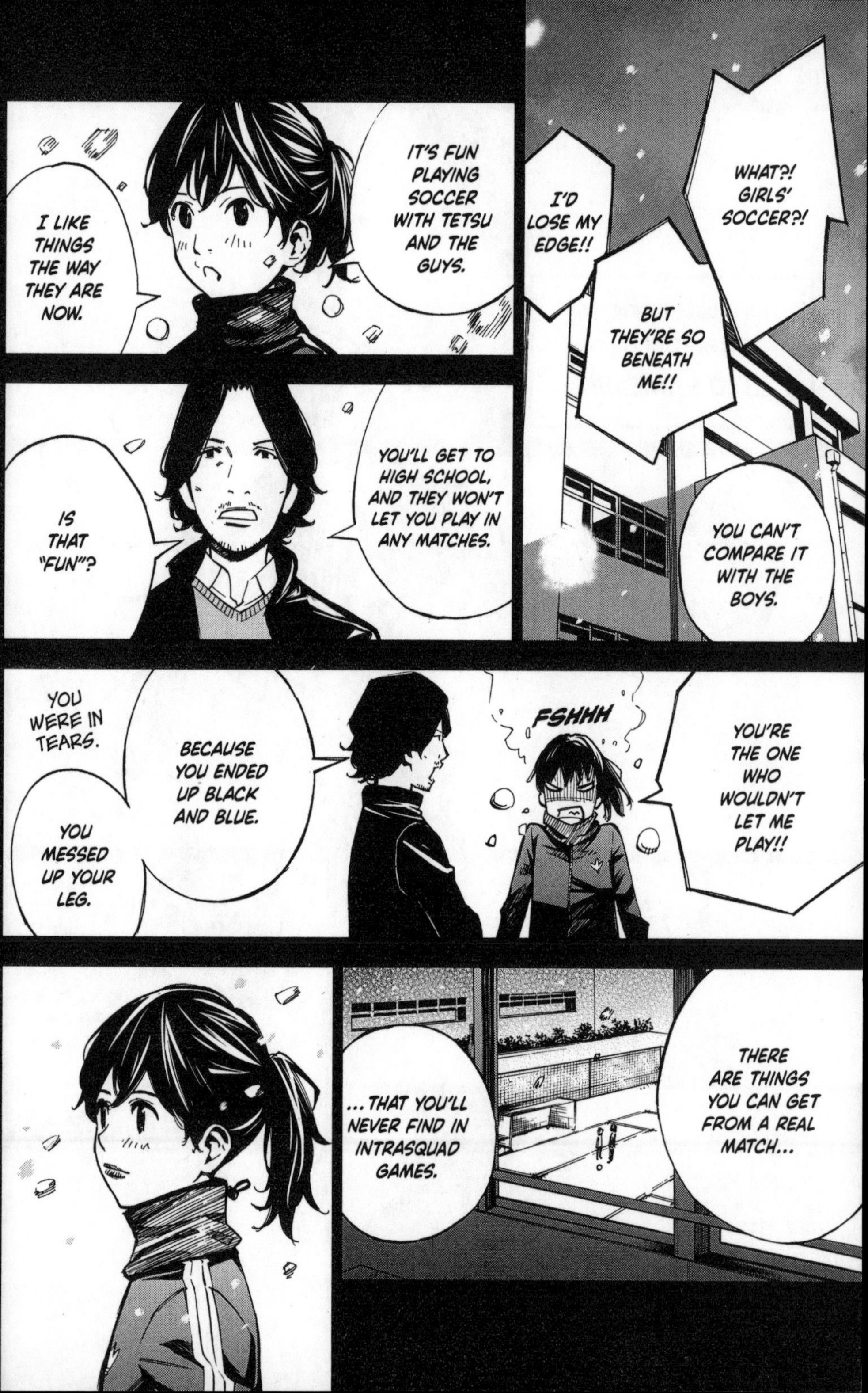
WHAT?! GIRLS' SOCCER?!
I'D LOSE MY EDGE!!
BUT THEY'RE SO BENEATH ME!!
YOU CAN'T COMPARE IT WITH THE BOYS.
IT'S FUN PLAYING SOCCER WITH TETSU AND THE GUYS.
I LIKE THINGS THE WAY THEY ARE NOW.
YOU'LL GET TO HIGH SCHOOL, AND THEY WON'T LET YOU PLAY IN ANY MATCHES.
IS THAT "FUN"?
YOU'RE THE ONE WHO WOULDN'T LET ME PLAY!!
FSHHH
BECAUSE YOU ENDED UP BLACK AND BLUE.
YOU WERE IN TEARS.
YOU MESSED UP YOUR LEG.
THERE ARE THINGS YOU CAN GET FROM A REAL MATCH...
...THAT YOU'LL NEVER FIND IN INTRASQUAD GAMES.

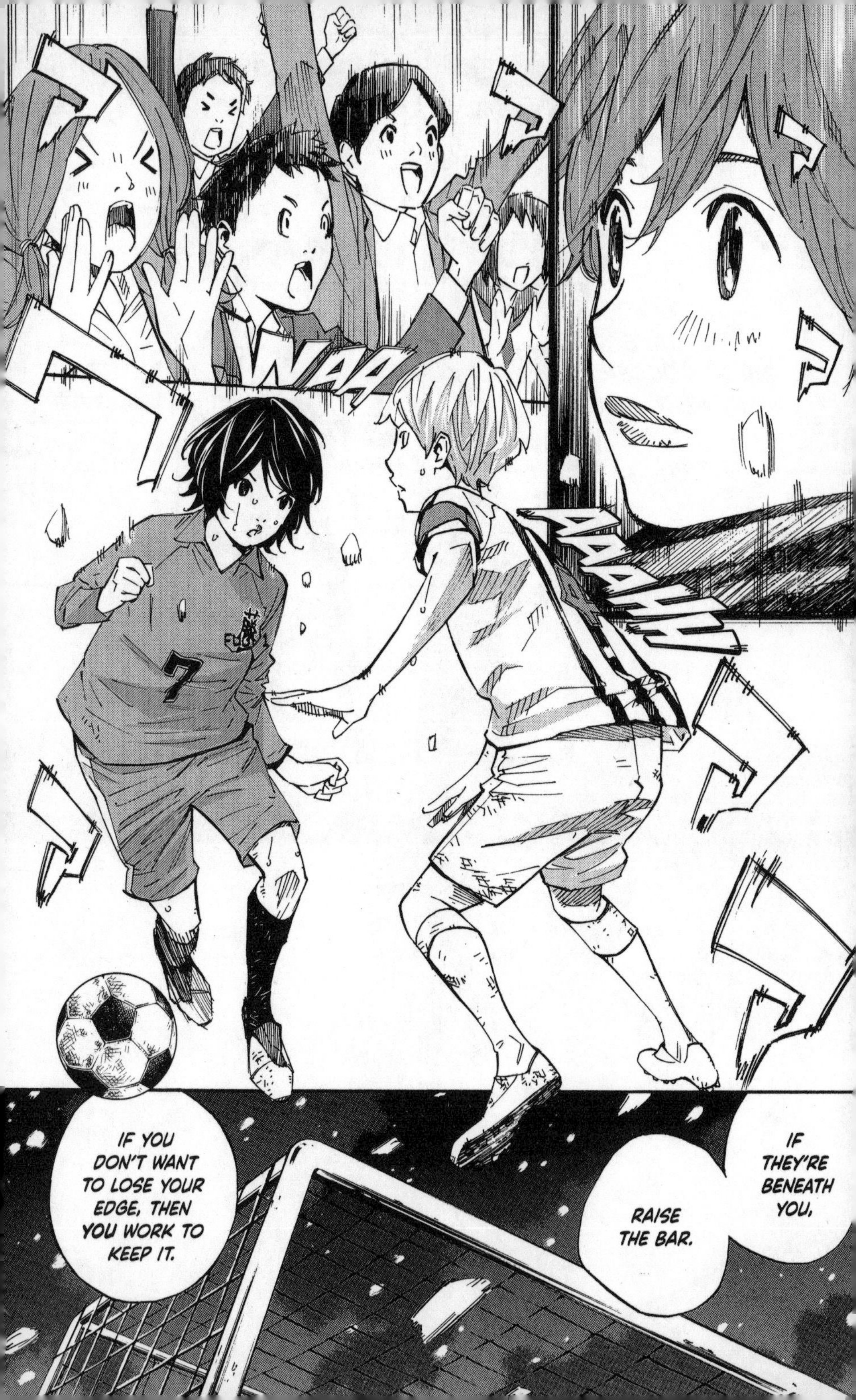
AAAHH
WAA
IF THEY'RE BENEATH YOU,
RAISE THE BAR.
IF YOU DON'T WANT TO LOSE YOUR EDGE, THEN YOU WORK TO KEEP IT.

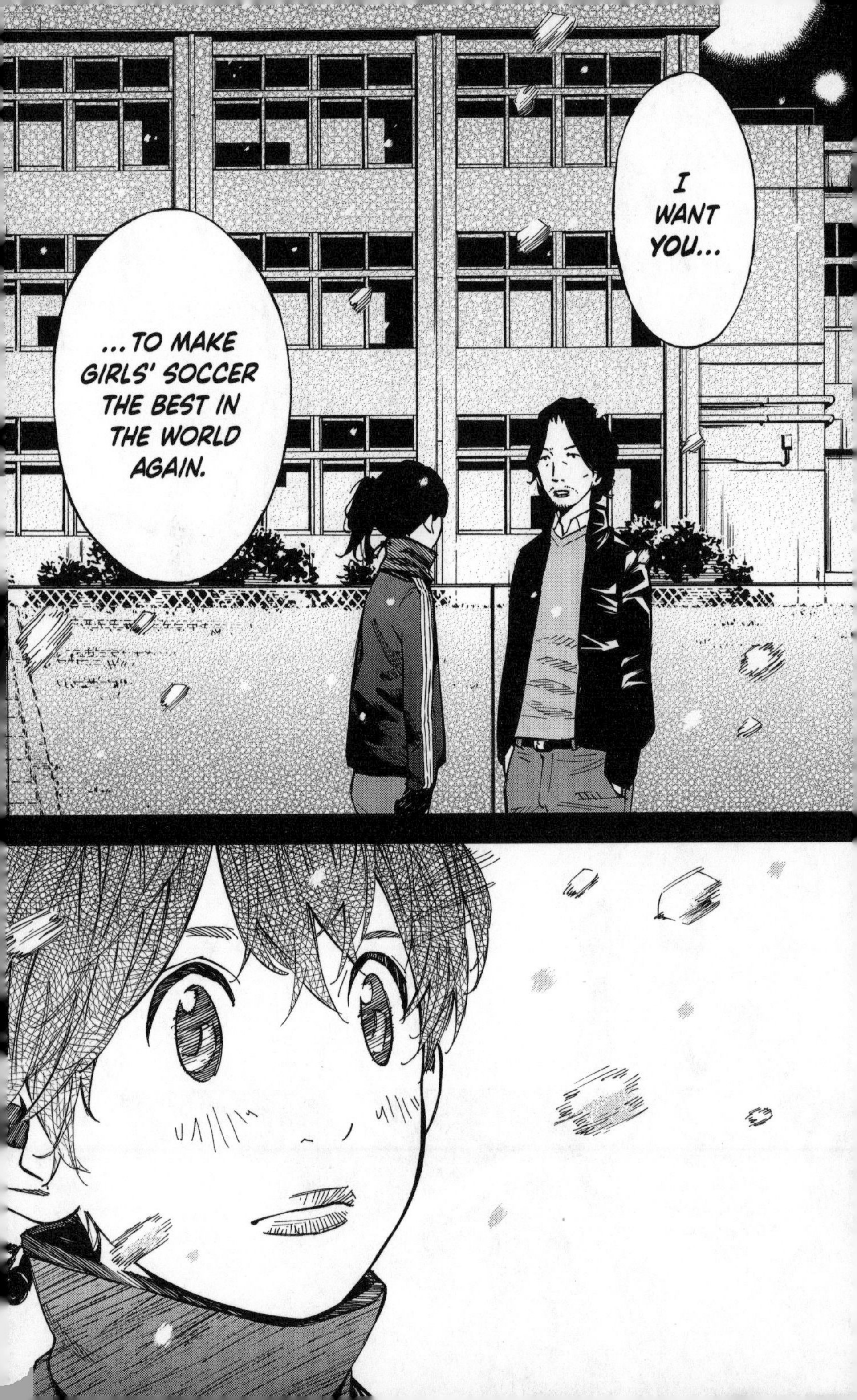
I WANT YOU...
...TO MAKE GIRLS' SOCCER THE BEST IN THE WORLD AGAIN.

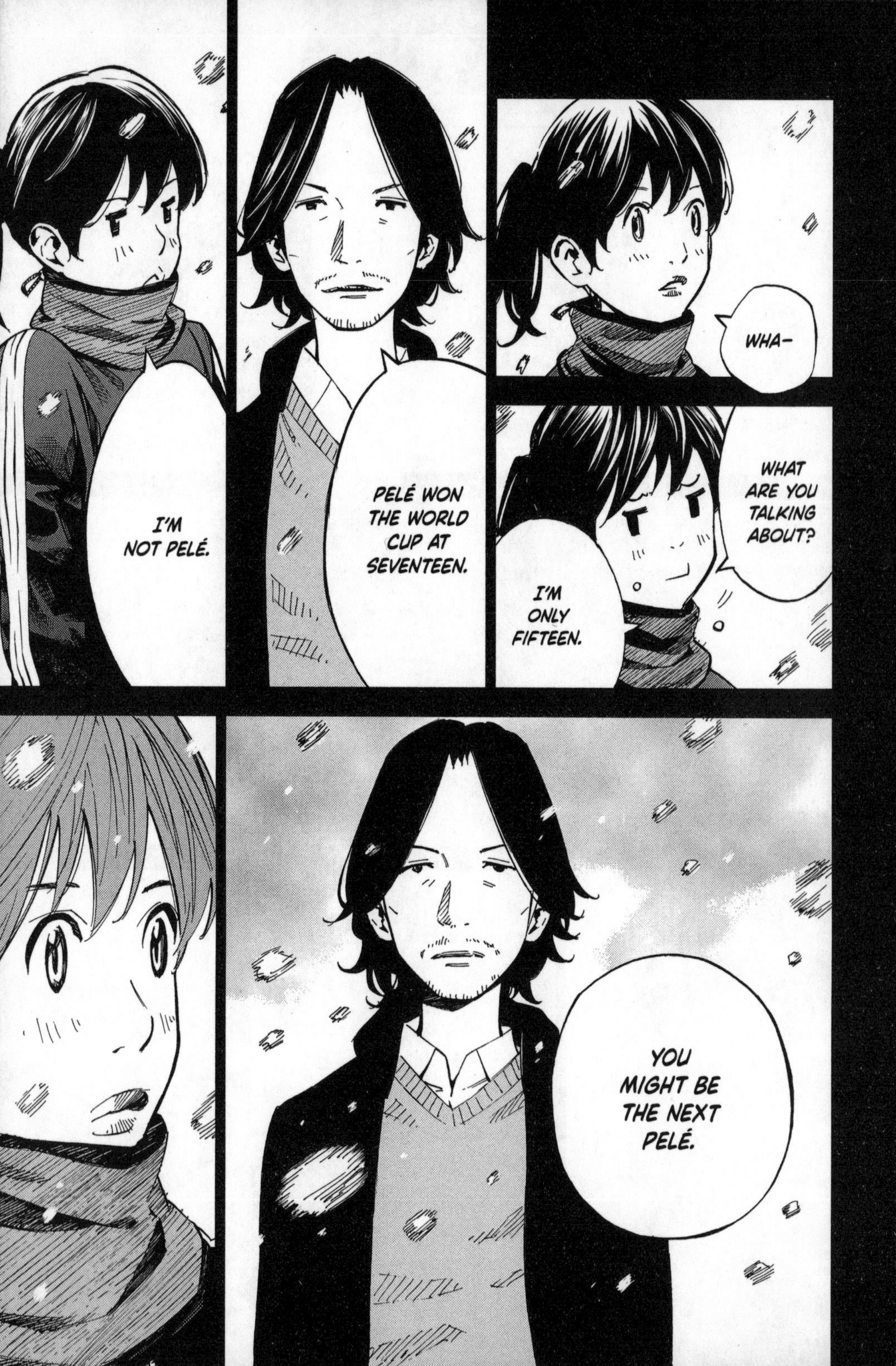
WHA-
WHAT ARE YOU TALKING ABOUT?
I'M ONLY FIFTEEN.
PELÉ WON THE WORLD CUP AT SEVENTEEN.
I'M NOT PELÉ.
YOU MIGHT BE THE NEXT PELÉ.

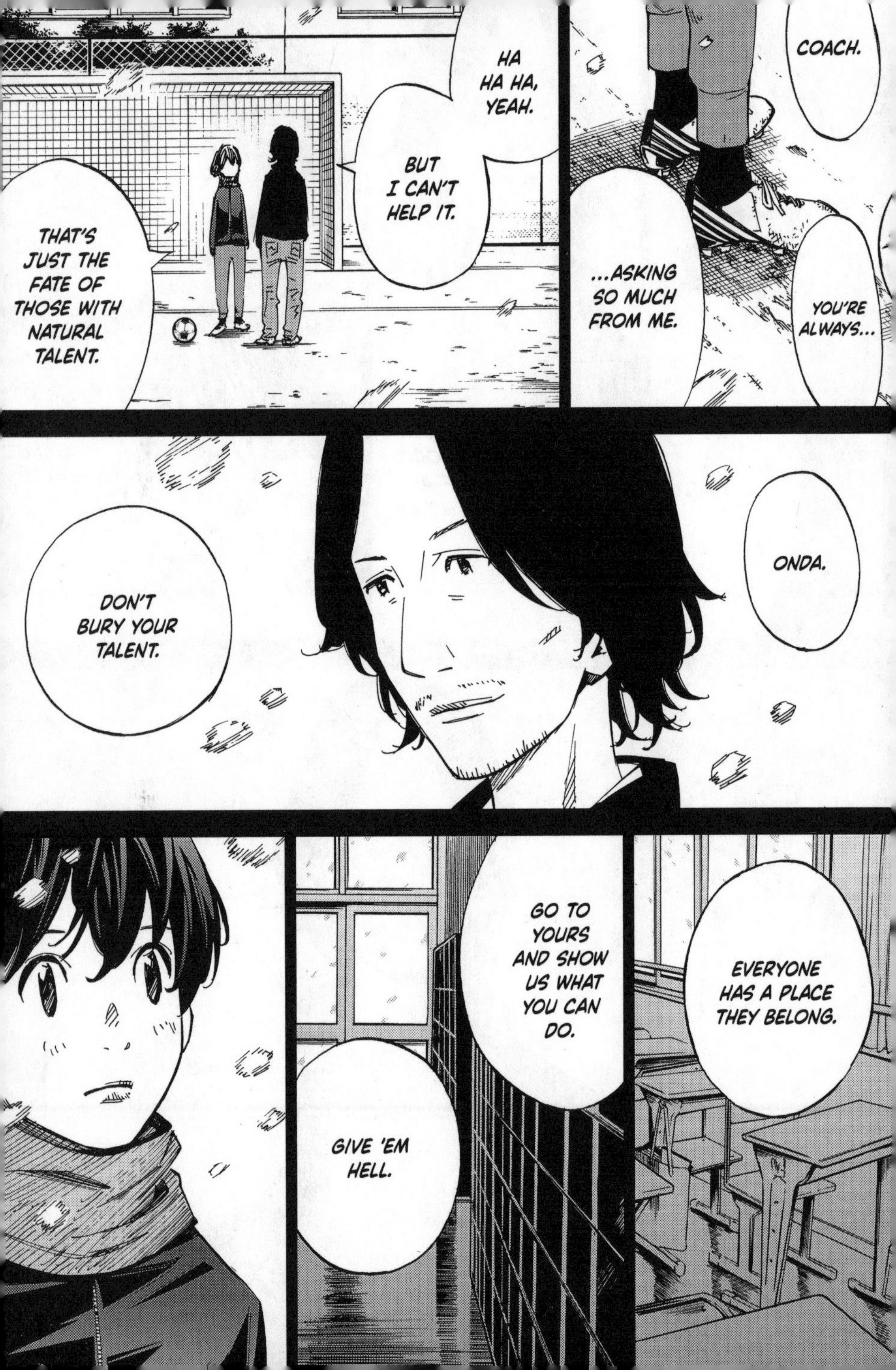
COACH.
YOU'RE ALWAYS...
...ASKING SO MUCH FROM ME.
HA HA HA, YEAH.
BUT I CAN'T HELP IT.
THAT'S JUST THE FATE OF THOSE WITH NATURAL TALENT.
ONDA.
DON'T BURY YOUR TALENT.
EVERYONE HAS A PLACE THEY BELONG.
GO TO YOURS AND SHOW US WHAT YOU CAN DO.
GIVE 'EM HELL.

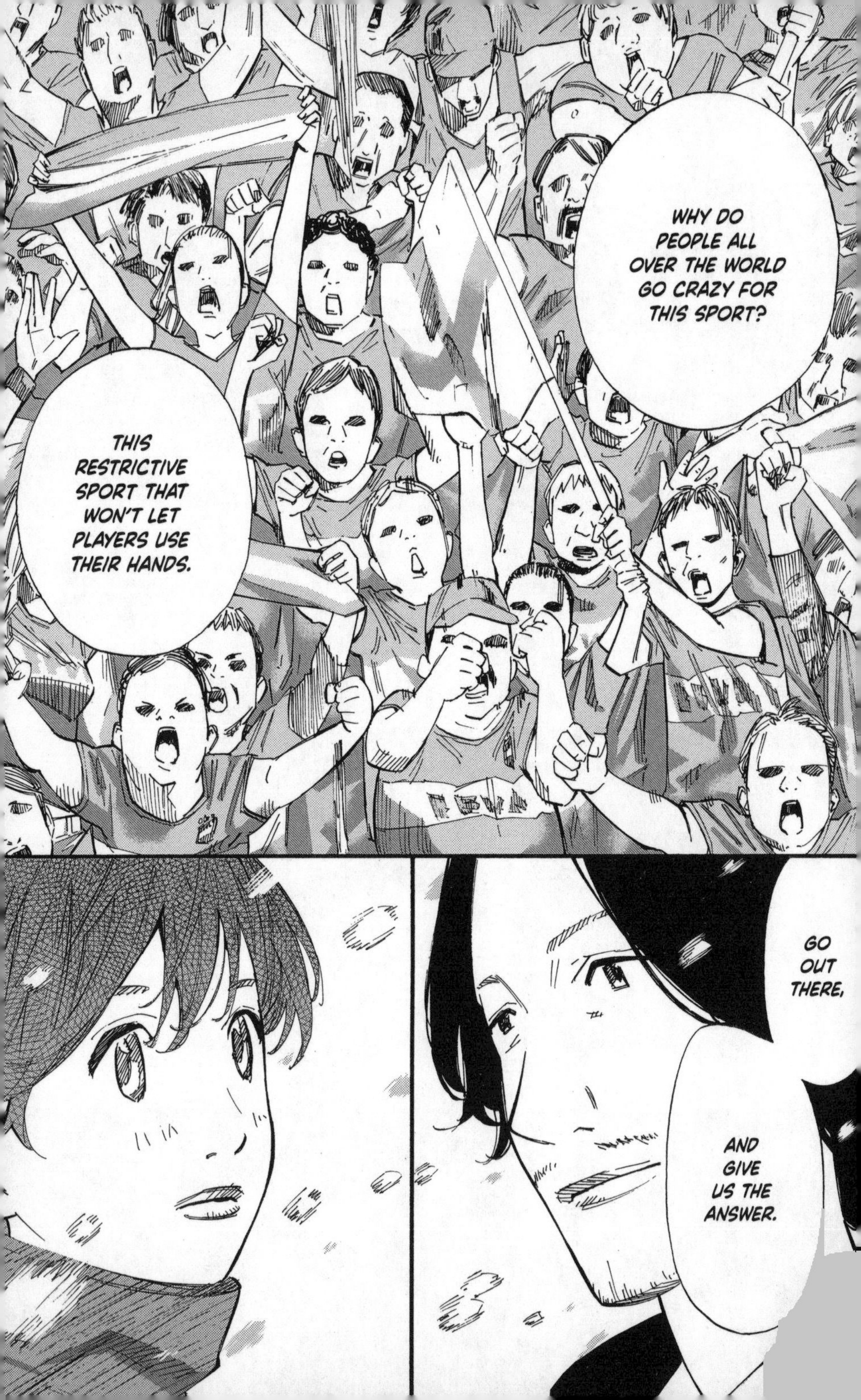
WHY DO PEOPLE ALL OVER THE WORLD GO CRAZY FOR THIS SPORT?
THIS RESTRICTIVE SPORT THAT WON'T LET PLAYERS USE THEIR HANDS.
GO OUT THERE,
AND GIVE US THE ANSWER.

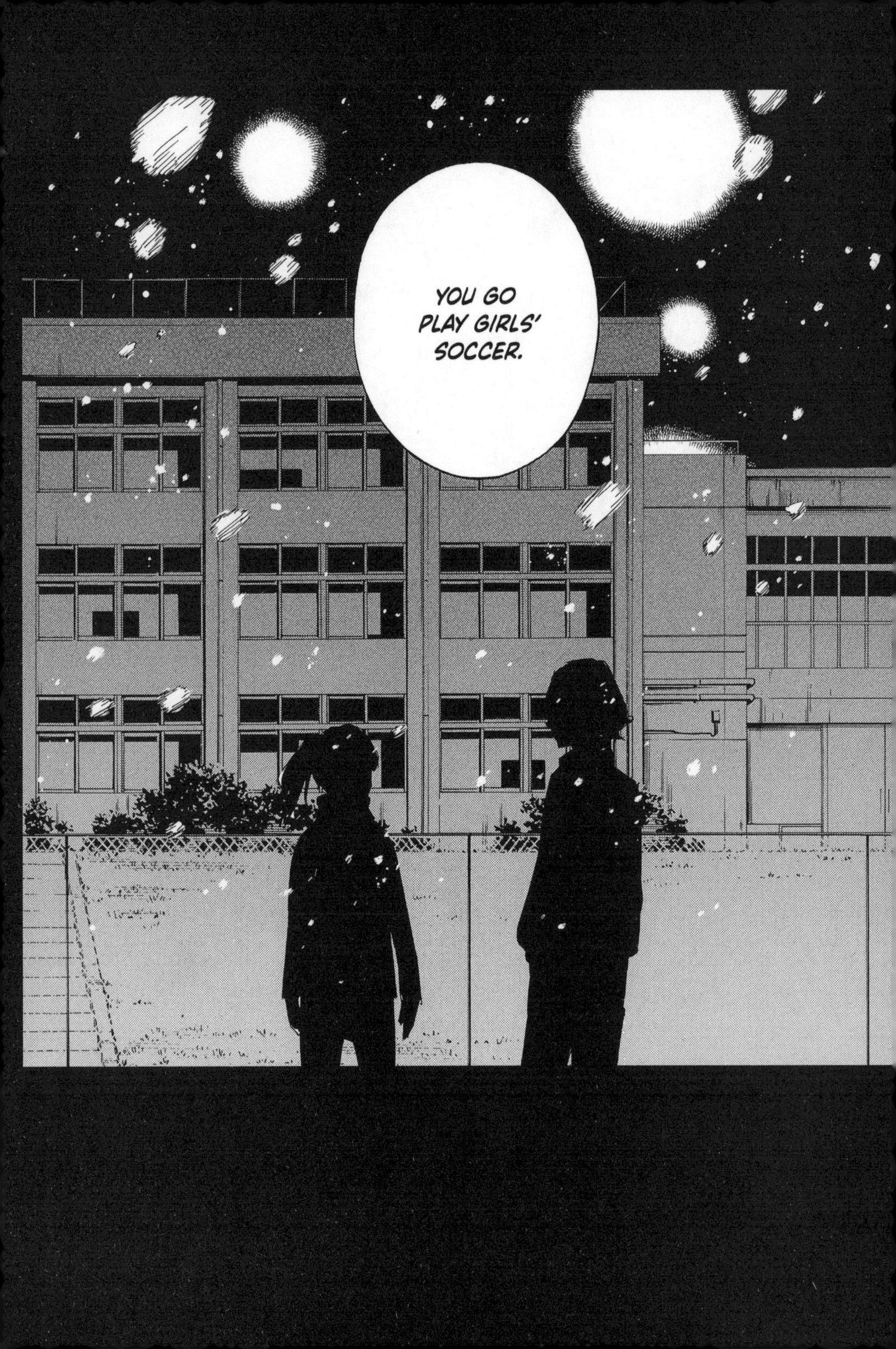
YOU GO PLAY GIRLS' SOCCER.

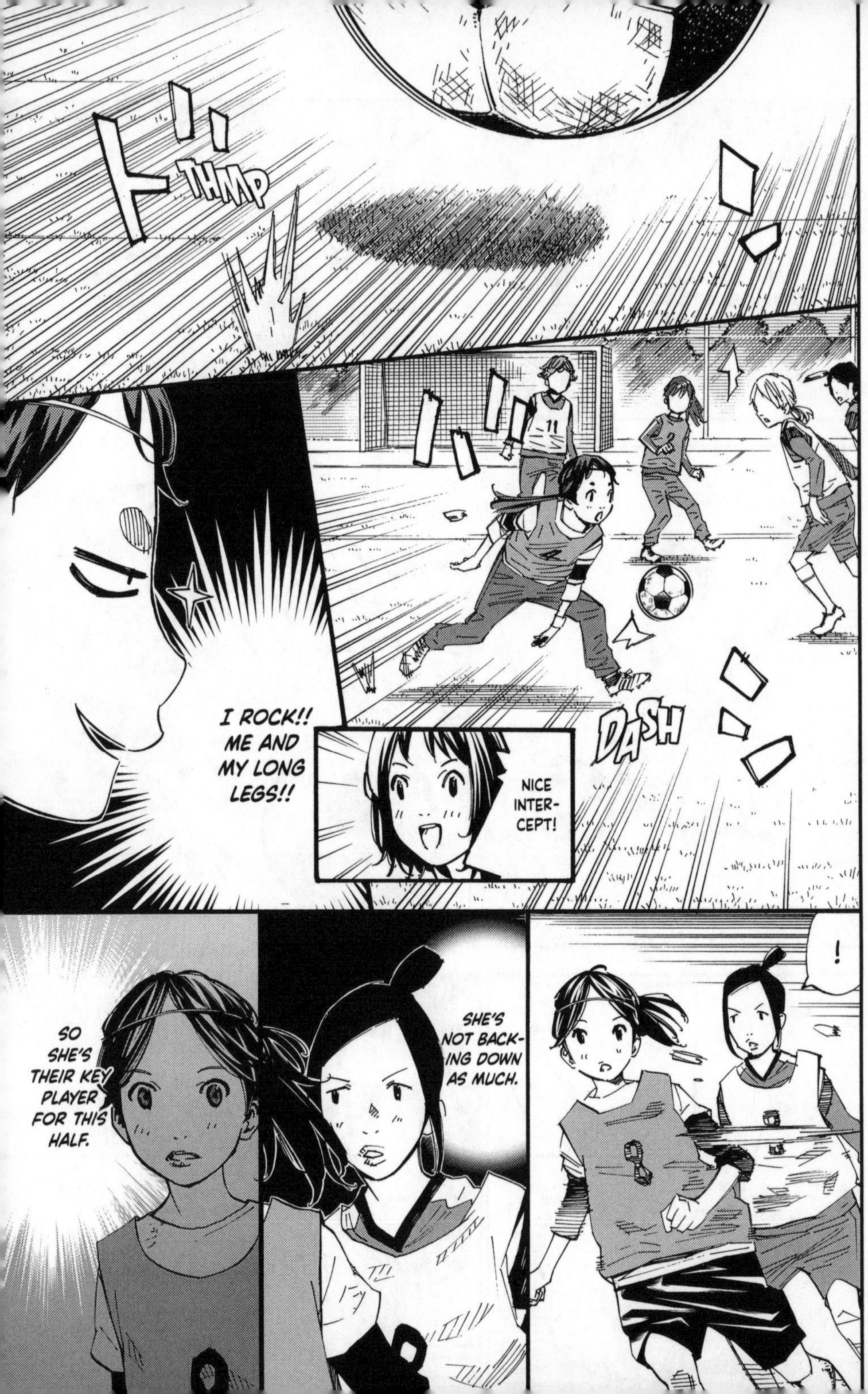
THMP
DASH
NICE INTER-CEPT!
I ROCK!! ME AND MY LONG LEGS!!
!
SHE'S NOT BACK-ING DOWN AS MUCH.
SO SHE'S THEIR KEY PLAYER FOR THIS HALF.

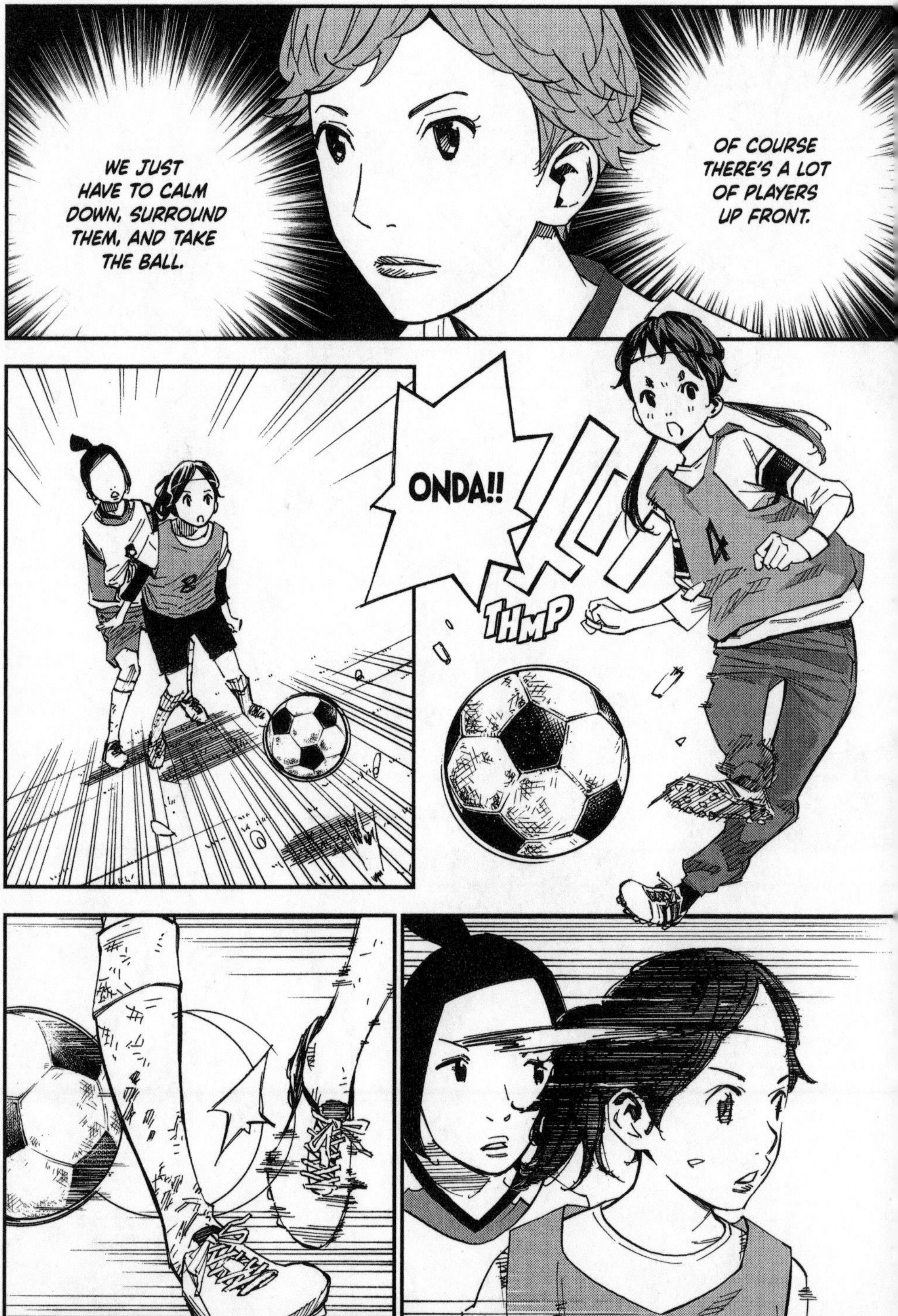
OF COURSE THERE'S A LOT OF PLAYERS UP FRONT.
WE JUST HAVE TO CALM DOWN, SURROUND THEM, AND TAKE THE BALL.
ONDA!!
THMP

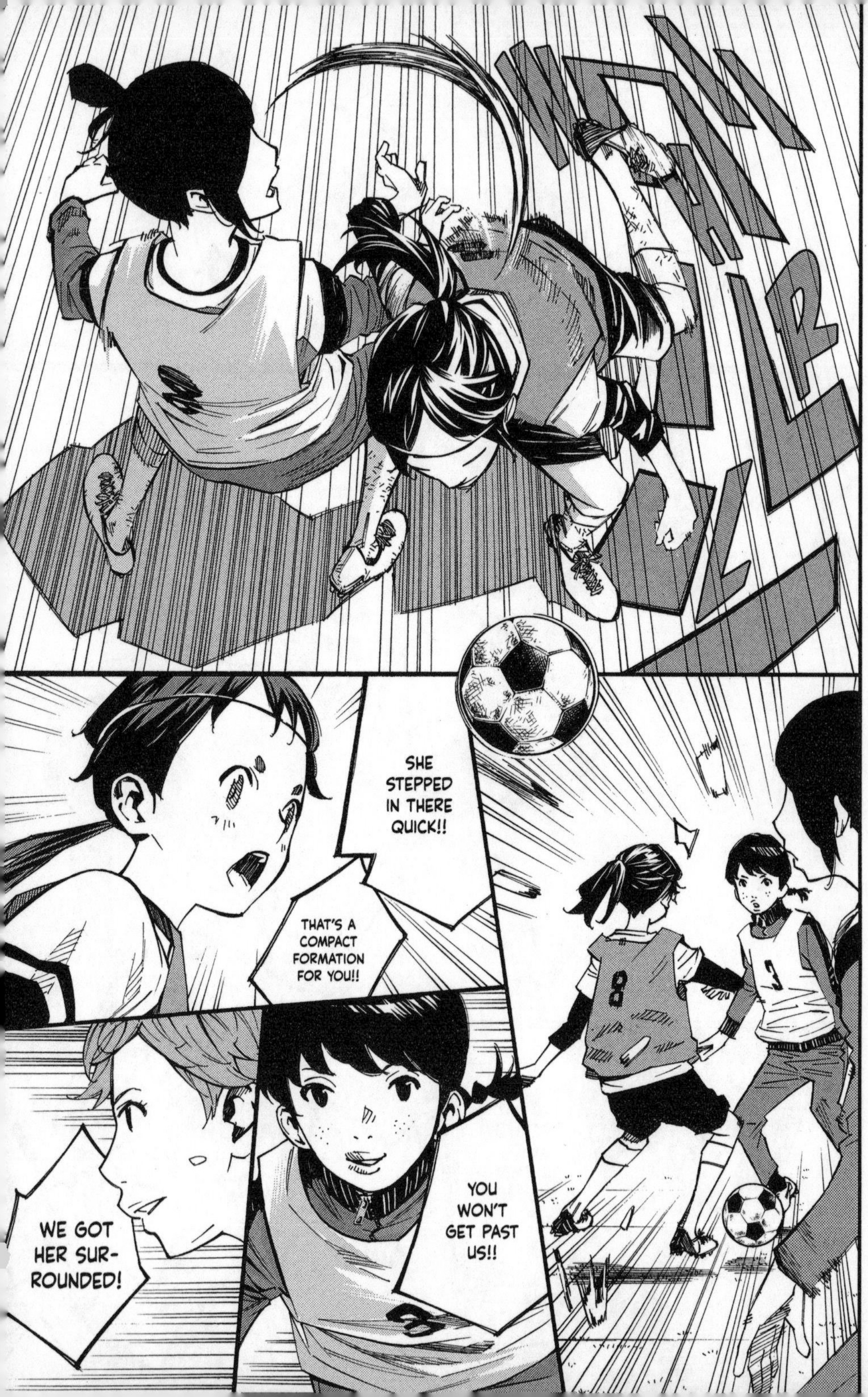
SHE STEPPED IN THERE QUICK!!
THAT'S A COMPACT FORMATION FOR YOU!!
YOU WON'T GET PAST US!!
WE GOT HER SUR- ROUNDED!

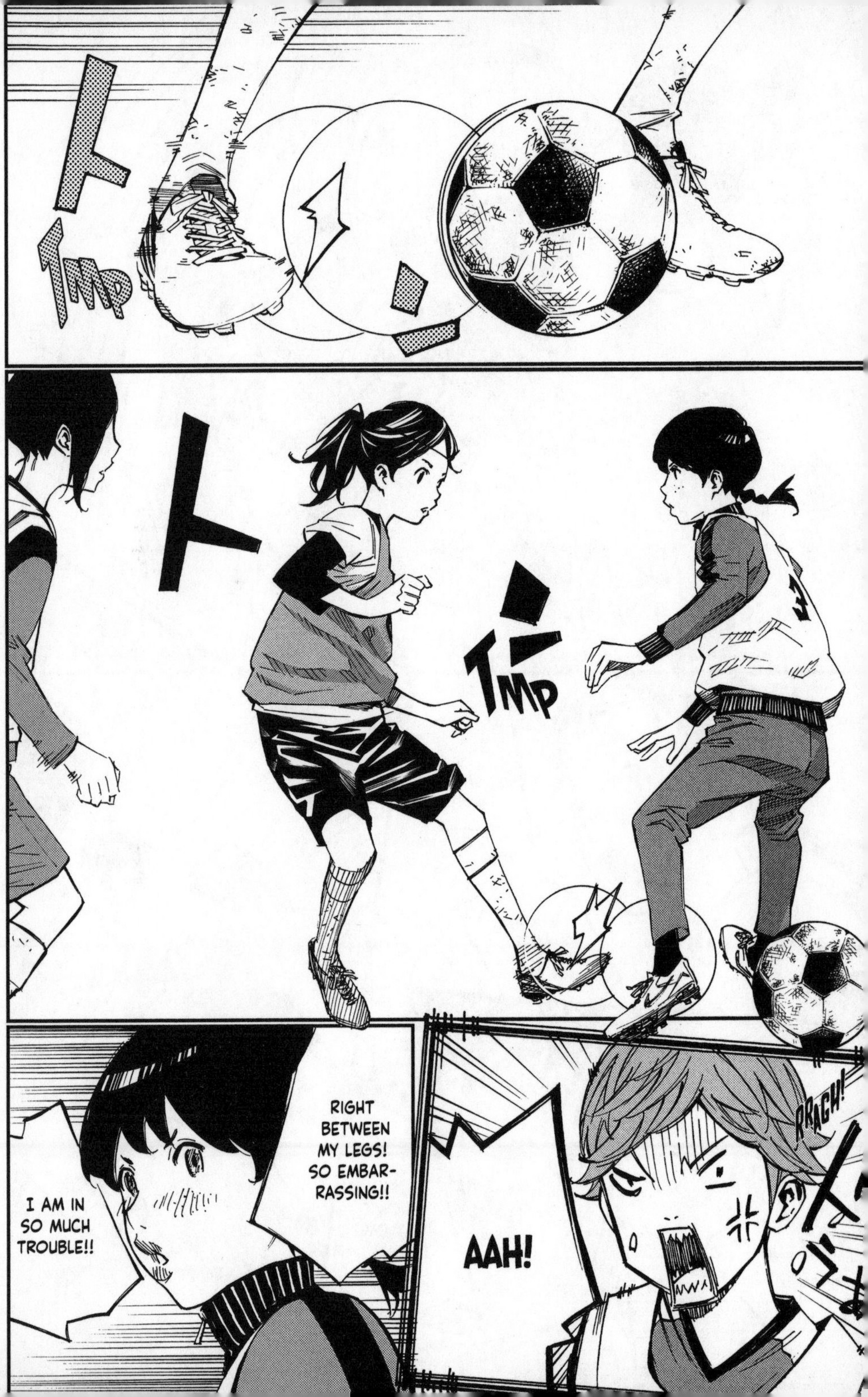
ト
TMP
ト
TMP
RRAGH!
AAH!
RIGHT BETWEEN MY LEGS! SO EMBARRASSING!!
I AM IN SO MUCH TROUBLE!!

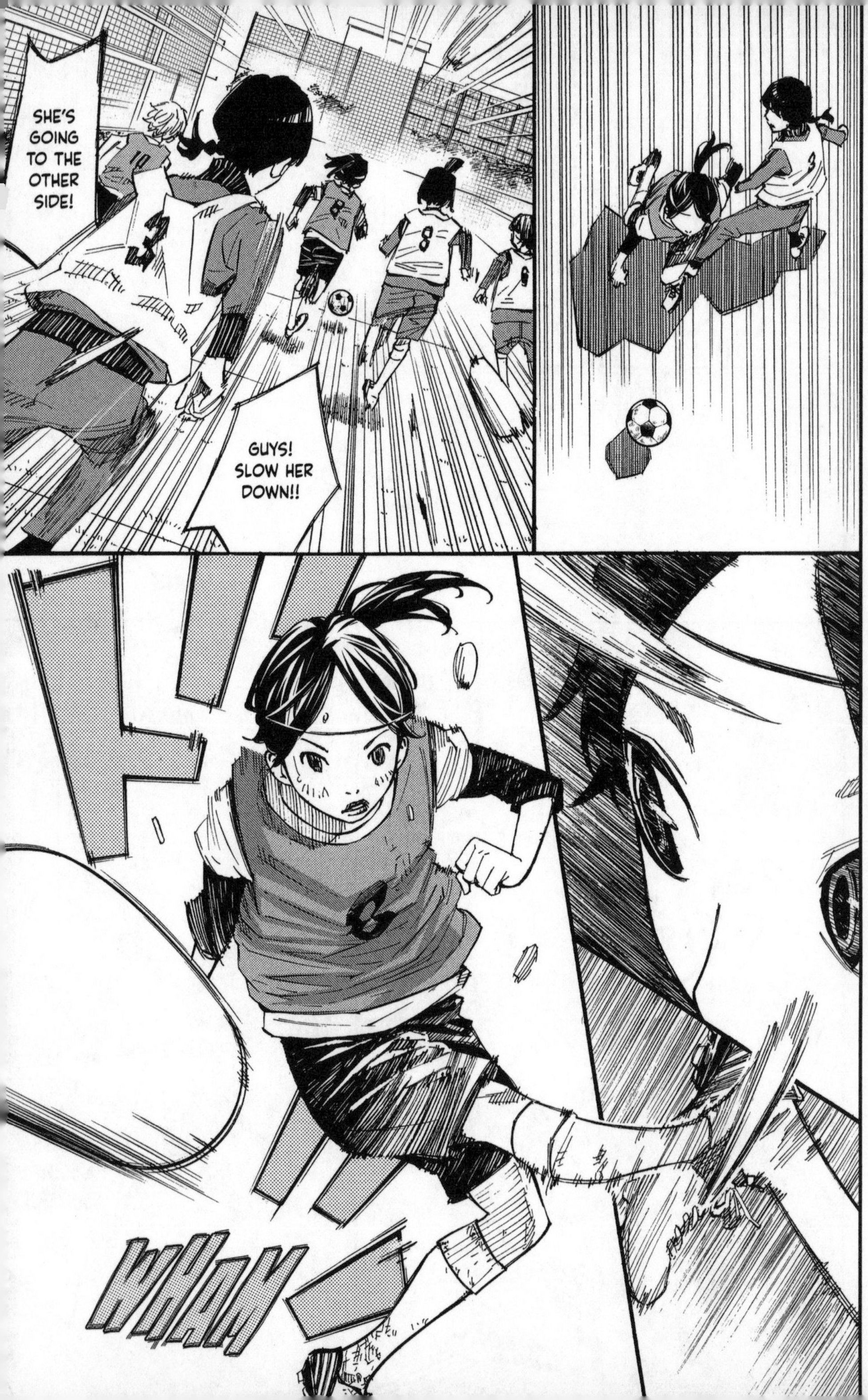
SHE'S GOING TO THE OTHER SIDE!
GUYS! SLOW HER DOWN!!
WHOA

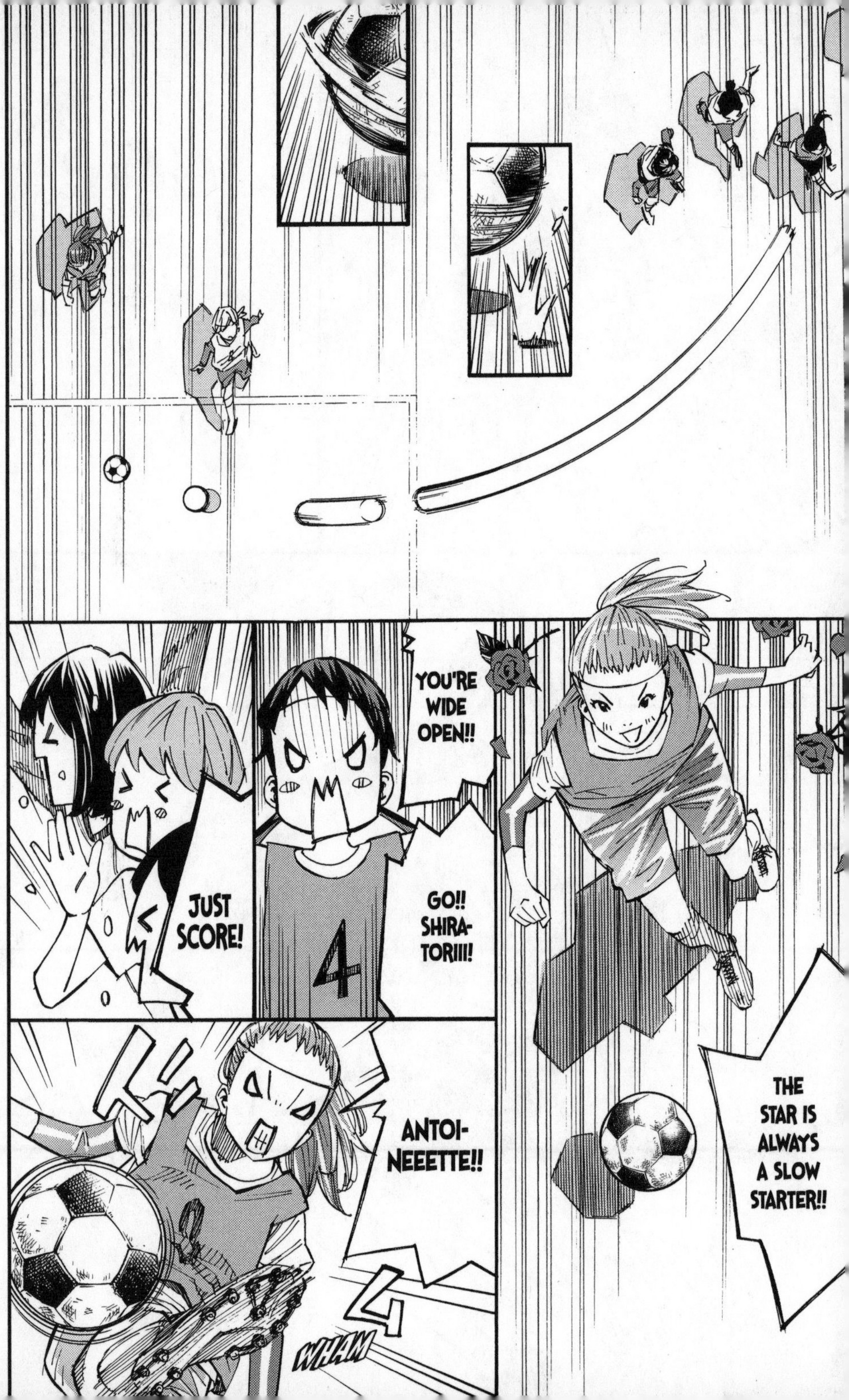

THE STAR IS ALWAYS A SLOW STARTER!!
YOU'RE WIDE OPEN!!
GO!! SHIRATORIII!
JUST SCORE!
ANTOI-NEEETTE!!
WHAM

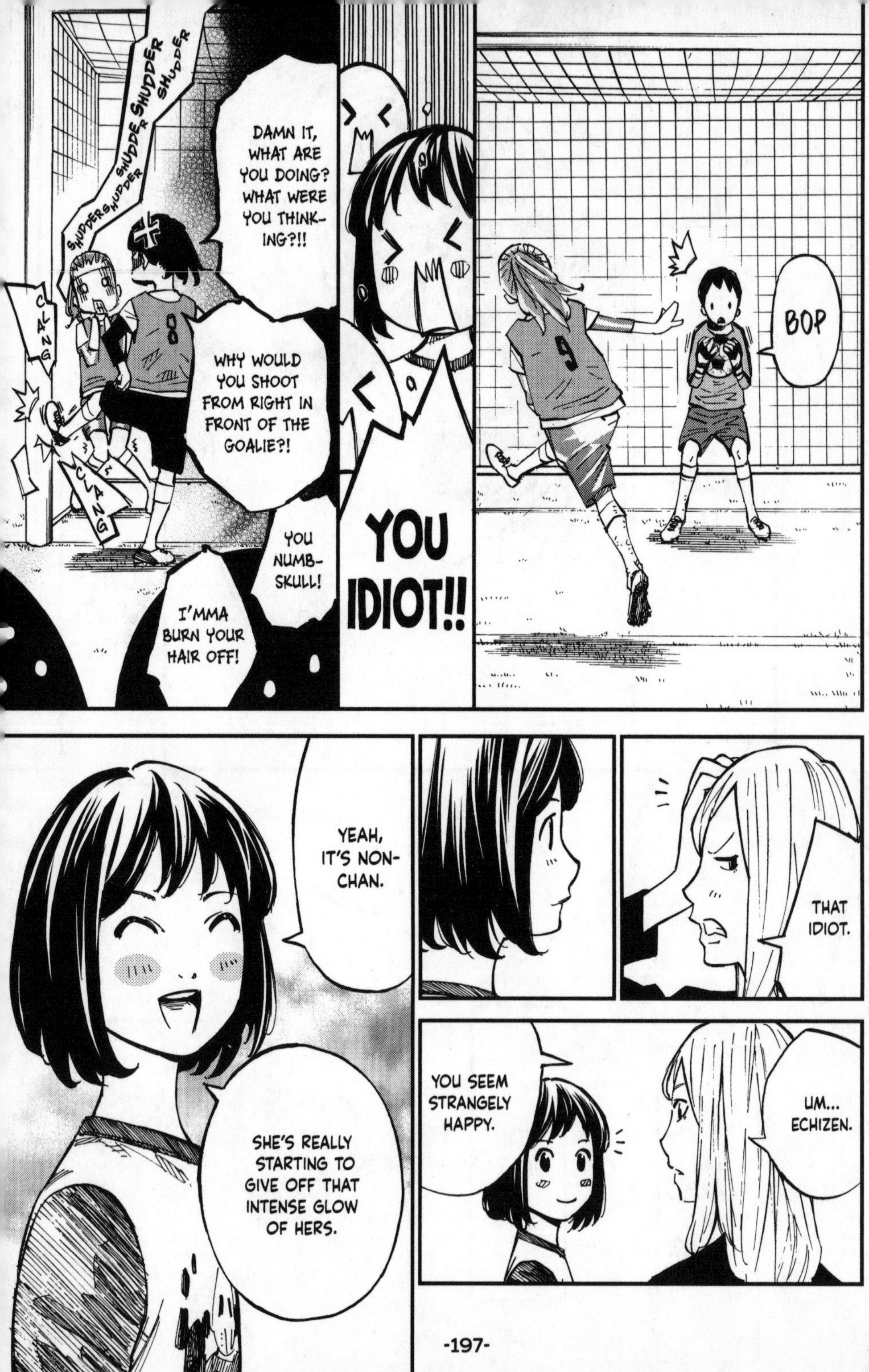
BOP
YOU IDIOT!!
DAMN IT, WHAT ARE YOU DOING? WHAT WERE YOU THINKING?!!
SHUDDERSHUDDER SHUDDER SHUDDER
CLANG
CLANG
WHY WOULD YOU SHOOT FROM RIGHT IN FRONT OF THE GOALIE?!
YOU NUMBSKULL!
I'MMA BURN YOUR HAIR OFF!
THAT IDIOT.
UM... ECHIZEN.
YOU SEEM STRANGELY HAPPY.
YEAH, IT'S NON-CHAN.
SHE'S REALLY STARTING TO GIVE OFF THAT INTENSE GLOW OF HERS.

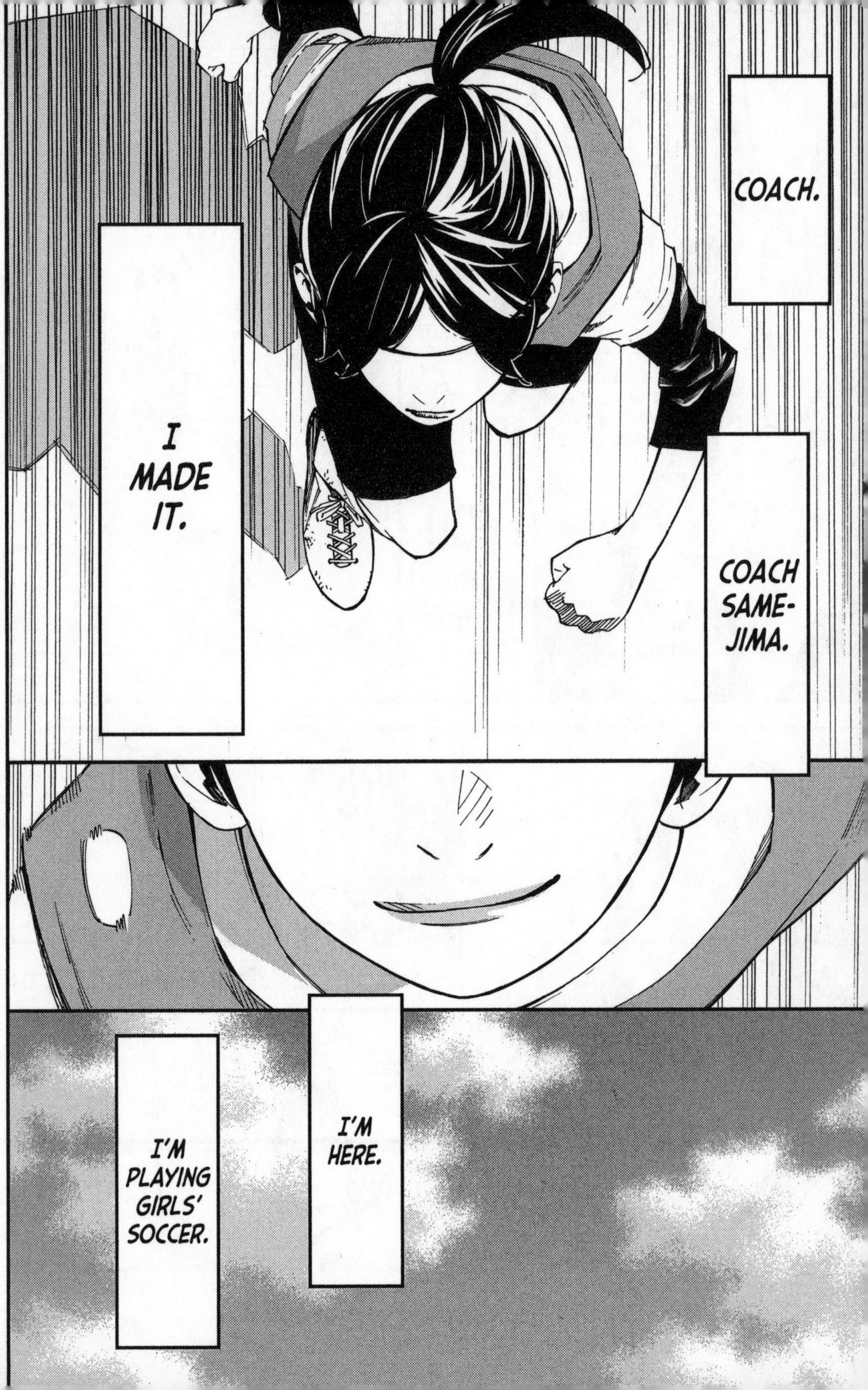
COACH.
COACH SAME-JIMA.
I MADE IT.
I'M HERE.
I'M PLAYING GIRLS' SOCCER.

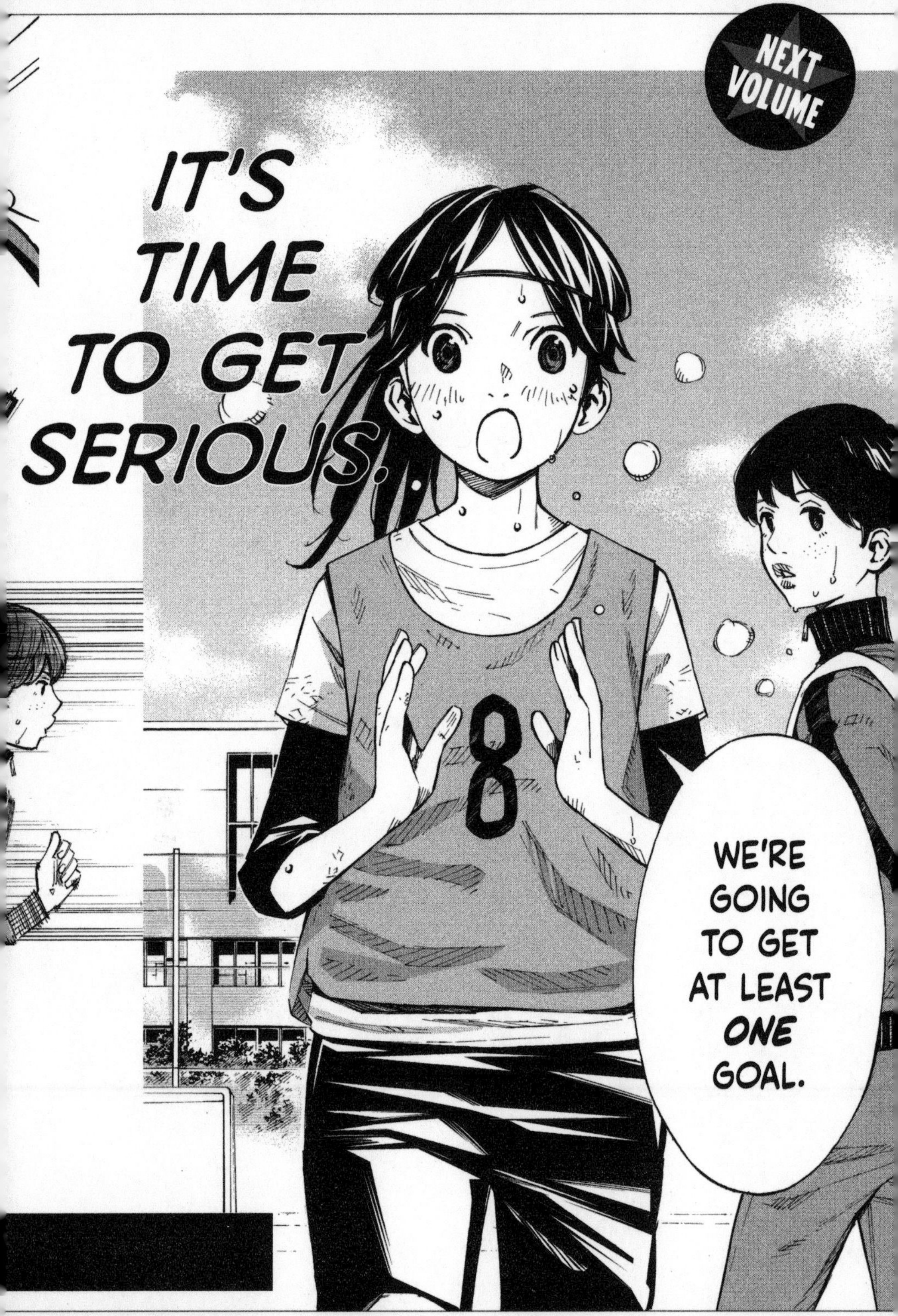
NEXT VOLUME
IT'S TIME TO GET SERIOUS.
WE'RE GOING TO GET AT LEAST ONE GOAL.

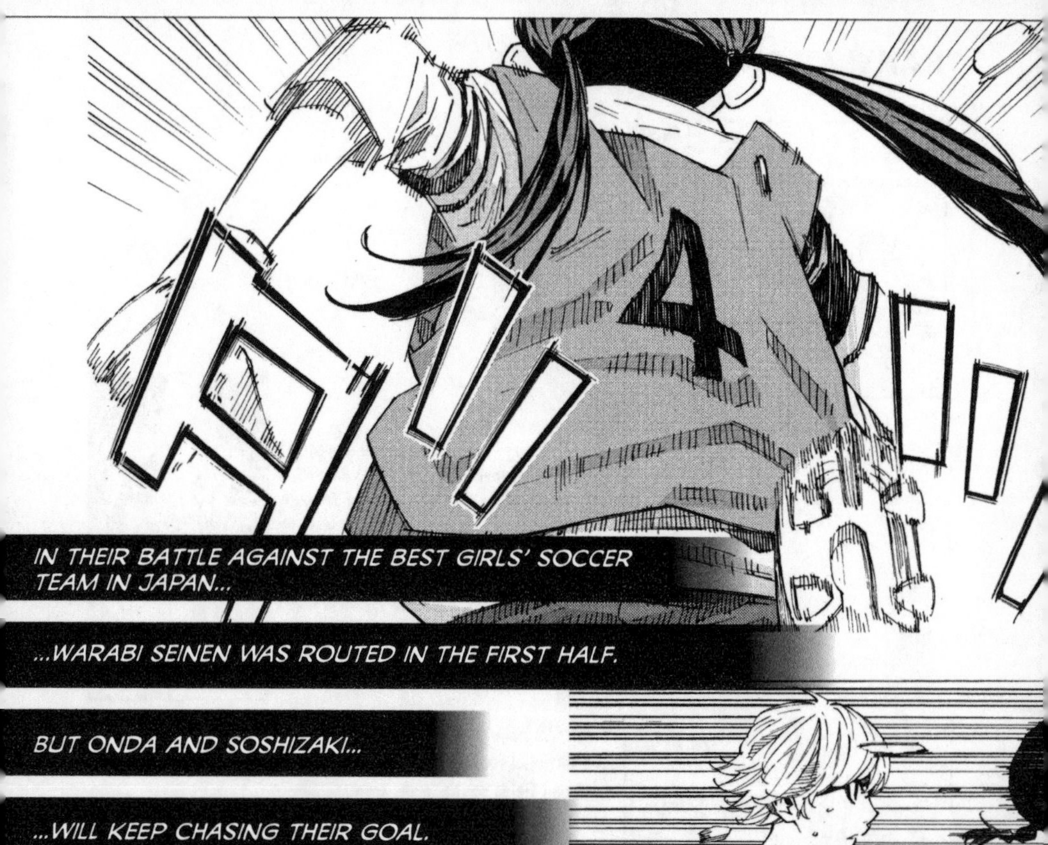
IN THEIR BATTLE AGAINST THE BEST GIRLS' SOCCER TEAM IN JAPAN...
...WARABI SEINEN WAS ROUTED IN THE FIRST HALF.
BUT ONDA AND SOSHIZAKI...
...WILL KEEP CHASING THEIR GOAL.
WITH EVERYONE PUSHING THEMSELVES TO THEIR LIMIT,
CAN SUÔ BREAK THROUGH...?

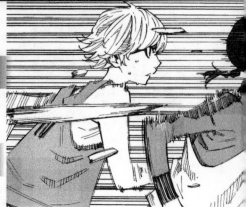

SAYONARA FOOTBALL

VOLUME 4

TRANSLATION NOTES

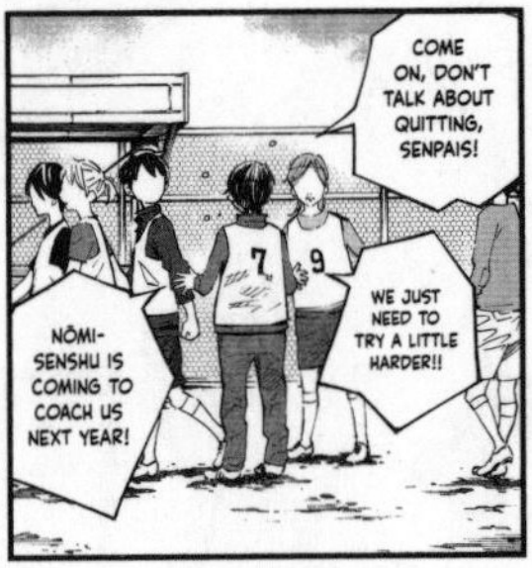
COME ON, DON'T TALK ABOUT QUITTING, SENPAIS!
WE JUST NEED TO TRY A LITTLE HARDER!!
NŌMI-SENSHU IS COMING TO COACH US NEXT YEAR!

Senshu, page 26
A name honorific indicating athletes, similar to "sensei" for doctors and teachers.

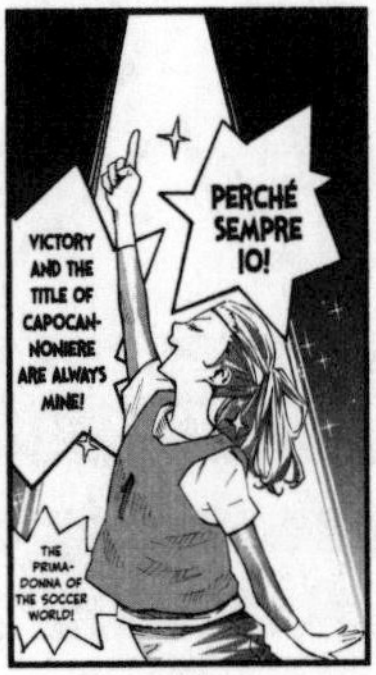
PERCHÉ SEMPRE IO!
VICTORY AND THE TITLE OF CAPOCANNONIERE ARE ALWAYS MINE!
THE PRIMA-DONNA OF THE SOCCER WORLD!

Perché sempre io, page 68
"Why always me?" in Italian. Mario Balotelli, a player for Manchester United, famously revealed a shirt bearing this phrase under his uniform as a celebration after scoring a goal in 2011. Capocannoniere is the title awarded to the highest goal-scorer each season in Italy's Serie A league.

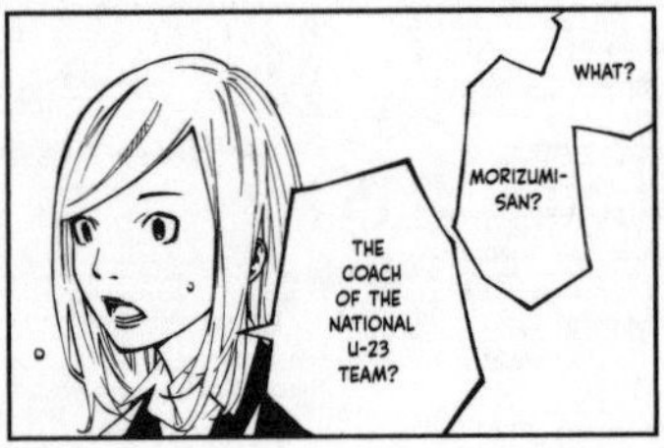
WHAT?
MORIZUMI-SAN?
THE COACH OF THE NATIONAL U-23 TEAM?

Under-23, page 81
The National Football Association of Japan fields youth teams from ages 15 to 23, in addition to the national team, for international competition.

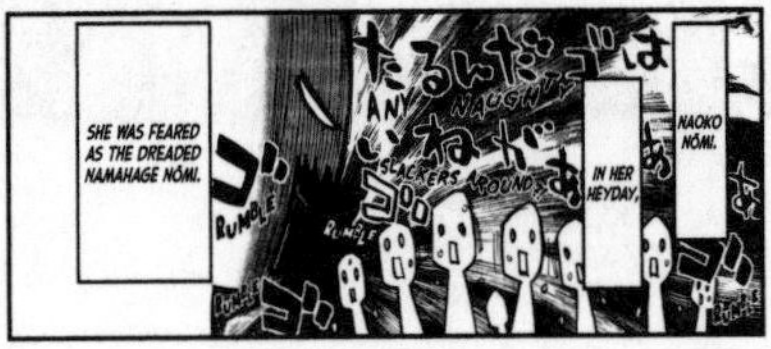
NAOKO NŌMI.
IN HER HEYDAY,
ANY NAUGHTY SLACKERS AROUND?
RUMBLE
RUMBLE
SHE WAS FEARED AS THE DREADED NAMAHAGE NŌMI.

Namahage, Page 87
These are a kind of demon from Japanese folklore, which are said to admonish those who are idle or lazy.

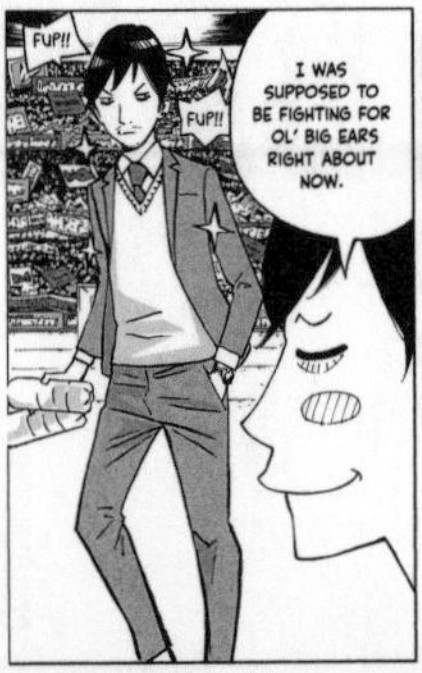
I WAS SUPPOSED TO BE FIGHTING FOR OL' BIG EARS RIGHT ABOUT NOW.
FUP!!
FUP!!

Big Ears, page 165
This is the nickname for the trophy given to the winners of the European Champion Clubs' Cup, given the overly pronounced shape of the actual cup's handles.

‹ KAMOME ›
SHIRAHAMA

Witch Hat Atelier

A magical manga adventure for fans of Disney and Studio Ghibli!

Witch Hat Atelier © Kamome Shirahama/Kodansha Ltd.

The magical adventure that took Japan by storm is finally here, from acclaimed DC and Marvel cover artist Kamome Shirahama!

In a world where everyone takes wonders like magic spells and dragons for granted, Coco is a girl with a simple dream: She wants to be a witch. But everybody knows magicians are born, not made, and Coco was not born with a gift for magic. Resigned to her un-magical life, Coco is about to give up on her dream to become a witch...until the day she meets Qifrey, a mysterious, traveling magician. After secretly seeing Qifrey perform magic in a way she's never seen before, Coco soon learns what everybody "knows" might not be the truth, and discovers that her magical dream may not be as far away as it may seem...

KC
**KODANSHA
COMICS**

Acclaimed screenwriter and director Mari Okada (*Maquia, anohana*) teams up with manga artist Nao Emoto (*Forget Me Not*) in this moving, funny, so-true-it's-embarrassing coming-of-age series!

When Kazusa enters high school, she joins the Literature Club, and leaps from reading innocent fiction to diving into the literary classics. But these novels are a bit more...*adult* than she was prepared for. Between euphemisms like fresh dewy grass and pork stew, crushing on the boy next door, and knowing you want to do that *one thing* before you die—discovering your budding sexuality is no easy feat! As if puberty wasn't awkward enough, the club consists of a brooding writer, the prettiest girl in school, an agreeable comrade, and an outspoken prude. Fumbling over their own discomforts, these five teens get thrown into chaos over three little letters: *S...E...X...!*

O Maidens in your Savage Season

Anime coming soon!

Mari Okada   Nao Emoto

KC
KODANSHA
COMICS

SAINT ☆ YOUNG MEN

A LONG AWAITED ARRIVAL IN PREMIUM 2-IN-1 HARDCOVER

After centuries of hard work, Jesus and Buddha take a break from their heavenly duties to relax among the people of Japan, and their adventures in this lighthearted buddy comedy are sure to bring mirth and merriment to all!

"Brilliant…the physical comedy and facial expressions will make you literally LOL."

—Sam Humphries
(host of *DC Daily*; writer, *Green Lanterns, Legendary Star-Lord*)

ıperback Original
2016 Naoshi Arakawa
021 Naoshi Arakawa

Published in the United States by Kodansha Comics, an imprint of
Kodansha USA Publishing, LLC, New York.

Publication rights for this English edition arranged through
Kodansha Ltd., Tokyo.

First published in Japan in 2016 by Kodansha Ltd., Tokyo
as *Sayonara watashi no Cramer*, volume 1.

ISBN 978-1-63236-965-9

Original cover design by Asakura Kenji

Printed in the United States of America.

www.kodanshacomics.com

9 8 7 6 5 4 3 2 1
Translation: Devon Corwin
Lettering: Allen Berry
Additional Layout and Lettering: Belynda Ungurath
Editing: PJ Hruschak
YKS Services LLC/SKY Japan, INC.
Kodansha Comics edition cover design by Adam Del Re

Publisher: Kiichiro Sugawara

Director of publishing services: Ben Applegate
Associate director of operations: Stephen Pakula
Publishing services managing editor: Noelle Webster
Assistant production manager: Emi Lotto, Angela Zurlo
Logo and character art ©Kodansha USA Publishing, LLC